# Frommer's

# Israel

## 5th Edition

## by Robert Ullian

Here's what the critics say about Frommer's:

"Amazingly easy to use. Very portable, very complete."

—*Booklist*

"Detailed, accurate, and easy-to-read information for all price ranges."

—*Glamour Magazine*

"Hotel information is close to encyclopedic."

—*Des Moines Sunday Register*

"Frommer's Guides have a way of giving you a real feel for a place."

—*Knight Ridder Newspapers*

WILEY

Wiley Publishing, Inc.

## About the Author

Educated at Amherst College and Columbia University, **Robert Ullian** is a writer whose work has appeared in publications ranging from *Esquire* and *Mademoiselle* to the *Boston Phoenix*. A recipient of a National Endowment for the Arts grant in fiction, he has taught art and writing at Hampshire College and the University of Massachusetts at Amherst and is the author of books on Venice, Bali, and Morocco, as well as coauthor of *Frommer's Israel Past & Present*.

Published by:

## Wiley Publishing, Inc.

111 River St.
Hoboken, NJ 07030-5774

ISBN 978-0-470-28969-3
Editor: Anuja Madar
Production Editor: Jonathan Scott
Cartographer: Andrew Dolan
Photo Editor: Richard Fox
Production by Wiley Indianapolis Composition Services

Front cover photo: Jerusalem: Tower of David & Jaffa Gate
Back cover photo: Red Sea, Eilat: Woman snorkeling, surrounded by sergeant major fish

For information on our other products and services or to obtain technical support, please contact our Customer Care Department within the U.S. at 800/762-2974, outside the U.S. at 317/572-3993 or fax 317/572-4002.

Wiley also publishes its books in a variety of electronic formats. Some content that appears in print may not be available in electronic formats.

Manufactured in the United States of America

5  4  3  2

# Contents

# List of Maps

## Acknowledgments

**Sadek Shweiki,** research assistant and multi-lingual translator, deserves very special gratitude. Born in Jerusalem, and educated at Hampshire College in Amherst, Massachusetts, where he majored in psychology and intercultural communication, he brings a careful understanding of Middle Eastern and Western societies to this book

I would also like to thank Patti Parson, Miki Azulay, Ilana Nadir, Sheryl Stein, Lauren Tayar, Fredi Engelberg, Judith and Chana Green, Dallal Shweiki, Patricia O'Donovan, Mike Abu Assab, Howard Isenberg, Jane Yacoubzadi, Henri Levy, Noam Bahat, Shlomo Morgon, Katherine Kopa, Su Neuman, Anas Maloul, Nomi Swartz, and Lyne, the Sophisticated Six-Year-Old (formerly the Traveling Toddler); all of whom contributed ideas, help, and enthusiasm to this edition.

Finally, I would like to thank my neighbors in Abu Tor, Jerusalem, who made me so welcome during the years I lived and worked there, and whenever I return. I hope readers of this book will find such friends in this very special land.

—Robert Ullian

## An Invitation to the Reader

In researching this book, we discovered many wonderful places—hotels, restaurants, shops, and more. We're sure you'll find others. Please tell us about them, so we can share the information with your fellow travelers in upcoming editions. If you were disappointed with a recommendation, we'd love to know that, too. Please write to:

*Frommer's Israel,* 5th Edition
Wiley Publishing, Inc. • 111 River St. • Hoboken, NJ 07030-5774

## An Additional Note

Please be advised that travel information is subject to change at any time—and this is especially true of prices. We therefore suggest that you write or call ahead for confirmation when making your travel plans. The authors, editors, and publisher cannot be held responsible for the experiences of readers while traveling. Your safety is important to us, however, so we encourage you to stay alert and be aware of your surroundings. Keep a close eye on cameras, purses, and wallets, all favorite targets of thieves and pickpockets.

---

## Other Great Guides for Your Trip:

*Frommer's Egypt*
*Frommer's Morocco*
*Frommer's Dubai*

## Frommer's Star Ratings, Icons & Abbreviations

Every hotel, restaurant, and attraction listing in this guide has been ranked for quality, value, service, amenities, and special features using a **star-rating system.** In country, state, and regional guides, we also rate towns and regions to help you narrow down your choices and budget your time accordingly. Hotels and restaurants are rated on a scale of zero (recommended) to three stars (exceptional). Attractions, shopping, nightlife, towns, and regions are rated according to the following scale: zero stars (recommended), one star (highly recommended), two stars (very highly recommended), and three stars (must-see).

In addition to the star-rating system, we also use **eight feature icons** that point you to the great deals, in-the-know advice, and unique experiences that separate travelers from tourists. Throughout the book, look for:

| | |
|---|---|
| *Finds* | Special finds—those places only insiders know about |
| *Fun Fact* | Fun facts—details that make travelers more informed and their trips more fun |
| *Kids* | Best bets for kids and advice for the whole family |
| *Moments* | Special moments—those experiences that memories are made of |
| *Overrated* | Places or experiences not worth your time or money |
| *Tips* | Insider tips—great ways to save time and money |
| *Value* | Great values—where to get the best deals |
| *Warning* | Warning—traveler's advisories are usually in effect |

The following **abbreviations** are used for credit cards:

| | | | | | |
|---|---|---|---|---|---|
| AE | American Express | DISC | Discover | V | Visa |
| DC | Diners Club | MC | MasterCard | | |

## Frommers.com

Now that you have this guidebook to help you plan a great trip, visit our website at **www.frommers.com** for additional travel information on more than 4,000 destinations. We update features regularly to give you instant access to the most current trip-planning information available. At Frommers.com, you'll find scoops on the best airfares, lodging rates, and car rental bargains. You can even book your travel online through our reliable travel booking partners. Other popular features include:

- Online updates of our most popular guidebooks
- Vacation sweepstakes and contest giveaways
- Newsletters highlighting the hottest travel trends
- Podcasts, interactive maps, and up-to-the-minute events listings
- Opinionated blog entries by Arthur Frommer himself
- Online travel message boards with featured travel discussions

# What's New in Israel, Jordan & Sinai

**A**s this edition of *Frommer's Israel* goes to press, tourism in Israel, Jordan, and Sinai is booming. Hundreds of thousands of travelers who for years have put off vacationing in the region have decided now is the time. Flights and hotels are fully booked, and after years of low tourism, when visitors could freewheel around the area without worrying about finding a rental car or a room, it is again necessary to plan ahead to nail down accommodations, especially your top choices in places where you really want to stay. With rooms at a premium, hotel rates have risen, and even more so for American travelers, already hit by a declining dollar. For years, Israel has held steady as a relatively affordable destination. Now, along with much of Europe, it has moved into a more expensive category.

But the Middle East travel scene is one of the most unpredictable in the world. A slight flare-up of tensions can lead to an unexpected tourism drop and a fall in prices. A major flare-up, and Israel, Jordan, and Sinai can empty of tourists as if by magic: It can take a year for prices, tourist numbers, and room occupancy to rebound.

Despite uncertainties, travelers are drawn to the region not only because of the powerful mystique of the three great Western religions—Judaism, Christianity, and Islam—but also because of the sheer beauty, variety, and magnificence to be encountered in these countries. After years without much momentum, the tourism infrastructure in Israel, Jordan, and Sinai is revamping and expanding to deal with thousands more visitors.

**PLANNING YOUR TRIP** Prices may be going up, but Israel has come up with an inexpensive, offbeat network of places to stay and things to do that give independent travelers a chance to have genuine, personal encounters with Israelis and with the land of Israel—experiences you couldn't get at any price. There's **ILH-Israel Hostels** (www.hostels-israel. com), a network of 20 unusual, quality-assured independent hostels and guesthouses across Israel, most with interesting, inventive managements that will help direct you to great local experiences. **Weekend** (www.weekend.co.il) is a website that offers all kinds of treks, nature walks, and activities throughout Israel, with coordinating, reasonably priced accommodations. The new **Jesus Trail** (www.jesustrail.com) offers a website that explains in detail beautifully planned walks that actually follow the footsteps of Jesus through the modern Galilee countryside, again with coordinating places for dining and lodging on your walking journey. The **Israel National Trail** (www. israelnationaltrail.com) provides similar, brilliantly planned information for hiking and walking throughout Israel. For more on planning your trip, see p. 49.

**GETTING THERE** **Delta Airlines** (www.delta.com), which a few years ago began direct service to Tel Aviv from its hub in Atlanta, began direct nonstop service from New York to Tel Aviv in 2008. At the same time, **El Al,** the national airline of Israel, announced a new cooperation/code-sharing agreement with **American Airlines** that will allow travelers to reach almost any major city in the U.S. on a single, cheaper ticket. With airline seats to Israel harder to nail down, **Air Canada,** an underused airline on the North America–Israel route, offering direct flights from Toronto to Tel Aviv, has been busy upgrading its cabins (and its business-class service, which was lagging when I last traveled from Israel on Air Canada in 2005). For travelers from the western half of the U.S., an Air Canada routing to Tel Aviv via Toronto can be an excellent option. For travelers from the U.K., a new choice of bargain, no-frill flights to Israel is in the offing, although scheduled airlines as of press time are opposing these initiatives.

**SETTLING INTO JERUSALEM**  For decades, Israel's moderate price-range hotels have been generally colorless, generic, and worn, with staffs that find it hard to crack a smile. Now, just in time for the U.S. dollar crunch, the Atlas hotels (www.atlas.co.il), a moderately priced Israeli hotel chain that has always been a cut above the competition, has really taken off. In 2008, Atlas's newly constructed 50-room **Harmony Hotel** (© 02/621-9999) opened its doors on the quaint Yoel Salomon Pedestrian Mall, right in the heart of downtown West Jerusalem. With spanking-new rooms, double-glazed windows, and a happy hour with complimentary wine and snacks each day, it promises a lively alternative to the five-star choices. Also in 2008, Dan Hotels (www.danhotels.com), the largest Israeli hotel chain, normally specializing in more expensive properties, opened its sparkling new **Dan Boutique**

Hotel (© 02/568-9999), a moderately priced choice with a rooftop deck overlooking the Old City. In East Jerusalem, the East Jerusalem YMCA has completely reconstructed its formerly institutional in-house hotel into a new midprice-range option, the comfortable and charmingly decorated **Legacy Hotel** at the East Jerusalem YMCA (© 02/627-0800; www.jerusalemlegacy.com). As hotel rooms fill up in West Jerusalem, more travelers for whom an Israeli atmosphere is not important will find themselves turning to places in East Jerusalem, where a number of hotels have been busy redecorating and updating.

Among the best of the new restaurants in the upper-moderate price range, you'll find the eclectic, surprising **Chakra** (© 02/625-2733), on Shlomzion HaMalka Street, a formerly nondescript street that's become lined wall-to-wall with trendy dining spots over the past few years. New kosher dining choices include **Eldad Vesayhoo** (© 02/625-4007), which for years was a nonkosher French-style standout with great luncheon specials, and **Eucalyptus** (© 02/623-2864), with a gourmet menu of traditional home-style Jerusalem recipes. **1868 Café** (© 02/672-5366) is a new near-gourmet dairy restaurant in a charming South Jerusalem location, serving fine fish, dairy meals, and wonderful desserts.

**EXPLORING JERUSALEM**  Much of the **Israel Museum** (www.imj.org.il) will be closed for renovations through 2009, but some parts of the museum complex will remain open to visitors, and some of the museum's collection will be exhibited at other venues in Jerusalem. Check the museum's website to see what's open and where.

The **Temple Mount/Haram Es Sharif** in Jerusalem's Old City, containing the magnificent Dome of the Rock and the

> **Warning    The West Bank**
>
> The West Bank, which includes the historic biblical towns of Bethlehem, Jericho, Hebron, and Nablus (biblical Shechem), is closed to Israeli visitors, and most Western governments have advised their citizens not to visit the area until the political situation improves. As a result, we do not cover the region in this book. Despite warnings, some travelers continue to visit the Church of the Nativity (birthplace of Jesus) in Bethlehem, mainly on organized Christian tours led by guides who are familiar with border crossing and security problems. At press time, the situation in other parts of the West Bank was so chaotic and unpredictable that virtually no tourists risked traveling there. In many cases, foreign insurance policies do not cover people traveling in areas where government travel warnings have been issued.

Al Aqsa Mosque (the third-holiest place of prayer in Islam), is open to visitors for 2 to 3 hours Sunday to Thursday mornings, and often for 1 hour Sunday to Thursday afternoons. For the latest information on visiting hours at this monumental site, check with Tourist Information. Since 2000, tourists have not been permitted to enter the Dome of the Rock or the Al Aqsa, but this situation may change during the time span of this edition.

For more on sightseeing in Jerusalem, see chapter 6, "Exploring Jerusalem."

**TEL AVIV**    Here the moderate-range Atlas Hotels (www.atlas.co.il) are really taking off with a series of properties that offer a bit of style and personality as well as helpful staffs. The Art Deco **Hotel Cinema** at Dizengoff Square (© 03/520-7100), built into a long-closed Bauhaus-style movie house, is probably Israel's most enticingly designed midrange hotel. Just next door, Atlas has freshly renovated its **Center Hotel** (© 03/526-6100), with a design theme reflecting Tel Aviv's Bauhaus architecture and a running video about the city's architectural history playing in the lobby. Not only that, but the Center Hotel lends complimentary bicycles to its guests for exploring around town. Atlas's pride, the **Melody Hotel**

(© 03/521-5300), across from the beachfront Tel Aviv Hilton, was totally renovated in 2007–08, and now sports designer rooms, a rooftop lounge deck, and the complimentary happy hour that now marks many of the Atlas properties. Atlas will open a new art-themed budget/moderate hotel, the **Art Hotel,** on Ben-Yehuda Street, a block from the beach, during the time span of this edition, and is busy upgrading its other Tel Aviv properties.

**Tel Aviv's restaurant scene** continues to offer stellar, world-class choices. The most dazzling new entry into the galaxy of luxury-level eateries is **Catit** (© 03/510-7001), where Chef Meir Adoni has created one of the richest, most lavish menus Israel has ever seen. **Goocha** (© 03/522-2886), a lively place specializing in tasty fish and seafood, wins my vote as the best new moderately priced restaurant, with branches on Dizengoff Street near the hotel district and on Ibn Givrol Street. The most important new development on the Tel Aviv dining scene is the formerly derelict, but now booming, **Old Tel Aviv Port,** which has become a nightly festival of promenading Tel Avivians exploring restaurants, bars, shops, and bakeries—many overlooking the sea. New places are constantly opening here, and the vast compound now hosts an interesting Friday flea market that's become a Tel Aviv institution. There are security checks at the entrances to the port area.

For other accommodations and dining choices in Tel Aviv, check out chapter 7.

**THE GOLDEN COAST**  The Roman and Crusader ruins of Caesarea are host to an ever-increasing number of fine restaurants overlooking the sea, where you can dine and enjoy the romantic ruins after 6pm, when the park at Caesarea officially closes. There are kosher and nonkosher choices. **Helena** (© 04/610-1018) is the best of the top-notch Caesarea choices: It's an elegant seafood restaurant with fabulous vistas, and has recently installed Amos Sion, one of the best young chefs in Israel, to oversee its kitchen. In Akko, the lovely, midrange boutique **Akkotel** (© 04/987-7100), built into a restored Old City mansion,

makes it possible to overnight with style in this picturesque walled city by the sea.

See chapter 8 for more information on accommodations, dining, and sightseeing options on the Golden Coast.

**JORDAN**  Sleepy Aqaba is now accumulating a luxury hotel scene. The new **Mövenpick Aqaba Hotel** (© 03/203-4020 in Jordan) is the most luxurious place to stay in Aqaba, but the neighboring new **Aqaba Intercontinental** (© 03/209-2222 in Jordan) is a very close second. Although they're luxury hotels, rates here are low compared to those in comparable Eilat hotels. With the addition of a new beachfront Marriott, Aqaba is becoming an increasingly good option for travelers looking for a day or two of seaside rest en route to or from Petra in southern Jordan.

See chapter 12, "A Side Trip to Petra," for the full details on this region.

# 1

# The Best of Israel, Jordan & Sinai

**A** journey to Israel is a journey to a place where the past and present call out to travelers in astonishing ways. There are layers of meaning everywhere you turn in this intense land, and why not? The history and legends of this country lie at the very heart of Western civilization's consciousness.

Israel is amazingly dramatic and diverse, the more so when you realize the entire country is the size of New Jersey. When you find yourself in the silent, haunting desertscape near The Dead Sea, spotting ibexes on sheer cliffs that are dotted with caves like those in which the Dead Sea Scrolls lay hidden for more than 18 centuries, it can be hard to believe that less than 60 minutes away is the 19th-century East European ghetto world of Jerusalem's Orthodox Mea Shearim quarter. A few blocks away from Mea Shearim you'll find the labyrinthine medieval Arab bazaars of the Old City, with ancient church bells and calls to prayer from the city's minarets punctuating your wanderings. Hop into a sherut (shared taxi) to Tel Aviv on downtown Jerusalem's Jaffa Road, and in less than an hour you're in a world of white skyscrapers, surfboards, and bikinis on the beach, with the Mediterranean lapping at your feet. Two hours to the north, and you can be exploring ruined Crusader castles in the green forests of the Galilee mountains.

As a visitor and long-term resident, I have had the opportunity to see Israel from a number of different perspectives. Thirty-five years ago, the country was an austere, no-frills society—Israelis lived with few luxuries, and the spartan life was part of the national ideology. Today, Israeli society is frenetically inventive, the country's economy is booming, the standard of living has skyrocketed, and many surveys rank Israel's per capita income among the top 20 in the world. Israel is becoming a nation with a lively sense of style and a taste for the good life. Luxury and better-quality hotel accommodations and resorts have popped up all over the country, and visitors will find an interesting array of fine restaurants and shopping opportunities geared to Israeli society at large rather than to visitors. With the Israeli-Jordanian and Israeli-Egyptian peace treaties, a journey to Israel can also easily include an excursion to the fabulous ancient Nabatean city of Petra in Jordan, or a diving or snorkeling odyssey off the Sinai Peninsula. But amid Israel's busy swirl of exoticism, ancient sites, shopping malls, and crowded highways, you can still find young, idealistic kibbutzim and communities in the Negev, where new immigrants and old-timers are reclaiming the land from the desert as they learn how to live on it, appreciate its wonders, and make it truly their own.

This book will help direct you, as an independent traveler, to some of the best and most authentic experiences Israel has to offer. Israel is an easy country to explore and get close to if you know the ropes. I hope to lead you to experiences that will be both personal and rewarding.

## 1  The Best Travel Experiences

- **Visiting the Dome of the Rock and the Temple Mount** (Jerusalem): Built by the early Islamic rulers of Jerusalem in A.D. 691 on the site of the Temple of Solomon, the Dome of the Rock is one of the most beautiful structures ever created. It is the crown upon a 4,000-year tradition of Western monotheistic belief. One can spend hours on the Temple Mount soaking up the atmosphere and the dazzling views. You might first visit the Temple Mount on a tour, but come back and experience the power of this extraordinary place on your own. See p. 173.

- **Journeying into the Past at Mea Shearim:** Mea Shearim is the Hassidic Jewish quarter of Jerusalem, little more than a century old, but in the dress and customs of its inhabitants and in its tangle of courtyards and alleyways, it is a miraculously surviving fragment of the world of Eastern European Jewry that disappeared forever into the Holocaust. A visitor to Mea Shearim may feel like a dreamer wandering the past. Many visitors will revere the strict discipline and religious devotion evident in Mea Shearim; others will be troubled by its many constraints. But a walk through these streets will give you insight into the powerful traditions that continue to make Israel unique. See p. 205.

- **An Evening Stroll through Old Jaffa:** The beautifully restored Casbah of Old Jaffa is probably the most romantic urban spot in the country, filled with galleries, shops, cafes, restaurants, and vistas of minarets and Crusader ruins set against the sunset and the sea. See p. 276.

- **Exploring the Eastern Shore of the Sea of Galilee:** The Sea of Galilee is Israel's greatest natural treasure, and its lyrical shores were the birthplace of Christianity. It is also almost miraculous in its loveliness—a sapphire/turquoise freshwater lake surrounded by the mountains of the Galilee and the Golan. The eastern shore is less developed and gives you a better chance to feel the lake's poetry. There are eucalyptus-shaded beaches where you can have a late afternoon swim and picnic and watch the silver-and-lavender twilight descend behind the mountains on the western shore of the lake, which sparkles with the lights of farm settlements and kibbutzim. See chapter 10.

- **Freewheeling in the Galilee:** This is the place to rent a car for a few days and explore Israel's most beautiful countryside—forested mountains, rushing streams, waterfalls, and oceans of wildflowers in late winter and early spring. Among the region's treasures are ruined Roman-era synagogues, Crusader castles, ancient churches, and the walled Casbah of Akko beside the Mediterranean. There are also the warm, sparkling waters of the Sea of Galilee to swim in from April to early November. See chapter 10.

- **Touching the Desert:** These are not just endless sandy wastes; the deserts of Israel encompass the unworldly and ethereal Dead Sea; the mysterious, abandoned Nabatean cities of Avdat and Shivta; the haunting fortress of Masada; canyon oases; and vast erosion craters that are geological encyclopedias of past eons. These landscapes were the crucible in which monotheism was born. Don't let the desert be just a 45-minute ride to The Dead Sea on a tour bus from Jerusalem. If you can, spend the night at

# Israel

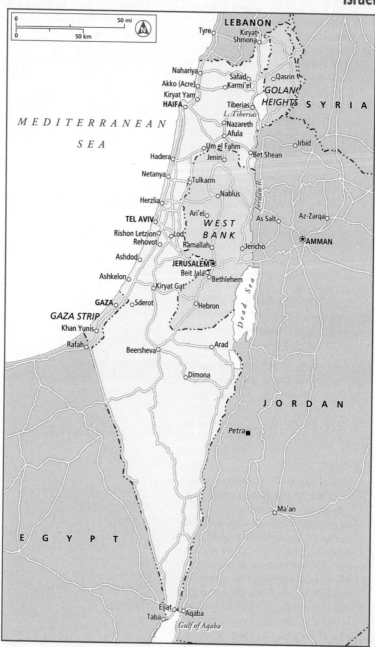

the guesthouse at the base of Masada before you make the ascent at dawn. Camp overnight in the dramatic Ramon Crater, or visit one of the inventive, idealistic Negev/Arava Valley kibbutzim. See chapter 11.

- **Snorkeling in the Red Sea:** The Red Sea, with its coral reefs, is an awe-inspiring natural aquarium. Rich with tropical marine life, it's one of the best places on earth for scuba diving and snorkeling. At the Coral Beach Nature Reserve just south of Eilat, there's enough to fascinate experts, yet wonders are accessible to all levels of swimmers—dazzling fish abound even in waist-deep water. Experienced divers can scuba dive at the Coral Island, a few miles down the coast from Eilat, or make an excursion into the Egyptian Sinai to the even more extraordinary reefs off Nuweiba, Dahab, and the legendary Ras Mohamed at Sharm el Sheik. See chapter 11.
- **Sampling the Music Scene:** Israel has an oversupply of magnificent musicians; even suburbs of Tel Aviv and small cities such as Beersheva are home to orchestras that would be the envy of many world capitals. You may find the Israel Philharmonic Orchestra performing at Tel Aviv's Mann Auditorium, or the acclaimed Rishon-Le-Zion Symphony Orchestra giving a visiting concert at the Haifa Auditorium. But also look out for an outdoor performance of *Carmen* in the Valley of the Sultan's Pool, just at the foot of the walls of Jerusalem; a night of Mozart at the 2,000-year-old Roman amphitheater beside the sea at Caesarea; Yemenite wedding singers or Arabic oudists performing at free municipal concerts inside Jerusalem's Jaffa Gate; Israeli African-American blues and jazz musicians at clubs in Tel Aviv; or festivals such as the Chamber Music Days at Kibbutz Kfar Blum, the Red Sea Jazz Festival in Eilat, or the Jacob's Ladder Folk Festival held each summer in the Galilee.

## 2 The Most Evocative Ancient Sites

People come to Israel to touch the past. The events that occurred here in ancient times and the stories and legends that arose in Israel are firmly planted in the minds of more than a billion people throughout the world.

- **City of David:** Now the Arab village of Silwan (in the Bible, Siloam), this is the oldest part of Jerusalem, located on a ridge that slopes downhill just south of the present Old City. David, Solomon, and the prophets walked here. By late Roman times, warfare had advanced to the point where this area was too low to be easily defended and it was left outside the walls of Jerusalem. The ancient gardens of Siloam inspired the *Song of Songs*. Now an overgrown orchard of fig and pomegranate trees, watered by the same Gihon Spring that was used by the prophets to anoint the kings of Judah, the gardens still stand at the foot of modern-day Silwan. The City of David is best visited on an organized tour or with a guide. See p. 213.
- **Northwest Shore of the Sea of Galilee:** This enchantingly lovely corner of the lake, in many ways the birthplace of one of the world's great religions, was the landscape of Jesus' ministry. Centering on the ruins of Capernaum (once a fishing town, and the site of St. Peter's house), and Tabgha, where the multitudes were fed with the Miracle of the Loaves and the Fishes, the shoreline is dominated by the Mount of Beatitudes.

Churches and archaeological excavations mark the locations of New Testament events. See chapter 11.

- **Bar'am Synagogue:** In the northern Galilee, near the Lebanese border, this is the best-preserved and perhaps most beautiful of the many ruined synagogues of antiquity. Built in the 4th century A.D., it was once the centerpiece of a small town in the breathtaking wooded mountains of this northern region. See p. 407.
- **Masada:** Located on an almost inaccessible mesa/plateau high above the shores of The Dead Sea, Herod built this legendary palace fortress in about 10 B.C. In A.D. 73, more than 75 years after Herod's death, it became the final stronghold of the First Revolt against Rome. Here the last Jews to live under their own rule (until the creation of the State of Israel in 1948) committed suicide on the eve of their conquest by Roman armies. Even without the drama of Masada's last stand, the site is one of haunting, audacious magnificence. See p. 444.

## 3 The Most Important Holy Places

The great sacred sites all possess extraordinary power, mystery, and beauty, at least partly conveyed upon them by centuries, if not millennia, of reverence. The ownership and histories of Israel's holy places are often a matter of contention and debate, not only among the three great monotheistic religions, but also among sects within these religions. These listings are in the order in which they appear in this book.

- **The Western Wall** (Jerusalem): Part of a vast retaining wall built by Herod around the Temple Mount, this is the most visible structure remaining from the Second Temple complex. Judaism's great legacy to the world is spiritual, but the massive stones of the Wall, each with its perfectly carved border, are testimony to the physical grandeur of the ancient Jewish world. Over the centuries, this enduring fragment of The Temple complex has come to symbolize the indestructible attachment of the Jewish people to the land of Israel. For more than 1,000 years, under Islamic governments, the Wall was the closest point that Jews were permitted to approach to the place where the ancient Temple of Jerusalem once stood. Because of the sanctity of the Temple Mount itself, very observant Jews do not go farther than the Wall to this day. See p. 172.
- **Dome of the Rock** (Jerusalem): A gloriously beautiful Islamic shrine, built in A.D. 691, covers the rock believed to have been the altar or foundation stone of the First and Second Temples. According to Jewish tradition, the rock was the altar upon which Abraham prepared to sacrifice Isaac; Islamic tradition holds that it was Abraham's first son, Ishmael, the father of the Arabic people, whom Abraham was called upon to sacrifice, either at this rock or at Mecca. The rock is also believed to have been the point from which the Prophet Mohammed ascended to glimpse heaven during the miraculous night journey described in the 17th Sura of the Koran. See p. 173.
- **Al Aqsa Mosque** (Jerusalem): On the southernmost side of the Temple Mount, built in A.D. 720, this is the third-most-important Muslim place of prayer after Mecca and Medina. See p. 174.
- **Church of the Holy Sepulcher** (Jerusalem): Christianity's holiest place, this church covers the traditional sites of the crucifixion, entombment, and

## Tips  Important but (Currently) Off-Limits Sites

Two very important religious sites in Israel are set in the chaotic West Bank. At press time this is an area for which the U.S. State Department has issued the highest warning against visiting (and we subsequently do not review anything in this area inside this book). Check the State Department website before you head out, and do not attempt to visit the following spots unless the warning has been lifted.

The **Tomb of the Patriarchs** in Hebron, on the West Bank, is the burial place of Abraham, Isaac, and Jacob, as well as their wives, Sarah, Rebecca, and Leah (Rachel, the second wife of Jacob, is buried in Bethlehem). It's surrounded by massive walls built by King Herod, and venerated by both Jews and Muslims. Rights to this place are a point of bitter contention between the Islamic and Jewish worlds.

The **Church of the Nativity** in Bethlehem marks the site of Jesus' birthplace. It is the oldest surviving church in the Holy Land; the Persians spared it during their invasion in A.D. 614 because, according to legend, they were impressed by a representation of the Magi (fellow Persians) that decorated the building.

resurrection of Jesus. Built about A.D. 330, the complex is carefully divided among the Greek Orthodox, Roman Catholic, Armenian Orthodox, Coptic, Syrian, and Ethiopian churches. See p. 181.

- **Mount of Olives** (Jerusalem): Overlooking the Old City of Jerusalem from the east, the mount offers a sweeping vista of the entire city. Here, Jesus wept at a prophetic vision of Jerusalem lying in ruins; in the Garden of Gethsemane, on the lower slope of the mount, Jesus was arrested; and the ridge of the Mount of Olives is the place from which, according to tradition, Jesus ascended to heaven. An encampment site for Jewish pilgrims in ancient times, the Mount of Olives contains Judaism's most important graveyard. See p. 209.
- **Baha'i Gardens** (Akko): At the northern edge of Akko, this site marks the tomb of the founder and

prophet of the Baha'i faith, Baha' Allah. As such, it is the holiest place for members of the Baha'i faith. See p. 319.

- **Baha'i Shrine & Gardens** (Haifa): The shrine was built to memorialize the remains of one of the Baha'i faith's martyrs, Bab Mirza Ali Muhammad, who was executed by Persian authorities in 1850. See p. 345.
- **Mount Sinai** (Sinai Peninsula, Egypt): Controversy still rages over which of the Sinai's mountains is the true site where the Ten Commandments were given to Moses, but the traditional identification of Mount Sinai is very ancient. An isolated Byzantine monastery at the foot of the mountain adds to the mysterious aura. The view from the top of Mount Sinai at dawn is among the most awe-inspiring sights you will ever see. See p. 481.

## 4  The Best Lost Ancient Cities

Israel and neighboring Jordan are filled with ruins of lost, ancient cities from every part of their long histories. In Herodian-Roman times, the population of Judea and the Galilee may have been around three million. Almost 2 millennia of wars, religious rivalries, persecutions, and misgovernment drove the population down to less than half a million by the start of the 19th century. Even knowledge of the location of many ancient sites was forgotten. Now, dazzling physical monuments to the past are being recovered at a rapid pace.

- **Caesarea** (on the coast between Tel Aviv and Haifa): Built by Herod as the great harbor and seaport of his kingdom, this was the splendid administrative capital of Roman Palestine. There are vast impressive ruins of the Roman city (including two theaters), as well as of the Crusader-era city, made all the more romantic by the waves lapping at the ancient stones. Caesarea was an important Byzantine Christian city, but it is not a biblical site. See p. 302.
- **Zippori** (Sepphoris, near Nazareth): Though not an overly dramatic site, this cosmopolitan Jewish-Hellenistic city, close to Nazareth, was the capital of the Galilee in Roman and Talmudic times. Especially interesting because it may have been familiar to Jesus, Zippori's highlights include a colonnaded street; a mosaic synagogue floor depicting the zodiac; and the beautiful mosaic portrait of a woman dubbed "the Mona Lisa of the Galilee," recently discovered in a late Roman-era villa. See p. 362.
- **Megiddo** (Armageddon, about 32km/20 miles southeast of Haifa): This town stood in the path of invading armies from ancient to modern times. It is an encyclopedia of Near

Eastern archaeology, with more than 20 levels of habitation from 5000 B.C. to A.D. 400 having been discovered here. Among the newest discoveries here are the detailed mosaic floor of a Byzantine-era church—perhaps the earliest building specifically designed as a church ever discovered. The famous ancient water tunnel of Megiddo, dug from inside the fortified town to the source of water outside the walls in the 9th century B.C., is a miracle of ancient engineering. See p. 367.

- **Korazim** (Galilee): A Roman-Byzantine–era Jewish town in the hills just northeast of the Sea of Galilee, this is a beautiful place, with sweeping views of the water. Portions of ruins still stand. A black basalt synagogue, with beautifully carved detailing, and some surrounding houses, also of local black basalt, give a good idea of what the more than 100 towns once located in this area must have been like. See p. 388.
- **Gamla** (Golan Heights): Little remains of this small Roman-era Jewish city located on a dramatic ridge in the Golan Heights. This site has a story chillingly similar to that of Masada—but the number of dead was far greater. In A.D. 67, at the beginning of the First Jewish Rebellion against Rome, Gamla was overrun by Roman soldiers, and as many as 9,000 townspeople flung themselves from the cliff, choosing death over subjugation. This dramatic site is especially beautiful amid late-winter wildflowers and waterfalls. A ruined synagogue, one of the few that can be dated from the Second Temple period, survives and is a good place for contemplation. See p. 419.

- **Bet Shean** (Jordan Valley): This place has been continuously inhabited for the past 6,000 years. A vast, Roman-Byzantine city with colonnaded streets and a theater that could house 5,000 people once stood here, although by the 19th century, Bet Shean was a small village. Remnants of earlier civilizations can be seen on the ancient *tel* (Hebrew for a mound composed of layers of cities) above the Roman ruins. See p. 421.

- **Petra** (Jordan): One of the great wonders of the world, yet forgotten for almost a thousand years, this legendary 2,000-year-old Nabatean city carved from the walls of a hidden desert canyon is now the highlight of excursion tours into Jordan from Israel. The entire Petra experience, including the trek into the canyon, has an air of adventure and mystery—especially if you plan 1 or 2 nights (or more) at Petra and give yourself time to get a feel for the place early in the morning and in the evening, before the hordes of visitors arrive. Petra and other treasures in Jordan are easily accessible from Israel by tour or independent travel arrangements. See chapter 12.

## 5 The Best Nature & Outdoor Experiences

Israel's diverse landscapes and unusual natural phenomena provide opportunities for interesting outdoor pursuits, many of which you might never have thought of in connection with a trip here.

- **Digging for a Day:** Joining an archaeological dig as a volunteer requires a definite commitment of time, money, and backbreaking labor. However, you can often arrange to dig for a day and get a close-up look at the hard work and thrills involved in bringing so much of Israel's history to light. Contact the Municipal Tourist Information Office in Jerusalem for current options. The digging season is during the dry summer months. See p. 85.

- **Hiking to Gamla:** A beautiful trail throughout the year, in late winter this 1- to 2-hour hike in the Golan takes you past wildflowers, streams, and waterfalls. The reward at the end of the trail is the dramatic ruined city of Gamla (see "The Best Lost Ancient Cities," above). The countryside is also dotted with prehistoric dolmens and Stone Age tombs. This walk brings you into contact with nature, archaeology, and a very moving piece of Israeli history. Plan additional time for the return walk, although a shorter trail is also available. See p. 419.

- **Camel Trekking in the Ramon Crater** (Negev): In the Negev Highlands, near Mitzpe Ramon, this geological encyclopedia can be visited on a speedy, bone-dismantling jeep tour or on a rather arduous hike. Or you can experience the mysterious quiet of the desert as you explore the crater accompanied by a guide, with a camel to carry your water and equipment. This traditional approach to trekking can be arranged for a variety of itineraries as well as for overnight camping and Bedouin-style cookouts. Travel agencies in Mitzpe Ramon can set it up for you at reasonable prices. See p. 451.

- **Diving and Snorkeling the Reefs of Eilat:** The Red Sea coral reefs are among the most interesting and easily accessible in the world; anyone who can swim even moderately well can snorkel and enjoy the underwater scene. Eilat is home to a number of diving schools offering short- and long-term programs, plus classes in underwater photography. Once you've seen the coral reef just off the shores of southern Eilat, you can graduate to a dive cruise of the more extensive reefs of the Coral Island. See p. 462.

- **Diving at Dahab** (Sinai Peninsula): Just across the border from Eilat are the Sinai Peninsula's extraordinary reefs and clear, light-filled waters. Reefs teeming with exotic marine life extend all the way down the coast; perhaps the most famous is the suicidal

Blue Hole, off the town of Dahab (but not recommended by this book). At the southernmost tip of Sinai, just beyond the resort center at Sharm el Sheik, is the reefy paradise of the Egyptian National Park at Ras Mohamed. Diving schools in Eilat and good Eilat travel agents and discounters can arrange diving-package excursions to Sinai. See p. 483.

## 6 The Best Beaches

Israel's four seas (the Mediterranean, the Sea of Galilee, The Dead Sea, and the Red Sea) offer an amazing variety of swimming experiences. The beaches of Israel look beautiful, but be careful about going in the water. Unusually strong riptides, whirlpools, and undertows along the Mediterranean coast can claim the strongest swimmer. Never swim in unguarded areas. Along much of the coast, especially north of Tel Aviv, the beaches seem sandy, but a few steps into the surf, and you're standing on a rocky shelf—not a good place to be when waves come crashing down. Pollution is also a serious problem, as it is throughout the Mediterranean. Israel's beach standards are much higher than those of most Mediterranean countries, but on many days, garbage from other countries swirls along the coast. At Nahariya, Akko, and the Poleg Nature Reserve (8km/5 miles south of Netanya), which have no sewage-treatment plants, I would hesitate to put a toe, no less my head, in the water. Expect beaches to be lively; Israelis play compulsive paddleball on any stretch of beach they're on, regardless of sleeping sunbathers in the line of fire. And watch out for sea urchins and stinging coral in the Red Sea and the burning medusas (jellyfish) that attack the Mediterranean beaches in July.

- **Gordon Beach** (Tel Aviv): Perhaps the most accessible place to sample

the Mediterranean, this free municipal beach has showers and a friendly mix of Israelis, new Russian immigrants, and tourists from luxury hotels. There are nearby places to take a break for a snack or meal, the sand is passably clean, and when the tide is clear, the beach is a pleasure. See p. 278 for more on the city's beaches.

- **Aqueduct Beach** (just north of Caesarea): An ancient Roman aqueduct gives this beach its name and travel-poster ambience. There are no showers or amenities except on summer weekends, when vendors sell drinks and snacks. Not good for swimming if the water is rough, but on calm days, as you float in the Mediterranean and gaze at the romantic ruins, you know it's not Blackpool or the Jersey Shore. See p. 305.

- **Ein Gev Resort Village Beach** (Sea of Galilee): The freshwater Sea of Galilee is warm and cleansing, spiritually as well as physically. You have to be a guest at the Ein Gev Resort Village to be allowed to use the beach here, but it's the prettiest one on the lake, with a date palm grove and thick lawns stretching down to the water, which is relatively free of foot-stubbing rocks. Just to the south of Ein Gev are several miles of eucalyptus-shaded beaches along the road (in summer there's a parking fee); they're rockier underwater, but very pleasant when not crowded with weekenders. Late afternoon often brings real breakers to the eastern shore of the lake; twilight here is soft and magical. See p. 391.

- **Ein Gedi Beach** (Dead Sea): Everyone should experience swimming in The Dead Sea, the amazing body of water at the lowest point on the face of the earth. Extremely high salt content makes you feel like a cork. and it's impossible to keep much of yourself underwater. The mineral-rich sea is believed to be therapeutic, but will sting any cuts on your skin, and if you stay in too long, you'll be pickled. Ein Gedi Beach offers freshwater showers as well as a cafe. Even in winter a desert dip may be possible. See p. 442.

- **Coral Beach Nature Reserve** (Eilat): The nature reserve has staked out a strip of beach alongside Eilat's best reefs. Here you can snorkel among dazzling fish and coral formations,

and even take interesting scuba expeditions. Snorkeling gear is for rent, and there are showers and changing areas. Not good for ordinary swimming—you must beware of burning coral and spiny sea urchins. See p. 460.

- **Dolphin Reef Beach** (Eilat): A good choice for everyday swimming in the Red Sea, Dolphin Reef is the most picturesque beach in Eilat, with thatched *palapas* and a resident dolphin population, free to come and go, leaping and frolicking not far from where people can swim. See p. 460.

- **Hilton Dahab Resort Beach** (Sinai Peninsula, Egypt): If you want to really beach out for a few days at a comfortable resort with a quiet, distant, end-of-the-earth ambience and views of the Arabia mountains facing you across the Red Sea, this is the place. The waters here offer good opportunities for swimming and snorkeling. See p. 483.

## 7 The Best Museums

Israel's museums are relatively new, innovative, and interactive. They display the discoveries of the past, of the self, and of nationhood that are happening so intensively every day in Israeli society. The most interesting museums are those that could only be found in Israel.

- **Israel Museum** (Jerusalem): Although it only opened in 1965, in 4 decades the Israel Museum has made its place on the world museum map. Its greatest treasures are beautifully exhibited and include a number of the Dead Sea Scrolls; a dazzling, all-encompassing collection of archaeological finds from Israel; a vast treasury of world Judaica and costumes; and excellent collections of primitive, pre-Columbian, European, and modern art.

There's also an enticing Children's Wing. Much of the museum will be closed for renovation through 2009. See p. 196.

- **L. A. Mayer Memorial Museum of Islamic Art** (Jerusalem): An undervisited treasure with an excellent collection of Islamic and Middle Eastern art, clocks, and well-chosen special and visiting exhibitions. See p. 198.

- **Sir Isaac and Lady Edith Wolfson Museum** (Jerusalem): Right in the heart of Jerusalem, this little-known gem consists of a large but intimate private collection of Judaica from all over the world. It is exhibited on the fourth floor of Heichal Shlomo, the Great Synagogue complex on King George Street. See p. 198.

- **Yad VaShem Memorial and Holocaust Museum** (Jerusalem): This large complex is a memorial to the six million Jews killed by the Nazis during World War II. A major focus of the complex is the new (2005) museum. Here, in ways that put a human face on the staggering numbers of victims, the history of the Holocaust is traced using actual film footage, videos of personal interviews with survivors, historical documents, artifacts, and personal items—some donated by survivors and accompanied by stories of unimaginable heartbreak. Other parts of the complex include an archive that gathers and stores information about individual victims, memorial structures, gardens, and commemorative installations. No visitor can leave here unaffected. See p. 199.

- **Bet Hatfutzot/Diaspora Museum** (Tel Aviv): Not a museum in terms of displaying actual genuine artifacts, Bet Hatfutzot is rather a vast ensemble of multimedia exhibits that illustrate the histories of Jewish communities throughout the world. It's fascinating and fun, and the special visiting exhibitions are always worthwhile. See p. 269.

- **Eretz Israel Museum** (Tel Aviv): This museum covers many aspects of the land of Israel, including its natural history, flora and fauna, archaeology, folklore, and traditional crafts. Highlights include a bazaar filled with craftspeople demonstrating skills from antiquity such as glass blowing, olive pressing, weaving, and pottery making; an extraordinary collection of ancient glass; and excavations of a *tel* (ancient mound) located right on the grounds of the museum. See p. 272.

- **Tel Aviv Museum of Art** (Tel Aviv): Notable for strong collections of Israeli and contemporary European (including Russian) art, as well as its Jaglom Collection of Impressionist and post-Impressionist art. There is a lively program of public events, performances, and special exhibitions. See p. 273.

## 8 The Best Luxury Hotels

The hotel scene in Israel is presently in the process of a change. After 6 years of a tourism slump, when almost no hotels were renovated or rooms redone, tourists are returning, and with them, carpenters, plumbers, and decorators to brighten establishments that had become worn and shabby. During the time span of this edition, many hotels we've described as needing to redecorate will probably do so. International chains have been better at keeping up standards and have already begun ambitious renovation programs. Although new hotel construction has been at a standstill in Israel since 2000, these plans are ready to go forward if the quiet security situation continues to hold. Inside Israel, hotel rates are beginning to rise in response to higher demand. In Jordan and Sinai, you'll find wonderful new hotels with rooms still going at bargain rates.

- **David Citadel Hotel** (Jerusalem; ℭ 02/621-1111). Rival to the King David (see below), this newest luxury hotel in Jerusalem is architecturally interesting, lively, and offers excellent food services, including a great sushi bar. Most of the light, modern rooms offer Old City views. See p. 126.

- **King David Hotel** (Jerusalem; ℭ 02/620-8888): Built in 1930 during the British Mandate, the King David has outlasted the British Empire and continues to sail on; it's elegant and up-to-date in every way. The Nubian, fez-adorned lobby attendants of the 1930s are no longer here, but the King David is thick with atmosphere and ambience, and VIPs from Henry Kissinger to Barbra Streisand seem to pop up here. The gardened swimming pool and views of the walls of the Old City are a real plus. See p. 126.

- **American Colony Hotel** (Jerusalem; © **02/627-9777**): This beautiful, atmospheric, gardened enclave was a 19th-century pasha's villa. As an international meeting place between the worlds of East and West Jerusalem, it attracts journalists, writers, archaeologists, and all sorts of VIPs. It's probably the most savvy, romantic spot in the Middle East. Some of the suites, furnished with antiques and traditional crafts, are as splendid as anything you'll find in the region, yet prices are comparatively reasonable. The hotel's Saturday-afternoon luncheon buffet is famous throughout the country. See p. 133.

- **Mount Zion Hotel** (Jerusalem; © **02/568-9555**): This lesser-known four-star standout features lovely gardens, interesting architecture, a large swimming pool, and the most dramatic vistas of the Old City, Himmom Valley, and the Mount of Olives of any Jerusalem hotel. See p. 131.

- **Tel Aviv Sheraton Hotel & Towers** (Tel Aviv; © **03/521-1111**): The most fun of Tel Aviv's luxury hotels—right on the beach, but steps away from the city's restaurant and gallery district—feels like an urban resort. The restaurants here are probably the best of any hotel in the country, topped off by the inventive (and kosher) **Olive Leaf** (p. 251). Mediterranean views from many of the guest rooms, complete with dazzling sunsets, are a plus, as is the very efficient business center. See p. 244.

- **Tel Aviv Hilton** (Tel Aviv; © **03/520-2240**): With an unequaled staff, business center, and CYBEX health club, the Hilton is the doyen of Tel Aviv's beachfront hotels. Suites and better-category rooms are beautifully furnished and decorated; the sheltered beach offers a resort atmosphere; and the kosher sushi bar hints at the Hilton's role as a center for business and tourism exchanges between Asia and the Middle East. See p. 248.

- **Dan Carmel Hotel** (Haifa; © **04/830-3010**): With sweeping views from its site at the top of the Carmel Range, as well as a careful staff and a relaxing, gardened pool enclave, this hotel, built in the 1960s and a bit dated for some, reigns as Haifa's best. The better guest rooms, with views of the bay, are nicely decorated and worth the extra money. Lower-category rooms still have a style that recalls the Eisenhower era. See p. 334.

- **The Scots Hotel** (Tiberias; © **04/671-0710**): With its 19th-century buildings, beautiful terraces, and gardens looking out on the Sea of Galilee, this well-run, four-star hotel seems almost like a villa on the Italian coast. Run under the auspices of the Church of Scotland, it welcomes visitors of all faiths. All rooms were totally rebuilt in 2004, but the "antique rooms" in an older building have special character. See p. 377.

- **Herods Palace Hotel Complex** (North Beach, Eilat; © **08/638-0000**): Opened in 1999, this blockbuster's public areas are the most sumptuous in Israel. With architectural touches echoing Middle Eastern traditions and staff at times costumed in "ancient" garb, the effect may seem a bit Hollywood-esque, but the gorgeous spa, the vast pool, and the excellent service are not fantasies. The Red Sea is steps away. See p. 468.

- **Four Seasons Sharm el Sheik** (Sharm el Sheik, Sinai, Egypt; ☏ 69/360-3555): This establishment is the most atmospheric and luxurious of Sinai's many new superluxury resorts. It's designed in a low-rise, garden style that suggests a whitewashed Egyptian/North African village. The Four Seasons offers rooms, suites, and private villas overlooking the Red Sea; a good snorkeling reef; diving, swimming, and snorkeling facilities; and every amenity you could want. See p. 484.
- **Mövenpick Resort Petra** (Petra, Jordan; ☏ 962-03/215-7111): Right at the entrance to Petra National Park (which makes more than one foray into Petra each day possible), the

Mövenpick is the best blend of contemporary and traditional Middle Eastern design in the region. Without being kitschy, public areas are atmospheric and exciting. The rooftop cafe at night is an easy place for travelers to meet and swap experiences under the stars. See p. 498.
- **Taybet Zaman Hotel and Resort** (Petra, Jordan; ☏ 962-03/215-0111): The stone houses and lanes of an abandoned Bedouin village in the mountains above Petra (a 20-min. drive away) have been turned into the rooms and passageways of a charming, atmospheric, quality resort. Vistas are awesome, and each room is uniquely decorated with Bedouin crafts. The village market is a shopping arcade, and local country musicians serenade at night. See p. 498.

## 9 The Best Value Hotels

This selection of hotel choices runs from splurges to economy strategies; each establishment offers something special.

- **Saint Mark's Lutheran Guest House** (Jerusalem; ☏ 02/626-8888): Beautiful, atmospheric, and immaculate, with gardens above the main Arab bazaar, this is the best possible place to stay in the Old City and one of the most remarkable little hotels in the country. See p. 121.
- **Jerusalem Inn Hotel** (Jerusalem; ☏ 02/625-2757): Just a short walk from the Old City, and 1½ blocks from Zion Square and the bustling Ben-Yehuda and Yoel Salomon malls, this small hotel offers tidy, no-frills doubles with a touch of style and excellent beds (blankets covered by duvet sheets). The management constantly upgrades rooms with new equipment, yet rates are kept reasonable for this level of quality. See p. 124.
- **YMCA Three Arches Hotel** (Jerusalem; ☏ 02/569-2692): This is in no way your average YMCA; instead, it's a respected hotel frequented by savvy travelers. You get a well-appointed double in a landmark building (designed by the same architect who created New York's Empire State Building), right across the street from the famed King David Hotel. Rooms are scheduled for updating. See p. 129.
- **Saint Andrew's Church of Scotland Guest House** (Jerusalem; ☏ 02/673-2401): With its own gardens and vistas of the Old City, this Church of Scotland hospice is one of the most dramatic vantage points in West Jerusalem. Rooms are simple but comfy, and open to guests of all faiths. Public areas are freshly renovated. See p. 132.
- **Jerusalem Hotel** (East Jerusalem; ☏ 02/628-3282): A small place run

by a well-informed, attentive family, the Jerusalem Hotel offers a pleasant garden restaurant with live music a number of times a week and a general atmosphere that makes it seem like a very affordable version of the renowned American Colony Hotel. See p. 137.

- **Hotel Cinema** (Tel Aviv; ⓒ **03/520-7100**): This new, amusingly inventive hotel, right on Dizengoff Square, is a monument to the Bauhaus and art moderne movements that are so much a part of Tel Aviv's heritage. Though it's great fun and centrally located, the Hotel Cinema is a few blocks from the beach, where most of the city's hotels are clustered. See p. 249.

- **Hotel de la Mer** (Tel Aviv; ⓒ **03/510-0011**): In a city with an oversupply of faceless medium-range hotels, this new little gem, just across the road from the beach, is a real find. The fresh, pleasant rooms are designed according to the principles of feng shui. See p. 247.

- **Ein Gev Resort Village** (Sea of Galilee; ⓒ **04/665-9800**): The Ein Gev kibbutz has bungalows, caravans, and basic doubles set amid eucalyptus and date palm groves right on the shores of the Sea of Galilee. It's a paradisiacal place to unwind and swim the warm waters of the lake. The kibbutz runs an excellent fish restaurant a mile down the road. Book this on a kibbutz package, and the price becomes very reasonable. See p. 391.

- **Vered HaGalil Guest Farm** (Galilee; ⓒ **04/693-5785**): Set in the hills a few miles north of the Sea of Galilee, this intimate, family-run place began as a simple horseback riding lodge and over 4 decades has slowly been turned into a small Garden of Eden. It offers a variety of rustic, charming accommodations and well-informed,

personal attention; you don't have to come here for riding, but if you do, the programs are probably the best in the country. See p. 393.

- **Ruth Rimon Inn** (Safed; ⓒ **04/699-4666**): In a country with few really romantic, atmospheric hotels, this inn, a collection of beautiful buildings from Ottoman times, is a winner and an example of what might be done elsewhere in the country. A stay here helps make the often-elusive magic of Safed more tangible. See p. 402.

- **Masada Guest House and Youth Hostel** (Masada; ⓒ **08/995-3222**): Right at the base of Masada, overlooking The Dead Sea, this new, beautifully designed Israel Youth Hostel Association establishment is virtually a hotel. The hostel gives you the option of overnighting in the desert and making the ascent to Masada in the cool dawn hours. See p. 448.

- **Kibbutz Ein Gedi Resort Hotel** (Kibbutz Ein Gedi, Dead Sea; ⓒ **08/659-4222**): A wonderful alternative to the big spa hotels along The Dead Sea, Ein Gedi Kibbutz is a beautiful, internationally recognized botanical garden of rare plants and trees that have been planted in a once-bleak piece of desert over the past 45 years. There are indoor and outdoor swimming pools; spectacular desert vistas; archaeological sites; and free use of the kibbutz's Dead Sea Spa and Dead Sea beach. Look for discounts on kibbutz packages. See p. 443.

- **Isrotel Ramon Inn** (Mitzpe Ramon; ⓒ **08/658-8822**): This efficient, comfortable hotel close to the wonders of the Ramon Crater opens up the interior of the Negev to travelers who do not want to stay in rudimentary accommodations. The staff will connect you to all kinds of hiking, biking, and nature activities, and the indoor swimming pool and outstanding home-style buffet are nice to come home to after a day exploring the desert. See p. 452.

- **Three Arava Valley Kibbutzim: Lotan, Yahel, and Ketura** (Arava Valley): Half an hour north of Eilat, these kibbutzim, founded largely by North Americans, are known for organic farming and inventive recycling projects. They offer wonderful programs in desert touring and ecology, a blanket of stars at night, simple accommodations, and delicious meals. Each is a paradise in it own way and a

chance for travelers to experience the vision and idealism at the heart of Israel's rebirth. See p. 455.

- **Isrotel Riviera Club** (Eilat; © 08/630-3666): A block from the beach, this informal hotel has units that can accommodate two to four people and are equipped with kitchenettes, TVs, and other useful amenities. Although not a kibbutz guesthouse, a room here can be booked as part of the Kibbutz Guest House Package (p. 90), making this the most affordable way to have nonscruffy accommodations in costly Eilat. See p. 470.

## 10  The Best Luxury Dining

Until the 1980s, it was almost considered anti-Zionist to spend money and effort on gourmet cuisine. Israel was a practical, egalitarian society, and good, healthful fresh food was all that was necessary to create a sturdy population. But people cannot live by falafel alone, and Israel has developed a group of truly fine, personal restaurants, many rooted in French tradition, but also exploring the cuisine traditions of Mediterranean cuisine.

- **Darna** (Jerusalem): Craftsmen and interior designers from Morocco were brought to Jerusalem to create this authentic, atmospheric glatt kosher restaurant that celebrates the traditions of Israel's large Moroccan Jewish population. The fine Moroccan cuisine matches the graceful service and ambience. Totally wonderful. See p. 142.
- **Canela** (Jerusalem): A chic, carefully designed, contemporary setting; a pianist at a white grand piano (Mon nights); and pampering service that includes valet parking are touches that help make this the best of the city's new crop of top-drawer kosher restaurants. The menu is Continental

and strong on meat; prices are not nearly as exorbitant as at the competition. See p. 151.

- **Arcadia** (Jerusalem): Jerusalem's most sublime French and Mediterranean restaurant offers a charming, unique setting and an ever-changing menu that's elegant and inventive without being pretentious or glitzy. See p. 154.
- **American Colony Hotel Arabesque Restaurant** (Jerusalem): The Saturday luncheon buffet in the Arabesque Restaurant is a Jerusalem tradition, with a romanticized atmosphere as well as a vast, all-you-can-eat buffet of excellent Middle Eastern and Continental choices. Sadly, this treat is only for lunch and only a once-a-week affair. See p. 133.
- **The Olive Leaf** (Tel Aviv): With an inventive menu of nouvelle cuisine that's actually hearty, filling, and prepared within the rules of kashrut, plus a view of the Mediterranean, this is the best hotel restaurant in Tel Aviv (in the Sheraton Hotel and Towers), and one of the three best kosher choices in Israel. The decor, like the

menu, is elegant without being phony or glitzy. Great luncheon deals. See p. 251.

- **Carmela Be Nachala** (Tel Aviv): Set in an antique, veranda-laden building that might have been transported from the 19th-century American South, this is a top choice for charm, ambience, and an ever-changing, inventive menu in the French/Mediterranean tradition. Half-portions are encouraged so you can sample more of the menu. See p. 255.
- **Orca** (Tel Aviv): Chef Eran Stroitman serves a constantly changing menu that's the toast of Tel Aviv, amid a marvelous 1930s art moderne setting. The downstairs bar is among the most chic in town (with amazing tapas); the restaurant's food is filling, delicious, and fascinating. See p. 256.
- **Catit** (Tel Aviv): Fabulous Chef Meir Adoni has created a menu filled with some of the richest, most lavish dishes in Tel Aviv to critical acclaim and awards. The setting is quiet and charming but not dramatic. See p. 259.
- **Cordelia** (Jaffa): Located in an eclectic and candlelit romantic Jaffa building, Cordelia is an example of food as theater and like nothing else in Israel. Chef Nir Zook's ever-changing menu is designed to surprise, amaze, shock, and usually please. See p. 266.
- **Mul Yam** (Tel Aviv): The seafood here is the freshest and most exotic in Israel, jetted in from all over the world, expertly prepared, and served in a comfortable, informal setting. Israelis love it. See p. 264.
- **Margaret Tayar's** (Jaffa): This place has an unpretentious terrace by the sea, and an internationally acclaimed chef who's a Tel Aviv legend and has won international acclaim. The prices are upper moderate, but Margaret can cook up a leisurely tasting feast

for you. See also "Best Moderate Dining," below (p. 267).
- **Yoe'ezer Wine Bar** (Jaffa): Set inside the cavernous arches of a Crusader-era building, this is a gourmand's paradise created by noted Israeli journalist and food writer Shaul Evron. Here, at your leisure, you can sample from an Elysian collection of European and Israeli wines, accompanied by wonderful breads and cheeses, or feast on a select menu of classic, richly prepared Continental cuisine. See p. 267.
- **Helena** (Caesarea): With vistas of the sea and a great young chef designing its menu, this restaurant, set amid the ruins of Caesarea, is the most romantic spot in Israel for a gourmet meal, especially when the sun sets over the Mediterranean. See p. 307.
- **Picciotto** (Zichron Yaacov): Named for its founder and former chef, an ex-fighter pilot who has moved on to the world of computers, this is a delightful Mediterranean restaurant set in a 19th-century cottage. It's not cheap, but by Israeli standards is a very good value. See p. 310.
- **Uri Buri** (Akko): Chef/owner Uri Yirmias is a man who knows where to get top-quality fish and seafood and how to prepare it, and who loves to see customers enjoying his dishes. Seaside sunsets and the ambience of Old Akko are extra pluses of this quality, informal place. See p. 320.
- **1872 Hashmura Restaurant** (Haifa): Named for the year in which the quaint stone mansion it occupies was built, this rustic French restaurant, strong on meat dishes, is an atmospheric choice for a special night out. It's also surprisingly affordable. See p. 342.
- **Decks** (Tiberias): With a setting that floats on the surface of the Sea of Galilee like a Fellini dream, Decks offers luxurious meats expertly grilled

over olive- and citrus-wood fires. As an extra, you get a complimentary post-dinner disco cruise. Decks is kosher and a great choice for a memorable evening at upper moderate prices. See p. 380.

## 11 The Best Moderate Dining

Israel is filled with interesting, affordable restaurants ranging from authentic ethnic and natural Mediterranean to kosher Indian or Mexican and gracefully inventive French. In order to be accessible to kosher diners, many Israeli restaurants offer vegetarian-only menus that are imaginative and affordable. The following is a selection of unusual choices for atmosphere, good food, and good value, but you'll find many other fabulous restaurants listed throughout this book.

- **Adom** (Jerusalem): An atmospheric old Jerusalem stone building houses a relaxed place with heavenly food and upper-moderate prices that should be higher (but don't tell them that). See p. 149.

- **Chakra** (Jerusalem): The decor here is inventive eclectic, and so is the cuisine—unique dishes created by a chef who loves spices and cooks his heart out, creating new tastes and mixing influences from all over the world. Besides the standard menu, there's a nightly tour de force of a dozen specials. See p. 152.

- **Village Green** (Jerusalem): This inexpensive vegetarian cafeteria right on Zion Square is virtually a public service, and is the best place in town for a healthy, hefty, fast meal. Lasagna, veggie pies, tasty soups, and salads by weight top the menu at this kosher L'Mehedrin restaurant. See p. 148.

- **Spaghettim** (Jerusalem): This fabulous restaurant offers a vast array of spaghettis in fantastic sauces loaded with fresh ingredients. The Jerusalem branch, set in an old Ottoman-era mansion with a delightful dining garden, is an especially romantic location, but there's also a branch in Tel Aviv. See p. 147 and 258.

- **Levan at the Cinémathèque** (Jerusalem): The view of the Old City walls from the terrace here is breathtaking, the crowd is intelligent and stylish, and the menu is very affordable. Salads, peasant sandwiches, and a good, reasonably priced pasta and fish menu are offered. In cold weather, the indoor dining room can be smoky, but in good weather, a meal or dessert on the terrace is a must. See p. 161.

- **Kohinoor** (Jerusalem): This kosher Indian restaurant provides a rare opportunity for kosher visitors to sample well-prepared Indian cuisine. The all-you-can-eat luncheon buffets are very affordable. The nonkosher Tandoori restaurants (Tel Aviv, Eilat, and Herzlia) of the same chain are equally excellent, elegant, and a good value. See p. 154.

- **Manta Ray** (Tel Aviv): On an empty stretch of beach between Tel Aviv and Jaffa, this beach pavilion is open to the sea, the sound of the waves, and the Mediterranean sunset. It serves great medleys of tapas, stylishly prepared fish and seafood, and is a good choice for breakfast or leisurely lunches and dinners. See p. 266.

- **Margaret Tayar's** (Jaffa): This is a small, authentic place a short walk from trendy Old Jaffa, with a covered terrace overlooking the sweeping Tel Aviv shoreline and a master cook who loves to see people enjoying her creations. Jaffa's fishers adore Margaret—she gets first choice of the catch. This is a one-woman tour de force whose hefty, unforced dishes (including exquisitely grilled fish) have been lionized in *Gourmet*. Always call to confirm hours. This is one of the very best restaurants in the country at any price. See p. 267.

- **Erez** (Herzlia): Erez Komarovsky has created a one-man world of contemporary Israeli cuisine served in a functional but bright, imaginative space. The entire concept draws on Israeli traditions of brashness, pragmatism, and a touch of poetry. It's always exciting, blessed with heavenly breads, and moderately priced, which makes the taxi ride up from Tel Aviv a worthwhile investment. See p. 293.

- **Abu Christo** (Old Akko): Fresh fish and a covered dining terrace right beside the sea give this restaurant a delightful Greek Island harborside ambience. You can put together a feast here, complete with Middle Eastern appetizers, for the price of a single main course elsewhere. See p. 320.

- **Ramon Inn Restaurant** (Mitzpe Ramon, Negev): This hotel restaurant serves the best food to be found from The Dead Sea to the outskirts of Eilat. The evening buffet (get there at 7pm) is filled with gently ethnic, home-style offerings. The large breakfast buffet, open to outsiders, offers exotic jams and fluffy, gourmet pita made less than a minute before it's on your plate. See p. 453.

- **Eddie's Hideaway** (Eilat): In a tourist town at the end of the earth, where most restaurants plan for customers they'll never see again, Eddie puts his heart into every meal and keeps coming up with Continental and Asian-touched menus that are delicious and inventive. See p. 474.

# 2

# Israel in Depth

To millions of Jews, Christians, and Muslims, Israel is the Holy Land where Solomon reigned in all his glory, where Jesus taught and performed miracles, and where Muhammad visited during a miraculous night journey.

Religion is the basis of Israel's political importance. Were it not for its sacred character, few people would choose to live on this narrow strip of land between the sea and desert. Jews have been living here since the time of Abraham, almost 4,000 years ago; Christianity began in the Galilee 2 millennia later. During the very early days of Islam in the 7th century A.D., before Mecca became a sacred city, the Prophet Muhammad advised Muslims to face in the direction of Jerusalem for prayers.

All three religions have battled to capture and hold the holy territory: Israelites fought Canaanites, Philistines, Assyrians, and Babylonians; Jews fought Hellenists and Romans; Byzantine Christians fought Zoroastrian Persians; and Muslim armies fought Crusaders. In the 20th century, Ottoman Turks were driven out by the British, and the British in turn were driven out by groups of Zionists and Palestinian Arabs.

Israel looms large in the great political happenings of our times. Realizing the ancient Jewish dream of a homeland and safe haven has meant the displacement of many Palestinians, which, in turn, has meant alienating the surrounding Arab countries in the already unstable Middle East. The problem of finding a truly fair solution to the many valid and conflicting claims on the Holy Land is one of the great challenges facing the Christian, Jewish, and Muslim communities in Israel and throughout the world.

## 1 The Lay of the Land

Israel is a surprisingly small country, but the land itself is remarkably varied and contains some of the earth's most unusual geological oddities. Depending on your itinerary, you are likely to find beaches; lush valleys; rugged, wooded mountains; rambling foothills; flat plains; snowcapped peaks; the hot wilderness that surrounds the mineral-saturated waters of The Dead Sea; desert regions; and the multicolored crags and crevices of the Negev. There are coral reefs teeming with rare marine life off Eilat and the Sinai Peninsula, and vast erosion craters in the Negev near Mitzpe Ramon that are geological encyclopedias

of the eons. The mineral-laden Dead Sea (in which it is impossible to sink) is by far the lowest point on the face of the earth—the dense atmosphere at this extremely low altitude is heavy with oxygen and beneficial to those with heart and respiratory problems; it also blocks some of the sun's rays and permits psoriasis sufferers to expose their skin for longer periods of time without risk of sunburn. The dramatic geology of the country also brings a varied climate. It can be a raw, cold, sleety January day in Jerusalem, in the Judean Mountains, and an hour away, at the Jordan Valley oasis of Jericho or at Ein Gedi, a canyon near The Dead Sea, it can be sunny, dry, and 75°F (24°C).

Israel is part of a land bridge connecting Africa and Asia. The below-sea-level Jordan Valley, running along the Israeli-Jordanian border, is a northern continuation of the Great Rift Valley of Eastern Africa, which runs through the Red Sea and surfaces at Eilat-Aqaba. Since prehistoric times, this has been a natural route of migration for birds, animals, and human beings. The enormously varied flora, fauna, and peoples who have come to inhabit this small region are a reflection of Israel's unique location and geological structure.

## ISRAEL TODAY

In 2008, Israel celebrated its 60th anniversary as an independent country, but its identity and future are still in the process of being shaped. The country today has fulfilled its mission of becoming a haven where persecuted Jews from all over the world can thrive, but the country's security remains at risk, and the long-term identity of Israel is still under construction. The country is nothing like it was at the time of its birth. In 1948, in the area of British Mandate Palestine that was to become Israel, there were approximately 680,000 Jewish residents and 840,000 Muslim and Christian residents. During the period of war that accompanied Israel's birth from 1948 to 1949, as many as 700,000 Palestinian Muslims and Christians fled or were expelled to the West Bank and East Jerusalem (which was occupied by Jordan) and to surrounding Arab countries. Approximately 180,000 Palestinian Christians and Muslims remained in Israel and became citizens of the newly formed state, with rights that were promised to be guaranteed in Israel's declaration of independence. At the same time, more than 300,000 Holocaust survivors in displaced persons camps throughout Europe poured into Israel, followed immediately by mass immigrations of the Jewish communities of Yemen and Iraq; and afterward by hundreds of thousands of Jews fleeing Egypt, North Africa, the former Soviet Union, and Ethiopia. The population of Israel now stands at 7,200,000: Approximately 5,400,000 Israeli citizens are Jewish; 1,450,000 are Arab Christians and Muslims; and 300,000 are of other backgrounds. In addition, in East Jerusalem, which Israel annexed in 1967, there are more than 250,000 East Jerusalem Palestinians who hold permanent Israeli resident IDs, but in most cases are not actual Israel citizens. The country is still learning how to function as a democratic, Jewish state that offers fair and equal opportunities to all its inhabitants, and the 25% of Israel's citizens who are not Jewish are learning how to exercise their democratic rights and how to forge identities that are both Arab (or international) and Israeli.

Israel is not yet a perfect society or democracy—but what nation has ever been forged from scratch in 6 decades, especially while facing the constant threat of war and attack? Meanwhile, every visitor to Israel can sense being in a vibrant, inventive society charging ahead in the arts, sciences, medicine, advanced technology, and style—a land of exotic peoples creating new identities and new strengths for themselves.

At the same time, despite the many failures on the road to peace and bitterness and radicalization among both Israelis and Palestinians, a majority among both peoples understands that a two-state solution with Israelis and Palestinians, living in peace and prosperity, is the best hope for the future. Much of the rest of the world watches and waits to play its part in helping to achieve this goal.

Recorded Jewish history dates from the time of Abraham, between 2000 and 1800 B.C. Many elements of the patriarchal chronicles have been reconfirmed as accurate by recent archaeological discoveries, but other elements of this enormously distant past may never be able to be historically documented. Modern scientific methods reveal that human beings have lived in the Holy Land since the Old Stone Age, some 600,000 years ago. But a history so deep and full of universal significance is almost impossible to grasp in its entirety. I've provided an outline of the major periods before 1917.

**A BRIEF LOOK AT THE PAST**  In Israel's museums and at Israel's archaeological sites, you will encounter the following terms used to define the many time periods in Israel's long history.

**Old Stone Age** (600,000–12,000 B.C.): Cave dwellers, hand axes, hunting, fire.

**Middle Stone Age** (12,000–7500 B.C.): Cultivation of grain, more sophisticated tools.

**Late Stone Age** (7500–4000 B.C.): First villages appear, including Jericho; animal husbandry, irrigation, and pottery begin.

**Chalcolithic (Copper) Age** (4000–3200 B.C.): Copper used in tools; towns grow; designs appear on pottery; a culture develops at Beersheva.

**Early Bronze (Canaanite) Age** (3200–2200 B.C.): Towns are fortified; temples and palaces built.

**Middle Bronze (Canaanite) Age** (2200–1550 B.C.): The Age of the Patriarchs; Abraham's travels; trade develops; the Hyksos invade Canaan and Egypt.

**Late Bronze (Canaanite) Age** (1550–1200 B.C.): Israel captive in Egypt; the alphabet develops; the Exodus from Egypt; Ten Commandments delivered on Mount Sinai; Israel conquers the Promised Land.

**Early Iron Age** (1200–1020 B.C.): Period of the Judges; Philistine invasion.

**Middle Iron Age** (1020–842 B.C.): The united monarchy under King Saul and King David (1000 B.C.); Jerusalem is capital of kingdom; in 961 King Solomon builds First Temple; golden age of Israelite culture and power.

**Late Iron Age** (842–587 B.C.): Period of the later kings and prophets; in 587, destruction of First Temple.

**Babylonian and Persian Periods** (587–332 B.C.): Israel captive in Babylon, followed by Persian domination; the

**Dateline**

- 600,000 B.C. Early human habitation of caves in Carmel Mountains near Haifa.
- 15,000 B.C. Appearance of farming settlements in the Galilee and Jordan Valley.
- 7000 B.C. Defensive wall built around Jericho in the Jordan Valley. Evidence of early centers for cult and fertility worship.
- 4500–3100 B.C. Towns develop at Bet Shean, Ein Gedi, Megiddo, and Beersheva.
- 3100 B.C. Start of early Canaanite era; development of cities.
- 1600 B.C. Hebrews enslaved in Egypt.
- 1250 B.C. Exodus of Hebrews under Moses. Early Canaanite-Hebrew alphabet begins to develop.
- 1100 B.C. Israelite tribes settle in much of Canaanite highlands; Israelite culture becomes pervasive. Philistine people from Aegean occupy Canaanite coast.
- 1025 B.C. Saul anointed first Israelite king by the prophet Samuel.
- 1004–1000 B.C. David, second king of Israelites, makes Jerusalem his capital;

*continues*

# History of Israel

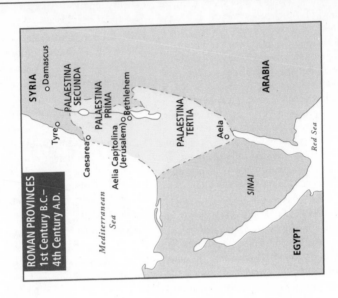

ROMAN PROVINCES
1st Century B.C.–
4th Century A.D.

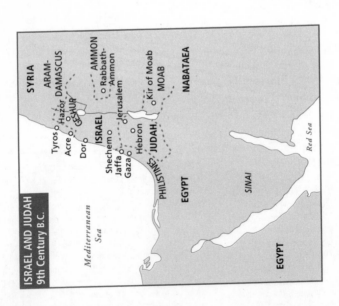

ISRAEL AND JUDAH
9th Century B.C.

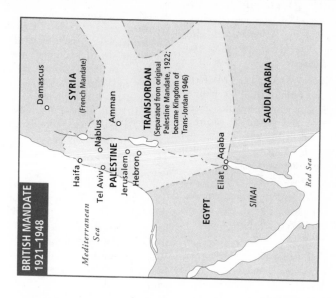

**BRITISH MANDATE 1921–1948**

Mediterranean Sea

Damascus ○

**SYRIA** (French Mandate)

Haifa ○
Tel Aviv ○ ○ Nablus
Jerusalem ○
Hebron ○ **PALESTINE**

Amman ○
**TRANSJORDAN**
(Separated from original Palestine Mandate, 1922; became Kingdom of Trans-Jordan 1946)

Eilat ○ ○ Aqaba

EGYPT

SINAI

SAUDI ARABIA

Red Sea

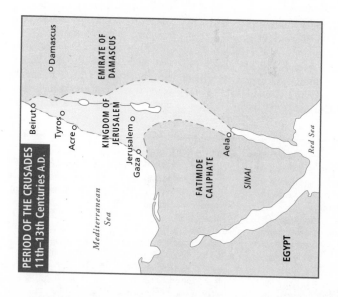

**PERIOD OF THE CRUSADES 11th–13th Centuries A.D.**

Mediterranean Sea

Beirut ○
Tyros ○
Acre ○
**KINGDOM OF JERUSALEM**
Jerusalem ○
Gaza ○

○ Damascus

**EMIRATE OF DAMASCUS**

Aela ○

**FATIMIDE CALIPHATE**

SINAI

EGYPT

Red Sea

Second Temple is built; times of Ezra and Nehemiah.

**Hellenistic and Maccabean Periods** (332–37 B.C.): Domination by Alexander the Great, by the Ptolomies and Seleucids; the Maccabean struggle; Hasmonean dynasty.

**Roman Period** (37 B.C.–A.D. 324): Herodian dynasty; birth of Jesus, his ministry, and crucifixion; wars against Rome; Second Temple and Jerusalem destroyed (A.D. 70); fall of Masada (73); Talmud and Mishnah compiled; Bar Kochba's revolt against Rome (132–35).

**Byzantine Period** (324–640): Jewish revolt, Byzantine domination; Jerusalem Talmud completed; Persian invasion and sack of Jerusalem (614); birth and rise of Islam in the Middle East.

**Arab Period** (640–1096): Jerusalem conquered by Islamic armies (638); Arab Empire capital first at Damascus, later Baghdad; joint Christian-Muslim protectorate of holy places; Christian pilgrimage rights curtailed.

**The Crusades** (1096–1291): First Crusade (1096–99), sack of Jerusalem, Crusader Kingdom under Godfrey of Bouillon. Second Crusade (1147–49): Saladin captures Jerusalem for Islam (1187). Third Crusade (1189–92); Fourth Crusade (1202–04).

**Mamluke and Ottoman Turkish Period** (1291–1917): Mongols and Seljuks replace Arabs and Byzantines as overlords of the Holy Land; Ottomans conquer Palestine; Suleiman the Magnificent rebuilds Jerusalem; Jews, expelled from Spain and Italy, welcomed into the Ottoman Empire; Napoleon's campaign in Egypt and Palestine (1799); movement to re-create a Jewish homeland led by Theodor Herzl (1860–1904), who published *The Jewish State;* the first Zionist Congress in Basel (1897).

**THE BRITISH MANDATE**  The Balfour Declaration in 1917 announced British support for the creation of a national home for the Jewish people in Palestine. In 1920, after Great Britain had captured the region of Palestine from the Ottoman Empire at the end of World War I, the League of Nations granted the British a "mandate" to govern Palestine, and Sir Herbert Samuel, a Jew, was named first British high commissioner. In 1922, Great Britain separated Trans-Jordan (present-day Jordan) from British Mandate Palestine and established a separate Arab country in that area.

Within Palestine, enormous progress was made during the first 20 years of British administration. Hospitals and schools were established in both Jewish and Arab areas, and in Jewish areas of the

---

begins conquest of territories from southern Syria to Eilat.

- **950 B.C.** King Solomon builds First Temple of Jerusalem.
- **928 B.C.** After death of Solomon, kingdom divided into Israel in the north, and Judah, with its capital at Jerusalem.
- **870–722 B.C.** Pagan religions flourish. Assyria conquers kingdom of Israel.

- **701 B.C.** Judah devastated by Assyrian invasion. Jerusalem, led by King Hezekiah and inspired by the prophet Isaiah, remains unconquered.
- **627–586 B.C.** Prophet Jeremiah in Jerusalem.
- **586 B.C.** Nebuchadnezzar destroys Jerusalem and Temple of Solomon. End of First Temple period. Jews exiled to Babylon.

- **540 B.C.** Babylon defeated by Persians. Jews allowed to return to Jerusalem.
- **515 B.C.** Second Temple built upon ruins of Solomon's Temple in Jerusalem.
- **445 B.C.** Ezra the Scribe begins public reading of Torah in Jerusalem.
- **332 B.C.** Alexander the Great conquers Judea. Hellenistic era begins.

country, dazzlingly modern, planned communities, both urban and agricultural, were built; much desolate land was reclaimed for agricultural use. The Arab population of Palestine resented British policy in the early 1920s, which encouraged Jewish immigration and the development of the Palestinian Jewish community, and almost immediately after the British Mandate took effect, political disorders developed. The era of the British Mandate was characterized by three-way disputes between British, Jewish, and Arab factions and by Arab attacks on Jewish communities, especially in 1921 and 1929. Jewish immigration increased during the early Hitler years. An Arab insurrection from 1936 to 1939 led the British, in 1939, to severely limit Jewish immigration before cutting it off entirely. Thus, during World War II, Jews seeking to escape the Nazi Holocaust in Europe were denied refuge in Palestine. After the outbreak of World War II, political tensions within Palestine diminished somewhat, and the area became an important Allied military base for the Middle East. However, the coming conflict was inevitable. In 1946, Arab and Jewish terrorism against the British increased, the King David Hotel was blown up by a Jewish underground group at odds with Ben-Gurion's more mainstream Zionist organization, and the cycle of violence rose to new heights.

In November 1947, with Britain abstaining, the United Nations General Assembly voted to partition Palestine into two separate states, one Arab and one Jewish. On May 14, 1948, with the Jewish parts of Jerusalem under Arab siege, fighting widespread across Palestine, and 400,000 Arab Palestinian civilians fleeing their homes, the British Mandate ended in shambles, and the State of Israel was proclaimed. Arab armies from surrounding states invaded the fledgling nation, but were pushed back, and the 1949 cease-fire lines left Israel in control of somewhat more territory than had been allotted to it by the UN partition. Only a very few Jewish areas fell to Arab armies. The Palestinian state proposed for those areas that remained under Arab control did not come into being. The West Bank and East Jerusalem, including the Old City, were annexed to the Kingdom of Jordan. Although most of the international community did not recognize this act, Jordan granted citizenship to all Palestinians under its control, the only Arab nation to do so. Egypt occupied but did not annex the Gaza Strip. Its inhabitants were declared stateless.

## THE MAKING OF AN INDEPENDENT STATE   In the beginning of the

---

- **167** B.C. Antiochus IV desecrates Jerusalem temple; outlaws Jewish religion.
- **164** B.C. Judah Maccabee captures Jerusalem; temple rededicated. Judea independent under Maccabee (Hasmonean) dynasty; borders greatly expanded.
- **63** B.C. Judea incorporated into Roman Empire.

- **37** B.C. Romans proclaim Herod the Idumaean king of Judea.
- **18** B.C. Herod begins vast renovation of Second Temple.
- **8–4** B.C. Jesus born in Bethlehem.
- A.D. **62** Completion of Herodian renovation of Second Temple.
- **66–73** Jewish revolt against Rome. Jerusalem and Second Temple captured by Rome and razed; Masada falls.
- **132** Second Revolt against Rome led by Bar Kochba; ruins of Jerusalem freed; temple service resumed.
- **135** Bar Kochba defeated. Hadrian orders Jerusalem rebuilt as Aelia Capitolina, a Roman city forbidden to Jews.

*continues*

State of Israel's history, there was enormous exhilaration but also a grim determination. The double weight of the horrors of the Holocaust and the enormous casualties suffered in the War of Independence from 1948 to 1949 drove the country to hang on, to protect every sand dune, to force life out of the desert, and to create a haven for any Jews who might ever again find themselves in danger. Life was austere in the newly won state. For years, food, clothing, razor blades, and paint were severely rationed as the country struggled to survive as well as to feed and shelter the thousands of new immigrants who arrived each month. In less than a decade, the nation's population quadrupled as hundreds of thousands of Holocaust survivors from Europe and Jewish refugees from the Middle East arrived and were absorbed. Hundreds of thousands more were added in the 1960s as the Jewish communities of North Africa fled to safer havens in France and Israel.

Slowly, with enormous effort, conditions grew more stable. Basic housing was built, uprooted people began to develop new identities, and although life was still spartan (Ben-Gurion and the founding fathers refused to allow television stations to be established in Israel, claiming that the nation had more important things to attend to), the country began to flourish. Modern farming and irrigation, along with dedication, made the desert bloom, and the long season ensured by the Mediterranean sun made marginal land wonderfully fruitful. Jaffa oranges, Israeli tomatoes and avocados, and the wines of Mount Carmel became famous. But even more important than its agriculture were Israel's developing industries (in a tide of history few Israeli pioneers could have foreseen, enormous areas of hard-won agricultural land are being plowed under to create new cities, highways, and industrial zones). Today the country manufactures its own tools and machinery, arms and airplanes, and is becoming an extremely important center for high-tech electronics. It also supports a burgeoning diamond and fashion industry—Israeli designs are highly regarded throughout the world. The Dead Sea, heavily saturated with minerals, has only begun to be exploited (though the price of mining this bonanza may be the destruction of The Dead Sea as one of the world's great natural wonders). Oil, however, must be imported. Israel's brilliant medical community, scientific establishment, and computer industries may one day benefit the entire region.

## WAR & THE SEARCH FOR PEACE

During the Suez War of November 1956,

- 160–300 Early Talmudic era. Classical synagogues built throughout Holy Land; Galilee center of Jewish population.
- 313–326 Emperor Constantine recognizes Christianity as new religion of Roman Empire. His mother, Queen Helena, visits Holy Land to identify sites of Jesus' life and ministry.

- 326–614 Hundreds of Byzantine churches and monastic communities built. Restrictions against Jews.
- 351 Jews of Galilee rebel against Byzantine/Christians.
- 400 Codification of Jerusalem Talmud.
- 614–629 Jerusalem conquered by Persians, recaptured by Byzantines.
- 638 Islamic conquest of Palestine. Omar Ibn El Khattab conquers Jerusalem.

- 691 Dome of the Rock built on Temple Mount.
- 720 Al Aqsa Mosque built on Temple Mount.
- 1008 Caliph Al Hakim destroys churches and prevents Christian pilgrimage.
- 1099 Crusaders conquer Jerusalem. Muslims and Jews massacred.
- 1187 Saladin recaptures Jerusalem from Crusaders.

Great Britain and France invaded Egypt in order to secure the Suez Canal, which Egypt had nationalized, and Israel (in coordination with the British and French reconquest of Suez) conquered Egypt's Sinai Peninsula and the Gaza Strip hoping to put an end to 9 years of Egyptian terrorist attacks on southern Israel. In exchange for the stationing of a United Nations peacekeeping force on the Egyptian side of the Israeli-Sinai border, and with promises of freedom to send its shipping through the Red Sea and the Suez Canal, Israel withdrew entirely from the Sinai Peninsula and Gaza in early 1957. Ten years of relative peace followed, punctuated by periodic Syrian sniper attacks on the Galilee from Syrian batteries on the Golan Heights.

Then, in May 1967, the United Nations peacekeeping force that had maintained security on the Israeli-Egyptian border for 10 years was unilaterally ordered out by Egypt's president, Gamal Abdel Nasser, in violation of international guarantees. At the same time, Nasser blockaded the port of Eilat on the Red Sea, economically strangling Israel, while from the Golan Heights, Syria stood ready to attack the Galilee. For Israelis, only too aware that the nation was less than 16km (10 miles) wide at Tel Aviv and that the Jordanian army in East Jerusalem was aimed point-blank at Jewish West Jerusalem, the agony of these weeks, while the Israeli government tried to rally international diplomatic support, was unbearable. The pace of Arab propaganda against Israel reached new pitches of frenzy and Arab armies mobilized to deliver what was claimed would be a crushing blow. The Israelis dug mass graves in the parks of Tel Aviv in preparation for the horrendous civilian casualties an Arab invasion would inflict.

In the early morning of June 5, 1967, Israel made a preemptive strike against the air forces of Egypt and Syria. At noon, Jordan, despite diplomatic pleas that it stay out of the conflict, began to shell West Jerusalem. In the Six-Day War that followed, Israel swept to an unimaginable victory, occupying the Sinai Peninsula, the Gaza Strip, the Golan Heights, East Jerusalem, and the entire West Bank. The Egyptian blockade of Eilat was broken. The Arab world was left in a state of shock. Suddenly Israel was no longer a struggling state hanging on tenaciously to its hard-won independence. Land areas had more than trebled. Infusions of new immigrants swelled the country's Jewish population. The economy was burgeoning and tourism was increasing at a rate greater than ever before. Israel's patriarch, David Ben-Gurion, by then in retirement,

- **1189–91** Third Crusade. Crusader Kingdom along coast with Akko as capital.
- **1240** Turkish armies plunder Jerusalem.
- **1261** Mongols devastate countryside.
- **1267** Post-Crusader Jewish community reestablished in Jerusalem.
- **1291** Mameluke conquest. Akko falls; end of Crusader Kingdom.
- **1517** Ottoman Turkish conquest of Jerusalem.
- **1538** Ottoman sultan Suleiman the Magnificent orders walls of Jerusalem rebuilt.
- **1550** Safed becomes center of Jewish scholarship and mysticism.
- **1569** Codification of normative Judaism (Shulchan Aruch) in Safed.
- **1776** Jezzar Pasha rebuilds Akko.
- **1799** Napoleon attacks but fails to win Akko.
- **1841** First Protestant mission in Jerusalem.
- **1863** First Hebrew newspaper in Jerusalem.
- **1870** Mikvah Yisrael, first agricultural school, founded.
- **1878** Petach Tikva, near Jaffa, and Rosh Pinna, in

*continues*

warned that all the conquered areas must be relinquished immediately, but in the euphoria of the day, his words made little sense to most Israelis.

For travelers, Israel, with its artifacts, excavations, and kibbutzim, always had a lot to offer. After the 1967 war, it had more. Most important of all, there was a united Jerusalem, the Western (Wailing) Wall, and the exotic Old City. For Christians, Israel became a synonym for the entire Holy Land. Both sides of Jerusalem were joined together. Concrete walls and barbed-wire fences that had divided the Israeli and Jordanian sides of the city became things of the past. In the early days of what most hoped would be a short and benign occupation, Israelis and tourists alike enjoyed the exotic bazaars and holy sites of East Jerusalem and the West Bank. Bethlehem, once virtually inaccessible from Israel, was only minutes away from Jerusalem. Jericho, believed to be the oldest city in the world, and Hebron, where the ancient Hebrew patriarchs were buried, were open to visits. In the north, the Golan Heights provided a double meaning: tranquillity in Galilee and a new area for tourist inspection.

In the south, there was a new accessibility to the great historic wilderness of Sinai. Eilat, once considered by Israelis as the end of the earth, awoke one morning with a deep and fascinating hinterland. The craggy isolation of the Santa Katarina Monastery, at the base of Mount Sinai where Moses was believed to have received the Ten Commandments, provided an unforgettable experience. Command cars, jeeps, buses, and airplanes began penetrating the desert that had once sustained the ancient Israelites during their 40-year odyssey from Egypt to the Promised Land.

In those days the mood was optimistic. No one questioned the premise that Israel was on the map for good. As the years passed, however, the Arab world continued to refuse to recognize Israel diplomatically, and the plight of the Palestinian refugees scattered throughout the Middle East continued to be ignored by the world at large. In the absence of a peace settlement that would trade most land captured in 1967 for peace, the occupation of the West Bank and the Gaza Strip began to seem less temporary. The small political movement for Jewish settlement of the Occupied Territories began to grow, although initially opposed by the Israeli government. Resentment among the Palestinians under occupation quietly rose.

The country experienced a sharp change in fortune in October 1973. The Yom Kippur War, a completely unexpected

Galilee, first Jewish farming settlements, founded.
- 1882 First aliyah from Europe and Jewish immigration from Yemen.
- 1897 First Zionist Congress in Basel.
- 1898 Herzl meets German kaiser in Jerusalem.
- 1909 Tel Aviv founded.
- 1911 First kibbutz founded at Degania in the Galilee.
- 1914 Jews from Russia and Allied countries expelled by Ottoman Turks.
- 1917 Balfour Declaration supporting Jewish national home in Palestine. British free Jerusalem from Turks.
- 1920 Official start of British Mandate.
- 1922 British create Trans-Jordan (now Jordan) from Palestinian lands east of the Jordan River.
- 1925 Hebrew University founded in Jerusalem.
- 1929 Arab-Jewish riots. Jews massacred at Hebron.
- 1936–39 Arab strikes and uprisings.
- 1939 British White Paper curtails Jewish immigration on eve of World War II.
- 1939–45 Six million Jews killed by Nazis in Europe.
- 1947 United Nations votes partition of Palestine into

simultaneous attack against Israel launched by Egypt and Syria, had a sobering effect on the entire nation. In the first days of the attack, the Golan Heights were almost retaken by Syria, and Egyptian forces, crossing the Suez Canal, overwhelmed Israeli troops in Sinai. More than 2,500 young Israelis were killed in 1 month, losses proportionately higher than the casualties the United States sustained during the entire Vietnam War. Egyptian and Syrian casualties were enormous. While the war ended with Israeli forces closer to Cairo and Damascus than ever before, the initial setbacks and the high cost in lives shook the nation's confidence and tarnished the images of its leaders. In a backlash, voters turned against the Labor Party, which had led the state since its founding, and elected a new government dominated by the right-of-center Likud led by Menachem Begin.

A few weeks after he assumed office in 1977, Prime Minister Menachem Begin quietly asked neutral intermediaries to arrange a meeting with Egypt's president Sadat anywhere in the world. This set in motion a series of events highlighted by President Sadat's dramatic visit to Jerusalem, the conclusion of a framework for the Middle East peace agreement in Camp David, and the treaty with Egypt in March 1979 terminating 30 years of war between the two countries. Accordingly, Israel withdrew from the Sinai, and Mount Sinai with the Santa Katarina Monastery reverted to Egypt. With the state of peace it remains open to tourists from Israel.

The hopes for a regional peace agreement, which the Egyptian-Israeli settlement raised, were not quickly realized. No additional Arab countries came forward to negotiate. The 1982 invasion of southern Lebanon put further strains on Israel's relations with its neighbors and provoked a great deal of debate in every sector of Israeli society. Triple-digit inflation and deteriorating relations with Palestinians in the Occupied Territories, as more land was appropriated for Jewish settlements, marked the early 1980s. The withdrawal from Lebanon and the economic stability achieved under Shimon Peres's brief tenure as prime minister from 1984 to 1986 promised better times, but in late 1987, the Palestinian population of the West Bank and Gaza decided it could no longer allow its future to be endlessly controlled by Israel. The Intifada, a grass-roots program of daily commercial strikes and demonstrations (both violent and nonviolent) against the military authorities, began. The Intifada continued through the early 1990s.

---

Jewish and Arab states. First Dead Sea Scrolls found.

- **1948** State of Israel declared. Five Arab countries attack.
- **1949–56** Cease-fire. Terrorist attacks on Negev from Egypt.
- **1956** Israel joins Anglo-French attack on Egypt. Conquers Sinai Peninsula.
- **1957** Israel returns Sinai. United Nations peacekeeping force installed in Egypt.

- **1967** Egypt expels peacekeeping force. Israel wins Six-Day War, occupies Sinai, Golan, West Bank, and Gaza.
- **1972** Palestinian terrorists massacre Israeli athletes at Munich Olympics.
- **1973** Egypt and Syria attack during Yom Kippur War.
- **1976** Israelis rescue Jewish hostages at Entebbe Airport.
- **1977** Likud wins elections. Sadat of Egypt comes to Jerusalem.

- **1979** Israel and Egypt sign peace treaty negotiated at Camp David.
- **1982** Israel invades Lebanon.
- **1984** Labor-Likud Coalition. Withdrawal from most of Lebanon. Aliyah of Ethiopian Jews.
- **1987** First Palestinian Intifada begins.
- **1989** Great Soviet aliyah begins.

*continues*

The year 1990 brought unexpected challenges to Israel, initially with a massive wave of 350,000 immigrants from the dissolving Soviet system, and in the summer of 1990, with the Kuwait crisis. Israel was not a direct participant in the Allied coalition against Iraq; however, in an attempt to win support for his policies throughout the Arab world, Saddam Hussein threatened to "incinerate half of Israel" with missile-borne chemical attacks if the Allied coalition moved against him. The United States asked Israel to refrain from retaliating if it came under attack and pledged that any Iraqi missile threat to Israel would be destroyed by American bombing within the first hours of war. Nevertheless, Israelis found themselves sitting in sealed rooms, experiencing scud missile attacks almost nightly for the entire 6 weeks of the Gulf War. Iraq's missiles turned out to be armed with high explosives instead of chemical weapons, but the ordeal of the scuds and their threat of chemical annihilation left its mark on Israeli society. Faced with the prospect of terrible chemical, bacteriological, and nuclear weapons in the future, many Israelis came to believe it was worth taking extraordinary risks to try to achieve peace. Other Israelis were more determined than ever to avoid any further concessions. The Oslo peace process began in 1991 under Likud prime minister Shamir and continued with greater hope after President Clinton arranged a White House peace process ceremony between the recently elected Prime Minister Rabin and Chairman Arafat in 1993.

**THE PEACE PROCESS STALLS**
Negotiating directly with Palestinians and with moderate Arab governments, Israel began a planned withdrawal from parts of the West Bank and Gaza in 1994. In the same year, a peace treaty was signed with the Kingdom of Jordan. The assassination of Prime Minister Rabin by a Jewish opponent of the peace process in November 1995 was a blow for those who hoped to create a new Middle East. An extraordinary gathering of world leaders for Rabin's funeral in Jerusalem showed the depth of concern throughout the world for the future of the Holy Land.

After the assassination of Prime Minister Rabin, hopes for peace between Israelis and Palestinians did not come to fruition. A new, violent Palestinian Intifada began in 2000. Tourism to Israel plunged, but by 2004, the security situation began to improve and tourism began to boom again. In 2005, Prime Minister Sharon evacuated all Israeli settlements in Gaza, but suffered a massive stroke before he could outline further plans. He was succeeded by his deputy prime minister, Ehud Olmert, who was elected in 2006 on a platform of continuing to build a separation barrier between Israel and the Palestinians, and further withdrawals of settlements from the West Bank.

## 3 Israel's Famous People

**Menachem Begin** (1913–92)   Born in Poland and an active Zionist, Begin arrived in Palestine during World War II, having lost much of his family in the Holocaust, and assumed command of an underground organization responsible for attacks against the British presence in Palestine. Condemned by Ben-Gurion and the Israeli provisional government for these tactics, Begin led the opposition to the Labor governments of 1948 to 1977. He became prime minister in 1977, and presided over the Camp David negotiations and peace treaty with Egypt in 1979. Though he approved the invasion of Lebanon in 1982, he resigned as prime minister in 1983 in despair about the war. He and Egyptian president Anwar Sadat received the Nobel Peace Prize in 1978.

**David Ben-Gurion** (1886–1973)   This Polish-born Zionist leader immigrated to Ottoman-ruled Palestine in 1906. Exiled by Ottoman Turks during World War I, he fled to the United States, where he met his wife, Paula. Ceaseless architect of the emerging Jewish state in the 1930s, he became Israel's first prime minister and led the country in the 1948 War of Independence. Deeply committed to the land, a visionary who believed Israel's future lay in the development of the desert, he retired to the Negev kibbutz of Sde Boker after his final term in office. In the euphoria after the 1967 war, Ben-Gurion urged magnanimous terms for a peace settlement, including the return of most conquered lands. He lived just long enough to see his country survive the onslaught of the Yom Kippur War in 1973.

**Abba Eban** (1915–2002)   South African–born, Cambridge-educated author, diplomat, and former foreign minister, Eban was noted for an eloquence and wit unrivaled among Western leaders since Winston Churchill. When asked by reporters about divisions between hawks and doves in the Israel cabinet during the tense days before the Six-Day War, he quipped, "The government of Israel is hardly an aviary." An Arabic scholar and a supporter of more moderate policies regarding the West Bank and Gaza, he is known for his PBS television series, *Civilization and the Jews.* Among his observations:

- **2004** Yassir Arafat dies in Paris; Mahmoud Abbas becomes president of the Palestinian Authority.
- **2005** Ariel Sharon evacuates Israeli settlements in Gaza, but suffers a debilitating stroke before he can further act on his agenda.
- **2006** Hamas is elected to a majority in the Palestinian legislature. In response, Western countries cut off all funding but humanitarian aid to the Palestinian Authority. Haifa and northern Israel heavily shelled during month-long war in Lebanon.
- **2007** Tourism returns to Israel at near record levels.

"History teaches us that men and nations behave wisely once they have exhausted all other alternatives."

**Teddy Kollek** (1910–2007) Indefatigable mayor of Jerusalem for 28 years, Kollek arrived in Palestine from Vienna during the rise of the Nazis in the 1930s, and was originally a member of Kibbutz Ein Gev. Leader of the One Jerusalem Coalition, his commitment to maintaining peace among the many ethnic and religious groups in the city was matched by his determination to adorn Jerusalem with every kind of artistic, cultural, and civic treasure possible. Amazingly accessible to the people of Jerusalem during his long tenure, Kollek often answered the municipal phones himself in the early morning hours before his staff arrived.

**Golda Meir** (1898–1978) Born in Russia, Meir emigrated to the United States as a child. As a young Milwaukee schoolteacher and ardent Zionist, she emigrated to British Mandate Palestine in 1921. Meir held many posts in the Labor Party and was famous for her personal courage: In 1948, on the eve of Israeli independence, she risked her life to travel to Jordan (disguised as an Arab woman) to plead with King Abdullah I not to make war on the new Jewish nation. Advised by Abdullah to wait a bit longer for independence, she shot back: "We've already waited 2,000 years." Prime minister from 1969 to 1974, Meir projected a grandmotherly image, often doing business with Israeli and foreign leaders in her kitchen. Her government was criticized for failing to detect the Egyptian and Syrian Yom Kippur surprise attack in 1973, and bore responsibility for heavy casualties.

**Yitzhak Rabin** (1922–95) Rabin was the first Israeli prime minister to be born in the land that was to become Israel. Originally a student of agronomy, he joined Palmach, the elite Haganah strike force, and served with Allied forces fighting in the Middle East during World War II. A brilliant strategist, as commander in chief of Israel's armed forces during the Six-Day War in 1967, he led the country to its greatest military triumph. Rabin's first term as prime minister, from 1974 to 1977, was distinguished by the successful raid on Entebbe Airport in Uganda, which rescued almost 100 Jewish and Israeli hostages. As defense minister in a Likud-Labor Coalition government, in 1987 he supported a hard line against Palestinian demonstrators, but came to be increasingly committed to creating a world in which Israelis and Palestinians could live side by side, "In dignity. In empathy. As human beings." Rabin was a modest, noncharismatic leader, and public faith in his caution and judgment enabled him to make concessions and territorial withdrawals in the search for peace. He was the recipient of the Nobel Peace Prize in 1995. Rabin was assassinated in November 1995 by an Israeli opponent to his policies.

**Boris Schatz** (1866–1932) Lithuanian-born court sculptor to the king of Bulgaria and ardent follower of Theodor Herzl, Schatz arrived in Jerusalem in 1906 and founded the Bezalel Academy of Arts and Crafts with the purpose of developing an indigenous artistic tradition for the nation he believed would one day be reborn. The Bezalel Academy planted the seeds for a modern cultural scene in Jerusalem, which had previously been a remote, religiously oriented community. Israel's extraordinary commitment to the arts is in no small part due to Schatz's vision of art as a necessary component of the emerging nation.

**Abraham Ticho** (1883–1960) Born in Moravia, Dr. Ticho arrived in Jerusalem in 1912 determined to battle the trachoma and other endemic eye diseases that caused thousands of cases of blindness among the local population. As founder and head of Jerusalem's first ophthalmic hospital, he became a modern

Jerusalem legend, working endlessly to save the eyesight of all who approached him (including Emir Abdullah, later king of Jordan). He was known for sometimes brusquely dragging off both Arab and Jewish children he spotted on the streets for treatment at his clinic. When he was stabbed and left for dead during the political unrest of 1929, thousands in Jerusalem's Jewish, Christian, and Muslim communities prayed for Dr. Ticho to recover. As one whose life's work was bringing light to others, Dr. Ticho was fascinated by Chanukah menorahs, sometimes accepting exotic Chanukah lamps in exchange for treatment. His remarkable collection of menorahs is now in the Israel Museum. The 19th-century mansion he shared with his wife, the artist Anna Ticho, is now a downtown branch of the Israel Museum.

**Yigael Yadin** (1917–84) A leading member of the Haganah during the 1940s, Yadin was responsible for drawing up and implementing Haganah's defense of Jerusalem in the War of Independence. After serving as chief of staff of the Israel Defense Forces until 1952, he devoted himself to archaeology, leading and writing about excavations at Hazor, Masada, and in the caves of the Judean Desert, and publishing extensively on the Dead Sea Scrolls. A brilliant lecturer, Yadin made archaeology so exciting and accessible to the Israeli people that he virtually became a national hero, and archaeology the national sport. Read Yadin's exciting, beautifully photographed book, *Bar Kochba,* and you'll understand why.

## 4 Architecture

Casting a shadow over all other structures in Israel are two that long ago vanished: the legendary First Temple, built by King Solomon in approximately 960 B.C. and destroyed by the Babylonians, and the Second Temple, originally put together on the ruins of the First Temple. In front of the First Temple, a Canaanite-style sanctuary building embellished with decorations of cedar, ivory, and gold, King Solomon is recorded in the Bible to have prayed: "The heavens, even the heaven of heavens, cannot contain Thee; how much less this house that I have built." The reconstruction of the Second Temple into a vast Hellenistic-style pilgrimage complex was begun by the Roman-installed King Herod in 18 B.C., not to be completed until A.D. 64, almost 70 years after Herod's death.

This ceremonial center did not endure for long. In A.D. 70, Jerusalem was destroyed by Roman armies. On the eve of this destruction, according to the Roman historian Tacitus, the Roman general, Titus, called a council to decide whether, in victory, Rome should destroy "the Temple, one of man's consummate building achievements." This hesitation on the part of the Romans to level the symbolic religious center of a stubbornly rebellious subject nation is an indication of the Herodian structure's grandeur and charisma. The Western Wall is part of the retaining wall system that held up the vast artificially created ceremonial plaza that surrounded the Herodian temple. A few architectural details found in archaeological excavations since 1967 have been identified with the structures that formed part of the Second Temple complex, but no fragment of the actual Second Temple building has yet been found.

Of all the ancient buildings that still stand in Israel, nothing is more incredible than the Dome of the Rock, built on the site of the First and Second Temples by the early Islamic rulers of Jerusalem in A.D. 691. The Byzantine architects who were commissioned to design the Dome of the Rock may have been inspired by the legends of the two vanished structures. In the 16th century it was adorned with Persian tiles by Sultan Suleiman the Magnificent. One of the world's most beautiful buildings, this shrine acts as a crown to a site that is both physically and spiritually sublime. With its golden dome, like a gilded balloon against the skies, offering intimations of ascension to the heavens (as Koranic tradition records the Prophet Muhammad did from this very spot), it combines simplicity with intricacy in a way that does equal justice to the monotheistic concept and the complex traditions associated with the site.

From the Crusader period, two remarkable Frankish Romanesque churches remain: the heavily restored Church of Saint Anne in Jerusalem, and the church in Abu Ghosh, near Jerusalem, which is more in its original state. Designed using Eastern and Western techniques to create marvelous acoustics, both are musical instruments to be played by the human voice: A single soprano in either will sound like a choir of angels.

The Street of the Chain and the Temple Mount in Jerusalem offer many examples of architecture from the Mamluke period, characterized by intricately carved arabesque stonework and Mamluke "stalactite"-adorned recesses over the doorways of its important buildings. The labyrinthine Old City of Akko, with its medieval khans and Ottoman Al-Jazzar mosque, deserves to be considered a national treasure. Unfortunately, the fascinating bazaars and residential quarters of Old Akko have been left in ill repair due to local political considerations.

The International Style of the 1930s and 1940s was brought to British Mandate Palestine by refugee architects who had studied at the Bauhaus and worked in the studios of Le Corbusier, Gropius, and Mies van der Rohe in Europe. Tel Aviv has one of the world's largest urban concentrations of such buildings, with their crisp white concrete curvilinear and blocklike shapes. These buildings were recorded in international architectural publications of their time as visionary gems, but a combination of civic unconcern and the fact that the sand-laden bricks used for construction did not weather well, has left many of these structures in a state of near ruin.

The British Mandate period also left an architectural legacy in Jerusalem, where the high commissioner issued an ordinance that all construction must be faced with Jerusalem stone. Both the YMCA building on King David Street (designed by the same American firm that did New York City's Empire State Building) and the Rockefeller Museum, designed by the noted British architect Austin S. B. Harrison, exhibit an interesting mixture of Art Deco, Byzantine, and Islamic themes.

The vast uninspired neighborhoods constructed after 1948 in Israel's main cities and development towns, hastily built to fulfill a practical need, dominate the landscape. Most Israelis detest these post-independence apartment blocks, locally known as egg boxes. Today renovation and restoration are necessary to save what architectural heritage Israel still possesses. The reconstruction of the old quarter of Jaffa and the Jewish Quarter in Jerusalem's Old City, along with the gentrifying of 19th-century Jerusalem neighborhoods such as Yemin Moshe, Ein Kerem, and the German Colony, have produced places with real charm and a sense of community. Other urban planning projects, such as the expanded routing of a major road system alongside the walls of Jerusalem's Old City (complete with pedestrian overpasses to the Jaffa Gate) and the piecemeal destruction of West Jerusalem's 19th-century Ha-Nevi'im Street neighborhood, may prove to repeat the kind of mistakes already made in many Western cities.

# 5 Language

Israel has two official languages: Hebrew and Arabic. English is widely spoken and understood, and Arabic is the daily language and language of instruction for Israel's Arabic citizens. But for Jewish Israelis, who comprise 83% of the country's population, the day-to-day language is Hebrew—the resurrected language of biblical times. Hebrew has only come to life again as a vehicle for everyday speech during the past 100 years. Although Hebrew ("the tongue of Canaan," according to the Prophet Isaiah) was the language of much of the time period of the Old Testament, it was gradually supplanted after the Babylonian Captivity (586 B.C.) by Aramaic, another Semitic language, which became the lingua franca of the region for the next 500 years. As Jewish history moved into the Diaspora, Jewish communities spoke Greek and Greek koine, Judeo-Persian, Latin and Arabic, Ladino—the late medieval Spanish of the Jewish community expelled from Spain in 1492 (spoken by many of their descendants to this day)—and expressive, irony-prone Yiddish, which the Jewish communities of northern Europe maintained and developed as they wandered deeper and deeper into eastern Europe over the centuries.

At the end of the 19th century, as Zionist leaders began to envision a return to Israel of Jews from all parts of the world, they wondered what language should be spoken in a Jewish homeland whose inhabitants' native tongues ranged from Yiddish, Russian, English, and Hungarian to Moroccan Arabic, Argentine Spanish, Urdu, and Uzbekistani. Many important leaders believed the official language of the Jewish homeland should be what at that time was considered the preeminent language of science, culture, music, medicine, and philosophy: in short, German. A handful of Zionists had other ideas.

When **Eliezer Ben-Yehuda** (1858–1922), a Polish-born linguist, came to Jerusalem in 1881, he believed that ancient Hebrew, used mainly as a liturgical language since the 5th century B.C., should be the language of the reborn Zionist vision. He codified Hebrew grammar, wrote the first modern dictionary, and coined words necessary for a modern vocabulary. Ben-Yehuda and his wife, also a linguist, spoke only Hebrew to their son, Itamar, who became the first primarily Hebrew-speaking person in the modern world.

From the initial determination of the Ben-Yehuda family and their friends, the Hebrew language, with its uniqueness and vitality, was brought back to life, changing and growing each day—the Israeli people's great communal work of art. Modern Hebrew is being stretched by the hour by its Israeli speakers as they take the language and vocabulary of a laconic, pastoral Iron Age civilization and reshape it to the needs of an enormously cosmopolitan, gregarious, heterogeneous society of the 21st century.

Written in its own alphabet, Hebrew must be transliterated into the Latin alphabet for non-Hebrew speakers. The varying ways in which Hebrew names are transliterated is sure to confuse you—most places seem to have several different names and spellings. Is it Jaffa, Joppa, or Yafo? Safed, Safad, Zfat, or Zefat? Lake Tiberias, the Sea of Galilee, or Kinneret Lake?

The confusion stems partly from Israel's long history, partly from myriad cultures and languages, and partly from Hebrew itself. Vowels are not normally written in Hebrew (this is also true of Arabic), and so in transliteration you get such unpronounceable words as Sde (for Sede) and Sderot (Sederot). Further confusions are added by sounds like the guttural "kh" sound, a rasping in the back of the throat usually rendered as "ch" but pronounced very differently from the "ch" in "church." You might come across "Hen" and "Chen," which are the same Hebrew word, pronounced more like "khen." How does one cope? The only way is to pronounce the word you want and compare it to the one you've found. If it sounds the same, it probably is: Mikveh Israel/Miqwe Yisra'el, Elat/Eilat, Tiberias/Teverya, and so on.

Arabic is the second official language of Israel, and English is Israel's major international language, so you will find that street and road signs are in Hebrew, Arabic, and English. English will work in virtually every shop, restaurant, and hotel in the country's three major cities, as well as most other places. If, however, you chance to encounter a storekeeper who speaks only Russian, Hebrew, Arabic, or one of the 17 or so other relatively common languages, just look for his 12-year-old son, who's studying English in school.

If you find yourself groping for another language, try French, German, or Yiddish. Many Israelis of Romanian origin know French, and Israelis from Morocco, Algeria, and Tunisia often speak fluent French.

You can use the Hebrew and Arabic glossaries at the back of this book as a crutch—you'll find that your stabs at speaking the native tongues will be warmly appreciated.

## 6 Religion

Israel is special, if not sacred, to more faiths than any other country in the world. Today for at least 15 different Jewish sects, several Christian sects, Muslims, Druze, Baha'is, Samaritans, Circassians, Karaites, Bedouins, and still others, Israel is holy, and although many of the groups claim the land as "their own," the differing faiths are practiced side by side. This calls for daily tolerance. For instance, many Jews from English-speaking countries find Israel isn't "Jewish" in the way they personally practice or understand Judaism. Christians traveling in Israel are often perplexed by certain Israeli Christian customs—entrance fees at holy shrines, or famous churches subdivided (with actual lines of demarcation on walls and floors) among different sects of Christianity. Protestants are often amazed to find most holy places tended by Greek Orthodox, Coptic, Syrian, and Catholic clergy. Catholics are surprised to find their Israeli counterparts functioning as Catholics did hundreds of years ago rather than following the modern practices of most of the Catholic world.

To Islam, the biblical patriarchs and Jesus were prophets, though not the final one. Islam, in some ways, is closer to Judaism and the nomadic-type culture of the patriarchs than to the Greek-influenced culture of Christianity. Islam is dedicatedly monotheistic: The profession of faith declares, "There is but one God, Allah, and Mohammed is His prophet." Muslims pray five times a day, fast in daylight hours during the month of Ramadan, make a pilgrimage to Mecca, and give alms. The Muslim Sabbath is from Thursday's sunset to sunset on Friday. However, the prohibition against work is less severe than in Judaism. Like Jews, Muslims are enjoined from eating pork. Gambling and drinking alcohol are also prohibited to Muslims, and they may not make paintings or sculptures of human beings or animals. Men may marry up to four wives, although this tradition is rarely practiced.

## 7 A Taste of Israel

Israel used to be a practical, early-to-bed and early-to-rise country, but in Tel Aviv, and increasingly elsewhere, late dining has become the trend. For travelers who want to get an early start in the morning, or want to take in an evening performance, Israel has become the land of the luncheon special—in many restaurants, the fabulous weekday lunch specials last until 5pm, or even later. Once the lunch deadline passes, the cost of a meal can double or even triple.

For those in a rush, or on a tight budget, the local falafel and *shwarma* sandwiches, stuffed breads, and the Iraqi-style *sabbiyah* (p. 157) are healthy and filling. In general, tip waitstaff 10% unless a service charge has already been added to the bill. When paying by credit card, leave the tip in cash so it can be picked up directly by your server.

Nonsmokers should be aware of the fact that lighting up is not nearly as frowned upon in Israel as it is in North America. This practice is gradually changing, but there are plenty of restaurants that won't even have a nonsmoking section.

If you have a hotel room with a fridge and keep kosher, or just want to have some food for Friday and Saturday, plan to shop for supplies on Friday, as shops and supermarkets will be closed for the Sabbath. A selection of nonkosher restaurants in big cities will stay open on the Sabbath.

For the scoop on kosher dining and Israeli cuisine, see p. 41.

### DINING CUSTOMS

**THE SABBATH (SHABBAT)** You will need to know a few things about Shabbat dining. On Friday afternoons and afternoons before holidays, shops, offices, and kosher restaurants close around 2pm in preparation for Shabbat (the Jewish Sabbath), which begins at sunset. Most restaurants don't reopen

until Saturday evening after dark. In summer, the Saturday evening reopening can be quite late. Depending on the volume of business, some restaurants may stay open beyond normal closing hours on Saturday night. An increasing number of nonkosher restaurants remain open on Shabbat in most cities.

Saturday's breakfast is usually provided by your hotel, but you will need to deal with Friday's dinner and Saturday's lunch. Most larger hotels will serve kosher Friday-night meals and Saturday lunches prepared before the Sabbath, but you generally need to reserve for these ahead of time, whether you're a guest of the hotel or not. By Saturday dinnertime, restaurants will be open again. If you're kosher and don't want to go to the expense of reserving Shabbat hotel meals, eat a hearty lunch on Friday and buy take-away supplies for Friday evening and Saturday lunchtime. A hotel room with a refrigerator comes in very handy for such purposes. For travelers who do not keep kosher, there's a good range of nonkosher restaurants in the major cities that will be open, though in smaller, religious towns such as Safed, there may be no Sabbath dining options outside of hotels.

**KOSHER FOOD** To those unfamiliar with kosher food, the prohibitions against eating pork, shellfish, and serving (and cooking) meat and milk products at the same meal are the most noticeable laws of kashrut (kosher dietary restrictions).

According to the rigorous regulations of kashrut, only peaceful animals that chew their cud and have cleft hooves, and birds that do not eat carrion may be used for food; and then, only if they have been killed instantly and humanely according to methods supervised by religious authorities. If there is reason to believe that an animal may have died in pain, or was diseased or injured, it cannot be considered kosher (which means no hunted animals). Only fish with fins and scales can be eaten, which means no shellfish or dolphins.

A restaurant may maintain a kosher menu, but if it prepares and cooks food or does business on Shabbat, it will generally not be able to receive a kashrut certificate. Many hotels prepare meals before Shabbat for their anticipated guests, and either serve cold Saturday meals or meals that have been kept warm on fires that were started before Shabbat.

Kosher restaurants that serve milk will not serve any food containing meat or poultry, although they are permitted to serve fish. This means that cheese lasagna must be meatless. In restaurants serving meat, your coffee will be served with milk substitute and desserts won't contain milk products.

In many cases, kosher restaurants may be 5% to 10% more expensive than comparable nonkosher restaurants. If kashrut is not a concern, you can save a bit by seeking out nonkosher places. Glatt kosher and mehadrin (especially stringent supervision of kashrut) often means an even higher price. Most kosher restaurants have adapted so skillfully to their constraints that you will notice nothing very unusual in your dining experience.

## CUISINE

For the first half of Israel's existence, food was supposed to be simple and healthy. Exotic spices and sauces were not Israeli; haute cuisine was regarded as indecent. It was virtually anti-Zionist to be into the many ethnic cuisines that flooded the country from the far corners of the earth. The Ministry of Absorption taught new immigrant housewives from Hungary, Morocco, and Kurdistan how to make healthy chopped Israeli salad, and for Friday night dinner, unadorned grilled chicken leg quarters or that *pièce de résistance* of Israeli cuisine, the breaded chicken cutlet schnitzel. Over the years, the chicken schnitzel has devolved into

something that can be heated up at streetside snack counters and served inside a pita with hummus and chopped salad, like a falafel—it's become the hamburger of Israel.

Today, Israel is in love with exotic and fine food, as well as good wines, and the country is awash with young, imaginative chefs trained at the best schools and restaurants in Paris, London, New York, and Los Angeles. It used to be that half the mothers in Israel dreamed their child might become a doctor, a violinist, or a concert pianist. Now gourmet chef has been added to that wish list. You'll find dozens of restaurants that are playgrounds for local chefs doing personal, inventive haute cuisine menus rooted in ancient local food traditions, immigrant recipes, and French, Mediterranean, nouvelle, and Asian traditions all blended together.

Tel Aviv is the center for designer eateries. For very reasonable prices during afternoon (lunch) specials, you can sample the creations of Israeli chefs receiving international acclaim. In these stylish restaurants (and in lots of moderate places, too), you might have a first course of shrimp falafel served with herbed, rich yogurt or a seviche with lentils in a Japanese lemon marinade, then go on to a nouvelle version of traditional oven-baked lamb served on a bed of lentils and cracked wheat seasoned with local Palestinian *zataar* but cooked Moroccan-style, with plums, apricots, and almonds. Everywhere in the country, standards are high and menus innovative.

Strangely, amid all this elegance, fusion, and attention to quality, it's hard to find a good chicken soup in Israeli restaurants. Trendy Tel Aviv is one of the few cities where you can find a few restaurants serving menus of old-world East European Jewish dishes such as potato latkes (pancakes), stuffed cabbages and derma (intestines), and matzo ball

## Israeli Street Food

Falafel and *shwarma* tucked into a pita with chopped salad and eaten on the run have become the national fast foods of Israel.

1. A quality falafel (spiced chickpea fritter) sandwich should contain at least four falafels and include your choice of a number of fresh salads.

2. Buy from places with a big turnover and fresh, hot falafels. You should be able to see falafels being fried; if the oil is dirty or idle, and not constantly boiling, move on.

3. A good, fresh salad bar is an indication of fresh falafel and *shwarma*.

4. A sandwich made with giant napkin-size Iraqi pita bread (available at stands in Jerusalem's Machane Yehuda and Tel Aviv's Hatikvah) costs half a shekel more and fills you up for most of the day.

5. *Shwarma* (spiced turkey or lamb on a spit) should be freshly sliced from the spit. If the proprietor must turn on the flame and heat the spit of *shwarma* for you, move on.

6. Many stands offer hummus (spiced chickpea paste) either as a separate sandwich choice or with falafel. Avoid it after 11am on a hot summer day.

7. Falafel sandwiches, especially with lots of essential *techina* sauce, tend to be messy. Grab tons of napkins—*techina* stains are forever. Pay extra for a place where you can sit.

soup. Good bagels and quality lox are hard to come by unless you find it at breakfast in a top luxury hotel—the combo didn't even hit Israel in force until a decade ago.

What is typical Israeli cuisine? It draws on Arabic traditions such as meze, or a vast array of spiced salads and spreads that opens a lavish Middle Eastern–style feast. It includes the Arabic falafel, still the stuff of fast-food life in Israel despite the recent arrival of McDonald's, Burger King, and Pizza Hut; it moves on to scrumptious *shwarma,* or seasoned meat cooked on a spit, and served with your choice of salads and sauces all tucked into a pita sandwich. Palestinian *zataar* (a traditional mix of local spices that includes dried hyssop and salt) flavors food throughout the country, and Arabic *sahlab,* a sweet milky drink traditionally served to passersby in bazaars, even turns

up in frozen gourmet form on the menus of Israel's luxury restaurants.

Like Arabic cuisine, Israeli cuisine favors lamb, grilled organ meats, and fresh grilled fish seasoned with *zataar,* sumac, and dill. Israeli grandmothers from Iraq and Kurdistan cook up lamb hearts stuffed with rice, almonds, and spices, simmered in curried apricot sauce; and *kubbe* (cracked wheat or semolina dumplings) stuffed with meat or vegetables and served in soups that are blends of exotic, tart, and sweet flavors. North African Israelis have made gourmet couscous dishes and *tagines* of lamb cooked with apricots, prunes, and raisins into favorites in homes and restaurants across the country. But Israeli cuisine is stretching to encompass other traditions as well. The skewers of grilled hearts, chicken, and gooselivers that workers love to eat in places such as Jerusalem's

Machane Yehuda vegetable market and at Tel Aviv's Etzel Street in the Hatikva district have evolved into an extraordinarily fine foie gras, which Israel exported to France, and which dominated the appetizer lists at quality restaurants all over the country until a ban on force-feeding of geese to create foie gras went into effect in 2007. Now the foie gras Israelis have come to love is either imported, or claimed to be so.

Israeli cuisine also means oysters jetted in from Brittany, kosher sushi bars, and kosher Thai cuisine. It also means the baklavaries and hummus parlors of Jaffa, Akko, Tel Aviv, and Jerusalem's Old and New cities. Hummus (mashed, seasoned chickpea paste) is beloved, and its consumption widespread. It's great with pita and heavenly on lafa, or fresh-baked Iraqi-style flat bread that is the size of a giant napkin and gets rolled, with fillings, into a very satisfying sandwich. Falafel with lafa is also a favorite Israeli treat—grab it when available as an alternative to a regular pita. For travelers, big, often very shareable fresh salads, available in cafes everywhere, may become mainstays, especially in hot weather. *Leben* and *eshel,* thin Israeli yogurts, are also good hot-weather choices, although fruit-flavored and custard yogurts are also available at

## Tips Dining Bargains

1. Look for weekday business lunch specials. In many restaurants they go on until 5 or 6pm. They give you great deals and an early start for getting to bed and up at dawn for another day's touring. Remember—after the witching hour when lunch turns to dinner, the price for the same dishes can double.
2. In Jerusalem, Tel Aviv, and Eilat, you'll find free tourist magazines and pamphlets loaded with coupons offering 10% discounts on many restaurants. Some of these places are quite good, and many are recommended by Frommer's. If nothing else, 10% takes care of the tip.
3. Amazingly, kosher restaurants are not all that easy to find in all parts of Israel. Check out www.eluna.com, a website that reviews tons of kosher choices all over the country. Not only do you get tips on what's good (remember, the restaurants reviewed on this site have a business arrangement with eluna), but you also get discount coupons and vouchers for dining spots that look promising.
4. Falafel and *shwarma* (grilled meat) sandwiches on pita used to be the staff of life for most Israelis and budget travelers, but in recent years, a fancier, more expensive Israeli dining scene has emerged. With food prices up and the U.S. dollar down, take to the streets. Israeli street food is great, and no eatery survives that isn't good. If you buy from a stand, look for a place with lots of fresh salads to add to your pita, and ask for a plastic bag to take your order away to your room—if you try falafel dining as you walk, half your meal will land in the gutter.
5. Fill up at breakfast. Israeli hotels offer vast morning buffets, and if you're discreet, and your hotel dining room is big and busy, there should be no problem slipping a few treats into your daypack for later in the day.

## Sampling the Grape

Israel's symbol has long been the familiar picture of the spies sent into Canaan by Moses returning with a bunch of grapes so huge they had to hang it from a pole to carry it. Now modern Israel is using grapes in a new way, to produce notable, prizewinning wines.

Information about Israeli wines is available in Jerusalem at the remarkable **Avi Ben Wine Store,** 22 Rivlin St. (℡ **02/622-3018**), and also at **Gaffen** wine shop, 42 Emek Refaim St. (℡ **02/561-9617**), in the German Colony. In Jaffa, the gourmet and atmospheric **Yoe'ezer Wine Bar** (℡ **03/683-9115**), opposite the Clock Tower on Yefet Street, offers a wonderful chance to sample fine Israeli and imported wines, accompanied, if you like, by excellent food (Yoe'ezer specializes in one of the most fabulous collections of Burgundian wines you'll ever find). The owner of Yoe'ezer Wine Bar, Shaul Evron, a noted Israeli journalist and food critic, is usually on hand in the evenings to offer careful advice and suggestions. His staff is also knowledgeable.

groceries and supermarkets. Arabic *labaneh*—a rich country yogurt, seasoned and served with pita, olives, and a drop of olive oil—is a summer dish you'll find in East Jerusalem, Old Akko, and Nazareth. For kosher travelers, Israel offers a rare chance to sample excellent kosher Indian food, as well as an array of kosher Italian, French, Chinese, and sushi restaurants.

But a big chunk of the Israeli cuisine experience is just being there. A great lamb chop, a plate of ordinary pasta, a grilled lamb kabob, or even a falafel sandwich becomes a memorable meal if it's served on a starlit dock stretching into the Sea of Galilee, or on a rooftop terrace in the heart of Jerusalem's Old City, with vistas of the Temple Mount and the roofs of the bazaars all around you. Israeli cuisine is an international food festival, only a small part of which is just like grandma used to make.

## ISRAEL'S WINE

The wine scene is fairly new in Israel. At one time, only parochial kosher wines of little interest to the outside world were produced, but since the 1980s, the wine industry in Israel has undergone a major revolution. The **Golan Heights** (Ramat Ha Golan) **Winery,** which opened at Qatzrin in 1983, set new standards of quality and inventiveness. Its 1984 cabernet sauvignon won a gold medal at the International Wine and Spirit Competition, and the winery has received the Chairman's Award for Excellence at Vinexpo three times. A wave of other new, smaller wineries throughout the country followed this success.

The Golan Heights Winery remains the leader in the climb toward new standards of excellence, concentrating on the production of cabernet sauvignon and merlot, as well as crisp, dry sauvignon blanc and chardonnay and a good semi-dry emerald Riesling. Golan Heights wines are produced in the Yarden, Gamla, and Golan series. Yarden is the most prestigious of the three, known especially for its deep red cabernet sauvignon, but all Golan Heights series are good.

**Carmel Mizrachi,** the largest winery in Israel, also underwent a quality revolution. Its Rothschild series is increasingly prestigious, and includes quality cabernet sauvignon and merlot, as well as chardonnay, emerald Riesling, and sauvignon blanc.

The smaller **Baron Winery** and the **Barkan Winery** are also worthy of note, as are the interesting wines of the Latrun

Monastery near Jerusalem and the wines of the West Bank's **Bet Jalla Monastery,** which are sold inside Israel at the Monastery at Bet Jimal, south of Beit Shemesh. The **Binyamina Winery,** near Zichron Yaacov, has recently begun producing quality wines. Among the up-and-coming "boutique" wineries, look for the **Dalton Winery** north of Safed, the **Amiad Winery** near Korazim northeast of the Sea of Galilee, the **Tzora Winery** in the hills west of Jerusalem, and the legendary **Margolit** wines, produced by the owner of an Italian restaurant in Jerusalem, which are generally available only by advance reserved purchase.

## 8 Recommended Books

### GENERAL BACKGROUND

Josephus's *The Jewish Wars* is on every English-speaking Israeli's bookshelf. A Jewish general in the Galilee during the revolt against Rome in A.D. 66—and an eventual traitor—Josephus was also a historian who provided volumes of historical commentaries and anecdotes about almost every area you'll see in Israel. *The Earthly Jerusalem,* by Norman Kotker (Scribner, 1969), is a graceful, wryly intelligent history of Jerusalem from earliest to modern times; *Jerusalem: City of Mirrors,* by Amos Elon, is another highly readable history of that city. *Jerusalem on Earth,* by Abraham Rabinovich (Macmillan, 1988), contains wonderful real-life stories about people in contemporary Jerusalem by one of the *Jerusalem Post's* finest human-interest writers.

### ARCHAEOLOGY

Yigael Yadin, the Israeli archaeologist whose father, Professor E. L. Sukenik of Hebrew University, identified the first fragments of the Dead Sea Scrolls in 1947, has written a beautifully photographed, thrilling book about the final archaeological search of the Dead Sea Caves in the early 1960s. The book, *Bar-Kokhba* (Harper & Row, 1971), reads almost like a novel and is available in bookstores throughout Israel and in most American libraries. Perhaps no other book allows you to share the excitement of each amazing discovery and lets you understand what archaeology means to those who love Israel. Yigael Yadin is also the author of books on the Masada and Hazor archaeological projects.

Other recommended books about archaeology include *Judaism in Stone,* by Hershel Shanks (Harper & Row, 1979), a heavily illustrated survey of ancient synagogues in Israel and the Middle East; and *In the Shadow of the Temple,* by Meir Ben-Dov (Harper & Row, 1985), a lavishly illustrated and photographed volume that details recent archaeological discoveries in the Jewish Quarter of Jerusalem.

### FICTION & POETRY

Israeli writers face the problem of creating literature in a language that was mainly used for prayer and religious study for more than 2,000 years. Working in a tradition so long interrupted, writers face many problems.

Among the Israeli writers most accessible to English-speaking readers are **Amos Oz,** whose early novel, *My Michael,* with its delicate narrative voice, has been beautifully translated into English; **Yehuda Amichai,** whose poetry is personal yet filled with evocative Israeli locales, imagery, and a graceful, visionary wit; and **Aharon Appelfeld,** who writes in the surreal, European tradition of Kafka. **S. Y. Agnon,** Israel's Nobel Prize–winning writer, worked in a disciplined Hebrew that drew intensively on a knowledge of east European legends and Jewish intellectual and religious history; try his novel, *The Bridal Canopy.* Emile Habiby is an award-winning writer from Israel's Arabic community; his wry approach can be sampled in *The Secret Life of Saeed, The Ill-fated Pessoptimist: A Palestinian Who Became a Citizen of Israel*. **Anton Shamas** displays an interesting blend of both Hebrew and Arabic style and sensibility. His novel, *Arabesques,* points to rich, new directions in which Israeli writing may develop. Among other outstanding modern novels are *The Smile of the Lamb,* by **David Grossman,** and *A Late Divorce,* by **A. B. Yehoshua.**

Murder mystery fans will find the works of **Baya Gur** interesting not only for their plots but also because they detail the many odd quirks of Israeli society. I especially like the books in the Detective Ohayon series, such as *The Bethlehem Road. Murder On A Kibbutz: A Communal Case* is another favorite. **Matt Beynon Rees,** a journalist from the U.K., writes about murder, politics, and intrigue inside the West Bank. His popular and revealing *The Collaborator of Bethlehem* is his most successful thriller in this genre.

For a sampling of Israeli poetry, read *The Modern Hebrew Poem Itself,* an anthology edited by Stanley Burnshaw (Holt, Rinehart and Winston, 1965); and *Poems of Jerusalem* (Harper & Row, 1988) and *Even a Fist Was Once an Open Palm with Fingers* (Harper Books, 1991), both by Israel's preeminent poet, **Yehuda Amichai.** The venerable and very moving **Taha Muhammed Ali** (who owns a tourist shop in Nazareth) writes poems of elegance and wisdom about the personal and political complexities of war and of being an Arab Israeli. His books, including *So What* and *Never Mind,* have been translated into English and Hebrew by Gabriel Levin, Yahya Hijazi, and Peter Cole. Israeli novelist David Grossman's *The Yellow Wind,* containing interviews with Palestinians just before the First Intifada, reveals the depth of despair and bitterness that has become a way of life for so many Palestinians.

## OTHER BOOKS

*Jerusalemwalks,* by **Nitza Rosovsky,** is filled with detailed, interesting guided walking tours in Jerusalem. Rosovsky's family has lived in Jerusalem for more than a century, and her anecdotal information is fascinating.

## 9 Recordings

The Oranim Zabar Troupe featuring Geula Gill orchestrated and performed many of the classic 1950s and 1960s Israeli songs that are known to Israeli folk dancers around the world. Look for "Shalom!" "Hora," and "On the Road to Eilat," all originally Electra recordings. This music, like Israel itself, was a synthesis of old and new traditions.

For the truly authentic stuff, look up ethnomusicologist Deben Bhattacharya, who compiled a wonderful four-record collection of traditional Israeli musicians from Morocco, Uzbekistan, Bukhara, Yemen, and other lands called *In Israel Today* (Westminster Recordings).

Israeli popular music reflects a lively, unusual blend of Western and Middle Eastern styles and sensibilities. Among Israel's all-time favorites to look for are Ethnix, a group that does Orientalized versions of Western dance rock; Zehava Ben, a wildly popular songstress of Jewish-Moroccan ancestry (her song, "Ketourne Massala," in collaboration with Ethnix, was one of Israel's biggest hits in recent years); the legendary Ofra Haza, who died suddenly in 2000, one of the first Israeli singers to break into the international market, with a repertoire that included both traditional Yemenite songs and rearrangements of these pieces into disco (*Shadai* is her most popular album: *Desert Wind* is geared to the dance market); and Yehuda Poliker, the son of a Holocaust survivor from the Greek community of

Salonika, whose bestselling *Enayim Sheli* (My Eyes) opened the door to Hebrew interpretation and rendition of Greek music. Finally, of special interest to Westerners is Ahinoam Nini (outside of Israel, she's know as "Noa"), who grew up in the United States and has returned to Israel to dazzle her homeland with her extraordinarily pure voice (she was invited to the Vatican to perform "Ave Maria" before the pope). Her original songs and renditions of classics range from witty to dramatic and reflect lively New York, English-language, Yemenite-Israeli sensibilities that are absolutely dynamite. *Bustan Avraham* (the Garden of Abraham), a group of Jewish and Arab Israelis that does gentle interpretations of traditional Middle Eastern music, is also very worth checking out.

## 10 Films

Israelis are in love with cinema, as evidenced by the fabulous cinémathèques and film archives in Jerusalem, Haifa, and Tel Aviv, and the mini-cinémathèques that have sprung up in smaller cities such as Eilat, Holon, and Herzlia. Documentary film played an important part in creating the image of the emerging Zionist dream in the 1920s and 1930s, but until recently, the Israeli film industry mainly produced rather heavy-handed comedies, melodramas, and dramas about the Israeli-Palestinian political situation. *Sallah,* a 1965 comedy about the absorption problems of Jewish immigrants from Arab countries, was the first Israeli film to have an international run; it starred Chaim Topol, who later starred in the American film *Fiddler on the Roof.* The Greek director, Costa-Gavras (who made the politically sensational *Z,* which examined the Greek military dictatorship of the 1960s) also turned his sights on the Israeli-Palestinian situation in the 1984 film *Hanna K,* starring Jill Clayburgh as a recent American immigrant to Israel who finds herself as the defense attorney for a mysterious Palestinian. Also check out the wry comedy *Goodbye New York,* by Amos Kollek (the son of Jerusalem mayor Teddy Kollek), staring Julie Hagarty as the most lost tourist ever to arrive in Israel. Interesting recent Israeli films include *Yana's Friends,* a bittersweet tale of new Russian immigrants in Tel Aviv at the time of the 1991 Gulf War, when Saddam Hussein was lobbing missiles into Israel each night that he threatened would contain chemical and biological weapons; and the 2007 international Israeli hit *The Band's Visit,* a social comedy about an Egyptian band on an official cultural tour of Israel that gets lost in the Negev desert. Nazareth director Elia Suleiman explores the quirks and difficulties of life in Israel's Arab community in his inventive comedies, *Chronicle of a Disappearance* and *Divine Intervention;* also check out the bittersweet *Rana's Wedding,* by Nazareth director Hani Abu Assad, about the sometimes comedic efforts of a young, modern East Jerusalem woman to get married so she can keep her Jerusalem resident status.

# 3

# Planning Your Trip to Israel

## Frommer's Planning Information

Israel is a tricky country to visit even when it's at its absolute best. It's a very small country in a politically sensitive part of the world, and whenever political tensions subside for a while, the floodgates open and the country is awash with a backlog of travelers who have been waiting to visit. Because Israel is so small, hotel rooms become extremely hard to find (and rates skyrocket). The minute tensions rise, or an act of terrorism occurs, tourism dips or disappears, and you have the entire country to yourself (hotel rates don't appear to go down—hoteliers try to get the most out of the few tourists who *are* around—but a bit of searching can turn up real bargains). Summer is high season in most parts of the country, and often very hot for intensive touring. Spring and autumn are ideal climate-wise, but visitors have to work around the Jewish High Holidays and the weeklong festival of Succot in the fall, plus the weeklong Passover holiday in the early spring and Shavuot in the late spring, when Israelis are on vacation, flights are full, rooms are scarce, and prices are at superhigh levels. At these times, it takes advance planning to book in where you want and when you want.

Citizens of western Europe, North America, Australia, and New Zealand are issued visas good for up to 3 months upon arrival at Israel's Ben-Gurion Airport. For security reasons, visitors whose passports indicate extensive travel to countries that are politically unstable or technically at war with Israel (such as Iran, Sudan, Afghanistan, or Lebanon) may be taken aside for questioning upon arrival in Israel, and in some cases denied entrance. Travelers with Israeli visa stamps in their passports may enter Egypt and Jordan, which have peace agreements and diplomatic relations with Israel; however, an Israeli visa stamp or any evidence of travel to Israel will generally preclude entrance into any other Arabic countries, except for Morocco and Tunisia. Travelers entering Jordan by land from Israel are issued a visa at the border for a fee. Travelers entering Sinai by land from Israel will receive a Sinai Only visa at the Taba Border Crossing. If you wish to travel into **Egypt beyond Sinai,** you must obtain an **All Egypt** visa from an Egyptian embassy or consulate ahead of time.

For travelers to Israel and Jordan, no special shots or vaccinations are necessary unless you are coming from an area of epidemic or infection. Water is drinkable throughout Israel; in Jordan and Egypt you must use bottled water.

For additional help in planning your trip and for more on-the-ground resources in Israel, please see the "Fast Facts, Toll-Free Numbers & Websites" appendix on p. 502.

---

**Tips    Tourism Info Hot Line**

Tourphone is an Israel Ministry of Tourism service available 24 hours a day, 7 days a week offering tourist information, directions, current entry and exit regulations at various border crossings, and assistance with emergencies and visa problems. Call *3888 from any Israeli telephone. Information is available in English and French.

---

## 1 Visitor Information

The Israel Ministry of Tourism maintains Israel Government Tourist Offices (IGTOs) in a number of countries throughout the world. The Ministry of Tourism's website (**www.tourism.gov.il**) has country-specific information for citizens of the U.S. and Commonwealth countries, as well as for many European countries. It also offers information about maps, special events in Israel, a schedule of conferences and conventions, information about tour groups, and special deals and advice for prospective visitors to Israel. On this website you'll also find the current rates of exchange vis-à-vis the new Israeli shekel.

For additional lively and very useful information, readers in the United States and Canada can contact the **Israel Government Tourism Office (IGTO) North American Information Center** (© **888/ 77-ISRAEL** [477235]; www.goisrael.com). **U.S.** offices are at 6380 Wilshire Blvd., Ste. 1718, Los Angeles, CA 90048 (© **323/658-7463**), and 800 Second

Ave., New York, NY 10117 (© **212/499-5650**).

**Canadians** can head to 180 Bloor St. W., Ste. 700, Toronto, ON M5S 2V6 (© **416/964-3784;** www.igto.ca; info@ igto.ca). For the **United Kingdom** and **Ireland,** the regional IGTO office is at UK House, 180 Oxford St., London W1D 1NN (© **0207/299-1111;** www. thinkisrael.com).

The **Jordan Tourism Board**'s official website (www.visitjordan.com) is probably the most efficient for any country in the Middle East. For travel information specific to Petra and its surrounding area, another helpful website is www.go2petra. com.

For travel forums filled with readers' reports, concerns, and discussions, go to the Frommer's Israel and Jordan message boards (www.frommers.com); and Trip Advisor (www.tripadvisor.com), which has lively forums on travel to Israel and Jordan.

## 2 Entry Requirements

### PASSPORTS

All travelers entering Israel, Jordan, or Sinai must present a valid passport with an expiration date not less than 6 months from the date of entry into those countries. Travelers from western Europe, Canada, the U.S., Australia, and South Africa will receive a visa upon entering Israel, Jordan, and Sinai; in order to enter

all of Egypt (beyond Sinai) by land from Israel, you must have an All Egypt visa, obtainable ahead of time at any Egyptian embassy or consulate. Visas for Israel are usually given for 3 months and can be renewed inside Israel at the Ministry of Interior in Jerusalem. Visas for Jordan are usually given for 30 days. Sinai Only visas to Egypt are generally good for 14 days.

> ### (Warning  Watch That Stamp!
>
> If you plan to visit Arab countries, ask for your visa stamp to be placed on a piece of paper separate from your passport when you enter Israel (if your passport is stamped by Israel, that stamp will close the doors to many Arab and Islamic countries for the duration of your passport). Israeli passport control personnel are accustomed to this request and in most cases will cooperate, but an occasional ill-tempered clerk may decide to make extra problems for you by stamping your passport. With political conditions the way they are, even in relatively friendly places such as Morocco, Egypt, or even Bali (a Hindu island in Muslim Indonesia), Israeli stamps in your passport could cause problems should you find yourself in a local police station, or when you show your passport in banks, hotels, or post offices.

*Note:* Visas to Jordan are given on the spot at the Sheikh Hussein Crossing from northern Israel and at the Rabin Crossing from Eilat (southern Israel); however, you must obtain a visa in advance from a Jordanian embassy if you plan to enter Jordan via the Allenby–King Hussein Bridge in the West Bank.

For information on how to obtain a passport, see **"Passports"** in the **"Fast Facts: Israel"** appendix (p. 502).

## VISAS

**ISRAEL**  Visas are given free to U.S., U.K., and Canadian citizens, without prior application, when they enter Israel at Ben-Gurion or Eilat International airports and show passports that are valid for at least 6 months beyond the time of arrival. The tourist visa is good for 3 months and can be extended for another 3 consecutive months at any office of the Ministry of the Interior (you may be asked to prove you have adequate funding for your extended stay). For residents of New Zealand, Australia, and Ireland, visas are issued free upon entry and are valid for 3 months. To work, study, or settle in Israel, you need the proper permit before arrival. If you enter Israel at an overland crossing from either Egypt (Sinai) or Jordan, you may receive a visa valid only for 30 days.

**JORDAN**  Travelers from Israel crossing into Jordan can obtain visas for a fee at border crossings. Visas to Jordan are generally valid for 1 month. For those travelers planning to enter **Jordan via the Allenby–Sheikh Hussein Bridge in the West Bank,** a visa must be obtained in advance in your country of origin or at the Jordanian Embassy in Tel Aviv, 14 Abba Hillel St., Ramat Gan (a suburb of Tel Aviv; *©* **03/751-7752**). Travelers from Israel crossing into Jordan at the Sheikh Hussein Bridge in northern Israel (not to be confused with the Allenby–King Hussein Bridge in the West Bank), or the Rabin Crossing near Eilat will be issued visas at the crossing point.

**EGYPT**  "All Egypt" visas for travelers entering Egypt from Israel by land at the Taba Border Crossing must be obtained in advance through the Egyptian Embassy in your home country, or at the Egyptian Embassy, 18 Basel St., Tel Aviv (*©* **03/544-1615**) or at the Egyptian Consulate in Eilat, 68 Hakfroni St. (*©* **08/637-6882**). "Sinai Only" visas for travelers planning to visit only Sinai are issued on the spot at the Taba Crossing. For those who wish to visit the Ras Mohammed National Park (outstanding snorkeling and diving reefs) at Sharm ek Sheik, Sinai, the All Egypt visa is required.

## MEDICAL REQUIREMENTS

Unless you're arriving from an area known to be suffering from an epidemic (particularly cholera or yellow fever), inoculations or vaccinations are not required for entry into Israel or Jordan.

## CUSTOMS
### WHAT YOU CAN BRING INTO ISRAEL

You can bring $200 (£100) worth of tax-free gifts into the country. You can also bring in 250 grams of tobacco, one bottle (⅘ quart) of liquor, and a reasonable amount of film. When you leave you can convert up to $3,000 (£1,500) back into foreign currency at the airport, so keep your bank receipts.

### WHAT YOU CAN TAKE HOME FROM ISRAEL

Note that you cannot take antiquities or archaeological artifacts out of Israel unless you have a certificate identifying the object, which will be provided to you by any licensed antiquities dealer.

**Canadian Citizens:** For a clear summary of Canadian rules, write for the booklet *I Declare,* issued by the Canada Border Services Agency (© **800/461-9999** in Canada, or 204/983-3500; www.cbsa-asfc.gc.ca).

**U.K. Citizens:** For information, contact **HM Customs & Excise** at © **0845/010-9000** (from outside the U.K., © 020/8929-0152), or consult their website at **www.hmce.gov.uk**.

**Australian Citizens:** A helpful brochure available from Australian consulates or Customs offices is *Know Before You Go.* For more information, call the **Australian Customs Service** at © **1300/363-263,** or log on to **www.customs.gov.au**.

**New Zealand Citizens:** Most questions are answered in a free pamphlet available at New Zealand consulates and Customs offices: *New Zealand Customs Guide for Travellers, Notice no. 4.* For more information, contact **New Zealand Customs,** the Customhouse, 17–21 Whitmore St., Box 2218, Wellington (© **04/473-6099** or 0800/428-786; **www.customs.govt.nz**).

## 3 When to Go

**CLIMATE**    The Israeli seasons are different from those in the United States and western Europe. Basically there are two seasons: winter (late Oct to mid-Mar), which is cool to cold and when the rains occur; and summer (Apr–Oct), which is warm to hot and virtually rain-free. Winter in Israel starts with showers in October and continues through periodic heavy rainfalls from November to March. Swimming is out in the Mediterranean during this time, except during occasional heat waves, although at times you can swim in Eilat and The Dead Sea in the winter. The Israeli winter doesn't normally involve snow, except for Mount Hermon on the Golan Heights. There could be occasional flurries in Jerusalem and the Upper Galilee (and the chance of a heavier snowfall two or three times a decade in Jerusalem). Jerusalem even had a .6m (2-ft.) snowfall in 1920, and two huge storms in the 1990s, so anything is possible. Luckily, even the biggest snowfall melts away in a few days. Tel Aviv and the coast don't get snow—people from those areas rush to Jerusalem to see it when it occurs.

During February and the beginning of March, the entire country seems to turn green from the winter rains, and wildflower displays in the Galilee and the Golan regions are truly spectacular. By late March, the flowers and the green will have faded. In the months that follow, the heat gathers intensity, reaching its peak in

July and August, when the only relatively cool spots are Jerusalem (at night) and the high mountains around Safed. The landscape is dry and parched by May, but by September temperatures fall off a bit.

Israel also experiences hot, dry desert winds at the beginning and end of the summer, although a *hamsin* can occur anytime from March to November. These southern and eastern winds are named after the Arabic word for 50, since the wind was traditionally believed to blow for 50 days a year. Thankfully, it doesn't. A *hamsin* (or *sharav*) heat wave means you must cut back on rushing around: Plan to be in air-conditioned museums, in the shadowy depths of a bazaar, or in the water during midday, and make sure you add to your water intake. Also, be sure to wear a hat and slather on sunscreen.

In winter, cold rain systems move in from the north. Because they are prevented from continuing south by the constant tropical highs over Africa, these storms can stall over Israel for days until they rain themselves out. Lots of warm socks, layered clothes (including a fleece liner), and a good raincoat and portable umbrella are what you need if you visit in winter. If you find a few days of your trip hampered by constant rain, your reward will be the chance to visit pine forests near Jerusalem and in the Galilee as fragrant and misty as those of the Pacific Northwest. In late winter, you'll see the countryside carpeted with wildflowers and a rare, fragile veil of greenery.

## Israel's Average Temperatures

|  |  | Jan | Feb | Mar | Apr | May | June | July | Aug | Sept | Oct | Nov | Dec |
|---|---|---|---|---|---|---|---|---|---|---|---|---|---|
| Jerusalem | °F | 43–53 | 44–57 | 47–61 | 53–69 | 60–77 | 63–81 | 66–84 | 66–86 | 65–82 | 60–78 | 54–67 | 47–56 |
|  | °C | 6–11 | 7–14 | 8–16 | 12–21 | 15–25 | 17–27 | 19–29 | 19–29 | 18–28 | 16–26 | 12–19 | 8–14 |
| Tel Aviv | °F | 49–65 | 48–66 | 51–69 | 54–72 | 63–77 | 67–83 | 70–86 | 69–89 | 59–83 | 54–76 | 54–77 | 49–66 |
|  | °C | 9–18 | 9–19 | 10–20 | 12–22 | 17–25 | 19–28 | 21–30 | 22–30 | 20–31 | 15–28 | 12–25 | 9–19 |
| Haifa | °F | 49–63 | 47–64 | 47–70 | 55–78 | 58–76 | 64–82 | 68–86 | 70–86 | 68–85 | 60–80 | 56–74 | 48–65 |
|  | °C | 8–17 | 9–18 | 2–21 | 13–26 | 15–25 | 18–28 | 20–30 | 21–30 | 20–30 | 16–27 | 13–23 | 9–18 |
| Tiberias | °F | 48–65 | 49–67 | 49–67 | 56–80 | 62–89 | 68–95 | 73–98 | 75–99 | 71–95 | 65–89 | 59–78 | 53–68 |
|  | °C | 9–18 | 9–20 | 11–22 | 13–27 | 17–32 | 20–35 | 23–37 | 24–37 | 22–35 | 19–32 | 15–26 | 11–20 |
| Eilat | °F | 49–70 | 51–73 | 56–79 | 63–87 | 69–95 | 75–99 | 77–103 | 79–104 | 75–98 | 69–92 | 61–83 | 51–74 |
|  | °C | 10–21 | 11–23 | 13–26 | 17–31 | 21–35 | 24–37 | 25–40 | 26–40 | 24–36 | 20–33 | 16–28 | 11–23 |

**ISRAEL'S CALENDAR(S)** If awards were given for "daily" confusion, or for having the maximum number of holidays a year, Israel would probably win them all. Israel "officially" operates on two separate systems for determining day, month, and year: the Jewish calendar, with its roots in ancient Canaanite and Babylonian tradition, dating from some 5,750 years ago, and the Gregorian calendar, used in most countries, including the United States. Recognized, but "unofficial," are even more calendars, such as the Julian (Julius Caesar) calendar, which runs 13 days behind the Gregorian; and the Muslim era, which counts the years from A.D. 622, when the Prophet Muhammad led the hegira from Mecca to Medina. Not only do these calendars disagree about dates, but also about whether time is measured by sun, moon, or a combination of the two, and when the year should start and end. (I've never calculated how many New Year celebrations occur each year in Israel, but I do know of at least three Christmases.)

**HOLIDAYS** Israeli holidays and events will affect your visit in several important ways. First, hotels and campsites will fill

## Tips Advice for a Rainy Day

There are very few storm drains in Israel, so streets become minirivers whenever it rains. Sturdy, rubber-soled shoes are a necessity. In Jerusalem and in areas of Old Tiberias, Jaffa, and Safed, the picturesque stone pavements and staircases become lethally slippery when wet. Walk on them as if they were covered with sheets of ice, and use railings provided on steep staircase passageways. Always check with tourist information offices or the Society for Protection of Nature before hiking in the desert in winter. The sun may be shining in the desert, but rain up in Jerusalem flows into the wadis (canyons) leading down to The Dead Sea and can build up into walls of water and boulders that sweep everything (including unwary tourists) away.

to capacity and rates will rise by as much as 20%. Next, transportation and restaurant service may be curtailed or completely suspended, and places of entertainment may be closed. On the other hand, a holiday is a special occasion, and you won't want to miss the events that may take place.

Israel is also a most confusing place when it comes to the weekly holiday schedule. Jews stop work at midafternoon on Friday; some Muslims at sundown on Thursday (although many shops remain open on Fri); most Christians all day on Sunday. In Tel Aviv, no buses run from late Friday afternoon until Saturday after sundown, although small private minibuses cover some of the main routes. In Jerusalem, buses run only in the Arab neighborhoods on Saturday; in Haifa, there's partial bus service on Saturday. In nonreligious Eilat, there is no public transport on Shabbat. Throughout the country, some shops open just as others are closing for a holiday.

Lots of religious holidays change dates each year. The entire Muslim religious calendar starts 11 days earlier each year—it's a lunar calendar. This means the Islamic holy month of Ramadan, when Muslims may not eat or drink during daylight hours (and when Western visitors may not visit the mosques on the Temple Mount in Jerusalem), slowly

migrates across the year. How to keep your wits amid all these openings and closings? Read the following information carefully.

**THE JEWISH SABBATH** The Bible states that the 7th day is one of rest—a time when no work can be done. For Orthodox Jews, this means no fires are lit, no human beings or animals can be made to work, no machines can be operated, no traveling can be done, no money handled, no business transacted. So officially that's the way it is in most of Israel, where the Sabbath, or Shabbat, is celebrated on Saturday. By 2 or 3pm on a Friday afternoon, depending on whether it's winter or summer (Shabbat begins at sundown), most shops have closed for the day. Buses and trains stop running at least an hour before Shabbat, and the movie houses are closed at night. There is a growing list of exceptions: In central Tel Aviv, many restaurants, cafes, discos, and theaters close on Friday afternoon for a few hours, but reopen on Friday night; Haifa has always had a quiet alternative Friday nightlife; and in Jerusalem, a number of cinemas and restaurants (nonkosher) remain open; recently the pub area around Jerusalem's Russian Compound has begun to boom, and Friday nights are very busy.

On Saturday, almost all shops throughout the country are closed (except in

Israel's Arab communities, including cafes and Arab or Christian establishments in Jerusalem's Old City) and nearly all transportation stops (only Haifa has limited municipal bus service at this time, and only taxis or small sherut companies ply in or between cities). Gas stations are mostly open on Shabbat, since few are located in religious neighborhoods. Most admission-free museums are ordinarily open for part of Shabbat; entrance tickets, when required, must sometimes be bought from private-duty guards outside the museum entrance. A few strictly kosher restaurants follow this same no-money-handling rule, accepting only advanced prepaid orders for Shabbat meals, which will often be cooked in advance and served tepid or cold; 99% of kosher restaurants, however, will be closed. Also, do watch for signs in restaurants or hotel dining rooms asking you not to smoke, so as not to offend Orthodox guests. (Lighting a cigarette or turning on a light switch is considered starting a fire, which is an act of work forbidden on Shabbat.)

Precise hours for the duration of Shabbat, which vary according to the time of sunset, are listed in the Friday *Jerusalem Post*. The restarting of buses and reopening of cinemas and restaurants can be quite late in summer, as Shabbat does not end until you can see three stars in the sky at one glance.

Most Israelis are not Sabbath observant and love to travel on their day off, so if you drive on Saturday, you'll find the roads to beaches and parks quite busy. About the only people who'll try to stop you are the ultrareligious Jews, such as those in Jerusalem's Mea Shearim section. There they tend to get violent about people who ignore their interpretation of Shabbat restrictions. Many streets in religious areas will be blocked with boulders; most ultra-Orthodox neighborhoods in Jerusalem and Bnei Brak, near Tel Aviv, have official permission to close their

streets to traffic. Don't even think of trying to drive in or up to such areas. You can be stoned, injured, and your vehicle damaged, and you will have no help from the police.

Israelis work 6 days a week, and as almost everything is shut down on Friday nights, Thursday and Saturday nights are for staying up late and partying. By nightfall on Saturdays, transportation services resume, and movie houses begin selling tickets for evening shows. By dark, all entertainment venues are usually packed full, including the many sidewalk cafes. Restaurants need about an hour after the end of Shabbat to assemble their staffs and prepare things before they open their doors to the public. You won't get the best possible meal at a restaurant on Saturday night—conditions are crowded, staffs are harried, and many items will have been prepared on Thursday or Friday.

## ISRAEL CALENDAR OF HOLIDAYS & EVENTS

Here's a general guide to when holidays and festivals occur in Israel. Keep in mind that a Jewish holiday that generally falls in March, say, may some years fall on a late date in February because Jews follow a lunar-based year. Note also that not all Jewish holidays are subject to Sabbath-like prohibitions and closings. Holidays on which things do close down are indicated by an asterisk (*). **Note:** *Celebration of each holiday commences at sundown on the evening before the date listed and ends at sundown of the last day shown.*

For updated information about holidays, special events, and festivals, check with your nearest IGTO office. In North America, call the **Israel Tourism Information Center** at © **888/77-ISRAEL** (477235), or check online at **www.goisrael.com**. For an exhaustive list of events beyond those listed here, check http://events.frommers.com, where you'll find a searchable, up-to-the-minute roster of what's happening in cities all over the world.

### January/February
**Israeli Arbor Day (Tu b'Shevat):** Thousands of singing and dancing

schoolchildren traipse off to plant trees all over the country. Synagogues and some restaurants have special Tu b'Shevat dinners. February 9, 2009; January 30, 2010.

## March

**Purim (Feast of Lots):** Recalling how Queen Esther saved her people in Persia (5th c. B.C.), this is an exciting time when folks, especially children, dress up in fancy or zany (or sometimes irreligious) costumes, have parties, parade in the streets, give food baskets, spray shaving cream at passersby, and generally make merry. In Jerusalem and Safed, which are considered walled cities, Purim is celebrated 1 day later than in the rest of the country. March 10, 2009; February 28, 2010.

## April

**Passover (Pesach)\*:** No bread, beer, or other foods containing leavening are obtainable for 7 days (8 days outside Israel), and hotel and restaurant meals may cost more because of the culinary complexities. Many restaurants simply shut down for this period. During the days just before the holidays, women furiously clean their kitchens, and houses in general, to render them spotless and free of any stray bits of leavening. The first night of the holiday is devoted to a Seder, a family meal and ritual recalling the exodus of the ancient Israelites from Egypt. (**Note:** In the Diaspora, the Seder is held on both the first and second nights of Passover; however inside Israel the Seder is held only on the first night.) Many hotels and restaurants have special Seders for tourists. The first and last days of this holiday are Sabbath-like affairs, which means the country more or less closes down. During the half-holiday days of the Passover week, many shops, museums, and services are on reduced schedules. As schools are shut, Israelis travel during this week. Reservations at

hotels, B&Bs, and kibbutzim are impossible to get unless you've booked well ahead, and rates are the highest of the year. April 9 to April 16, 2009; March 30 to April 5, 2010.

**Holocaust Memorial Day (Yom Ha-Shoah)\*:** This marks the time of the year in 1945 when the last of the concentration camps in Europe were liberated and the Holocaust came to an end. All places of entertainment are closed. As the day begins (like all Jewish days, at nightfall), most restaurants are closed, although public transportation continues and most shops and businesses are open. At 10am on Yom Ha-Shoah, a siren sounds throughout the nation, and a period of silence is observed in memory of the six million Jews who perished. A special memorial ceremony is held at Yad VaShem in Jerusalem. Some places for simple meals and snacks are open during the day. April 21, 2009; April 11, 2010.

**Memorial Day\*:** One week after Yom Ha-Shoah, the nation remembers its war dead. Restaurants and places of public entertainment are closed, but transportation operates and most shops are open. Again, at 11am, a siren sounds, and a period of silence is observed. Throughout the country, memorial services are held. April 28, 2009; April 18, 2010.

**Independence Day:** The day after Memorial Day, Israel commemorates the day in 1948 when the British Mandate ended and the State of Israel was proclaimed. It is celebrated with house parties and municipal fireworks at night. April 29, 2009; April 19, 2010.

## May/June

**Lag b'Omer:** Ending 33 days of mourning, this is an especially happy celebration for the Hassidim, who leave Jerusalem and other cities at this time to sing and dance around bonfires at the Meiron tomb of the mystical Rabbi Shimon Bar Yochai, in Galilee. There are also pilgrimages made by Jews to the tombs of great rabbis. Children around the country sing, dance, and light evening bonfires. May 12, 2009; May 2, 2010.

**Jacob's Ladder Country, Folk, and Blues Festival** (usually at Kibbutz Nof Ginossar): This important event is held in the Galilee for 3 days in mid-May. Everything from contemporary and classic folk to Celtic is offered. For information, call © **04/696-2231,** or visit **www.jlfestival.com**.

**Shavuot (Pentecost)\*:** The early-summer harvest celebration is a joyous time, a special favorite of agricultural settlements. It is often marked by plays, entertainment, and children dressed in white, wearing floral crowns. Since it also recalls the receipt of the Ten Commandments, as well as the bringing of the "first fruits" to The Temple, it is observed as a religious holiday. Dairy foods such as blintzes and cheesecakes are traditionally prepared for the holiday, and at synagogues throughout the country, as well as at the Western Wall, the Torah is studied throughout the night. May 29 to May 30, 2009; May 19 to May 20, 2010.

**Abu Gosh Music Festival:** A new festival held in the Arab-Israeli village of Abu Gosh, in the hills west of Jerusalem. Classical and religious music is performed in the village's two churches; there are street performances and arts and crafts. It's held each year at Shavuot and Succot.

**Israel and Jerusalem Festivals of the Performing Arts:** In late spring, two festivals of extraordinary music groups, theater, and dance companies come from all over the world to perform. For exact dates and programs, check with the Israel Ministry of Tourism website (www.goisrael.com).

## July/August

**Tisha b'Av:** The fast day on the ninth day of the Jewish month of Av is a time set aside to remember the destruction of the First and Second Temples, which by ominous coincidence were destroyed on the same calendar day in the years 586 B.C. and A.D. 70, respectively. Entertainment facilities are closed. Many restaurants are closed. July 30, 2009; July 20, 2010.

**Israeli Folkdance Festival** (Karmiel, in the Galilee): Jewish ethnic dancers come from around the world for this festival held in early July.

**Jerusalem International Film Festival:** Increasingly prestigious, with many offerings from both mainstream and exotic countries. It takes place at the Jerusalem Cinémathèque in the first 2 weeks in July. For more information, call © **02/672-4131,** or visit **www.jer-cin.org.il**.

**Jerusalem Arts and Crafts Festival:** Held in the Sultan's Pool in the valley outside the western walls of the Old City, the contemporary Israeli craft booths are not usually of a high level, but the large International Craft Section is excellent. Performances by Israeli musicians every night. Late July.

**Red Sea Jazz Festival** (Eilat): This increasing acclaimed international jazz festival is held in Eilat for 4 days in either July or August. Go to **www.red seajazzeilat.com** for program information, tickets, and hotel and travel packages for the festival.

## September/October

The **Jerusalem International Chamber Music Festival:** Held at the YMCA Concert Hall and produced by the Jerusalem Symphony Orchestra under the directorship of pianist Elena

Bashkirova, this festival offers an array of internationally famous musicians performing classical chamber music. For information, check out **www.jcmf. org.il**.

**Ramadan:** During the holy month of Ramadan, Muslims do not eat or drink during daylight hours, but at night many parties are held. Most places serving food in Arab communities will be closed during the day; Islamic sites and mosques are closed to non-Muslims during the entire month. The Islamic holy month begins approximately 10 days earlier each year, and the exact first and last days depend on astronomical sightings in Saudi Arabia, therefore the following dates are approximate to within a day: August 22 to September 21, 2009; August 11 to September 10, 2010. **Eid Al Fitr,** the biggest holiday in the Islamic year, is celebrated the day Ramadan ends, and 2 or 3 days immediately following. On Eid Al Fitr, many shops are closed.

**Rosh Hashanah (Jewish New Year)*:** The start of the High Holy Days. Because the Jewish calendar starts in September or October, that's when New Year falls. It is a 2-day religious festival, not an occasion for revels but rather for solemn contemplation and prayer. Almost everything in the Jewish sector of the country is closed. September 19 and 20, 2009; September 9 and 10, 2010.

**Yom Kippur (Day of Atonement)*:** On the 10th day of the Jewish year, the High Holy Days culminate in the most solemn of Jewish holidays. Observant Jews spend nearly the whole day in synagogue. Places of worship are crowded, but the large synagogues reserve seats for tourists, and some of the larger hotels organize their own services. Yom Kippur is a fast day, but hotel dining rooms serve guests who wish to eat. Everything comes to a standstill; even television and radio stations suspend broadcasting. September 28, 2009; September 18, 2010.

**Succot (Feast of Tabernacles)*:** This 7-day holiday recalls how Moses and the children of Israel dwelled in "booths" (or "succot") as they left Egypt to wander in the desert. Observant families have meals and services in specially built, highly decorated yet simple huts, located outside in gardens or on balconies. Succot is also a harvest festival and thus an agricultural and kibbutz favorite. On the first and last days of Succot, Sabbath-like restrictions are observed. October 3 to October 10, 2009; September 23 to September 30, 2010.

**Simchat Torah*:** As Succot ends, Jews rejoice as they complete the yearly cycle of reading the Torah (the first five books of the Bible); street festivities in Jerusalem and Tel Aviv mark this day. Cantors read the final verses of the Torah in synagogues around the country and then immediately start again at its beginning. October 11, 2009; October 1, 2010.

## November

**Olive Festival:** In recent years, both Jewish and Arab communities in the Galilee have come to mark the November olive harvest period with at least a dozen local festivals of traditional foods, music, crafts, and dance. It's partly a genuine grass-roots reawakening of ancient traditions, and partly aimed at both Israeli and foreign tourists. Check with the Nazareth and Akko tourist information offices for the best listings.

**Jacob's Ladder Winter Folk Festival** (Kibbutz Nof Ginossar): A new indoor winter version of the 30-year-old (summer) Jacob's Ladder Folk Festival (see above). It's held on the shores of the Sea of Galilee. For information, call © **04/696-2231,** or visit **www.jlfestival.com**.

## December

**Chanukah:** Celebrates the victory of the Maccabees over Syrian Greeks and the consequent rededication of The Temple in 164 B.C. For 8 days, this history-based holiday is marked by the nightly lighting of the Chanukah, or eight-branch menorah (as opposed to the traditional seven-branch menorah, which was lit in The Temple and is a more ancient symbol of the Jewish people). December 22 to December 29, 2008; December 12 to December 29, 2009.

**Eid Al Adha:** The second-biggest Islamic holiday commemorates Abraham's near-sacrifice of his son. Animals are sacrificed, big family feasts are held, children receive gifts and new clothes, many shops in Arab neighborhoods are closed, and mosques are closed to tourists. The holiday changes according to the lunar calendar. December 9, 2008; November 28, 2009.

**International Choir Concerts:** These take place in Bethlehem on December 24. The Christian Information Centre (**www.christusrex.org**), inside Jaffa Gate, has information about these programs and about security conditions in Bethlehem.

**Liturgica (Jerusalem):** A week of choral music organized by the Jerusalem Symphony Orchestra in late December. For program information, go to www.jso.co.il/index-english.php.

## 4 Getting There & Getting Around

### GETTING TO ISRAEL
#### BY PLANE

Flights from North America and most flights from elsewhere land at Israel's main international airport, **Ben-Gurion** (TLV), partway between Tel Aviv and Jerusalem. Ben-Gurion Airport is approximately 20 minutes from Tel Aviv and 45 minutes from Jerusalem. At press time there were plans to recode the airport with a code indicating Jerusalem. The other international airport is Eilat, at the southern tip of Israel, but it is mainly used for direct charter flights from Europe to Eilat and a very few scheduled flights from inside Israel to Eilat.

A number of airlines operate nonstop flights from North America to Israel. Additionally, most European airlines offer direct connections through their home cities between a host of cities in North America and Israel. If you're traveling a long-haul route from North America, the airline you choose, and time of your flight, can have a major effect on your trip. If you have very few days to travel and want to start your trip the minute your workweek ends on Friday, you'll lose a day on El Al or Israir, because they currently do not fly on the Jewish Sabbath. If you're good at sleeping on airplanes, you may want a night flight; if you're not a strong in-flight sleeper, a daytime flight may get you to Israel in better shape to enjoy your vacation. The flight to Israel is a long 11 hours from the East Coast of North America. Upgrading to business class, especially if you can work it on frequent-flier miles, can be a very good investment and help you to avoid the effects of jet lag and sleeplessness. Finally, check the land arrangements that various airlines may offer for your time in Israel. An airline that offers great hotel package deals with your ticket can save you considerable money, or allow you to stay at top-quality hotels at bargain rates.

**El Al Israel Airlines** (© **800/223-6700** or 212/768-9200; www.elal.co.il) is still tops as far as getting you to Israel from North America as directly and conveniently as possible. It offers up to 28 nonstop flights a week to Tel Aviv's Ben-Gurion Airport (TLV) from New York's JFK Airport and is the only airline that offers first-class service on nonstop flights between New York and Israel. It also offers daily nonstop service from Newark (EWR), except Friday, when El Al never flies. El Al is the only airline that offers direct flights to Tel Aviv with no change of planes from Miami, Los Angeles, and Chicago. Two nonstop flights a week leave from Miami, and El Al is the only airline offering nonstop flights from Los Angeles to Tel Aviv (three times a week). El Al now sports a newly designed, upgraded platinum class, which replaced a far less luxurious business class. The airline also offers a discount for children age 11 and under traveling with two parents or adults. It's always worth checking with El Al to see about companion fare specials and upgrade deals, which are usually offered when travel to Israel is low. *Note:* El Al now has a code-sharing agreement with **American Airlines,** opening up all kinds of frequent-flier possibilities and allowing for many new connections and stopovers for points in North America and Europe.

*An added bonus:* Thanks to its close connections to the Israeli travel industry, El Al offers a variety of fabulous land-package arrangements (no other airline even comes close), but these packages can only be purchased with a round-trip North America–Israel El Al ticket.

Discount carrier **Israir Airlines** (© 877/ **ISRAIR-1** [477-2471] or 516/593-1785; www.israirairlines.com) is a recent addition to the New York-Tel Aviv airline scene. It plans to fly daily, except on the Jewish Sabbath, and promises to be a bit less expensive per ticket than El Al and a bit more no-frills. At press time, Israir had suspended service, but may be back on the New York-Tel Aviv route in summer 2009.

**Continental Airlines** (© 800/231-0856; www.continental.com) offers daily nonstop service between Newark Liberty International Airport and Tel Aviv. Its upscale business-elite class is probably the best of this category serving Israel, so if you have the cash or miles to burn, it's your best bet. Unlike El Al and Israir, Continental flies to Israel on Friday.

**Delta Air Lines** (© 800/241-4141; www.delta.com) began daily nonstop service between New York's JFK Airport and Tel Aviv in 2008. It also offers direct service between Atlanta and Tel Aviv, making it much easier for travelers in the South, Midwest, and West to make good connections to Atlanta and then on to Israel. The business-class section is a very worthwhile upgrade. Delta flies to Israel on Friday.

**Air Canada** (© 888/712-7786; www.aircanada.ca) has daily service from Toronto or Montreal to Tel Aviv, making it the best option for most Canadians. It also may be a good option for passengers from the U.S. Midwest, even with a necessary change of planes in Toronto or Montreal. Air Canada does fly on Friday. In 2008, Air Canada renovated its cabins and upgraded its business class, which was not up to par when I last flew on this airline.

If you want to combine your trip to Israel with a stopover in Europe (or just want to break up your flights so you can stretch your legs on the ground), look into the national airline of the country of your choice; there may be good deals available. Many European carriers are partnered with U.S.-based airlines, so you can use frequent-flier miles accumulated on domestic routes on the flight from Europe to Israel. Some of the European carriers that offer flights to Israel include **British Airways** (© 800/247-9297 in the U.S., or 0870/850-9850 in the U.K.; www.british-airways.com); **Swiss International Airlines,** with the shortest layovers and best connections between flights from North America and Israel (℡ 877/FLY-SWIS [359-7947] in the U.S., or 0845/601-9056 in London; www.swiss.com); **Lufthansa,** with the best first-class service, including a first-class lounge with complimentary bedrooms in Frankfurt Airport (℡ 800/645-3880 in the U.S., or 0870/837-7747 in the U.K.; www.lufthansa.com); and **Alitalia** (℡ 800/223-5730; www.alitalia.com). The latter is a major carrier of passengers between North America and Israel, and offers excellent land and hotel arrangements if you want to do a stopover in Italy or combine a pilgrimage to Rome with a journey to Jerusalem. **Austrian Airlines** (www.aua.com) gives you the chance for a stopover in Vienna, but its business-class service from Vienna to Tel Aviv consists of a plain coach seat and a slightly upgraded meal—not a good way to spend the last 4 hours of a flight from North America and a waste of money or frequent-flier points.

### Arriving at Ben-Gurion Airport

Modern **Ben-Gurion International Airport** (℡ 03/975-5555; www.ben-gurion-airport.com), at Lod on the outskirts of Tel Aviv, serves all of Israel, though there are small regional airports scattered throughout the country. After landing and passing through immigration and security, you'll proceed into the arrivals hall for baggage claim. There are lots of people around to help you here, including a fully staffed tourist office and a hotel reservations desk. Once you pass through this hall, you go through Customs and enter the main terminal, where you'll find shops, currency exchanges, car-rental desks, and airport transportation services.

**GETTING TO JERUSALEM**  The highly recommended **Nesher Taxis and Sheruts** (℡ 02/625-7227), located outside the main arrivals hall, will take you and your baggage from Ben-Gurion Airport to any address in Jerusalem via a

sherut (a shared taxi van) for NIS 45 ($11/£5.60) per person. The 45-minute trip into town will be a bit longer than by private taxi, but you don't have to argue with a taxi driver over fares and service is door-to-door.

The fixed-price rate for a **private taxi** to any destination in the main part of town is about NIS 260 ($65/£33). The price is higher at night and during Shabbat. You'll be whisked off directly to your destination, which could be nice after a long flight and the trudge through passport control, baggage pickup, and the airport terminal. A private taxi always means a bit more of a chance of an argument over fares, which isn't the best introduction to Israel.

**Egged buses** run from Ben-Gurion to the Central Bus Station in Jerusalem for approximately NIS 20 ($5/£2.50). From the station you need to take a bus or taxi to your final destination. The savings are not that great over a sherut, and if you have baggage this can be very difficult. There is no bus service from around 11pm to around 6am.

For more on transportation into Jerusalem, see "Arriving," in chapter 5.

**GETTING TO TEL AVIV**  **Trains** leave Ben-Gurion Airport for the Arlosoroff Train Station in Tel Aviv two times an hour from 3:30am to 11pm. Fare is NIS 16 ($4/£2). From there you'll need to take a local taxi. You're not too far to most Tel Aviv hotels, but with baggage, jet lag, and brutal summer heat, it's not walkable. For information and the latest train schedules, see **www.israrail.org.il/english**.

The set **taxi** fare to Tel Aviv is approximately NIS 135 ($34/£17); rates are higher at night and during Shabbat.

For more information on getting to Tel Aviv, see "Orientation," in chapter 7.

### LONG-HAUL FLIGHTS: HOW TO STAY COMFORTABLE

- Your choice of airline and airplane will definitely affect your legroom.

For international airlines, the research firm Skytrax has posted a list of average seat pitches at **www.airline quality.com**.

- More-desirable coach seats on the long haul flights to Israel are often reserved for regular customers or available only for a surcharge. Even passengers with disabilities or medical notes are not always given priority for better seats over those who have preferred customer standing with some airlines. If you have medical reasons for being assigned a better seat, start working on it early, don't take no for an answer, and keep bugging your airline!

- Emergency exit seats and bulkhead seats typically have the most legroom. Emergency exit seats are usually left unassigned until the day of a flight (to ensure that able-bodied people fill the seats); it's worth checking in online at home (if the airline offers that option) or getting to the ticket counter early to snag one of these spots for a long flight. Many passengers find that bulkhead seating offers more legroom, but keep in mind that bulkhead seats have no storage space on the floor in front of you.

- To have two seats for yourself in a three-seat row, try for an aisle seat in a center section toward the back of coach. If you're traveling with a companion, book an aisle and a window seat. Middle seats are usually booked last, so chances are good you'll end up with three seats to yourselves. And in the event that a third passenger is assigned the middle seat, he or she will probably be more than happy to trade for a window or an aisle. Direct flights to Israel are generally heavily booked so don't count on this strategy.

- To sleep, avoid the last row of any section or the row in front of an emergency exit, as these seats are the least likely to recline. Avoid seats near highly trafficked toilet areas. Avoid seats in the back of many jets—these can be narrower than those in the rest of coach. Or reserve a window seat so you can rest your head and avoid being bumped in the aisle.

## GETTING AROUND BY CAR

***Note:*** You cannot take a rental car into or out of Israel. Cars rented in Israel are not generally insured for damages or liability if taken into the West Bank.

In the main Israeli cities, such as Tel Aviv, Haifa, and Jerusalem, a car is not only unnecessary, it's a burden. Parking is very difficult; taxis, sheruts, and buses are efficient and reasonably priced, and these cities are filled with such arcane driving regulations as NO LEFT TURNS FOR NEXT 7 BLOCKS, SUN–THURS 11AM–2PM. The police will definitely be waiting for you to make a left turn on the sixth block (which you probably weren't counting anyway because you were probably lost).

A car becomes necessary if you want to explore the Galilee, the sites along the coast, such as Caesarea or Akko, or freewheel in the desert. There won't be parking or traffic nightmares in the countryside, and distances are short, so you can take in many sites. Road signs are almost always in English; don't panic if on a major highway a sign is only in Hebrew—the next sign up or the one beyond will usually have the information you need in English. Your rental car agency will provide you with maps of Israel that are sufficient for most travelers. If you want something more detailed, bookstores will carry MAPA and CARTA driving maps of Israel. Corazin maps, available in Tiberias and around the Sea of Galilee, are especially made for tourists and are filled with notes on sites you might want to visit. They don't show every road—just those that take you to places of interest to travelers.

## DRIVING RULES

**Seatbelt use** for drivers and all passengers is mandatory. Although Israel honors American, Canadian, and U.K. driver's licenses, if you plan to drive in other countries you might want to have an international driver's license, which should be obtained in advance in your hometown. **Speed limits** are 50km (31 miles) per hour in towns and urban areas; 90km (56 miles) per hour on intercity roads unless otherwise posted.

The local automobile club, **MEMSI** (© **03/564-1122**), has its main office in Tel Aviv at 20 Rehov Ha-Rakevet. The Jerusalem office of MEMSI is at 31 Ben-Yehuda St. (© **02/625-9711**). MEMSI offers very detailed road maps, some of which are in English. If you're renting a car, your rental agency will take care of roadside breakdown problems.

If a visitor's foreign car registration is valid and the driver is in possession of a valid driver's license, a car may be brought into Israel for a period of up to 1 year. No customs document or customs duty deposit is required. Due to the many hostile countries that surround Israel, and for security reasons, very few foreign vehicles are actually brought into Israel. Almost all tourists find it easier to rent a car in Israel.

This is a tough country for autos. Auxiliary roads are rarely wide and straight, and once you're off the main highways, you're faced with winding, narrow mountain roads, particularly in the Golan Heights and the Negev. Also be aware that among Israeli drivers, brashness on the road is the national sport. Drivers are often aggressive and impatient; tailgating is the norm, not the exception.

Other hazards? Rains bring up loose gravel and dirt and make for unstable, slippery conditions. Flash floods occur in the desert during the rainy season, often gutting low sections of the highway. Most unusual are the road and street closings on Shabbat in the Orthodox Jewish neighborhoods of West Jerusalem. In Mea Shearim and other ultrareligious Jerusalem neighborhoods, roads are blockaded to prevent passage of cars, as driving is forbidden in these areas during the Jewish Sabbath. Vehicles attempting to enter these streets, or even approaching them, will be stoned and possibly destroyed.

## RENTING A CAR

In general, you'll do best by scouting things and reserving a car in advance of your arrival in Israel. Car-rental agencies, both international and local, rent small cars for about $45 to $70 (£23–£35) a day, depending on the season, the company, and the size of the car, and whether you've booked an advance-payment special package from your own country. Apply ahead of time for the discount cards that most international car-rental companies currently offer. At the very least, they may get you an automatic upgrade. Remember, if you plan to travel in the summer, or drive to the Negev and Eilat, you'll want a car with air-conditioning that **really** works (if you deal with a rent-a-wreck outfit, which I don't advise, there may be no air-conditioning at all).

The largest Israeli car-rental firm is **Eldan** (© **800/938-5000** or 888/243-5326 in the U.S. and Canada, or 212/629-6090 in New York, or 08/951-5727 in the U.K.; www.eldan.co.il) and is always worth looking into. Its fleet of cars is larger and more varied than those of the international agencies and it often has discount specials. Eldan also offers more offices and service centers throughout the country than any of its competitors, so if you have a breakdown, you have a better chance of getting a replacement quickly. Other major car-rental companies in the country are **Avis** (© 800/331-1212 in the continental U.S.; www.avis.co.il), **Budget** (© 800/527-0700 in the U.S.; www.budget.co.il), **Europcar** (© 877/940-6900 in the U.S.; www.europcar.com), **Hertz** (© 800/654-3131 in the U.S.; www.hertz.com), and

**Thrifty** (© 800/367-2277 in the U.S.; www.thrifty.com). These companies all have rental desks at Ben-Gurion Airport.

Driving is one of the best ways to see Israel, but it can be expensive if you don't shop around and book in advance from your own country or find a car-rental package through your airline ticket or hotel package. The very cheapest cars are often not available, even though their rental prices are widely publicized by agencies. Your best deal will be on a weekly, unlimited-kilometer basis. As the deductible on the agency-provided collision insurance is a staggering $750 to $1,000, you'll want to protect yourself against that much liability for damage to the car. Unless you're renting a car with the special MasterCard world card (which will cover the mandatory Collision Damage Waiver/CDW at many agencies), you must initial the little block that shows you want the collision damage waiver insurance, which will cost about $15 per day (be sure to ask exactly how much before you sign on the dotted line). If you book in advance from your own country, and pay with a gold MasterCard, get a letter from the rental agency verifying that your credit card has covered the CDW payment and have it with you when you rent your vehicle in Israel. A balance sheet of what you'll actually end up paying for a lower mid-price range car rental with automatic transmission may look like this:

| | |
|---|---|
| Basic weekly charge, unlimited kilometers $50 (£25) per day | $350 (£175) |
| Collision Damage Waiver, 7 days at $18 per day | $126 (£63) |
| Mandatory Third Party Liability, 7 days at $15 per day | $105 (£53) |
| Gasoline, 100 liters at $2 (£1) per liter ($8/£4 per gal.) | $200 (£100) |
| Total | $781 (£391) |

These figures are an average of going rates, and the total works out to about $112 (£56) per day for a simple automatic transmission car. Do not be misled by firms offering extremely low daily rental rates, such as $6 or $8. The daily rental rate can be only a small portion of the total rental bill, which also includes the collision damage waiver and the kilometer charge. Again, travel packages and advance shopping and payment can often get you a better deal.

Your best bet for a bargain may be a package purchased with your flight. El Al's "Sunsational" hotel/car package, with unlimited mileage (available only to El Al passengers), is generally unbeatable. At times, certain El Al or Sheraton Hotel packages include a free rental car for 5 days. In many cases you'll want to upgrade the kind of car offered. Reserving and prepaying from the United States through the Israel Tourism Center or a travel discounter can also cut costs.

Some smaller Israeli companies offer no rental charge on Shabbat, although you do have to pay Saturday insurance (if it is a religious company, you may be on your honor not to drive on Shabbat). Others offer free transportation from the airport to your hotel if you want to start the rental later in your trip. Companies offering such services are often more expensive, but you may find these extras worthwhile. **Warning:** Beware of local companies that offer to waive rental fees and insurance on Shabbat. If your parked car is vandalized or stolen or hit by another car on Shabbat, you're in big trouble.

It's a good idea to reserve a car as far in advance as possible. Except in holiday periods, a day in advance should be enough time to secure some kind of vehicle, but keep in mind that cars with automatic transmission are often in short supply. The earlier you reserve, the more certain you can be of getting the car you want, when you want it. *A bright note:*

## *Tips*  Money-Saving Car Rental Tips

At press time, only the MasterCard world card (not the gold or platinum card) still covers the CDW (collision damage waiver) when you rent a car in Israel. It could pay to get a world card before traveling to Israel (at press time Master-Card charged 1% commission on debit transactions overseas, whereas many other cards charge 3%). Eldan, the largest Israeli car-rental company, rents the Toyota Prius, as do some international rental agencies. Daily rental and insurance for the Prius is a bit more than for comparable-size cars, and it's hard to nail one down, but with gasoline prices on the rise, this gas-saving hybrid could be a good investment—especially if you plan to do a lot of driving.

There's often a shortage of cars in the least expensive class: If you reserve one in advance, and the cheapest class is not available, there's a chance you may get bumped up at no additional charge.

Almost every major car-rental company has a Jerusalem office on King David Street, between the Hilton and King David hotels; in Tel Aviv, the offices are on Ha-Yarkon Street, between the Dan and the Sheraton hotels. If you don't happen to pass the agency you want, your hotel or any travel agent will be glad to arrange the rental.

**SPECIAL CONSIDERATIONS**   Visitors should deal only with reputable rental companies, only sign contracts after reading them thoroughly in a language they completely understand, and make sure of proper and full insurance coverage. If you are asked to sign a part of your contract written in Hebrew, make certain it is explained to you and note in writing beside your signature that you do not read Hebrew. The rate of car theft in Israel is very high—you do not want to be held responsible for the cost of an entire car.

*Note:* No cars rented in Israel are insured for travel in the West Bank and Gaza, although most companies do permit travel on Hwy. 1, the main east-west highway from Jerusalem to The Dead Sea, and Route 90, the main north-south road along The Dead Sea and the Jordan

Valley from near Jericho to Tiberias, as well as southward along The Dead Sea. Clarify these regulations each time you rent a car and get explicit instructions as to how to get to these roads in the West Bank, making sure not to stray anywhere else in the West Bank with your rental car. Also, clarify whether your car is insured for East Jerusalem, should you drive or inadvertently stray there.

Be sure to go with the car-rental worker who makes note of dents and marks when you rent your car. Insist that every mark be noted on your contract, including marks on rubber bumpers—no matter how unimportant they may seem. If they're not indicated on the contract, you'll be charged for them when you return the car.

Age minimums for rentals vary from company to company, but you usually must be 21 years old to rent or drive a rental car in Israel. Seniors over 75 or 80 may have some difficulty finding an agency that will rent to them. Check American companies in the United States for their rental policies in Israel. You may pay more for insurance if you're under or over a certain age.

## PARKING & TOLLS

There is only one toll road in Israel: the presently under-construction Pan Israel Highway (Hwy. 6), which will eventually run the length of the country from north to south. At present, only the northern and central portions of this road are open. There are no toll bridges in Israel. The number of cars in Israel has quadrupled during the past few years, so Israel now has real, honest-to-goodness traffic jams and a parking problem in the big cities. In Jerusalem, Tel Aviv, Tiberias, and other main cities, when you park on streets in downtown areas during daylight hours you'll either pay for parking with a meter, or you must display a parking card in the passenger window. This is a strip of paper with punched tabs for the hours of the day. You tear a tab to designate the month, day, and hour when you parked. Cards can be purchased at newsstands or from lottery ticket vendors. Parking on many residential streets in Jerusalem and Tel Aviv will soon be by residential sticker only. At most hotels in major cities, you'll have to pay to park in an adjacent municipal lot or the hotel's own lot (fees are usually reasonable but rates vary according to day or night and Shabbat). Most country (rural) hotels in Israel have free parking.

*Note:* Do not park illegally anywhere or *you will get towed;* parking enforcement officials in Israel are quick and *very* thorough.

## GASOLINE (PETROL)

Gasoline comes in 91 octane and 96 octane varieties and costs about $2 (£1) *per liter.* Rental cars are often "required" to have the higher-octane gas. These gas prices work out to about $8 (£4) per U.S. gallon. As in Europe and North America, the price of gasoline has been skyrocketing.

Gas stations are plentiful enough on main roads, though on Saturday some of them are closed and those that are open often add a surcharge.

## BREAKDOWNS/ASSISTANCE

On Saturday and Jewish holidays, it's virtually impossible to have a flat tire repaired in the Jewish sections of Israel, but your rental car company will provide you with numbers to call in case of emergencies and road service. Bigger companies usually have better service.

Check out Orbitz, Hotwire.com, Travelocity, and Priceline.com, all of which offer competitive online car-rental rates. For additional car-rental agencies, see the appendix, "Fast Facts, Toll-Free Numbers & Websites" (p. 502).

## BY TRAIN

**Israel Railways** (www.israrail.org.il/english) has been undergoing a steady process of revival and expansion for more than a decade. Tel Aviv is the rail hub of Israel. A rail line along the Mediterranean coast connects Tel Aviv to Haifa and Nahariya in the north; a second line connects Tel Aviv to Ben-Gurion Airport; a third line goes from Tel Aviv to Beersheva; and a fourth line goes from Tel Aviv to the western outskirts of Jerusalem. Service along the coast is fast and frequent; the Beersheva and Jerusalem lines are slow and less frequent, and there is service at least every hour from Ben-Gurion to Tel Aviv from around 5:45am to around 11pm. The Israel Railways website gives current schedules and prices. Trains do not run on the Sabbath.

The **Arlosoroff Street Station in Tel Aviv** is a short taxi ride to most hotels; the **Jerusalem Train Station,** on the western edge of the city, is not a convenient place to enter Jerusalem, especially with luggage. You'd do better arriving in Jerusalem by the much faster Egged buses from Tel Aviv or by sherut (shared taxi van), both of which bring you closer to the center of town and to a wider range of municipal buses.

## BY BUS

Intercity buses are the fastest and easiest way of traveling between the major cities of Israel (although traffic jams in recent years have led the country to resuscitate its almost forgotten train service along the Jerusalem–Tel Aviv–Haifa corridor). Buses between Jerusalem, Haifa, and Tel Aviv depart very frequently—at peak times as fast as each bus fills up. The Jerusalem–Tel Aviv fare is NIS 23 ($5.75/£2.90). For less frequent buses, such as Tel Aviv or Jerusalem to Eilat (fare NIS 80/$20/£10), you must book your ticket in advance.

## BY SHERUT

A sherut (shared taxi van) is a good way to travel between Jerusalem and Tel Aviv and between Tel Aviv and Haifa. Sheruts leave as fast as they fill up from Rav Kook Street in Jerusalem (just across Jaffa Rd. from Zion Square) to just in front of the New Central Bus Station in Tel Aviv; and from Tel Aviv to Haifa. If you're in downtown Jerusalem, sheruts save you going all the way to the Jerusalem Bus Station and dragging baggage or getting lost in the vast multilevel Jerusalem and Tel Aviv bus stations. Sherut fares are a fraction less than bus fares. Sheruts leave from in front of the Tel Aviv Bus Station for Haifa, but there is less demand for this route, and the sheruts can take a while to fill up. Because sheruts carry fewer passengers than buses, and there is time to scrutinize passengers, many Israelis feel sheruts are a bit less likely to be terror targets than buses.

## BY PLANE

Distances in Israel are not great, and with the time you'd spend to get to the airport, go through security, and go through the arrival process and transfers at your destination, you could probably just drive. The 4-hour drive from Tel Aviv or Jerusalem to Eilat, through what some consider boring desert landscape, is the most popular route to replace with a flight, but airport transfers and hassles cut down on the time you'll actually save. If you can afford it, and if traveling overland on hot days just isn't your cup of tea, then by all means use Israel's inland air service **Arkia** (© 09/863-3480 or *5758 for reservations in Israel; www.arkia.co.il). There are no flights on Shabbat, but otherwise daily flights connect Tel Aviv with **Eilat** and **Rosh Pina** (Safed/Tiberias), and Haifa with Eilat. Other flights are scheduled according to demand, as the seasons change. A round-trip flight from Tel Aviv to Eilat, for example, costs approximately $160 to $280 (£80–£140). You can book flights on Arkia through your home travel agent; booking direct on its website often saves you a few dollars: in North America, **Israir** (© 877/ISRAIR-1 [477-2471] or 516/593-1785; www.israirairlines.com) also flies within Israel, including connecting service from Ben-Gurion Airport to Eilat.

Arkia also sponsors popular bargain packages from Tel Aviv and Jerusalem to Eilat, including airfare and accommodations. Or you can design your own tour, gather a group of people, and charter an Arkia aircraft, from nine-seaters to Boeing 737s. You can book tickets and check flight schedules at any travel agency or on Arkia's website.

## 5 Money & Costs

### CURRENCY

The basic unit of currency is the **New Israel Shekel (NIS)**. At press time, both the value of the U.S. dollar and the value of the shekel were extremely volatile, and this situation may continue for some time. We estimate the shekel-dollar exchange rate to be approximately **NIS 4** to $1 (50p), or **NIS 1 to 25¢ (13p)**; all prices in this guide were calculated at that exchange rate.

The shekel is divided into 100 agorot, and the smallest denomination you will encounter is a copper-colored 5-agorot coin, but these are hardly in circulation anymore. There are 10-agorot copper-colored

| What Things Cost in Israel | NIS | US$ | UK£ |
|---|---|---|---|
| Cup of coffee | 6.00–20.00 | 1.50–5.00 | 0.75–2.50 |
| Municipal bus fare in most cities | 5.60 | 1.40 | 0.70 |
| Overnight at a moderate-price hotel (no swimming pool) | 560.00–880.00 | 140.00–220.00 | 70.00–110.00 |
| Meal at moderate-price restaurant | 60–100 | 15.00–25.00 | 7.50–13.00 |
| With wine add | 40.00 | 10.00 | 5.00 |
| Liter of gasoline | 8.00 | 2.00 | 1.00 |
| Daily *International Herald Tribune* | 11.00 | 2.75 | 1.40 |
| Falafel sandwich | 12.00–18.00 | 3.00–4.50 | 1.50–2.25 |

coins, and larger, copper 50-agorot (half-shekel) coins, all useful for bus fare. The 1-shekel coin is a tiny silver buttonlike object that is extremely easy to lose. Hang onto a few 1-shekel coins: Pay phones in restaurants and hotels often only take 1-shekel coins instead of the cheaper per-call telephone cards. There are also 2-, 5- and 10-shekel coins, as well as 20-, 50-, and 100-shekel notes. *Note:* The new, small 10-shekel coins are not popular, as they are easily lost and counterfeit 10-shekel coins abound. How can you tell a phony 10-shekel coin? If the rims are smooth or only irregularly grooved, it's bad. Israelis are adept at passing bad 10-shekel coins at busy places and slipping away before being noticed—a useful skill for travelers to develop. Otherwise, you're out approximately $2.50 (£1.25).

Exchange counters at Ben-Gurion Airport generally offer poor rates of exchange. ATMs give standard rates. After such a long flight, you might prefer to avoid possible lines at the airport by exchanging at least some money—just enough to cover airport incidentals and transportation to your hotel—before you leave home (though don't expect the exchange rate to be ideal). You can exchange money at your local American Express or Thomas Cook office or at your bank. American Express also dispenses traveler's checks and foreign currency via **www.americanexpress.com** or ⓒ **800/807-6233,** but they'll charge a $15 (£7.50) order fee and additional shipping costs.

## ATMs

International ATM debit cards will only work at Israeli ATMs specifically marked to accept them. These machines usually have decals for PLUS, Cirrus, Visa, MasterCard, or international flags on them.

---

*Tips* **Small Change**

When you change money, ask for some small bills or loose change. Petty cash will come in handy for tipping and public transportation and taxis (Israeli taxi drivers never seem to have change when a foreigner tries to pay). Consider keeping the change separate from your larger bills so that it's readily accessible and you'll be less of a target for theft.

## The Shekel, the Dollar & the Pound

At this writing NIS 1 is estimated to equal approximately 25¢/13p, or NIS 4 to $1; NIS 8 to £1. Although the dollar is currently low, it is expected to rebound against the shekel if and when the U.S. economy improves. As currency rates fluctuate, the value of a shekel may not be the same when you travel to Israel. For up-to-the-minute currency exchange rates, go to **www.oanda.com**. The following table should be used only as an approximate guide:

| NIS | US$ | UK£ | NIS | US$ | UK£ |
|---|---|---|---|---|---|
| 1.00 | 0.25 | 0.13 | 20.00 | 5.00 | 2.50 |
| 2.00 | 0.50 | 0.25 | 25.00 | 6.25 | 3.13 |
| 3.00 | 0.75 | 0.38 | 30.00 | 7.50 | 3.75 |
| 4.00 | 1.00 | 0.50 | 40.00 | 10.00 | 5.00 |
| 5.00 | 1.25 | 0.65 | 50.00 | 12.50 | 6.25 |
| 6.00 | 1.50 | 0.75 | 100.00 | 25.00 | 12.50 |
| 7.00 | 1.75 | 0.88 | 125.00 | 31.25 | 15.63 |
| 8.00 | 2.00 | 1.00 | 150.00 | 37.50 | 18.75 |
| 9.00 | 2.25 | 1.13 | 200.00 | 50.00 | 25.00 |
| 10.00 | 2.50 | 1.25 | 500.00 | 125.00 | 62.50 |
| 15.00 | 3.75 | 1.88 | 1,000.00 | 250.00 | 125.00 |

In Jerusalem and Tel Aviv, these ATMs are easy to find in heavily touristed areas, but in other cities they are few and far between, so stock up on shekels while you can. You can use your credit card to receive cash advances at ATMs. Keep in mind that credit card companies protect themselves from theft by limiting maximum withdrawals outside their home country, so call your credit card company before you leave home. And keep in mind that you'll pay interest from the moment of your withdrawal, even if you pay your monthly bills on time.

Many five- or six-digit PINs will work at Israeli ATMs that accept foreign ATM cards, but some longer PINs do not. Check with your bank as to whether your card will function in Israel. The easiest and best way to get cash away from home is from an ATM (automated teller machine). The **Cirrus** (© 800/424-7787; www.mastercard.com) and **PLUS** (© 800/843-7587;

www.visa.com) networks span the globe; look at the back of your bank card to see which network you're on, then call or check online for ATM locations at your destination. Be sure you know your personal identification number (PIN) and daily withdrawal limit before you depart. *Note:* Remember that many banks impose a fee every time you use a card at another bank's ATM, and that fee can be higher for international transactions ($5/£2.50 or more) than for domestic ones (where they're rarely more than $2/£1). In addition, the bank from which you withdraw cash may charge its own fee (Israeli banks presently charge a nominal fee of NIS 3 (75¢/40p) for each withdrawal). To compare banks' ATM fees within the U.S., use **www.bankrate.com**. For international withdrawal fees, ask your bank. *Note:* At press time Visa was planning to impose a 3% commission on all foreign withdrawals made with Visa/ATM debit cards. At press time the fee on withdrawals using a MasterCard debit card is 1%.

## TRAVELER'S CHECKS

Traveler's checks are accepted at fewer and fewer shops, hotels, and restaurants in Israel—credit cards are becoming the more popular payment option. If you carry traveler's checks, be prepared to cash them mainly in banks or with money-changers, and not at the greatest exchange rate. Still, traveler's checks offer extra protection against theft or loss. You can buy traveler's checks at most banks. They are offered in denominations of $20, $50, $100, $500, and sometimes $1,000. Generally, you'll pay a service charge ranging from 1% to 4%.

The most popular traveler's checks are offered by **American Express** (© **800/807-6233,** or 800/221-7282 for cardholders—this number accepts collect calls, offers service in several foreign languages, and exempts Amex gold and platinum cardholders from the 1% fee); **Visa** (© **800/732-1322;** AAA members can obtain Visa checks for a $9.95 fee for checks up to $1,500 at most AAA offices or by calling © **866/339-3378**); and **MasterCard** (© **800/223-9920**).

**American Express, Thomas Cook, Visa,** and **MasterCard** offer **foreign currency traveler's checks,** which are useful if you're traveling to one country, or to the euro zone; they're accepted at locations where dollar checks may not be.

If you carry traveler's checks, keep a record of their serial numbers separate from your checks in the event that they are stolen or lost. You'll get a refund faster if you know the numbers.

## CREDIT CARDS

Credit cards are another safe way to carry money. They also provide a convenient record of all your expenses, and they generally offer relatively good exchange rates. You can withdraw cash advances using your credit cards at banks or ATMs, provided you know your PIN. Keep in mind that you'll pay interest from the moment of your withdrawal, even if you pay your monthly bills on time. Also, note that many banks now assess a 1% to 3% "transaction fee" on **all** charges you incur abroad (whether you're using the local currency or your native currency).

*Note:* **Visa** currently offers a "Support Israel" HAS Advantage card that gives you points toward travel to Israel for each dollar you spend. For information, go to **www.hasadvantage.com**. That said, a **MasterCard world card** (not the gold or platinum card) automatically covers collision damage waiver fees and

---

### (Tips  Keeping Flush

Don't wait until you're down to your last shekel if you're using ATMs to keep yourself funded. International ATM connections sometimes go down, and Israeli banks have a way of having sudden 1-day wildcat strikes. Remember that ATMs will not be restocked during Shabbat, and there's usually a run on ATMs on Friday, so stock up before the Israeli weekend or holidays.

Have more than one ATM card with you—recently one of the largest banks in America placed a sudden block on all its ATM transactions in Israel and a dozen other countries because of high ATM fraud levels—and their customers in Israel were left stranded. Check with your bank to see if any of the countries you plan to visit are under an ATM block, and inform your bank security service of your travel plans so that ATM card charges overseas will not be refused as suspicious.

> ⌒ *Warning* **Bad Notes**
>
> Black-market street dealers sometimes try to pass off pre-1985 old shekel notes in denominations of 500 and 1,000. These notes have **no value** and are not in circulation, although their design is exactly like current notes of lower denominations. Be certain that all currency notes you accept are clearly marked "New Sheqels" in English.

offers better insurance coverage on car rentals in Israel than does a gold or platinum Visa card.

For tips and telephone numbers to call if your wallet is stolen or lost, see "Lost & Found" in appendix A. The most commonly accepted credit cards in Israel are Visa, MasterCard, and American Express. Diners Club is somewhat less universally accepted.

## 6 Health

### STAYING HEALTHY
#### GENERAL AVAILABILITY OF HEALTHCARE

Israel is blessed with an oversupply of doctors and contains a network of well-equipped, modern hospitals and Magen David Adom clinics, where you can get emergency treatment for flu, fevers, fractures, and upset stomachs, as well as for more serious emergencies. You are never far from good medical care. If need be, your hotel can arrange a house call with a licensed local physician who will be delighted to have a private case (and private payment). Pharmacies are well stocked, and you'll encounter many international name brands, but drug prices outside of Israeli insurance plans—even for nonprescription medicines such as aspirin or basic anti-diarrhea medicines—are comparatively high. Jordan and Sinai are not as well covered with major hospitals. Private consultation with a local physician will usually be relatively inexpensive.

The United States **Centers for Disease Control and Prevention** (© **800/ 311-3435;** www.cdc.gov) provides up-to-date information on health hazards by region or country and offers tips on food safety. The website **www.tripprep.com,** sponsored by a consortium of travel medicine practitioners, also offers helpful advice on traveling abroad. You can find listings of reliable clinics overseas at the **International Society of Travel Medicine** website, www.istm.org.

### HEALTH & FOOD CONCERNS

**WATER** Tap water is safe and drinkable in Israel, except at The Dead Sea. There, even some luxury hotels have special taps on each floor that you must go to for drinking water. Although Israeli water is safe, the presence of various minerals in the water may make you a bit queasy. For this reason, bottled water could be a good investment, though in small amounts and for teeth brushing, local water is fine.

In Jordan and Egypt (Sinai), *tap water is not drinkable.* Bottled water is essential.

**KOSHER FOOD** In Israel, at least half of all restaurants are kosher, although some may not have official kashrut certificates (in many cases because they do business on the Sabbath). All Israel hotels serve kosher food, with the exception of Christian guesthouses and hotels in Arabic areas of Jerusalem and Nazareth. In some secular areas of Tel Aviv, kosher restaurants, certified or not, can actually be hard to find. If you're lactose intolerant, note that kosher meat restaurants use no dairy products at all, not even for desserts. For more on kosher food, see p. 41.

**VEGETARIAN FOOD**   The summer heat is especially conducive to lighter meals, and vegetarians will be delighted to find many vegetarian restaurants and venues serving vegetarian dishes throughout Israel. As kosher restaurants cannot serve both dairy and meat dishes, many add an array of vegetarian dishes to broaden their menus. There are also many traditional vegetarian dishes available at restaurants in Jordan and in Egypt.

**BUGS, BITES & OTHER WILDLIFE CONCERNS**   **Scorpions** are always something to be aware of in desert and Mediterranean regions. If bitten by a scorpion, get emergency medical treatment *immediately.* Scorpions do not go out of their way to attack, but they love damp, warm places, and you can get bitten if you happen to put a hand or foot where one of them is resting. Check carefully when entering showers, bathrooms, or other damp places in the desert or countryside. There's minimal danger in the cities, but at beaches and in the countryside, take some simple precautions. Always shake out towels at the beach or pool before drying yourself; shake out shoes and socks before putting them on. If you're staying in simple places in the desert, shake out your sheets before getting into bed. Orange groves may look inviting, but big, mean snakes think so, too; avoid the temptation to stroll or picnic in them. In the Jordan Valley, there is a rare but very ugly skin infection called **"Rose of Sharon"** that's hard to control and will scar unless you get medical treatment—don't hesitate to see a doctor about any unusual or persistent bug bites or skin eruptions.

There is **rabies** in the countryside, and wild animals should be avoided. Dogs that are clearly well-tended pets are okay, but keep away from stray dogs and kittens and the urban refuse bin cats, no matter how friendly or hungry they may seem.

When snorkeling or diving in the Red Sea, remember that many coral formations are not only sharp, but they can burn. It is illegal to touch or walk on any coral—not only for your safety, but for the protection of the coral, which can be easily broken and killed. **Spiny sea urchins,** covering the underwater floor in many places, are the bane of snorkelers. Getting your foot impaled on one of these spines can wreck a vacation. It's best to wear foot coverings and try to avoid stepping anywhere near a sea urchin—and note that it's very easy for a wave or current to glide you right onto one. Study photo charts of fish before snorkeling, and memorize those that are poisonous to touch, especially the stonefish or rockfish, with their billowing, diaphanous fins that appear to be so delicate.

**RESPIRATORY   ILLNESSES**   The Dead Sea, far below sea level, has the thickest, most oxygen-rich atmosphere on the face of the earth. Those suffering from asthma, allergy, heart, or pulmonary problems often find the dry, pollen-free, oxygen-rich atmosphere helpful. The Negev city of Arad, with its dry, pollen-free air, is especially known as a place that is helpful to those suffering from asthma, or who have allergies to pollens and mold.

**SUN EXPOSURE**   Sunburn and dehydration are problems throughout the region, but especially in the desert in summer. Although the air is dry, paradoxically, you often don't feel thirsty. Force yourself to drink a minimum of four 1.5-liter bottles of water a day as you travel the area in summer, more if you are in the desert. Sunscreen is a must, though you need less of it at The Dead Sea because the thicker atmosphere screens out the sun.

## WHAT TO DO IF YOU GET SICK AWAY FROM HOME

Any foreign consulate can provide a list of area doctors who speak English. If you get sick, your hotel desk can direct you to the nearest Magen David Adom clinic or can recommend a local doctor. We list hospitals and emergency numbers under "Fast Facts," in the individual destination chapters.

If you suffer from a chronic illness, consult your doctor before your departure. Pack **prescription medications** in your carry-on luggage, and carry prescription medications in their original containers, with pharmacy labels—otherwise they won't make it through airport security. Also carry copies of your prescriptions in case you lose your pills or run out. Don't forget an extra pair of contact lenses or prescription glasses. Carry the generic name of prescription medicines, in case a local pharmacist is unfamiliar with the brand name.

We list **additional emergency numbers** in appendix A, p. 503.

# 7 Safety

## STAYING SAFE

Israel is a low-crime country. Some of the major dangers you will encounter are car-related. Israeli drivers, though no worse than drivers in some other countries, aren't renowned for sound driving practices. Blatant tailgating is the unnerving way of life here. Car theft and theft of belongings from rental cars is also a major problem. Some rental car companies require you to use a steering wheel lock, and it is *never* a good idea to leave valuables in your car. Keeping baggage out of sight in the trunk helps a bit, but a parked rental car is an irresistible magnet for thieves.

When traveling in Jordan or in East Jerusalem and Arab cities inside Israel, travelers should not carry or drink alcohol (which is forbidden by Islam) in public, and modest dress is expected of both men and women. Women traveling alone must realize they are visiting Muslim societies, where the very fact of being unaccompanied by a man will be regarded as suspicious and provocative. Extremely modest dress is essential. All behavior must be very guarded, and all visitors should be aware of conservative Muslim sensibilities. Gay and lesbian travelers are advised to be unusually discreet when visiting these areas.

## SECURITY

Terrorism has become a problem everywhere in the world, and Israelis have become expert in dealing with it. Despite the news of the past few years, the chance is actually greater that you'll be involved in a traffic mishap while in Israel. In Jerusalem, security guards now prowl the bus stops, checking and intercepting suspicious-looking people before they can board a bus. Guards conduct bag and body checks at the entrances to shopping malls, markets, shops, cafes, restaurants, transportation hubs, and hotels. You'll find security guards at most major restaurants. Always keep alert and be aware of suspicious persons, especially if they are well bundled in coats or jackets when the weather is not cold.

## CULTURAL ETIQUETTE

**In ultra-Orthodox Jewish neighborhoods,** such as Mea Shearim, in Jerusalem, it is considered provocative for men and women to walk hand in hand, or even in close proximity. Long sleeves and skirts for women and long trousers for men are considered proper dress. No tank tops. **In Arab areas,** male travelers must not approach women to ask for directions or for any other purpose (women travelers may approach local women). It is provocative to be seen carrying or drinking alcohol in public, as the use of alcohol is forbidden by Islam.

## 8 Specialized Travel Resources

### TRAVELERS WITH DISABILITIES

Most disabilities shouldn't stop anyone from traveling. There are more options and resources out there than ever before.

Inside Israel, there's been a slow but ongoing effort to provide access for visitors with disabilities—even at sites famed for their inaccessibility, such as Masada. Atop the dramatic plateau of Masada, a new network of wheelchair-accessible pathways was completed in 2000. At least some trails in a number of Israel's **national parks and nature reserves** (www.parks.org.il) have been made wheelchair accessible over the past few years. In addition to **Masada,** other national parks and sites with special-access facilities include **Ashkelon National Park, Gamla Nature Reserve,** and the **Hula Reserve,** as well as the **Knights Hall** in Akko. National parks and sites that will have some amount of special-access provisions by 2009 include: **Zippori, Tel Hai,** the **Soreq Stalactite Cave,** and the **Ein Fasha Beach** at The Dead Sea. Street crossings and public restrooms throughout the country rarely offer easy access. Some institutions located in difficult sites, such as the **Israel Museum** and **Jerusalem Cinémathèque,** have provisions for handicap access, but you must call in advance to be able to use these facilities.

*Access in Israel: A Guide for People Who Have Difficulty Getting Around,* by Gordon Couch, in cooperation with the Pauline Hephaistos Survey Project, published by Quiller Press, is an invaluable guide to special needs accessibility conditions in airports, hotels, restaurants, parks, museums, and other sites in Israel. Sights in places such as Jerusalem's Old City are arranged according to location, so you can easily plan what places you want to visit in a given area. Note, however, that it does not rate all hotels, restaurants, and sites, and in a few instances, as new access projects have been completed, this edition is already out-of-date. *Access in Israel* can be ordered by contacting the Access Project (39 Bradley Gardens, West Ealing, London, W13 8HE, United Kingdom; gordon.couch@virgin.net). There is no charge, but a contribution of $15 (£7.50) is welcome to cover mailing costs. This book is not offered for sale and is only obtainable by contacting the Access Project.

In 2004, the Israeli Association for the Advancement of Accessibility, in cooperation with the Israeli Ministry of Tourism, published a more current and thorough book, *Access Unlimited: Your Guide to Israel,* by Dr. Judith Bendel, Zvi Gur, and Ariel Kalkuda. A complete labor of love, written by Israelis who know their country well, this book is extensive, professional, and savvy. I cannot praise this book too highly. Assessments for blind and visually impaired travelers are included. Entries are alphabetical, rather than by location, which makes it necessary to have a working knowledge of the neighborhood or area you are visiting. At present, this book can be obtained without charge through the Israel Ministry of Tourism in your region well in advance of your trip. For more information, go to the Access Unlimited website at **www.access-unlimited.co.il**, or fax **972-9-7650-430.**

*One caveat:* There are a few errors in both these books. An example: In *Access Unlimited,* the pool at the Sheraton Moriah Tel Aviv Hotel is listed as accessible, when in fact a narrow spiral staircase presently in use makes access unusually difficult. Those who make reservations at the Sheraton Moriah and hope to use the pool may find themselves disappointed. Although these editions are extremely helpful as planning tools, readers should call ahead to confirm and clarify all information.

Many travel agencies offer customized tours and itineraries for travelers with

## *Tips* Accessibility Assistance

**Yad Sarah** (© **972/2-644-4633** from outside Israel; www.yadsarah.org) is Israel's largest voluntary organization. It lends medical equipment, crutches, and wheelchairs; arranges airport and intercity transportation; helps prepare and equip hotel rooms for special needs; and offers advice for travelers to Israel with special needs. All services are free, although deposits are required for equipment. Advance planning and reservations are required to get the most help from Yad Sarah, but it's also a great resource for sudden or last-minute emergencies.

disabilities. **Access-Able Travel Source** (© **303/232-2979;** www.access-able.com) offers extensive access information and advice for traveling around the world with disabilities.

**Avis Rent a Car** has an "Avis Access" program that offers such services as a 24-hour toll-free number (© **888/879-4273**) for customers with special travel needs; special car features such as swivel seats, spinner knobs, and hand controls.

Organizations that offer assistance to travelers with disabilities include **Moss-Rehab** (www.mossresourcenet.org), which provides a library of accessible-travel resources online; the **American Foundation for the Blind** (AFB; © **800/232-5463;** www.afb.org), a referral resource for the blind or visually impaired that includes information on traveling with Seeing Eye dogs; and **SATH** (Society for Accessible Travel & Hospitality; © **212/447-7284;** www.sath.org; annual membership fees: $45 adults, $30 seniors and students), which offers a wealth of travel resources for all types of disabilities and informed recommendations on destinations, access guides, travel agents, tour operators, vehicle rentals, and companion services.

For more information specifically targeted to travelers with disabilities, the community website **iCan** (www.ican online.net/channels/travel) has destination guides and several regular columns on accessible travel. Also check out the quarterly magazine *Emerging Horizons* (www.emerginghorizons.com; $14.95 per year, $19.95 outside the U.S.); and *Open World* magazine, published by SATH (see above; subscription: $13 per year, $21 outside the U.S.).

## GAY & LESBIAN TRAVELERS

Israel has come a long way since the 1980s, when laws regarding homosexual activity were removed from the books. A decision by the government to award pensions of deceased military officers to their surviving partners, regardless of sex or of marital status, was a landmark in changing attitudes. However, an open gay scene has only really emerged in trendy Tel Aviv, which *Out* has called the "most gay-friendly city in the Middle East" (this may seem faint praise, but Tel Aviv *is* mellow by most world standards). A score of bars, cafes, and clubs offer a constantly changing calendar of theme nights and parties. For the past several years, Tel Aviv, as well as more conservative, traditional Jerusalem, has hosted official gay pride parades. The Jerusalem parades, however, have been marked by violence and (in a rare display of unity) condemnation by leading Muslim, Christian, and Jewish religious authorities. Eilat, somewhat like Tel Aviv, has developed a general attitude of tolerance; mild-mannered Haifa stands somewhere between Tel Aviv and Jerusalem.

Resource organizations include the **Association for GLBT in Israel,** 28 Nachmani St., Tel Aviv (© **03/620-5590;** office@glbt.org.il); **CLAF** (Community of Feminist Lesbians in Israel; © **054/531-9855**); and the **Political Council for GLBT Rights in Israel** (© 03/613-2418).

**Support and Crisis Lines:** The White Line for emotional counseling (© **03/732-5560**) is open daily from 7:30 to 11:30pm; **Someone Listens** (© **03/516-7236**) is the info and counseling line for the Association for GLBT; and Gay-friendly Psychologists and Therapists is at © **03/516-7235.**

**Minerva,** 98 Allenby St., Tel Aviv (© **03/560-3801**), is a relatively venerable and centrally located bar that was once a lesbian meeting point, but now has a gay section and is pan-sexually friendly and savvy. It's open daily from 10pm until very late. For more information, see p. 286.

In Jerusalem, things are quieter but opening up. There is a very active place called Open House at 2 Ha Soreg St., 2nd floor (© **02/625-3191**); Ha Soreg Street is 2 blocks east of Zion Square off Jaffa Road.

Note that in the Palestinian/Arabic communities throughout Israel, and in East Jerusalem, the West Bank, Jordan, and Egypt, any kind of openly gay or lesbian behavior is completely forbidden both by custom and by law. Extreme caution and the lowest possible profile are advised. Similar discretion must be observed in the Jewish ultrareligious and Hassidic neighborhoods of Jerusalem north of Jaffa Road (such as Mea Shearim); in the Old City of Jerusalem; in Safed, which has a largely religious population; and in small, less-touristed Israeli towns where the character of the population may not be clear.

For more gay and lesbian travel resources, visit www.frommers.com.

## SENIOR TRAVELERS

Mention the fact that you're a senior when you make your travel reservations. Although most major airlines have canceled their senior discount and coupon book programs, some Israeli hotels, especially those in international chains, still offer lower rates for seniors, especially during off season. Israeli pensioners get discounts on admission to museums and national parks, and your foreign senior ID may move a guard to give you the senior rate for an Israeli, though the discount is negligible compared to the effort and possible confrontation.

The **Association of Americans and Canadians in Israel (AACI)** sponsors many social activities and tours for seniors (see "For Long-Term Visitors," below).

Members of **AARP** (formerly known as the American Association of Retired Persons), 601 E St. NW, Washington, DC 20049 (© **888/687-2277;** www.aarp.org), get discounts on hotels, airfares, and car rentals. AARP offers members a wide range of benefits, including *AARP The Magazine* and a monthly newsletter. Anyone 51 and older can join.

Many reliable agencies and organizations target the 50-plus market. **Elderhostel** (© **877/426-8056;** www.elderhostel. org) arranges study programs for those aged 55 and over (and a spouse or companion of any age) in the U.S. and in more than 80 countries around the world. Most courses last 5 to 7 days in the U.S. (2–4 weeks abroad), and many include airfare, accommodations in university dormitories or modest inns, meals, and tuition.

Recommended publications offering travel resources and discounts for seniors include: the quarterly magazine *Travel 50 & Beyond* (www.travel50andbeyond. com); *Travel Unlimited: Uncommon Adventures for the Mature Traveler* (Avalon); *101 Tips for Mature Travelers,* available from Grand Circle Travel

(© **800/221-2610** or 617/350-7500; www.gct.com); and *Unbelievably Good Deals and Great Adventures That You Absolutely Can't Get Unless You're Over 50* (McGraw-Hill), by Joann Rattner Heilman.

## FAMILY TRAVELERS

*Frommer's Israel* has, as a member of its research team, a savvy 6-year-old trilingual Jerusalemite named Lyne, who has explored the country with me endlessly since she was 4 weeks old. She has included some of her favorite places and things in our Children's Itinerary (she insisted on omitting some of her favorite places, such as the Tisch Family Zoo in Jerusalem, where she accidentally fed my hat to a giraffe with traumatic consequences). See p. 212. Also see "Especially for Kids" on p. 211.

To locate accommodations, restaurants, and attractions that are particularly kid-friendly, see the "Kids" icon throughout this guide. For a list of more family-friendly travel resources, see the experts at www.frommers.com.

## WOMEN TRAVELERS

For women travelers, Israel proper is not too different from Europe or the United States. Army service is universal for non-religious Israelis, and many younger Israeli men may seem more macho and pressing than Europeans or Americans, but that's usually because you're a tourist and a woman—and all alone. Hebrew is a language that stylistically prefers directness over guile, and when translated into English, some Israelis may seem amazingly blunt, or at least brash.

It's important to remember to dress modestly when visiting holy places of Judaism, Islam, and Christianity, or ultra-Orthodox Jewish neighborhoods, such as Mea Shearim in West Jerusalem. In Mea Shearim, women should not wear trousers or jeans (shorts are forbidden there for men as well as women). At least knee-length skirts (the longer the better) and blouses that do not leave shoulders and upper arms exposed are strongly advised. The penalty for immodest dress can be getting spat on, pelted with pebbles, or worse. The police generally do not take action against religious Jews who attack immodest visitors to their neighborhoods.

East Jerusalem, the Old City of Jerusalem, the West Bank, Jordan, and Egypt are largely Arabic societies, and unless women travelers are guarded in their dress and behavior, there's a good chance there will be insults and unwanted advances. Women in Islamic societies do not venture far from their houses unless they are in the company of a husband, relatives, or at least one other woman; women travelers may seem to be breaking the rules of propriety simply by being alone. It is always best to try to have at least one traveling companion, male or female, with you if possible. Modest dress and behavior also helps to avoid unwanted attention. In Middle Eastern society, except in the all-tourist Sinai resorts, a woman alone, seen drinking in public, or walking on the streets with a bare midriff or shorts, is not respectable, and will often not receive even common courtesy.

Check out **Journeywoman** (www.journeywoman.com), a real-life women's travel-information network where you can sign up for a free e-mail newsletter and get advice on everything from etiquette and dress to safety; or the travel guide *Safety and Security for Women Who Travel* by Sheila Swan and Peter Laufer (Travelers' Tales), offering common-sense tips on safe travel. For general travel resources for women, go to www.frommers.com.

## STUDENT TRAVELERS

Israel is a student-friendly country. There are all kinds of student flights and discount airfares to Israel, and if you're from a Jewish-American family, you may even be eligible for a free trip to Israel under the **Birthright (*Taglit*) Program** (www.birthrightisrael.com), which provides the gift of first-time, peer-group, educational tours of Israel (airfare included) to Jewish adults ages 18 to 26. More than 40,000 people have taken advantage of this program, which is designed to encourage Jewish identity and connection with the State of Israel (waiting lists are long, so plan well in advance).

Even for independent travelers, there are discounts for students at museums, national parks, and railroads, although train discounts are minimal. Check out the **International Student Travel Confederation** (ISTC; www.istc.org) website for comprehensive travel services information and details on how to get an **International Student Identity Card (ISIC),** which qualifies students for substantial savings on rail passes, plane tickets, entrance fees, and more. It also provides students with basic health and life insurance and a 24-hour help line. The card is valid for a maximum of 18 months. You can apply for the card online or in person at **STA Travel** (© **800/781-4040** in North America, 132-782 in Australia, 0871/2-300-040 in the U.K.; www.statravel.com), the biggest student travel agency in the world; check out the website to locate STA Travel offices worldwide. If you're no longer a student but are still under 26, you can get an **International Youth Travel Card** (IYTC) from the same people, which entitles you to some discounts. **Travel CUTS** (© **800/592-2887;** www.travel-cuts.com) offers similar services for both Canadians and U.S. residents. Irish students may prefer to turn to **USIT** (© **01/602-1904;** www.usit.ie), an Ireland-based specialist in student, youth, and independent travel.

## FOR LONG-TERM VISITORS

The **Association of Americans and Canadians in Israel (AACI)** is mainly for North American immigrants to Israel, but you can join the AACI or participate in many of its social activities, lectures, theater performances, and tours even if you're only planning to be in the country for a month or two, or only considering the possibility of immigrating to Israel. The AACI sponsors get-togethers on American holidays, English tutoring for new Ethiopian immigrants, singles events, counseling on retirement in Israel, and legal advice, and generally promotes the well-being of the country's English-speaking community. AACI offices in Jerusalem, 6 Mane St. (© **02/561-7151;** fax 02/566-1186), and in Netanya, 28 Shmuel Ha-Naziv St. (© **09/833-0950**), are especially active, but there are branches throughout the country, including Haifa, Tel Aviv, and in the Negev. Check the "In Jerusalem" and the "Tel Aviv City Lights" supplements to the Friday *Jerusalem Post* for their list of activities. The AACI website is at **www.aaci.org.il**.

## 9 Sustainable Tourism

**In Israel,** the enormously active and inventive **Society for Protection of Nature in Israel,** or SPNI (www.spni.org), sponsors projects that protect the environment and promote awareness of threats to the natural beauty of the county, the urban landscape, and the ecological balance of the region. SPNI offers a program of superb walks, hikes, tours, 1-day to weeklong trips, and lectures about issues of conservation. Most tours are in Hebrew, but this is a very English-friendly organization with an English-language affiliate, the American friends of SPNI (www.aspni.org).

**Bustan Ha Shalom (Orchard of Peace;** www.bustan.org) is a partnership of Jewish and Arab Israeli eco-builders, architects, conservationists, and farmers working together on sustainable community action, largely on behalf of Israel's formerly nomadic, Bedouin community. Among its many activities, the organization is concerned with conserving the traditional Bedouin way of life, encouraging the production and sale of traditional Bedouin crafts, and protecting the civil and political rights of Bedouin; it hosts volunteer projects such as tutoring, and building straw bale medical centers, homes, and playgrounds for Bedouin settlements.

The **Jewish Coalition for Service** (www.jewishservice.org/vol_israel.html) can plug you into many projects in Israel, including Bustan's 10-week Green Apprenticeship Program (you don't have to be Jewish).

## ECO-TOURISM

Israel has a number of collective and cooperative (kibbutz and moshav) communities that practice organic farming, recycling, and host programs in eco-tourism. **Kibbutz Lotan,** in the dramatic Arava Valley (Southern Negev), is a kibbutz founded in the 1980s by American immigrants to Israel who have taken the lead in showing Israelis how to create environmentally gentle, sustainable desert communities, organic farming, and exciting architecture based on natural and recycled materials. Lotan, together with neighboring kibbutzim **Yahel** and **Ketura,** has set up programs of desert eco-study, eco-hikes, birding, meditation, relaxation, and massage that are truly excellent, especially in tandem with the chance to live in and observe these communities. See p. 455 for information on these kibbutzim. **Succah in the Desert** (p. 453), in the central Negev highlands just outside Mitzpe Ramon, is one of the few eco-accommodations in Israel—it is very simple but has charm and mystique. Also in Mitzpe Ramon, the **Isrotel Ramon Inn** is one of Israel's few environmentally friendly major hotels (p. 452).

The organic farming community of **Klil,** near the northwestern border of Israel, does not have overnight accommodations for tourists, but is filled with artists and craftspeople who have built unusual homes and studios. It also hosts a ceramics workshop that helps preserve and encourage the artistry of traditional Ethiopian Jewish potters (p. 322).

In Jordan, the **Royal Society for the Conservation of Nature** (www.rscn. org.jo) maintains a careful network of nature reserves and a sustainable tourism base among the tribal people of the magnificent, wild Dana Nature Reserve.

**Sustainable tourism** is conscientious travel. It means being careful with the environments you explore and respecting the communities you visit. Two overlapping components of sustainable travel are **eco-tourism** and **ethical tourism.** The **International Ecotourism Society** (TIES) defines eco-tourism as responsible travel to natural areas that conserves the environment and improves the well-being of local people. TIES suggests that eco-tourists follow these principles:

- Minimize environmental impact.
- Build environmental and cultural awareness and respect.
- Provide positive experiences for both visitors and hosts.
- Provide direct financial benefits for conservation and for local people.
- Raise sensitivity to host countries' political, environmental, and social climates.
- Support international human rights and labor agreements.

You can find some eco-friendly travel tips and statistics, as well as touring companies and associations—listed by destination under "Travel Choice"—at the **TIES** website, www.ecotourism.org. Also check out **Ecotravel.com,** which lets you search for sustainable touring companies in several categories (water based, land based, spiritually oriented, and so on).

While much of the focus of eco-tourism is about reducing impacts on the natural environment, ethical tourism concentrates on ways to preserve and enhance local economies and communities, regardless of location. You can embrace ethical tourism by staying at a locally owned hotel or shopping at a store that employs local workers and sells locally produced goods.

**Responsible Travel** (www.responsibletravel.com) is a great source of sustainable travel ideas; the site is run by a spokesperson for ethical tourism in the travel industry. **Sustainable Travel International** (www.sustainabletravelinternational.org) promotes ethical tourism practices, and manages an extensive directory of sustainable properties and tour operators around the world.

In the U.K., **Tourism Concern** (www.tourismconcern.org.uk) works to reduce social and environmental problems connected to tourism. The **Association of Independent Tour Operators** (AITO; www.aito.co.uk) is a group of specialist operators leading the field in making holidays sustainable.

**Volunteer travel** has become increasingly popular among those who want to venture beyond the standard group-tour experience to learn languages, interact with locals, and make a positive difference while on vacation. Volunteer travel usually doesn't require special skills—just a willingness to work hard—and programs vary in length from a few days to a number of weeks. Some programs provide free housing and food, but many require volunteers to pay for travel expenses, which can add up quickly.

For general info on volunteer travel, visit **www.volunteerabroad.org** and **www.idealist.org**. Specific volunteer options in Israel are listed above, and under "Special-Interest Trips," below.

Before you commit to a volunteer program, it's important to make sure any money you're giving is truly going back to the local community, and that the work you'll be doing will be a good fit for you. **Volunteer International** (www.volunteerinternational.org) has a helpful list of questions to ask to determine the intentions and the nature of a volunteer program.

## ANIMAL-RIGHTS ISSUES

The Dolphin Reef in Eilat is a beach where humans can swim only as far as a net—from which they can watch wild dolphins frolicking in the open sea. The Dolphin Reef takes swimmers beyond the net in carefully escorted groups, without boats or propeller vehicles. The dolphins, in the open sea, are free to approach or not—depending on their mood. Compared to other "swim with dolphins" programs I've seen in other countries, Eilat's Dolphin Reef seems protective of the dolphin's freedom and unobtrusive (p. 460). For information on animal-friendly issues throughout the world, visit the **Tread Lightly** website at www.treadlightly.org. For information about the ethics of swimming with dolphins, visit the **Whale and Dolphin Conservation Society** website at www.wdcs.org.

## GREEN DINING

A relatively new organization in Israel has begun to issue the Tav Chevrati Seal of Social Justice to restaurants that treat workers fairly and provide careful, personal assistance to customers with disabilities. **In Jerusalem,** restaurants listed in this book that have received the Tav Chevrati Seal include Keshet, in the Jewish Quarter of the Old City; Joy Grill, Coffee Mill, and 1868 Café in the German Colony; Eldad Vesayhoo, Aroma, Babette's Waffles, Darna, Dr Lek's Ice Cream, Eucalyptus, Marakiyah, Village Green, Little Jerusalem at Ticho House, La Guta, Moshiko's Falafel and Shwarma, and Chakra in Downtown Jerusalem; and Orna and Ella, and Gordon Inn Pub in Tel Aviv.

## 10 Packages for the Independent Traveler

El Al (www.elal.com) offers incredible deals on hotel and car-rental packages that are only available with the purchase of a round-trip El Al ticket to Israel.

For more information on package tours and for tips on booking your trip, see www.frommers.com.

## 11 Escorted General-Interest Tours

With escorted tour companies, your entire trip is arranged door-to-door, site-to-site, and meal-to-meal. One of the largest packagers of escorted tours to Israel is **Isram** (www.isram.com). There are often large groups, but everything is preplanned, taken care of, and controlled—you just sit back and relax. **Gate 1 Travel** (www.gate1travel.com) is another major packager that puts together escorted and independent tours at good prices. As with Isram, hotel choices may not be the most atmospheric or memorable, but they will be solid and adequate for each price category. **Margaret Morse Tours** (www.margaretmorse tours.com) specializes in quality, fully escorted group tours that may be a bit higher in price, but often include a more

thoughtful choice of details and accommodations.

Israel is an unusual destination in that it has so many synagogues and churches, as well as major Jewish and Christian organizations, that sponsor group tours and missions to the Holy Land. It's always worthwhile to check with your synagogue or church as to what organized group tours they can direct you to. These package tours have the added advantage of zeroing in on sites and events that are of special interest to your own traditions and background. For more information on escorted general-interest tours, including questions to ask before booking your trip, see www.frommers.com.

Go to the Israel Ministry of Tourism website, www.goisrael.com, for a full listing of recommended tour companies.

## 12 Special-Interest Trips

### ACADEMIC TRIPS & LANGUAGE CLASSES

**LANGUAGE SCHOOLS** In order to absorb enormous numbers of new immigrants over the past 5 decades, Israel has developed intensive Hebrew-language programs, centered around an institution called an *ulpan*. If you plan an extended visit to Israel, you should know that a good many kibbutzim operate *ulpanim* that are based on the principle of working for your education, room, and board. In exchange for half a day of Hebrew-language classroom instruction, you work the other half-day in a job assigned by the kibbutz—in the fields, kitchen, or

wherever you are needed. For more information on kibbutz *ulpan* programs, go to **www.kibbutzprogramcenter.org**.

Throughout Israel there are also many nonkibbutz *ulpan* programs in which foreign visitors, for a tuition fee, can study the Hebrew language. Tel Aviv, Jerusalem, and Haifa have *ulpanim* where you pay a fee and study beside new immigrants from Ethiopia, Argentina, Uzbekistan, Denmark, and the far corners of the world. There are 3-, 8-, 12-, and 20-week courses that are very reasonably priced. For more information, go to the **World Zionist Organization Israel Programs** website at www.wzo.org.il. **Ulpan Akiva,** PO Box

## Private Guides

Israel is an easy country for English speakers to explore on their own, but if you are considering hiring a private guide for part of your visit, it's necessary to plan well in advance. The county has a system of licensed guides who have completed an extensive program of preparatory training. Private guides arrange all the logistics of travel during the times they are under hire, and can take you to major sites as well as out-of-the-way places efficiently. For those with little time, this can be a restful way to get a great deal done in-depth. The government licensing program has helped to raise the general quality of guides in Israel, but you still may find yourself engaging a guide whose personality or politics don't exactly mesh well with yours. Or, despite English-language requirements, you may encounter a guide who is not especially articulate. Some guides may be dramatic, with almost theatrical personalities. These guides can be fascinating, but you may find yourself having to keep your eyes glued to your guide out of politeness, while you are unable to look around or experience your surroundings.

Beware of guides who are on cellphones taking other bookings and receiving calls from home as they drive you through pristine deserts in their Land Rovers, which can destroy the atmosphere of a tour. Check ahead of time about a guide's policy on turning off his cellphone. It is a good idea to ask friends who have visited Israel for personal recommendations, and to discuss plans with a prospective private guide by phone in order to get a feel for his or her approach before making a commitment. Most good professional guides have put together a brochure or video that will give you an indication of their styles and approaches.

Approximate rates for a private guide are $270 (£135) per day for a Jerusalem tour by foot and taxi, $300 to $400 (£150–£200) a day for a licensed and insured guide with a vehicle within Israel. There can be extra charges for more than 8 hours per day and for off-road trips and use of off-road vehicles. If your guide accompanies you overnight, the fee should include the cost of his or her hotel room (in many places, a licensed guide will receive a discount—your guide will know where he can be put up at a discount rate). If you engage an Israeli guide to arrange excursions into

6086, Netanya 42160, Israel (© **09/835-2312/3;** fax 09/865-2919; www.ulpan-akiva.org.il), offers programs for nonimmigrants as well, and is world famous for intensive, live-in programs in both Hebrew and Arabic for varying periods of time in a pleasant seaside community. Ulpan Akiva supplements its language programs with a full range of field trips and social and cultural activities. Ulpan Akiva arranges for accommodations. Dining facilities at its campus are kosher. Courses at Ulpan Akiva are accepted for credit at a number of American universities.

## BIKING TOURS & HOLIDAYS

**Israel MTB** (www.israel-mtb.com) offers escorted mountain-biking tours of varying levels of difficulty through carefully chosen landscapes ranging from a half-day to a week, and include transportation

Jordan and to accompany you on these trips, the rate could be $660 to $700 (£330–£350) per day, including a vehicle and hotel accommodations.

Following are some guides with unusual background qualifications and specialties in nature, archaeology, and active tours. If they are not able to meet your time specifications or interests, they may be able to refer you to other guides who will better match your needs.

American-born **David Perlmutter**, POB 8015, Jerusalem 91080, Israel (✆ 054/420-1353; david@israeladventure.com), was a guide for the Society for Protection of Nature in Israel and helped design that organization's hikes and tours. He specializes in mountain-biking, hiking, and off-road tours in a comfortable four-wheel-drive vehicle in Israel and Jordan as well as photography, wine and culinary, and cultural tours.

**Judy Stacey Goldman**, Gan Rehavia Aleph, no. 6, 92461 Jerusalem (✆ 02/624-5827; fax 02/623-3834; judebob@netvision.net.il), is the coauthor of *The Underground Guide to Jerusalem* and *The Underground Guide to Tel Aviv*, two lively insider books on the country's two major metropolitan areas. She also coauthored (with Joan Nathan) *The Flavor of Jerusalem,* a very personal, classic book on Israeli cuisine. Goldman was born in Canada.

**Richard Woolf** (✆ 04/693-5377 or 050/589-4647; www.israwebs.com/woolf) specializes in the Galilee, where he has lived for almost 40 years. He was born in the U.K. and provides a comfortable vehicle for touring. **Sam Salem** (✆ 054/215-8441; guide.holy@gmail.com) is a member of Jerusalem's Christian community whose specialties include Bethlehem, Jericho, the Old City of Jerusalem, and the Temple Mount. He has unusual access and connections to many special sites.

**Rabbi Jeffrey Bearman**, POB 11022, Jerusalem 91110 (✆/fax 02/676-5197; rabbjeff@netvision.net.il), is a Reform rabbi (somewhat unusual in Israel) and a licensed guide. **Davide Silvera** (✆/fax 03/516-5265; cellphone 050/535-3555; www.gebus.com) speaks Italian, English, and French. **Susan Lamdan** (lamdans@netvision.net.il) is a guide in the Jerusalem area with excellent reader feedback. **Madeline Lavine** (✆ 054/450-4098; madl@zahav.net.il) specializes in tours of historic Jerusalem neighborhoods, both in the Old and New cities.

to and from biking areas, support crew, and accommodations. Prices range from $120 to $1,200 (£60–£600). Customized tours can also be arranged. Most tours are in the desert and southern part of the country.

**CMBC, the Carmel Mountain Bike Club** (www.geocities.com/Colosseum/Arena/9765/cmbchome.htm), is a group of Haifa-area cycling enthusiasts, including Jon Lipman, who maintain a detailed English-language website and will be happy to share advice and information on activities, bike rides, and tours with fellow cyclists. For further information about mountain biking in Israel, go to the site for Israel Bike Trails (www.israelbiketrails.com).

## PHOTOGRAPHY

**Dimui Photo Tours** ✦ (www.dimui.com) offers carefully planned, very upmarket, luxury priced photo tour itineraries of Israel, custom designed to encompass sites of striking photographic and historical interest. Groups are small; each tour is accompanied by world-class, recognized photographers and draws on their experience and knowledge of the secrets of the landscape. Instruction sessions are included. The logistics guide is excellent, accommodations are top quality, be they urban hotels; atmospheric, restored Turkish-era mansions; or air-conditioned tents in the desert, and interesting gourmet meals are provided.

## ADVENTURE & WELLNESS TRIPS

The **Society for Protection of Nature in Israel** (www.aspni.org), known as SPNI, offers a wide range of excellent, well-planned nature and camping hikes and tours throughout Israel and beyond. Most tours are in Hebrew, but the guides are among the best in the business, and are generally fluent in English (as are most Israeli participants), so English speakers will not be left out. SPNI also offers a selection of tours in English.

**Israel Challenge** (www.israelchallenge. com) specializes in adventure tours that include rappelling, mountain climbing, biking, hiking, and canyoning, all imbued with special Israeli national spirit. They work with small family groups or with groups of up to 60. The programs can be custom designed, and include extras such as end of the day massages and desert feasts with live music.

**Desert Eco Tours** (www.desertecotours. com) offers diving tours of Sinai and the Red Sea, as well as jeep, safari, and camel tours; 1-day diving and snorkeling cruises; and camping trips in the Negev, Jordan, and Egypt. **Red Sea Sports** (www.redseasports.co.il), based in Eilat, offers a 1-week diving tour of the best spots in the Red Sea, plus programs of diving instruction and day tours to Mount Sinai. The emphasis of both Desert Eco Tours and Red Sea Sports is adventure, although they can also put together very comfortable accommodations packages.

**Women Walkers** (www.womenwalkers. com) is an American-based company that organizes four escorted hiking tours to Israel for women only. The 10-day tours do not include airfare, but do include well-chosen and planned hikes in all areas of the country, accompanied by guides, as well as transportation to and from hiking sites and interesting, comfortable accommodations. Groups are rarely larger than 10, and hikes are of varying degrees of difficulty. Itineraries change every year.

## FOOD & WINE TRIPS

**CULINARY TOURS**    At press time, schedules of specialty tours are only starting to revive after years of low tourism. The Ministry of Tourism (www.goisrael.com) can direct you to culinary tours as they are scheduled. A good culinary tour includes learning the stories of the cooks as well as the recipes. I strongly urge readers interested in Israeli cooking and culinary tours to read the classic, *The Flavor of Jerusalem,* by Joan Nathan and Judy Stacey Goldman, which places its recipes among the family who created them. (Goldman is also on our list of recommended private guides, p. 82).

## VOLUNTEER & WORKING TRIPS

**Volunteers for Israel,** 330 W. 42nd St., no. 1618, New York, NY 10036 (✆ **212/ 643-4848;** fax 866/514-1948; www.vfi-usa.org/about.html), arranges volunteer support positions in both civilian and military organizations in Israel. Assignments may include hospital work, typing, repair work, and KP duty with noncombat sectors of the Israeli military. We've had letters from readers in all age groups over 20 testifying to interesting experiences in this program; after you fulfill your 3-week obligations, you are eligible for a special El Al discount fare. Application to this program requires a nonrefundable $100 (£50) fee.

**ARCHAEOLOGICAL DIGS**   You can volunteer to work at an archaeological dig if you are 18 or older, prepared to stay for at least 2 weeks, and capable of doing strenuous work in a hot climate. You will have to pay your own fare to and from Israel. Most excavations take place between June and October, but there are off-season digs. Lectures are given at some sites, and some offer academic credit for the work. If you'd like to join a dig, it's best to inquire as far in advance as possible. Even very short-term volunteer projects may be arranged.

The best summary of current digs is found each year in the January/February issue of the magazine *Biblical Archaeology Review*, PO Box 7026, Red Oak, IA 51591, available at many libraries and newsdealers. *Biblical Archaeology Review's* listings include exactly who to contact for information about joining each specific dig, as well as estimates on expenses for volunteers and a description of each dig's recent finds. The **Israel Ministry of Tourism North American InfoCenter** (© **888/77-ISRAEL** [477235]) will also give you general, updated information about finding a suitable dig.

The **Biblical Archaeology Society**, 4710 41st St., NW, Washington, DC 20016 (© **800/221-4644** or 202/364-2636; www.bib-arch.org), which publishes the *Biblical Archaeology Review*, organizes archaeology-based study tours of Israel and the surrounding region. The **Israel Archaeological Society**, 467 Levering Ave., Los Angeles, CA 90024 (© **800/477-2358** or 310/472-9449; archaeology@mindspring.com), is another organization concerned with this field—they will send you schedules of their tours and events.

## SPECIAL PROGRAMS
**PLANT A TREE**   If you'd like to plant a tree in Israel with your own hands, just call © **800/223-484** (toll-free) anywhere in Israel to arrange it. You can also check out **www.treesfortheholyland.com** for more information. The cost per tree is $18 (£9).

**JEWISH-ARAB DIALOGUE PROGRAMS**   One out of every five Israeli citizens living inside the pre-1967 boundaries of Israel is Arab. There are a growing number of dialogue and intercultural understanding projects inside Israel for Israeli Arabs and Jews; you will often find Israelis from English-speaking countries, armed with democratic traditions and experience living in multicultural societies, at the forefront of these projects. Visitors to Israel may observe these organizations and participate in lectures and tours that illuminate the problems and possibilities that exist for dialogue and understanding; students and professionals, including educators, psychologists, creative artists, and social workers, can also volunteer to participate in these programs. This can be an offbeat but interesting way to encounter one of the most hopeful sides of Israeli society.

**Neve Shalom/Wahat al Salaam,** 99761 Doar Na Shimshon, Israel (© **02/991-5621;** visitor programs 02/991-2222, ext. 101; www.nswas.com), is a unique Israeli-Palestinian cooperative village near Jerusalem that sponsors programs for visiting youth groups, including meetings with Jewish and Palestinian youth; programs for peace-oriented groups, focusing on area peace organizations; and tours for pilgrim groups, focusing on religious sites and the Holy Land's significance to Judaism, Christianity, and Islam. Neve Shalom/Wahat al Salaam (which means "Oasis of Peace") has an international conference and visitor center, guesthouse, and restaurant on its premises, and offers half- and full-day lecture programs for NIS 50 to

NIS 100 ($13–$25/£6.25–£13) per person. Individuals and groups of fewer than 15 people will be added to larger groups.

**New Israel Fund & Shatil Volunteer Programs,** 1101 14th St. NW, 6th floor, Washington, DC 20005 (© **202/842-0900;** www.nif.org), is concerned with human rights, intercultural understanding, and education programs inside Israel. It sponsors professional exchange, volunteer, and intern projects; social change fellowships; as well as village volunteer-in-residence programs for teaching English, medical, business, and other skills.

## 13 Staying Connected

### TELEPHONES

Israel's public telephones are mostly for phone cards only. A few public phones take one-shekel coins, and one-shekel coins are needed for pay phones in neighborhood groceries and restaurants. Many convenience groceries and newsstands sell **prepaid calling cards** in denominations ranging from NIS 18 to NIS 100 ($4.50–$25/£2.25–£13). Even if you've made cellphone arrangements, it can be a good idea to have a low-denomination calling card as backup.

For **reversed-charge or collect calls,** and for operator-assisted overseas or person-to-person calls, dial © 188.

For **local directory assistance** ("information"), dial © 144; 1-700 and 1-800 numbers are toll-free. All operators speak some English and if necessary will connect you to a special English-speaking operator. Phone calls from your hotel will be ridiculously expensive.

### CELLPHONES

In order to decide what kind of cellphone option you need, you have to think about how you plan to use your phone. If you want to mainly keep in touch with your family at home, you might want to rent a phone that will work in Israel but see if it can be set up with a number in your local home calling area, so calls to and from your family will be local. In the U.S., a company such as Talk'n'Save (www.talkn save.net) can do this for you.

**Amigo** (www.amigo-us.com) is another company that will rent a phone to you that is ready to go for use in Israel—no worries about compatibility with SIM cards or installing them. Amigo's rates are $1 per day and calls from Israel to the U.S. are 12¢ per minute. They'll ship your phone to you before you leave for Israel, and you ship it back to them on your return. For a phone user calling the States daily and making only a few calls inside Israel, the cost, including shipping, could be around $75 for a 2-week rental. Most companies offer repair service in Israel, though not on Shabbat.

Many travelers find arranging for a phone to be delivered in advance is easier than buying or renting or trying to add a SIM card when you arrive at Ben-Gurion Airport, exhausted, jet-lagged, and in a line at a cellphone counter behind 20 other arriving passengers. If you plan to visit Israel for multiple visits or a long period of time, buying a phone is an option; comparison shop. If you go to www.israelsims.com, you'll find deals for purchasing an unlocked cellphone for about $50; they'll ship it to you ahead of your trip and also sell you a Cellcom card for whatever amount you feel you'll need. You'll know your phone number ahead of time, and be ready to phone as soon as you hit Ben-Gurion.

**Cellular Abroad** (www.cellularabroad. com/israel) rents cellphones for many overseas destinations. They have multiple-country packages that could allow you to use your phone on excursions to Jordan and Sinai.

At the main **Arrivals Concourse at Ben-Gurion Airport** after picking up your baggage and clearing Customs, you'll see the **Telecommunications Center,** where all major mobile and satellite phone providers have desks. You probably won't be in shape to do comparative cellphone rental shopping after a 12-hour flight, so advance planning is useful. **Cellcom** (ℂ *123; www.cellcom.co.il/cultures/ he-il/roamers_info) is the largest provider in the country, followed by **Pelephone** (ℂ *166; **www.pelephone.co.il**) and **Orange/Partner** (ℂ 800/054-054; www. orange.co.il).

Two other possibilities are **Israel Phones** (www.israelphones.com) and **Tikshoret Besheva** (ℂ 972/2-652-2353; fax 972/3-684-4392; yossch@netvision. net.il). Both companies will deliver a cellphone to your hotel or apartment. Daily rates (subject to change) are approximately $1 (50p) a day with an optional additional charge for insurance. With Tikshoret Besheva, incoming calls are free; calls within Israel to Cellcom or land phones begin at 25¢ (13p) a minute; calls to the U.S., Canada, or the U.K. begin at approximately 40¢ (20p). Prices are lower after 9pm and, with some plans, on the Sabbath. *Note:* In the Jordan Valley and The Dead Sea area, which are the lowest points on earth and far below sea level, cellphone communications are not usually optimum.

## VOICE-OVER INTERNET PROTOCOL (VOIP)

If you have Web access while traveling, consider a broadband-based telephone service (in technical terms, **voice-over Internet protocol,** or **VoIP**) such as Skype (www.skype.com) or Vonage (www.vonage.com), which allows you to make free international calls from your laptop or from a cybercafe. Neither service requires the people you're calling to also have that service (though there are fees if they do not). Check the websites for details.

## INTERNET & E-MAIL
## WITH YOUR OWN COMPUTER

Downtown West Jerusalem from the post office on Jaffa Road to the Ben-Yehuda Mall, up to King George Street, and the adjacent Yoel Salomon, Rivlin Street and Jerusalem Courtyard neighborhoods are Wi-Fi (wireless fidelity) access zones: Cafes and restaurants are filled with locals and travelers communing with their computers. Large areas of downtown Tel Aviv and Haifa are Wi-Fi access zones.

In addition, many hotels, cafes, and retailers are providing Wi-Fi zones where you can get high-speed connection without cable wires, networking hardware, or a phone line (see below). For dial-up access, most business-class hotels throughout the world offer dataports for laptop modems, and a few thousand hotels in the U.S. and Europe now offer free high-speed Internet access. In addition, major Internet service providers (ISPs) have **local access numbers** around the world, allowing you to go online by placing a local call. The **iPass** network also has dial-up numbers around the world. You'll have to sign up with an iPass provider, who will then tell you how to set up your computer for your destination(s). For a list of iPass providers, go to **www.ipass.com** and click on "Individuals Buy Now." One solid provider is **i2roam** (ℂ 866/811-6209 or 920/235-0475; www.i2roam.com).

Wherever you go, bring a **connection kit** of the right power and phone adapters, a spare phone cord, and a spare Ethernet network cable—or find out whether your hotel supplies them to guests.

*Note:* In **Israel** you will need an adapter addition for your computer's electric plug that will match up with Israel's round-hole electric sockets. Most small appliances will operate on a two-prong adapter plug, but some appliances and some Israeli electrical outlets require three prongs. For **Jordan and Sinai,** it's a good idea to have both a two- and a three-round-prong adapter. Many hotels will lend them out, or you can buy one for under a dollar at most electric appliance or hardware stores. Electric current in Israel is 220 volts—make sure you have an automatic internal current adapter or an external adapter designed especially for your computer or it will get fried.

To find public Wi-Fi hot spots at your destination, go to **www.jiwire.com**; its Hotspot Finder holds the world's largest directory of public wireless hot spots.

## WITHOUT YOUR OWN COMPUTER

It's hard nowadays to find a city in Israel that *doesn't* have a few cybercafes. The Jaffa Road/Ben-Yehuda Mall area of downtown Jerusalem and lower Ben-Yehuda Street in Tel Aviv, near the main Tel Aviv hotel district, are well stocked with Internet cafes and centers. Even amid the labyrinths of the Old City of Jerusalem, there's **Mike's Center,** Suq Khan es Zeit Street (the main road from the Damascus Gate southward)—Mike's is located above the Abu Assab Carot and Orange Juice Shop and offers private booths (air-conditioned in summer) for you to work in.

Aside from formal cybercafes, most **hotels and hostels** have at least one computer with Internet access. Rates will not be great, but at the end of a long day, the convenience could be worth the price. Avoid **hotel business centers** unless you're willing to pay exorbitant rates.

For help locating cybercafes and other establishments where you can go for Internet access, see "Internet Access" in appendix A (p. 505).

## 14 Tips on Accommodations

You'll find a wide range of accommodations in Israel, ranging from hotels to guesthouses to self-catering apartments. There is no official accommodations rating system in the country, but the detailed listings in this book include information on hotel amenities and facilities that will help you decide what hotels will fit your needs.

## A NOTE ABOUT SEASONS

Israel's hotels fill up during certain seasons and holidays, and you should be prepared with advanced reservations, secured by a deposit. Generally speaking, hotels are busiest during July and August, and on the major Jewish and Christian holidays such as Passover, Easter, Rosh Hashanah, Yom Kippur, Chanukah, and Christmas. Rates skyrocket during these times and rooms can be very scarce if you don't book well in advance. For detailed information, and a full list of holiday dates, see the "Israel Calendar of Holidays & Events," earlier in this chapter.

Off season is generally November through February (except for Chanukah/Christmas/New Year's). It is, however, the busiest season in Eilat, which has almost perfect, sunny weather when it's chilly up north.

## HOTELS

With a few exceptions, Israeli hotels in all price categories tend to lack atmosphere and architectural style—many of the country's hotels could as easily be in Cleveland, Ohio, as in Jerusalem or Tiberias. In our hotel listings, we note the establishments that are unusual and *do* have character. When Israeli hotels get the right mix of location, ambience, architecture, and service, they are memorable—examples include the King David, American Colony, and Mount Zion hotels in Jerusalem; the Cinema Hotel in Tel Aviv, and the Scots Hotel in Tiberias.

Some hotels and B&Bs offer full or half board, which can be a good way to save on meals during your trip. Full board means that you get breakfast, lunch, and dinner, while half board includes breakfast and one main meal (usually dinner).

Because of the tourism slump of the past few years, when Israeli hotels filled their rooms with guests on special cut-rate packages, many top and moderate hotels have not been able to budget renovations and were rather run-down at press time. As tourism to the region revives, renovation programs should improve this situation.

Israel is a very informal place, and a tradition of careful service does not usually exist at most Israeli hotels. Where you do find good service, consider yourself blessed. Once you accept that there is no use getting frazzled by this situation (and just let yourself get out and enjoy the country), the happier you will be.

## MAJOR HOTEL CHAINS

Israel has a number of leading chains that American travelers may not be familiar with. **Dan Hotels** (✆ 03/520-2552; www.danhotels.com), Israel's most prestigious chain, has several locations spread throughout the country and a reputation for personal service. Its most famous property is the legendary King David Hotel, but in addition to its higher-priced properties, it has recently opened moderate-range hotels in Jerusalem and Haifa. **Isrotel** (✆ 08/638-7799; www.isrotel.co.il) is an Israeli chain that has developed well-run, imaginative properties that fit into and serve the special interests of their locales. Their hotels range from the top-notch Royal Beach in Eilat to the all-suite business-oriented Isrotel Tower in Tel Aviv and the desert-trek-oriented Ramon Inn in Mitzpe Ramon. The relatively new **Fattal Hotels** (www.fattal-hotels-israel.com) manages a number of hotels at The Dead Sea, Eilat, and Haifa. Its hotels range in price from moderate to deluxe, and some are all-inclusive, targeting Israeli-package tourists. Its top-of-the-line property is Le

Méridien at The Dead Sea, the most luxurious of The Dead Sea hotels. **Atlas Hotels** (✆ 03/542-5555; www.atlas.co.il) is a well-run, moderate-to-budget hotel chain that offers properties with style and service in Tel Aviv, Jerusalem, and Eilat; its most unique property is the inventive Cinema Hotel in Tel Aviv.

Many kibbutzim have established hotels and holiday resorts amid the most beautiful settings of the Israeli countryside. All of the hotels in the **Israel Kibbutz Hotel Chain** (✆ 888/669-5700 in the U.S.; www.kibbutz.co.il) have swimming pools, and rooms are generally comfortable and meet upper-moderate standards. There are 7-day reduced-rate packages available for this chain's hotels, with car rental included.

A number of international hotel chains, well-known to American and British travelers, are also represented in Israel. **Sheraton Hotels** (✆ 800/325-3535; www.sheraton.com) is the largest of these and runs the most luxurious hotel in the country; reservations for the Le Méridien hotels in Haifa, Eilat, and The Dead Sea can be made through the Sheraton network. **Hilton Hotels** (✆ 800/HILTONS [445-8667]; www.hilton.com) has deluxe hotels in Tel Aviv and Eilat, and four excellent resorts with some of the most experienced staffs in Sinai.

## HOTEL PACKAGES

**AIRLINE PACKAGES** Some of the best bargains in Israeli hotel accommodations are offered by El Al, the national carrier of Israel, but you can only buy them in conjunction with the **"Sunsational Israel"** package. Details and prices constantly change, but the bargains are unbeatable and can include 5 nights at Jerusalem's centrally located Jerusalem Tower Hotel or Tel Aviv's excellent (almost beachfront) Basel Hotel, starting at $60 (£30) a night per person, double occupancy. With this deal, you also get a

Hertz manual transmission rental car (there is a 35¢ per kilometer charge plus insurance; an automatic transmission car can be ordered for a higher price). El Al also offers a **Sheraton Moriah Hotel Flexi package** that gives you accommodations at deluxe Sheraton Hotels across Israel, including the Sheraton Plaza Jerusalem, starting at $110 (£55) per night for a double. El Al's more expensive **"Dantastic"** packages include accommodations at the luxury Dan Hotel chain at considerable savings. Look at all plans carefully and compare them before making a selection.

**KIBBUTZ PACKAGES**   The **Kibbutz Guest House Package** is especially enticing; it lets you explore the real Israeli countryside while overnighting at comfortable kibbutz hotels, holiday villages, and less-expensive guesthouses that have swimming pools or beaches, and invariably lovely settings. There are amazingly well-priced minimum 7-night deals, which include a double room and breakfast (double occupancy) and a middle-grade Avis rental car (with unlimited mileage and manual transmission). For extra charges you can book a package that gives you a choice of more luxurious car and better kibbutz accommodations.

Although all accommodations in the kibbutz hotel and holiday village network are the equivalent of those you'd find in midrange hotels, you'll find great variety in the general setup and character of each facility. You'll be amazed at the sheer drama of many of the kibbutz sites, from such desert retreats as Ein Gedi (set in a botanical garden of rare trees and plantings, perched above The Dead Sea near the fortress of Masada), to places like Ye'elim, adjacent to the Negev's Hai Bar Wildlife Reserve. There are semiluxury resorts such as the lovely Kfar Blum, or the hotel at the Orthodox Kibbutz Lavi; there are also simpler holiday villages such as Nasholim, on

the shores of the Mediterranean, or Ein Gev, on the Sea of Galilee. Many kibbutzim in the program are just a few minutes' drive from Jerusalem or within easy distance of Tel Aviv.

You can arrange for a kibbutz land package (including the **Kibbutz Association Fly and Drive Package**) independently of any airline ticket by calling, in the U.S. and Canada, the **Israel Tourism Center** (✆ **888/669-5700** or 201/703-9111). You may add additional days to the Kibbutz Hotel Chain Plan at rates far below those you could book independently and then move on to independent arrangements for the rest of your trip. If you're traveling alone, there's a single supplement (subject to the package you choose), and for families there are special children's rates.

## BED & BREAKFASTS

Unlike the network of kibbutz hotels and holiday villages, which are really midrange country hotels, and the kibbutz resorts, which are often quite separate from the actual kibbutz, **Kibbutz Country Lodgings** (www.kibbutz.co.il) consists of a growing network of smaller kibbutz and moshav communities that run simple guest bungalows or buildings, or kibbutz families who have guest room facilities in their own houses. Rates can be as low as $90 (£45) per night for a double room with a comfortable bedroom and private bathroom in interesting countryside locations. Best of all, you get a chance to see a bit of real kibbutz life. This is an especially good option if you want to keep your accommodations expenses down and put the savings into a rental car for freewheeling independent travel. For a commission of approximately $50 (£25), the Israel Tourism Center (✆ **888/669-5700** in the U.S.) will make reservations for you at other kibbutz and bed-and-breakfast places. Most travel agents specializing in Israel can book packages for you with the Kibbutz Hotel Chain or Kibbutz Country Lodgings. Local tourist information offices in the Galilee can also give you lists of guesthouses at moshavim (cooperative communities) in the area.

The Israel Tourism Center can also make bed-and-breakfast arrangements through the **Good Morning Jerusalem** bed-and-breakfast rental office. There is a $50 (£25) commission for this service, but you save the expense and bother of international phone calls and faxes. For bed-and-breakfast accommodations in Jerusalem (see chapter 5) and Tel Aviv (see chapter 7), there are rental services that will make note of your requirements and preferences and try to match them to a room in their listings. Reservations for these rooms, ranging in price from about $90 to $120 (£45–£60) for a double, can be made from overseas.

At tourist information offices in Tel Aviv, Jerusalem, and many other Israeli cities, you can use a computer bank to access lists of accommodations in private homes for any area in the country. The information disbursed by these computers is rather lean—just a list of names, addresses, and phone numbers, but with a few phone calls, you can usually come up with something. If you're looking at local listings, the staff at the tourist information office may be willing to direct you to places they know to be especially good. For summers, weekends, and holidays, it is always best to reserve ahead.

## YOUTH HOSTELS

The concept of youth hostels is right at home with the traditional Israeli preference for a functional, practical lifestyle and congenial atmosphere in which travelers can meet freely and easily. Israel's wonderful network of official **Israel Youth Hostel Association Hostels**, or **IYHA Hostels** (© 1-599/510-511; www.iyha.org.il/eng) offers simple, inexpensive accommodations in many dramatic and rustic sites throughout the country. IYHA hostels often offer the only available accommodations in remote areas of the country, or in areas along hiking routes. The hostels at Mitzpe Ramon, in the Negev, overlooking the Ramon Crater; and at Ein Gedi, beside The Dead Sea, provide great bases for hiking those areas. The Masada Hostel, at the foot of Masada, is *the* place to overnight if you want to make a predawn ascent onto Masada and watch the sun rise over The Dead Sea before the day's tour buses start arriving. Other IHYA hostels, such as the small, rustic retreat at Poriya, on an orchard-covered hill overlooking the Sea of Galilee near Tiberias, are great bargain options.

In the past few years, the IYHA has been busy upgrading its network of facilities. Many hostels are set up with a maximum of four to six beds per room; a large percentage of these rooms now have private shower/bathrooms and can easily be converted into doubles or family rooms. Dining facilities now offer meals

---

## *Tips* **Great Guesthouses**

Many of the accommodations listed on the **Christian Information Centre** website (http://198.62.75.1/www1/ofm/cic/CICmainin.htm) are among the most atmospheric and unusual choices in Israel (some of the best guesthouses are listed in detail in this book). Rates are very reasonable; rooms are comfortable but simple; atmosphere is quiet; buildings are usually 19th century in decor; and in most cases, guesthouses welcome visitors of all faiths without questions.

far superior to the once spartan youth-hostel fare.

Hostels offer rock-bottom prices and a friendly welcome to all. Age is no barrier, nor is membership. Having a youth hostel membership card, however, does give you certain advantages, such as better rates at the hostels, plus discounts at some restaurants, national parks, historical sites, museums, and on buses and trains. Only hostels bearing the triangular sign are authorized by the Israel Youth Hostels Association. It is advisable to book in advance.

*Note:* Not all youth hostels take foreign currency, and it's a good idea to check the availability of space (especially in summer months) before arriving. The IYHA also has 14-, 21-, and 28-day bargain-price tours and car-rental packages. Fax, write, or inquire at the Jerusalem office for further information.

Israel Hostels, or ILH (www.hostels-israel.com), is an independent network of 20 interesting, independent hostels, inexpensive hotels, B&Bs, kibbutz guesthouses, and other unusual, inexpensive places to stay throughout Israel. The managements are almost always friendly, well-informed, and personal.

## LANDING THE BEST ROOM

Somebody has to get the best room in the house. It might as well be you. You can start by joining the hotel's frequent-guest program, which may make you eligible for upgrades. A hotel-branded credit card usually gives its owner "silver" or "gold" status in frequent-guest programs for free. Always ask about a corner room. They're often larger and quieter, with more windows and light, and they often cost the same as standard rooms. When you make your reservation, ask if the hotel is renovating; if it is, request a room away from the construction. Ask about nonsmoking rooms, rooms with views, rooms with twin, queen- or king-size beds. If you're a light sleeper, request a quiet room away from vending machines, elevators, restaurants, bars, and discos. Ask for a room that has been most recently renovated or redecorated.

If you aren't happy with your room when you arrive, ask for another one. Most lodgings will be willing to accommodate you.

For tips on surfing for hotel deals online, visit www.frommers.com.

# 4

# Suggested Itineraries

Without a doubt, Jerusalem is the most fascinating place in Israel, so if you have very limited time, plan to spend much of it there. Distances are not great in Israel, and it is possible to get a quick taste of the desert, the Mediterranean coast, and even the Sea of Galilee on organized day trips from Jerusalem. But if you want to visit Eilat or get a real feel for the Galilee, then you're going to have to get on the road and move around the country. And to do that without needing a vacation after your vacation, you're going to need at least a week to check out the country's highlights. To help you make the best of your time, you'll find three itineraries in this chapter. The first two are for the time-dependent traveler who can spend only a week or two in Israel. The last one is specifically designed for families.

*Note:* Renting a car in the big cities such as Jerusalem and Tel Aviv is self-defeating—traffic and parking are a nightmare. But getting to amazing places in the countryside can be difficult without a rental car—especially if you have limited time. Although public transportation is an option in Israel, all of these itineraries are designed for those who'll have access to a car while in the country.

## 1 The Regions in Brief

It doesn't take much time to get from one region of Israel to another (at some points it's only 16km/10 miles wide), but you'll find the country is enormously varied. A quick review of the landscape will help you to decide where to spend your time.

**JERUSALEM** The jewel in the crown. The city is many worlds: modern and timeless; Jewish and Arab; religious and nonreligious. The walled, labyrinthine Old City has been named a World Heritage Site; in addition to being a perfectly preserved town with more than 4,000 years of history, it contains the great holy places of Judaism, Christianity, and Islam—the Temple Mount with the Dome of the Rock and the Al Aqsa Mosque, the Western Wall, and the Church of the Holy Sepulcher. Highlights of the New City include the remarkable Israel Museum, which houses the Dead Sea Scrolls, and Yad VaShem, the haunting Holocaust Memorial and Museum.

**THE DEAD SEA** Easy to visit for a day using Jerusalem as your base, The Dead Sea, the lowest point on the earth, is also a good place to visit for a few days as part of a jaunt into the Negev Desert. The almost impregnable Herodian Fortress of **Masada,** the most dramatic ancient site in the country, is perched on a plateau above The Dead Sea. It was here that the last Jewish resisters against Rome committed suicide rather than surrender. The beautiful canyon oasis of **Ein Gedi** is another attraction, as is the unique experience of trying to sink in the mineral-heavy Dead Sea. The southern Israeli shore of the sea is now lined with world-famous spa/hotels, offering therapeutic and beauty packages.

**THE NEGEV**    The southern part of Israel (nearly two-thirds of the country) is desert and semidesert; it contains beautiful **nature reserves,** and is great for hiking and nature tours. This part of the country, least visited by tourists, is perhaps the most mysterious. Long famous for its coral reef and laid-back snorkeling and diving, **Eilat,** at the southern tip of the Negev, is a world unto itself—a mirage rising out of the sand with dozens of new high-rise megahotels and fancy restaurants grouped on the city's few miles of Red Sea shoreline. The **Sinai Coast of Egypt,** a bit farther south and easily accessible from Eilat, offers reefs that are more spectacular, a landscape more dramatic and less developed, and hotels that are considerably less expensive.

**TEL AVIV**    Full of energy and verve (many wonder how it can be in the same country as Jerusalem), Tel Aviv has great restaurants, good beaches, and three inventive museums: the Diaspora Museum, the Eretz Israel Museum, and the Tel Aviv Museum of Art. From April to October, Tel Aviv is a good first stop in Israel—you can spend a day or two at the beach recovering from jet lag before plunging into the rest of the country.

**THE MEDITERRANEAN COAST**    If you want to relax on the beach, get to know this area, also known as the Golden Coast. **Netanya,** in the midcoast region, is a favorite of older, long-term English- and French-speaking travelers. It has lots of hotels in all price ranges, and many apartments and studios for rent. The ruined Roman- and Crusader-era city of **Caesarea** is the most dramatic archaeological site along the coast; farther north, the Old City of **Akko,** with its bazaars, cafes, and minarets beside the Mediterranean, is the most exotic site. **Kibbutzim** and moshav holiday villages, from Nasholim, south of Haifa, right up to the northernmost coast, are good spots for a pleasant beach break from touring.

**HAIFA**    Israel's third major city offers a spirit and face quite different from Jerusalem or Tel Aviv. It is a business and industrial city, but it's so beautifully laid out on a stepped mountain overlooking the harbor that it's quite memorable. Haifa makes a good urban base for exploring the northwestern part of the country.

**THE GALILEE**    Israel's northern region is lovely countryside, with forested mountains and olive groves dotted with Arab cities and towns, kibbutzim, and the remains of ancient ruined cities, synagogues, and churches. At the heart of the Galilee is the freshwater **Sea of Galilee,** a lyrically beautiful body of water made all the more special by its association with both New and Old Testament sites. The Galilee offers great hiking and nature trails, but it's also a good place to rent a car for a few days and freewheel.

**THE WEST BANK/PALESTINIAN AUTHORITY AREAS**    This was a countryside of classic biblical landscapes and ancient sites, but 20 years of political turmoil and war has made the West Bank difficult to visit at the best of times, and outright dangerous at the worst of times. As of press time the governments of most Western countries advise against visiting this area until the political situation improves. It's best to consider this area off-limits when planning your itinerary.

**PETRA, JORDAN**    Israel's neighbor offers dramatic, totally unspoiled landscapes as well as magnificent sites from ancient times, such as the legendary rock-hewn city of **Petra,** in the southern part of the country. Luxury hotels here are a bargain compared to those in Israel. The less-developed Jordanian side of The Dead Sea is dotted with hot springs, and now contains a number of relaxing spa hotels that offer a variety of unique therapeutic and beauty treatments. **Wadi Rum,** south of Petra, offers opportunities for camping and hiking with Bedouin guides in one of the most dramatic desertscapes in the world.

## 2 Israel in 2 Weeks

This itinerary will allow you time to enjoy the beauty and variety of landscapes and to interact with a variety of places. You'll swim in four seas (Mediterranean, Galilee, Dead, and Red) and have a solid block of time to explore the jewel in the crown, Jerusalem, in a personal way.

### Day ❶: Settling into Tel Aviv & Exploring Old Jaffa

From May to October, you can recover from jet lag by beaching and swimming in the sparkling, warm Mediterranean. Head from Ben-Gurion Airport to a hotel close to the sea; top choices include the **Tel Aviv Sheraton Hotel & Towers** (p. 244) or the less-expensive **Hotel de la Mer** (p. 247). Lots of sunlight will help get you into the rhythm of Israeli time. In the cool of the evening, explore the **Old City of Jaffa** with its medieval streets, galleries, and eateries overlooking the sea. Dine at **Margaret Tayar's** (p. 267) by the sea, the romantic **Cordelia** (p. 266), or the authentic **Dr. Shakshuka** (p. 268).

### Day ❷: Inventive Tel Aviv

Indulge in an Israeli buffet breakfast at your hotel, and then take in the ambience of the country's quintessential Israeli city. Spend at least a few hours at Tel Aviv's unique **Diaspora Museum** (p. 269). Swim as the sun plummets into the Mediterranean, and then head to the Tel Aviv Port, recently recycled into a stylish seaside boardwalk, for an evening of people-watching, dining, shopping, dancing, and drinking.

### Day ❸: Up the Coast to Haifa

Make **Haifa** your base—hotels at the top of the Carmel Mountains have breathtaking vistas, and there are many dining choices in Haifa after a day of touring the countryside, from the artists' village of Ein Hod to the walled Arabic port city of **Akko.** Akko is famous for ancient bazaars, mosques, and harborside restaurants such as **Uri Buri** and **Abu Christo.**

**Kibbutz Lohammei HaGetaot,** founded by survivors of the Holocaust, combines past tragedy and hope for the future: It contains an important **Holocaust Museum,** set amid the orchards and fields where the descendants of those few who survived have made their lives. Farther north, visit the grottoes and white seaside cliffs at **Rosh Ha-Niqra.**

### Day ❹: Freewheeling the Galilee

Move inland across the northern Galilee. Base in the mystic, mountaintop city of **Safed,** in or near **Nazareth** or at **Metulla** amid orchards and greenery at the northernmost tip of Israel, or at a kibbutz guesthouse in the Galilee. Visit the ancient ruined synagogue at **Bar'am** (the best preserved in Israel) and the **nature reserves and springs** at Baniyas and Tel Dan, with their freezing waters. Dine at a rustic spot such as **Dag Al HaDan,** a trout farm restaurant set amid streams, where the fish on your plate was alive and swimming while you were parking your car.

### Day ❺: The Sea of Galilee

Circle the shoreline of this mysterious and lovely lake with its New Testament sites at Tabgha, Capernaum, Kursi, and the Mount of Beatitudes, where the Sermon on the Mount was given. The eastern shore south of Ein Gev has quiet eucalyptus-shaded beaches. Overnight at the Scots Hotel or Sheraton (p. 377 and 376) in **Tiberias,** or **Kibbutz Ein Gev** (p. 382), with its date palm–shaded beach. Dine at scrumptious **Decks** in Tiberias (p. 380), and afterward dance on an evening party boat.

## Day ❻: More Galilee

While you're based at the Sea of Galilee, explore the wild, beautiful Golan Heights; hike to **Gamla** (p. 419) with its tragic history and ruined Herodian-era synagogue; or visit the **Golan Heights Winery** and museums in Katzrin (p. 418). Or, visit **Nazareth's Church of the Annunciation** and Nazareth's replica of a biblical village: nearby **Kana,** with two churches marking the miracle of water turned to wine; and ruined Zippori, the Hellenistic metropolis close to the then-tiny Nazareth of Jesus' childhood. Have a late swim in the lake and dine around the Sea of Galilee.

## Day ❼: Drive from Sea of Galilee to The Dead Sea

Travel south through the Jordan Valley visiting the vast archaeological park of Roman-era **Bet Shean** or the Crusader castle ruins at **Belvoir,** or make a short stop at the famous zodiac mosaic floor of the 5th-century **Bet Alpha Synagogue** at **Kibbutz Heftziba.** Overnight at **Kibbutz Ein Gedi Resort Hotel,** with its lavish botanical gardens overlooking The Dead Sea, the **Masada Hostel,** or the deluxe **Le Méridien Spa Hotel.**

## Day ❽: Luxuriate at The Dead Sea & Explore Masada & Ein Gedi

Explore the legendary Herodian fortress of **Masada** where the last Jewish resisters against Rome chose suicide over surrender; try to sink in the unearthly Dead Sea. Try the famous therapeutic mud, mineral, and massage treatments at The Dead Sea hotel spas or Kibbutz Ein Gedi Spa. Or hike the Ein Gedi Reserve, a canyon oasis where David hid from King Saul. Hope for a Bedouin cookout night at Kibbutz Ein Gedi, or have a relaxing evening Dead Sea mineral bath or treatment (p. 438).

## Day ❾: Drive to Eilat for Diving & More

**Snorkel** Eilat's coral reef with its exotic Indian Ocean fish or view the fish at the aquarium or from a glass-bottom boat. Enjoy Eilat's busy restaurant scene and nightlife. Overnight at (luxury) **Herods Palace** Tower Floor with gourmet snack buffet; or (budget) **Isrotel Riviera Club** (p. 470). Or, overnight at the less expensive **Ambassador Hotel,** right next to great snorkeling at Eilat's **Coral Beach National Park.** For kids, there are camel rides and the **Dolphin Reef** (p. 460), where you can watch wild dolphins. Eilat Center is a fast-food shopping mall with arcades and games to keep kids busy.

## Day ❿: Drive to Jerusalem

En route to Jerusalem (4 hr.), stop at **Timna Park**'s desert landscapes, or look around **Kibbutz Lotan**'s inventive desert buildings and organic farm—you may want to overnight here and get the feel of a genuine, creative kibbutz. In Jerusalem, return the rental car and take an evening walk to the **Jewish Quarter** of the Old City and the **Western Wall.** Dine and window-shop in the New City.

---

### *Tips* Jerusalem Sightseeing

Tailor the Jerusalem suggestions in this tour to the days sites are open. The Temple Mount is closed to visitors Friday and Saturday; much of West Jerusalem shuts for Shabbat. There are wonderful concerts, performances, and lectures (many in English). Check the Friday *Jerusalem Post* or the newspaper *Ha'aretz* for listings.

## Day ⑪: The Old City

Get up early and go into the **Old City** to see the **Temple Mount.** The Temple Mount, with the magnificent **Dome of the Rock** and **Al Aqsa Mosque,** is open only Sunday to Thursday 9 to 11am and sometimes in the early afternoon. It's a highlight of any journey to Jerusalem, and should not be missed. Exit the Old City via the Damascus Gate and sample the interesting foods for sale along the way. Take a round-trip taxi to the **Mount of Olives,** which is best visited in the morning, when the sun will be behind you as you look (and photograph) west to the panorama of the Old and New Cities. Afterward, explore the Old City bazaars; the **Crusader Church of St. Anne,** with its exquisite acoustics; and the **Holy Sepulcher Church.** Eat dinner and then do some gift shopping or attend a concert in West Jerusalem.

## Day ⑫: The New City

Take **Egged Bus no. 99's** NIS 40 ($10/£5) Jerusalem Highlights tour. Visit the **Israel Museum** or **Yad VaShem Holocaust Memorial & Museum** (or both). Then visit the **Mahane Yehuda** produce market—colorful and filled with great places for falafel, mixed grill, hummus, and other treats. Walk over to **Mea Shearim** via Ethiopia Street, and explore this 19th-century world of East European Jewry. Dine in and explore the gentrified German Colony/south Jerusalem neighborhoods, or walk in charming, restored Yemin Moshe.

## Day ⑬: More of New Jerusalem

Choose from the **Knesset,** with its Chagall panels; **Hadassah Hospital Ein Kerem,** with world-famous Chagall stained-glass windows; and a host of small museum gems in chapter 6. Take an excursion to bucolic **Ein Kerem** (p. 206), village of John the Baptist, or to **Mini Israel,** 45 minutes from Jerusalem, where you can see miniatures of almost every place you've visited (at twilight the buildings' interior lights go on). Enjoy dinner and entertainment in West Jerusalem.

## Day ⑭: Your Favorites in Jerusalem

Browse the Old City—it's endlessly fascinating, or if you haven't done so, visit (or revisit) Yad VaShem or the Israel Museum. Choose a place with a view or special menu for your farewell dinner, then do some final shopping before heading off to the airport.

## 3 8 Days in Northern Israel with Young Kids

If you're coming from North America, the long flight and jet lag are likely to leave a kid either semicomatose or in a very negative state of mind. But Israel is a kid-friendly country, and exploring it though a child's eyes will add new levels of meaning to your journey. The country is a tale of two halves. Southern Israel is filled with a plethora of attractions and sites geared to kids, from camel trekking in the **Ramon Crater** to floating in **The Dead Sea.** Even archaeological sites such as Masada are filled with adventure and drama for young ones. Touring the northern part of Israel with a child, however, needs more careful planning. Only the most pious child will enjoy darkened holy places, the rubble of archaeological sites, and being hounded by shopkeepers in the bazaar trying to sell child-size crowns of thorns. ("How many you need? What size you take?") So I've designed this itinerary to help you navigate the northern spots without taxing you or your child's patience.

And to make sure I kept a child's perspective in mind, *Frommer's Israel* has as part of its team an inquisitive, golden-haired, 6-year-old moppet named Lyne, who lives in

Jerusalem, attends a bilingual school, and has been checking out restaurants, zoos, museums, and hotels with me since she was a 4-week-old in a Snugli, charming the staff of a kosher Indian restaurant in Jerusalem. Lyne may be more patient than most kids her age, but she knows what kids like. Her picks are included in this itinerary.

### Days ❶ & ❷: Jerusalem's Old City

A hotel with a pool is a necessity; the **Inbal Hotel** (p. 127) has one open year-round, and is next to Liberty Bell Park, with a playground. *Lyne's Pick: Mount Zion Hotel (p. 131), because you can jump from the kids' pool to the big pool in one step, and there are often Jerusalem and visiting kids to play with.* Spend your morning in the Old City, exploring the bazaar and Jewish, Christian, and Islamic holy sites. *Lyne's Pick: The Crusader-era Church of Saint Anne (p. 180, where groups and individuals of all religions are welcome to try out the exquisite acoustics with religious songs of any tradition).* Father Michel from Canada, who oversees the church, is very welcoming, and "Frère Jacques" (preferably in French) qualifies as religious and sounds great; break between verses to let the echoes reverberate. Check the Via Dolorosa between the fourth and fifth Stations of the Cross for a shop selling simple toys from the days when "Made in Japan" meant "Broken in 5 Minutes!" Lyne loves to shop here. *Kanafeh* (an ancient sweet cheese pizza) at **Jaffar and Sons Pastry Cafe** (p. 142) on the Suq Khan es-Zeit Bazaar is a big hit.

### Day ❸: Jerusalem's New City

Visit the **Israel Museum** (p. 196). *Lyne's Picks: The ancient and modern objects that line the entrance path to the museum; the Children's Museum; the wall of Chanukah menorahs from all over the world in the Judaica Wing; and the Billy Rose Sculpture Garden filled with works by Picasso, Rodin, and others.* For older children, the **Bible Lands Museum** (p. 193), next to the Israel Museum, contains fascinating, interactive computer explanations of scarabs and ancient inscriptions, and brings ancient artifacts to life. Move on to the excellent **Tisch Family Zoological Gardens** (p. 212). Have dinner at **Ticho House** (p. 201), where there is a parklike garden for kids to run around in between courses.

### Day ❹: To the Galilee

Drive north through Jordan Valley. Stop to swim at **Sachne** (p. 424), with its water park for kids; **Belvoir** Crusader castle (p. 421); and **Hammat Gader** hot springs (p. 389), with its alligator farm, vast ruins of ancient baths, and a good Thai restaurant. Overnight at **Kibbutz Ein Gev Resort Village** (p. 391) in a family bungalow set in a date-palm grove beside the Sea of Galilee. Take a swim in the lake, then dine at Ein Gev on incredibly fresh Saint Peter's fish.

### Day ❺: The Galilee

Swim in the lake at Ein Gev's beautiful beach before moving on to a family bungalow at Lyne's absolutely favorite Israeli

---

### ⒯Tips Kids' Activities

No matter where you travel with your kids, always check the Friday *Ha'aretz/Herald Tribune* and *Jerusalem Post,* and check in with Tourist Information offices everywhere. Especially in summer, there's usually an array of street performers at night on Jerusalem's Ben-Yehuda Mall or Tel Aviv's beach promenade, puppet shows, and special museum exhibits and activities aimed at kids.

## (Kids) Lyne's Other Kid-Friendly Picks in Israel

**Uri Buri** (Akko; p. 320)  One of the few restaurants with gourmet food and an atmosphere relaxed enough to tolerate kids. Lyne loves Uri's calamari (chewy and no bones) and tender coquilles St. Jacques *a la plancha.*

**Abu Christo** (Akko; p. 320)  Kids can feed pita bread to fish swimming in the sea from their table while parents eat the very fresh catch of the day.

**Dan Caesarea** (Caesarea; p. 306)  Set amid vast, lush gardens, with an enormous pool and a kid-size basketball court, this is a fun place to relax for a day or so while taking in the region. The nearby ancient ruins of Caesarea (p. 304) come alive with a modern, multimedia presentation.

**Dan Carmel Hotel** (Haifa; p. 334)  The energetic children's summer staff and evening entertainment captivated Lyne, and the swimming pool is deliciously warm by August. The Dan Hotels' children's clubs are excellent throughout the country.

**Kibbutz Shefayim Guest House** (north of Tel Aviv; p. 292)  This place has a kids' water park and a swimming pool with artificial waves and a sandy bottom. Lyne also likes walking along the wild cliff-side paths overlooking the Mediterranean and watching the sunset.

**Alpaca Farm** (Mitzpe Ramon; p. 451)  You can interact with the weird, gentle animals that are always ready to eat Alpaca snacks from your hands. Within an hour of leaving, Lyne felt we needed to go back to get more alpaca information for the guidebook.

**Kibbutz Lotan** (north of Eilat; p. 455)  Lyne was charmed by the inventive structures of natural and recycled materials, the sitting areas and solar teahouse in the organic fields, watching falling stars in the desert sky at night, and the swimming pool with a large shallow area.

**Herods Palace Hotel Complex** (Eilat; p. 468)  This hotel has the largest adult and kids' pools in the country, as well as children's activities and a staff that Lyne adored. Not at all stuffy, although it's the most deluxe hotel in Eilat. Manager Adi Maor, who has a good eye for what will delight children, has set up a new children's center at the less-expensive, neighboring **Sheraton Moriah Eilat** (p. 470).

**Taybet Zaman Hotel and Resort** (Petra; p. 498)  The entire Petra experience is exciting for kids. The unique Taybet Zaman hotel, created from a traditional Bedouin village, is charming and itself an interesting place to explore.

hotel, the **Vered HaGalil Guest Farm** (p. 393) in the hills overlooking the northern side of the Sea of Galilee. Lyne loves to visit the beautiful horses here before breakfast. Explore the nearby ruined Roman-era Jewish village of **Korazim** (p. 388), then ride the quiet Galilee countryside on Vered HaGalil's beautiful horses. (*Lyne's Pick: a gentle, dark-brown pony named Choco.*) Dine at **Decks** (p. 380) in Tiberias (where Lyne, usually not a meat eater, downed a baby lamb chop and some salmon perfectly grilled on citrus- and olive-wood fires). *Lyne's Pick: Evening party boat on* *the Sea of Galilee, with everybody dancing to Israeli and Arabic music—you get a free voucher for a boat ride with dinner at Decks.*

### Day ⑥: To Tel Aviv via Nazareth and Caesarea

Explore **Nazareth Village** (p. 360), with its replicas of biblical-era houses and synagogue; then head off to explore the vast seaside **Roman and Crusader ruins at Caesarea** (p. 304), with its great multimedia presentation. Check into a beachfront hotel in Tel Aviv before dining at **Margaret Tayar's** (p. 267) in Jaffa, which has acclaimed food and a fabulous vista, and is *very* informal, so kids can prowl around between courses. Take an evening stroll through romantic Old Jaffa.

### Day ⑦: Tel Aviv

See the **Eretz Israel Museum**'s (p. 272) exhibitions of living crafts, its planetarium, and ancient glass; there's a great museum shop for kids and adults. *Lyne's Pick: The restored houses you can go into from 1100 B.C.* For older kids, move on to the **Diaspora Museum** (p. 269); for younger kids, try the wonderful drivethrough **Safari Park** (p. 275); kids find

the thriving giraffe herd fascinating. Take a late-afternoon Mediterranean swim. Dine on great hamburgers or chicken wings at **Mike's Place** (p. 285); on sweet potato quiche at **Shalvata** (p. 286), whose tables are actually in the sand; or have quality seafood for dinner at the beachfront **Manta Ray** (p. 266) in south Tel Aviv. Finish your day off with dessert at the **Chocolate Bar** (p. 263). *Lyne's Pick: Visit kosher Roy Chocolate, where, by prearrangement, it is sometimes possible to do participate in Belgian chocolate-making and sculpting (p. 263).*

### Day ⑧: Back to Jerusalem

Stop at **Mini Israel** (p. 230), located between Tel Aviv and Jerusalem, where kids can explore miniatures of virtually every landmark they've visited in Israel. Stop off in Jerusalem for last-minute shopping and a goodbye dinner in West Jerusalem, or *Lyne's Pick: Try the informal rooftop **Papa Andreas** restaurant (p. 140) in the Old City, which has incredible vistas.* Head off to Ben-Gurion Airport for a late-night flight home, or overnight in Jerusalem and then fly home the next morning.

# 5

# Settling Into Jerusalem

No one will ever be able to pinpoint what makes Jerusalem so special. The mountains, the wind, and the extraordinary light may be part of its appeal. Three thousand years ago, King David, the warrior-psalmist of the Bible, made Jerusalem his capital. Perhaps he saw the poetry of the place as it was then. The Gihon Spring flowed through a paradise of gardens nestled at the foot of the Kidron Valley. From there a long, narrow ridge rose steeply northward, filled with stone houses perched precariously on its sides. At the top of the ridge, seemingly hanging in the heavens, was the threshing floor of Araunah, which David purchased as the site of The Temple his son, Solomon, would one day build. Overlooking everything were the vast groves of the Mount of Olives, an ocean of silver leaves shimmering in the sun and wind, the source of the city's wealth; over the ridge of the Mount of Olives, the sun rose each day. From its crest, the view opened onto the desert, stretching over barren mountains and down steep wadis eastward to The Dead Sea. Into this wilderness, with great ceremony, the scapegoat was released each year, carrying with it Jerusalem's sins.

For more than 1,000 years after the time of King David, Jerusalem was the physical as well as the spiritual capital of the Jewish world. Jews longed for the city, whether the splendid Jerusalem of King Solomon or the ruined Jerusalem of the Babylonian Captivity. Jews fought and died for the redemption of Jerusalem during the Maccabee Revolt in 167 B.C., and

were rewarded with a miraculous victory over the Hellenistic Seleucids of Syria (the lights of Chanukah commemorate their victory to this day). It was at the dazzling and legendary Jerusalem built by King Herod that hundreds of thousands of Jews prayed during pilgrimage festivals, and thousands perished during the great revolt against Rome in A.D. 70. Sixty-five years later, defending the ruins of Herodian Jerusalem, hundreds of thousands more died during the Bar Kochba Revolt in A.D. 135. To this day, ancient Jerusalem remains the dream at the heart of Jewish civilization and well beyond. Almost half the world now knows the refrain, "Pray for the Peace of Jerusalem." The sagas of this city's endless struggles and the legends of its charismatic inhabitants lie at the heart of the consciousness of Western civilization.

Although the brief physical grandeur of Herodian Jerusalem long ago vanished in the ravages of warfare and time, the city's mystique has expanded far beyond anything that could have been dreamed of in ancient times. The most awesome holy places of Judaism, Christianity, and Islam have come to dot the Old City and its nearby hills. During the centuries of the Crusades, Jerusalem was the ethereal vision that moved the armies of Europe and Islam. But for almost 700 years after the Crusades ended, the actual city of Jerusalem existed mostly as a shadowy, forgotten backwater, slowly falling into ruin and decay. Not until the 19th century did the city again begin to come alive and reemerge from behind its walls.

During the years of the British Mandate (1918–48), the modern incarnation of Jerusalem developed as a quiet religious center, tourist attraction, and university town in a remarkably beautiful mountain setting. Nineteen years of division by war, barbed wire, and minefields (1948–67) brought Jerusalem's gentle renaissance to a temporary halt. With the city's reunification in 1967, however, Teddy Kollek, the city's world-renowned (former) mayor, began a 25-year crusade to make sure Jerusalem would not merely exist or even thrive but would absolutely shine.

## 1 A Brief History

**JERUSALEM TODAY**   Jerusalem today is a busy place. A state-of-the-art light-rail system is under construction, running from points all over the Judean Hills right down the middle of central Jerusalem's main thoroughfare, Jaffa Road. New construction is going on everywhere, bringing new industry, new highways, and, in the next few years, a whole new hotel scene. Since 1967, a constant stream of new civic delights—museums, festivals, concerts, and performance programs—has turned an austere outpost in the Judean hills into a lively, Mediterranean city with cafes, pubs, and restaurants packed to the brim with activity. The newly created pedestrian streets of the downtown center are flooded with strollers and, especially in summer, you'll find a nightly air of festive celebration.

A walled city is always a small town at heart, and for the past century, even as Jerusalem expanded beyond its walls and across the surrounding hills, it remained in spirit a small town: inward looking, personal, intensely involved in its local gossip and also with its thundering history. Now, for good or for ill, Jerusalem stands on the verge of becoming a true metropolis rather than the small city of exotic neighborhoods and religious communities the world has known since the 1920s. What Jerusalem is turning out to be like in the 21st century is a point of international interest and concern. For 3,000 years, through splendor and desolation, the earthly Jerusalem has always been a place that mirrored its extraordinary legend. Is this New Jerusalem able to maintain its mystique with a major highway system routed just 9m (30 ft.) from the walls of the Old City, so that visitors have to climb a pedestrian overpass in order to enter the Jaffa Gate? Or with many of the eccentric, small-scale 19th-century neighborhoods of the New City, and their quaint networks of pedestrian streets, courtyards, and Ottoman-era mansions (underappreciated in a town with Herodian, Byzantine, and Omayyid treasures to preserve) slated to be demolished and replaced with office blocks? A new wave of 30 skyscrapers is planned for the previously low-rise center of West Jerusalem, and the city has already seen the arrival of such worldly establishments as Pizza Hut, McDonald's, and Toys "R" Us. At what point will Jerusalem begin to seem like anywhere else?

The city is at a crossroads politically and socially as well as physically. Will it ever in some way be a shared capital for Palestinians and Israelis? Will the religious Jewish community become the demographic and ruling majority in West Jerusalem and, if so, what will happen to the museums, parks, entertainment, and cultural institutions created by the city's secular community over the past 30 years? Should developers be allowed a free hand to Manhattanize Jerusalem, or should limits be placed on the future growth of the city?

Jerusalem has been a holy city for 3,000 years, far eclipsing the length of time that any other place has borne such a title. It is also a holy city for all three great religions of the Western world: Judaism, Christianity, and Islam. Optimists believe that city

# Historic Jerusalem

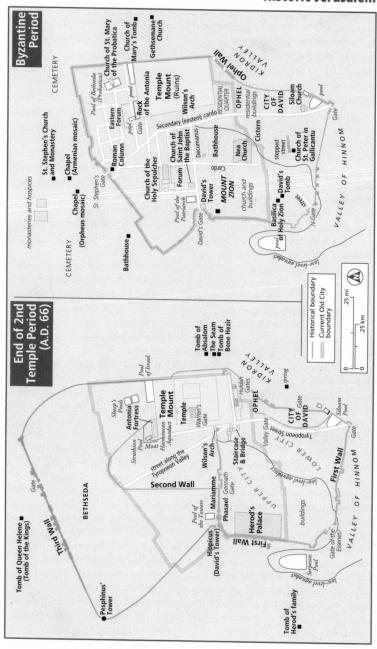

## Byzantine Period

monasteries and hospices

CEMETERY

CEMETERY

St. Stephen's Church and Monastery

Chapel (Orpheus mosaic)

Chapel (Armenian mosaic)

St. Stephen's Gate

Roman Column

Pool of Bethesda (Probatica)

pool

Eastern Forum

pool

Church of the Probatica

Church of St. Mary of the Probatica

Church of Mary's Tomb

Gethsemane Church

Rock of the Antonia

Temple Mount (Ruins)

Wilson's Arch

Gate

Secondary (eastern) cardo

KIDRON VALLEY

Ophel Wall

RESIDENTIAL QUARTER

OPHEL

residential buildings

Decumanus

Church of Saint John the Baptist

Bathhouse

Cistern

CITY OF DAVID

Siloam Church

Church of the Holy Sepulcher

Church of the Forum

Cardo

Nea Church

stepped street

Church of St. Peter in Gallicantu

pool

Bathhouse

Pool of the Patriarch

David's Tower

MOUNT ZION

church and buildings

David's Tomb

Street

Basilica of Holy Zion

pool

N-Gate

Gate

David's Gate

low-level aqueduct

VALLEY OF HINNOM

## End of 2nd Temple Period (A.D. 66)

Tomb of Queen Helene (Tomb of the Kings)

Gate

Psephinus' Tower

Third Wall

BETHESDA

Sheep's Pools

Pool of Israel

Antonia Fortress

Struthian Pool

Hasmonean Aqueduct

Moat

Temple Mount

Temple

Warren's Gate

Tomb of Absalom

The Seam

Tomb of Bene Hezir

KIDRON VALLEY

spring

Huldah Gates

OPHEL

street along the Tyropoeon Valley

Second Wall

Wilson's Arch

Staircase & Bridge

Valley Gate

Tyropoeon Street

CITY OF DAVID

Siloam Pool

LOWER CITY

Gate

Mariamme

Phasael

Gennath Gate

UPPER CITY

low-level aqueduct

Pool of the Towers

Hippicus (David's Tower)

First Wall

Herod's Palace

First Wall

buildings

Gate of the Essenes?

Serpents Pool

VALLEY OF HINNOM

low-level aqueduct

Tomb of Herod's family

Historical boundary

Current Old City boundary

.25 mi

0

.25 km

0

N

103

planners and real estate developers will find a way to turn a mysterious walled holy city into a fast-paced holy megalopolis. For now, in many ways, the city walks a tightrope between its legend and the rapidly encroaching world of the 21st century.

**AN ANCIENT CITY**   Jerusalem is one of the world's oldest continuously inhabited cities. It was in existence long before it was first mentioned in Pharaonic records of the 2nd millennium B.C., or in the Bible.

Genesis relates that Abraham, in the shadowy period of approximately 1800 B.C., visited Melchizedek, "king of Salem," one of the first-known references to Jerusalem. However, for the next 800 years the city played no part in biblical or Jewish history. Then, in 1004 B.C., King David, the Israelites' great poet-warrior, captured Jerusalem, which was a small Jebusite/Canaanite city perched on a narrow hill just to the south of the present Old City walls. The city was considered neutral territory, situated on land not controlled by any of the 12 tribes of Israel, and seemed an ideal choice for a capital that would not exacerbate tribal rivalries. David brought the Ark of the Covenant to Jerusalem from his former capital, Hebron. On the Ophel, a stretch of ascending land between the settlement of Jerusalem and the high place that was to become the Temple Mount, David built his palace and declared that henceforth Jerusalem would be the capital.

Under the reign of David's son Solomon, Jerusalem grew in importance. The Bible records that it was the center of a brief-lived empire that stretched from southern Syria to the Gulf of Eilat. African ivory and gold, cedar from Lebanon, spices, textiles, and pottery from distant lands adorned Jerusalem's houses and were bargained for in its markets. The queen of Sheba came to Jerusalem with her entourage, bearing unimaginable treasures in exchange for Solomon's wisdom; tradition says she returned to her distant homeland (possibly in Africa) bearing his child. With the aid of Phoenician architects and artisans sent by his ally, King Hyram of Tyre, Solomon built the **great Temple** (960 B.C.) and constructed a more magnificent palace (although the Bible records the grandeur of Solomonic Jerusalem with awe, the city would actually have been a small, densely packed early–Iron Age settlement covering no more than several acres).

Under Solomon's visionless successors, the kingdom split in two: the larger kingdom of Israel to the north and the smaller kingdom of Judah to the south, with Jerusalem remaining the capital of small, struggling Judah.

The House of David continued to reign in Jerusalem for 3½ centuries. Some of the Davidic rulers dispensed social justice and encouraged religious revivals under the influence of the great prophets; some of the kings turned to the worship of other gods. Invaders came and retreated. The northern kingdom of Israel, ruled by a succession of non-Davidic Jewish/Israelite dynasties, fell to Assyria in the late 8th century B.C. and vanished from history, its population dispersed throughout Assyria's great empire. The Assyrian armies then stormed across Judah, destroying its towns and cities.

Only Jerusalem was able to avoid defeat and destruction, thanks to one of the most miraculous and fateful engineering feats in history. An underground tunnel was dug in 701 B.C. by King Hezekiah (with the encouragement of the Prophet Isaiah) from inside the city's walls to Jerusalem's water source, the Gihon Spring, located in a valley outside the walls. The workers, digging from each end of the proposed tunnel, frantically hacked through the bedrock of Jerusalem in a wildly curving S-shaped route, somehow managing to meet, thereby creating underground access to the Gihon Spring (which was then camouflaged) before the dreaded Assyrians arrived to lay siege to the city. With its hidden water supply Jerusalem was able to withstand the Assyrian siege and was saved. The fragile beginnings of Western monotheism, precariously taking root in 8th-century-B.C. Jerusalem, were not swept away into the dustbin of history. Perhaps more than any other structure built by human beings, **the water tunnel of King Hezekiah,** which still exists today (see "East Jerusalem Attractions," in chapter 6), changed the course of history.

In the next century, the messages of Isaiah and Jeremiah, and the religious reforms of King Josiah, strengthened Judean Judaism, so that unlike the religion of the Northern Kingdom of Israel, it would be able to survive both the defeats and exiles that lay ahead.

Jerusalem was conquered by the armies of Nebuchadnezzar, king of Babylon, who in 586 B.C. destroyed The Temple, sacked the city, and carried most of Jerusalem's inhabitants into exile in Babylonia. But Babylonia soon fell to the Persians, and in 540 B.C. King Cyrus of Persia allowed the Jews to return to their homeland and rebuild a modest Second Temple. Only a small remnant of the exiles chose to leave what had become a comfortable, cosmopolitan Jewish community in Babylonia and resettle the ruins of Jerusalem. The next centuries were remarkably quiet, and it was during this period that many believe the core of postbiblical Jewish religion and tradition was created in Jerusalem.

**THE HELLENISTIC PERIOD**    The city fell under the domain of Alexander the Great in 331 B.C. A continuation of Hellenistic rule later passed to the Syrian-based Seleucids, and it was against their attempts to forcibly Hellenize the Jews that the Maccabees, a priestly family from the Judean village of Mod'in, led their famous revolt between 167 and 141 B.C. The festival of Chanukah marks the miraculous recapture and rededication of the Jerusalem Temple during the revolt against the Seleucids.

For the next century, Jerusalem was the capital of an independent Jewish Commonwealth ruled by the increasingly Hellenized descendants of the Maccabees, who are known to history as the Hasmonean dynasty. To some Jews, however, including those who gravitated toward the ascetic Essene sect, the legendary House of David remained the spiritual and eternal royal dynasty; the Hasmoneans and the priesthood they controlled were merely transient temporal authorities. In the minds of many Jews living 2,000 years ago, the dichotomy between the spiritual and earthly Jerusalem, nurtured through centuries of psalmists, prophets, and the Babylonian exile began to take on new, mystically intense meaning. This dichotomy, with its many interpretations, has remained part of the Western world's concept of Jerusalem into modern times.

**THE ROMAN OCCUPATION**    Pompey claimed Jerusalem for Rome in 63 B.C., and in 37 B.C. Herod (whose Idumaean father converted to Judaism) was appointed king of Judea by the Romans. Perhaps in an effort to make himself loved by his reluctant and resentful subjects, or perhaps to impress his Roman overseers with his industry, Herod rebuilt Jerusalem and designed a palatial temple area that dwarfed the original Temple of Solomon and replaced the less-grand Second Temple.

Herod died in 4 B.C. The city that he had built, with its fortress, towers, aqueducts, water reservoirs, and vast temple complex, was the Jerusalem that Jesus knew. Herod's great temple complex, initially opposed by many Jews who felt it was too Roman in its grandeur, became a symbol of Jewish national and religious aspirations and a constant flash point in Jewish opposition to Roman rule. As never before, The Temple became a center for Jewish pilgrimage from Judea, the Galilee, Babylonia, Persia, and all parts of the Roman Empire; more than 100,000 pilgrims could be accommodated in Jerusalem during the great festivals of Passover, Succot, and Shavuot. To a greater extent than ever, religion was Jerusalem's major industry, and it was increasingly big business. During this period, rabbinical Judaism was also developing, grounded in study, prayer, synagogues, and careful analysis of ethical and ritual rules governing Jews everywhere. This component of Judaism flourished alongside the priestly cult, which was centered on daily prayers and sacrifice at The Temple in Jerusalem.

It was to this city that was a magnet for the ancient Jewish world that Jesus came to celebrate Passover, and it was in Jerusalem that Jesus was imprisoned and crucified by Pontius Pilate, the Roman procurator. According to most Christian traditions, the Church of the Holy Sepulcher marks the site of the crucifixion and burial of Jesus, and the Via Dolorosa is the way Jesus trod, carrying the cross, from prison to Golgotha.

The Jewish rebellion against Roman rule in A.D. 66 drove the Roman occupiers from Jerusalem, and brought the Roman armies of Titus and Vespasian to reconquer Jerusalem. In A.D. 70, Rome laid siege to Jerusalem, starved out the population, destroyed the city and its Temple, and killed or sold into slavery most of its surviving inhabitants. The Roman 10th Legion was stationed beside the ruins of the Jaffa Gate for more than 60 years to prevent Jews from filtering back and reestablishing their city.

There is evidence, however, that a very small number of Jews and early Christians (who were considered to be a Jewish sect) may have continued to live in the ruins of Mount Zion, where they provided services for the 10th Legion's camp. During these decades, Jews were permitted to visit Jerusalem to mourn its destruction, and were still able to identify the exact locations of specific buildings and holy sites among the acres of ruins. Talmudic lore records that a group of rabbis walking on the Temple Mount noticed that a fox had made its lair in the wreckage of the Holy of Holies. Aging witnesses to Jesus' last days in Jerusalem would have been able to pass on their memories of where events took place to a younger generation. Although the city was now desolate, the powerful charisma of Jerusalem continued to grow.

Bar Kochba's revolt in A.D. 132, triggered by the decision of the Emperor Hadrian to rebuild Jerusalem as a non-Jewish Roman outpost, returned the ruined city to the Jews for 3 short years. The Temple site was rededicated, though probably not rebuilt, and daily sacrifice was reinstated. The revolt ended in A.D. 135 with even greater military disaster for the Jews than the revolt of A.D. 70. According to some estimates, half a million civilians died in each of the revolts against Rome, numbers unheard of in ancient warfare. Hadrian leveled the ruins of Jerusalem, sowed the land with salt, and, with an entirely different city plan and arrangement of streets, built a Roman city called "Aelia Capitolina" in honor of the imperial family and the Roman god Jupiter Capitolina. Hadrian filled Aelia Capitolina with pagan temples and barred Jews from residing in the city for all time. Herod's vast Temple Mount platform, and its great retaining walls, too massive and still too politically sensitive to demolish, were among the few features from Herodian Jerusalem that remained. According to some historians, a Roman temple (or at least, an altar) may have been installed on the site of the Jerusalem Temple itself. Jews were generally allowed into the city only to visit the ruins of the Temple Mount and only on the ninth day of the month of Av, the anniversary of The Temple's destruction.

The building of Aelia Capitolina was an attempt to make Jerusalem into just another provincial city on the fringe of the Roman Empire. Today, you can still see elements from this alien interlude in Jerusalem's history, including a fragment of **the colonnaded Cardo,** Aelia Capitolina's main north-south thoroughfare, which was

## Impressions

*Jerusalem: the city which miraculously transforms man into pilgrim; no one can enter it and remain unchanged.*

—Elie Wiesel

uncovered by archaeologists in the 1970s. The basic layout of the present-day Old City, divided into quadrants by perpendicular intersecting market streets leading from the Damascus and Jaffa gates, is inherited from this time, as is the Arabic name for Damascus Gate (Bab-el-Amud, or "Gate of the Column"), recalling a towering, long-lost column that once stood inside the gate to serve, in traditional Roman fashion, as a distance marker.

**THE BYZANTINES** Jerusalem's 200-year stint as an ordinary town ended with Emperor Constantine, who converted the Roman Empire to Christianity and turned Jerusalem into a Christian holy city. He built the **Church of the Holy Sepulcher** in approximately A.D. 330, and the Byzantine emperor, Justinian, 200 years later, renovated and enlarged it. Jerusalem regained its ancient name, and again became an extraordinary destination for religious pilgrimage from all over the ancient world—this time by followers of a new religion. The city was filled with churches, monasteries, convents, and daily religious processions. Jews were forbidden to reside in Byzantine Jerusalem, but the tradition, begun after the Bar Kochba Revolt in A.D. 135, of allowing Jews to visit the city and mourn the loss of The Temple, continued. At times, Jews were allowed only to view the city from the Mount of Olives. In A.D. 614, the pre-Islamic Persians (who were then mostly Zoroastrians) captured Jerusalem from the Byzantines. They destroyed the churches and monasteries of the city, including the Holy Sepulcher, and left the corpses of thousands of the city's defenders and martyrs to be eaten by vultures—an act still remembered and commemorated with horror by Jerusalem's Christian communities. After 25 years of warfare, the Byzantines recaptured Jerusalem in A.D. 629, and had only just begun to rebuild the Christian presence in the city when the armies of a new religion—Islam—swept out of the desert.

**ISLAM & THE CRUSADES** Caliph Omar, second successor to Muhammad, began the Muslim occupation of Jerusalem in A.D. 638. In the decades after his death, according to his wishes that the Temple Mount not lie in ruins, with its sacred rock exposed to the elements, Caliph Abd el-Malik built the masterpiece **Dome of the Rock** (A.D. 687–91) marking the spot from which the Prophet Muhammad, in his miraculous night journey, rose from the earth to glimpse paradise. By A.D. 720, the **Al Aqsa Mosque,** Islam's third-holiest sanctuary, had been built at the southern edge of the Temple Mount. Under the tolerant rule of the early Muslims, Jews were again allowed to reside in Jerusalem and the Christian community continued to flourish.

Around the year A.D. 1000, the mad Caliph Al Hakim, ruling from Egypt, began a wave of anti-Christian persecution that culminated in the burning of the Church of the Holy Sepulcher. Feudal Europe responded with the Crusades, and in the wars that followed, the mystical concept of Jerusalem was burned more strongly than ever into the traditions of both Christianity and Islam. After the initial success of the **First Crusade** in 1099, Jerusalem changed hands several times between Crusaders and Muslims (most notably under Saladin). The Crusader Church of Saint Anne (A.D. 1147), with its near miraculous acoustics, is Jerusalem's great architectural treasure from this era.

## Saints & Warriors: Caliph Omar & Saladin

Islamic forces have conquered Jerusalem twice: in A.D. 638, and again in 1187, when it was recaptured after 88 years of Crusader rule. Both times, the warriors who won Jerusalem were among the most extraordinary men Islamic civilization has ever produced. In each case, Jerusalem was captured without resort to a final military onslaught, and in each case, although these leaders stayed only briefly in Jerusalem, their association with the city came to be regarded as the crowning triumphs of their lives.

**Omar ibn el Khattab** (d. 644), the second successor to the Prophet Muhammad, was a warrior of great saintliness who eschewed all luxuries and dressed in a simple rough-spun cloak. According to legend, when the Byzantine ambassador came to Medina to seek an audience with Caliph Omar, he was directed to a hill outside the city. There he found only a man alone, asleep on the ground under a palm tree, using his dusty sandals for a pillow. When the ambassador was told that this was the caliph, he responded, "Great Omar, you are truly a ruler of peace and justice unequaled to be able to go unprotected among your people in such a way."

Accepting the peaceful submission of Jerusalem from the Byzantine patriarch Sophronius in A.D. 638, Omar declined an invitation to pray in the Church of the Holy Sepulcher for fear that in future times, any place in which he had prayed would be turned into a mosque. According to tradition, the tolerant and visionary Omar permitted Jews to reside in Jerusalem again; initiated the cleaning of the Temple Mount, which had been used as a garbage dump for 300 years; and ordered the transformation of Jerusalem into an Islamic as well as a Jewish and Christian holy city. Omar's redemption of the Temple Mount as a holy place eventually led to the building of the

Hundreds of architectural fragments from Crusader buildings, in secondary use adorning Mamluke and Ottoman period buildings throughout the Old City, attest to the massive destruction inflicted on the city during these centuries. The entire Jewish population of Jerusalem was massacred when Crusader armies captured the city in 1099, but by the year 1260, not long after the Crusaders had been dislodged, a small Jewish community was reestablished. The Mamlukes, an Egyptian dynasty, added Jerusalem to their empire in 1244. Over the next 2½ centuries, Jerusalem was slowly filled with Mamluke mansions, religious buildings, and covered markets, all notable for tall, "stalactite"-ornamented doorways and careful stonework.

**TURKISH RULE** In 1517, the Ottoman Turks, also Muslims, took control of Jerusalem. In an aesthetic stroke of genius, the 16th-century Ottoman rulers faced the deteriorating exterior of the Dome of the Rock with dramatic cobalt blue and turquoise ceramic tiles from Persia and Anatolia. The Ottomans also rebuilt the magnificent walls around Jerusalem in 1538, but these largely ceremonial fortifications (gunpowder and cannon had made such defensive structures obsolete) surrounded a depopulated community devastated by centuries of Crusader wars and struggling to survive. By the early 19th century, the city's population, estimated to have been close

Dome of the Rock, a lasting monument to his brief, radiant encounter with Jerusalem.

**Saladin** (1137–93), of Kurdish origin, was the sultan of Egypt, Syria, Yemen, and Palestine, founder of the Ayyubid dynasty, and the most romantically heroic of all Islamic generals. Saladin's moral leadership and passion, rather than overwhelming tactical advantage, brought his disparate forces to victory over the Crusaders at the Horns of Hittin, near Tiberias, on July 4, 1187. Three months later, Jerusalem surrendered under Saladin's siege. In contrast to the massacre of Muslims and Jews that had accompanied the Crusader conquest of Jerusalem in 1099, Saladin's victory was marked by chivalry and compassion. Native Christians were allowed to remain in the city; those of Crusader origin were offered safe passage with their goods out of the country via Akko on payment of a ransom of 10 dinars each. As Saladin and his brother watched the wealthy, including the Crusader patriarch and his retinue, depart with treasure-laden wagons, leaving thousands of unransomed poor to be sold into slavery, they announced a donation to ransom 7,000 poor Christians, thus shaming the patriarch into matching their generosity. In one of the many historical coincidences fraught with meaning to Jerusalemites, Saladin conquered the city on October 2, 1187, the anniversary of the Prophet Muhammad's miraculous night journey from Mecca to Jerusalem, and his ascension from the Temple Mount to the heavens. The selfless Saladin, in the great tradition of early Islamic leaders such as Omar ibn el Khattab, lived without personal wealth or luxury, and died without even enough money to pay for his grave.

to 100,000 in Herodian times, had shrunk to less than 15,000. Only in the second half of the 19th century did the city begin to come alive again, with its Jewish, Christian, and Muslim communities spreading into neighborhoods beyond the walls of the Old City.

In the last decades of the 19th century, as the European powers vied for influence in this strategic portion of the floundering Ottoman Empire, each government planted its flag in Jerusalem under the guise of vast church-related construction projects. The number of monuments to European nationalism that date from this brief era is amazing. Germany's massive neo-Romanesque Dormition Church and Monastery on Mount Zion recalls Worms Cathedral overlooking the Rhine; the delicate, Renaissance-inspired Holy Trinity Church in the Russian Compound echoes the late-15th-century Cathedral of the Assumption in the Kremlin; St. George's Cathedral in East Jerusalem, completed in 1912, is an enclave of neo-Gothic Britain built from Jerusalem stone, with a bell tower and cloister that calls to mind a fragment of Magdalene College at Oxford that somehow dropped into the Middle East. The exotically medieval Russian Church of Saint Mary Magdalene with its gilded onion-shaped domes transformed the vista of the Mount of Olives. Florentine, Ethiopian, and

---

**Impressions**

*Jerusalem of gold, of copper, of light . . . To all your songs, I am the harp.*
—Popular Israeli song

---

French architecture sprang up across the city in the form of hospitals, churches, convents, and pilgrimage facilities.

**THE BRITISH ARRIVE** Turkish rule lasted exactly 400 years, until General Allenby marched through Jerusalem's Jaffa Gate at the head of a British regiment in the final year of World War I. Under the British Mandate (1918–48), the New City blossomed and much of downtown West Jerusalem took on its basic shape. Landmarks such as the YMCA, the King David Hotel, the Rockefeller Museum in East Jerusalem, the original Hadassah Hospital and Hebrew University on Mount Scopus, the art moderne Central Post Office on Jaffa Road, Saint Andrew's Church near Abu Tor, and West Jerusalem's King George Street all stand as monuments to that era. The Rechavia neighborhood, with its streamlined buildings and curving balconies designed in the International Style by refugee architects from Germany, and the exotic mansions built for the city's leading Arabic families in the adjacent neighborhood of Talbeyeh, are also part of Jerusalem's British Mandate–era heritage.

**TO THE PRESENT DAY** In November 1947, the United Nations voted to establish two states in Palestine: one Jewish, the other Arab. Jerusalem was to remain a united, international city, independent of either proposed state. In spite of this decision, by early 1948 the Jewish sector of Jerusalem found itself under siege by Arab forces and suffered shelling and bombardment for many weeks. Eventually, Israeli forces secured a narrow strip of mountainous land (the Burma Rd.), which connected the Jewish part of Jerusalem to the rest of Israel, and the siege was broken. The State of Israel was established in the 1948 War of Independence, but the cease-fire lines left Jerusalem split down the middle, from north to south, by a wall of concrete, barbed wire, and minefields. The modern western section of the city remained in Israeli hands, but the Old City, including the Jewish Quarter (from which all Jews had been expelled) and the modern Arab neighborhoods north of the Old City (along with the rest of West Bank), were annexed by the Kingdom of Jordan.

In the Six-Day War of 1967, East Jerusalem came under Israeli control and the city was reunited once again. But the distinctions left by 2 decades of division still remain: Downtown East Jerusalem and the Old City are predominantly Palestinian (Christian and Muslim Arabs), and West Jerusalem is predominantly Israeli.

## 2 Orientation

### ARRIVING

**BY PLANE** A reasonably priced way to get to Jerusalem from Ben-Gurion Airport is by **sherut** (shay-*root*), a van shared by eight passengers with a fixed per-person rate. The current fare is NIS 45 ($11/£5.60) per person, baggage included. The sherut stand, run by **Nesher Sheruts,** is to the left as you exit the arrivals area of the terminal building. Confirm that the destination of the Nesher van is Jerusalem, give your luggage to the driver, and climb in. When all the seats are claimed, the van will take off. The driver must, without charging an extra agora (a single small-denomination coin), take you from the airport to the hotel or residential address of your choice anywhere in

Jerusalem. If you're lucky, you'll be the first in the van to be dropped off at your destination. If not, you'll find yourself on an odyssey through parts of Jerusalem you would never normally see, but you *will* get to your destination. If you are with a group of three or four people, it could pay to take a taxi.

The fixed-price rate for a **private taxi** is about NIS 260 ($65/£33). If you happen to have four people in your party (standard taxis take only up to four passengers, and the fourth passenger is at the driver's discretion), the cost for this most convenient option is really little more than that of a sherut. Remember that if you have a lot of baggage, it may not fit into one cab. Agree on a definite price ahead of time. Taxi drivers do not expect tips, but if you have a number of heavy bags, the driver may quote a slightly higher fare. If your driver doesn't charge extra for help with bags, offer a NIS 10 ($2.50/£1.25) tip. Rates after 9pm and on Shabbat and Jewish holidays are higher. All major car-rental companies have offices at Ben-Gurion Airport.

For the return trip to the airport, your hotel will be glad to call in advance (reserve about 2 days before your departure) and make an appointment for a sherut to pick you up. If you want to make your sherut reservation in person, the office of **Nesher Taxis and Sheruts** (✆ **02/625-7227**), known for its extremely reliable airport service, is upstairs at 23 Ben-Yehuda St., near King George Street. The company will pick up round-the-clock, 7 days a week, but if you need transport to the airport on the Sabbath, you must make your reservation by Thursday—the Nesher office is closed on Shabbat.

**BY TRAIN**    On weekdays, 20 trains a day arrive from Tel Aviv at Jerusalem's Malha Station, on the far western edge of the city. From there, you must take a municipal bus into the center of town. Officially the trip takes and hour and 30 minutes; the fare from Tel Aviv to Jerusalem is NIS 20 ($5/£2.50) with small discounts for children and students; children 4 and under with adult are free. For current schedules and fares, go to www.israrail.org.il, and click on "English."

**BY BUS**    There is direct, scheduled bus service from most major cities to Jerusalem. Between Tel Aviv and Jerusalem, buses leave as soon as they are full; the trip takes about 1 hour; fare is NIS 20 ($5/£2.50). Most buses arrive and depart from Jerusalem's **Central Bus Station,** which is at the western entrance to the city, right on Jaffa Road. From there, you can easily pick up municipal buses to all parts of West Jerusalem. *Tip:* After depositing most passengers, Egged intercity buses from Tel Aviv and Haifa arriving in Jerusalem after 8pm generally continue down Jaffa Road to the center of town, making additional request stops along the way. The buses then stop at the corner of Agron Street and the beginning of King David Street, and at the corner of Agron Street and King George Street. Check with your bus driver; if you're going to the center of town, this is a convenient, free option.

Arab-owned van buses to **Bethlehem** (as far as the Crossing Point from Jerusalem into Bethlehem) leave from a bus station across the street and a block east of the Damascus Gate. At press time, bus no. 22 went to the Bethlehem crossing. Returning from Bethlehem, you can request to be let off at Jaffa Gate or the New Gate (if you are staying in West Jerusalem). Fare is NIS 6 ($1.50/75p).

**BY CAR**    Route 1 (Hwy. 1) is the main road to Jerusalem from Tel Aviv and Ben-Gurion Airport; it runs right into Jaffa Road, downtown West Jerusalem's main street. Signs at the entrance of the city direct you to the downtown center, via a slightly circuitous route, as private cars are barred from most of Jaffa Road near the city entrance. If you're going to the Renaissance, or other hotels on Herzl Boulevard, or points in the extreme western part of the city, follow signs for Herzl Boulevard/Government Center.

The newer, often less-busy Hwy. 443 toward Tel Aviv runs parallel to the north of Route 1 and leads you to the northern part of Jerusalem. Parts of it traverse territory lined by high cement security walls, so you don't see much of the landscape. If you're coming from or headed toward points on the coast north of Tel Aviv, this is the fastest route.

From the Sea of Galilee, The Dead Sea, or Eilat and the Negev, the most direct route is Route 90, which follows the Jordan Valley. From Route 90, turn onto Route 1 just south of Jericho, and make the steep ascent up to Jerusalem. At the edge of the city, follow signs to the Center. This will take you to the northern walls of the Old City, approaching Damascus Gate. Keep right if you're heading for the center of West Jerusalem, and left for East Jerusalem.

**Parking** is difficult in Jerusalem. Many hotels have very limited or no parking facilities. There are parking garages at Hillel and Yoel Solomon streets in downtown Jerusalem; outside Jaffa Gate on Mamilla Street; and on Mamilla Street under the Hilton Hotel. There are metered streets throughout the center of town: You must purchase parking tickets in advance from kiosks, and display your parking ticket, with the appropriate time marked, in order to avoid fines. Your car-rental agent will show you how to use the parking ticket system. In Jerusalem, it is much easier to use public transportation or taxis. The Old City is only accessible by foot.

All major **car-rental agencies** are clustered on 2 long blocks of King David Street, beginning at Agron Street.

## VISITOR INFORMATION

There's a **Ministry of Tourism** information desk (© 03/971-1145) in the arrivals hall of Ben-Gurion International Airport. The staff will provide city maps and brochures (which you must buy), and answer your questions. A hotel reservations desk nearby can also help you find a room for the night before leaving Ben-Gurion for Jerusalem.

In the Old City, there's a **Tourist Information Office** just inside Jaffa Gate, a few steps down on the left (© 02/627-1422). At press time, the hours were Sunday to Thursday from 8am to 5pm and Friday from 8am to 1pm; in summer, there may be Saturday hours. This office sells maps and booklets, but there is a shelf with free maps and tourist brochures as well. Look for the Jerusalem Menus booklets, with discount coupons for many of the restaurants recommended by this book. The office also rents a recorded walking tour of the Old City for NIS 50 ($13/£6.25) per day plus a security deposit.

The **Christian Information Centre** (© 02/627-2692; http://198.62.75.1/www1/ofm/cic/CICmainin.htm) at the far end of the square inside Jaffa Gate offers all kinds of useful information about tours, Christian hospices, group tours to Bethlehem, and religious services. It's open Monday, Wednesday, Friday, and Saturday 8:30am to 5:30pm; Tuesday and Thursday, 8:30am to 4pm; and Saturday 8:30am to noon.

If you're surfing the Web, the **Ministry of Tourism** is at www.goisrael.com, and the **Municipality of Jerusalem** site is www.Jerusalem.muni.il.

**MAPS & PUBLICATIONS** Maps of Jerusalem are available at the Tourist Information Office inside the Jaffa Gate and cost NIS 5 to NIS 20 ($1.25–$5/60p–£2.50), depending on the type you choose. It also sells books on travel in Israel, but check your planned purchases carefully—I bought a book of Israeli road maps only to find that it was totally out-of-date (the office was kind enough to give me a refund). The office also offers a shelf of free pamphlets and information, including the always-useful Jerusalem Menus publications, with their restaurant discount coupons. Most major hotels have a counter with a selection of these free flyers and pamphlets, and good free maps that are sufficient for the requirements of most tourists. The Tourist Information Office may also have the booklet schedule for the Cinémathèque, and for art, cultural, and performance events throughout the city. If your hotel doesn't have a good selection, check out the lobbies of other major hotels. Car-rental agencies have general maps of Israel, and can often provide more detailed maps of cities. **Steimatzsky's Bookstore** at Jaffa Road next to Zion Square (and other local bookstores) will have many current road maps.

*Note:* Many current maps printed in Israel no longer show the demarcation line between the West Bank and the pre-1967 Israeli border. Without a map showing this demarcation line, it is a bit easier to possibly stray into the West Bank, which at press time was under State Department/Foreign Office Travel advisories, and where most rental cars are not insured. Be careful and always get clear directions before setting out anywhere near that zone.

The *International Herald Tribune* contains the entire daily English-language edition of *Ha'aretz,* Israel's most respected newspaper—almost the entire newspaper is translated on the spot each day into English. The Friday *Ha'aretz* contains a detailed section on events in Jerusalem and throughout the country. The *Jerusalem Post* has a daily listing of city events, but the Friday (weekend) edition is your best bet. Like *Ha'aretz,* it contains an exhaustive list of the week's activities throughout Israel. Another source of information is the free monthly *Events in the Jerusalem Region,* prepared by the Tourist Information Office and available at various tourist office locations and in many hotel lobbies.

## CITY LAYOUT

To get around Jerusalem easily, it helps to understand how the city has grown. In the mid-1800s, Jerusalem was still a walled medieval city—a tortuous maze with sewage running down the streets. After the mid–19th century, Christian pilgrims and Zionist settlers began to create neighborhoods outside the city walls. From 1948 to 1967, Jerusalem was further divided when modern West Jerusalem remained under Israeli jurisdiction while the Old City and downtown East Jerusalem became part of the Kingdom of Jordan. Although the city has been united under Israeli control since 1967, Jerusalem is still three different cities in one: the Old City, the newer Israeli city of West Jerusalem, and the newer Arab city of East Jerusalem.

Due east of the Old City, the Kidron Valley lies between ancient Jerusalem and the long ridge known as the Mount of Olives (Et-Tur in Arabic). On the slopes of the mount, facing the Old City, is the Garden of Gethsemane. Farther down the valley, south of the Old City walls, is the Arabic town of Silwan, where the earliest settlement of Jerusalem developed more than 5,000 years ago. This is where the Jerusalem of King David and King Solomon was located in ancient times; today it is a densely inhabited East Jerusalem neighborhood.

# NEIGHBORHOODS IN BRIEF

**THE OLD CITY** The Old City is easily defined: It is the area still enclosed within the grand walls built by the Ottoman Turkish sultan, Suleiman the Magnificent, in 1538. The Old City is divided into four quarters: the **Muslim Quarter,** the **Christian Quarter,** the **Armenian Quarter,** and the **Jewish Quarter.** Seven gates provide access through the massive walls; two of these are important for the visitor. The **Jaffa Gate**

(Sha'ar Yafo in Hebrew, Bab el-Khalil in Arabic), at the end of the Jaffa Road (Derech Yafo), is the main access to the Old City from West Jerusalem. **Damascus Gate** (Sha'ar Shechem in Hebrew, Bab el-Amud in Arabic) is the main access from East Jerusalem (if you get lost in the Old City's labyrinthine alleys, just ask for either gate).

Except in the Jewish Quarter, the dominating motif here is Arab: The food is Arabic, the language is Arabic, and customs are Eastern.

**WEST JERUSALEM** To the west and south of the Old City, this modern Israeli city is a huge area of residential, commercial, and industrial development punctuated by high-rise hotels and office towers. Extending far to the south and west, and encroaching on the east, the "New City" (as it's sometimes called) includes the Knesset and the government precinct on the western edge of town; one of Hebrew University's two large campuses; the Israel Museum; and, on a distant western hilltop, the Hadassah Medical Center. Broad avenues twist and turn along the tops of the Judean Hills to connect West Jerusalem's outlying quarters with the century-old downtown area.

**Downtown West Jerusalem** is centered on Zion Square (Kikar Ziyon), where Jaffa Road intersects with Ben-Yehuda Street. A few short blocks west of Zion Square is King George V Avenue (known as King George St. or Rechov Ha-Melech George), which joins Ben-Yehuda and Jaffa Road to form a **Downtown Triangle.** Many of the hotels, restaurants, and businesses of interest are in or near this triangle. **Ben-Yehuda Street** is now a bustling pedestrian mall filled with souvenir,

jewelry, and Judaica shops; cafes; and places to grab a quick snack. Evenings, especially in good weather, Ben-Yehuda becomes a mecca for younger travelers and young Israelis. A quainter pedestrian mall network, centering on **Yoel Salomon Street,** runs off Zion Square at the foot of Ben-Yehuda Street. This area is known as **Nachalat Shiva.** Its renovation has transformed Jerusalem's evening ambience from that of a quiet mountain town to a lively, gregarious Mediterranean-style city where people like to stroll and rendezvous in cafes. This small enclave of old West Jerusalem is being preserved, but other 19th-century neighborhoods in West Jerusalem are slated for demolition and will be replaced by large office blocks.

**EAST JERUSALEM** Not as modern and sprawling as its western counterpart, East Jerusalem is nevertheless a bustling modern cityscape lying north of the Old City. Its compact business, commercial, and hotel district starts right along the Old City's north wall on **Sultan Suleiman Street,** which runs from Damascus Gate to Herod's Gate, and then downhill to the Rockefeller Museum. **Nablus Road** (Derech Shechem in Hebrew) runs northeast from Damascus Gate to the American Colony Hotel; **Saladin Street** (Salah ad-Din in Arabic), the area's chief shopping thoroughfare, starts at Herod's Gate and meets Nablus Road near the American Colony Hotel. The triangle formed by these streets encloses the heart of downtown East Jerusalem. This area is quiet at night, and is only beginning to recover economically from the years of the Intifada.

## 3 Getting Around

**BY BUS**    Here are some of the most important destinations, and the buses that take you there:

| | |
|---|---|
| Abu Tor (and Old Railroad Station): | 6, 7, 8, 21, 30, 38, 48 |
| American Colony (East Jerusalem): | 23, 27 |
| Bet Ha-Karem: | 6, 14, 17, 18, 20, 21, 24, 27 |
| Damascus Gate (Old City): | 27 |
| East Jerusalem: | 23, 27, 99 |
| Ein Kerem: | 17 |
| German Colony (South Jerusalem): | 4, 14, 18, 24 |
| Ge'ula Quarter: | 3, 9, 39 |
| Hadassah Hospital at Ein Kerem (Chagall Windows): | 19 |
| Israel Museum: | 9, 17, 24, 99 |
| Jaffa Gate (Old City): | 3, 19, 20, 30, 80, 99 |
| Jewish Quarter (Old City): | 1, 38 |
| King George V Avenue | 4, 7, 8, 9, 14, 31, 38, 48 |
| Mount Scopus: | 9, 23, 26, 28 |
| Mount Zion: | 38 |
| Yad VaShem: | 13, 17, 18, 20, 23, 24, 27, 39, 40, 99 |
| Zion Square: | 6, 13, 15, 18, 20, 21 |

Bus drivers make change, sell single and multiple tickets and passes, and speak English.

A single full-fare city bus ticket costs NIS 5.60 ($1.40/70p). But if you ask the driver for a *kartisiya* (that's kahr-tee-*see*-yah), he'll sell you a pass good for 20 trips, plus one extra trip for free. You'll be amazed at how quickly you can use up a *kartisiya*. The pass is punched each time you board a bus. If two of you are traveling together, just tell the bus driver "pamayim" (twice) as you hand him the *kartisiya*, and he'll punch two fares. Students pay reduced fares and can buy a special discount *kartisiya* as well. If you pay for a normal, single fare, *keep the receipt the driver gives you until you exit the bus*. Occasionally you may be asked to produce it as proof you've paid.

There is a city bus station near Damascus Gate on Nablus Road for destinations in East Jerusalem and surrounding Arabic communities.

### Bus 99: Jerusalem's All City Circle Route

At press time Jerusalem's special **Red Double-Decker Tourist Bus** left four times daily from in front of Safra Square on Jaffa Road, Sunday to Thursday, starting at 9am. It stops at 29 major sites throughout the city, and is a great way to sit back and get a feel for the city. Audio explanations of the route and sites are available in eight languages. The fare for the **all-city circle route** (approx. 2 hr.; no getting off the bus) is NIS 45 ($11/£5.60). **All Day Passes,** allowing multiple stop offs, is NIS 65 ($16/£8.10), but you have to coordinate reentering the bus with the route schedule. Tickets can be bought at many hotels (your hotel can also make a reservation for you); for further information, go to www.egged.co.il. Click on "English," then on "Tourism."

**BY TAXI OR SHERUT** Sheruts travel the main bus route from Sederot Herzl to Jaffa Road and Zion Square on Shabbat; they charge a shekel per person more than standard bus fare. The trick is finding one with room and flagging it down. Private taxis will take you throughout the city and charge higher night and Shabbat rates. The standard initial drop is approximately NIS 10 ($2.50/£1.25), but this rate is always rising. By law, the meter (ha-*sha*-on) must be turned on, and you will be given a printed receipt (ka-ba-*lah*) at your destination, but when taxi drivers see a foreigner, many will ask for a set price before starting. Except during the most terrible rush hour traffic jam, you'll always do better with the meter. Unfortunately, on a rainy Friday night, if the driver claims his meter is broken, you may not want to argue. In central Jerusalem, a daytime ride should not be much more than NIS 25 to NIS 30 ($6.25–$7.50/£3.10–£3.75). Legal fare schedules rise after 9pm and on Shabbat (sundown on Fri to sundown on Sat). Taxi drivers do not expect tips; at most, if your driver claims to have no change, round off the fare to the nearest shekel. Your driver may charge extra if he assists you in dragging baggage into or out of a building. If he doesn't charge for this, a tip of a few shekels is warranted.

**ON FOOT** Central Jerusalem and the Old City are compact and easy to walk. It is difficult to get to museums and the Knesset area at the Western side of town by foot, as distances are relatively far, and pedestrian facilities along the access roads are not good.

---

## *FAST FACTS:* Jerusalem

*Airport Transportation* Call **Nesher Taxi-Sherut** (© 02/625-7227). The office is closed for reservations on Shabbat; however, Nesher's taxi and sherut service to Ben-Gurion does run during the Sabbath and can be reserved ahead of time. Call before Friday morning if you need a seat on an airport sherut from Friday afternoon to Sunday.

*American Express* The office at 18 Shlomzion HaMalka St. (© 02/624-0830) is open Sunday to Thursday 9am to 5pm and Friday 9am to 1pm. Exchange rates, especially for American Express traveler's checks, are relatively good and there is no commission charge. Lost or stolen American Express traveler's checks can be reported 24 hours daily by calling toll-free (© 800/940-3211 or 03/636-4416).

*Area Code* The area code is **02.**

*Babysitters* Ask at the front desk of your hotel.

*Bus Information* Call © 02/530-4704 for municipal bus information, including **bus no. 99,** the red, double-decker All City Circle tourist bus that makes a circuit of 29 sites throughout Jerusalem. For schedules and routes, go to www.egged.co.il.

*Car Rental* Most offices are on King David Street between Agron Street and the King David Hotel. Options include **Avis,** 22 King David St. (© 02/624-901); **Budget,** 23 King David St. (© 02/624-8991); **Eldan,** 24 King David St. (© 02/625-2151); **Hertz,** 19 King David St. (© 02/623-1351); and **Perry,** 36 Keren Hayesod St. (© 02/561-9690).

*Consulates* See appendix A.

*Currency Exchange* Banking hours are 8:30am to noon or 12:30pm; on Sunday, Tuesday, and Thursday also from 4 to 5pm. There are many banks on Ben-Yehuda

Street, Jaffa Road, and King George V Avenue. **Money-changers,** which are legal and offer slightly better rates than banks, will change money in less time with no commission. In East Jerusalem, a number of money-changer offices are on Saladin Street; in the Old City, these offices can be found inside Damascus and Jaffa gates; they are generally open daily from 9am to 5 or 6pm. In West Jerusalem, **Change Point,** a convenient money-changing office, has branches on the Ben-Yehuda Mall near Zion Square, open Sunday through Thursday from 9am to 8pm and on Friday from 9am to 1pm.

**ATMs** connected to the major international networks can be found at Zion Square and on the Ben-Yehuda Mall. You must use ATMs with the Cirrus, Sum, PLUS, or other international connection indicated, or that specifically say that foreign ATM cards can be used. *Tip:* Even if you have a bank that doesn't charge for foreign withdrawals (many savings banks offer this service) if it's a Visa debit card, Visa will charge you 3%.

*Dentists & Doctors* Ask your hotel or consulate for a list of English-speaking doctors and dentists. For a centrally located, American-trained and -certified dentist, try Dr. Mat Weiner, 1 bar Kinora St. (© **02/567-1167**), 2 blocks north of Jaffa Road. For dental first aid and to reach an on-duty dentist, call © **02/625-4740.**

*Drugstores* The *Jerusalem Post* lists under "General Assistance" the names and addresses of duty pharmacies that stay open nights and on Shabbat.

*Emergencies* To call the **police,** dial © **100.** Dial © **101** for Magen David Adom (Red Shield of David), Israel's emergency first-aid **ambulance** service. Magen David Adom has a clinic in Romema, near the Central Bus Station, and also a mobile intensive-care unit (© **02/652-3133**) on call 24 hours a day. For **medical emergencies** requiring hospitalization, dial © **102.**

*Events Information* For details on special performances and events in Jerusalem, call the **city hot line** (© **02/531-4600**), or go online to **www.jerusalem.muni.il**.

*Hospitals* Hospital emergency rooms are open daily, 24 hours. Bring your passport and have a means to pay the fees. In central Jerusalem: **Bikur Holim Hospital,** Strauss Street near Jaffa Road (© **02/646-1111**): At the western edge of the city: **Shaarei Tze dek Hospital,** Sderot Herzl, Bayit VeGan (© **02/655-5111** or emergency room 02/655-5508). **Hadassah Hospital,** Ein Kerem (© **02/677-7111**). For information on possible Blue Cross–Blue Shield coverage at Hadassah Hospital, Ein Kerem, call © **02/677-6029.**

*Hot Lines* **Helpline** (Milev Center for Crisis Counseling; © **800/654-1111**) offers English-speaking counselors for all problems and age groups. You can call the Jerusalem Rape Crisis Center at © **02/625-5558** daily, 24 hours. The Mental Health Hot Line (Eran) can be reached at © **02/561-0303** from 8am to 11pm; if this office is closed, call © **03/523-4819** in Tel Aviv. English is spoken, and visitors are welcome to call.

*Libraries* The **American Cultural Center Library** (© **02/625-5755**) is on Keren Hayesod Street, between Agron Street and the Dan Panorama Hotel. It's open Sunday through Thursday from 10am to 4pm.

*Liquor Laws* East Jerusalem is largely Muslim; Islamic law forbids the use of alcohol. Drinks are served in hotels that cater to Western visitors, but unless an

East Jerusalem or Old City restaurant offers a wine list with its menu, assume that alcohol is not available. Do not attempt to drink outdoors or in public places in East Jerusalem or the Old City.

*Lost Property* Unattended objects stand a good chance of being zapped by the bomb squad. Check with the local police, and try to retrace your steps.

*Luggage & Storage Lockers* Bags are best stored at your hotel. Be prepared for a security check before storing.

*Newspapers & Magazines* In addition to the *Jerusalem Post* and the *International Herald Tribune,* which includes *Ha'aretz* in English (see "Maps & Publications," earlier in this chapter), the twice-monthly *Jerusalem Report* magazine has become Israel's English-language answer to *TIME* and *Newsweek. Eretz* magazine, beautifully written and photographed, focuses on nature, history, and travel in Israel.

*Photographic Needs* The downtown King George Street/Ben-Yehuda area abounds with 1-hour photo-developing shops. Prices are comparable to nondiscounted developing in the United States. To avoid X-ray problems at the airport, it's a good idea to develop film before leaving Israel. **Photo Prisma** at 44 Jaffa Rd. (© 02/623-4796), just across from Zion Square, has an English-speaking staff and an excellent reputation for stocking fresh film as well as for fast, quality developing and digital services.

*Police* Dial © **100.** Border police in military uniforms carrying highly visible weaponry and patrol Ben-Yehuda Mall and other central areas. (*Note:* They fine jaywalkers.)

*Post Office* Jerusalem's Central Post Office (© **1-700-500171**) is at 23 Jaffa Rd., near the intersection with Shlomzion Ha-Malka Street. General hours for all services are Sunday to Thursday from 7am to 7pm; limited services (telephone and telegraph) are open nights and on Shabbat. East Jerusalem has its own main post office, which is now a branch, opposite Herod's Gate at the corner of Saladin Ibn Sina and Sultan Suleiman streets.

In the Old City, the post office is a few steps from Jaffa Gate, up past the Citadel of David and next to the gate of the Christ Church Anglican Hospice. A branch in West Jerusalem is on Keren Kayemet Street half a block from the corner with King George V and the Jewish Agency.

*Radio* News in English is on **Voice of Israel Radio** at 7am, 1:10pm, and 8pm on AM 576 and 1458 kHz.

*Religious Services* The **Christian Information Centre** (© **02/627-2692**), inside Jaffa Gate on Omar Ibn El-Khattab Square near the Christ Church Hospice and opposite the entrance to the Tower of David, has a list of all Christian services. The center is open Monday through Saturday from 8:30am to 1pm; closed Sunday and holidays. *This Week in Jerusalem,* available free at major hotels, lists Reform, Conservative, and Orthodox Jewish synagogues. Because of security regulations, which vary according to the level of warnings from week to week, independent Muslim tourists who do not have Israeli IDs or advance security clearance may not be allowed into the Al Aqsa compound on Friday (when only Muslims are allowed onto the Temple Mount for Fri prayers) unless they are with an official group or have made prior arrangements with the Waqf (Islamic Trust controlling access to the Temple Mount/Haram es Sharif complex).

*Safety* Jerusalem is a low-crime city, but be aware of pickpockets in the crowd crushes of the Old City and avoid the deserted bazaars after dark. While political demonstrations in West Jerusalem are passionate but usually safe, it is advisable to avoid demonstrations in East Jerusalem or in the Old City. Keep alert at all times. Get away from and report any unattended or suspicious object immediately.

*Telegrams, Telex & Fax* There are telex and fax services at the Central Post Office, 23 Jaffa Rd. Inside the Old City, the **Bookshelf,** Jewish Quarter Road (© **02/ 626-0473;** fax 02/627-3889), offers excellent fax service and will even notify you after-hours about any fax responses you may receive. For telegrams, dial © **171.**

*Telephones* See appendix A. Information is © **144.** Collect calls are © **142.**

*Toilets* In the Old City, signs read wc or oo, and indicate public restrooms. In West Jerusalem, restaurants and cafes are your best option.

## 4 Where to Stay

Israel has tons of upscale hotels, but inexpensive and moderately priced hotels are in short supply, especially in Jerusalem. There are a few hotels with atmosphere and ambience in every price category, but most choices are generic and bland. With the tourism slump from 2000 to 2005, most hotels fell behind in updating, but as tourism returns, worn rooms should start to be tended to again. Since 2001, official rack rates for hotel rooms have become fantasies—except during important Jewish holidays. The eleventh commandment now reads: You shall not pay full price at a hotel.

Many hotels listed here can be booked as part of El Al, or other packages, or through the Internet and discounters, at substantially lower prices. Especially in off seasons, there are discounts to be found in all price categories if you plan ahead through a good travel agent. Jerusalem's hotels are busiest at Passover and Easter, in September or October during the Jewish High Holidays (Rosh Hashanah, Yom Kippur, Succot, and Simchat Torah), and at Christmas. Many hotels consider July and August regular season.

*Note:* All official hotel prices in Israel are quoted in U.S. dollars. Foreign travelers are expected to pay by credit card or foreign cash; if you pay the equivalent amount in shekels, you must also pay an additional value-added tax (VAT) of 15.5%.

**Christian hospices or guesthouses** are a good alternative to hotels—Jerusalem abounds with them, and guests of all faiths are welcome. Guesthouses were originally built to accommodate the pilgrims and tourists who began to arrive in great numbers in the 1880s. Many are housed in atmospheric 19th-century building complexes with evocative Jerusalem architecture and style. Atmosphere is, of course, sedate; better hospices are like extremely well-run small hotels, with comfortable private rooms with bathrooms. St. George's, Jerusalem's Anglican guesthouse (see later in this chapter), has a bar, but most do not. *Tip:* Unmarried couples can forget about sharing a room at most Christian guesthouses. You might be able to fudge separate last names on passports, but no visible wedding ring, no double room at most places, especially if you're under 25.

**Bed-and-breakfast accommodations** in a private home or apartment are an interesting alternative to a hotel. Prices are considerably lower than hotels, and you have the chance to experience the lifestyle of one of the city's many unusual neighborhoods. Hosts are often senior citizens with lovely, spacious (by Israeli standards) homes, and a genuine interest in working with visitors from abroad.

A room in an apartment that has its own private bathroom should be about $50 (£25) for a single and $90 (£45) for a double, with breakfast and service included. A small studio or private flat would be about $120 (£60) for two people; long-term rates are available. Really unusual places with private entrances, gardens, views, and especially nice decor, or accommodations for families, could be much more.

**Rental Agencies: Good Morning Jerusalem,** 17 Ezrat Israel St., Jerusalem (℘ 02/ 623-3459; www.accommodation.co.il), is a bed-and-breakfast and holiday apartment rental agency. With listings all over Israel, including in Jerusalem, they will reserve accommodations for you and try to match your requirements regarding noise, neighborhood, kashrut, and so on, to the listings they have available. (The office cannot vouch for the kashrut standards of any particular household, and accepts the claims of its participating hosts.) The office is open Sunday to Thursday from 9am to 5pm and Friday from 9am to 1:30pm. With advance notice, the office can make arrangements to meet or facilitate nighttime arrivals. You can also reserve an entire apartment for yourself (rate is according to number of people; 1-week minimum stay) from Good Morning Jerusalem through the **Israel Tourism Center,** or **ITC** (℘ **888/669-5700** or 201/556-9669 in the U.S. and Canada; israelhotels@worldnet.att.net). There is a $35 (£18) fee for this service, but you save on overseas phone bills and can discuss the neighborhood and kind of apartment you would like.

**Home Accommodation Association of Israel** (www.bnb.co.il) is an affiliation of 24 homeowners, many with very unusual properties and locations. You deal directly with the property owners: The website includes contact information, photos, and descriptions for each property.

**Jewish Home Swap** (www.jewishhomeswap.com) is a free service that gives people an opportunity to save on vacation costs by exchanging their homes with other people. The emphasis here is on homes with kosher kitchens and locations close to Jewish religious services.

## THE OLD CITY

The advantage to staying in the Old City is that you feel the rhythms and hear the sounds of this extraordinary (and largely car-free) place—the calls to prayer from the minarets, the medley of bells from the city's ancient churches. You'll watch the bazaars come to life in the morning and slowly close down for the night; you'll catch glimpses of street life that a visitor based in the New City would never see. You won't come across any high-rise (or even low-rise) luxury palaces in the Old City, just a few inexpensive to moderately priced hotels, hospices, and hostels. The crime rate in the Old City, as in all of Jerusalem, is low, but the streets here (except for parts of the Jewish Quarter) are deserted at night and can seem intimidating. You'll need a spirit of adventure and an enjoyment of labyrinths and Casbah-like alleyways in order for this to be the right part of town for your base.

### NEAR JAFFA GATE
**Inexpensive**
**Christ Church Guest House**   This is a great location, just inside the Jaffa Gate. Through big iron gates you'll find a flagstone courtyard with trees and benches, a 150-year-old English-style church that now houses a Protestant/Messianic congregation,

and very simple single, double, and triple rooms with private bathrooms in a series of atmospheric 19th-century buildings. The gates close at 11pm and stay locked until 6am, except by special arrangement. This guesthouse is heavily booked during the summer months and for Christian holidays—reserve well in advance for these times. Very reasonable meal plans can be arranged. The Guest House also runs the nearby inexpensive Coffee Shop and organizes tours and lectures oriented toward the Protestant Messianic movement; however, those guests who are not evangelical are under no pressure to join. A protected parking area is an added feature, although the management does not take responsibility for cars parked there.

Jaffa Gate (PO Box 14037), Jerusalem 91140. © 02/627-7727. Fax 02/627-7730. www.cmj-israel.org. $100 (£50) double. Rate includes breakfast. MC, V. Limited free parking. **Amenities:** Dining room.

**Gloria Hotel**   The Gloria is very moderately priced, with modern facilities and an excellent location just inside Jaffa Gate. The entrance is up a flight of steps; from there an elevator takes you up one more level to the hotel desk, where an English-speaking clerk awaits you. The lobby is spacious but simple, with lots of Jerusalem stone and a scattering of local crafts as decorative touches. The rooms, last renovated in 1987, are relatively large and quiet and have either twin or double beds and central heating. The dining room, where you'll find the breakfast buffet, overlooks the Tower of David and West Jerusalem. In 1999, a new 22-room annex was added across the street from the main building; ask to see these new rooms before deciding which you prefer. Small amenities may not be available, but the Old City ambience, good management, and excellent location are big pluses.

Latin Patriarchate St. (PO Box 14070), Jerusalem. © 02/628-2431. Fax 02/62-2401. www.gloria-hotel.com. 94 units. $80–$120 (£40–£60) double. Discounts in off season. Higher rates for Christmas and Easter. Rates include breakfast. AE, V. Limited free parking. Bus: 20. About 80 ft. inside Jaffa Gate, turn left on Latin Patriarchate St.; hotel is on the right. **Amenities:** Dining room; bar. *In room:* A/C, TV.

**Saint Mark's Lutheran Guest House** ⚡   The most beautiful, atmospheric place to stay in the Old City (and perhaps in all of Jerusalem), this well-run guesthouse occupies a series of restored stone buildings and terraced gardens overlooking the main bazaar, a 4-minute walk from Jaffa Gate. Here, guests can experience the atmosphere inside the Old City walls from a secluded oasis that has breathtaking views of the Dome of the Rock. Rooms (renovated in 2003) are of Jerusalem stone and simply furnished but comfortable; most bathrooms have showers only. The site is shared by, but separated from, the Evangelical Lutheran Hostel. Although this part of the Old City, bordering the Jewish Quarter and the Jaffa Gate, is safe, a drawback for some might be the idea of walking to the guesthouse at night. Visitors of all backgrounds are welcome. Free coffee and tea are served. Call for directions before arrival and arrange a baggage porter to meet you.

Saint Mark's Rd. (PO Box 14051), Old City, Jerusalem. © 02/626-8888. Fax 02/628-5107. www.luth-guesthouse-jerusalem. com. 23 units. Regular season (June 16–Sept 14 and winter except Christmas and Easter) $120 (£60) double. Rate includes breakfast. Extra charge for Christmas, Easter, and Jewish holidays. Cash only. Bus: 20 to Jaffa Gate. **Amenities:** Dining room; lounge; garden; use of kitchen in hostel. *In room:* Fridge, heat in winter, fan in summer.

## NEAR DAMASCUS GATE
### Inexpensive
**Austrian Hospice** ⚡   This large building, located in the Muslim Quarter between the Damascus and Lions' gates, was built in 1857 and served as a hospital from 1948 to 1985; now it's been renovated and restored to its original use as a guesthouse for

pilgrims and visitors. The Hospice's gardens, terraces, fabulous rooftop vistas of the Old City, careful security, and dedicated staff are all real pluses. The feeling here is quiet but friendly, with visitors from all backgrounds welcome. Rooms are furnished simply but are comfortable and heated in winter; bathrooms have showers only. Inexpensive dorms are in the basement. A Viennese coffee shop on the premises serves great *Sacher torte,* strudel, and light meals; half-board is available. Call ahead for information on **wheelchair access** (unusual in the Old City). Curfew is 10pm, but late-entry permission can be obtained.

37 Via Dolorosa (PO Box 19600), Jerusalem 91194. © 02/626-5800. Fax 02/627-1472. www.austrianhospice.com. 34 units, plus dormitory facilities. $130 (£65) double. Rate is based on the value of the euro and includes breakfast. Cash only. **Amenities:** Cafe. *In room:* Hair dryer.

## WEST JERUSALEM

The Zion Square/Ben-Yehuda Mall area is the place to stay if you want to be in the midst of the city's lively restaurants, cafes, and bars, and in an area where you can stroll, shop, and people-watch in the evenings. A number of hotel choices are a few blocks farther south, in the King George Street/King David Street triangle, within walking distance or a short bus ride of Zion Square. Farther south you'll find a number of pleasant hotels in the interesting neighborhoods of Abu Tor and the German Colony (you'll need a bus or taxi to get to Zion Square, but it's less than a 5-min. ride). The outlying Bus Station/Sderot Herzl area on the western side of town is the fourth major West Jerusalem hotel area. It can be a 20-minute or more bus ride into Zion Square from this area, and you'll need a taxi on Shabbat; the better distant hotels offer shuttle service into town.

### ZION SQUARE, JAFFA ROAD & BEN-YEHUDA MALL

Step out of your hotel, and you'll be right in the heart of the downtown shopping-and-restaurant district, with a great variety of cafes, window-shopping, and people-watching possibilities. The area is noisy, and in summer, discos add to the roar of traffic.

#### Moderate

**Harmony Hotel** *(Finds)*   A promising moderate choice (opened in 2008, as *Frommer's Israel* went to press, and inspected while still under construction), the six-story Harmony has a fabulously central location on a charming pedestrian street filled with interesting cafes, restaurants, and shops just off Zion Square. Rooms are brand-new with fresh, duvet-covered beds; lobby reception is 24 hours; there's a daily complimentary happy hour, with wine and canapés; and Atlas Hotels management indicates style and quality service. Street noise may be a problem, but windows are double-glazed, and in summer your air conditioner will be on. There are two elevators; one is programmed for Shabbat. Taxis can take you right to the hotel despite the pedestrian street location. Opening-year specials may make this the hottest moderate-range hotel in town.

6 Yoel Salomon St., Jerusalem. © 02/621-9999. Fax 02/621-9998. www.atlas.co.il. 50 units. $190–$220 (£95–£110) double. Rates include breakfast. Look for promotional specials. AE, DC, MC, V. Parking (fee). Bus: 6, 18, 20, or 21. **Amenities:** Dining room; Internet facilities. *In room:* A/C, cable TV, free Wi-Fi, fridge, coffeemaker, hair dryer, safe.

**Jerusalem Tower Hotel**   This modern hotel, set on the upper floors of a high-rise office tower, is as central as you can get in Jerusalem, but offers minimal personality and style. You enter through a small lobby on the ground floor of an office tower 2 short blocks from Zion Square; guest floors are accessed by two busy elevators. Rooms are compact but modern and well planned; many offer sweeping views (try to get a room facing the Old City).

# Where to Stay in Downtown West Jerusalem

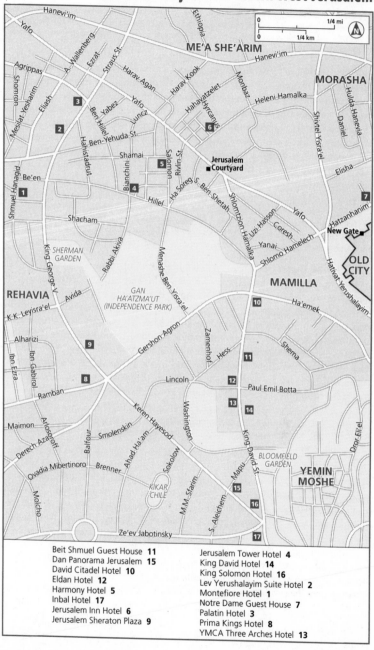

Beit Shmuel Guest House **11**
Dan Panorama Jerusalem **15**
David Citadel Hotel **10**
Eldan Hotel **12**
Harmony Hotel **5**
Inbal Hotel **17**
Jerusalem Inn Hotel **6**
Jerusalem Sheraton Plaza **9**

Jerusalem Tower Hotel **4**
King David Hotel **14**
King Solomon Hotel **16**
Lev Yerushalayim Suite Hotel **2**
Montefiore Hotel **1**
Notre Dame Guest House **7**
Palatin Hotel **3**
Prima Kings Hotel **8**
YMCA Three Arches Hotel **13**

33 Hillel St., Jerusalem. © **02/620-9209.** Fax 02/625-2167. www.towerhotels.com. 120 units. $150–$200 (£75–£100) double. Rates include breakfast. Web and package discounts often available. AE, DC, MC, V. Fee parking. Bus: 6, 18, 20, or 21 and all buses to Zion Sq. **Amenities:** Dining room; bar; room service; laundry service. *In room:* A/C, TV, hair dryer, safe.

### Lev Yerushalayim Suite Hotel (Kids)

Lev Yerushalayim means "heart of Jerusalem," and this tower complex is indeed located in the heart of West Jerusalem, right across the street from the intersection of King George Street and the Ben-Yehuda Mall. The pleasant suites consist of a contemporary living room/kitchenette and bedroom freshly decorated in soft colors and soundproofed against the roar of downtown traffic. The suites are a good choice for families; extra sleeping space is available on convertible living-room sofas, with a surcharge of $15 (£7.50) per night for each additional guest. The fully equipped kitchenettes include a microwave oven and refrigerator. All food service is glatt kosher.

18 King George St., Jerusalem. © **02/530-0333.** Fax 02/623-2432. http://levyerushalayim.co.il. 97 units. $160–$220 (£80–£110) double. 7-day minimum stay. Rates do not include 15% service. Additional charge for Jewish and Christian holidays or for stays less than 7 days (subject to availability). Rates include breakfast. AE, DC, MC, V. Indoor parking (fee). Bus: 4, 7, 9, or 14. **Amenities:** Dining room; cafe; bar; room service; laundry service. *In room:* A/C, TV, kitchenette (kosher), hair dryer.

### Notre Dame Guest House ★

Located in a beautifully restored landmark just steps away from the walls of the Old City, convenient to West and East Jerusalem municipal bus routes, the massive Notre Dame complex is a center for Roman Catholic institutions and pilgrim groups, but all travelers seeking a tranquil atmosphere with expertly managed accommodations are welcome. Public areas are spacious, with Jerusalem stone architecture. Rooms are simple but comfortable, and many share a terrace balcony. Some rooms are equipped for travelers with disabilities. A coffee shop, open daily from 9am to 11pm, serves light, reasonably priced meals. La Rotisserie, a luxury restaurant patronized by savvy Jerusalemites, is also on the premises (at press time only open Sat–Sun). In summer there's a Thursday night Middle Eastern barbecue.

PO Box 20531, Jerusalem (at the end of Jaffa Rd.). © **02/627-9111.** Fax 02/627-1995. www.notredamecenter.org. 145 units. $100–$140 (£50–£70) double. Rates include breakfast. MC, V. Free parking. Bus: 19 or 20. On Paratrooper's Rd., opposite New Gate. **Amenities:** Restaurant; coffee shop; laundry service; dry cleaning; nonsmoking rooms. *In room:* A/C, hair dryer.

## Inexpensive

### Jerusalem Inn Hotel ★ (Value)

This is the best, brightest little budget hotel in town, with a great location on a relatively quiet street, a 3-minute walk from Zion Square and less than 10 minutes from the Old City. Rooms are reached by stairway (there are three floors). Most rooms are compact, but all are well planned (some with small balconies), brightened by framed art posters, and furnished with new, comfortably firm beds (duvet sheets cover the blankets—a luxury in a budget hotel). The hotel works well for both single travelers and families; larger rooms can be arranged for four or five people. All rooms have private bathrooms with glass-enclosed stall showers (in this price category, most other hotels offer only shower sprays that flood your entire bathroom). Some doubles have larger bathrooms or more space—check before making your choice. Israeli breakfast is in a pleasant garden room, but there's no lobby.

7 Hyrcanos St., Jerusalem. © **02/625-2757.** www.jerusalem-inn.com. 23 units. $90–$150 (£45–£75). Rates include breakfast. Rates are higher during Passover, Succot, and Christmas. Long-term discounts in low season. MC, V. Bus: 18, 20, or 21 and all buses to Zion Sq. On Jaffa Rd., coming from Zion Sq., turn left on Helena Ha-Malka St., then left on Hyrcanos. **Amenities:** Breakfast room. *In room:* A/C, cable TV, free Wi-Fi, fridge, safe.

## Hotel Rates in Israel

Israeli hotel rates have officially been quoted in U.S. dollars for decades, although this policy may change if the dollar remains unstable. Hotel bills paid in foreign currency or with foreign credit cards by non-Israelis are not subject to 15.5% VAT; if possible, always pay for your room with a credit card. If you pay in shekels, you will have the VAT added to your bill. A few B&Bs and small hotels may post a shekel price list. If they do, check if paying in foreign currency will allow them to eliminate your VAT.

**Palatin Hotel**   This centrally located hotel, set on a pedestrian street just off Jaffa Road, has been a landmark for budget travelers for decades. Standard rooms can be extra small (there is also a higher-priced category of slightly larger rooms); mattresses are thin; and basic decor always seems to cling to the 1960s, even though the property has been updated from time to time. Reception and the dining room, where a buffet breakfast is served, are up a long flight of stairs from the street level, which doesn't make this a great choice for those with disabilities. Tea and coffee are available free of charge to guests all day. The newly created pedestrian mall makes this very central location a bit quieter at night than you might expect, but light sleepers should beware.

4 Agrippas St. ℂ 02/623-1141. www.hotel-palatin.co.il. 28 units, all with bathroom or shower. $100–$150 (£50–£75) double. Rates include breakfast. AE, DC, MC, V. **Amenities:** Dining room; free Internet desk. *In room:* A/C, TV, fridge (on request), hair dryer, safe (on request).

## KING GEORGE STREET & KING DAVID STREET

A few blocks from the Ben-Yehuda/Zion Square triangle you'll find a group of hotels along the southern reaches of King George Street, which becomes Keren Hayesod Street. About a kilometer (½ mile) from Zion Square, Keren Hayesod runs into King David Street, and there's another cluster of hotels going north back toward the center of town. The distance to Zion Square from most of these hotels is walkable, but because it is uphill and in the hot sun, many will want to take a bus or taxi, particularly after a hard day's touring. Nearby are Liberty Bell Park, charming Yemin Moshe, and the Cinémathèque, with its hillside of neighboring cafes and restaurants.

### Very Expensive

**David Citadel Hotel** 🏨🏨 *Kids*   Centrally located at a busy intersection, Jerusalem's newest luxury hotel (1998) does not have the tranquil buffering gardens of its rival, the King David, but unlike other new hotels in town, it has a distinctive architectural style that mixes Jerusalem stone and traditional arches with sleek postmodern design and views of the Old City. The mood is younger and livelier than the King David's, and food services, directed by Chef Eric Attias, are more innovative, including an excellent kosher sushi bar and nightly theme buffets (p. 158). Rooms are done in natural textiles and come in a number of sizes; all have views of the Old City and extra amenities, including bathrooms (many with both tubs and stall showers) stocked with special Ahava Dead Sea cosmetics. The CYBEX fitness center is the best in Jerusalem; the large, heated pool is open all winter, with a water entrance from inside. *Tip:* In summer, much of the pool falls under cool shadows after 3pm.

7 King David St. ℂ 02/621-1111. Fax 02/621-1000. www.tdchotel.com. 384 units. $440–$630 (£220–£315) double. AE, DC, MC, V. Parking (fee). Bus: 6, 18, or 21. **Amenities:** Restaurant; cafe; bar; sushi bar; heated outdoor pool; children's pool; health club; spa; sauna; steam room; children's activities; concierge; travel desk; shopping arcade; salon; business center; 24-hr. room service; nonsmoking rooms; synagogue; rooms for those w/limited mobility. *In room:* A/C, TV, dataport, minibar, coffeemaker, hair dryer, safe.

**King David Hotel** ★★★ *Kids*    The luxurious King David is Jerusalem's status address, built in 1930 as a regional companion to the legendary Shephard's Hotel in Cairo. Shephard's was destroyed during anticolonialist riots in the early 1950s, and the King David, too, has suffered the trials of history. In 1946, its south wing, housing British military headquarters, was blown up by a Jewish underground organization. The entire wing of the building was rebuilt, but if you look closely, you can see differences in the stone.

The King David continues to be a perfectly maintained symbol of a bygone era (including a rather formal staff), but its reputation and list of diplomatic and celebrity guests continues to grow. The lofty Egyptian-esque/Canaanite Art Deco public rooms should be experienced for their own sake; the view from the gardened swimming pool and terrace (where Paul Newman and Eva Marie Saint had a rendezvous in the 1960 film *Exodus*), offers great vistas toward the walls of the Old City.

Guest rooms were completely redone in 1997 and 1998, with the total number reduced so that individual rooms are now larger. Furnishings are of dark-grained woods that suggest the lavish tropical veneers of the 1930s; many bathrooms sport a glass-enclosed shower as well as a tub. You pay extra for rooms with Old City/garden views, but they're definitely special. The gigantic breakfast buffet is justly famous; nearby exclusive tourist, Judaica, and jewelry shops await King David guests. Discounters and package tours can get you into the King David for considerably less than the rack rates.

23 King David St., Jerusalem 94101. ℂ 02/620-8888. Fax 02/620-8882. www.danhotels.com. 237 units. $380–$460 (£190–£230) standard double with street view; $440–$630 (£220–£315) deluxe double and double with Old City view. Rates include breakfast. AE, DC, MC, V. Bus: 6, 18, or 21. **Amenities:** Restaurant; dining room; cafe; outdoor pool; tennis court; fitness and massage center; sauna; hair salon; business center; shopping arcade; room service; nonsmoking rooms; synagogue. *In room:* A/C, TV, dataport, minibar, hair dryer, safe.

## *Kids* Family-Friendly Hotels

At the **Dan Hotel Chain,** which in Jerusalem includes the **King David** (p. 126) and the **Dan Panorama** (p. 127), up to two children can stay free in a room with their parents; the only charge is for breakfast. To keep the little ones busy, try **Ramat Rachel** (p. 132), which offers a big pool and playground facilities. The **Mount Zion Hotel** (p. 131) has a roomy in-season pool (visited by interesting local families with kids), as well as a children's pool. A number of its rooms are extra large and can accommodate families.

**Lev Yerushalayim** (p. 124), right in the center of town, is a suite hotel—all rooms include a kitchenette and a living area containing a couch that converts into a bed. In the luxury category, the alcove rooms at the new **David Citadel Hotel** (p. 126) offer extra space for families planning to bunk together. The **Inbal Hotel** (p. 127) offers year-round swimming and is next to Liberty Bell Park, with a playground for young children.

> **Tips**  **Pricing Discounts**
>
> Hotel prices in Israel are not cheap, but the eleventh commandment for travelers to Israel is: Thou shalt not pay full price. Packages and discounters, or travel agents specializing in Israel, can get you into many of the most interesting Israeli hotels at prices far lower than the rack rates. For general tips on getting hotel discounts, see p. 88.

## Expensive

**Dan Panorama Jerusalem** *Kids*    The Dan Panorama is around the corner from the King David Hotel and a 10-minute walk or quick bus ride to Ben-Yehuda Mall (the bus stop is at the hotel's front door). Although carefully run and centrally located, it's less fancy than the nearby King David and lacks the King David's gardens and views. The elegant public areas glisten. Standard rooms are comfortable and many have been recently renovated: superior rooms are more spacious, with newer decor. The staff is friendly and efficient; there's a small rooftop pool. As at all Dan Hotels, there is variation in rack rates for rooms, depending on the type of view.

39 Keren Hayesod St., Jerusalem. ✆ 02/569-5695. Fax 02/623-2411. www.danhotels.com. 292 units. $230–$380 (£115–£190) double. Up to 2 children 17 and under stay free in parent's room. Rates include breakfast for adults 18 and over. Discounts available on Dan Hotel packages. AE, DC, MC, V. Parking (fee). Bus: 4, 7, 8, 14, or 48. **Amenities:** Restaurant; dining room; rooftop pool; health club; Jacuzzi; sauna; children's activities (seasonal); room service; non-smoking rooms. *In room:* A/C, cable TV, fridge (on request), hair dryer, safe.

**Inbal Hotel** *Kids*    For decades this was the popular Laromme Hotel. The 1980s-style Inbal was originally slated to be a skyscraper, but public pressure demanded it be redesigned as a low-rise that would not clash with the city's skyline. The result is an interesting structure set at the edge of Liberty Bell Park (a plus for children) and built around a balconied atrium lobby. A new Executive Lounge was opened in 2008, but other public areas and guest rooms need updating. Rooms come in two sizes; the larger (maximum) rooms are spacious, with luxurious bathrooms, and cost about $70 (£35) additional for a double. There are 14 well-appointed suites. The outdoor pool is covered with an air balloon and heated for winter swimming. *Tip:* Guests get triple El Al points for each stay.

3 Jabotinsky St., Jerusalem. ✆ 02/675-6666. Fax 02/675-6777. www.inbal-hotel.co.il. 308 units. $440–$550 (£220–£275) double. Rates include breakfast. AE, DC, MC, V. Free parking. Bus: 4, 8, 9, 14, 17, or 48. **Amenities:** 3 restaurants; bar; heated outdoor pool; children's pool; fitness center; Jacuzzi; business services; shopping arcade; salon; room service; massage; laundry service; nonsmoking rooms; synagogue; rooms for those w/limited mobility. *In room:* A/C, TV, minibar, hair dryer, safe.

**Jerusalem Sheraton Plaza**    This 1970s 22-story tower is the top hotel closest to the Ben-Yehuda Mall area, though it's still a 5-minute walk away. Always bustling, the public areas have recently been renovated. Rooms are moderately spacious and have balconies; those facing southeast (additional charge) have spectacular views of the Old City. Those facing north, though missing out on the Old City, have sweeping vistas of the area. Club Floor rooms receive special staff service. The hotel's entrance plaza is below street level; to leave by foot entails climbing a hill or stairway. The dining here (all glatt kosher), originally designed by Chef Shalom Kadosh (hailed as the high priest of glatt kosher), is very good and attracts many observant guests. Beds are new, comfy Sheraton "Sweet Sleepers."

47 King George St., Jerusalem. ☎ **800/325-3535** in the U.S., or 02/629-8666. Fax 02/623-1667. www.sheraton.co.il. 300 units. $350–$400 (£175–£200) standard double. AE, DC, MC, V. Parking (fee). Bus: 4, 7, 9, or 14. **Amenities:** Restaurant; dining room; cafe; bar; outdoor seasonal pool; massage room; sauna; shopping arcade; salon; business center; children's center in summer; laundry service; nonsmoking rooms; synagogue. *In room:* A/C, TV, Wi-Fi, minibar, coffeemaker, hair dryer.

## Moderate

**Eldan Hotel** 🔶   Run by Eldan, Israel's largest car-rental company, the Eldan opened in 1999 in a great location across from the King David. Public areas shine and the dining is all glatt kosher. Rooms are average size and are up-to-date in amenities and style; most have bathrooms with tubs, though eight rooms have stall showers. Staff are friendly and efficient. The lack of a swimming pool is the only minus. *Tip:* You can get a small rate discount if you rent an Eldan vehicle, or vice versa.

24 King David St., Jerusalem. ☎ **02/567-9777.** Fax 02/624-9525. www.eldanhotel.com. 76 units. $190–$240 (£95–£120) double. Rates include breakfast. AE, DC, MC, V. Limited free parking. Bus: 6, 18, or 21. **Amenities:** Restaurant; dining room; bar; fitness room; business center; room service; laundry service; nonsmoking rooms. *In room:* A/C, TV, dataport, minibar, safe.

**King Solomon Hotel**   Although situated at the fork of busy King David and Keren Hayesod streets, the design of this modern hotel, built in the 1980s, manages to keep street noise to tolerable levels. The entrance is on a service driveway between the two thoroughfares and opens onto an airy, multilevel stone-floor lobby. Room furnishings are blandly modern, but superior rooms and suites are spacious and updated; some offer excellent views. The large rooftop pool, with a view of the Old City walls in the distance, is quite spectacular. Dining facilities are glatt kosher. The hotel is within walking distance of Yemin Moshe, the German Colony, and the Cinémathèque, but you'll probably want to take a bus to the Ben-Yehuda Mall area. In off season, special packages sometimes offer double rooms for around $130 (£65).

32 King David St., Jerusalem. ☎ **02/569-5555.** Fax 02/624-1774. www.kingsolomon-hotel.com. 148 units. $220–$330 (£110–£165) double. Higher rates for Passover, Succot, and Dec 15–Jan 20. Rates include breakfast. AE, DC, MC, V. Free parking. Bus: 5, 18, or 21. **Amenities:** Restaurant; dining room; cafe; bar; rooftop pool; salon; room service; laundry service; synagogue. *In room:* A/C, TV, minibar, hair dryer, safe.

**Montefiore Hotel** *(Value)*   Built in 1998 and operated until 2006 under a different name and management, this bright hotel is on a quiet street 1½ blocks from the very central intersection of King George and Ben-Yehuda streets. If the new management turns out to be good, this hotel will offer great value. Rooms are not large, but they're relatively new (they were touched up and recarpeted in 2006), quiet, and pleasant. Each has two narrow beds that are arranged together to form a double bed. Mini-refrigerators can be rented for an additional fee, and use of the lobby safe is a small extra fee per day. The dining room is beautifully designed; after breakfast it morphs into an Italian restaurant. Food services throughout the hotel are glatt kosher. Off season, in late fall and winter, rates can drop as low as $90 (£45) for a double room.

7 Schatz St., Jerusalem 94267. ☎ **02/622-1111.** Fax 02/624-8420. www.montefiorehotel.com. 48 units. $140–$180 (£70–£90) double. Rates include breakfast. AE, DC, MC, V. Bus: 4, 8, 9, or 19. **Amenities:** Restaurant; dining room; laundry service; free Wi-Fi in lobby. *In room:* A/C, TV, fridge (fee).

**Prima Kings Hotel**   Location is the big plus for this hotel: It's next door to the Great Synagogue/Heichal Shlomo building (p. 203), and a 10-minute walk from the Ben-Yehuda area. A good supermarket is half a block away. The lobby and lounge areas have a light, garden feel. They were designed in the late 1980s and have occasionally been updated. Rooms have been more recently redone; they are functional rather than gracious, and rather small. The hotel is often used by tour groups and is available at discounts through package consolidators. You enter the hotel on Ramban Street; note that this busy intersection suffers from a high level of traffic noise. Try for a rear room. Food service is glatt kosher.

60 King George St., Jerusalem. ℂ **02/620-1201.** Fax 02/620-1211. www.prima.co.il. 187 units. $175–$275 (£88–£138) double. Rates include breakfast. AE, DC, MC, V. Bus: 4, 8, 9, or 48. **Amenities:** 2 restaurants; dining room; cafe; bar; room service; laundry service; nonsmoking rooms; synagogue. *In room:* A/C, cable TV w/pay movies, minibar, hair dryer, safe.

**YMCA Three Arches Hotel** ⟨★⟩ ⟨*Value*⟩  This historic landmark (p. 204) opened in 1933 and was designed in an Art Deco, Byzantine-Islamic style by Arthur Loomis Harmon, who also designed New York's Empire State Building. It is a center for lectures, performances, and classes as well as an excellent, very pleasant hotel. Public areas are atmospheric, and the panoramas of Jerusalem from the Y's tower are magnificent—if you stay here, try to see it at different times of day. The YMCA's elegant terrace is one of the most popular fair-weather dining places in town. Guests also have use of a 1930s-style indoor swimming pool and a fitness room. All guest rooms were totally redone in the early 1990s and now sport modern bathrooms but increasingly fraying room decor. Unfortunately, as with many Israeli hotels, rooms are now due for renovation, though the atmosphere, facilities, staff, and location still make this an unusual and affordable choice.

26 King David St. (PO Box 294), Jerusalem 91002. ℂ **02/569-2692.** Fax 02/623-5192. www.ymca3arch.co.il. 56 units. $150 (£75) double. Rate includes continental breakfast. AE, MC, V. Bus: 6, 18, or 21 to King David St. **Amenities:** Restaurant; dining room; cafe; indoor pool; fitness room; room service; laundry service; library/lounge. *In room:* A/C, TV, hair dryer.

### Inexpensive

**Beit Shmuel Guest House** ⟨*Value*⟩  With a great location, this large, modern complex, designed by renowned architect Moshe Safdie, offers views of the Old City; a network of terraces, gardens, and courtyards; and a full schedule of lectures, concerts, and cultural activities on the premises under the sponsorship of the World Union for Progressive (Reform) Judaism. There is a hostel section containing rooms with private bathrooms that can be arranged for two to six people, and a newer Beit Shimshon Guest House with 11 better rooms for up to four guests. Visitors of all faiths and ages are welcome. The complex can seem a bit institutional and be noisy during nighttime concerts; many hostel rooms are worn from heavy use. Call ahead for arrangements on wheelchair access. It's heavily booked with groups in summer and Jewish holidays, when rates are higher. Reserve far ahead.

13 King David St., Jerusalem (entrance around the corner at 3 Shamia St.). ℂ **02/620-3473** or 620-3456. Fax 02/620-3467. www.beitshmuel.com. 50 units. Beit Shimshon Guest House $143 (£72) double; Beit Shmuel Hostel $85 (£43) double. Rates include breakfast. AE, MC, V. Bus: 6, 18, or 21 to 1st stop on King David St. *In room:* A/C, TV.

**Rosary Convent Guest House and Hostel**  For spotless, simple, but pleasant accommodations, an excellent choice is the Rosary Convent, set back from the road in a quiet garden located around the corner from the Sheraton Plaza Hotel and across the street from a Supersol supermarket. Rooms are airy, with high ceilings, but can be chilly on very cold winter nights; bathrooms are shared, but private bathrooms may be available during the time span of this edition. The gate to the complex closes at 10pm; if you plan to be out later, you must try to make arrangements with the management ahead of time.

14 Agron St. (PO Box 54), Jerusalem. ℂ **02/625-8529** or 623-5581. Fax 02/623-5581. 23 units, all with shared bathroom. $90 (£45) double. Rate includes breakfast. Cash only. Bus: 4, 7, 9, 14, or 19. **Amenities:** Breakfast room.

## WESTERN EDGE OF CITY/SDEROT HERZL

Stretching from the area of Jaffa Road near the Central Bus Station to the area of Sderot Herzl that runs toward the residential neighborhood of Beit Ha-Kerem, this area offers modern expensive and moderate choices. There's not much that's interesting within walking distance of most of these hotels, and the highway system in the area does not lend itself to excursions by foot. But they are all close to major bus routes into the center of town; the better, more distant hotels offer free shuttle service to various points in the city. This area is not far from the Knesset and Government Center, the Hebrew University's Givat Ram Campus, and the Israel Museum.

### Expensive

**Crowne Plaza**   For more than 20 years, this landmark tower on a hill at the western edge of the city was the Jerusalem Hilton, and some Jerusalemites still refer to it as such, which makes for confusion. Public areas, though spacious, are a bit jumbled. Panoramic views from the guest rooms, most with small balconies, are a plus, but the rooms themselves, though comfortable and well equipped, are not remarkable. Crowne rooms offer use of a lounge with snacks, and pampering attention. The location is perfect for conventions at the neighboring Binyinei Ha-Uma Convention Center, and the shopping arcade is good, but you're far from West Jerusalem's cafe-and-restaurant scene. The excellent (kosher) **Kohinoor Indian** restaurant (p. 154) is on the premises.

Givat Ram, Jerusalem. © 02/539-0808. www.h-i.co.il. 397 units. $205–$275 (£103–£138) double. Rates include breakfast. Up to 2 children 18 and under stay free in parent's room, except during high season and in Crowne-level rooms. AE, DC, MC, V. Parking (fee). Bus: 6, 20, 21, or 48 or any bus to Central Bus Station. **Amenities:** Restaurant; dining room; cafe; bar; small outdoor pool; miniature golf; tennis courts; health club; sauna; Jacuzzi; children's activities in season; playground; free downtown shuttle; business center; shopping arcade; room service; laundry service; nonsmoking rooms; synagogue; rooms for those w/limited mobility. *In room:* A/C, TV, minibar, coffeemaker, hair dryer, safe.

### Moderate

**Ramada Jerusalem**   There are two separate high-rise towers in this well-equipped 1980s-built hotel; the less-expensive tower is sometimes closed during off season, and then everyone gets the attractive deluxe rooms. Public areas are spacious and serve as a conduit between the two sections, with hundreds of tiny star lights creating a romantic, almost sculptural effect at night. The large indoor and outdoor swimming pools, tennis courts, and the excellent health club are major strong points. However, the hotel's service is not as strong, and the decor in many rooms is wearing thin. Restaurant facilities are glatt kosher. Except in high season, you'll often find a discount policy: Stay 7 nights and pay only for 6. This is the farthest hotel from the center of town on Sderot Herzl, but there's a free downtown shuttle service; from here you can walk to Mount Herzl and Yad VaShem.

6 Wolfson St., Jerusalem. © 02/659-9999. www.ramada.com. 625 units. From $250 (£125) double. Look for AAA and other discounts. Rates include breakfast. AE, DC, MC, V. Free parking. Bus: 5, 6, 14, 18, 20, 21, or 48 to Herzl Blvd. at Rupin Bridge. **Amenities:** Restaurant; dining room; cafe; bar; indoor and outdoor swimming pools; children's pool; tennis courts; Jacuzzi; sauna; playground; business center; room service; massage; laundry service; nonsmoking rooms; synagogue. *In room:* A/C, TV w/pay movies, dataport, minibar, fridge (on request), hair dryer, safe (most rooms).

## FARTHER WEST: EIN KEREM
### Inexpensive

**Sisters of Sion Convent** *(Finds)*   Located in the village of Ein Kerem, with its terraced hillsides, gardens, and orchards, this hospice is a quiet, atmospheric retreat a half-hour bus ride from downtown Jerusalem. Not all guests are religious; some travelers come for the tranquillity and charm of Ein Kerem, which was the birthplace of John the Baptist. The convent itself is a lovely, well-kept ensemble of atmospheric buildings set in a walled orchard. Rooms are very simple but spotless. Meals, which can be arranged on a pension plan, are beautifully prepared. Rates are slightly higher on weekends; reservations are essential. Although bus no. 17 into Jerusalem sometimes runs only once an hour, the sisters can provide you with the schedule so you won't have to wait.

Ha-Oren St., Ezor "D," Ein Kerem, Jerusalem. © 02/641-5738. Fax 02/643-7739. 34 units, 23 with private bathroom, 8 with shared bathroom. $120 (£60) double. Rate includes breakfast. Cash only. Bus: 17 to Ein Kerem. **Amenities:** Dining room.

## SOUTH JERUSALEM

South of the King George Street/King David Street area, you'll likely use buses or taxis to get to the center of town, although you may find the half-hour walk interesting. Two atmospheric hospices are located in the Abu Tor and German Colony neighborhoods. Hebron Road, with views of the Old City, also offers two hotel choices. A half-hour municipal bus ride from the center of town, you'll find a large kibbutz hotel in the Judean mountains on the edge of the desert.

### EXPENSIVE

**Mount Zion Hotel** ★★ *Finds* *Kids*　With vistas that outdo even the King David's, this is Jerusalem's most architecturally interesting hotel, composed of renovated 19th- and early-20th-century Jerusalem stone buildings that have been carefully blended into a modern complex with terraces, gardens, and a beautiful swimming pool. The entire structure is built on a cliff-side shared by Jerusalem's fashionable Cinémathèque—you enter the hotel from the top and work your way down six levels. Most rooms have been recently renovated and are decorated with Moroccan touches that fit nicely with the old stone walls. Suites are equipped with kitchenettes and minibars; many rooms have minifridges. A fabulous two-story garden villa that can accommodate an extended family starts at about $2,000 (£1,000) a night. Look for the hotel's authentic 19th-century *hammam* (therapeutic Ottoman-era hot bathroom/steam room). *Tip:* For romance and views and the exotic, renovated executive and junior suites in the heavily redone Citadel are among the most dazzling in Jerusalem and worth the extra charge. In terms of service and amenities, this is a four-star hotel.

17 Hebron Rd., Jerusalem 93546. © 02/568-9555. Fax 02/673-1425. www.mountzion.co.il. 140 units. $240–$400 (£120–£200) double. Rates include breakfast. Extra charge for Old City–view rooms. AE, DC, MC, V. Free parking. Bus: 7, 8, 21, or 48. **Amenities:** Dining room; lobby bar/cafe; outdoor pool; exercise room; Jacuzzi; sauna (fee); Turkish steam room (fee); massage room. *In room:* A/C, TV, Wi-Fi, kitchenette (suites only), fridge (in some), hair dryer, safe.

### MODERATE

**Dan Boutique Hotel** *Value*　Totally renovated in 2008, this moderate-price, newest addition to the Dan Hotels was originally planned as a residential hotel. There's a variety of room sizes (some quite large) and arrangements, which makes this a good choice for families. Everything shines and is up-to-date, in both public areas and in well-appointed guest rooms (including widescreen plasma TVs). Better rooms are on floors five to eight; there are 14 roomy suites. No pool, but a rooftop sun deck with lounges has great views of the Hinnom Valley and Old City. Nearby bus stops offer schedules that will take you all over the city.

31 Hebron Rd., Jerusalem. © 02/568-9999. Fax 02/673-4066. www.danhotels.com. 126 units. $150–$220 (£75–£110) double. Rates include breakfast. AE, DC, MC, V. Limited free parking. Bus: 7, 8, 21, or 48. **Amenities:** Dining room; cafe; bar; fitness center; laundry service; synagogue. *In room:* A/C, cable TV, fridge, safe.

**Ramat Rachel Hotel** *(Kids* More like a resort than a hotel, this is the only kibbutz guest facility within the reach of Jerusalem's municipal bus routes. Ramat Rachel offers its visitors a vast swimming pool (heavily patronized by Jerusalemites in summer), night-lit tennis and basketball courts, a playground, and views of Bethlehem and the Judean desert. For those who want to relax as well as sightsee, or for families with children, this is a unique choice. There are 60 newer rooms, and all rooms (including refurbished older rooms) have been brightened with colorful textile creations by noted artist Calman Shemi. Some rooms have balconies. Seven rooms are designed for travelers with disabilities, and there is wheelchair access to all hotel facilities. All dining facilities are glatt kosher. Service is above average for a kibbutz establishment.

Kibbutz Ramat Rachel, Jerusalem 90900. ℂ 888/669-5700 in the U.S., or 02/670-2555. Fax 02/673-3155. www.ramatrachel.co.il. 164 units. $176–$230 (£88–£115) double. Jewish holidays extra. Discounts available through Kibbutz Hotel Chain/ITC 7-day packages. Rates include breakfast. AE, DC, MC, V. Free parking. Bus: 7. **Amenities:** Dining room; cafe; bar; Olympic pool; indoor heated pool; fitness center; spa; Jacuzzi; sauna; playground; airport transportation; business center; salon; massage; laundry service; nonsmoking rooms; 7 rooms for those w/limited mobility. *In room:* A/C, TV, minibar, hair dryer.

## INEXPENSIVE

**Little House in Bakah** Set in a beautiful landmark early-20th-century stone mansion facing busy, highwaylike Derech Hebron, the Little House in Bakah is something of a misnomer, as it's large and impressive. It contains simple and affordable guest rooms and a dining room, an Internet cafe, and a friendly lobby lounge. There's also a new annex of family suites of varying sizes. Don't expect luxury, but rooms are comfortable and pleasant enough; 13 of the smaller rooms are for singles. The pluses are relatively low room rates, affable management, general atmosphere of camaraderie, and the proximity to the interesting, partly gentrified little streets of the German Colony–Bakah neighborhood. The minuses are the traffic noise (try for a room at the back) and the long schlep from the center of town. Discount for long-term stays.

Hebron Rd. at Yehuda St., Jerusalem. ℂ 02/673-7944. Fax 02/673-7955. www.o-niv.com/bakah. 38 units. $150–$170 (£75–£85) double. Rates include breakfast. MC, V. **Amenities:** Dining room; cafe/bar; limited room service; laundry service. *In room:* A/C, TV, Wi-Fi.

**Saint Andrew's Church of Scotland Guest House** *(★ (Value* Situated on a small hill, the banner of St. Andrew waving from its tower, and surrounded by a garden with panoramic views of Mount Zion and the Old City, this guesthouse is only a few steps to buses to all points in town. Rooms are simple but freshly renovated and spotless, and one ground-floor room is available for those with disabilities. There's a garden, sun porch, and pleasant lounge well stocked with reading material and a new dining room where you can make free tea or coffee all day. The building is adorned with beautiful examples of Armenian ceramic tiles from the 1930s, which were created by Jerusalem's famous Palestinian Pottery Workshop. The efficient and friendly Scottish staff offers a hearty evening dinner when groups are in. Sunbula, a nonprofit shop selling fine Palestinian embroidery and local crafts, is also on the premises, and the beautiful Jerusalem Cinémathèque is across the road.

Church of Scotland, PO Box 8619, Jerusalem. ℂ 02/673-2401. Fax 02/673-1711. www.scotsguesthouse.com. 20 units. $115–$140 (£58–£70) double. Rates include breakfast. MC, V. Free parking. Bus: 4, 8, or 48 along King George V Ave. or Keren Hayesod St., or 6, 18, or 21 from Central Bus Station or Jaffa Rd.; railroad station or Khan Theater stop. **Amenities:** Dining room; lounge; laundry service; Wi-Fi; 1 room for those w/limited mobility. *In room:* A/C, coffeemaker, hair dryer (on request).

# NORTH JERUSALEM
## EXPENSIVE
**Regency Jerusalem**   Designed by one of Israel's foremost architects, the Regency (opened in 1987) was considered one of the city's finest hotels. Set on the lower slopes of Mount Scopus, the hotel's seven arcaded courtyards and multilevel atrium lobby settle gracefully across the landscape, with marvelous vistas of the city in the distance. The immediate neighborhood is not interesting for strolling, but a free shuttle bus takes you to downtown West Jerusalem. Room decor is wearing thin, but the basic design of the hotel is daring and tasteful. The fitness center is among the best in town; the swimming pool is roomy, although not very deep, and often loaded with outsiders. In 2001, the Israeli minister of tourism was murdered in this hotel, which caused tourists and Israelis to shy away for a number of years. Rates are comparatively low for what you get; look for discount deals.

32 Lehi St., Jerusalem. © 02/533-1234. Fax 02/532-3196. www.regency.co.il. 503 units. $210–$240 (£105–£120) double. Rates include breakfast. AE, DC, MC, V. Bus: 4. **Amenities:** Restaurant; dining room; cafe; bar; outdoor swimming pool; fitness center (fee); sauna; steam room; in-season children's activities; playground; floodlit basketball, tennis, volleyball courts; free shuttle to downtown Jerusalem; business center; large shopping arcade; salon; room service; laundry service; concierge-/club-level rooms; synagogue. *In room:* A/C, TV, minibar, hair dryer, safe.

# EAST JERUSALEM
With the construction of the Olive Tree Hotel, the Grand Court, and the Jerusalem Novotel, the axis of good hotels in East Jerusalem has shifted to the extreme western edge of this part of town. For decades, most of East Jerusalem's hotels had been located in and around Saladin Street, the bustling main shopping thoroughfare of the area. These hotels, like the neighborhood in general, have not aged well, and a band of new, upper-moderate hotels is being built just to the east of Hwy. 1, which divides the eastern and western parts of the city. This area is relatively convenient to West Jerusalem and has always been home to East Jerusalem's best and most vibrant hotels—the legendary American Colony Hotel, and the moderate Jerusalem Hotel—as well as the best Christian guesthouses (Notre Dame and St. George's). East Jerusalem's best restaurants are also beginning to accumulate in this area. There are still a few good hotel choices left in East Jerusalem's downtown center, and also on the Mount of Olives, with its wonderful views. Most of East Jerusalem's hotels are within walking distance of the Damascus Gate.

The atmosphere of downtown East Jerusalem is Palestinian, and the genuine helpfulness and hospitality found in many of East Jerusalem's hotels is very much in the Arabic tradition. As a rule, East Jerusalem hotels offer good value and are somewhat less expensive than those in the western part of town. Be forewarned, however, that the area is relatively dead at night, and that many of the cheaper hotels not listed here are run-down and smoky.

Most East Jerusalem hotels raise their prices by 20% to 25% during the Christmas and Easter holidays.

## EXPENSIVE
**American Colony Hotel** 𝕬𝕬𝕬   The former home of a Turkish pasha, and later in the 19th century the center for a "colony" of American and Swedish Protestants, this romantic hotel with beautiful gardens is in a class by itself. Popular with journalists, scholars, archaeologists, and diplomats, the American Colony has become almost as legendary as Rick's Cafe in Casablanca. At the center of Jerusalem's history for more than a century (a white bedsheet from the American Colony was Jerusalem's flag of

# Where to Stay & Dine in Jerusalem

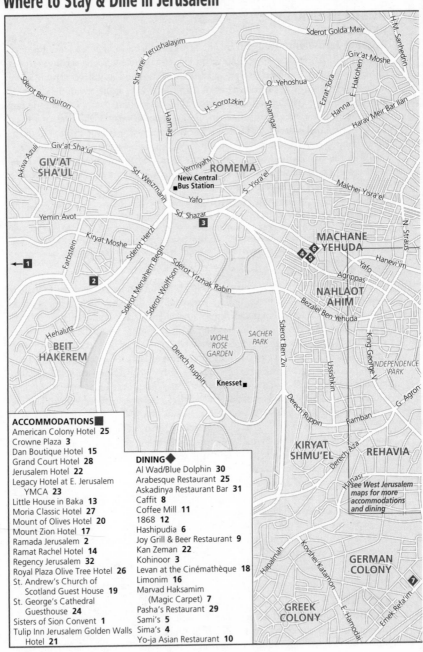

**ACCOMMODATIONS** ■
American Colony Hotel **25**
Crowne Plaza **3**
Dan Boutique Hotel **15**
Grand Court Hotel **28**
Jerusalem Hotel **22**
Legacy Hotel at E. Jerusalem
    YMCA **23**
Little House in Baka **13**
Moria Classic Hotel **27**
Mount of Olives Hotel **20**
Mount Zion Hotel **17**
Ramada Jerusalem **2**
Ramat Rachel Hotel **14**
Regency Jerusalem **32**
Royal Plaza Olive Tree Hotel **26**
St. Andrew's Church of
    Scotland Guest House **19**
St. George's Cathedral
    Guesthouse **24**
Sisters of Sion Convent **1**
Tulip Inn Jerusalem Golden Walls
    Hotel **21**

**DINING** ◆
Al Wad/Blue Dolphin **30**
Arabesque Restaurant **25**
Askadinya Restaurant Bar **31**
Caffit **8**
Coffee Mill **11**
1868 **12**
Hashipudia **6**
Joy Grill & Beer Restaurant **9**
Kan Zeman **22**
Kohinoor **3**
Levan at the Cinémathèque **18**
Limonim **16**
Marvad Haksamim
    (Magic Carpet) **7**
Pasha's Restaurant **29**
Sami's **5**
Sima's **4**
Yo-ja Asian Restaurant **10**

*see West Jerusalem maps for more accommodations and dining*

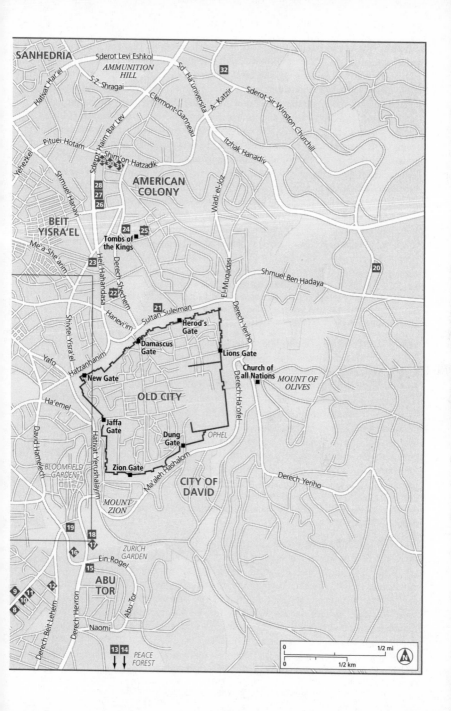

SANHEDRIA

Sderot Levi Eshkol

AMMUNITION HILL

S.Z. Shragai

Hativat Har'el

Sderot Haim Bar Lev

Pituei Hotam

Sd. Ha'universita

Clermont-Ganneau

**32**

A. Katzir

Sderot Sir Winston Churchill

Yehezkel

Shmuel Hanavi

Shimon Hatzadik

**29**
**30**
**31**

AMERICAN COLONY

Itzhak Hanadiv

Wadi el-Joz

**28**
**27**
**26**

BEIT YISRA'EL

Me'a She'arim

**24** **25**

Tombs of the Kings

**23**

Heil Hahandasa

Derech Shechem

**22**

El-Muqadasi

Shmuel Ben Hadaya

**20**

Hanevi'im

Sultan Suleiman

**21**

Shivtei Yisra'el

Yafo

Hatzanhanim

New Gate

Herod's Gate

Damascus Gate

Lions Gate

Derech Yeriho

Church of all Nations

MOUNT OF OLIVES

Ha'emel

OLD CITY

Derech Ha'ofel

Jaffa Gate

Dung Gate

OPHEL

David Hamelech

BLOOMFIELD GARDEN

Zion Gate

Ma'aleh Hachalom

CITY OF DAVID

Derech Yeriho

MOUNT ZION

Hativat Yerushalayim

**19**
**18**
**17**

**16**

ZURICH GARDEN

Ein Rogel

**15**

ABU TOR

**9** **11**
**8** **10**
**12**

Derech Beit-Lehem

Derech Hevron

Naomi

Abu Tor

**13** **14**

PEACE FOREST

| 0 | | 1/2 mi |
| 0 | | 1/2 km |

surrender to General Allenby's approaching British forces in 1917), the hotel offers walled courtyards, public areas decorated with splendid Armenian ceramics, intricately painted antique wooden ceilings, and other authentic old Jerusalem touches. The more costly executive Pasha rooms and suites are in the original building and feature antiques juxtaposed with modern bathrooms; some rooms are decorated with mother-of-pearl cocktail tables and copper trays, and have ornate gold-and-blue hand-painted ceilings. The less-expensive, but comfortable and spacious, business rooms and the smaller economy rooms are mostly in the hotel's newer, less august wings. Although less exotic in decor, they share the American Colony's magical ambience and are surrounded by luxuriant plantings. Within each room category there can be great variation, so ask to see different rooms if possible. Even if you can't afford this kind of luxury, you might want to treat yourself to the elegant and vast Saturday luncheon buffet in the Arabesque room or the charming garden cafe for a light meal or dessert. The bar hums with atmosphere and genuine intrigue. The hotel is style without glitz, and regarded as a meeting point for Palestinian and Israeli business, political, and journalistic contacts. The swimming pool is too small for a place of this size, but you can cool off in it.

Nablus Rd. (PO Box 19215), Jerusalem 97200. ✆ 02/627-9777. Fax 02/627-9779. www.americancolony.com. 92 units. $325–$465 (£163–£233) double. Rates include breakfast and service charge. AE, DC, MC, V. Limited free parking. Bus: 27. **Amenities:** Restaurant; dining room; cafe; bar; outdoor pool; children's pool; fitness center; Jacuzzi; sauna; business center; room service; massage; babysitting; laundry service; dry cleaning; Wi-Fi. *In room:* A/C, TV, high-speed Internet access, minibar or fridge, hair dryer, safe.

**Grand Court Hotel**   Heavily booked by package tours since it opened in 2005, this hotel—the third largest in the city—is one of three blockbusters lined up along Hwy. 1, right on the East/West Jerusalem dividing line. The overall design has many good points—light, spacious public areas; a rooftop terrace with a pool that doesn't fall into chilly afternoon shade; and standard guest rooms that are fresh and comfortable. Rooms for travelers with disabilities are available. Readers report kinks not yet ironed out in the hotel's food and general service, especially when tour groups are in. It may take some time until a staff that can handle such a massive hotel is in place, but it has potential. It's within walking distance of the Damascus Gate and East Jerusalem restaurants, but a taxi ride from the center of West Jerusalem. Food is kosher.

15 St. George St., East Jerusalem. ✆ 02/591-7777. Fax 02/591-7778. www.grandcourt.co.il. 442 units. $180–$280 (£90–£140) double. AE, DC, MC, V. **Amenities:** Dining room; cafe; bar; rooftop pool; fitness room; summer children's club; salon; nonsmoking rooms; synagogue; rooms for those w/limited mobility. *In room:* A/C, TV, dataport, minibar, coffeemaker, hair dryer, safe.

**Royal Plaza Olive Tree Hotel**   Opened in 2000, this large, contemporary, eight-story structure represents a new generation of Jerusalem hotels aimed at package and group tours. Public areas evoke a few old Jerusalem architectural touches (with an olive tree as the hotel atrium's centerpiece). Rooms, though comfortable and relatively new, are not memorable; superior rooms are larger and contain a fold-out sofa; one-bedroom suites include Jacuzzi bathtubs. You're within walking distance of East Jerusalem's restaurants and the Old City, but it's a taxi ride or a very long walk to the downtown center of West Jerusalem. Food is kosher.

23 St. George St., Jerusalem 46752. ✆ 02/541-0410. Fax 02/541-0411. www.olivetreehotel.com. 304 units. $260–$330 (£130–£165) double. Rates include breakfast. Discounts for stays more than 7 nights. AE, DC, MC, V. Free parking. Bus: 27. **Amenities:** Dining room; cafe; bar; indoor pool; fitness room; Jacuzzi; summer children's club; salon; nonsmoking rooms; rooms for those w/limited mobility. *In room:* A/C, TV, dataport, minibar, hair dryer, safe.

## MODERATE

**Moria Classic**    From the outside, this hotel, which opened in 2000, looks like a massive, sparkling new twin of its neighbor, the Olive Tree Hotel. There are, however, some differences: The public areas have fewer Jerusalem architectural touches, the swimming pool is outdoors, and there's a charge to use the fitness room. Rooms are comfortable and have refrigerators, and there are special rooms for travelers with disabilities. Because of its size, the hotel gets many tour groups—great rates are available through packagers or Internet discounters. The Old City and East Jerusalem's downtown are within walking distance, but it's a schlep (or a taxi ride) to West Jerusalem's center. Food services are kosher.

9 St. George St., Jerusalem. ℂ 02/532-2000. Fax 02/532-0011. www.hotels.co.il. 397 units. $170–$240 (£85–£120) double. Rates include breakfast. AE, DC, MC, V. Bus: 27. **Amenities:** Restaurant; bar; seasonal pool; fitness room; room service; laundry service; nonsmoking rooms; club-level rooms; synagogue; rooms for those w/limited mobility. *In room:* A/C, TV, dataport (some rooms), minibar, hair dryer, safe.

## INEXPENSIVE

**Jerusalem Hotel** ★★ *(Finds*    This increasingly popular gem of a hotel, run by the very hospitable, well-informed Saadeh family, is a real winner. It's housed in an old stone mansion with thick walls, high ceilings, and a garden cafe. A meeting place for writers, journalists, and savvy travelers over the years, the Jerusalem Hotel has come to be known as an economy version of its neighbor, the famed American Colony Hotel just up Nablus Road. Rooms, last redone in 1997, have exposed Jerusalem stone walls; handcrafted, traditional Egyptian furniture; and good bathrooms. The restaurant offers good Middle Eastern and Continental dishes in both the garden and in a traditional dining room with low tables and pillow-covered divans. On Saturday evenings (when tourism is normal), the hotel serves an excellent Lebanese buffet ($16/£8) with salads, vegetarian dishes, and six hot dishes, plus excellent traditional Middle Eastern oud (lute) music; in summer, look for great Saturday evening all-you-can-eat barbecues. Thursday evenings, there's live Western music, ranging from soft jazz to classical. The management can help with tours to Bethlehem and points in the West Bank, conditions permitting (at the moment, I don't recommend it).

The entrance at 4 Antara Ben-Shadad St. is off Nablus Road, on a side street facing the north side of the Egged East Nablus Road Bus Station. The garden and a very high Plexiglas shield screen out the small bus station, which is closed by late afternoon.

Nablus Rd. (entrance at 4 Antara Ben-Shadad St.), Jerusalem. ℂ/fax 02/628-3282, or 800/657-9401 for reservations in the U.S. www.jrshotel.com. 15 units. $100–$145 (£50–£73) double. Rates include breakfast. AE, DC, MC, V. Bus: 27. **Amenities:** Restaurant; dining room; tour desk; Wi-Fi. *In room:* A/C, TV, hair dryer.

**Legacy Hotel at East Jerusalem YMCA**    Completely reconstructed and opened in 2008, the YMCA's formerly institutional hotel facility is now very stylish, up-to-date, and comfortable. Near the American Colony Hotel, and a 10-minute walk to the Damascus Gate, this is now a bright, moderately priced option. The character of the East Jerusalem YMCA is not nearly as all-encompassing and binational as at the landmark, atmospheric West Jerusalem YMCA on King David Street, but for the moment, its guest rooms outdo those at the King David Street Y. Some rooms have balconies and Old City views; junior and one-bedroom suites are beautifully designed, with balconies and great vistas. There's an indoor swimming pool (heavily used by locals), and the food service is quite good. There's an airport shuttle service for NIS 50 ($13/£6.25).

29 Nablus Rd., Jerusalem. ℂ **02/627-0800.** Fax 02/627-7739. www.jerusalemlegacy.com. 49 units. $150–$220 (£75–£110) double. Rates include breakfast. MC, V. Free parking. **Amenities:** 3 restaurants; dining room; indoor pool; fitness room; squash; basketball and volleyball courts. *In room:* A/C, cable TV, minibar, safe.

**St. George's Cathedral Guesthouse** ⭐ *(Value)* This well-run Anglican/Episcopal establishment offers private rooms housed in a cloister around an English garden. Accommodations are simple; they were redecorated in 1996 (new bathrooms were also installed at that time), and the ambience is both evocative and comfortable. Rooms vary, so ask if you can have a look at a few before taking one. There's a charming Jerusalem stone bar in the basement, and the entire very British enclave seems like the setting for a chapter of *The Jewel in the Crown.* The staff is knowledgeable and very helpful.

To find it, walk up Nablus Road, and you'll be approaching Saint George's Cathedral on the right. The hotel is in the cathedral compound, where Nablus Road and Saladin Street meet. Bus no. 27 comes right to the door of Saint George's (bus noise may be a problem for some).

20 Nablus Rd. (PO Box 19018), Jerusalem. ℂ **02/628-3302.** Fax 02/628-2253. 24 units. $100–$120 (£50–£60) double. DC, V. Bus: 27. **Amenities:** Dining room; bar. *In room:* A/C.

**Tulip Inn Jerusalem Golden Walls Hotel** Conveniently located close to the Damascus Gate, on the side of the Damascus Gate bus station (rooms on that side tend to be noisier), this three-story, modern building has views of the Old City walls (across the street); views from the roof are spectacular, and the hotel plans to develop the roof as a place for guests to visit. It's not an opulent place, and much of the decor looks 1970-ish, but it can be a good deal when rates are negotiable.

Sultan Suleiman St., Jerusalem 97200. ℂ **02/627-2416.** Fax 02/626-4658. asmin@pilgrimpal.com. 103 units. $160–$240 (£80–£120) double. AE, DC, MC, V. Bus: 27. **Amenities:** Restaurant; bar; limited room service. *In room:* A/C, TV, hair dryer.

## MOUNT OF OLIVES

To the east of downtown East Jerusalem, the Mount of Olives is a bit out of the thick of things, but some returning visitors wouldn't dream of staying anywhere else. It's a downhill walk to the Old City and East Jerusalem, and there's no public transport over to West Jerusalem, so you may find yourself resorting to taxis, especially at night. But your rewards for staying in this area include incredible views of Jerusalem and almost bucolic, spiritual surroundings. *Note:* Women should not walk on the Mount of Olives unescorted at any time.

**Mount of Olives Hotel** This friendly, family-run hotel offers marvelous, panoramic vistas; an atmospheric location amid the gardens of the Mount of Olives; and proximity to the many churches on the Mount. Rooms are simply furnished, but comfortable and centrally heated; the Plus rooms are worth the few dollars more. The downside is a tough climb up to the hotel and the distance from both Old and New cities—you'll need taxis, especially at night, when the Mount of Olives is dark and empty. Jewish taxis from the New City may refuse to take you all the way. Ask about room no. 317 (the panorama room), with an especially fabulous view of the Old City—usually booked by TV news crews. There is a TV lounge.

53 Mount of Olives Rd., Jerusalem. ℂ **800/762-9295** in the U.S., or 02/628-4877. Fax 02/626-4427. www.mtolives. com. 61 units. $68–$98 (£34–£49) standard double. Rates include continental breakfast. AE, DC, MC, V. At top of hill on Mount of Olives Rd., turn right and pass through Arab village of Et-Tur, and continue past 2 hospitals. Russian church will be on left; hotel is at bend in road to left. **Amenities:** Dining room; lounge.

## OUTSIDE THE CITY
### INEXPENSIVE

**Neve Shalom-Wahat al Salaam Hotel and Hostel** *Finds*  This village of peace (its name means "oasis of peace" in both Hebrew and Arabic) is located in the countryside near the Latrun Monastery, between Tel Aviv and Jerusalem, just where the plain of Ayalon begins to rise into the mountains of Judea (the ancient borderland between the Israelites and their longtime enemies, the Philistines). The village, with its sweeping vistas, was founded as a place where Israeli Jews and Israeli Arabs could live together in friendship and understanding, and over the years its inhabitants have turned their community effort into a national center for learning and dialogue. The modern, low-rise hotel, originally built for study seminars, is now open to the public, and visitors are welcome to spend a night or two here within a 25-minute drive of both Jerusalem and Tel Aviv, enjoying the lovely countryside and getting a feel for this unusual project. The simple but comfortable rooms are modern, and have private bathrooms with showers. Guests have use of a TV room. A delicious home-style lunch or dinner vegetarian buffet can be arranged, and you can join a lecture (if offered in your language) for a modest fee. A large swimming pool and adjacent toddlers' pool are set amid gardens and vistas of the countryside. Although not a kibbutz, Neve Shalom-Wahat al Salaam can be included as an overnight choice in the Kibbutz Hotel Chain discount packages, which can be reserved in the U.S. and Canada by calling *C* **888/669-5700.**

Buses and sheruts between Tel Aviv and Jerusalem will let you off at the Latrun Junction. You must prearrange with Neve Shalom for a pickup near the junction.

Doar Na Shimshon 99761. *C* **02/991-7160.** Fax 02/991-7412. www.nswas.org. 39 units. $120–$160 (£60–£80) double; higher on Jewish holidays. Rates include breakfast. AE, DC, MC, V. **Amenities:** Dining room; lounge; pool; children's pool; holistic massage. *In room:* A/C.

## 5 Where to Dine

Jerusalem has a huge selection of restaurants, dairy bars, lunch counters, snack shops, delicatessens, and cafes.

In the Old City and East Jerusalem, you'll find mostly Middle Eastern cuisine. Pork is prohibited to Muslims, as it is to Jews, but you will find pork and shellfish in East Jerusalem restaurants catering to tourists or Christian Arabs. There are no kosher restaurants in East Jerusalem or in the Old City except in the Jewish Quarter. The Old City has plenty of snack stands and inexpensive Arab restaurants. Most Old City eating places are open daily from late morning to 5 or 6pm.

In West Jerusalem, the dining scene is quite different. Downtown West Jerusalem has tons of restaurants and places for a quick meal, and most places are open until very late at night. You'll find pedestrian streets that are wall-to-wall eating places, but thanks to the years of terror attacks (2000–03), many of the best restaurants in town have moved to hidden courtyards; to quiet, slightly out-of-the-way streets; and to old Ottoman-era mansions surrounded by walled gardens. Almost every restaurant or cafe has a security guard at its entrance (and many charge a security fee that's worth the peace of mind). The many ethnic restaurants (Yemenite, Israeli, Kurdish, Eastern European) that travelers loved have mostly gone. Like Tel Aviv, Jerusalem has an oversupply of personal, vaguely French/Mediterranean restaurants overseen by talented, inventive chefs. Meals are interesting, of good quality, and not cheap, but almost all restaurants offer incredible business lunch specials from noon until 5 or 6pm that make them very affordable.

---

**⟨Tips** **Catching Restaurants at Their Best**

Saturday night is very big for dining out in Israel, but because kosher restaurants often prepare food for Saturday night on Thursday before closing for the Sabbath, and because nonkosher restaurants will not have received fresh fish and vegetables for 2 days, you won't find restaurants at their best. If you're going to splurge at a top restaurant, do it midweek.

---

**SABBATH DINING**   Kosher restaurants usually close by 2 or 3pm on Friday for Shabbat. The following nonkosher restaurants, described in detail later in this chapter, have Friday evening or Saturday afternoon hours, and provide a good variety of choices. In downtown West Jerusalem: Adom, Barood, the restaurant at the King David Street YMCA, Sakura, Spaghettim, Zuni, McDonald's, and Arcadia. In South Jerusalem: Levan at the Cinémathèque. In East Jerusalem: American Colony Hotel, Blue Dolphin, Askadinya, Pasha, and Kan Zeman at the Jerusalem Hotel.

## THE OLD CITY
### NEAR JAFFA GATE
**Inexpensive**

**Armenian Tavern** ⓖ ARMENIAN   The prettiest restaurant in the Old City is housed in a newly restored room with exposed stone walls, Crusader-era arched ceilings, an indoor fountain, rustic wooden tables, and panels of hand-painted Armenian tiles that are a feast for the eye. The home-style food is prepared with special Armenian herbs and seasonings that give each dish a slightly novel taste. Inexpensive appetizers are great here—choose from delicate home-style meat pizzas (small but delicious) and a range of cold salads, soups, and stuffed vegetables. The pepper salad and the cucumber-and-yogurt salad are excellent. Main courses are mildly exotic and always delicious. Friday nights, special traditional dishes are brought in from the kitchen of the owner's and neighboring family's homes—you can have a fine home-style feast. Background music is Armenian and Greek. Wine and beer, rarities in Old City restaurants, are added attractions.

79 Armenian Orthodox Patriarchate Rd. ⓒ 02/627-3854. Reservations necessary Fri–Sat evenings. Main courses NIS 40–NIS 65 ($10–$16/£5–£8.10). AE, DC, MC, V. Tues–Sun 11am–10:30pm. After entering Jaffa Gate, turn right at the Tower of David (Citadel). Continue straight; restaurant is on the right, down a flight of stairs.

**Papa Andreas** ⟨Moments⟩ MIDDLE EASTERN   In good weather, the rooftop dining terrace of this restaurant offers a spectacular day, evening, or night view of the Old City, with the Dome of the Rock and the Temple Mount in the distance. The menu includes tasty medleys of Middle Eastern appetizers, grilled meats, *shwarma,* and even pasta and pizza. Nothing on the menu is dramatic, but the view makes up for that. Service is friendly, attentive, and the management doesn't mind if you linger to enjoy the twilight and the evening prayer calls. Bring a warm sweater if you plan to eat dinner on the roof—even Jerusalem summer evenings get chilly—but the vistas make the cold and the climb up several flights of stairs worthwhile.

64 Aftimos St., Muristan Bazaar. ⓒ 02/628-4433. Reserve if you want a table with a great view. Main courses NIS 39–NIS 80 ($9.75–$20/£4.90–£10). MC, V. Daily 8am–midnight.

## IN THE BAZAARS & NEAR DAMASCUS GATE

While there are not many restaurants in this area, you can find many Arabic pastry shops, places grilling whole chickens (which can be carved and packed in aluminum foil for takeout), and fresh juice bars. Wander from Damascus Gate along Suq Khan es-Zeit Street, which bears to the right at the fork.

### Inexpensive

**Abu Assab Refreshments** FRESH JUICES   The best place in the Old City for fresh orange, grapefruit, and carrot juice (often as sweet as cantaloupe juice), Abu Assab always purchases the best of the crop. Have yours at the juice bar, or follow the tiny staircase upstairs for table service. It's located ¾ of the way from Damascus Gate to the Cardo, on the right side.

Suq Khan es-Zeit Bazaar. No phone. NIS 6–NIS 10 ($1.50–$2.50/75p–£1.25). Cash only. Sat–Thurs 9am–5pm; Fri 9am–3pm.

**Abu Shukri** ✿ Value HUMMUS   This restaurant, one of the best and most afford-able in Jerusalem, can be found where the Via Dolorosa and Al Wad Road meet. It's famous for hummus (mashed, seasoned chickpeas eaten with pita bread) that is so spectacular that in more tranquil times, people in Jordan used to send out for it in insulated ice chests, and lines of Israelis waited for tables on Saturday afternoons. This is a bring-your-own-napkins kind of restaurant, and the Formica tables may be cracked and broken, but the hummus has been written up in newspapers and period-icals ranging from the *New York Times* and *Condé Nast Traveler* to *Playboy* magazine. Try your hummus with whole chickpeas in olive oil, or with brown beans (called *fool*) or roasted pine nuts (my favorite), and be sure to ask for the pita bread to be served hot (included in the price). I like to order a small plate of chopped salad and mix it in with the hummus; falafel here is fresh and spicy. In 1999, Abu Shukri began to add meat to its menu—you can get excellent grilled kabobs, *shwarma,* and *kubbe* (cracked wheat dumplings stuffed with meat). Mint tea is a good beverage choice.

63 Al Wad Rd. ✆ 02/627-1538. Main courses NIS 20–NIS 40 ($5–$10/£2.50–£5). Cash only. Daily 8am–4:30pm (later on Sat).

**Amigo Emil** ✿ Finds INTERNATIONAL/ARABIC   This friendly place with its sparkling tables, glasses, and goblets, is set on a quiet bazaar street at the edge of the Christian Quarter. It's a good choice for a Western-style meal and a break from the bus-tle of the Old City. You can order chicken wings in barbecue sauce; omelets; old-fash-ioned chicken soup; meat lasagna; boneless, breaded chicken breast stuffed with Israeli cheese; a meze of Arabic appetizers; a nice chicken curry; spicy Lebanese-style fish; or grilled meats. There are special touches, such as delicious *carabage halab* (a wonderful Arabic pastry made by the owner's family); fresh tangerine juice in season; and good espresso. The dining rooms offer atmosphere, with arches and exposed, ancient stone walls. As this is a Christian-owned establishment, there's a wine and beer list.

El Khanka St. Bazaar (left side as you go downhill). ✆ 02/628-8090. Main courses NIS 32–NIS 70 ($8–$18/£4–£8.75). AE, MC, V. Mon–Sat 10am–9pm. From David St., near Jaffa Gate, turn left onto Christian Quarter Rd.; at the end, turn left onto El Khanka.

**Families Restaurant** MIDDLE EASTERN   For decades, this restaurant, owned by the Abdulatif family, has been one of the few where you will see both Arabic fam-ilies and tourists dining (when I was a student, the sign in the window unfortunately read: ABDULATIF'S RESTAURANT AND FAMILY BUTCHERY). The *shwarma,* which you can see at the front counter, is probably the best in the bazaar—you can order a *shwarma* sandwich filled with your choice of salads or a more expensive plate to eat at a table, or take it away. There are also soups and traditional oven dishes such as hummus and meat casseroles, but the *shwarma* is the thing for a fast, tasty meal. The large, arched-ceiling dining room probably goes back to the time of the Crusades. *Tip:* If you order the top-notch *shwarma* sandwich or plate, go to the counter and point out which accompanying salads you would like.

Suq Khan es-Zeit Bazaar. No phone. Main courses NIS 30–NIS 40 ($7.50–$10/£3.75–£5); *shwarma* sandwich NIS 18 ($4.50/£2.25). Cash only. Daily 8am–6pm. Coming from direction of Jaffa Gate, it will be on the right about 30m (98 ft.) after the turn for Via Dolorosa.

**Jaffar and Sons Pastry Cafe** ARABIC PASTRY   People flock to Jaffar for a wonderful Middle Eastern dessert called *kanafeh,* which you will see being cut from large pizzalike trays. A recipe with origins that date from ancient times, *kanafeh* is mildly sweet cheese, grains, and pistachios baked in a very light honey syrup and served (optionally) with a bit more honey syrup on top. Buy a ticket at the cashier's counter for an order of *kanafeh,* and take a table (drinking glasses are communal—you'll probably prefer bottled soft drinks or water); your order of *kanafeh* will soon be delivered to you. A newly renovated cafe of polished gray marble has unfortunately replaced the old domed-ceiling rooms. You can ask to have your order boxed for takeout (bring your own napkins and plastic forks, and take your *kanafeh* off to some interesting spot for a picnic). It's absolutely delicious when warm.

Suq Khan es-Zeit Bazaar. No phone. Items NIS 12 ($3/£1.50). Cash only. Daily 9am–5pm. From Damascus Gate, bear right at the fork in the road, and continue into the narrow bazaar. Jaffar is the 2nd large pastry shop with glass windows on the right.

### THE JEWISH QUARTER

This part of the Old City is home to a number of kosher fast-food spots on Jewish Quarter Road, where you can have a bowl of soup (usually made from powder) or a slice of kosher pizza or quiche. I like a bagel shop at the Seven Arches, near the Burnt House. On Jewish Quarter Road you'll also find two (nonkosher) old-fashioned Arabic-style bread bakeries where you can buy warm, freshly baked pita and big sesame bread rolls, which are tasty to snack on as you explore the Old City. Ask the baker for a tiny, free package of *zataar* (local spices) to flavor the bread in the traditional Middle Eastern style.

**Keshet** VEGETARIAN/DAIRY   Probably the best kosher choice in the Old City, Keshet serves a variety of quiches, salads, soups, omelets, and even potato latkes (pancakes) and delicious fresh-squeezed fruit juices. It's air-conditioned and there are outdoor tables for people-watching at the edge of busy Hurva Square.

Tiferet Israel St., in the corner of Hurva Sq. ☎ 02/628-7515. Main courses NIS 40–NIS 60 ($10–$15/£5–£7.50). MC, V. Sun–Thurs 9am–7pm in summer, to 5 or 6pm in winter; Fri 9am–2pm.

## WEST JERUSALEM
### BEN-YEHUDA & YOEL SALOMON PEDESTRIAN MALLS & ZION SQUARE
#### Expensive

**Darna** ★★ MOROCCAN   The owner of Darna, a successful Jerusalem restaurateur who came to Israel from Morocco as a youth, decided to create a fabulous, authentic Moroccan restaurant after he revisited North Africa in the early 1990s and was dazzled by the beauty of his one-time homeland. Moroccan designers and craftsmen were

# Where to Dine in Downtown West Jerusalem

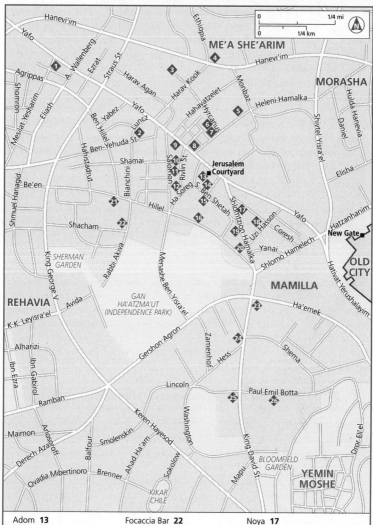

| | | |
|---|---|---|
| Adom **13** | Focaccia Bar **22** | Noya **17** |
| Angelo **6** | Gabriel **15** | Sakura Japanese Restaurant **13** |
| Arcadia **1** | Hess **5** | Sea Dolphin **15** |
| Barood Bar Restaurant **13** | Hillel Espresso Bar **8, 21** | Shanty **10** |
| Canela **19** | International Restaurant | Spaghettim **16** |
| Chakra **20** |   at the YMCA **25** | Te'enim Vegetarian Cuisine **26** |
| Dagim BaChatzer **13** | Katy's **14** | Terra Restaurant & Bar **15** |
| Darna **7** | Korusin Restaurant **2** | Tmol Shilshom |
| David Citadel Hotel **23** | La Guta **12** |   Bookstore Cafe **8** |
| 1868 **24** | Little Jerusalem Restaurant | Vaquiero **4** |
| Eldad Vesayhoo **13** |   at Ticho House **3** | Village Green **9** |
| Eucalyptus **6** | Marikiyah **18** | Zuni Restaurant/Café/Bar **11** |

brought to Jerusalem to create just the right setting, and top chefs were imported to supervise the intricacies of classic Moroccan cuisine prepared within the bounds of kashrut. The result is a memorable place that delights the eye and the taste buds without being hokey or touristy. The *dechicha* (spiced barley and lamb soup served with dates) and the meze of Moroccan salads are wonderful and very reasonably priced, as is the *pastilla*, a sweet phyllo pie traditionally made of pigeon, but (thankfully) done here with Cornish hen. These courses alone would make a fine light dinner, but for main courses, the couscous dishes and the *tagines* (lamb or chicken cooked with dried fruits or vegetables in covered clay pots) are my favorites, as is the Safi-style sea bream. There are also unusual specialties such as a rich but light *tagine* of brains with lemon, saffron, and egg. Service is in a graceful Moroccan style, and carefully chosen background music seems to echo the medinas of Fez and Marrakech. For two people, soups, the meze, and one main course or one set menu plus a main course could be adequate. This glatt kosher restaurant is one of the best dining experiences in Israel.

3 Hyrcanos (Horkanos) St. ✆ **02/624-5406.** Reservations necessary. Main courses NIS 100–NIS 170 ($25–$43/£13–£21); business lunch NIS 80 ($20/£10); set-menu dinner starting at NIS 175 ($44/£22); menu gastronomique (tasting menu) NIS 240 ($60/£30). AE, DC, MC, V. Sun–Thurs 12:30–3:30pm and 6:30pm–12:30am; Sat after Shabbat–midnight.

**La Guta** ✿ FRENCH/MOROCCAN   A bit more unusual than more expensive luxury kosher choices, and set in charming, whitewashed, arched-ceiling rooms of a 19th-century building, La Guta offers meals in a Franco/North African tradition from the very personal kitchen of Mrs. Guta Ben Simhon. Everything served here is unique. Look for terrine de foie gras in scallion confiture; foie gras in cherry tomato jam; mullet filet in olive and herbs; goose thigh in forest berries; and a variety of sumptuous meat dishes, such as beef filet stuffed with foie gras, served in port-wine sauce. Interestingly seasoned salads round out the menu. On Tuesday, you can sample Guta's couscous. Desserts are worthwhile, and there's a good wine list.

18 Rivlin St. ✆ 02/623-2322. Reservations required. Main courses NIS 80–NIS 120 ($20–$31/£10–£16); fixed-price lunch specials from NIS 70 ($18/£8.75); fixed-price dinners and Sat fixed-price dinner specials from NIS 100 ($25/£13). AE, DC, MC, V. Sun–Thurs noon–4pm and 6:30–11pm or later (last order at 10pm); Fri noon–2pm; Sat after Shabbat.

## Moderate

**Eucalyptus** ✿✿ *(Finds)* JERUSALEM HOME-STYLE   Chef/owner Moshe Basson is famous throughout Israel and beyond as a "food archaeologist" who reconstructs the home-style dishes of Jerusalem's many cultures and traditions. His menu includes a remarkable array of herbs, spices, and cooking techniques like nothing else in the country, and has been praised by food critics worldwide. If you love cooking, try to arrange to come when Moshe is present—he loves to explain the history and preparation secrets of the many salads, soups, and rustic dishes on his worthwhile tasting menu (Moshe's talented co-chef, Sufian, will also be happy to offer explanations). Signature dishes include figs stuffed with chicken in tamarind sauce; sorel soup; ingria (a meat stew with sweet-and-sour eggplant); a wonderful lamb stew served under a pita dough crust; lamb served over smoked green wheat; and interesting ethnic fish dishes. On occasion, Moshe's international award-winning couscous is served. The traditional *ma'aluba*, a baked chicken and rice dish, is usually made with chicken legs and thighs, but if you like light chicken, ask if it can be substituted. Meat is the strong point here, but many dishes can be made in vegetarian form. There are unusual, traditional desserts as well. Dishes can be ordered a la carte, but the tasting menu is highly recommended. There are discounts at lunch.

7 Horkanos St., Jerusalem. ⓒ **02/623-2864.** Reservations recommended. Main courses NIS 75–NIS 110 ($19–$28/ £9.40–£14). AE, DC, MC, V. Sun–Thurs noon–4pm and 6–10:30pm. Check for possible evening hours after Shabbat.

**Vaqueiro** SOUTH AMERICAN   This all-you-can-eat, kosher-meat restaurant in the South American tradition has a decidedly South African twist and is one of Jerusalem's popular upper-moderate-priced dining spots. Sample from a large all-you-can-eat menu of meats brought to your table fresh from the oven or fire. At lunch there are two menus: a one-time-around sampling of six meats; and for NIS 25 ($6.25/£3.10) more, all-you-can-eat privileges. But the real strength of the restaurant is at dinner, where the all-you-can-eat expands to 10 meat courses that change nightly, but may include rib-eye steak; chicken wings in peach sauce; goose legs in orange sauce; Bobotee (a South African dish of oven-baked dark turkey and dried fruit); flaky empanadas; or even a whole, juicy, honey-basted American-style turkey. There is an array of salads and vegetables (most with a South African twist); the salmon alternative is definitely not Vaqueiro's strong point. Wines and tempting desserts are wheeled around on carts and are not included in the fixed price. Cape Brandy Cake (one portion can easily be shared by up to four after a dinner like this) is the dessert of choice. Located in a charming 19th-century mansion separated from the street by a walled garden, Vaqueiro offers both atmosphere and security.

54 Hanevi'im St. ⓒ **02/624-7432.** Reservations necessary. Fixed-price dinner NIS 140 ($35/£18). AE, DC, MC, V. Sun–Thurs noon–4:30pm and 6–11pm; Sat after Shabbat.

### Inexpensive

**Angelo** ✪ KOSHER ITALIAN   The most superb, freshly made pasta in Jerusalem is served at this cozy kosher-mehadrin place run by Angelo, an immigrant from Rome. The ravioli and the gnocchi are elegantly tender, and there's cannelloni filled with ricotta and smoked salmon that I especially like. Angelo's sauces are truly alive with flavor and quality (I love his spicy fresh tomato sauce rich with tasty cherry tomatoes). If you arrange ahead of time, Angelo can sometimes prepare special Roman Jewish dishes. Meat is not served here, but there are a daily fresh fish special and a number of Italian dessert choices including *pannecotta* and tiramisu made fresh each day. Look for daily lunch deals.

9 Hyrcanos (Horkanos) St. ⓒ **02/623-6095.** Reservations recommended. Main courses NIS 45–NIS 80 ($11–$20/ £5.60–£10). AE, DC, MC, V. Sun–Thurs noon–11pm; Sat after Shabbat–midnight. Closed Fri. The restaurant is 2 short blocks from Zion Sq., parallel to Jaffa Rd.

**Focaccia Bar** *Value* ITALIAN/MEDITERRANEAN   A 19th-century cottage with a large dining garden (covered and heated in winter) is the setting for this very popular, informal meeting place. In a corner of the garden, a brick *taboon* (oven) turns out focaccia and pizza. You can order generous hot salads filled with stir-fried veggies and chicken or goose breast, plus soups, cold salads, pizzas, pastas, or stylish appetizers such as fried calamari or a plate of smoked salmon with quail eggs, cream cheese, and raw vegetables. The clientele ranges from professors to families to teeny-boppers, the atmosphere is lively, and the place gradually becomes an alfresco bar late on summer nights.

4 Rabbi Akiba St. ⓒ **02/625-6428.** Main courses NIS 36–NIS 60 ($9–$15/£4.50–£7.50). AE, DC, MC, V. Daily 9am–2am.

**Hess** DELI/SWISS   An interesting combination of European delicatessen and Franco-German-Swiss-Jewish cuisine, Hess is the brainchild of a well-known Swiss kosher sausage producer. There's home-style corned beef and tongue, both served either hot or in sandwiches with Dijon mustard, and there are sausages and salamis.

You'll also find very substantial dinners such as pan-fried veal liver or foie gras, or oven-baked lamb. The place is simple, but standards are very high.

9 Helene HaMalka St. ✆ 02/625-5515. Reservations suggested. Main courses NIS 40–NIS 120 ($10–$30/£5–£15). MC, V. Sun–Thurs 11am–11pm.

**Hillel Espresso Bar** MEDITERRANEAN   Along with its neighbor Aroma, this is a stylish hangout for Jerusalem's coffee drinkers, but it's also famous for terrific, Mediterranean-style sandwiches made with great breads, wonderful cheeses, herbs, spices, and other ingredients. The "Hillel" (house) sandwich consists of sun-dried tomato, fried eggplant, feta cheese, basil, and nuts; other interesting sandwich combos include smoked salmon; smoked tuna; or omelet with goat cheese, tomato, and scallion. There are also salads, good cakes, quiches, and a soup of the day. As the place is kosher, there's no meat. Takeout makes this a good choice for picnics or a meal on the run. A second very popular branch of Hillel Espresso Bar is located at the corner of Jaffa Road and Helene HaMalka Street.

8 Hillel St. ✆ 02/624-7775. Meals NIS 26–NIS 36 ($6.50–$9/£3.25–£4.50). MC, V. Sun–Thurs 7am–1am; Fri 7am–2pm.

**Korusin Chinese Restaurant** GLATT KOSHER CHINESE   A convenient, compact, two-story place on Lunz Street near the bottom of the Ben-Yehuda Mall, Korusin is an interesting change of pace in a town with few Asian choices. It serves chicken, duck, meat, and vegetarian dishes prepared in a variety of traditional Chinese styles. The sushi here is very good, as are the soups. There are lunch specials until 6pm. It may expand to larger premises, but for now, Korusin is always busy, and the narrow stairs to the upper level may be difficult for those with limited mobility.

Lunz St. in Ben-Yehudah Mall. ✆ 02/624-2042. Main courses NIS 55–NIS 80 ($14–$20/£6.90–£10). AE, DC, MC, V. Sun–Thurs 11am–10pm; Fri 11am–2pm; Sat after Shabbat–11pm.

**Little Jerusalem Restaurant at Ticho House** ★★ *Finds* *Kids* VEGETARIAN/ FISH   You'll be amazed when you come upon this large hidden oasis, its gardens and terrace cafe set right in the center of downtown West Jerusalem—it's especially wonderful for outdoor dining in summer. Built in 1880 as a private villa, Ticho House (p. 201), around 1912, became the home of artist Anna Ticho and her husband, Dr. Abraham Ticho, a legendary ophthalmologist dedicated to wiping out endemic eye disease. At the in-house kosher restaurant you can dine indoors or on the garden terrace. The menu features crepes; soups (onion soup served in a loaf of bread is a favorite); sandwiches (melted cheese and herbs is a specialty); hefty, fresh salads filled with quality ingredients; vegetable pies, pastas, and casseroles; and a variety of more pricey fish dishes (go for denise or bream rather than the imported salmon). Many people come just for the desserts, which are excellent.

Saturday evenings, Ticho House offers a "Viennese Night," with a wonderful string quartet playing waltzes, and an all-you-can-eat buffet of blintzes and Viennese pastries; on Tuesday evenings, there's live jazz, and in addition to the regular menu, you can choose a wine-and-cheese buffet that includes soup and salad. Ticho House is sometimes closed for private parties, so always call ahead. Service is friendly and presided over by Nava Bibi, the very attentive director who keeps Ticho House's traditions alive.

Abraham Ticho St., off Ha Rav Kook St. ✆ 02/624-4186. Reservations necessary. Main courses NIS 40–NIS 90 ($10–$23/£5–£11). DC, MC, V. Sun–Thurs 10am–midnight; Fri 10am–2pm; Sat after Shabbat–11:45pm.

## (Kids) Family-Friendly Restaurants

**Moshiko's** (p. 156), on the Ben-Yehuda Mall, is the best *shwarma* stand in town (and their falafel is good, too)—it's messy but delicious enough to entice most kids and offers outdoor tables in good weather (never give a kid a falafel sandwich to eat on the run unless you've brought a wardrobe of disposable clothes for him). In winter, when there are no tables, this is a poor option. **Eldad Vesayhoo** (p. 150), in the Jerusalem Courtyard, off Jaffa Road, has the best-priced elegant lunch specials in town (Sun–Thurs until 5:30pm), which works out well for American families that don't want to keep late hours. Very speedy service comes with Eldad's luncheon specials, so kids don't get too impatient. **Little Jerusalem Restaurant at Ticho House** (p. 146) offers more leisurely service, but kids can get up and run around in the garden in between courses. The **Village Green** (Kids) (p. 148) is a busy, reasonably priced self-service vegetarian cafe with lots of healthy choices. Kids love the tofu burgers, the lasagna, and the delicious desserts, many of which are made without sugar. The hot and cold salad bar includes spaghetti and is sold by weight, so you can buy very small amounts for tiny appetites.

**Shanty** ✿ INTERNATIONAL   Located in the heart of the city's restored 19th-century restaurant district, this pub is a Jerusalem favorite—cozy, atmospheric, affordable, and serving great food. The menu includes everything from roast beef sandwiches, fresh fish, and baby back ribs to *biriyani*, goulash soup, and patai noodles. Hefty stir-fried salads filled with chunks of hot chicken or marinated livers mixed with mild herbs and spices are affordable and are meals in themselves, as is the rich sweet-potato soup and the special in-season mango soup. This is a favorite spot for wine, a salad, soup, desserts, and conversation. Shanty also offers outdoor seating in good weather and a well-stocked bar.

4 Nahalat Shiva. ✆ **02/624-3434.** Main courses NIS 25–NIS 70 ($6.25–$18/£3.10–£8.75). MC, V. Sun–Thurs 7:30pm–after midnight; Fri 11am–3pm and 9:30pm–after midnight; Sat after Shabbat–after midnight. On Yoel Salomon St., turn into the alleyway to the side of the Ceramics gallery at 11 Yoel Salomon. At the end of the alley, turn left into the courtyard. The security guard for Shanty, Mike's Place, and Tmol V'Shilshom Bookstore Café is at the end of the courtyard.

**Spaghettim** (Value) ITALIAN   Housed in a spacious room at the modern Beit Agron Journalists' Building, this restaurant offers a stylish, hearty menu of al dente spaghetti served with your choice of more than 50 sauces. The sauces are divided into three categories based on tomatoes, olive oil, or cream. Each sauce is generously filled with fresh herbs and vegetables. My favorites are *pollo zingara* (sliced breast of chicken, peppers, fresh mushrooms, garlic, hot chili, and red wine); *bianco* (peas, lemon, dill, garlic, and hot chili); the mild or peppery Alfredos; and pollo coriander, almost Indian in its exotic richness. As a first course, I strongly recommend the minty salad Panzanella—easily shareable—and a loaf of fresh-baked house bread (extra charge). For dessert, or as a meal in itself, you might want to try one of the sweet spaghettis, ranging from *arancio* (fresh orange, butter, cream, and liqueur) to chocolate or poppy seed. Imported and Israeli wines are available, and there's even whole-wheat pasta for those who want a healthy choice. There are two Spaghettims in Tel Aviv, and other branches may be opening across the country.

Inside Beit Agron, 35 Hillel St. © 02/623-5547. Main courses NIS 39–NIS 70 ($9.75–$18/£4.90–£8.75). AE, DC, MC, V. Daily noon–1am.

### Tmol Shilshom Bookstore Cafe ★ (Finds VEGETARIAN

Set in cozy 19th-century rooms lined with books, this place has an eccentric style, welcoming spirit, and one of the most interesting and well-prepared vegetarian menus in town. Among the specialties are spiced sweet-potato soup, pumpkin ravioli in herbed cream sauce, and a spicy tomato-and-egg *shakshouka* (a traditional Jerusalem recipe). There are hefty casseroles, salads, and sandwiches on house breads—everything from bagels and lox with cream cheese to an elegant fresh trout stuffed with feta cheese served in a special orange sauce. You'll find lots of wines and interesting alcoholic and nonalcoholic drinks to linger over: teas, coffees, hot chocolate with rum, and even *sahlab*, a traditional Middle Eastern drink. Delicious cakes and Ben & Jerry's ice cream make this a good dessert stop as well. The cafe is a favorite of students and travelers of all ages (in the afternoon you can sit here for hours or even bring your laptop); it's gay-friendly and at night it's even a popular first-date choice for religious Israelis. There are often evening readings or talks in Hebrew or English, plus live music. Stop by and pick up the monthly schedule of events.

5 Yoel Salomon St. © 02/623-2758. Main courses NIS 40–NIS 80 ($10–$20/£5–£10). AE, DC, MC, V. Sun–Thurs 9am–after midnight; Fri 9am–1pm; Sat after Shabbat. In rear courtyard of Yoel Salomon St.; enter from alley at 11 Yoel Saloman St. (next to Ceramics Gallery). Cafe is at far left and upstairs.

### Village Green ★ (Kids (Value VEGETARIAN

Even with two levels of dining rooms and tables spread out onto the plaza at the Jaffa Road end of Rivlin Street, it's still sometimes hard to fit everyone into this popular kosher L'Mehedrin restaurant. Portions are big, delicious, and reasonably priced. Grab a tray and proceed to the counter, where English-speaking staff will explain the changing array of freshly baked vegetable pies in whole-wheat crusts, quiches, lasagnas, buckwheat burgers, and grilled tofu served with herbs or spicy peanut sauce. You can order just a cup of cold yogurt, garlic, and cucumber soup beautifully flavored with dill, or a full meal with your choice of a personally constructed salad, steamed vegetables, brown rice (all priced by weight so you can take as much or little as you want) or hot soup, and choose from a selection of great breads and desserts (including sugar-free). Some macrobiotic foods are offered; however, microwave ovens are used. At mealtimes, the place can be a madhouse, with long lines at the buffet and checkout, but otherwise this is a great choice for a non-time-consuming meal.

Beit Yoel, corner of Jaffa Rd. and Rivlin St. © 02/625-1464. Full meal NIS 30–NIS 42 ($7.50–$11/£3.75–£5.25), priced by weight. MC, V. Sun–Thurs 9am–10pm; Fri 11:30am–3pm; closed Sat.

### Zuni Restaurant/Café/Bar FRENCH/INTERNATIONAL

Open 24/7, this stylish, friendly place with a young spirit is located in the upstairs rooms of an old stone building on the Yoel Saloman pedestrian street. It serves a wide range of light and heavy meals, or you can just stop by for elegant soup, a good coffee, a California-style wrap, or an unusual salad. It works as a spot for lunch on a rainy Saturday afternoon, or an interesting place for evening drinks and talk. Excellent brunches are served till late. Lunch (until 4pm) is 30% off the regular menu price.

15 Yoel Salomon St. © 02/625-7776. Main courses NIS 40–NIS 100 ($10–$25/£5–£13). AE, MC, V. Daily 24 hr.

## Getting Connected in Jerusalem

Jerusalem offers a wide variety of atmospheric places to get online. Charges are usually NIS 6 to NIS 10 ($1.50–$2.50/75p–£1.25) for 15 minutes. In West Jerusalem, the entire, lively downtown area from the post office on Jaffa Road, including the Ben-Yehuda–Yoel Salomon Pedestrian Mall area up to King George Street, is a Wi-Fi zone. If you've got a Wi-Fi–equipped laptop with you, just set up in one of the many cafes or restaurants with everyone else. In the Old City of Jerusalem, the best (and possibly the cheapest) place is **Abu Assab's Internet Cafe,** above the venerable Abu Assab Orange and Carrot Juice Shop, at 172 Suq Khan es Zeit St. (the main thoroughfare running from Damascus Gate south; ℂ **02/628-2486**). It offers private, air-conditioned booths, is open daily 9am to 10pm, and has discount plans and unique advantages such as fresh-squeezed orange, grapefruit, and carrot juice (the best in town) to keep you alert and healthy while surfing. You can also have your laundry done while you browse. In the Jewish Quarter, the little **Bookshelf Bookstore,** 2 Jewish Quarter Rd. (ℂ **02/627-3889**), is an interesting center of neighborhood activity, with two computers tucked in among the books. It's overseen by a very helpful owner who came to Israel from California. It's open Sunday to Thursday from 10am to 6pm and Friday from 10am to 2pm.

## JERUSALEM COURTYARD

The quaint, somewhat hidden **Jerusalem Courtyard,** filled with some of the city's best-loved restaurants, can be reached through the covered gate just east of 31 Jaffa Rd., and also from the broad covered stairs at the end of Rivlin Street. There are security guards at both entrances to the courtyard.

### Moderate

**Adom** 🎖🎖 *Finds*  FRENCH/MEDITERRANEAN    This is my favorite moderately priced restaurant in Jerusalem. Chef Daniel Uman's wonderful menu ranges from hearty to exquisite; the Jerusalem stone dining rooms are spacious and atmospheric, the service friendly, and the music carefully chosen. The dinner menu varies daily, but among starters, look for excellent fish and meat carpaccios in fine olive oils and herbs; cannelloni filled with brie, leek, walnuts in a pepper-*zataar* sauce of local seasonings; lamb and pine-nut risotto with hot salad; and rustic pâtés and soups (including a great crab bisque with scallops and shrimp; or in winter, a lavish chestnut soup). My favorite main course is a signature dish of shrimp in truffle oil and Dijon mustard, served on a bed of wild rice and tiny local beans. But also look for the T-bone lamb in olive oil and herbs, made with the most delicious lamb in Israel; fresh fish (the simple salmon filet is wonderful); seafood paellas and risottos; or the very generous, affordable and delicious house schnitzel. There's even a reasonably priced children's platter, and a humungous gourmet hamburger served with aioli, sun-dried tomato, and other extras. House breads and cheese platters are excellent—the toasted nut bread goes well with the pâté. The bar is great, and a good house wine is served by the glass at a reasonable price. After 10pm, when Adom becomes a bar and gathering point, there's a special menu of half-courses and tapas. Desserts are worthwhile.

In the Jerusalem Courtyard, entered via 31 Jaffa Rd. © **02/624-6242**. Reservations recommended. Main courses NIS 60–NIS 130 ($15–$33/£7.50–£16). AE, DC, MC, V. Sun–Fri 6:30pm–after midnight; Sat 1pm–after midnight.

### Barood Bar Restaurant ★ *Finds* CONTINENTAL/SEPHARDIC This cozy,

authentic little place has real charm and spirit. It offers an always-changing daily menu of home-style choices such as pork spareribs with a rosemary barbecue sauce, or goose breast in an oyster sauce, but the Balkan/Sephardic home-style dishes are the most interesting. Look for leek stew with meat and plums, Sephardi-style stuffed cabbage, or an oven-baked casserole of spicy meatballs with eggplant. There are also interesting appetizers such as pickled quail eggs or *pastelikos* (tiny breads) filled with meat and pine nuts, eaten with hard-boiled egg and spiced salad. Barood is a great choice for a Friday-night or Saturday-afternoon meal. There's often a party atmosphere late Friday afternoons and Saturday nights (and sometimes live music). The bar serves an amazing range of alcoholic and nonalcoholic drinks and is also a simpatico place for meetings. Despite antismoking laws, the atmosphere is still sometimes nicotine rich; in summer, nonsmokers may want to dine alfresco, in the pleasant Jerusalem Courtyard.

Jerusalem Courtyard. © **02/625-9081**. Reservations suggested. Main courses NIS 50–NIS 70 ($13–$18/ £6.25–£8.75); complete lunch specials Sun–Thurs noon–5pm from NIS 55 ($14/£6.90). AE, DC, MC, V. Mon–Sat 12:30pm–1am.

### Dagim BaChatzer FISH A very promising new kosher fish restaurant set in an

atmospheric, century-old building, Dagim BaChatzer (Fish in the Courtyard) serves a selection of drumfish, grouper, mullet, salmon, trout, bass, and St. Peter's fish (here called tilapia), all fried, grilled, or baked in a traditional stone oven (your choice). A meal begins with a meze of 10 interesting Middle Eastern salads served with fresh-from-the-stone-oven herbed focaccia. Main courses are cooked to perfection and served with earthy fried potatoes or steamed fresh vegetables. No meat is served, but nonfish eaters can order salads and pastas. There's a full wine list, and you can order house wine by the glass. The rich, dairy pastries and desserts are excellent. The evening menu is offered at a discount during lunch, and there are special fish each day according to the fishermen's catch.

In courtyard off 31 Jaffa Rd. © **02/622-2524**. Reservations suggested at night. Main courses NIS 80–NIS 100 ($20–$25/£10–£13). AE, MC, V. Sun–Thurs noon–midnight; Fri noon–1 hr. before Shabbat; Sat 1 hr. after Shabbat–midnight.

### Eldad Vesayhoo ★ *Kids* *Value* FRENCH/MEDITERRANEAN This busy,

recently-turned-kosher restaurant, with a few extra tables set outside in summer, is famous for its terrific and elegant lunch specials offered Sunday to Thursday until 5:30pm and until 3pm on Friday. It's also famous for its meats—at lunch you can get a two-course lunch special that includes the best chunk of sirloin in town, cooked as you want it, served with your choice of wonderful sauces; an excellent goulash; or flavorful lamb kabobs or chicken, all served with a choice of French sauces, rice or potato, and vegetable. The lunch choices also include pasta and fresh fish. At night (when it's not good for kids), there's a large a la carte menu with prices that triple the lunch special rates, and many special dishes not offered at lunch. Goose-filled dates; gooseliver in Calvados; and veal brains in lemon parsley sauce are among the rich samplings. For vegetarians, there are good pastas. Lunchtime service is very speedy (which kids like), so you don't have to plan for a long repast if your time is short.

Jerusalem Courtyard. ✆ **02/625-4007.** Reservations recommended for dinner. Main courses NIS 54–NIS 140 ($14–$35/£6.75–£18); fixed-price dinner from NIS 80 ($20/£10); 2-course lunch specials from NIS 50 ($13/£6.25). AE, DC, MC, V. Sun–Thurs noon–midnight; Fri noon–3pm.

**Sakura Japanese Restaurant** ⚐ JAPANESE    Designed to suggest a typical, small-town restaurant in Japan, Sakura is believed by many to be the best Japanese restaurant in Israel, with standards that outdistance anything available in trendier Tel Aviv. The menu varies according to the seasonal availability of sushi fish, which is flown in almost daily from New Zealand, the Pacific Northwest, and the North Atlantic. There are traditional first courses such as miso soup and wakame salad, and a selection of main courses that includes very fresh shrimp tempura, soba noodle dishes, salmon teriyaki, mussels in a sweet-and-sour sauce, and mixed sushi and sashimi platters. There's also a special fresh fish of the day as well as moderately priced lunch specials.

Jerusalem Courtyard. ✆ **02/623-5464.** Main dishes, sushi, and sashimi NIS 15–NIS 90 ($3.75–$23/£1.90–£11). DC, MC, V. Daily noon–midnight.

## OFF & ON SHLOMZION HAMALKA STREET

**Shlomzion HaMalka Street,** running south for 2 blocks from Jaffa Road to David Street, is lined with very stylish restaurants and bars. Since 2001, it's become the most stylish dining address in town. Restaurants here pride themselves on not having "quaint" Old Jerusalem architectural style. Late on Thursday, Friday, and Saturday nights the establishments of the street morph into a wall-to-wall party. Each bar has its own style, personality, and special food offerings—Jerusalem not being a town of heavy drinkers. Just party-hop and prowl. Look for **Sol Tapas Bar,** serving more than 70 tasty tapas each night; and **Osho,** probably the most upscale bar in Jerusalem, with an elegant menu and a vast selection of drinks. Adjacent streets are also filling up with excellent eateries. The following are some of the best dining bets.

### Expensive

**Canela** ⚐ FRENCH/CONTINENTAL    This sleek upscale restaurant is striving to become Jerusalem's foremost kosher choice for meetings, celebrations, and that special night out. There have been changes in chefs and menus (on one visit, the dishes that arrived at the table were prepared somewhat differently from the way the menu and waiter described them, but the meal was still enjoyable). The restaurant's design is quietly luxurious, with specially commissioned furniture and decorative details. Visually, each dish is beautifully presented. A changing menu is filled with classic dishes, but you'll always find one or two playful choices, such as seared tuna in spicy caramel or roasted eggplant with green *techina* and walnuts. Main-course meat dishes, such as a country ragout of slow-cooked lamb, eggplant, and chickpeas, or grilled sirloin with a mustard-brandy demi glace, are better bets than the fish selections. A special pastry chef and kitchen turns out excellent desserts. There's a graceful, well-stocked bar. Live music plays on Monday nights starting at 10pm. Late in the evening, when the restaurant morphs into a bar/bistro, smaller portions of the menu's highlights can be ordered at NIS 50 ($13/£6.25) a plate. Two-course luncheon specials start at NIS 86 ($22/£11). Service is careful. Valet parking is a unique touch.

8 Shlomzion HaMalka St. ✆ **02/622-2293.** Reservations necessary. Main courses NIS 90–NIS 180 ($23–$45/£11–£23). AE, DC, MC, V. Sun–Thurs noon–4pm and 6pm–midnight (last order at 11pm); Fri 11am–3pm; Sat after Shabbat–midnight.

**Katy's** FRENCH    For decades a favorite with Jerusalemites for an intimate, special night out, this is the traditional French restaurant of Katy Ohana, who sometimes draws on North African and local traditions to create her culinary style. The menu can change daily. The eggplant and goat cheese with basil, and mushrooms, salmon, and seafood with caviar sauce are among Ohana's well-known appetizers. Duckling with black currant sauce and her wonderful gooseliver are the acknowledged main-course specialties. Ohana's wonderful, buttery brioches are a local legend. Servings are usually hefty. Lately, there have been all kinds of fixed-price specials that are far lower than the prices quoted below.

2 Ha-Soreg St. ℭ 02/623-1793. Reservations recommended. Main courses NIS 95–NIS 150 ($24–$38/£12–£19); complete fixed-price meal NIS 180 ($45/£23). Add 15% service. AE, DC, MC, V. Daily 12:30–4:30pm and 6:30pm–midnight.

## Moderate

**Chakra** ★★ *Finds* ECLECTIC/ASIAN FUSION   An eccentric, informal place that started the Shlomzion HaMalka Street revolution (it was the first on the block—the other restaurants flocked in to share Chakra's success), Chakra offers some of the most interesting meals in town at any price. This is the personal creation of chef-owner Ilan Garousi, who has filled his menu with his own interpretations of seasonings and ideas he's picked up from all over the world. Ilan's enthusiasm and energy are boundless: To his standard menu, he adds about 12 nightly main-course selections and all kinds of dynamite appetizers, depending on what's fresh and available in the market. Come with friends so you can sample and share. You might find a Bokaharian soup made with chickpeas, lamb-meat dumplings, and sweet-and-sour dried berries; shrimps on grilled figs; or lighter-than-air fish kabobs in coriander. Or you could find tempura shrimp or chicken filled with rice and minced lamb spiced with cumin. Spicy, delicious European and central Asian meat stews abound. Desserts are inventive and worth trying. The menu is divided into "Land" and "Sea," rather than into first and main courses, and some listings are appetizers or tapas-style dishes. The waiters will translate. The crowd is locals in-the-know and a smattering of tourists from the nearby King David and David Citadel hotels. Prices are very fair, and most people come away dazzled. Tasting medleys of small dishes can be arranged. The noise level on weekends and busy nights is a problem for some.

18 Shlomzion HaMalka St. ℭ 02/625-2733. Reservations helpful. Main courses NIS 55–NIS 110 ($14–$28/£7–£14). AE, MC, V. Daily 7–11pm. No sign—as you go downhill on Shlomzion HaMalka, it's the last place on the right before you hit King David St.

**Gabriel** ★ FRENCH/CONTINENTAL   A sophisticated kosher restaurant that doesn't play games of glitz and pretentiousness, Gabriel is a great place for a hefty but very stylish meal. During the dinner hour, it's small and intimate; later it becomes more of a tapas bar and meeting place. You'll find standard and very good French-style first courses, and a fresh fish selection among the main course choices, but Gabriel's strong point is meat, from a thick filet steak served in Marsala and ginger sauce to a kosher chicken *cordon bleu* filled with smoked goose breast and chicken liver, served in a Dijon mustard sauce. All main courses come with a selection of side dishes; presentation is elegant, but the emphasis is also on a tasty, filling meal. Lighter luncheon fixed-price menus (house bread, plus first and main course) start at NIS 70 ($18/£8.75). Golan wines are served by the glass or decanter, and desserts vary from day to day.

7 Ben Shetah St. ℭ 02/624-6444. Reservations suggested. Main courses NIS 70–NIS 110 ($18–$28/£8.75–£14). AE, DC, MC, V. Sun–Thurs noon–5pm and 7pm–midnight; Fri noon–3pm; Sat after Shabbat–after midnight.

## Coffee & People-Watching

Jerusalem cafe life is thriving. The Ben-Yehuda Mall, the adjacent and more picturesque Yoel Salomon Mall, and Jaffa Road across from Zion Square are filled with cafes that are great for people-watching. You can order giant, eminently shareable salads as well as quiches, pasta dishes, soups, sandwiches, rich desserts, pastry, and of course, coffee. If you just want coffee, make sure there are no minimum charges. **Cafe Rimmon,** at the lower end of Ben-Yehuda Mall, is an ideal spot for watching Jerusalem life pass by.

A great cup of coffee, probably the best in town, can be found 2 blocks south of Ben-Yehuda Mall, at **Aroma,** on the corner of Hillel Street and Rabbi Akiva Street. It's a busy counter with a few tables, but it's a Jerusalem institution, serving good, inexpensive sandwiches as well. It's open 24/7.

**Jaffa Road,** across from Zion Square and eastward to Helene Ha Malka Street, has recently developed into Jerusalem's new "coffee row." **Aroma** has set up a second branch here with tables on the sidewalk (a third **Aroma** is at 34 Emek Refaim St., in the picturesque German Colony). A block to the east, **Hillel Expresso Café** and the **Coffee Bean,** an import from California, face off on opposing corners of Helene Ha Malka Street, both with lots of sidewalk and inside tables, and excellent salads, sandwiches, quiches, and desserts. They're all in Jerusalem's free Wi-Fi access zone and dotted with laptop users. **Tmol Shilshom Bookstore Cafe,** 5 Yoel Salomon Mall (p. 148), is an atmospheric retreat, its walls lined with books, where patrons read and browse, write letters, log on to the Internet, or just linger over coffee, soup, salad, wine, or cake.

**Noya** ★★ *(Finds* CONTINENTAL    Opened just at press time, this showcase for the legendary Chef Ginadi is the best gourmet choice for meat (especially lamb) in Jerusalem; it also offers an excellent menu of fish. Ginadi's famed focaccia, served with smoked eggplant puree, is divine. Great luncheon specials available until 6pm. Kosher lemehedrin.

3 Shlomzion Hamalka St. ⓒ 06/625-7311. Main courses NIS 90–NIS 150 ($23–$43/£12–£22). AE, DC, MC, V. Sun–Thurs noon–midnight; Friday 11am–1:30pm; Sat after Shabbat–midnight.

**Sea Dolphin (Dolphin Yam)** SEAFOOD    It used to be hard to find good fish in a Jerusalem restaurant. Now, this moderately priced, nonkosher establishment (owned by a family that's been bringing fresh fish from the coast up to Jerusalem for decades) serves a wide range of seafood as well as very fresh grilled or fried fish. It's stylish but very informal, and always busy. Each main course comes with a large, refillable meze of 10 salads and appetizers, but there are also good seafood soups and fresh fish and seafood appetizers. You have your choice of many simple and complex sauces with main courses, but if you order fish, I'd ask for the sauce on the side and use just enough so that the freshness of the fish is not overwhelmed. Remember to ask for local fish that is sure to be fresh. There are lunch specials and discounts (and a smattering of meat and veggie choices for those who don't eat things from the sea).

9 Ben Shitah St. ⓒ **02/623-2272.** Reservations helpful. Main courses NIS 60–NIS 110 ($15–$28/£7.50–£14); lunch (Sun–Fri noon–5pm) NIS 50–NIS 70 ($13–$18/£6.25–£9). AE, DC, MC, V. Daily noon–midnight.

**Terra Restaurant & Bar** ★★ MEDITERRANEAN    Set in intimate rooms with stone walls and arches, this little hideaway turns out elegant, gracefully inventive dishes at prices that are not out of sight. There are all kinds of haute cuisine meat and seafood tapas and unique appetizers, such as stir-fried chicken livers with chestnuts and brandy. There's fish and pasta among the main courses, but the seafood and meat dishes are the more interesting choices. My favorites are shrimp baked in a terra cotta vessel with herbed saffron virgin olive oil, and calamari stuffed with seafood and feta cheese in a wine and garlic sauce. The menu constantly changes, but look for mussels steamed in champagne, shallots, and herbs, and rib-eye steak in smoked whiskey sauce. There are wonderful sorbets and pies on the dessert list, and a carefully composed bar and wine list. Business lunch specials are offered from noon to 5pm.

3 Ben Shitah St. ℂ 02/632-5001. Reservations useful. Main courses NIS 70–NIS 110 ($18–$28/£9–£14); lunch specials vary daily. AE, DC, MC, V. Daily noon–5pm and 7pm–midnight.

### Inexpensive

**Marakiyah** Ⓥalue SOUP    This little "souperia" looks like an outpost in Berkeley, Cambridge, or New York's East Village—a mix of assorted old tables, chairs and sofas, candlelight, mellow background music, and garage and attic-sale decor. *Marak* means "soup" in Hebrew, and the menu consists of very good vegetarian soups (a different selection every night), served with bread and pesto. Among the standards are sweet potato; lentil with wine; spicy Yemenite tomato, onion, and cheese; and tomato with anise. Great *shakshuka,* a spicy egg-and-tomato dish, rounds out the hot menu. There's coffee, tea, pies, wine, and beer by the half-liter, and lots of leisurely conversation. There's also a rear patio, and live jazz Monday and Wednesday nights after 10pm when the Marakiyah gets really busy, with a mixed, but university-oriented, clientele.

4 Koresh St. (behind the Jaffa Rd. Central Post Office). ℂ 02/625-7797. Soup and bread NIS 25 ($6.25/£3.10); half-liter of wine NIS 19 ($4.75/£2.40). Cash only. Sun–Thurs 7pm–3am; Sat after Shabbat–3am.

## WEST OF KING GEORGE V AVENUE
### Expensive

**Arcadia** ★★★ FRENCH/MEDITERRANEAN    Acknowledged as the finest restaurant in Jerusalem, this little hideaway (reached through an offbeat little 19th-c. pedestrian lane) has understated, minimalist decor, a dining garden, and top reviews from Israeli and foreign food writers. Chef Ezra Kedem doesn't perform flashy inventive tricks with food; instead, quality, skill, and natural grace mark his dishes. The content of the French/Mediterranean menu constantly changes and is done with a light touch that matches the decor. Among the appetizers, you may find a dish of oven-roasted shrimp with a citrus sauce and basil flowers; a saffron-scented seafood soup; or herbed lamb ravioli on beet-root salad. For main courses, there's almost always a slow-cooked, rustic dish of baby lamb prepared in different ways; prime rib for two; something different and interesting, such as pan-sautéed duck livers on a bed of warm lentil salad; and an array of simple, carefully prepared fresh fish and seafood (the sea bass in wild sage butter is wonderful). The wine list is especially good, drawing on Israeli boutique wineries, as well as imports. Fixed-price two-course luncheons begin at NIS 90 ($23/£11), and there is a fixed-price, two-course dinner for NIS 160 ($40/£20) that includes service (but not Arcadia's delicious house bread). With either of these you'll be tempted to add a very worthwhile wine, a dessert, or an upgrade on a first or second course. In my experience, the serving staff has not been strong in explaining details of menu choices, and pigeons can make dining under the trees in the garden fraught with danger. But with its blend of quality and gentle magic, Arcadia is unequaled, especially at night.

10 Agrippas St. ✆ 02/624-9138. Reservations recommended. Fixed-price dinner NIS 160–NIS 240 ($40–$60/ £20–£30). AE, MC, V. Mon–Fri 12:30–3pm and 7–10:30pm; Sat 1–3pm and 7–10:30pm. Closed Sun. In the lane between 63 Jaffa Rd. and 10 Agrippas St., 2 blocks west of King George St.

## Moderate

**Kohinoor** ★★ KOSHER INDIAN    With its decorative Southeast Asian artifacts and attentive service, this kosher branch of Tel Aviv's famous Tandoori Restaurant creates a graceful atmosphere of Anglo-Indian elegance. The sumptuous and affordable luncheon buffet is a chance for kosher travelers to become acquainted with one of the world's great cuisines. At dinner, you might want to start your meal with *zafrani lassi,* a refreshing, chilled "yogurt" drink. The boneless tandoori chicken dishes are succulent and flavorful. I was amazed by the fine *nawabi korma,* a boneless chicken prepared in lightly creamed and seasoned saffron sauce based on soy instead of milk in order to conform to kashrut regulations. There are examples of the cuisines of many regions here—a wonderful array of South Indian dishes with coconut milk sauces has just been added to the menu. Everything is of very high quality, but served with very moderate spicing: If you want fiery traditional Indian seasoning, just let the staff know. The menu is marvelous at explaining dishes, and contains a virtual cookbook of special recipes. Very much worth the trip over to the Crowne Plaza Hotel.

In the Crowne Plaza Hotel. ✆ 02/658-8867. Reservations recommended. Main courses NIS 40–NIS 90 ($10–$23/ £5–£11); lunch buffet NIS 60 ($15/£7.50). AE, DC, MC, V. Sun–Thurs noon–4pm and 6pm–midnight; Fri noon–4pm; Sat after Shabbat–midnight. Bus: 18, 20, or any bus to Central Bus Station.

## AGRIPPAS STREET & MAHANE YEHUDA

Walk a few blocks up Agrippas Street, and you'll find yourself surrounded by no-frills restaurants and hole-in-the-wall places serving generous portions of grilled meats, *shashlik* (chunks of meat on a skewer), and kabobs (which in Israel consist of ground meat on a skewer).

## Inexpensive

**Hashipudia** MIDDLE EASTERN    *Shipudia* means "skewer," and this restaurant specializes in skewers of beef or lamb, chicken hearts and livers, chicken or goose breast, and that *pièce de résistance* of skewered meats: gooseliver. Most of the skewers are around NIS 40 ($10/£5) and come with your choice of two side dishes. You can put together the combination of your choice, and as an added treat, Hashipudia makes wonderful fresh Iraqi pita bread on the spot each evening in a traditional oven. A lunch special of salad or soup, main course, baklava, and tea or coffee is offered for NIS 60 ($15/£7.50). A full range of economically priced soups, and stuffed vegetables as well as more expensive steaks, chops, and fish makes this one of the best restaurant choices in the Agrippas Street neighborhood. *Tip:* Don't confuse this with Shipudei HaGefen, on Agrippas Street.

6 Ha-Shikma St. ✆ 02/625-4036. Main courses NIS 28–NIS 80 ($7–$20/£3.50–£10). AE, DC, MC, V. Sun–Thurs noon–midnight. Head west on Agrippas St. Ha-Shikma St. is a right turn after the market.

**Sami's** MIDDLE EASTERN    Sami's is the rival of longtime mixed grill champion, Sima's, its across-the-street neighbor (see below). There are partisans on both sides as far as taste goes. Sami's, with its polished marble floors and walls and adequate seating, has certainly elevated *me'orav Yerushalmi* (Jerusalem mixed grill) to a new standard of elegance. You may even be allowed to order a hefty small-size mixed-grill sandwich and eat it at a table, although the rule of Agrippas Street is that unless you order a meal, you don't get a plate (your sandwich comes in a paper bag). Steaks, kabobs, schnitzels, and salads are all excellent. Prices include pita, olives, and pickled vegetables.

## Street Meals

**Falafel &** *Shwarma*   My favorite falafel is on the corner of Agrippas Street and the wide uncovered pedestrian street of the Machane Yehuda market (on your right as you walk up Agrippas St. from King George: It's the first broad market street past the covered market area). Here you'll find a **Yemenite falafel counter** serving well-spiced falafel fritters and all kinds of salads, pickled vegetables, sauces, and condiments. For a bit extra, you can ask for your falafel to be wrapped inside an enormous Iraqi pita instead of a plain pocket pita, which makes for a very filling meal. Best of all, you can carry your sandwich across Agrippas Street and through one of the entrance portals to the old Nahalot neighborhood, where you'll find a small playground with benches. There, under the scrutiny of the local cats, you can sit down and enjoy your meal (bring your own napkins). This park is also a good place to bring a takeout mixed-grill sandwich from **Sima's** or **Sami's** farther down Agrippas Street. I always like to slice a few little plum or cherry tomatoes from the market into my takeout sandwiches.

At the corner of Agrippas and King George streets, you'll find a large and very busy **falafel and** *shwarma* **place** with mountains of chopped salads. Here you'll have to eat standing on the sidewalk like a normal Israeli, but without the local skill of not dripping falafel sauce all over yourself and not having half your sandwich land in the gutter. The falafels are average, but the spot is convenient, open until 10pm or later from Sunday to Thursday (until 2pm Fri), and the turnover is fast, which ensures freshness. **Moshiko's,** at the lower end of the Ben-Yehuda Mall, does Jerusalem's best *shwarma* sandwiches. Quality is tops, portions excellent, and if you can nail down one of Moshiko's outdoor tables, you can people-watch and not lose half your sandwich on the ground.

On the north side of Hanevi'im Street, opposite its intersection with Havatzelet Street, is a hole-in-the wall place selling what many Jerusalemites consider the **best falafel** in town. See if you agree. If you're willing to walk a few blocks west of King George Street to **Falafel Bar,** at 70 Jaffa Rd., you'll find the only falafel stand in Jerusalem run by a new American immigrant (and possibly the only one run by a woman). Yehudit Cohen taught creative writing in America, and her falafel and *shakshouka* (a spiced egg dish) are terrific.

The **Gate Cafe,** just inside the Damascus Gate, on an upstairs covered terrace on the left, serves fabulous extra-spicy **hand-built** *shwarma,* a kind of *shwarma* not made on a spit. It's different, authentic, and memorable.

**Bagels   Bagel Corner,** 41 Jaffa Rd. (© 02/624-4115), right at Zion Square, sells a variety of freshly made bagels ranging from onion and garlic to wholewheat and cheese for approximately NIS 4 ($1/50p) each. They're more breadlike than traditional American bagels, but they're tasty. They also sell bagel sandwiches made with a wide variety of cream cheeses, lox, and other fillings. It's open Sunday to Thursday, 24 hours; on Friday until 2pm; and on Saturday after Shabbat. In the Jewish Quarter of the Old City, you can pick up your bagels at a similar shop beside the Seven Arches, near the Burnt House Museum.

*Burekas*  The block of shops on Hanevi'im Street opposite Havatzelet Street includes a bakery with a sidewalk window counter where you can order fresh-from-the-oven potato, spinach, or cheese *burekas,* as well as miniature cheese or fruit Danish-style pastries. You can find *burekas* throughout the city, but they're always more of a treat when fresh. The Machane Yehuda market is another good place for freshly baked *burekas.* The **English Bakery,** on Jaffa Road opposite Zion Square, has quality *burekas* and very nice sweet pastries and cookies.

**Stuffed Breads   Samboosak Bakery/Café,** Jaffa Road next to the Coffee Bean on the corner of Helene HaMalka Street, is filled with fresh-from-the-oven Middle Eastern breads stuffed with savory cheeses and herbed vegetables, as well as hearty little Middle Eastern pizzas, sandwiches, muffins, and cookies. Great for a cheap, on-the-run takeout meal.

**Sabbiyah**  This traditional (and tasty) Iraqi-Jewish sandwich is a big local favorite. The best place to pick one up is the **Sabbiyah,** a stand at 24 Ben-Yehuda St., on the right side as you walk uphill on the first block past the pedestrian zone. Owner Aviad will tuck eggplant, cooked egg, spicy mango, green pepper, fresh herbs, and other things into his mother's fabulous fluffy "cloud" pita (whole-wheat or white). It all costs under NIS 16 ($4/£2).

**Fresh Roasted Nuts   Yaavetz Street,** a small pedestrian passageway running between Jaffa Road (half a block east of King George St.) and the Ben Hillel Street section of Ben-Yehuda Mall, has two shops selling absolutely the best fresh-roasted nuts in town. My favorite is the shop at the far end of the street from Jaffa Road, just at the foot of the steps leading up to the Ben-Yehuda Mall. Prices on the signs are usually quoted for 1 kilo; divide by 10, and you'll have the price for 100 grams, which is a reasonable-size bag for one person to carry around for fortification on a day's sightseeing.

**Take-Home Meals   Dishes,** a storefront with no street number on Jaffa Road across from Safra Square, is a little place with hot counters laden with fresh-off-the-stove pots of homemade Iraqi *kubbe,* soups, couscous, wonderful meat, chicken and fish patties, stuffed vegetables, and many other foods from Middle Eastern Jewish cuisines. Point to what looks interesting, put together a meal, and take it back to your hotel room. Everything is delicious and authentic; a very full meal is usually NIS 32 to NIS 50 ($8–$13/£4–£6.25).

**Ice Cream   Dr Lek,** at the end of Yoel Salomon near Hillel Street, is a local chain offering exotic flavors; **Dream and Cream,** Lunz Street, in the Ben-Yehuda Mall, is international and serves very rich ice cream; and at the corner of Lunz and Ben-Yehuda streets you'll find a popular place (no name, but you won't be able to miss it) that offers a choice of 25 kinds of fruits, nuts, and chocolates that they'll whip up into a fresh frozen yogurt for you on the spot.

**Belgian Waffles   Babette's** ✸, at Shammai Street near Yoel Saloman Street, is a Jerusalem legend. The place is a closet, and the waffles are takeout only, with many possible toppings. Lines form outside the door. It's open evenings only—look for a window with purple shutters.

80 Agrippas St. ℂ **02/625-0985.** Main courses NIS 40–NIS 70 ($10–$18/£5–£8.75). AE, DC, MC, V. Sun–Thurs 11am–midnight; Fri 11am–3pm; Sat after Shabbat–midnight.

**Sima's** ✿ MIDDLE EASTERN    Sima's is my favorite place on the street, and a local legend for its wonderfully seasoned Jerusalem Mixed Grill, which comes with chips (french fries), salad, bread, and condiments if you order it as a platter. I like the mixed grill better in its less-expansive pita sandwich form. Sima's is often mobbed, so a takeout mixed-grill pita sandwich could be a good bet. You must order a platter meal rather than a sandwich in order to qualify for table service at busy times. Best not to think about which iron, vitamin B and cholesterol-rich organs may be lurking in the mixed grill (most of which is chicken and lamb). Sima's fame has led to a branch opening in trendy Tel Aviv. *Tip:* I like to slice a small, fresh market tomato into my mixed grill sandwich.

82 Agrippas St. No phone. Main courses NIS 40–NIS 70 ($10–$18/£5–£8.75). Cash only. Sun–Thurs 9am–11pm; Fri 9am–1pm; Sat after Shabbat–midnight.

## NEAR THE YMCA & KING DAVID HOTEL
### Expensive
**Chef's Special Night at the David Citadel Hotel** ✿✿ *Finds* FRENCH/ MEDITERRANEAN    Thursday night is Chef Eric Attias's special night at the spacious, quietly luxurious dining room of the David Citadel Hotel. At this once-a-week pleasure, Eric Attias (who before 2001 directed the kitchen at the David Citadel's Le Divellec Restaurant, the most spectacular and lavish kosher restaurant I've ever encountered in Israel) offers a dinner buffet that includes a large, exquisite Mediterranean antipasti table (which would be a fine meal in itself) plus your choice of a first course, main course, dessert, and coffee or tea (served with assorted liquored truffles). Though only a small glimpse of what his restaurant was like, this is one of the best kosher choices in Jerusalem for a very special meal, and an excellent choice for anyone who loves fine dining. The menu changes seasonally. You might start with a rustic soup of smoked duck and bean. Then go on to a delicate *tagine* of lamb, slow cooked (in classic Moroccan style) with dried fruits served on baked barley and buckwheat; or Attias's special roasted shoulder of veal filled with dried fruits served on wild saffron rice. The roasted breast of chicken is heavenly, filled with pistachios and pine nuts, served on Moroccan tanzia. There are always an interesting fish creation and a filet of beef dish served with an elegant twist. On other nights, the hotel's dining room serves lively theme-night buffets, but the Chef's Special Night is the jewel in the crown, and an amazing deal.

In the David Citadel Hotel, 7 King David St. ℂ **02/621-1111** daytime, or 621-2020 evening. Reservations necessary. Fixed-price dinner NIS 140 ($35/£18). Add 15.5% VAT. AE, DC, MC, V. Thurs 7–10:30pm.

**1868** FRENCH    Opened in 2004, this luxury kosher restaurant, seemingly aimed at tourists from the deluxe King David and David Citadel hotels across the street, has gone through a number of staff and chef changes. It's getting a lot of PR and strives to be known as the best gourmet kosher restaurant in the world (with commensurate prices). I, however, find 1868 to be somewhat uneven, as do friends and Frommer's readers. There's an ambitious French menu dotted with elegant starters, and main courses of fish, poultry, and hefty steaks (the steaks tend to get cooked more well-done than many customers request). The food is good, but not more exceptional than at other top-class kosher restaurants elsewhere in the city that are less pricey. There's an impression of ambience and dignity in the 19th-century Jerusalem stone dining rooms, which is an important component of a special dinner, but on closer look, many elements of the decor are rather tacky and faux elegant. The wine list, too, is good, but overpriced. There is a nine-course tasting menu that allows you to sample the rich, complex dishes of the kitchen, including interesting desserts; the price is approximately NIS 480 ($120/£60) per person including wine.

10 King David St. ℂ **02/622-2312.** Main courses NIS 110–NIS 170 ($25–$43/£13–£21). AE, DC, MC, V. Sun–Thurs 5:30–11:30pm; Sat after Shabbat.

**Moderate**
**International Restaurant at the YMCA** ✸ CONTINENTAL   The dining terrace at this landmark has been a favorite Jerusalem meeting place for decades, and the dining room is decorated in an Islamic Art Deco style of the British Mandate era, with an Ottoman-Turkish fireplace. The food is pleasant, but not exceptional, although at press time, with the end of the long tourism slump, the restaurant was reinvigorating itself with a fine Saturday luncheon buffet in winter, and a barbecue on Saturday afternoons in summer. The menu starts with brunches, coffee, and cakes; it goes on to include salads and quiches, and vegetable, meat, and shrimp pies. More ambitious and pricier fish and steak courses top the selections. There is also a complete wine list. The "Y" is open every day and it is very central, making it convenient as well as atmospheric.

26 King David St. ℂ **02/623-1154.** Reservations recommended evenings. Main courses (which include side dishes) NIS 70–NIS 110 ($18–$28/£8.75–£14). AE, DC, MC, V. Daily 8am–midnight.

**Te'enim Vegetarian Cuisine** ✸ *Finds* VEGETARIAN   Owner Patrick Melki, who comes from the south of France, has designed the menu of this vegetarian restaurant with real style. In addition to the standard fare, he has added an array of special meals from different parts of the world. The numerous salads range from Mediterranean classics to Chinese and Indian. Tofu dishes are house specialties. The restaurant, tucked away on a road that curves behind the King David Hotel, offers vistas of the walls of the Old City. Desserts, including fruit pies and carrot cake, are homemade, and each choice is just a bit original.

In the Zionist Confederation House, 12 Emile Botta St. ℂ **02/624-0090.** Main courses NIS 45–NIS 90 ($11–$23/£5.60–£11). AE, DC, MC, V. Sun–Thurs noon–10pm. From King David St., follow Emil Botta St. past parking lot. Look for sign on right to Zionist Confederation House.

## SOUTH JERUSALEM
### GERMAN COLONY & BAKA
**Moderate**
**1868 Café** ✸ KOSHER DAIRY/FISH   Set in a charming old stone bungalow in the leafy, gentrified neighborhood of Baka, this is an excellent, somewhat more affordable affiliate of the exclusive 1868 meat restaurant. You come here to treat yourself to lavish textures and tastes. The cafe serves scrumptious breakfasts until noon and wonderful pastries and both light and major meals throughout the day: salads, pastas, quiches, and fish in carefully prepared sauces. Portions are not large, but everything is gourmet, or close to it.

34 Bethlehem Rd. ℂ **02/672-5366.** Reservations necessary for dinner. Main courses NIS 50–NIS 90 ($13–$23/£6.25–£11). AE, DC, MC, V. Sun–Thurs 7am–midnight; Fri 7am–1 hr. before Shabbat; Sat 1 hr. after Shabbat–midnight.

**Joy Grill & Beer Restaurant** ✸ GRILL   This attractive, busy place has a young, friendly spirit. It serves a gigantic menu of stylishly prepared meats, although you can find a vegetarian stir-fried noodle dish tucked into the menu. There are daily specials written on a blackboard (ask your waiter to fill you in), such as an excellent, mildly exotic filet mignon marinated in red wine and coconut milk, but you'll also find a broad selection of more standard beef, lamb, and poultry dishes. Joy's offerings range from flavorful lamb burgers (best not to order well-done, or even medium, as they tend to be dry) and a variety of chicken wings, to duck in passion-fruit gravy and filet mignon in tamarind sauce and garlic confit. An excellent side salad comes with the Joyburger, and the delicious herbed french fries and garlic sweet potatoes are worthwhile side dishes. Fruit sorbets are the dessert of choice. Joy Grill prides itself on its 20 kinds of beers.

24 Emek Refaim St. ⓒ 02/563-0033. Reservations usually necessary. Main courses NIS 45–NIS 110 ($11–$28/£5.60–£14). AE, DC, MC, V. Sun–Thurs noon–midnight; Fri noon–3pm; Sat after Shabbat.

### Inexpensive

**Caffit** CAFE    Thanks to its busy garden terrace, this has long been the main watering hole for the gentrified German Colony. The large salads, served with a basket of rolls and herb butter, are popular. Pastas, crepes, bagels and lox, vegetable pies, focaccia, and sweet-potato pancakes (with sour cream) round out the lighter menu. Main courses of pan-fried sea bream or Saint Peter's fish are new attractions. People often come here just to sit and talk over a piece of cake, crepes, or ice cream while sipping a glass of wine or other alcoholic beverage.

35 Emek Refaim St. ⓒ 02/563-5284. Main courses NIS 40–NIS 90 ($10–$23/£5–£11). DC, MC, V. Sun–Thurs 7am–1am; Fri 7am–2pm; Sat after Shabbat. Bus: 4, 14, or 18.

**Coffee Mill** COFFEE    One of the many little neighborhood places that make the German Colony special, the Coffee Mill's walls are lined with 70 kinds of beans and tons of teas. They'll prepare a cup of Guatemalan, Ethiopian, Sumatran, mint chocolate, almond, or butterscotch coffee for you, as well as exotic teas. Sandwiches are rather plain; the simple, homemade cakes and pies are quite tasty.

Emek Refaim St. ⓒ 02/672-5491. Coffees and teas NIS 16–NIS 20 ($4–$5/£2–£2.50); sandwiches NIS 22–NIS 26 ($5.50–$6.50/£2.75–£3.25). AE, MC, V. Sun–Thurs 7:30am–8pm (until 10pm in summer); Fri 7:30am–3pm. Bus: 4, 14, or 18.

**Marvad Haksamim (Magic Carpet)** *Value* EUROPEAN/ISRAELI    It's hard to get a lunch or dinner table at this bustling no-frills place, known for heaping plates of fresh, home-style food. Turnover is fast, however, and you'll be rewarded for waiting. Your meal comes with Yemenite tomato purée and a large freshly baked loaf of flat, flaky Yemenite salouf bread (a very small extra charge and very worthwhile). Main-course offerings include big portions of goulash, schnitzel, chicken, brisket, or grilled meats served with your choice of potatoes, rice, pasta, vegetables, or salad. You probably won't need a first course to fill up, but in case you want a light meal, you can have a plate of five kinds of house salads or stuffed vegetables. There are also rich Yemenite calf's foot, or pumpkin, potato, and meat soups as well as Kurdish-style *koubeh* soups and European blintzes (including liver blintzes) that make the menu a bit exotic. Service is attentive and speedy. This is an extremely good value.

The downtown branch's new location is in the Lev Yerushalayim Suite Hotel (p. 124), 2nd floor in the plaza, behind King George Street.

42 Emek Refaim St. ⓒ 02/567-0007. Main courses NIS 42–NIS 80 ($11–$20/£5.25–£10). AE, MC, V. Sun–Thurs 10am–10pm; Fri 10am–3pm.

**Yo-ja Asian Bar-Restaurant** CHINESE    This glatt kosher Asian-style restaurant specializes in noodle and dim sum dishes, although it offers meat, poultry, and vegetarian dishes as well. There is an open kitchen, so you can watch the Chinese cooks at work, and a dining terrace in a rear garden. Always delicious, Yo-ja's noodles are a chewy, earthy, in-house interpretation of Asian noodles, served in Thai, curried, Szechuan, and other styles. The doughy dim sum are tasty, as are the soups. You'll also find Peking duck (order in advance) and Szechuan rib-eye steak. The kitchen will do authentically fiery Szechuan and Hunan spicing on request.

25 Emek Refaim St. ⓒ 02/561-1344. Main courses NIS 45–NIS 90 ($11–$23/£5.60–£11). AE, DC, MC, V. Sun–Thurs noon–11pm; Fri noon–3pm; Sat after Shabbat.

## HEBRON ROAD

The magnificent hillside overlooking the Old City has developed a number of lively restaurants and cafes. The beautiful stone Haas Promenade, or Tayelet, which winds along the hillside comes with its own cafeteria and an elegant restaurant, as well as out-of-the-way spots on the grass where you can bring your own picnic. Just before twilight is an especially nice time to come, when the Old City and the Judean Hills sink into a powdery mysteriousness. To get to this neighborhood, take bus no. 5, 6, 7, 8, 21, or 48 to the railroad station, or bus no. 4, 14, or 18 and ask for the stop nearest the Cinémathèque.

### Moderate

**Limonim** ⊕ CONTEMPORARY    Located on the upper floor of an old stone *caravanserai* (a caravan inn) from Ottoman times, this kosher restaurant serves one of the most interesting menus in town. You might want to start off with a house medley of hot and cold appetizers. Everything among the wide-ranging, inventive menu choices has its own special twist: The Israeli salad is laced with citrus fruit and topped with a pomegranate dressing; meat patties and leek/spinach patties are baked in sauces of dried fruit and cinnamon; veal chops are grilled in vanilla oil; and chicken wings are prepared in honey or with spicy mango sauce. There are many stir-fried vegetarian and meat dishes, as well as fish dishes, and hot and cold salads with unusual house dressings (*Limonim* means "lemons," and the restaurant is especially proud of its dried lemon sauces). Portions are large and there are a few daily specials worth asking about. The sorbets are a good dessert option and there's a good selection of Israeli wines. Limonim can be a bit uneven, and its dishes sometimes too inventive for some tastes, but most visitors will be very happy here.

In the Jerusalem Khan (opposite the Old Train Station), Remez St. ⓒ 02/671-9502. Main courses NIS 48–NIS 120 ($12–$30/£6–£15). AE, DC, MC, V. Sun–Thurs noon–midnight; Sat after Shabbat–midnight.

### Inexpensive

**Levan at the Cinémathèque** ⊕ ITALIAN/MEDITERRANEAN    With dazzling views of the Old City walls, Mount Zion, and the ancient City of David, the terrace of this restaurant has been an absolute must for a meal or coffee and dessert, from late April until November (and whenever the weather is warm enough in winter). Unfortunately, during recent renovations the terrace was enclosed with dark glass that takes away from the view, and a horizontal, eye-level metal strip now bisects the panorama. Still, the darkened vista is out there and maybe the Cinémathèque will someday undo the damage. The menu here lets the freshest vegetables, finest herbs, and wonderful breads and cheeses speak for themselves. You can feast on a country salad and an order of freshly baked house bread (served with fresh herbs and olive oil, and highly recommended); or try the soups, homemade pastas, and excellent country-style sandwiches. There's a full bar with a good array of wines.

Hebron Rd. ⓒ 02/673-7393. Reservations recommended (essential for terrace seating). Main courses NIS 45–NIS 90 ($11–$23/£5.60–£11). AE, DC, MC, V. Daily 10am–after midnight.

## BORDER OF EAST & WEST JERUSALEM

Shimon Hazadik Street, a quiet, once-residential street of stone bungalows running just off Hwy. 1, is becoming a new restaurant row. It's easily accessible to both West and East Jerusalemites, being just a few doors east of Hwy. 1, the unofficial dividing line between the two halves of Jerusalem.

## Moderate

**Al Wad/Blue Dolphin** ✦ LEBANESE    There are two restaurants in one here: Al Wad, which offers very good Arabic-style food, and the Blue Dolphin, which specializes in very fresh fish and seafood. For seafood, the management asks you to call a day ahead and discuss the menu so they can order in the freshest possible items. Go for the local fish: baby sea bass; lebrak or denise from the Red Sea; or Saint Peter's fish from the Sea of Galilee (avoid the imported salmon steak). Among the appetizers, the mixed seafood platter for two (NIS 130/$33/£16) is a meal in itself, highlighted by delicate Jaffa crabs and fresh shrimp in a dill cream sauce. Salads are large, laced with mint and seasonal touches such as pomegranate seeds; they're generous enough to split. Main dishes come with herbed vegetables and mashed potatoes. Traditional Lebanese dishes from the Al Wad side of the kitchen can also be ordered. The place is charming, with a garden terrace and an indoor section of rough Jerusalem stone, and arched doorways and windows. There is a separate dining section with a bar for those who want alcoholic drinks with their meal.

7 Shimon Hazadik St. ℂ 02/532-2001. Reservations recommended. Main courses NIS 60–NIS 100 ($15–$25/ £7.50–£13). AE, DC, MC, V. Daily noon–11pm.

**Askadinya Restaurant Bar** ✦ CONTINENTAL    Askadinya offers one of East Jerusalem's most inventive menus, filled with dishes that are fun and delicious. You might start with spiced pumpkin soup filled with herbs and shrimp, or a large, interesting salad. Main courses include lamb cutlets in a sauce of mustard, capers, and sliced palm hearts; and steak filet medallions in raisin-and-caramel sauce topped with crumbled banana and apricot. There are also traditional choices, such as veal *cordon bleu*, as well as a good array of pastas, poultry, and fish dishes. You can come here for light meals, coffee, and dessert, or for the pleasant outdoor bar. There's a courtyard for summer meals, and a cozy stone dining room for colder weather. On Thursday evenings, there's live classical music.

11 Shimon Hazadik St. ℂ 02/532-4590. Reservations recommended. Main courses NIS 45–NIS 90 ($11–$23/ £5.60–£11). AE, DC, MC, V. Wed–Mon noon–midnight; Tues 7pm–midnight. 1 block east of Hwy. 1, and 4 long blocks north of the Olive Tree Hotel.

**Pasha's Restaurant** ARABIC    This restaurant offers many homemade specialties that just aren't offered elsewhere in Jerusalem. Among the appetizers are wonderful lamb spleens stuffed with parsley, garlic, and meat; great *kubbe* (cracked wheat dumplings fried and filled with meat or vegetables); fried goat cheese; sautéed lamb brains; as well as hummus flavored with thin slices of fried lamb. The perfectly grilled skewers of cubed lamb, chicken breast, and liver are moist and tasty, but the traditional oven dishes such as *mansaf* (seasoned lamb cooked with pine nuts and almonds, served on rice with an earthy Bedouin yogurt) and *musakhan* (chicken baked with onion and local spices, and served on special fresh-baked flat bread) are worth trying. The meze of salads is good, and the Arabic pastries are homemade. After dining, you can order a *nargeila* (hookah) to smoke in a number of flavors. Pasha's is located in a charming 1920s stone bungalow with a dining garden that is closed and heated in cold weather. *Note:* Another chain with the same name has opened a restaurant in the city; to differentiate, the Pasha's reviewed here is in East Jerusalem.

13 Shimon Hazadik St. ℂ **02/582-5162.** Reservations recommended evenings. Main courses NIS 44–NIS 80 ($11–$20/£5.50–£10). AE, DC, MC, V. Daily noon–midnight. 1 block east of Hwy. 1 and 4 blocks north of the Olive Tree Hotel.

## EAST JERUSALEM
### Expensive
**American Colony Hotel Arabesque Restaurant** ★ CONTINENTAL/MIDDLE EASTERN   The legendary **Saturday luncheon buffet** at this hotel restaurant is a truly marvelous feast. The meal includes all-you-can-eat soup, salads, fish, chicken, lamb, and beef dishes (as well as coffee and desserts). A whole chilled salmon, rich and beautifully prepared, is often the centerpiece of the spread, but there are surprises each week, such as fresh calamari or Brittany mussels. This is a great place to dine after spending Saturday morning in the bazaars of the Old City. The ambience, simple yet mildly exotic, harks back to a romanticized British Empire. For other meals, the Arabesque Restaurant runs from average to interesting, with such unusual touches as curried banana soup or spicy South African ostrich stew. There is always a menu of fine traditional Middle Eastern dishes. *Tip:* For lighter (and lower-priced) meals in a similar atmosphere, try the moderately priced **Courtyard Café,** also in the American Colony Hotel. A light repast will run you somewhere in the NIS 32 to NIS 80 ($8–$20/£4–£10) range.

Off Nablus Rd. ℂ **02/627-9777.** Reservations recommended. Main courses NIS 90–NIS 160 ($23–$40/£11–£20); Sat buffet NIS 160 ($40/£20). Add 15.5% VAT. AE, DC, MC, V. Daily noon–3pm and 6:30–10:30pm; Sat noon–3pm.

### Inexpensive
**Kan Zeman** ★ MIDDLE EASTERN   In good weather, the vine-covered garden here is one of the most pleasant spots for a leisurely meal in East Jerusalem. Jerusalemites and travelers from both sides of the city come here to enjoy the ambience. Highly recommended is Friday night when there is live traditional Arabic music. The daily menu includes Arabic and Western salads, an interesting home-style *shwarma,* grilled meats, and a few traditional oven-baked specialties. The delicious *shrak shwarma* is a very generous plate of seasoned chicken or meat served inside a Palestinian tortilla-like wrap with salad and chips on the side. In really cold weather, the garden restaurant moves indoors to a Bedouin-style dining room.

In the Jerusalem Hotel, 4 Antara Ben Shadad St. ℂ **02/628-3282.** Main courses NIS 35–NIS 60 ($8.75–$15/£4.40–£7.50). MC, V. Daily 11am–11pm. On a side street off Nablus Rd. facing the north side of the Egged East Bus Terminal.

## IN THE COUNTRYSIDE WEST OF JERUSALEM
### Moderate
**Kela David** MEDITERRANEAN   Set in a vineyard, Kela David (David's slingshot) is a wonderful place for country appetizers and wine, and also for a major meal. For a light repast, the plate of cheese and peppers, toasted in olive oil, garlic, and rosemary, and served with fabulous homemade bread and kalamata olives, is shareable and under NIS 45 ($11/£5.60). The olive, onion, and health breads are sensational. Herbed lamb or chicken, slow roasted on hot stones in a traditional *taboon* (stone oven) for 12 hours, head a list of main courses that also includes gooseliver in white-wine sauce, as well as trout, pastas, and steak. Salads, desserts, and coffees are excellent. Virgin olive oil (not importable into the United States) and local wines are for sale.

Hwy. 38 (Beit Shemesh–Beit Guvrin Hwy.), Givat Yishaiahu. ℂ **02/999-4848.** Main courses NIS 40–NIS 120 ($10–$30/£5–£15). AE, DC, MC, V. Mon–Sat 10am–10pm. Look for a pink house in a vineyard to the left of Hwy. 38 as you travel southward toward Beit Guvrin.

# 6

# Exploring Jerusalem

Jerusalem possesses much that is striking and beautiful, but more than most great destinations, it demands a sense of vision as well as eyesight. In the Hebrew language, you do not say you will "go to Jerusalem." The idiom is to "ascend" or "go up" to the city. It is not merely the city's altitude that is alluded to in this phrase.

Jerusalem today is adorned with an enticing network of museums, concerts, and performances, as well as with the archaeological treasures of its past, almost miraculously rediscovered and displayed in ways that interact with the daily life of the city. There are three main sightseeing areas in Jerusalem: inside the Old City's walls; downtown East Jerusalem; and West Jerusalem, the "New City."

## 1 The Old City

The Old City is enclosed by a 12m-high (40-ft.) wall built in 1538 by Suleiman the Magnificent, the greatest of the Ottoman Turkish sultans (some portions of the wall, in fact, are more than 2,000 years old). The existence of this wall, which gives unity and magnificence to the Old City, is something of a miracle. According to legend, Sultan Suleiman, who never visited Jerusalem, had a dream that he would be devoured by lions unless he rebuilt the walls that had lain in ruins around Jerusalem since the Crusader wars of the early 13th century. So disturbing was this dream to the sultan that he sent his architects from Istanbul to reconstruct Jerusalem's walls. Either through ignorance, or because the architects hoped to keep some of the building funds for themselves, the new walls did not include the southern part of Mount Zion, which had been inside Jerusalem's defenses in earlier times. When the sultan learned of the architects' omission, he had them beheaded.

There are eight gates in the Old City fortress wall. The main gates are the **Jaffa Gate,** entered from Mamilla-Agron Street or Jaffa Road, and the **Damascus Gate,** entered from Ha-Nevi'im Street or Nablus Road. Israelis call Damascus Gate Sha'ar Shechem; the Arabic name is Bab el Amud. On the eastern side of the Old City, the **Golden Gate,** traditional entrance point for the Messiah, has been walled up for centuries.

The Old City itself is divided into five sections: the **Christian Quarter,** the **Armenian Quarter,** the **Muslim Quarter,** the **Jewish Quarter,** and **Temple Mount** (Mount Moriah), the latter including the Western (Wailing) Wall, the Dome of the Rock, and Al Aqsa Mosque. The Dome of the Rock and the Al Aqsa Mosque were built from A.D. 690 to 720, 600 years after The Temple was destroyed by Rome. Throughout the Islamic world, this complex is called **Haram es Sharif,** or the Noble Sanctuary.

### THE JAFFA GATE

The citadel tower, beside the Jaffa Gate, is called the **Tower of David** ✶, although historically this site was developed 800 years after David died. Three massive towers built

# FREE Gift with Membership

**Give this card to a friend** or relative to sign up for an AARP membership, *and* they'll get a FREE Classic Courier just for joining.

**Prefer the Classic Courier for yourself?**
You can use this card to renew your own AARP membership, and we'll send *you* the FREE gift!

□ 1 year/$16
□ 3 years/$43
□ 5 years/$63

□ Check or money order enclosed, payable to AARP. (No cash please.)

□ Please bill me later.

**Or, to join or renew now, visit www.aarp.org/ATMoffer**

Name _____ Apt. _____

Address _____

City _____ State _____ Zip _____

DOB ____ / ____ / ____
    MONTH  DAY   YEAR

Spouse/Partner Name _____

DOB ____ / ____ / ____
    MONTH  DAY   YEAR

**JEZATM**

**AARP**®

# BUSINESS REPLY MAIL
FIRST-CLASS MAIL   PERMIT NO 3132   LONG BEACH CA

POSTAGE WILL BE PAID BY ADDRESSEE

**AARP MEMBERSHIP CENTER**
PO BOX 93156
LONG BEACH CA   90809-9893

by Herod on the foundations of Hasmonean fortifications originally stood on this spot. Just to the south, close to the protection of the garrison in the Jaffa Gate's tower, would have been Herod's palace. After the destruction of Jerusalem by the Romans in A.D. 70, the foundations of the towers guarding the Jaffa Gate were among the few structures not deliberately obliterated on orders from Rome. They were left standing to show there had once been a city that had been no pushover to subdue. Each of the subsequent rulers of Jerusalem, from Romans and Byzantines to Muslims, Crusaders, and Ottoman Turks, has rebuilt the fortifications beside Jaffa Gate, though none have come close to the scale of Herod's towers. The Ottoman Turks built a mosque here, and its minaret still dominates the complex.

The **Tower of David Museum of the History of Jerusalem** ⊛, Omar Ibn el Khatab Square (© **02/626-5333;** www.towerofdavid.org.il), now fills the citadel, hosting well-chosen, often very exciting temporary art and history exhibits, performances, and tours. Although some of the permanent exhibits look like illustrations from a school text-book, they are useful teaching tools. The structure of the citadel itself, with its great views of the New and Old cities, is fascinating. The courtyard of the citadel has also been a venue for concerts and for performances of plays by contemporary Israeli writers. From April to October, a sound-and-light show that narrates Jerusalem's history in 40 minutes is presented in English on Saturday at 9pm and on Monday and Wednesday at 9:30pm. Bring warm clothes for evening performances. If the special performances and events are revived, look for discount admission packages to the museum, the mystery performance, and the sound-and-light show for children, students, and seniors. Admission to the tower costs NIS 30 ($7.50/£3.75); there's an additional charge for special exhibits and tours, and there are discounts for children and on holidays. The museum is open Sunday to Thursday 10am to 5pm and Saturday 10am to 2pm.

A breach in the city walls beside Jaffa Gate was made for the visit of Kaiser Wilhelm II and his entourage in 1898. Here the leader of the British forces, General Allenby, liberating Palestine from Ottoman rule, entered Jerusalem in 1917. Today, this breach allows automobiles to enter the area of the Old City just inside the Jaffa Gate.

If you head straight into the **bazaar** (the *suq*) from the Jaffa Gate, you'll enter David Street, bustling with shops selling religious crafts and souvenirs, maps, and household items. On your left, at the entrance to David Street, is the **Petra Hotel,** which in its heyday (1874–1910) was Jerusalem's most elegant accommodations for visitors. Although the Petra Hotel is now a backpacker's hostel, the view from the roof is one of the most spectacular in Jerusalem, with the Dome of the Rock perfectly centered in front of you and the entire Old City at your feet. Ask to visit the roof at the desk just inside the lobby on the second floor; the fee is NIS 5 ($1.25/60p) per person. After this overview, you'll have a better idea of where things are in the maze you're about to enter.

If your first destination is the Church of the Holy Sepulcher, then take the first left off David Street, called Christian Quarter Road. Follow this road until you come to St. Helena's Road, a stepped bazaar on the right that will lead you down to the entrance to the church.

If the Western Wall and the Temple Mount are your first goal, continue straight along David Street. It makes a quick jog to the right and then to the left in the heart of the covered bazaar, where it changes its name to Street of the Chain (Silsileh, Shal-shelet). Follow the street downhill as the bazaar continues. Eventually, a right on a small side street marked Ha-Kotel leads to the Western Wall. If you go straight down

# Jerusalem: Old City

Convent of
the Sisters
of Mary

Bus
Station

Nablus Rd.

Ha'nevi'im

Damascus
Gate

Sheikh
Lu'lu
Mosque El-

Es-

El Jabz

Sheikh

El-Kan ayes

Al-Wad

Shivtei Yisra'el

Notre Dame
Church & Center

Hatzahanim

CHRISTIAN
QUARTER

Suq Khanes-Zeit

El-Tuta

Via
Dolorosa

New
Gate

Er-Rusul

Ethiopian
Patriarchate

El-Khanqa

Et-Taqiya

French
Hospital

New Gate St

Casa Nova

Terra
Sancta

St. Francis St.

Greek
Patriarchate Rd.

Christian Quarter Rd.

Holy
Sepulcher

Es-Saraya

Mamilla

Jaffa Road

St-Peter

St-Dimitri

St George

Pool of
Hezekiah

Muristan
Bazaar

El-El-Hakari

St Patriarchate Rd.

David St.

Suq El-Bazar

Tifer

Jaffa Gate

Citadel

St-Mark

Jewish Quarter Road

et
Yisra'el.

Arts and
Crafts Lane

Armenian Patriarchate Rd

Ararat

James

Or Hayim

St

El-Malak

Beir El-

ARMENIAN
QUARTER

Hati

Hativat Etzioni

Zion
Gate

CHRISTIAN
CEMETERY

MOUNT
ZION

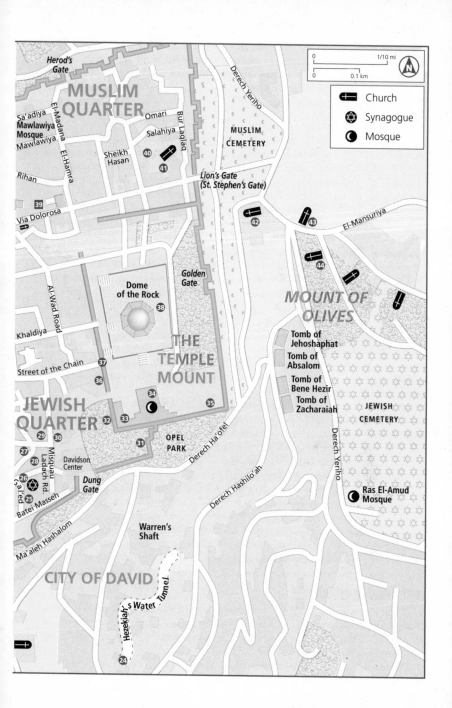

the Street of the Chain, however, you arrive at the Gate of the Chain, an entrance to the Temple Mount, otherwise known as the Noble Enclosure (Haram es Sharif), with the Dome of the Rock and Al Aqsa Mosque its main attractions. At present, entrance to the Temple Mount for tourists is permitted only through the Mograbi Gate, just to the right of the Western Wall.

## ARMENIAN QUARTER

As you enter Omar Ibn el Kattab Square on David Street, you'll see a road heading off to the right, past the moat. This route is the Armenian Patriarchate Road, leading into the Armenian Quarter, a quiet residential area centered around Armenian religious structures. Armenia was the first nation to adopt Christianity, predating Emperor Constantine's conversion of the Roman Empire by several decades. From that time on there has always been an Armenian presence in Jerusalem.

In the Armenian Quarter are many hidden enclaves and ancient buildings, including the **Church of the Holy Archangels,** from the early medieval period, and the **Gulbenkian Library,** containing more than 4,000 illuminated manuscripts, some of which can be seen during special exhibits. Access to these sites is variable.

The splendid **St. James Cathedral,** entered through the Armenian Monastery on Armenian Patriarchate Road, dates from the 11th and 12th centuries and is built on the site of earlier churches. It commemorates the place where James the Elder, son of Zebedee, was put to death by order of Herod Agrippas I in A.D. 44 (Acts 12:2). The cathedral also contains the tomb of James, the oldest brother of Jesus and first bishop of the Jerusalem Christian community. This James was the author of the Epistle of James and was stoned to death in A.D. 62. The cathedral, with its rich interior of hanging lamps, censers (for burning incense), and ceremonial objects, may be visited for services daily from 3 to 3:30pm.

The **Helen and Edward Mardigian Museum of Armenian Art and History** (© 02/628-2331, ext. 228) displays a magnificent collection of artifacts and religious objects as well as a chronicle of Armenian history. It's open Monday to Saturday from 10am to 4:30pm; admission is NIS 5 ($1.25/60p).

The Armenian Patriarchate Road follows the inside of the Old City wall and winds around to the left, passing the Zion Gate, the Jewish Quarter parking lot (inside the Old City walls), and eventually leading downhill to the Western Wall, and above the Western Wall, the Temple Mount (Haram es Sharif) and the Dome of the Rock.

*Tip:* The intricacies of the secluded Armenian Quarter are difficult to explore on your own. Aram Khatchadourian (PO Box 14003, Old City, Jerusalem; © 050/735-1859), a licensed guide and member of Jerusalem's Armenian community, gives full- or half-day private walking tours of the Armenian and other quarters of the Old City, with a special emphasis on the Armenian Quarter.

## THE JEWISH QUARTER

Let's take a detour through the Jewish Quarter on our way to the Western Wall and Temple Mount. By doing so, you'll save an uphill walk, as the wall lies well below most of the quarter. But first, some history and information about this part of town and its relationship to the other parts of the Old City.

The Jewish Quarter lies directly west of the Temple Mount and sits on a higher hill than the Temple Mount itself. With the exception of the sacred Temple Mount, the entire original city of Jerusalem from the time of David (1000 B.C.) was outside the walls of the present Old City, just downhill and to the south. Over the centuries, ancient Jerusalem spread northward, up the slope. By the time of King Hezekiah, around 700 B.C., much of the uphill area now occupied by the Jewish Quarter had become a new addition to the city, surrounded by the Broad Wall. But the wall and its many towers were not strong enough to keep out Nebuchadnezzar of Babylon, who conquered and laid waste to Jerusalem in 586 B.C.

Jews returned to Jerusalem after the Babylonian Captivity, but it took centuries for the city to regain its former size. In the late Second Temple period, Jerusalem again expanded uphill, and the area that is now the Jewish Quarter was inhabited once more and developed into an aristocratic and priestly residential neighborhood, with many luxurious mansions overlooking the Temple Mount. The main market street of Hero-dian Jerusalem developed at the bottom of the Tyropoean (Cheesemakers') Valley, which separates the heights of the present Jewish Quarter from the Temple Mount. The market street continued northward to the Damascus Gate. In order for thousands of religious pilgrims to make their way to the Temple Mount without becoming entangled in the crush of the market, two massive pedestrian staircases and overpasses were constructed above the market street. By the 1st century A.D., Herodian Jerusalem had expanded farther northward, beyond the present Old City's northern wall and the Damascus Gate. A new, bustling upper market developed where the present Suq Khan el Zeit market leads toward the Damascus Gate. The original City of David, the old-est part of town, came to be known as the Lower City.

Jerusalem was again leveled in A.D. 70 by Roman armies (the remains of houses burned in that conflagration have been uncovered in what is now the Jewish Quarter); 65 years after the Romans destroyed Jerusalem, they (and later their Byzantine succes-sors) rebuilt the city. You can visit several recently uncovered vestiges of Byzantine times in the Jewish Quarter, including the **Nea Church,** and the southern end of the city's colonnaded north-south thoroughfare, the **Cardo Maximus.** Jews were forbidden to reside in Jerusalem during the long Byzantine period, which began in A.D. 326, and many Jewish inhabitants of the area allied themselves with the then-pagan Persians, who conquered and occupied Jerusalem from A.D. 614 to 629. The Byzantines returned, fol-lowed quickly by the Muslims, who conquered Jerusalem in A.D. 638. Under their more tolerant rule, a permanent Jewish community was reestablished in the northeast quad-rant of the Old City, on the site of the present Muslim Quarter. The Crusaders con-quered Jerusalem in 1099 and celebrated their triumph by massacring most of the city's Jewish population as well as thousands of Muslims and local Christians.

In 1267, after the Crusaders were driven from Jerusalem, a small Jewish commu-nity reestablished itself in the ruins of what is now the Jewish Quarter. This area has been the center of the Jewish community in the Old City ever since.

The Jewish Quarter's most recent destruction came during and after the 1948 war with Jordan, when all the synagogues and most other buildings in the quarter were severely damaged, and over the next 2 decades fell into almost total ruin; many were systematically demolished. Since the Israeli conquest of the Old City during the 1967 war, the quarter has been rebuilt and revitalized. Although some original buildings have been carefully re-created, and many new structures were designed to blend in with them, the basic nature of the current Jewish Quarter is quite different from the impoverished, densely populated neighborhoods that existed here before 1948.

Following St. James Road (a left turn off Armenian Patriarchate Rd.) to where it becomes Or Hayim Street, you'll come to the **Old Yishuv Court Museum,** 6 Or Hayim St. (✆ **02/628-4636**). This museum displays artifacts and crafts typical of

Ashkenazi and Sephardic communities in the Jewish Quarter from the middle of the 19th century to the end of Turkish rule in 1917. Admission is NIS 14 ($3.50/£1.75), and it's open Monday to Thursday from 9am to 2pm.

The **Cardo Maximus** is a recently excavated 2nd- to 6th-century-A.D. street that was Roman and Byzantine Jerusalem's main market and processional thoroughfare, once bordered by stately columns and lined with portico-shaded shops. What you see now, about 2m (8 ft.) lower than the level of the bordering contemporary Jewish Quarter Road, dates from the Byzantine period. The original street is said to have been laid out by the Roman emperor Hadrian (A.D. 117–38) when he rebuilt the city as Aelia Capitolina after the Bar-Kokhba Revolt of A.D. 132 to 135. In late Byzantine times, the Cardo was extended southward and served as the processional route between the Holy Sepulcher and the Nea, Jerusalem's two largest churches of that era.

The southern portion of the Cardo is open to the sky; the rest is beneath the modern buildings of the Jewish Quarter. At the end of Or Hayim Street, you can visit the open area of the Cardo; its imposing columns, found by archaeologists, have been reerected. As you walk northward along the reconstructed Cardo, where modern tourist shops have been installed, you can see on your right the walled-up facades of Crusader-era shops built into arches. In this restored section you can look down well-like structures that reveal how far above the original level of the land the city has risen in its constant rebuilding on the ruins of each wave of destruction. You'll also see fragments of the city's defensive walls dating from the First Temple period, about 700 B.C.

Parallel to the Cardo is the Jewish Quarter Road. At the far side of the parking lot at the southern end of Jewish Quarter Road are the ruins of the **Nea Church,** long sought by archaeologists and only uncovered 2 decades ago. The Nea (or "New" in Greek) was Byzantine Jerusalem's largest and second-most important church after the **Church of the Holy Sepulcher.** Built by Justinian in A.D. 543, the Nea was destroyed either by an earthquake in the late 6th century or during the Persian conquest of A.D. 614. So complete was the Nea's eradication that its precise location was only discovered during excavations in the 1980s. Some historians theorize that the many marble columns needed to build the vast Nea may have been salvaged from the ruins of the Herodian temple, which had lain abandoned after its destruction in A.D. 70. Procopius, a contemporary Byzantine historian, reports a bit skeptically that the columns needed to build the Nea had magically appeared "on a hill" near the construction site as if from heaven. If the Nea's columns had indeed been taken from the Temple Mount, then outraged Jews who aided the Persians in their conquest of the city in A.D. 614 may have made a special effort to demolish a building constructed from pieces of their ruined temple. Ironically, these building materials may have returned to the Temple Mount in the 7th century when the Islamic conquerors of Jerusalem reused material from the city's many ruined Herodian and Byzantine structures to build the Al Aqsa Mosque and the Dome of the Rock. To the untrained eye, unfortunately, there is not much to see, but these few recently discovered fragments of the long-lost Nea provide a physical basis to one of Jerusalem's great and elusive legends.

Many Jewish Quarter buildings from other times are today recalled by only a single arch, doorway, or minaret. You can inspect the haunting arches, altar, apse, and ruined cloister from the once lost **Crusader Church of Saint Mary of the Teutonic Knights** (1128) on Misgav Ladach Street. If you enter the ruins, walk back to the apse, where the windows frame a wonderful view of the Temple Mount. Across from the entrance to the church is a small covered square known as **Seven Arches.** In the pre-1948 Jewish Quarter, Seven Arches was the heart of a lively market packed with vegetable vendors and customers. Rebuilt in its original form after 1967, Seven Arches no longer hosts a market and seems to perform no function. To the west, you'll see the minaret from the **Sidnah Omar Mosque,** and beside it a single, broad, graceful arch, rebuilt from the remains of the **Hurva Synagogue,** which was once the great synagogue of the Jewish Quarter; its domed roof was a Jerusalem landmark. The name, meaning "ruin," recalls its difficult and unfortunate history. The original Hurva was built in the 17th century with Ottoman permission, but was soon destroyed by Ottoman decree. Over the centuries, the name "hurva" became attached to the desolate site where the synagogue had been built with so much hope and pride. In the 1850s, a new synagogue was authorized and built. Heavily damaged in the 1948 war, it was destroyed after the Jordanians captured the Jewish Quarter. Since 1967, there have been a number of movements and plans (including one by visionary American architect Louis Kahn) calling for a new Hurva Synagogue. At press time, a new Hurva, with its dome matching the arch of the original synagogue, was finally under construction.

Between the minaret and the Hurva is the **Ramban Synagogue** of Rabbi Moshe Ben-Nachman, who helped reconstitute the Jewish community of Jerusalem in 1267, after it had been obliterated by the Crusaders. You'll also want to take a look at the complex of four small **Sephardic synagogues** named for Rabbi Yochanan Ben-Zakkai, whose school, according to tradition, occupied this site during the Second Temple period. One of the four is named for the rabbi himself, another for Eliyahu Ha-Navi (Elijah the Prophet); the other two are the Central Synagogue and the Istanbuli Synagogue. During Muslim rule, no church or synagogue was allowed to exceed the height of the nearest mosque, so to gain headroom, the floors of these synagogues were laid well below ground level. The synagogues are open Sunday to Thursday from 9:30am to 4pm, and Friday from 9:30am to noon. Admission is NIS 12 ($3/£1.50).

The **Tiferet Israel (or Yisrael) Synagogue** (Ashkenazi, or Eastern European Jewish) was founded by Nisan Bek and inaugurated in 1865. Dedicated to the Hasidic rabbi Israel Friedmann of Ruzhin (the synagogue's name means "Glory of Israel"), it was destroyed after the War of Independence and was recently restored.

Moving eastward across the Jewish Quarter in the direction of the Western Wall, you can visit two remnants of the neighborhood's elegant Herodian past.

The **Herodian Quarter Wohl Museum** (© 02/628-3448) contains archaeological excavations, done in the 1970s, of the wealthy residential quarter of Herodian Jerusalem. It includes remains of a palatial mansion with painted faux marble walls, mosaic floors, an atrium pool, and ritual bath installations indicative of the prevailing standard of living and religious observance in this affluent quarter. Admission is NIS 14 ($3.50/£1.75), or by combined ticket with Burnt House (see below) NIS 26 ($6.50/£3.25). It's open Sunday to Thursday from 9am to 5pm and Friday 9am to 1pm.

The **Burnt House** (© 02/628-7211) is a remnant of the destruction of Jerusalem by the Romans in A.D. 70. The wealthy Upper City, site of the present Jewish Quarter, held out for a despairing month after the Lower City and Temple Mount fell. From these heights, the inhabitants of the Upper City stood on their roofs and watched with horror as The Temple went up in flames. When the Romans finally decided to storm the Upper City, they found little resistance; much of the population was dead or near death from disease and starvation. The Burnt House chillingly brings to light the day when the Romans burned the Upper City. In the 1970s, when archaeologists excavated what had been the kitchen or workroom of this building, they found the forearm bones of a young woman amid the debris. As diggers continued to excavate the area of the room that lay where the arm pointed, they uncovered a wooden spear, almost as if the young woman had been reaching for this weapon when she met her death. Most tantalizing of the household artifacts found on this site is a set of weights marked with the name "Bar Kathros," a priestly family mentioned in the Talmud (and also in an ancient folk song as one of the wealthy families that oppressed the poor). Historians know the House of Bar Kathros was responsible for the manufacture of incense for The Temple. The excavated house, now preserved beneath modern buildings, is a museum with a brief slide show about the site. The entrance to the house is marked on a modern door in Seven Arches off Misgav Ladach Road (ask if you have difficulty finding the door). The house is open Sunday to Thursday from 9am to 5pm and on Friday from 9am until noon. Admission is NIS 14 ($3.50/£1.75); a combined ticket to Burnt House and Herodian Quarter Wohl Museum can be purchased for NIS 26 ($6.50/£3.25).

## THE WESTERN WALL ★★★

This is known in Hebrew as the Kotel Ha-Ma'aravi. It was formerly called the "Wailing Wall" by European observers because for centuries, Jews came here to mourn the loss of their temple. It is the holiest of Jewish sites, a remnant of the monumental Herodian retaining wall that encloses and still supports the Temple Mount.

For centuries the wall stood 18m (59 ft.) above the level of the earth and 27m (89 ft.) long, towering over a narrow alley 3.6m (12 ft.) wide that could accommodate only a few hundred densely packed worshipers. In 1967, immediately after the Six-Day War, the Israelis bulldozed the Moors Quarter facing the wall to create a plaza that could accommodate tens of thousands of pilgrims. They also made the wall about 2m (7 ft.) higher by digging down when building the plaza and exposing two more tiers of the Wall's ashlars (squared stones) that had been buried by accumulated debris for centuries. At the southern end of the Wall, away from the area reserved for prayer and worship, archaeologists since 1967 have uncovered spectacular remains from various periods.

At the prayer section of the Western Wall, grass grows out of the upper cracks. The lower cracks of the chalky, yellow-white blocks have been stuffed with bits of paper containing prayers. Orthodox Jews can be seen standing at the wall, chanting and swaying. Visitors of all religions are welcome to approach the Wall and to pray silently beside it (both Pope John Paul II and the Dalai Lama have come to pray here as pilgrims). Men who would like to go to the Wall must wear a hat or take a head covering, at no cost, from a box beside the entrance to the prayer area. Women may borrow shawls and short-skirt coverings, but it is best to come with a longish skirt and long sleeves. A separate section at the extreme right of the Western Wall is reserved for women, who are not allowed into the men's section in keeping with Orthodox Jewish tradition. On some days, you may encounter a number of professional beggars who can make a visit to the Wall difficult. Giving charity at a time of pilgrimage is an ancient Jewish tradition, but many travelers find it best to avoid the Western Wall charity seekers and instead make a donation to an organized charity at a later time. Services are held here daily; no photography or smoking is permitted on the Sabbath and some Jewish holidays.

The exposed lower courses of the Western Wall are composed of enormous rectangular ashlars, or carefully carved stones, each dressed only with the recessed borders typical of Herodian-era stonework. The sides of these monumental ashlars have been carved with such precision that they rest perfectly against and on top of each other, without mortar. Over the millennia, the fine straight lines and margins of some of the ashlars have eroded away.

The Wall was built by King Herod just before the time of Jesus and is part of a structure that retains the western part of Temple Mount and the vast, artificial ceremonial plaza Herod created on the Temple Mount itself. These retaining (as well as defensive) walls surround the western, southern, and eastern sides of the Temple Mount. The largest of the ashlars is 3.6m (12 ft.) high and 14m (46 ft.) long and weighs approximately 400 tons. According to Josephus, the Roman Jewish historian, construction of the walls took 11 years, during which time it rained in Jerusalem only at night, so as not to interfere with the workers' progress.

In the right-hand corner of the women's prayer area, beside a protruding newer building, you can see an area of the Wall composed of small, rough stones. These stones block a fragment of a Herodian-era door to the Temple Mount, today called Barclay's Gate after the 19th-century American consul who first identified it. To the south of the earthen ramp leading up the Temple Mount, you can see a fragment of large stonework protruding out of the Wall. This is **Robinson's Arch,** all that remains of a great stairway, set on arches, which passed over the busy market street at the foot of the Western Wall, and led directly into the Great Stoa on the southern side of Temple Mount.

The Western Wall is actually much higher and longer than the portion you can readily see today. For an idea of how high the original construction was, and what the level of the earth was 2,000 years ago, enter the doorway located between the men's restrooms and the public telephones on the plaza's northern side. Both men and women can enter free upon request, Sunday, Tuesday, and Wednesday from 8:30am to 3pm, Monday and Thursday from 12:30 to 3pm, and on Friday from 8:30am to noon; closed Saturday. Enter the dark labyrinth of vaults and chambers, pitfalls (now rendered safe by lamps, grates, and barriers), and passages. Inside, the continuation of the Wall is clearly visible. Shafts have been sunk along the Wall to show its true depth. The arches in this artificial cavern date from various eras, ranging from Herodian (37 B.C.–A.D. 70) to Crusader (1100–1244). The platform is behind a prayer room filled with Orthodox worshipers. The prayer room is off-limits to women, except in the viewing area.

A special walk into recently excavated tunnels alongside the Western Wall can be arranged by making an appointment with the **Western Wall Heritage Foundation** (© 02/627-1333; www.thekotel.org). Admission is NIS 28 ($7/£3.50); special tours are extra.

## TEMPLE MOUNT (HARAM ES SHARIF)—DOME OF THE ROCK ✸✸✸

Take the rising pathway to the right of the Western Wall, which leads to the Temple Mount, one of the most historic and sublime sites in the world. In the Islamic world, this is the Haram es Sharif, the Noble Sanctuary, and one of its crowning architectural achievements. After David conquered Jerusalem, he purchased the flat rock at the top of Moriah from Arunah the Jebusite, who had used it as a threshing floor. Some historians theorize that the name Arunah, a dialect variation of the name Aaron, may indicate that Arunah was a Canaanite priest, and the site a Canaanite holy place. The Bible (2 Chron. 3) relates that "Solomon began to build the house of the Lord at Jerusalem on Mount Moriah." The more modest Second Temple (Solomon's was destroyed by Nebuchadnezzar in 586 B.C.) was originally built by returnees from the Babylonian Captivity between 525 and 515 B.C., and later, shortly before the time of Jesus, Herod enlarged and rebuilt it into the most massive religious complex in the eastern Roman Empire. The vast Temple Mount you see here is an artificially created,

---

**Tips   Scheduling a Visit to the Temple Mount**

At press time, tourists could only visit the Temple Mount/Haram es Sharif from Sunday to Thursday from 7:30 to 11am and from 1:30 to 2:30pm. It is best to arrive at least an hour ahead of closing time. Although visitors may walk around on the Temple Mount, take photographs, and enjoy the vistas, for now entry into the Dome of the Rock, the Al Aqsa Mosque, and the Islamic Museum is not permitted. Longer visiting hours and permission to enter the buildings on the Temple Mount may be restored during the time span of this edition. The Temple Mount is always closed to non-Muslims on Friday and during the entire holy month of Ramadan.

---

flat, stone-paved platform, about 12 hectares (30 acres) in area, built by Herod to accommodate vast numbers of pilgrims in ancient times. Herod's temple complex was destroyed by the Romans in A.D. 70. All structures on the Temple Mount today, including the Dome of the Rock and the Al Aqsa Mosque, are Islamic holy places and religious institutions built after the Muslim conquest of A.D. 638.

There is no charge to enter the Temple Mount compound. You must not, however, wear shorts or immodest dress in the compound. (If your outfit is too revealing, guards may be willing to provide you with long cotton wraps, or they may ask you to return another time with more modest clothing.) Visitors are allowed on the Temple Mount by permission of the Islamic religious authorities, and are asked to obey instructions given by the guards.

There is an admission fee of NIS 38 ($9.50/£4.75) to go inside the two mosques and the Islamic Museum. If the buildings are again open to foreign visitors, I highly recommend that you invest in the combined admission ticket, which may be purchased from a stone kiosk between Al Aqsa and the Dome of the Rock. If visiting hours are lengthened, you may usually remain on the Temple Mount, but cannot enter the Dome of the Rock or the Al Aqsa Mosque during the midday prayers.

**Al Aqsa Mosque** ✹✹, the third-holiest place of prayer in the world for Muslims after Mecca and Medina, is the first large edifice you'll come to. Completed in approximately A.D. 720, it is among the oldest mosques in existence and also among the most beautiful—a vast broad basilica originally nine naves wide (it was rebuilt somewhat smaller after the Crusades). It was in front of the graceful porticos of the Al Aqsa that King Abdullah I of Jordan was assassinated in 1951, by gunmen who felt he was attempting to create a basis for eventual peace in the area. He died here in the presence of his then 15-year-old grandson, the late King Hussein of Jordan.

**Note:** Although at press time the interiors of the Al Aqsa and the Dome of the Rock were closed to visitors, the following information is provided in case they are reopened.

A mosque is a sacred enclosure open to air and light (as opposed to the dark interiors of pagan-era temples). Because a mosque is a sacred precinct, you must remove your shoes before entering. This tradition is very ancient, going back to the time when Moses, approaching the Burning Bush in the Sinai, heard the voice of God telling him to take off his shoes. You must also leave handbags and cameras outside, so you might want to come with a partner who can watch these things for you. Try to stash your wallet and identification papers into a pocket.

# Temple Mount (Haram es Sharif)

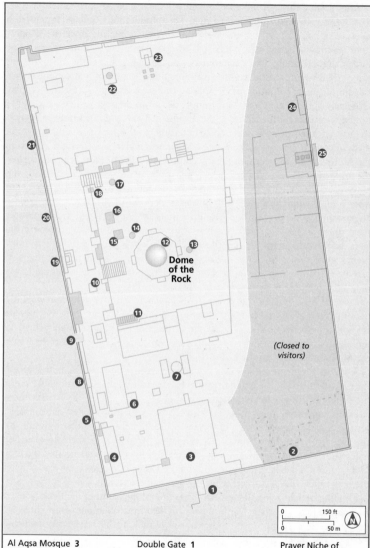

Dome
of the
Rock

(Closed to
visitors)

| | | |
|---|---|---|
| 0 | | 150 ft |
| 0 | | 50 m |

Al Aqsa Mosque **3**
Bab el-Nazir **21**
Bab el-Qattanin (Cotton
   Merchants' Gate) **19**
Dome of Hebron **16**
Dome of St. George **18**
Dome of the Ascension **15**
Dome of the Chain **13**
Dome of the Rock **12**
Dome of the Spirits **17**

Double Gate **1**
El-Kas **7**
Fountain of Qaitbay **10**
Fountain of
   Sultain Suleiman **23**
Gate of the Chain **9**
Golden Gate **25**
Iron Gate (Bab el Hadid) **20**
Islamic Museum **4**
Moroccan Gate **5**

Prayer Niche of
   the Prophet **14**
Quabbat Suleiman **22**
Solomon's Stables
   (underground) **2**
Solomon's Throne **24**
Summer Pulpit **11**
Ticket Office **6**
Western Wall **8**

After passing through the portico, you will enter a broad open hall with chandeliers, its floor covered with Oriental rugs. The mosque's lofty ceilings, supported by a forest of varied columns, are embellished with early Islamic and Byzantine design. Up front, past rows of great marble pillars, is a wood-partitioned platform reserved for the Jordanian royal family. The extraordinary wooden-stair pulpit of the Al Aqsa Mosque, one of Islam's great artistic treasures for more than 7 centuries, was commissioned by Saladin for the rededication of Al Aqsa as a mosque after the Crusader occupation. Originally built by master artisans from Syria, it was destroyed when a mentally disturbed Australian tourist set fire to the Al Aqsa in 1969, and it has been painstakingly reconstructed by craftspeople retrained in techniques that have not been used for hundreds of years. A separate women's prayer chamber, in blue, is at the right. As you enter the Al Aqsa, you face south, in the direction of Mecca. **Mihrabs,** or prayer niches on the southern wall, remind worshipers of the **qibla,** or direction they must face during prayers, which are performed five times a day. During the five daily prayers, the Al Aqsa is filled with worshipers who in unison perform the rituals of prostration that accompany Islamic prayer. Non-Muslim visitors are not permitted inside mosques at these times. In between prayers, when visitors are allowed to enter, you will find a large, serene space, with perhaps a few individual worshipers at various places on the floor. Unlike most churches and synagogues, mosques contain no pews or chairs. Visitors are invited to view the architecture and design details of the building; however, they are requested not to engage in any prayers.

Leave Al Aqsa, reclaim your shoes and belongings, and turn right. You will only be permitted to walk to the end of the building, but at the far end of the vast pavement is a corner in the city walls. Some say this is the "pinnacle of the Temple" where Satan took Jesus to tempt him (Matt. 4:5). In the distance, you can get a marvelous view of the Mount of Olives and the Kidron Valley.

A stairway leads to the so-called **Solomon's Stables,** perhaps first misidentified by the Crusaders. Today, these subterranean chambers are popularly believed to have been the stables for King Solomon's thousands of horses. The "stables" are actually the substructure supporting this portion of Herod's vast, artificially created ceremonial platform that is the present surface of the Temple Mount. To add to the confusion about the site, many Muslims believe the "Solomon" referred to is the Ottoman Sultan Suleiman (Solomon) the Magnificent, who rebuilt the walls that surround the present Old City and did extensive repair work on the Dome of the Rock during his reign in the mid-1500s. (For security reasons, this area will probably be closed to visitors.)

Heading straight across Temple Mt. Plaza toward the Dome of the Rock, you'll pass **El-Kas,** the fountain where Muslims perform their ritual ablutions before entering the holy places. It is equipped with a circular row of pink marble seats, each of which has a faucet. The fountain is not for use by non-Muslims.

The exterior walls of the dazzling **Dome of the Rock** ✸✸✸ are covered with a facade of Persian blue tiles, originally installed by the Ottoman sultan Suleiman the Magnificent in the mid–16th century. In 1994, under the auspices of Jordan's king Hussein, the great dome was completely reconstructed and regilded with 80 kilograms (176 lb.) of 24-karat gold. The Dome of the Rock is reached by climbing the broad ceremonial stairs that lead to a decorative archway and a raised center portion of the Temple Mount complex. The Dome of the Rock's interior is every bit as lavish and intricate as the outside. Plush carpets line the floor, and stained-glass windows line the upper ceiling. Again, visitors must remove their shoes and leave them, along with their cameras and bags, on shelves before entering the shrine.

Everything in this beautiful Muslim sanctuary, built in A.D. 691, centers on the rock that occupies the middle of the shrine. According to Islamic tradition, this rock is the spot from which the Prophet Muhammad ascended to view paradise during the Night Journey described in the 17th Sura of the Koran. Tradition holds that when the Prophet rose, the rock tried to follow, and although it failed, the cave beneath the rock was formed. Footprints of Muhammad are pointed out on the rock.

Next to the rock, a few strands of the Prophet Muhammad's hair are kept in a latticework wooden cabinet. A stairway leads under the rock to a cavelike chamber; according to tradition, this is the Well of the Souls, where it is said the souls of all the dead are gathered. Glass partitions have been erected to stop pilgrims from eroding the sacred rock—for centuries it was chipped away by the faithful who wanted to bring home a memento.

Jewish tradition holds that on this rock occurred the supreme act of faith that stands at the very foundation of the Jewish religion: Abraham's near sacrifice of Isaac. Genesis 22 relates how Abraham, in approximately 1800 B.C., followed God's instructions to go to Moriah and sacrifice Isaac, his beloved son. Isaac, unaware of the dreadful command, followed in his father's steps and asked, "Behold the fire and the wood, but where is the lamb for a burnt offering?" Abraham responded, "God will provide for the sacrifice," as he built the altar on the rock and prepared to bind his son. At the final moment, the voice of God intervened and ordered Abraham to lower his knife. Approximately 900 years later, in 960 B.C., the Temple of Solomon was constructed either on or beside this rock. For the next millennium, the First and Second Temples were located on this site.

From the flat courtyard surrounding the two mosques you have a wonderful view. To the south are the Valley of Jehoshaphat (Valley of Kidron) and the UN Government House (Mount of Contempt) on the hill. To the east are the lower slopes of the Mount of Olives, the Russian Magdalene Church, with its many onion-shaped golden domes, and the Tomb of the Virgin. Midway up the Mount of Olives is a large modern white structure with many levels of arcades that seem built into the side of the slope. This is the vast Mormon Center, constructed in the 1980s and considered to be one of the most beautiful examples of contemporary architecture in Jerusalem. On the crest of the Mount of Olives, above the Church of Mary Magdalene, you'll see the high-steepled Russian Monastery and the Dome of the Ascension, marking the place from which Jesus ascended to heaven. Farther to the right and a bit downhill is the gray, tear-shaped dome of Dominus Flevit, which commemorates the spot where Jesus wept as he saw a vision of Jerusalem in ruins. Indeed, from the time of the city's destruction in A.D. 70 until the building of the Dome of the Rock in A.D. 691, Jews traditionally stood near this spot and viewed the actual ruins of the Temple Mount. To the right, on the southern crest of the ridge, is the modern Seven Arches Hotel, built during Jordanian times on the ancient Jewish cemetery of the Mount of Olives.

Your combined entrance ticket also admits you to the **Islamic Museum,** in the southwest corner of the Temple Mount complex, to the right of the Al Aqsa Mosque. The museum is filled with architectural details, including capitals and carved stonework from earlier structures on the Temple Mount as well as ornamental details from earlier periods of the Al Aqsa Mosque's existence.

## DUNG GATE, SILWAN (THE CITY OF DAVID) & THE JERUSALEM ARCHAEOLOGICAL PARK

The gate in the city wall near the Temple Mount is Dung Gate, which leads downhill to the Arab neighborhood of Silwan, site of Jerusalem and the ancient City of David as it existed around 1000 B.C. Until the medieval era, Silwan was encompassed within the walls of Jerusalem; only when the walls of the city shrank to their present configuration, and the city wall separated Silwan from the rest of the city, was the Dung Gate built. For centuries, the gate was just a small doorway in the wall, but in recent years it has been widened to accommodate cars and buses. Jerusalemites claim that the gate is named for the debris from each consecutive destruction of Jerusalem that was dumped out into the valley below. Silwan today is as crowded as in ancient times—its houses now climb the sides of a steep cliff at the edge of the Mount of Olives. Silwan is where the original settlement of Jerusalem developed in prehistoric times beside the **Gihon Spring.** Its streets are where the prophets walked, and the events of First Temple Jerusalem took place.

By the 2nd century B.C., the growing city of Jerusalem was expanding uphill and northward, onto the site of the present Old City. The newer Upper City was the more affluent part of town; the older Lower City was densely populated and poor. In the centuries after the Roman destruction of Jerusalem in A.D. 70, the population of Jerusalem had so greatly decreased and the technology of warfare had progressed to such a point that the original City of David was no longer militarily defensible. It was left outside the walls of the city and by medieval times had sunk to the status of a small, sporadically settled village known as Silwan. So completely forgotten was the site of the original city that until late in the 19th century, most historians and visitors believed the Jerusalem of the First Temple period had been located on the site of the present Old City.

In Silwan you can visit the underground water tunnel and the collection **Pool of Siloam** (in Hebrew, Shiloah) built by King Hezekiah in 701 B.C.; this remarkable structure hid Jerusalem's water supply from the Assyrians and saved the city from destruction. At the southern end of Silwan (which takes its Arabic name from the biblical pool of Siloam), just beyond where the walls of old Jerusalem would have been, are ancient overgrown gardens of pomegranates and figs still watered by the **Gihon Spring.** These gardens, originating in prehistoric times, most likely occupy the site of the gardens of the kings of Judah and may be the site of the walled gardens that inspired the Song of Songs. It was to a tent beside the Gihon Spring that David initially brought the Ark of the Covenant, the pivotal first step in Jerusalem's transformation into a holy city. Here the ark had rested until the Temple of Solomon was built to house it. The Bible also records that King David was buried inside this city; if so, his tomb should be somewhere in Silwan rather than at the site on Mount Zion that has been venerated since at least medieval times. Normally, under Judaic law, burials are not permitted within the walls of a city, but the Bible records that an exception was apparently made for King David. Archaeologists are still searching for evidence of the Davidic burial site, but the Lower City was extensively quarried for building stone in the centuries after the Roman destruction, and the true location of David's tomb, legendary for its powers, remains one of Jerusalem's mysteries.

You can enter daily from 9am to 5pm, for free, and follow the paths along the steep hillside past the excavation site. However, under current political conditions, it is best to visit this area with an organized tour. **Zion Walking Tours** (② 02/652-2568; fax 02/628-7866) offers tours that depart from the Tower of David inside the Jaffa Gate; ask at the tourist office for information. **Archaeological Seminars Ltd.** (② 02/627-3515) and **SPINI** (② 02/625-2357; fax 02/625-4953) lead guided tours of the City of David. See "Organized Tours," later in this chapter, for more information.

*Moments* **The Hidden Wall**

For centuries the small stretch of the Western Wall of the Temple Mount used for Jewish prayers was the only part of the Herodian Temple Mount complex non-Muslims could actually approach and touch. The once-important southern wall of the Temple Mount was largely hidden by accumulated earth and debris, and by later buildings that rose and fell with each successive wave of history. Now excavations have made the southern wall and extreme southern part of the Western Wall accessible all the way down to the Herodian street level. At a quiet time of day, when no tour groups are trudging through, you can sit in the shade of an ancient shop doorway and contemplate the charisma and enormity of the Herodian ashlars. Wild capers grow out of the monumental walls. If you look up near the extreme southern end of the Western Wall where the level of earth would have been centuries ago, you can see a large ashlar on which, probably in the Byzantine era (before Islamic times), archaeologists believe a Jewish pilgrim to the ruined Temple Mount carved the Hebrew words from Isaiah 66:14: "And when you see this, your heart shall rejoice, and your bones shall flourish like an herb." For 1,500 years, this visitors messa ge lay hidden and forgotten in the earth.

## THE JERUSALEM ARCHAEOLOGICAL PARK

**The Southern Wall of the Temple Mount and the Davidson Center** ★★   The Jerusalem Archaeological Park just outside the southern wall of the Temple Mount offers an opportunity to explore the monumental ruins of the Herodian Temple Complex and later Byzantine/Islamic structures that have been uncovered here during the past 3 decades. When The Temple was in existence (before A.D. 70), the southern wall of the Temple Mount was the main route for approaching The Temple. A broad staircase, mentioned in Talmudic writings, ended in a broad esplanade, which was wide enough to provide access to the two sets of gates that once existed, fragments of which can still be seen. From the gates, pilgrims would have proceeded through tunnels that dramatically emerged onto the surface of the sacred enclosure not far from The Temple building itself. Visitors to the park can now stand on the Broad Stairs (the gates are now blocked by later construction, but traces are still visible) and walk on the Herodian market street that ran along the western side of the Temple Mount. They can also explore the ruins of Herodian-era shops along the market street (they were part of the complex and rents may have gone toward the upkeep of the Temple Mount), and see where the great staircase to the Temple Mount once stood, supported by a series of arches that spanned the market street below. The excavations have also uncovered Byzantine-era structures that once stood beside the partly destroyed southern wall of the Temple Mount, and the impressive walls of early Islamic palaces (ca. 8th c. A.D.) that took their place.

The **Davidson Exhibition Center** at the archaeological park gives you the chance to take a virtual tour of the Temple Mount as archaeologists believe it might have appeared to a pilgrim in Herodian times (late 1st c. B.C. until the Roman destruction of Jerusalem in A.D. 70). Located in the ruins of an early-8th-century Islamic palace uncovered by archaeologists at the foot of the Temple Mount, the Davidson Center contains a small museum with artifacts found at the site, as well as videos and computer information on the Temple Mount's history. The video and digital re-creation of the

Herodian Temple Mount are interesting, but there are a number of anachronistic and questionable details (see if you can spot them). There are 1-hour audio tours of the center (which is already relatively self-explanatory) and also of the archaeological park (worthwhile for those who want to understand all the details of the site). Private guides can be booked in advance for NIS 160 ($40/£20) per person, but a map and the recorded audio tour of the site, available at the Davidson Center, is sufficient for most visitors.

Entrance from near inside of Dung Gate. © 02/627-7550. www.archpark.org.il. NIS 30 ($7.50/£3.75) adults; NIS 16 ($4/£2) students, children, and seniors. Sun–Thurs 8am–5pm; Fri 8am–2pm. Closed Sat. Bus: 1, 2, 38, or 99.

## THE MUSLIM & CHRISTIAN QUARTERS

**Church of Saint Anne and the Pools of Bethesda** ★★    Sixty meters (197 ft.) inside the Lion's Gate, on your right, is a wooden doorway leading to a hidden garden enclave where you'll find this beautiful 12th-century Crusader church, erected in honor of the birthplace of Anne (Hannah), the mother of Mary. It is built next to the Bethesda Pool, the site where Jesus is believed to have healed a paralytic. As the church is just a few hundred feet east of the Sanctuaries of the Flagellation and the Condemnation, at the beginning of the Via Dolorosa, you might want to visit it before following the Stations of the Cross. Saint Anne's acoustics, designed for Gregorian chant, are so perfect that the church is virtually a musical instrument to be played by the human voice. Pilgrim groups come to sing in the church throughout the day, and you, too, are welcome to prepare a song of any religion—only religious songs are permitted. The church's acoustics are most amazing when used by a soprano- or a tenor-range solo voice. *Tip:* If you want to try the acoustics (and if you're not a soprano or tenor), "Amazing Grace," sung with pauses between the lines to allow for the echo, will sound truly powerful in this 900-year-old church; so will "Silent Night."

Lion's Gate (Saint Stephen's Gate). Admission NIS 10 ($2.50/£1.25). Mon–Sat 8am–noon and 2–5pm (until 6pm in summer); closed Sun.

## VIA DOLOROSA

This is the **Way of the Cross,** traditionally believed to be the route followed by Jesus from the Praetorium (the Roman Judgment Hall) to Calvary, which was the scene of the Crucifixion. Over the centuries, millions of pilgrims have come here to walk the way that Jesus took to his death. Each Friday at 3pm priests lead a procession for pilgrims along Via Dolorosa (starting in the Monastery of the Flagellation at the tower of Antonia, not far from the Lion's Gate). Large wooden crosses are carried by some of those in the procession and prayers are said at each of the 14 Stations of the Cross. The Via Dolorosa begins in the Muslim Quarter, in the northeast corner of the Old City, and winds its way to the Church of the Holy Sepulcher in the Christian Quarter.

You can enter the **Sanctuaries of the Flagellation and the Condemnation,** where Jesus was scourged and judged. In the sanctuaries are some of the original paving stones of the Lithostrotos. Hours are year-round daily from 8am to noon; also 2 to 6pm from April through September and 1 to 5pm from October through March.

The Sanctuary of the Condemnation marks the first Station of the Cross. As you leave the sanctuary to follow the Via Dolorosa, keep in mind that each Station of the Cross is marked by a small sign or a number engraved in the stone lintel over a door. Paving stones on the Via Dolorosa itself have been set in a semicircular pattern to mark those stations directly on the street. Other stations are behind closed doors;

knock and a monk or nun will probably be there to open up for you. There's a rest-room opposite Station 3.

The following is a quick guide to the Stations of the Cross:

**Station 1:** Jesus is condemned to death. **Station 2:** Jesus receives the cross (at the foot of the Antonia). **Station 3:** Jesus falls for the first time (Polish biblical-archaeological museum). **Station 4:** Jesus meets his mother. **Station 5:** Simon the Cyrene helps Jesus carry the cross. **Station 6:** Veronica wipes Jesus' face. **Station 7:** Jesus falls the second time (at bazaar crossroads). **Station 8:** Jesus consoles the women of Jerusalem. **Station 9:** Jesus falls the third time (Coptic Monastery).

The five remaining Stations of the Cross are inside the Church of the Holy Sepulcher (see below). **Station 10:** Jesus is stripped of his garments. **Station 11:** Jesus is nailed to the cross. **Station 12:** Jesus dies on the cross. **Station 13:** Jesus is taken down from the cross and given to Mary. **Station 14:** Jesus is laid in the chamber of the sepulcher and from there is resurrected.

## CHURCH OF THE HOLY SEPULCHER AT GOLGOTHA

The church is divided among the six oldest Christian sects: Roman Catholic, Armenian Orthodox, Greek Orthodox, Egyptian Coptic, Ethiopian, and Syrian Orthodox. Each denomination has its own space—right down to lines drawn down the middle of floors and pillars—and its own schedule of rights to be in other areas of the church at specific times. The decor, partitioned and changed every few feet, is a mixture of Byzantine and Frankish Crusader styles.

You can observe the various stations inside the church—the marble slab at the entrance is the Stone of Unction, where the body of Jesus was prepared for burial; the site of Calvary on the second floor; and the early-19th-century marble tomb edifice enclosing the actual cave of the sepulcher.

After the Roman emperor Constantine converted to Christianity and made Christianity the religion of Rome in A.D. 326, his mother, Queen Helena, made a pilgrimage to the Holy Land and located what was believed to be the tomb from which Jesus rose. Further excavation nearby uncovered the True Cross, which became the most sacred relic of the Christian world until it was carried off by the Persians in A.D. 614. It was over this tomb that Constantine built the first Holy Sepulcher Church, a complex of classical structures, which was enlarged by Justinian 200 years later. Fire, earthquake, the 7th-century Persians, and a mad 11th-century Muslim caliph destroyed much of the great, classical church, but the Crusaders rebuilt it in the 12th century—a mixture of Byzantine remnants and medieval Frankish reconstruction that was far less grand than the original. The church has been restored many times and is currently being renovated. In 1997, the renovated interior of the great dome covering the sepulcher was unveiled. It is bright, fresh, and, to some visitors, a bit incompatible with the antiquity of the place. Its design motifs had to be neutral, avoiding incorporating any of the special traditions of the branches of Christianity that control different areas of the building.

If you're in Jerusalem during Easter week, you can attend many of the fascinating services based on ancient Eastern church traditions that are held at the church. Most notable are the Service of the Holy Fire, the dramatic pageant called the Washing of the Feet, and the exotic midnight Ethiopian procession on the part of the church under Ethiopian jurisdiction—the roof. No admission fee; modest dress required.

**Lutheran Church of the Redeemer**   Kaiser Wilhelm II of Germany made his pilgrimage to Jerusalem in 1898 to dedicate the Church of the Redeemer, a Protestant church just outside the gates to the Church of the Holy Sepulcher. Ottoman-Turkish permission to allow construction of a Protestant church at such a prestigious location symbolized the growing alliance between Germany and the Ottoman Empire, one that would continue through World War I. The church has become a venue for concerts and performances of organ music; the view from the tower (no elevator, and a steep climb of more than 200 steps) is exceptional.

Between Muristan Bazaar and Suq Khan es Zeit Bazaar ℭ 02/627-6111. Admission to tower NIS 5 ($1.25/60p). Mon–Sat 9am–1pm and 2–5pm. English services Sun 9am.

## DAMASCUS GATE & THE BAZAARS

The Damascus Gate, largest and most magnificent of all the entrances to the Old City, is the main route into the Old City from East Jerusalem. Once you are inside the gate, cafes, shops, and market stalls line a wide-stepped entrance street going downhill; Arabs sit inside and out smoking water pipes and watching you as you watch them. The game they're playing is *shesh-besh,* a sort of backgammon. Music emanates from coffeehouses and shops. Whether you take **El-Wad Road** (the Valley Rd.) to the left or **Suq Khan es-Zeit** (the Market of the Inn of the Olive Oil) to the right, the way becomes very narrow and confusing. Unlike the markets near the Jaffa Gate, which cater primarily to visitors, this part of the bazaar is an authentic market used by the people of East Jerusalem. You'll see stalls of spices and coffees, blacksmiths, craft shops, pastry and bread bakeries, shops selling sneakers and children's wear, butcher stalls, tiny one-chair barber establishments, shoe stores, and fruit-and-vegetable stands.

Suq Khan es-Zeit eventually becomes the covered **Suq el Attarin,** or Bazaar of the Spices, now mostly a clothing bazaar. In other centuries, this covered market was lined with open sacks of curry, cocoa, sesame, pepper, saffron, and all kinds of beans, dried herbs, medicines, and vegetables. Parallel and to the right of this central market street is the covered Suq El-Lahhamin (the Butchers' Bazaar), its pavement often slippery with puddles of blood.

If you continue walking straight, eventually Suq El Attarin will cross David Street, and soon thereafter it becomes the recently excavated and renovated Cardo (the main street of Roman and Byzantine Jerusalem), which runs through the restored Jewish Quarter. The area, incidentally, is well patrolled by police officers.

## THE OLD CITY RAMPARTS

A good place to explore is the walk on the **Old City Ramparts.** You can enter the wall route at Jaffa Gate. The views are thrilling, but an entire circuit of the walls (about 4km/2½ miles) is no longer permitted as part of the circuit skirts the Temple Mount. Underneath the present Damascus Gate, the Roman-era gate, to the left and below, has been excavated. Within this classical, triple-arched gate (which may have been extant in Jesus' time) there's a small museum (closed at press time), displaying laser reconstructions of the original gate and worth a quick visit if it's open. Again, notice how much lower ground level was before 2,000 years of destruction and rebuilding.

**Note:** It's not a great idea for anyone to walk alone on the ramparts at any time of day. The ramparts are at times patrolled by groups of unruly local kids and unsavory illegal "guides."

The entry ticket costs NIS 18 ($4.50/£2.25) for adults, NIS 10 ($2.50/£1.25) for children, and is good for 2 days (3 days if you buy on Fri). The ramparts are open Saturday to Thursday from 10am to 4pm and Friday 9am to 2pm.

0 ____ 60 ft
0 ____ 20 m

**Rotunda**

**Katholikon**

**Golgotha**

**Atrium**

**Entrance**

1 Stone of Unction
2 Chapel of Forty Martyrs and bell-tower
3 St. John's Chapel and Baptistery
4 St. James's Chapel
5 Place of the Three Marys (Armenian Orthodox)
6 Angel's Chapel
7 Holy Sepulcher
8 Coptic Chapel
9 Jacobite Chapel (Syrian Orthodox)
10 Tomb of Joseph of Arimathea (Abyssinian)
11 Franciscan Chapel (R.C.)

12 Altar of Mary Magdalene (R.C.)
13 Arches of the Virgin
14 Christ's Prison (Greek Orthodox chapel)
15 Chapel of Longinus (Greek Orthodox)
16 Chapel of Parting of Raiment (Armenian Orthodox)
17 St. Helen's Chapel (Armenian Orthodox)
18 Chapel of Discovery of Cross (R.C.)
19 Medieval cloister
20 Chapel of the Mocking
21 Chapel of Adam (Greek Orthodox)
22 Site of tombs of Godfrey of Bouillon and Baldwin I

23 Altar of Crucifixion and Stabat Mater Altar (Greek Orthodox)
24 Altar of the Nailing to the Cross (R.C.)
25 St. Michael's Chapel
26 St. John's Chapel (Armenian Orthodox)
27 Chapel of Abraham
28 Chapel of the Agony of the Virgin and Chapel of St. Mary of Egypt
29 Tomb of Philippe d'Aubigny
30 Latin Choir (R.C.)
31 Navel of the World
32 Greek Choir

## Via Dolorosa

Damascus Gate

Street of the Valley (El Wad Road)

Street of Damascus Gate (Tariq Bab El Amud)

Lithostrotos

Convent of the Sisters of Zion

Our Lady of the Spasm

Ecce Homo Arch

Church of the Condemnation (Franciscan Monastery)

Lion's Gate (St. Stephen's Gate)

St. Marys Street

City Wall

Chapel of the Flagellation (Franciscan Monastery)

Greek Orthodox Convent of St.Charlambos

**Church of the Holy Sepulcher**

Coptic Patriarchate

Via Dolorosa

Sug Khan Ez-Zeit

Church of St. Veronica

Ethiopian Monastery

Church of the Redeemer

The Muristan

### Stations of the Cross

1 Jesus is condemned to death.
2 Jesus receives the Cross.
3 Jesus falls for the first time.
4 Jesus meets his grieving mother.
5 Simon of Cyrene helps Jesus carry the Cross.
6 Veronica wipes the face of Jesus.
7 Jesus falls for the second time.

8 Jesus speaks to the daughters of Jerusalem.
9 Jesus falls for the third time.
10 Jesus is stripped of his garments.
11 Jesus is nailed to the Cross.
12 Jesus dies on the Cross.
13 The body of Jesus is taken from the Cross.
14 Jesus is laid in the Holy Sepulcher.

## Schindler's Grave

Thanks to the making of the film *Schindlers List,* Oskar Schindler, the German businessman who fervently worked to save the lives of Jewish slave laborers during the Holocaust, has become world famous. His final resting place, arranged by those who owed their lives to him, is in a graveyard on Mount Zion. Exit the Zion Gate, turn left, cross the road, and continue downhill around to the right to a Christian cemetery (many of the graves have Arabic inscriptions). The grave of the often puzzling but heroic Oskar Schindler is in the lower tier, marked by the many stones left on it (per Jewish tradition) by visitors.

## STREET OF THE CHAIN

Perpendicular to the Suq El Attarin–Cardo market is the Street of the Chain, which runs gently downhill to the **Gate of the Chain,** the most important entrance to the Haram es Sharif, or Temple Mount. This was the great residential street of medieval Islamic Jerusalem. It starts out as a typical market passageway, but as you get closer to the Haram, you'll begin to notice monumental, richly ornamented doorways of Mamluke period mansions and buildings decorated with carved stonework in "stalactite" patterns over the entryways. You can only surmise this area's affluent past; like much of the Old City, the neighborhood is overcrowded and has not yet benefited from programs of preservation and renovation.

## MOUNT ZION

This important location can be easily spotted as you approach the walls of the Old City from the west or the south. The building with a round squat tower is the Dormition Abbey, and near this site is King David's Tomb and the Room of the Last Supper (Coenaculum) above it. To reach **King David's Tomb,** walk out Zion Gate, proceed down a narrow alley bounded by high stone walls, and turn left. Although this place has been venerated as the site of David's burial, the tradition can only be traced back to early medieval times; many believe the tomb would have been located in the ancient City of David, south of the present Old City. The building is open daily, including the Sabbath, from 8am to 5pm; until 2pm on Friday. Men should cover their heads when entering the room; modest dress and head scarves are advisable for women.

Near King David's Tomb (in fact, in the same building) is a doorway and flight of stairs leading to the **Coenaculum (Upper Room),** where Jesus sat with his disciples to celebrate the Passover Seder, the Last Supper. Again, the room's authenticity is based on many centuries of veneration; however, some question this tradition. It is open daily from 8:30am to 4pm.

In the cellar of a building (71) near King David's Tomb is the **Chamber of the Holocaust,** an eerie room lit by candles and dedicated to the memory of the six million Jews slain by the Nazis. The chamber, a private memorial and museum, is open for visits Sunday to Thursday from 9am to 4pm and on Friday to 1pm.

Close by is the graceful **Dormition Abbey** (℃ **02/671-9927**), completed in 1910 by the German Benedictine Order on the spot where, according to tradition, Mary fell into sleep before her burial and assumption into heaven. Inside the church are an elaborate golden mosaic; a crypt containing interesting religious artwork; and a statue of Mary, around which are chapels donated by various countries. From the tower of the church there's a fabulous panoramic view. It's open daily from 8am to noon and 2 to 6pm. The Dormition Abbey at times is a dramatic venue for public concerts.

## WALKING TOUR | THE OLD CITY

| | |
|---|---|
| **Start:** | The Jaffa Gate. |
| **Finish:** | The tour has three options: The first will take you to the Jewish Quarter and the Western Wall, the second to the Islamic shrines and mosques on the Temple Mount, the third to an unusual Christian enclave on the roof of the Church of the Holy Sepulcher. |
| **Best Times:** | Sunday to Wednesday from 8am to 3pm. |
| **Worst Times:** | Shabbat, Muslim holidays, Friday, or after 3pm when the Dome of the Rock is closed. |

This is a meandering walk that will get you to some major sites, offbeat vista points, and authentic refueling stops, but the Old City is a vast, intricate Chinese box of experiences, as unplanned and exotic as the 4,000-year history of Jerusalem itself. One way to enjoy the texture of this sublime hodgepodge is simply to plunge in and wander, chancing upon hummus parlors and holy sites, ancient bakeries and antique Bedouin embroideries. I will clue you in to a bit of Jerusalem's history and local lore as we move along.

**FROM THE JAFFA GATE TO THE CARDO** The first part of the walk takes you to the Cardo, where the walk divides into three possible options. We begin at:

---

### ❶ Jaffa Gate
Before you enter Jaffa Gate, which is the traditional entrance to the city for visitors from the West, check out the stones from many eras that make up the present Old City wall, which was erected by order of the Ottoman-Turkish sultan Suleiman the Magnificent in 1538. Some stones have been dressed with carefully cut flat borders surrounding a raised, flat central area (the boss) in the style of King Herod's stonecutters and probably dating from 2,000 years ago. You will see this style again in the monumental stones of the Western Wall, a retaining wall for the vast artificial platform that Herod constructed to surround the original Jerusalem Temple site with room for the thousands of Jews who made the pilgrimage from all over the ancient world. You will notice other kinds of stones with flat borders and rougher raised bosses. These are in the pre-Herodian style of the Hasmoneans (the Maccabees) who were the

last Jewish rulers of Jerusalem until modern times, with the exception of Bar Kochba, who conquered the ruins of the city during the Second Jewish Revolt against Rome in A.D. 132 to 135. You will also see rough ashlars of the Byzantine era, as well as the virtually undressed stones of Crusader and medieval times. In each of the upper corners of the closed decorative archway to the left of the Jaffa Gate, notice stones carefully carved into a leaf design, which are believed to have come from a long-destroyed Crusader church. The walls of Jerusalem, like the city itself, are composed of stones used again and again, just as many of the legends and traditions of the city reappear and are reassembled by each successive civilization and religion.

Inside the gate, on the left, is:
### ❷ The Tourist Information Office
Here you can pick up free maps, information, and tourist publications.

# Walking Tour: The Old City

1 The Jaffa Gate
2 Government Tourist Information Office (GTIO)
3 New Imperial Hotel
4 The Petra Hotel
5 The view from the Petra Hotel roof
6 Suq El Hussor
7 Stone rooftop
8 Cardo
9 Hurva Synagogue
10 Herodian Quarter Excavations
11 Crusader Church of St. Mary
12 Western Wall
13 Archeological excavations at the southern foot of the Temple Mount
14 Southern wall of the Old City
15 The Temple Mount
16 Al Aqsa Mosque
17 Dome of the Rock
18 Islamic Museum
19 Suq El Attarin Bazaar
20 Suq Khan Es Zeit
21 Ethiopian Compound and Monastery
22 Crafts shop
23 Ethiopian Chapel
24 Chapel of the Archangel Michael
25 Church of the Holy Sepulcher

## Walking Tour Routes

—·—·— Option 1
·········· Option 2
— — — Option 3

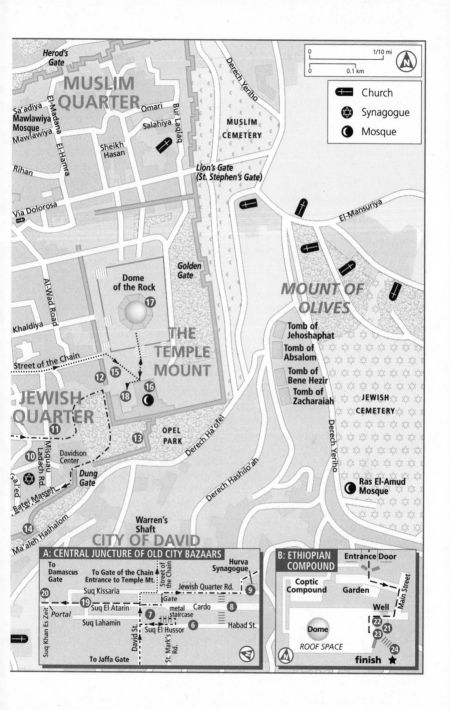

**Herod's Gate**

## MUSLIM QUARTER

Sa'adiya
**Mawlawiya Mosque**
El-Madana — El-Hamra
Mawlawiya

Omari
Salahiya
Bur Lajlaq

Sheikh Hasan

Rihan

Via Dolorosa

Khaldiya

Al-Wad Road

Street of the Chain

### JEWISH QUARTER

Misquau Ladach Rd.

Ga'ed

Batei Massel

Ma'aleh Hashalom

**Lion's Gate (St. Stephen's Gate)**

**MUSLIM CEMETERY**

**Derech Yeriho**

El-Mansuriya

**Golden Gate**

**Dome of the Rock** 17

## THE TEMPLE MOUNT

12  15
18  16

11
13

**OPEL PARK**

Davidson Center

**Dung Gate**

**Warren's Shaft**

## CITY OF DAVID

10
14

### Legend
- Church
- Synagogue
- Mosque

0    1/10 mi
0    0.1 km

## MOUNT OF OLIVES

Tomb of Jehoshaphat
Tomb of Absalom
Tomb of Bene Hezir
Tomb of Zacharaiah

### JEWISH CEMETERY

Derech Yeriho

Derech Ha'ofel

Derech Hashilo'ah

**Ras El-Amud Mosque**

---

**A: CENTRAL JUNCTURE OF OLD CITY BAZAARS**

To Damascus Gate

To Gate of the Chain Entrance to Temple Mt.

Street of the Chain

**Hurva Synagogue**

Suq Kissaria

Jewish Quarter Rd. 9

20

19    Suq El Atarin

Gate
metal staircase
Cardo    8

Suq Lahamin    7    6    Habad St.

Portal
Suq Khan Es Zeit

David St.
St. Mark's Rd.
Suq El Hussor

To Jaffa Gate

---

**B: ETHIOPIAN COMPOUND**

Entrance Door

Coptic Compound

Garden

Main Street

Well

Dome

ROOF SPACE

22  21
23
24

**finish** ★

Enter the archway on the left to the arcade of:

### ❸ The New Imperial Hotel

Built in the 1880s, this was, in its time, the most luxurious hotel in Jerusalem. In the 19th century, the now largely deserted arcade was a private bazaar for hotel guests, where the beggars, lepers, cripples, and "riffraff" of Jerusalem could be neatly excluded. Slightly uphill and in the center of the arcade is a broken streetlamp mounted on a cylindrical stone that was uncovered when the foundations for the New Imperial were dug. The Latin lettering, "LEG X," records a marker for the camp of the Tenth Legion Frentensis, which conquered and destroyed Jewish Jerusalem in A.D. 70. Flavius Josephus wrote that after The Temple and the buildings of Jerusalem were systematically razed and the surviving inhabitants led off to slavery, death, and exile, the Tenth Legion encamped beside the ruins of the Jaffa Gate for 62 years to guard the ruins against Jews who might try to filter back and reestablish the city. The discovery of this marker in proximity to the Jaffa Gate confirms Josephus's account. The once-elegant New Imperial, as it drifted into seediness, became a spot for romantic assignations during the British Mandate period. Characters played by Bogart (if not Bergman) would have felt at home.

Next door is the:

### ❹ Petra Hotel

The first modern hotel built in the Old City in the 1870s, the once elegant Petra, now reduced to the status of a hostel, is popular with backpackers. Herman Melville and Mark Twain probably stayed in an earlier structure on this site (the old Mediterranean Hotel) during their visits to what was then a decrepit warren of ruins filled with lice-covered beggars and crazed religious fanatics. Neither Melville nor Twain found Jerusalem a pleasant place to stay.

Enter at the far right as you face the building, climb the stairs to the second floor lobby of the Petra, and ask the person at the desk for permission to see:

### ❺ The View from the Petra Hotel's Roof

Be sure to show this book; admission is about NIS 5 ($1.25/60p) per person. From the lobby, climb two more long flights of stairs, and emerge from the creaky wooden attic stairs onto the roof with its strange series of curved stone domes. Turn left, up a few steps and left again, and you will face one of the Old City's great panoramas—perfectly aligned, with the golden Dome of the Rock (site of the First and Second Temples) in the exact center of the vista, with the roofline of the city spread out below you. This is where photographers come for postcard views. The roof used to be a quiet, contemplative spot, but guests of the hostel make the roof into a wall-to-wall sleeping bag encampment in summer.

As you look eastward toward the Temple Mount, you'll see the Mount of Olives across the horizon behind the Dome of the Rock. In ancient times, this now-barren ridge was a natural olive grove, and its cultivation was one of the sources of ancient Jerusalem's wealth. The green area of the ridge, just behind the Dome of the Rock, is the Garden of Gethsemane (Gethsemane is the anglicized version of the Hebrew word for "olive press"), where Jesus was arrested after the Last Supper. This is the western side of the Mount of Olives ridge. On the eastern side, out of view, is the site of the village of Bethany where Lazarus, who was raised from the dead by Jesus, and his sisters, Mary and Martha, lived. Jesus may have been making his way to their house after the Passover dinner at the time of his arrest.

The Dome of the Rock was built in A.D. 691. According to legend, the saintly warrior Omar Ibn El Khattab, who conquered Jerusalem for Islam in A.D. 638, was greeted by the Christian archbishop Sophronius at the Jaffa Gate. Sophronius surrendered the city peacefully to Omar, and then offered to lead the new ruler on a tour of his conquest. The first thing Omar Ibn El Khattab asked to see was "the Mosque of Suleiman," or the place where Solomon's Temple had once stood. The vast ceremonial platform surrounding the site of the ancient Jewish temple was one of the few architectural landmarks of Herodian Jerusalem that the Romans had found too difficult to eradicate when they destroyed the city in A.D. 70. Three hundred years later, as Christianity triumphed over Roman paganism, the Temple Mount was one of the places in the city left purposely in ruins (perhaps symbolically) by the Byzantine Christians. By the time of the Muslim conquest, the Temple Mount had become the garbage dump for Jerusalem and the surrounding area. Omar Ibn El Khattab was so saddened by the sight of the ancient holy place defiled and in ruins that he removed his cloak and used it to carry away debris. Sophronius prudently followed Omar's example. Later Muslim authorities ordered the most beautiful building to be placed over the rock. The silver-domed Al Aqsa Mosque, on the southern edge of the Temple Mount, also commemorates this event.

Just below the Petra's roof is a large empty rectangular area, the Pool of Hezekiah, misnamed centuries ago for the Judean king whose hidden water system saved ancient Jerusalem from Assyrian onslaught in 701 B.C.; the pool is actually a disused reservoir for a water system constructed in Herodian and Roman times. To the north, you will see the great silver dome of the Church of the Holy Sepulcher, built over the site venerated for almost 2,000 years as the place of Jesus' crucifixion and entombment. In the far distance, beyond the walls of the Old City, on the northern part of the Mount of Olives ridge, the small city is the complex of the Hebrew University and Hadassah

Hospital on Mount Scopus. To your right (south), inside the walls of the Old City, are the domes of the Armenian Cathedral of Saint James, the roofs of the Armenian and Jewish quarters of the Old City, and 8km (5 miles) to the south, beyond the hill of Abu Tor (believed to have been the Hill of Evil Counsel as well as the site of the Blood Acre purchased for a potters' field with Judas Iscariot's 30 pieces of silver) is Bethlehem, birthplace of King David and of Jesus.

**Leave the Petra Hotel and continue down David Street to:**

### ❻ Suq El Hussor

This former basket bazaar, which once sold the big, traylike olive-twig baskets older Palestinian women sometime still balance on their heads, filled with grapes, fruits, and vegetables, is now a small covered street of ordinary shops, but it leads to a great view.

**About 18m (59 ft.) on the left side of Suq El Hussor, you'll notice an open metal staircase. Climb the staircase, and you'll be on:**

### ❼ The Stone Rooftop of the Covered Markets

Here you'll discover a different world above the bustling labyrinths of the bazaars. The broad rooftop area straight ahead covers the exact center of the Old City, where the four quarters meet. At the right time of day, if you listen carefully, you will hear emanating from the large dome on your right the unmistakable sound of a game of billiards; this dome at the very heart of the Holy City covers a billiard parlor. In Crusader times, this large structure housed the city's bourse or exchange. From this rooftop, you can clearly see the architectural distinctions among the four quarters of the walled city: the orange-tile-roofed Christian Quarter to the northwest; the dome-roofed Muslim Quarter with its many television antennas to the northeast; the new stonework of the Jewish Quarter to the southeast, rebuilt by the Israelis after they reoccupied the Old City in 1967 (this area is devoid of antennas; its inhabitants receive cable); and, to the southwest, the older stone buildings of the Armenian Quarter. Again, through the maze of TV antennas, you get an interesting chance to photograph the lavish Dome of the Rock.

**Descend the metal staircase, and backtrack on Suq El Hussor to David Street. Turn right onto David Street. The next right on David Street leads to the:**

### ❽ Cardo

The restored and renovated section of Roman and Byzantine Jerusalem's main market street is now filled with stylish modern shops.

At this point you have three choices for the rest of your tour.

### THE FIRST OPTION: THE JEWISH QUARTER
You could easily wander the streets of this beautifully reconstructed area for a number of hours.

**Walk south on the Jewish Quarter Road to the:**

### ❾ Hurva Synagogue

This site was home to the Jewish Quarter's main synagogue from the 16th to the mid–20th century, but all you see today are ruins from the most recent incarnation's destruction by the Jordanians in 1948. There are plans in the works to rebuild it exactly as it stood before it was destroyed. For more on this site, see p. 171.

**TAKE A BREAK**
A slice of kosher pizza, a falafel, a light meal, or wonderful Arabic bread fresh from the bakery oven is all available on the section of the Jewish Quarter Road beyond the Hurva Synagogue.

**Walk across the square behind the synagogue, and you'll see signs for the:**

### ❿ Herodian Quarter

The present Jewish Quarter, on a hill opposite the Temple Mount, was the aristocratic residential part of Jerusalem in Herodian times. During the 1970s, intensive archaeological excavations were carried out here while the Jewish Quarter was being rebuilt. The ruins of large mansions were found with facilities for *mikvot* (ritual baths) and with mosaic floors ornamented by simple geometric designs (in strict keeping with the Mosaic commandment against graven images).

**Take Tiferet Israel Street, which runs from the northeastern corner of the big square to the end, where you will come upon the:**

### ⓫ Crusader Church of Saint Mary

In the extensive ruins of this Crusader-era church, once hidden beneath buildings from later times, you can explore the ruined cloister and the basilica, with a view of the Temple Mount and the Mount of Olives framed in the window of the central apse.

**Turn right at the church and make a left to the great staircase, which descends down to the:**

### ⓬ Western Wall

The Herodian retaining wall for the western side of the Temple Mount was built by Herod the Great more than 2,000 years ago. It's a remnant of the outer courtyard of the Jerusalem Temple, and the holiest place of prayer in Jewish tradition. See p. 172.

**Between the Western Wall and the Dung Gate, you can enter the area of the:**

### ⓭ Archaeological Excavations

Set at the southern foot of the Temple Mount, these excavations are accessed through the Davidson Exhibition Center (p. 179), which shows video programs depicting what the Jerusalem Temple would have been like in the years before its destruction in A.D. 70. Self-guided audio tours take you to various points along the southwestern and southern walls of the Temple Mount, where you can study the grandeur of this structure away from the crowds at prayer at the Western Wall.

**From the excavations, take the road inside the city wall uphill to the:**

### 14 Southern Wall of the Old City

Here you'll find a lovely view down into the valley below, which was the site of the original City of David 3,000 years ago.

**You will see a parking lot inside the city walls; cross it and turn right into a pathway that becomes Habad Road. Follow Habad Road to the far end. Or Hayim Street is a left turn off Habad Road. Continue uphill until the road ends at the Armenian Patriarchate Road. A right turn onto this road will get you back to the square inside the Jaffa Gate.**

**SECOND OPTION: THE TEMPLE MOUNT** From the Cardo, if it is not a Friday, and not after 11:30am, continue straight onto where David Street seems to end.

**Turn right, then quickly take the first left, a continuation of David Street called the Street of the Chain. Continue down this road to the great green door (the Gate of the Chain) at the end, which leads directly onto the:**

### 15 Temple Mount

The Temple Mount (in Arabic, Haram es Sharif) is open for visitors until 3pm. Give yourself ample time to walk around the ceremonial plaza and enjoy the views of the Mount of Olives. At press time the Al Aqsa Mosque and the Dome of the Rock on the Temple Mount were not open to the public, but if entering them is again permitted, non-Muslims must buy admission tickets (approx. NIS 38/$9.50/£4.75, and well worth the fee) from a small stone kiosk to the right of the Al Aqsa Mosque, which will admit you to both mosques and to the museum (you may be asked to wait outside during noonday prayers). It is permissible to take photographs outdoors on the Temple Mount, but you cannot bring a camera into mosques or shrines.

**Walk diagonally to the right after entering the Gate of the Chain to the southern end of the Temple Mount to:**

### 16 Al Aqsa Mosque

This is the main Islamic prayer hall on the Temple Mount.

**In the center of the Temple Mount is the:**

### 17 Dome of the Rock

You can't miss its lavish exterior tiles and its golden dome.

**At the southwest corner is the:**

### 18 Islamic Museum

This museum houses a collection of Islamic artifacts from earlier periods on the Temple Mount.

**THIRD OPTION: THE BAZAARS & THE CHURCH OF THE HOLY SEPULCHER** This walk begins at the intersection of David Street and the Cardo.

**Turn left into the narrow, covered:**

### 19 Suq El Attarin Bazaar

The Spice Market was covered during the time of the Crusaders, who perhaps could not bear the blazing summer sun of the region. It's actually an additional segment of the Cardo, once the great Roman north-south market and ceremonial street. The Roman Cardo, originally broad and colonnaded, evolved over centuries into the present warren of narrow, parallel bazaars (including the Butcher's Bazaar, with its dangling skinned sheep heads and gutters of blood, parallel just to the left) that runs all the way north to the Damascus Gate. El Attarin is now mostly populated by clothing and sneaker shops.

**Follow this covered market street until you exit from the covered portion, through a nondescript portal, and continue straight on. The next section of the street, no longer roofed over but covered by shop awnings, is:**

### 20 Suq Khan es-Zeit (the Market of the Inn of the Olive Oil)

Probably since Herodian-Jewish times, this area has been a major food market—the Frankish Crusaders called this the

*Malcuisinat,* or Street of Bad Cookery, unhappy with the many Middle Eastern specialties sold here. You will notice pastry shops displaying mysteriously radiant mountains of baklava arranged on top of glowing light bulbs and flashlights; the peanut baklava filling is sometimes dyed green to approximate the more costly pistachio. There are also chewy rolled pancakes filled with nuts or sweet cheese, served in a honey syrup; other shops sell dried fruits or dark globs of fruit- and nut-filled nougat. There are also hibachis cooking kabobs and *shashliks,* and rotisserie chicken to go. Any of these places are good bets for snacks.

---

**TAKE A BREAK**
**Abu Assab Refreshments,** a busy Old City landmark, sells fresh orange, grapefruit, and carrot juice, and is the least expensive and best of its kind in town. It's a good place to stave off dehydration and fill up on vitamins, and you can order the juices straight or in any combination. You can stay downstairs for a quick break, or go upstairs where there is table service. Mike, the British-educated manager, who is often at the downstairs carrot juice counter, will translate the Arabic price list.

---

A short way along the same side of the street is a stone staircase. Climb the staircase to the top, turn left, and follow the lane to the end, turn right, and follow the street around through the Coptic Convent and onto the:

### ㉑ Ethiopian Compound & Monastery

It's located on the Church of the Holy Sepulcher's roof with the protruding dome in the center. Through the windows of the dome you will be able to see the **Chapel of Saint Helena** inside the Holy Sepulcher Church below; you'll even be able to smell the church incense, and at times, hear services and prayers.

The Ethiopians use this roof area each year on the Saturday midnight eve of Easter Sunday for one of the city's most exotic religious processions. The Ethiopian Patriarch, with a great ceremonial African umbrella, circumambulates the dome, followed by monks beating ancient drums—so large that they must be carried by two men—and by chanting white-robed pilgrims. The procession then retires to a leopard-skin tent (nowadays made of canvas in a leopard-skin pattern) to chant and pray through the night. This very moving ceremony is open to the public, and many Jerusalemites make it a point to attend each year.

The compound is spread across the sprawling segments of the roof of the Church of the Holy Sepulcher. Note that here on this ancient roof entire trees and gardens grow, among them the olive trees (or offshoots of olive trees) in which Abraham supposedly found the ram he offered in sacrifice after God freed him from the commandment to sacrifice Isaac. Beside the expanse of the roof surrounding the dome are the living quarters of the tiny, walled, fortresslike monastery. Visitors may not enter this monastery compound, but you can look into the lane at the entrance to the monastery: The low round-walled buildings and trees offer a distinctly African feeling. For centuries, the Church of the Holy Sepulcher has been divided among the six oldest factions of Christianity, and in the most recent division, the Ethiopian Church, with roots dating from the 4th century A.D., got the roof. Both Ethiopian monks and a lay community have inhabited this location for centuries (you can often smell the wonderful spicy cooking of the communal kitchen). Note the church bells hanging in the ruined Gothic arches of the Crusader-era church structure to the right and above the tiny main street.

To the left of the doorway into the monastery lane, you will find the community's well, with a shaft running down through the Holy Sepulcher Church

---

(running water has obviated the need for the well, but the Ethiopians still have the right to a certain amount of water from it each day).

Opposite the well is a small, sometimes open door leading to a:

**㉒ Crafts Shop**

It's usually closed, but at times you can find Ethiopian crafts and hand-painted icons for sale.

From this door continue around the corner to the large ancient wooden door leading to the:

**㉓ Ethiopian Chapel**

This structure was probably built in medieval times. Here, if a monk is in attendance, you will be shown crucifix-shaped holy books written in ancient Ge'ez (the sacred language of Ethiopia), and you will have time to take in the paintings (unfortunately done by European religious painters rather than by traditional Ethiopian religious artists) that depict the Queen of Sheba visiting King Solomon in approximately 940 B.C. Charmingly, the artist decided to depict an anachronistic group of 18th-century Hasidic Jews among King Solomon's entourage. From the traditionally believed union of the queen and King Solomon, the royal Ethiopian family is said to have

descended (one of the emperor of Ethiopia's titles was "the Lion of Judah"), and in 1935, when Emperor Haile Selassie was forced to flee the Italian invasion of his country, he took up residence in Jerusalem, "the land of my fathers." There is a tray for contributions at the back of the chapel.

Continue to the rear of the chapel and down the staircase to the:

**㉔ Chapel of the Archangel Michael**

In this ancient chapel, with its carved and inlaid wood paneling, the community of Ethiopian monks gathers in late afternoon for prayers (4pm in winter; 5pm during daylight saving time). It is sometimes possible for visitors to sit in the rear of the chapel and listen to the traditional Ethiopian chanting, which is extremely beautiful.

The ancient wooden door of the chapel leads outside to the main entrance plaza in front of the:

**㉕ Church of the Holy Sepulcher**

Now that you've seen the roof, you are ready to journey through the very special interior. (See p. 181 for a detailed description of the church.) After visiting the church, make your way back through the bazaars to David Street and the Jaffa Gate.

## 2 West Jerusalem Attractions

### MUSEUMS

**Ammunition Hill Memorial and Museum**   At the top of Givat Ha-Tachmoshet (Ammunition Hill), between Sheikh Jarrah and Ramat Eshkol, the site of a bloody battle in 1967, this museum is dedicated to the reunification of Jerusalem and to those who died in the Six-Day War. You can walk through bunkers and trenches, and five exhibition halls full of weapons, maps, battle plans, and more.

Ammunition Hill. ℂ **02/582-8442.** Admission NIS 16 ($4/£2); half-price for students and children. Sun–Thurs 9am–5pm; Fri 9am–1pm. Bus: 4, 9, 25, 28, or 99.

**The Bible Lands Museum** ★★   This museum, opened in 1992, was founded by Dr. and Mrs. Elie Borowski, who donated an incomparable private collection of ancient Near Eastern artifacts as the nucleus of an institution that would survey cultures surrounding the ancient Judeo-Israelite world.

This is an art lovers' museum: Visitors will be amazed by the beauty of the objects on display. In the words of Dr. Borowski, a noted Near Eastern scholar and adviser to museums who carefully built his collection over a period of 40 years, "Each of the

# Jerusalem Attractions

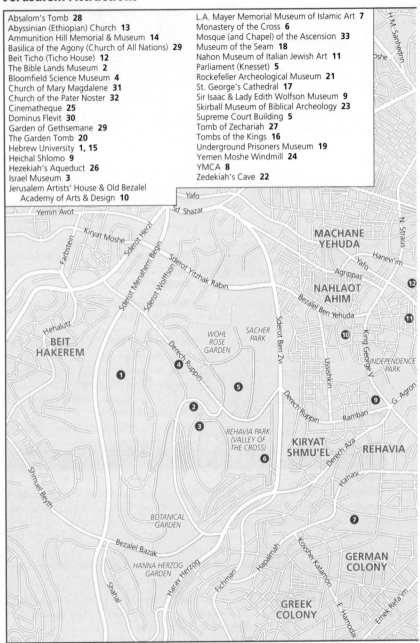

Absalom's Tomb **28**
Abyssinian (Ethiopian) Church **13**
Ammunition Hill Memorial & Museum **14**
Basilica of the Agony (Church of All Nations) **29**
Beit Ticho (Ticho House) **12**
The Bible Lands Museum **2**
Bloomfield Science Museum **4**
Church of Mary Magdalene **31**
Church of the Pater Noster **32**
Cinematheque **25**
Dominus Flevit **30**
Garden of Gethsemane **29**
The Garden Tomb **20**
Hebrew University **1, 15**
Heichal Shlomo **9**
Hezekiah's Aqueduct **26**
Israel Museum **3**
Jerusalem Artists' House & Old Bezalel
   Academy of Arts & Design **10**

L.A. Mayer Memorial Museum of Islamic Art **7**
Monastery of the Cross **6**
Mosque (and Chapel) of the Ascension **33**
Museum of the Seam **18**
Nahon Museum of Italian Jewish Art **11**
Parliament (Knesset) **5**
Rockefeller Archeological Museum **21**
St. George's Cathedral **17**
Sir Isaac & Lady Edith Wolfson Museum **9**
Skirball Museum of Biblical Archeology **23**
Supreme Court Building **5**
Tomb of Zechariah **27**
Tombs of the Kings **16**
Underground Prisoners Museum **19**
Yemen Moshe Windmill **24**
YMCA **8**
Zedekiah's Cave **22**

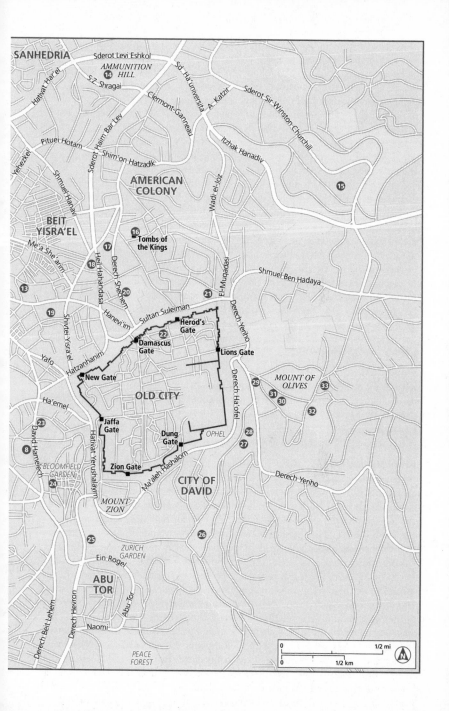

objects has its time in history, its location in space, its meaning in religion and daily life, and last but not least, its beauty and artistry."

The museum is arranged chronologically: Artifacts from differing cultures that existed at the same time are displayed side by side. Themes such as religious worship, trade, communication, and transportation are examined in ways that bring the objects to life and give you a personal, human insight into life in the times they represent.

Museum highlights: the **Assyrian ivories** from Nimrud (ca. 800 B.C.), including a masterpiece winged griffin delicately grazing on foliage; and the 4th-century-A.D. **sarcophagus of Julia Latronilla,** with its bas-relief depiction of the life of Jesus (among the earliest known representations of Jesus and of elements of Christian theology). Other objects catch the eye with their charm, vitality, or mysterious beauty: an Egyptian cosmetics container in the shape of a swimming girl (ca. 1550 B.C.); a Minoan terra-cotta sarcophagus, freely painted in bright colors with folk motifs; a 1st-century-A.D. Roman painted linen shroud with the serene, ethereal image of a woman covering its length. A special section of the museum is devoted to cylinder seals and scarabs; a remarkable computer/video program brings these minute works of art to life with detailed, fascinating explanations. There are also visiting exhibitions and new donations.

The Bible Lands Museum hosts a wonderful program of Saturday evening concerts (including wine and cheese) that often features many of the country's most talented new immigrants. Admission for concerts is NIS 80 ($20/£10); discounts for students.

25 Granot St., beside the Israel Museum. © 02/561-1066. www.blmj.org. Admission NIS 32 ($8/£4); discounts for students. Sun–Tues and Thurs 9:30am–5:30pm; Wed 9:30am–9:30pm; Fri 9:30am–2pm. Call ahead for a schedule of English-language tours. Bus: 9 or 17.

**Bloomfield Science Museum**   Another of the city's brand-new attractions, this is a hands-on museum with many state-of-the-art exhibits that may be of special interest to children and young adults. It's a possible option for a rainy-day activity, but not particularly special to Israel or Jerusalem.

Rupin St. at Givat Ram. © 02/561-8128. Admission NIS 32 ($8/£4); students NIS 20 ($5/£2.50). Mon and Wed–Thurs 10am–6pm; Tues 10am–8pm; Fri 10am–1pm; Sat 10am–3pm. Bus: 9, 24, or 28.

**Israel Museum** ★★★   *Note:* Through at least 2009, the permanent galleries of the museum will be closed for renovations. This includes the Judaica Wing; the Archaeological galleries; and the permanent exhibits of European, Asian, pre-Columbian; and primitive art. What will be open includes the Shrine of the Book (with the Dead Sea Scrolls); the miniature model of Ancient Jerusalem; the outdoor Billy Rose Sculpture Museum; the Youth Wing; and one pavilion for temporary exhibits. Some of the museum's collection will be exhibited at other venues throughout the city, including Ticho House and the Rockefeller Museum. Check the museum website for updated information.

Opened in May 1965, this complex is an outstanding example of modern Israeli architecture. There are five main components: the Bezalel Art Museum, the Samuel Bronfman Biblical and Archaeological Museum, the Billy Rose Art Garden, the Shrine of the Book, and the always lively and fascinating Children's Wing. All sections of the museum are worthy of a world-class institution, but the Shrine of the Book (containing the Dead Sea Scrolls), the Judaica Wing, and the Archaeological Museum are unique and laden with treasures not found anywhere else in the world.

The **Bronfman-Bezalel complex,** in the main building and adjoining wings, houses a bookstore and gift shop in its lower level, as well as a snack bar and auditorium. Outside, to the left of the stairs, is the moderately priced museum cafeteria.

In this part of the museum, you'll find the **Judaica Wing** ✯✯✯, composed of an unequaled collection of ceremonial artifacts from Jewish communities throughout the world. In one gallery, there are scores of fascinating Chanukah lamps from Europe, Asia, and North Africa, each reflecting the architecture and design traditions of their places of origin. There are also silver Torah finials from around the world, ceremonial spice boxes, beautifully ornamented plates and trays for Passover Seder, and containers for the *etrog,* a citron fruit that is part of the Succot tradition. Other rooms contain illuminated manuscripts from Iran, Poland, and Italy and a vast exhibit of costumes worn by Jews in the lands of the Diaspora, all displayed among the artifacts and elements of architecture that surrounded the daily life of each community. There is an entire reconstructed interior of a 17th-century Italian synagogue from the Veneto region, as well as a delicately painted German *succa* (temporary harvest structure) from the 18th century in which a wealthy family would have dined outdoors, according to tradition, during the harvest festival of Succot. The recently transferred interior of a synagogue from Cochin, India, is one of the museum's newest treasures. Adjacent to the Judaica Wing, the museum also exhibits European period rooms, and beyond that, rooms devoted to European art and contemporary Israeli art.

The **Archaeology Wing** ✯✯✯ contains the world's largest collection of objects found in Israel. Among the most dramatic highlights drawn from thousands of years of history and prehistory are powerful stone and clay masks from Neolithic through early Canaanite periods; the mysterious and elegantly wrought hoard of copper wands, scepters, crowns, and other objects (possibly ceremonial maces) from the Chalcolithic (Copper Age) sanctuary of a forgotten people (ca. 3500 B.C.), uncovered in the 1960s, where they were hidden in the depths of a cave overlooking The Dead Sea; and the illustrated mosaic floors and architectural elements of ancient Byzantine-era Jewish and Samaritan synagogues ranging from Hebron to the Galilee, including a delicately carved stone chancel screen and a massive stone seat reserved for the most honored member of an ancient Jewish congregation.

Other important galleries expand the scope of the museum and are very worth visiting. One contains a beautifully chosen collection of **pre-Columbian Central American art** from 2000 B.C. to A.D. 1550; another has an exceptional collection of **primitive and tribal art.** A gallery adjacent to the Archaeology Wing houses a beautiful collection of ancient glass; in addition, there is the **Walter and Charlotte Floersheimer Pavilion for Impressionist and Post-Impressionist Art** with works by Corot, Monet, Renoir, Degas, Gauguin, Matisse, and others. The new **Weisbord Pavilion,** just across the walk from the museum's entrance building and gift shop, houses a small collection of works by Rodin as well as visiting exhibits of modern art.

Another remarkable part of the museum is an archaeological garden between the Shrine of the Book and the Youth Wing complex. It contains classical Greco-Roman sculptures, sarcophagi, and mosaics, most of which were discovered and excavated in Israel.

The **Billy Rose Art Garden** ✯✯✯, on a 8-hectare (20-acre) plot, has been impressively landscaped by the renowned Japanese-American artist Isamu Noguchi. In the garden of semicircular earth-and-stone embankments is a 100-piece sculpture collection, which contains both classical and modern European, American, and Israeli works. Artists represented include Rodin, Zorach, Henry Moore, Picasso, Maillol, and Israeli sculptors, such as Channa Orloff.

Then there's the **Shrine of the Book** ✯✯✯, with its distinctive onion-shaped top, contoured to resemble the covers to the clay containers in which the Dead Sea Scrolls were discovered. In addition to housing the prized Dead Sea Scrolls and the Bar Kochba letters, the underground shrine is the exhibition site for additional finds from Masada and other sites around The Dead Sea in which Jewish fugitives from the wars against Rome hid their most precious possessions.

On Saturday or holidays, you have to buy your tickets just outside the museum from a local ticket agent. The museum is located south of the Knesset.

Ruppin St. © 02/670-8811. www.imj.org.il. Admission NIS 40 ($10/£5); special 2-entry and multiple-entry tickets available. Sat–Mon and Wed–Thurs 10am–5pm; Tues 4–9pm; Fri 10am–2pm. Bus: 9, 17, 24, or 99.

## L. A. Mayer Memorial Museum of Islamic Art ✦

This is another worthwhile jewel of a museum, with a strong permanent collection of Islamic art and consistently superb visiting exhibitions. A wonderful collection of Palestinian costumes and embroidery, the great national folk craft of the region, tops the exhibits of local art; the Islamic jewelry gallery is an additional pleasure. The museum also houses a large and fascinating international collection of clocks, including the famous Salomons collection of Breguet watches from Paris dating from 1769 to 1823. A collection of Islamic carpets was added in 1999.

2 Ha-Palmach St. © 02/566-1291. www.islamicart.co.il. Admission NIS 20 ($5/£2.50). Sun–Mon and Wed–Thurs 10am–3pm; Tues 10am–6pm; Fri–Sat 10am–2pm.

## Museum of the Seam

Right on what had been the no man's land between East and West Jerusalem, this old Turkish-era mansion was turned into a fortress and used as an Israeli command post during the 1948 War of Independence and up until 1967. Until 1999, the museum was dedicated to the history of divided Jerusalem. Now the museum has become sociopolitical contemporary, attempting to establish dialogue, understanding, and coexistence between Israelis and Palestinians, using lectures, art exhibits, and state-of-the art media displays. The museum hosts special education groups daily from 9am to 3pm, but call ahead to confirm, as this can change.

To get here, from East Jerusalem, continue up Nablus Road; you'll pass East Jerusalem's American consulate building. Nablus Road goes to the right of the consulate. Detour left across the busy Rte. 1 highway to Tourjeman Post on the highway's western side. From West Jerusalem, it's on the edge of Mea Shearim.

Shivtei Israel, Saint George St. and Nablus Rd. (Rte. 1). © 02/628-1278. www.coexistence.art.museum. Admission NIS 25 ($6.25/£3.10). Sun–Thurs 9am–5pm; Fri 9am–2pm. Bus: 1, 11, or 27.

## Nahon Museum of Italian Jewish Art (Finds)

This museum contains the transported interior of the beautiful 18th-century synagogue of Conegliano Veneto, near Venice, which is open for services on Friday evenings and on Saturday mornings. The exhibits cover the scope of Italian Jewish life and contain ritual objects from medieval times to the present; you may be able to visit the on-site workshops of a special team of Italian and Israeli artisans working to restore and preserve these treasures of Jerusalem's Italian Jewish community. The garden and plaza in front of the complex seems to be a small piece of Italy itself.

27 Hillel St. © 02/624-1610. www.jija.org. Admission NIS 10 ($2.50/£1.25). Sun–Wed 9am–2pm; Thurs 9am–1pm. Services Fri evening and Sat morning.

## Sir Isaac and Lady Edith Wolfson Museum ✦

For many years, one of the city's hidden treasures has been this vast, outstanding private collection of antique Chanukah menorahs, paper cuts, kiddush cups (ceremonial wine goblets), wedding contracts, mezuzzot (sacred parchment holders, affixed to the doors of Jewish households), and other items of Judaica hidden away on the fourth floor of the Heichal Shlomo–Great Synagogue complex. In keeping with contemporary museum trends throughout the world, the Wolfson apparently exhibits only a few objects from its regular collection, where dozens of items were once shown. The main attractions are well-chosen temporary exhibits of antique and contemporary Judaica coordinated to Jewish holidays according to the time of year. Although mostly composed of antique objects, the collection also includes works of contemporary Judaica by such craftspeople as Oded Davidson and Danny Azulai, whose workshops can be visited in downtown Jerusalem.

In Heichal Shlomo, King George St. ℂ 02/624-7908. Admission NIS 25 ($6.25/£3.10). Sun–Thurs 9am–3pm. Bus: 4, 7, 8, 9, or 48.

**Skirball Museum of Biblical Archeology**    For archaeology buffs, this handsomely displayed collection, largely of objects discovered at Tel Dan in the north, is a worthwhile stop. There's a pleasant library attached—stocked with English periodicals—that's a good place to read, write, and collect your thoughts. If you're pressed for time, however, it's skip-worthy.

Hebrew Union College, 13 King David St. ℂ 02/620-3333. Free admission. Sun–Thurs 10am–4pm; Sat 10am–2pm.

**Underground Prisoners Museum**    Housed in the 19th-century Russian pilgrimage hostels that later served as British Mandate Jerusalem's Central Prison, this museum documents the prison conditions suffered by many who fought for Jewish immigration to British Mandate Palestine and for the establishment of a Jewish state.

Off Safra Sq., near Shivtei Israel St. ℂ 02/623-3166. Admission NIS 10 ($2.50/£1.25). Sun–Thurs 8:30am–4pm.

## MEMORIALS

**Mount Herzl**    Mount Herzl is located at the end of the Bet Ha-Kerem section of Jerusalem. It is the memorial for Theodor Herzl, who predicted and worked for the founding of Israel until his death in 1904. A large black monolith marks Herzl's interment. Herzl's wife and his parents are buried there, too. The cemetery also contains the graves of Golda Meir, Levi Eshkol, and other important leaders. The final resting place of Yitzhak Rabin is also here.

Down the road from the Herzl cemetery, inside an entrance made of orange stone, is a military cemetery for those who have fallen in the country's many wars.

The on-site **Herzl Museum** (ℂ **02/651-1108**) explores the life and work of the founder of modern Zionism with an inventive new 1-hour video production, and contains a replica of Herzl's Vienna study with his own library and furniture. No admission fee.

Accessed on Herzl Boulevard. Free admission. Park Apr–Oct daily 8am–6:30pm (Nov–Mar until 5pm); museum Sun–Thurs 9am–5pm, Fri 9am–1pm. Bus: 17, 17A, 18, 20, 21, 23, 24, 26, 27, 39, 40, or 99 to Herzl Blvd.

**Yad VaShem Memorial and Holocaust Museum** ✹✹✹    Down the road from Mount Herzl is a ridge called Har Ha-Zikaron (Mount of Remembrance). This is Israel's great memorial and place of commemoration for the millions who perished in the Holocaust and whose graves, both known and unknown, are distant from these hills. The vast, sprawling complex contains many sections. Perhaps the most central is the new **Holocaust Museum,** opened in 2005 and probably the most wide-ranging museum of the Holocaust in the world. Housed inside a long, tunnel-like structure that finally ends in a panoramic terrace with vistas of the Judean Mountains, this new museum is designed to help give a personal dimension to the overwhelming six million human beings who fell victim to the Nazis. Moving video testimonies by survivors dot the long, meandering line of exhibits that detail the suffering of Jewish communities throughout Europe, from the beginning of the Nazi persecution to its horrific end. There are diary excerpts, personal photographs, letters, and, at times, the only remaining mementos of loved ones that have been bravely donated to Yad VaShem by elderly Holocaust survivors. This museum and its vast exhibit replaces Yad VaShem's original museum, built in the 1960s.

Other elements of Yad VaShem include the **Avenue of the Righteous Among the Nations,** lined with trees planted in tribute to each individual gentile who helped save Jewish lives during the Nazi era—many of these heroes sacrificed their own lives and the lives of their families. Here you'll find trees honoring those who tried to save Anne Frank and her family in Amsterdam, and a tree in honor of Princess Alice of Greece (mother-in-law of Britain's queen Elizabeth II), who hid a Greek Jewish family for over a year in Athens. The heavy entrance gate to the **Hall of Remembrance,** designed by two of Israel's leading sculptors, Bezalel Schatz and David Polombo, is an abstract tapestry of jagged, twisted steel. Inside is a huge stone room, like a crypt, where an eternal flame sheds somber light over the plaques on the floor commemorating Bergen-Belsen, Auschwitz, Dachau, and other camps.

Very important to the work of Yad VaShem is the **Hall of Names,** which contains more than three million pages of testimony, as well as the names, photographs, and personal details of as many of those who perished in the Holocaust as Yad VaShem has been able to gather. Visitors are invited to contribute information they might have about relatives and friends in order that no victim will be forgotten.

On the crest of the western slope of the **Mount of Remembrance** stands a 6m-high (20-ft.) monument dedicated to the 1.5 million Jewish soldiers among the Allied forces, partisans, and ghetto fighters. Below the monument one can see the vast sculptural memorial called the **Valley of the Destroyed Communities,** commemorating the 5,000 European Jewish communities that disappeared during World War II. There is a special memorial to the **Children of the Holocaust** that is hauntingly moving, donated to Yad VaShem by a husband and wife whose own young child was murdered by the Nazis. It commemorates more than 1.5 million murdered children.

Across the hill is an archive building that has the most complete library, research, and education center dedicated to this topic. The new Main Entrance Pavilion contains a cafeteria and an extensive bookstore.

On Har Ha-Zikaron. 🅒 02/675-1611. www.yadvashem.org.il. Free admission. Sun–Thurs 9am–4:45pm, Fri 9am–1pm; Hall of Names Sun–Thurs 10am–2pm, Fri 10am–1pm; archives and library Sun–Thurs 9am–3pm. Closed Sat and Jewish holidays. Bus: 17, 18, 20, 21, 23, 27, or 99.

## CHURCHES & MONASTERIES

Rechov Ha-Nevi'im (Street of the Prophets) was the "Christian street" of 19th-century West Jerusalem, and still has a variety of churches and missionary societies. From Zion Square, in the heart of downtown Jerusalem, cross Jaffa Road and go up the hill on Ha-Rav Kook Street. Opposite the intersection of Ha-Rav Kook and Ha-Nevi'im streets is the entrance to the narrow, high-walled Ethiopia Street, [0]with its 19th-century stone mansions. Here you'll find the splendid **Abyssinian (Ethiopian) Church.** The elegant building with the Lion of Judah carved into the gate above the courtyard is the spiritual home of the Coptic Ethiopian clergy. The lion symbolizes the meeting of the Queen of Sheba, the Ethiopian empress, and King Solomon, from whom she traditionally received the emblem. The interior of the turn-of-the-20th-century circular church is filled with a wonderful array of icons and paintings; although none are in the Ethiopian tradition, many were chosen for their charm and native beauty. Bungalows for clergy and pilgrims from Ethiopia surround the church enclave.

**Notre Dame de France** is on Shivtei Israel Street at Zahal Square, just opposite New Gate in the Old City walls. The Assumptionist Fathers built this monastery in 1887 to serve as a pilgrim's hostel. The monumental buildings of the complex, on the old border between East and West Jerusalem, were badly damaged during heavy fighting in the 1948 war. Part of the complex, restored in the 1970s, serves as a hospital, a restaurant, a hotel, and a pilgrimage center.

**Saint Andrew's Church of Scotland** was built by the people of Scotland in 1929 and was dedicated by General Allenby, who liberated Jerusalem from the Ottoman Empire in 1917. This Presbyterian Church is situated on a hilltop near Abu Tor and the Jerusalem railroad station. Also at the top of Abu Tor, and built over the foundations of a medieval church, is the **Greek Orthodox Monastery,** called the "Church of Evil Counsel." It contains catacombs and crypts. Private cottages on the grounds are rented to fortunate Jerusalemites, including one of the country's most talented and respected poets.

The **Russian Orthodox Holy Trinity Cathedral** is just off Jaffa Road. This white multidomed architectural gem in the Renaissance style was originally constructed after the Crimean War for pilgrims of the Russian Orthodox faith (see Russian Compound, below).

There are also a number of interesting churches and monasteries in Ein Kerem and Rechavia (see "Exploring West Jerusalem Neighborhoods," below), and in Abu Ghosh (see section 10, later in this chapter).

## MORE ATTRACTIONS

**Beit Ticho (Ticho House)** *Finds*    You'll be amazed when you come upon this large hidden oasis with its gardens and terrace restaurant/cafe right in the center of downtown West Jerusalem—it's especially wonderful for outdoor dining in summer. Loved by Jerusalemites, both for its beauty and its history (and also as a meeting place), Ticho House was built in 1880 as a private villa for the Aga Rashid Nashishibi. Later it became the home of artist Anna Ticho and her husband, Dr. Abraham Ticho, a legendary ophthalmologist (p. 225) who maintained his surgery there. The building is now a downtown branch of the Israel Museum, complete with a handy museum gift shop. There's a permanent exhibit of Anna Ticho's controlled, powerful charcoals and drawings, as well as visiting exhibitions arranged by the museum. Upstairs, Dr. Ticho's consulting office is preserved, filled with his international collection of antique Chanukah lamps. Especially moving are the notes to Dr. Ticho, preserved under glass on his desk, from members of the Arab, Jewish, and British communities after he was seriously wounded during the political unrest of 1929. Ticho House hosts poetry and fiction readings, intimate theater and music performances, and a Friday morning concert series.

Off Harav Kook St. © **02/624-5068.** Free admission. Exhibit rooms Sun–Thurs 10am–5pm (Tues until 10pm), Fri 10am–2pm, Sat after Shabbat–5pm; restaurant Sun–Thurs 10am–midnight, Fri 10am–3pm, Sat after Shabbat.

**Chagall Windows at Hadassah Medical Center** *★★*    The largest medical center in the Middle East, the Hadassah Hebrew University Medical Center stands on a hilltop several miles from downtown Jerusalem. The center contains a medical school, nursing school, hospital, dental and pharmacy schools, and various laboratory buildings. The hospital's synagogue contains Marc Chagall's 12 exquisite stained-glass windows

## Two Dreams Restored

Israel's earlier branch of Hadassah Hospital is on Mount Scopus, overlooking Jerusalem's Old City. Opened in 1938, in an ultramodern building designed by Erich Mendelssohn and funded by Hadassah supporters throughout the world, it was the pride of the Jewish community of British Mandate Palestine and the embodiment of a dream to bring quality medical care to all in Jerusalem, "without regard to nationality or religion." But at the time of the cease-fire at the end of Israel's War of Independence in 1948, Hadassah Hospital on Mount Scopus found itself a small Israeli-held bastion in middle of Jordanian-controlled East Jerusalem, protected by international agreement but cut off from Israeli-held West Jerusalem. So a new Hadassah Hospital was built in Ein Kerem at the far western edge of Jerusalem, where it would be relatively safe in case fighting again broke out. Ironically, when the Six-Day War erupted in 1967, one of the first places hit by Jordanian bombardment was the new hospital. When Marc Chagall learned that the windows he had created for the hospital's synagogue had been damaged, he promised to replace them, making them "more beautiful than ever." He more than succeeded. Today, Hadassah Mount Scopus is again open, and both Hadassah hospitals serve all the communities of Jerusalem.

depicting the blessings that Jacob, on his deathbed, bestowed to each of his 12 sons (Gen. 49:1–27). The sons of Jacob became the founders of the Twelve Tribes of Israel.

Call for information about complete 5-hour tours of the medical center, or for the short tour of the Chagall windows.

Ein Kerem. ☏ 02/641-6333. Admission and tour of Chagall windows NIS 14 ($3.50/£1.75); discount for students and seniors. Sun–Thurs 8am–1:15pm and 2–3:45pm; Fri and eves of holidays 8am–12:30pm. Bus: 19 or 27 from Jaffa Rd.; 19 from Jaffa Gate, Agron St., King George V Ave., or Bezalel St.

**Hebrew University, Givat Ram Campus**    Located on two Jerusalem campuses, Hebrew University is one of Israel's most dramatic accomplishments, with more than 18,000 students spread across this and the Mount Scopus campus. Built to replace the university's original Mount Scopus campus, which was cut off from West Jerusalem from 1948 to 1967, the Givat Ram Campus now houses the university's science departments and functions in tandem with the Mount Scopus Campus, which was reclaimed in 1967 during the Six-Day War.

Take special architectural note of the Belgium House Faculty Club, La Maison de France, the physics building, and the huge Jewish National and University Library (partly inspired by LeCorbusier's Villa Savoye in Poissy, France) at the far end of the promenade. And don't miss the mushroom-shaped synagogue behind the library and the futuristic gym. The synagogue, with its dome supported by eight arches, was designed by Heinz Rau (one of the designers of Brasilia) and the important Israeli architect, David Reznik; Reznik's imprint dots the city—he designed Jerusalem's Hyatt Regency Hotel and codesigned the Mormon Center on Mount Scopus.

You can stop for lunch in the cafeteria of the administration building, or in the Jewish National and University Library, which contains a vast stained-glass window depicting images of Jewish mysticism.

Givat Ram campus (West Jerusalem). ☏ 02/688-2819. Free university tours Sun–Thurs 11am from Visitors Center in the Sherman Building. Bus: 9, 24, or 28 to modern Givat Ram campus.

**Heichal Shlomo**   Facing the large main park, Gan Ha-Atzma'ut, this imposing complex includes the Great Synagogue and the former Seat of the Rabbinate, designed in a rather vague imitation of what was believed to be King Solomon's Temple. Weekly programs—religious and folk songs, lectures, and readings—mark the end of Shabbat and the beginning of the new week. For times of traditional religious services, check at Heichal Shlomo, your hotel, or a tourist information office. The Wolfson collection of Judaica (see Sir Isaac and Lady Edith Wolfson Museum, above), one of the world's finest, can be seen on the fourth floor.

58 King George V Ave. No phone. Heichal Shlomo free admission; Wolfson museum NIS 10 ($2.50/£1.25). Sun–Thurs 9am–1pm; Fri 9am–noon. Bus: 4, 7, 8, 9, or 48.

**Jerusalem Artists' House and Old Bezalel Academy of Arts and Design**   Many cultural activities center on the Jerusalem Artists' Association. Exhibitions of art, evenings of chamber music, concerts, readings, jazz, and art lectures are scheduled each year (for specifics, check with the tourist office or at the office here); there's an expensive restaurant (Cezanne) and a very good, affordable vegetarian restaurant (the Village Green). On the main floor, paintings and sculptures of more than 500 artist members are sold (if you buy, they'll ship your purchases). Upstairs and throughout the building are general exhibitions in August and the spring; special exhibitions, featuring about three artists at a time, change every 3 weeks during the rest of the year. Note the beautifully carved outside doors, the crenelated roof and dome, and the garden sculpture. The present Bezalel School is at Hebrew University.

12 Shmuel Ha-Nagid St. ✆ 02/625-3653. Free admission. Sun–Fri 10am–1pm and 4–7pm; Sat 10am–1pm. Bus: 4, 7, 8, 9, 19, or 48.

**Parliament (Knesset)**   This modern landmark—called by some West Jerusalem's Acropolis, by others an airport terminal with no runway—houses magnificent mosaics and tapestries by Chagall, as well as Knesset sessions that run the gamut from funereal to the most rowdy in the democratic world. The entryway, a grillwork of hammered metal, is the work of Israeli sculptor David Polombo, who did the dramatic doors at Yad VaShem. **You must have your passport with you,** and you will be subject to a careful security search. Always call ahead to check current schedule. *Tip:* The Knesset may not be the mother of parliaments, but it now has a dress code for visitors: No sandals, jeans, collarless T-shirts, shorts, or bare midriffs. Ben-Gurion himself would not have passed muster on certain days.

Government Quarter—Kiryat Ben-Gurion, Kaplan St. ✆ 02/675-3333. Free guided tours on Sun and Thurs 8:30am–2:30pm; viewing of Knesset sessions Mon or Thurs 4–9pm, Wed after 11am. Closed Jewish holidays. Bus: 9, 17, 24, 28, or 99.

**Russian Compound**   Once this 19th-century series of structures surrounding the beautiful Russian Orthodox Holy Trinity Cathedral was the world's largest "hotel"; it could accommodate 10,000 Russian pilgrims at one time (until World War I, Russians composed the largest block of pilgrims in the Holy Land). Today, this neglected but architecturally striking enclave serves as a municipal parking lot and an Israeli prison; at visiting times, families of prisoners can often be seen huddling outside the police barricades. Around the back, near the entrance to the prison, a low iron fence surrounds a monumental Herodian-era column abandoned in the process of being carved directly from bedrock—it apparently cracked and was abandoned, but its size has led to speculation that it may have been meant to adorn The Temple complex. The Underground Prisoners Museum (p. 199) is housed in part of the Russian Compound complex behind Safra Square. There are plans to restore the pilgrimage buildings, and to turn the parking lots into gardens and the complex into luxury and moderate hotels. Today it remains an oddly romantic touch of St. Petersburg right in the heart of Jerusalem.

As you walk along Jaffa Road from Zion Square, look up to your left (north), before the main post office, and you'll see the Russian Orthodox Cathedral.

Off Jaffa Rd. near Zion Sq.

**Sanhedrian Tombs**    Go up Shmuel Ha-Navi, off Shivtei Israel Street, to northeast Jerusalem's beautiful public gardens of Sanhedria. Here you look at the Tombs of the Sanhedria or the Tombs of the Judges, where the judges of ancient Israel's "Supreme Court" (during the 1st c. A.D., before the Romans destroyed Jerusalem and banned Jewish residence in the area) are buried. The three-story burial catacomb is intricately carved from rock.

Sanhedria. Free admission. Gardens daily 9am–4 or 5pm; tombs Sun–Fri 9am–4 or 5pm. Bus: 2 from Jaffa Gate.

**Supreme Court Building**    In a country starved for good modern architecture, the new Supreme Court Building, opened in 1992, is a major hit with Israelis and visitors alike. The contemporary design of the building incorporates traditional Middle Eastern motifs of domes, arches, and passageways, all set up to create interesting interplays of shadow and light. Call for the current schedule of English tours that highlight the building's design and the traditions of the court.

Next to Knesset. ✆ 02/675-9612. Sun–Thurs 8:30am–2:30pm; free tours in English Sun–Thurs at noon. Bus: 9, 17, 24, 28, or 99.

**YMCA**    One of the most outstanding landmarks in the city, the YMCA was built in the early 1930s with funds donated by a Montclair, New Jersey, philanthropist named James Jarvie. Designed by the architectural firm that did New York City's Empire State Building, the building is an interesting mixture of Art Deco, Byzantine, and Islamic styles. This is probably the most amazing YMCA in the world. On the first floor you'll find a replica of the London room in which the YMCA was founded in 1844. The 46m (151-ft.) **YMCA Tower** ★★ (Mon–Sat 9am–2pm) offers one of the most dramatic panoramas of the city. Notice the six-winged bas-relief seraph that ornaments the center of the tower's facade; the tower also houses the only carillon in the Middle East. Concerts played on the tower bells, especially at midnight on New Year's Eve, are among the city's little-known pleasures. Built by Christian, Jewish, and Muslim workers and artisans, the YMCA is a meeting place for all the city's communities. The complex includes a swimming pool, tennis courts, athletic fields, lecture and concert halls, a gymnasium, a restaurant, and one of the best hotels in Jerusalem.

24 King David St. ✆ 02/625-7111. Free admission; small donations for tower entrance. Tours Mon–Sat 9am–3pm. Bus: 5, 6, 18, or 21.

## 3 Exploring West Jerusalem Neighborhoods

**YEMIN MOSHE** ★    In the 1850s, British philanthropist Sir Moses Montefiore, with the help of Judah Touro from New Orleans, built the nucleus of this residential quarter, the first outside the walls of the Old City, in an effort to bring indigent Jews from the Old City into a more healthful environment. The project included a now-famous windmill for grinding flour. Despite its magnificent view and graceful architecture, the neighborhood remained poor for more than a century.

Today, Yemin Moshe is a picturesque, beautifully restored neighborhood—an architectural treasure and one of the most elegant addresses in town. There are no shops, but the views are spectacular. It's a fascinating place for an early-evening or winter-afternoon stroll; however, a noontime walk in the hot July sun is not recommended. The steep pedestrian-street staircases of Yemin Moshe may make it a bit difficult for some.

Down one of the first flights of staircases is the **Yemin Moshe Windmill,** which houses a museum dedicated to Sir Moses Montefiore. It is open Sunday to Thursday from 9am to 4pm, and until 1pm on Friday. Admission is free. Below the windmill is the original row of **old stone buildings (Mishkanot Sha'ananim),** the first Jewish houses built outside the walls of the Old City since ancient times. Ornamented by Victorian ironwork porches, the buildings are now used as a residence by visiting artists and diplomats.

A replica of the Liberty Bell in Philadelphia stands in the center of Jerusalem's **Liberty Bell Garden,** not far from the windmill. The 2.8-hectare (7-acre) garden has a picnic area, vine-covered trellises, a large children's playground, and an entertainment area. You may wonder why a copy of the Liberty Bell has been made into the centerpiece of a Jerusalem park. The words inscribed on the American original were spoken by one of Jerusalem's most famous inhabitants, the Prophet Isaiah, more than 2,500 years before the Declaration of Independence was written: "Proclaim liberty throughout the land, and to all the inhabitants thereof." It was with these words that Israel's independence was announced in 1948.

**MEA SHEARIM** 🏃🏃    This area, a few blocks north of Jaffa Road, is populated by Hasidic and ultra-Orthodox Jews of East European origin. It is a world unto itself, and a visit here is like going back in time to the world of religious eastern European Jewry that existed before the Holocaust. Originally built in the late 19th century as a semi-fortified agricultural community in what was at that time open countryside, about a mile beyond the walls of the Old City, the neighborhood consists of numerous courtyards designed to be defended against unruly Bedouin marauders. In the 20th century, the area came to be inhabited by Hasidic rabbinical courts and followers of the many Hasidic sects that emigrated to Jerusalem from Europe. Some married women in this area, according to strict East European Orthodox tradition, wear wigs and scarves over their shaved heads. A number of residents speak only Yiddish in conversation, as Hebrew is considered too sacred for daily use. Some don't even recognize the laws of the Israeli government, believing that no State of Israel can exist before the coming of the Messiah. Demonstrators protesting such issues as medical autopsies, driving on Saturday, and coed swimming pools have clashed with police. The neighborhood is filled with synagogues, yeshivas, and small workshops and shops selling religious objects.

Architecturally, Mea Shearim has the feel of an 18th-century Polish ghetto, the more so because of the traditional dress and lifestyle of its residents. Visitors to this area are requested to dress modestly (no shorts, short skirts, uncovered arms or shoulders for women; slacks for men). Men and women are advised not to walk in close proximity (certainly not hand in hand), and visitors are advised to stow away cameras and to be very discreet in taking photographs. No inhabitant of Mea Shearim will voluntarily pose for snapshots, and there have been incidents in which improperly dressed visitors have been spat upon or stoned.

**GERMAN COLONY & BAKA**    About 1.6km (1 mile) south of downtown West Jerusalem, these two picturesque neighborhoods, filled with overgrown gardens, are undergoing a process of gentrification. For many years, the old cottages and mansions (built at the start of the 20th c. by German Protestants and affluent Arabic families) housed Israelis from exotic places such as Kurdistan and Morocco, but more recently, members of Jerusalem's American, British, and Latin American immigrant communities have been moving in. The two charming neighborhoods offer family-run restaurants and shops that tend to reflect the area's ambience. **Emek Refaim Street** (a southern continuation of King David St.) is the German Colony's main artery; a walk down **Yehoshua Ben Nun Street,** which runs parallel to Emek Refaim 1 block to the west beginning at **Rachel Immenu Street,** gives you a better idea of the neighborhood's interesting residential architecture. Because of the area's newfound popularity, modern apartment buildings are being squeezed into every possible garden and empty lot. Much of the area was saved from demolition through efforts lead by Sara Fox Kaminiker, who came to Israel from the United States and served on the city council under the administration of Teddy Kollek (Sara Fox Kaminiker's book of walking tours, *Footloose in Jerusalem,* which includes this neighborhood, is highly recommended—it's currently out of print, but you might be able to find it online or at smaller bookstores).

In Baka, the main street is **Derech Bethlehem.** On many of the narrow side streets running off this thoroughfare, you'll find eccentric examples of Arabic mansions and 1930s bungalows. For those who like architecture, the quiet back streets of both neighborhoods are good places to meander by bike.

**RECHAVIA-TALBEYEH**   A turn to the west from King George V Avenue, at either the Jewish Agency compound or the Kings Hotel, will bring you into Jerusalem's most beautiful residential section, with its middle- and upper-class, tree-lined streets. Rechavia's glory is its collection of 1930s International Style apartment buildings and houses. Talbeyeh, just to the south, is filled with elaborate villas and mansions built mainly by Jerusalem's Arab Christian community in the 1920s and 1930s. Abandoned when their original owners fled in 1948, these houses are now inhabited by Israelis. **Hovei Zion Street** is lined with examples of these gracious homes.

Sights in the area include the **prime minister's residence,** at the corner of Balfour and Smolenskin; and the **Alfasi grotto** (also called the "Tomb of Jason"), on Alfasi Street, a frescoed and inscribed tomb discovered by builders while they were digging foundations (daily 10am–4pm). The medieval **Monastery of the Cross,** in the Valley of the Cross outside Rechavia, was built by Gregorian monks in the 11th century and is now maintained by the Greek Orthodox Church. According to tradition, the beautiful monastery is located on the spot where the tree stood from which the cross was made. If you don't want to walk down the rocky hillside from Rechavia to the monastery, take bus no. 9 or 17. The monastery is open Monday to Friday from 9am to 4pm. Admission is NIS 5 ($1.25/60p). At the southern edge of Rechavia, in Kiryat Shmuel, is **Bet Ha-Nassi,** the president's residence. You can look through the gates, but except for receptions, it is not open to the public.

**EIN KEREM**   This ancient village, in a deep valley at the western edge of Jerusalem, is traditionally regarded as the birthplace of John the Baptist. Now incorporated into Jerusalem, you can reach it in less than 30 minutes by bus no. 17 from King George Street or Jaffa Road. The lanes and gardens of Ein Kerem (Well of the Vineyard) are lovely; the old Arabic-style houses have been grabbed up and renovated by some of the city's most successful and famous inhabitants; and high above the area, on the crest of the mountains, is the vast Hadassah–Ein Kerem Medical Center (not accessible from Ein Kerem itself). Ein Kerem contains a number of 19th-century European churches, convents, and monasteries. Most important is the **Church of Saint John** in the center of town, marking John the Baptist's birthplace (daily 6am–noon and 2–5pm); on request you can see the grotto beneath the church with its Byzantine mosaic. On Ma'ayan Street, you'll find the **Church of the Visitation** (daily 8–11:45am and 2–5pm), commemorating the visit of Mary to her cousin Elizabeth, the mother of John the Baptist. It was often depicted in medieval and early Renaissance paintings as a scene in which the two expectant women touch each other's stomachs, and according to legend, the two infants jumped for joy inside their mothers' wombs when Mary and Elizabeth met. Below the Youth Hostel off Ma'ayan Street is a mosque and minaret marking the well from which Mary drew water; farther along the ridge is the Russian Convent, known as the **Moscobiyah,** a fascinating enclave of 40 Jerusalem stone buildings scattered among a wooded area of pines and cypresses. The nuns live in small ocher-painted houses reminiscent of wooden cottages in Russia. You can make an appointment to visit by calling ✆ **06/625-2565** or 02/541-2887. Bring a snack or canteen along, or you can pick up something in the grocery at the center of town. Restaurants here look appealing, but meals are expensive and nothing special. The times for return to Jerusalem should be posted at the bus stop in the center of Ein Kerem; you may have to wait in downtown Jerusalem for up to 30 minutes until the infrequent bus no. 17 to Ein Kerem picks you up.

**MACHANE YEHUDA**    The Old Market Quarter—liveliest on Wednesday and Thursday—is off Jaffa Road, 1km (½ mile) west of Zion Square. In a square off Machane Yehuda and Jaffa Road, there is a war memorial commemorating the "Davidka," an improvised weapon used in the defense of Jerusalem.

## 4 East Jerusalem Attractions

You can probably cover the major sights of East Jerusalem in half a day. As you go along **Saladin Street** from the north, toward the Old City walls, you'll pass the **Ministry of Justice** on the right. Farther down, across the street in a tree-shaded compound, is the famed **Albright Institute of Archaeological Research.** Just past it on the left, you'll find **Az-Zahra Street,** a modern thoroughfare of clothing and appliance stores, bookshops, restaurants, and hotels, leading to the Rockefeller Museum.

**The Garden Tomb**    This 1st-century tomb, discovered in 1867 by Dr. Conrad Schick, is very similar to the biblical description of the tomb of Jesus. In 1883, the very "Kiplingesque" General Gordon (later to die in the siege of Khartoum) visited the tomb on his way to Egypt, and in a fit of pique over the exclusion of Protestant services from the Church of the Holy Sepulcher, had a vision that this site outside the Damascus Gate was the real tomb of Jesus. The tomb was finally excavated in 1891, and whether it is the correct place or not, it certainly meets some of the specifications: close to the site of the crucifixion; outside the walls of the city; hewn from the rock; a tomb made for a rich man; and situated in a garden. As late as the early 20th century, the nearby hill that Gordon identified as Golgotha (Calvary), or according to the New Testament, "the Place of the Skull," was indeed eerily shaped like a skull, but construction and quarrying have obscured this impression.

To get here, head up Nablus Road (Derech Shechem), opposite Damascus Gate. Look for the side street named Conrad Schick Street on the right.

Conrad Schick St. ✆ **02/628-3402.** Free admission (donations accepted). Mon–Sat 8am–12:15pm and 2:30–5:15pm; Protestant service in English Sun 9am. Bus: 27.

**Rockefeller Archaeological Museum** ⭐   Located near Herod's Gate, and named for John D. Rockefeller, who financed its construction with a gift of $2 million in 1927, the Rockefeller is a treasury of regional archaeological objects ranging from the Stone Age to the 18th century. Among the Rockefeller's highlights are the original bas-relief stonework that once adorned the entrance to the Church of the Holy Sepulcher; the 9th-century carved wooden panels and ceiling beams of the Al Aqsa Mosque; and richly ornamented early Islamic architectural details from the 8th-century Hisham's Palace near Jericho.

Much of the collection was excavated in Ashkelon, Acre, and Galilee by American and English archaeologists during the first half of the 20th century. Pottery, tools, and household effects are arranged by periods—Iron Age, Persian, Hellenistic, Roman, and Byzantine. There is also a special gallery of Egyptian antiquities; in the south gallery's Paleolithic section are the bones of Mount Carmel Man.

The museum's eclectic 1930s design is a Jerusalem landmark that combines elements of Byzantine, Islamic, and Art Deco, and includes a beautiful, recently renovated cloister garden set around a reflecting pool. The building was damaged during the Six-Day War, but the museum's displays were barely affected. Luckily, there was no damage at all to the many Dead Sea Scrolls, at that time kept for study in the museum, which was in the area of Jerusalem under Jordanian control. The Rockefeller is now a branch of the Israel Museum. At press time the museum was closed for renovation through 2010, so check before you go.

Sultan Suleiman St. ☎ 02/628-2251. www.english.imjnet.org.il. Admission NIS 26 ($6.50/£3.25). Discount joint admission to Israel Museum available. Mon and Wed–Thurs 10am–3pm; Sat 10am–2pm; closed Tues and Fri. Bus: 1 or 2.

**Saint George's Cathedral**   Neo-Gothic towers adorn this compound, which also includes an excellent travelers' guesthouse and the headquarters for the Anglican archbishopric, with jurisdiction extending as far across the Middle East as Sudan. It's a rare architectural enclave for this part of the world, recalling the courtyards of Oxford or Cambridge. Feel free to pass through the courtyard for a look. The complex also contains a religious college, a school, a small garden, and residences. There is a small exhibit of beautiful Palestinian textiles on display as well.

Nablus Rd. Free admission. Daily 9am–4pm. Bus: 27.

**Tombs of the Kings**   Behind Saint George's, on the left side as you head down Saladin Street, is a gate marked "Tombeau des Rois." About 6m (20 ft.) down a stone stairway, you'll see a hollowed-out courtyard, with several small cave openings. Inside one are four sarcophagi, covered with carvings of fruit and vines. Despite the name, the tomb is for the family of Queen Helena of the Mesopotamian province of Adiabene, who converted to Judaism in Jerusalem around A.D. 50.

Saladin St. Admission NIS 5 ($1.25/60p). Mon–Sat 8am–12:30pm and 2–5pm. Bus: 27.

**Zedekiah's Cave**   Follow the Old City walls to the east of Damascus Gate, and you'll soon come to the entrance leading under the walls into Zedekiah's Cave, or Solomon's Quarries, which tradition calls the source of the stones for Solomon's Temple. Because of this, the cave is of special importance to the worldwide Order of Masons, which claims spiritual descent from the original builders of the First Temple. Jewish and Muslim legends claim that tunnels in those caves extended to the Sinai Desert and Jericho. The quarries got their name because King Zedekiah was supposed to have fled from the Babylonians through these tunnels in 587 B.C., only to be later captured near Jericho. An illuminated path leads you far back into the caves and under the Old City.

Near the Damascus Gate. Admission NIS 10 ($2.50/£1.25). Daily 10am–4pm. Bus: 27.

## MOUNT SCOPUS, MOUNT OF OLIVES & VALLEY OF KIDRON

You can reach the Mount of Olives Road either by driving north up Saladin Street or by taking a left turn at the wall, just past the Rockefeller museum. For Hebrew University Mount Scopus campus, take bus no. 4A, 9, or 28 from downtown West Jerusalem.

**MOUNT SCOPUS**    From Sheikh Jarrah (on Nablus Rd.), the road heads past the Mount Scopus Hotel and proceeds, gradually curving, past Shepherds Hotel. At the bend in Mount Scopus Road, to your left, you'll see the **Jerusalem War Cemetery,** the resting place for British World War I dead. You are now on Mount Scopus–Har Hatsofim, which means "Mount of Observation." It was here that the Roman armies of Titus and Vespasian camped in A.D. 70 and observed the city under siege as they planned their final attack.

About 90m (295 ft.) down the ridge, you'll find the **Mount Scopus Hadassah Hospital** on the left. The **Hebrew University on Mount Scopus,** which opened on April 1, 1925, is now one of the largest institutions of higher learning in the Middle East. It is mostly housed in a vast fortresslike megacomplex designed by David Reznik. The design seems to reflect the university's past experience. At the end of the War of Independence in 1949, the cease-fire lines found Israeli defenders still holding out at Hebrew University and Hadassah Hospital, two important Jewish institutions deep in the heart of Jordanian-controlled East Jerusalem. For the next 19 years, these two bastions were resupplied by monthly Red Cross convoys, and a new Hadassah Hospital and Hebrew University had to be built in West Jerusalem. Since 1967, the hospital and campus have been restored to their original functions and greatly enlarged. From the Truman Research Institute (a pink stone building) there's a sweeping view of both the New and Old cities. Tours are conducted Sunday to Friday at 11am from the Sherman Building.

**VIEWS OF JERUSALEM**    The road skirting the ridge proceeds past the high-towered Augusta Victoria Hospital—an Arab Legion bastion during the Six-Day War—the Arab village of Et-Tur, the Mount of Olives, the Jewish Cemetery, and the Seven Arches Hotel. The best views of Jerusalem are from Hebrew University on Mount Scopus, the Jewish graveyard on the Mount of Olives, and the Seven Arches Hotel. For optimum viewing and photographs, come in the morning, when the sun is behind you.

**MOUNT OF OLIVES** ★★    Here you'll find six churches and one of the oldest Jewish cemeteries in the world. It was this cemetery that religious Jews had in mind when they came to die in the Holy Land through the start of the 20th century. Start down the path on the right, and you'll come to the Tombs of the Prophets, believed to be the burial place of Haggai, Malachi, and Zechariah. Many Jews have believed, and perhaps still do, that from here the route to heaven is the shortest, since God's presence is always hovering over Jerusalem; others have held that here, on the Mount of Olives, the resurrection of the dead will occur.

Farther up the road, on the southern fringe of Et-Tur, stands the **Mosque (and Chapel) of the Ascension** (ring the doorbell for admission), marking the spot where Jesus ascended to heaven. Interestingly, this Christian shrine is under Muslim control. Muslims revere Jesus as a prophet. However, they do not believe Jesus to be the son of God, nor do they believe that Jesus died on the cross.

## The Peoples' Princess

Among the thousands of people who have found their final resting place on the Mount of Olives, one of the most recent and unusual is Princess Alice of Greece, mother of Prince Philip, Duke of Edinburgh, and mother-in-law of Queen Elizabeth II. Born in Windsor Castle in 1885, the great-grand-daughter of Queen Victoria, Princess Alice at an early age was diagnosed as being almost totally deaf. Carefully trained in lip reading, she was fluent in both English and French; later in life she also mastered Greek.

In 1903, Princess Alice married Prince Andrew, son of King George of Greece, and devoted her life to helping others. During the 1912 Balkan War, she worked as a nurse close to the battlefront, caring for sick and wounded Greek soldiers. During this time, both the princess and King George stayed in the home of the family of Haim Cohen, in the northern Greek city of Trikkala, near the war zone. Alice was fascinated by the family's warmth and traditions. The princess's friendship continued when Cohen later became a member of the Greek parliament. By the late 1930s, the Greek royal family was no longer in power, but Princess Alice remained in Athens, wearing the habit of a nun as she became increasingly committed to a life of religion and charitable work.

In 1943, during the Nazi occupation of Greece, Princess Alice learned that the widow and children of Haim Cohen were desperately trying to escape deportation to the death camps in Poland. At the risk of her life and with the help of two servants, Princess Alice hid her Jewish friends on the grounds of the royal palace in Athens for 13 months until Greece was liberated. Princess Alice died at Buckingham Palace in 1969, and in 1988, in accordance with her dying wish, was reinterred at the **Church of St. Mary Magdalene** on the Mount of Olives. In 1994, Prince Philip and his sister, Princess Sophie, traveled to Jerusalem to receive Yad VaShem's Medal of Honor of Righteous Among the Nations, awarded to their late mother. A tree in memory of Princess Alice has been planted at Yad VaShem.

Just a few steps away is the **Church of the Pater Noster,** built on the traditional spot where Jesus instructed his disciples in the Lord's Prayer. Tiles along the walls of the church are inscribed with the Lord's Prayer in 44 languages. The Carmelite Convent and Basilica of the Sacred Heart are on the adjoining hill.

From up here you can see a cluster of churches on the lower slopes of the Mount of Olives. All can be reached either from here or from the road paralleling the fortress wall, diagonally opposite Saint Stephen's Gate (Lion's Gate).

If you head down the path to the right of the Tomb of the Prophets, you'll come to **Dominus Flevit** (daily 8am–noon and 2:30–5pm), which is a relatively contemporary Franciscan church that marks the spot where Jesus wept over his vision of the future destruction of Jerusalem. Next, the Russian Orthodox **Church of Mary Magdalene,** with its onion-shaped spires, was built in 1888 by Czar Alexander III (Tues and Thurs 10–11:30am). Call ✆ **02/628-4371** for more information.

The Roman Catholic **Garden of Gethsemane** (Apr–Oct daily 8:30am–noon and 3pm–sunset; in winter daily 8:30am–noon and 2pm–sunset) adjoins the **Basilica of the Agony (Church of All Nations);** it's in the courtyard where Jesus supposedly prayed the night before his arrest. The church's gold mosaic facade shows God looking down from heaven over Jesus and the peoples of the world. The church was built by people from 16 different nations in 1924. Next door, past beautifully tended gardens of ancient olive trees and bougainvillea, is the **Tomb of the Virgin,** which is a deep underground chamber housing the tombs of Mary and Joseph. The tomb is open daily 8am to noon and 2:30 to 5:30pm.

**VALLEY OF KIDRON**    The Valley of Kidron is between the Mount of Olives and the Old City walls. It runs south, between Mount Ophel (where David built his city) and the Mount of Contempt. Just under the wall here, roughly in front of Al Aqsa Mosque, are two tombs: **Absalom's Tomb** and the **Tomb of Zechariah.** At one time, religious Jews would throw stones at Absalom's tomb (Kever Avshalom) in condemnation of Absalom, who rebelled against his father, King David. Scholars attribute Absalom's Tomb to Herodian times—it is Jerusalem's only relatively intact structure from before the Roman destruction in A.D. 70.

The Valley of Kidron is also known as the Valley of Jehoshaphat. The Book of Joel records that the judgments will be rendered here on resurrection day: "Let the heathen be awakened, and come up to the Valley of Jehoshaphat, for there will I sit to judge all the heathen round about." Muslims hold to a similar belief. They believe Muhammad will sit astride a pillar under the wall of the Dome of the Rock. A wire will be stretched from the pillar to the Mount of Olives, opposite, where Jesus will be seated. All humankind will walk across the wire on its way to eternity. The righteous and faithful will reach the other side safely; the rest will drop down in the Valley of Jehoshaphat and perish.

About 180m (591 ft.) down the valley is the **Fountain of the Virgin,** at the Arab village of Silwan. Water from the spring (the Gihon) anointed Solomon king and served as the only water source for ancient Jerusalem. During the Assyrian and Babylonian attacks (8th c. B.C.), King Hezekiah constructed an aqueduct through which the waters could be hidden inside the city, an extraordinary engineering feat at the time. **Hezekiah's Aqueduct** is still there (underneath the church commemorating the spot where Mary once drew water to wash the clothes of Jesus). It's about 480m (1,575 ft.) long, and the depth of the water is from .5 to 1m (1½ ft.–3 ft.). The walk takes about 40 minutes; take a flashlight or a candle with you. You can walk through from Sunday to Thursday between 8:30am and 3pm, on Friday and holiday eves until 1pm. Entrance is free, but give the caretaker a tip. It is best to visit Silwan and Hezekiah's tunnel with a tour group (see section 6, below for information). Above the **Gihon Spring** lie the ruins of King David's city (see "Dung Gate, Silwan [The City of David] & the Jerusalem Archaeological Park," earlier in this chapter).

## 5 Especially for Kids

The **Train Puppet Theater** in Liberty Bell Park offers programs (in Hebrew, but nonetheless interesting) for children and hosts an International Puppet Theater Festival every other year. Call ✆ **02/561-8514** for information, or check the listing in Friday's *Jerusalem Post.* Also see "Jerusalem After Dark," later in this chapter. The **Israel Museum's** lively **Children's Wing** has great exhibits, many of them hands-on; workshops in recycled materials; and a library of fabulous children's books you can sit and read. See "Museums" in section 2, earlier in this chapter.

**The Time Elevator**   This is a 30-minute, multimedia, semivirtual reality history of Jerusalem presented in a former auditorium refitted with special chairs and a floor that provides special motion effects. It's not good for younger children or for those who do poorly on roller coaster rides. The presentation itself is interesting, but expensive for what you get. The show is repeated about every 40 minutes.

Beit Agron, Hillel, and Rivlin sts. ℂ 02/625-2227. Admission NIS 50 ($13/£6.25). Sun–Thurs 10am–8pm.

**The Tisch Family Zoological Gardens**   Jerusalem's biblical zoo has recently moved into this new, beautifully landscaped site at the western edge of the city, with a state-of-the art open design that blends into the surrounding countryside. Emphasis is on creatures mentioned in the Bible or native to Israel, but there are also now many animals, large and small, from the far corners of the world. Children will enjoy the friendly waterfowl and the camel encampment (camel and pony ride facilities are planned). There is a pleasant safari-style refreshment facility on the grounds. In summer, during the heat of the day, most animals are inactive; the zoo is at its best in cooler weather. Prepare for a 10-minute walk from the bus stop. Admission ends an hour before closing time.

Manahat, Jerusalem. ℂ 02/675-0111. www.jerusalemzoo.org.il. Admission NIS 42 ($11/£5.25) adults; NIS 34 ($8.50/£4.25) children. Sat–Thurs 9am–6pm (until 5pm in winter); Fri 9am–4pm. Bus: 26, 33, or 99.

## 6 Organized Tours

As a general rule of thumb, make certain that your tour guide is officially licensed by the Ministry of Tourism. Also, on any guided tour that includes holy places, you must dress modestly. This means no shorts (men or women), no sleeveless shirts or blouses, and women should have a head covering.

**BUS TOURS**   The red, double-decker **Jerusalem Circular Line Egged bus no. 99** (ℂ *2800; www.egged.co.il) offers a 2-hour tour that passes the most-visited sights in the city, from the Mount of Olives to Yad VaShem. The bus leaves from in front of Safra Square at 10am, Sunday to Friday; there are no Saturday buses. A single tour ticket is NIS 45 ($11/£5.60); there are earphone cassettes at each seat with channels for route descriptions in English and seven other languages. It is always wise to check with the Egged website for the latest information on bus no. 99's timetable and route and about bookings.

**GUIDED WALKING TOURS**   Free municipal walking tours in English are offered Saturday at 10am from 32 Jaffa Rd.; check with the **Tourist Information Office** at Jaffa Gate (ℂ 02/628-0382) or Safra Square (ℂ 02/625-8844) for current information. The Jaffa Gate office also rents recorded, self-guided walking tours for approximately NIS 45 ($11/£5.60) per day.

The **Society for the Protection of Nature in Israel (SPNI)** 🌟🌟, 13 Helene Ha-Malka St. (ℂ 02/624-4605 or 02/625-2357), offers excellent walking tours within Jerusalem as well as hikes and tours of the surrounding countryside. A 1-day tour is approximately NIS 180 ($45/£23). In July and August, SPNI often has 3-hour late-afternoon Summer Neighborhood Tours that are inexpensive or free and built around themes such as food, architecture, ethnic diversity, or specific geographic areas. Some of the tours end with a concert in a hidden garden or courtyard. Call SPNI for details and meeting points.

Various commercial concerns will take you on guided tours of the city that emphasize its history and archaeology. Most of these are 3-hour excursions in small groups with other visitors—but remember, you'd need a long, very full day to really get an idea of all the city's quarters and traditions. **Jerusalem Walks in English** (© 02/540-1641) does a twice-weekly morning tour from Jerusalem's New City through the Jewish Quarter to the Western Wall for NIS 50 ($13/£6.25). **Archaeological Seminars Ltd.,** 34 Habad St. in the Jewish Quarter (© 02/627-3515), will guide you through the Jewish Quarter, Temple Mount, the Temple Mount excavations, the City of David (Ophel), or the Christian and Muslim quarters of the Old City. Tours run Sunday to Thursday and cost around NIS 96 ($24/£12) per person for a 3-hour itinerary. For information on schedules, various itineraries, and the chance to "dig for a day" at an archaeological site, phone or stop at the office.

**Zion Walking Tours** (© 02/628-7866) will show you the historical and archaeological highlights of the Old City or the Mount of Olives. Half-day tours depart from the Tower of David and run from NIS 60 ($15/£7.50), with senior and student discounts. **Walking Tours Ltd.** (© 02/652-2568) also offers 3- to 4-hour itineraries for around the same price.

## 7 Outdoor Pursuits & Sports

**CYCLING**    Jerusalem is a hard city to bike in, with steep hills, insane traffic, and drivers who traditionally ignore cyclists (or worse). Bikes can be rented at Rochim Bikes, 88 Agrippas St. (© 02/623-2598). Day rates start at NIS 40 ($10/£5). It's at the corner of Mani Street, and the staff can offer advice, warnings, and news of local biking activities.

**HEALTH CLUBS**    The best is the CYBEX fitness center at the **David Citadel Hotel** (© 02/621-1111). The **Jerusalem Regency** (© 02/533-1234) also offers good health club facilities.

**JOGGING**    Jerusalem, with its many hills, is not the easiest place for unplanned jogging. I like to use the roads and pathways in the Bloomfield Gardens, just above Yemin Moshe. A very useful but hard-to-find paperback, *Carta's Jogger's Guide to Jerusalem,* by Morton H. Seelenfreund (ask at Steimatzky bookstores), costs less than NIS 40 ($10/£5) and offers maps and many good ideas.

**SWIMMING**    You have a choice of many pools. One of the cheapest (but also most crowded) is the **Jerusalem public pool,** 43 Emek Refaim St. (© 02/563-2092). On Friday, Saturday, and holidays, Israelis pack the pools. Admission is NIS 60 ($15/£7.50). It's open from 8am to 5pm in summer only.

A more convenient, although more expensive, option is to pay the visitors' rate to use a pool at one of the city's hotels. In central Jerusalem, the **Inbal Hotel** (© 02/675-6666) has a covered pool open year-round. The **David Citadel Hotel** (© 02/621-1111) has a heated outdoor pool open year-round, with direct water access from its CYBEX fitness center, but in winter this can be a chilly option. Admission policies vary according to time of year and rate of occupancy, but range from NIS 80 ($20/£10) and up. Prices are higher Friday and Saturday.

In good weather, the outdoor pools at the **Mount Zion Hotel** (© 02/568-9555) and the **King David Hotel** (© 02/620-8888) offer lovely gardens, kiddie pools, and spectacular views of the Old City's walls. Outsider admission to the pool at the King David depends on how full the hotel is, so call ahead.

**TENNIS**    Reservations are always needed to secure a court. The **YMCA,** King David Street (© **02/569-2692**), is a good, central place to play if you have your own equipment. It is open Monday to Saturday 8am to sunset and costs approximately NIS 40 ($10/£5) per hour. Prices are higher on the weekends. The **Hebrew University at Mount Scopus** (© **02/581-7579**) has 10 lighted courts and rents equipment at similar prices. It's open Sunday to Thursday 7am to 10pm and Friday and Saturday 7am to 5pm.

## 8 Shopping

### THE SHOPPING SCENE
Jewelry, Judaica, and local Israeli crafts and art objects are the most interesting items for shoppers. Many shops in the Ben-Yehuda area, as well as in the Jewish Quarter of the Old City, sell reproductions of cast-bronze antique wall menorahs from North Africa, medieval Italy, and Eastern Europe. The designs are authentic and decorative. There is no lack of modern menorahs, mezuzahs, dreidels, candleholders, and embroidered yarmulkes, as well as objects for Passover, Succot, Shabbat, and synagogue services. *Tip:* It is possible to bargain a bit at most tourist shops in West Jerusalem. In times when tourism is down, you can ask if it's possible to do a bit better on the price; unfortunately, while the U.S. dollar is at record lows, offering to pay in dollars will get you nowhere. Very few of the stores on Ben-Yehuda Street or King David Street will allow you to return an item if you see something nicer or at a better price elsewhere, so shop carefully. Shops in Mea Shearim often have a better selection and better prices.

There are also many outstanding individual shops that sell original art, jewelry, glass, and ceramics. Most of our listings are for places where you can find handmade items and purchase them directly from the artisans who make them.

**HOURS, SALES TAX & SHIPPING**    Tourist shops are generally open Sunday to Thursday from 9am to 7pm, although some shops close from 1 to 4pm for siesta. On Friday, shops are open from 9am to 2pm.

There is no sales tax; however, unless otherwise stated, the value-added tax (VAT) of 15.5% is included in the price. Always ask about VAT exemptions when paying in foreign currency. Some expensive tourist shops will give you voucher forms, good for VAT refunds on items costing more than $50 when presented at Ben-Gurion Airport just before you leave the country. See appendix A for more information.

Merchants are generally cooperative about packing your purchases securely for shipping or for the plane ride home. If you decide to mail purchases home, remember to bring strong tape with you to the post office, as all packages must be inspected for security and Customs before they can be sealed. You must also bring your passport to the post office for identification when you mail packages.

### SHOPPING A TO Z
#### ART
**Israel Museum Gift Shop**    An exciting selection of posters is on sale here. Also, check out reproductions of Anna Ticho's charcoal and pen-and-ink landscapes and Shalom of Safed's vibrant primitive paintings, as well as high-quality reproductions of Judaica and antiquities at reasonable prices. Ruppin St. © **02/670-8811.** A smaller Israel Museum Gift Shop is in downtown Jerusalem at Beit Ticho (p. 201).

**Jerusalem Artists' House Gallery**    Housed in the Ottoman-Turkish buildings of the original Bezalel Academy of Art and Design (the school has now moved to the Hebrew University campus), this remarkable cooperative gallery, sponsored by the Jerusalem Municipality and the Israeli government, represents more than 500 juried Israeli artists, ranging from the famous and established to the newest and most promising. Upstairs, you'll find a changing array of one-person and group exhibits. The staff of the Artists' House can put you in touch with any artist whose work interests you, and they will arrange for the shipping of your purchase. The gallery is open Sunday to Thursday from 10am to 1pm and 4 to 7pm, Friday 10am to 1pm, and Saturday 11am to 2pm. 12 Shmuel Ha-Nagid St. ℂ 02/625-2636.

## BASKETWARE

Jerusalem's once roaring basket market, the **Suq El Hussor,** is gone, but you can still find a few locally made, primitive **olive-twig baskets,** a Jerusalem and regional tradition that is thousands of years old. At press time, the only shop where a few real olive-twig baskets could be found was a small hole-in-the-wall place on the right side of Christian Quarter Road in the Old City, between David Street and St. Helena Street. The owner, a small man with a small mustache, is one of the toughest bargainers in town. Rough, almost bird's nest–like in texture, these baskets look great when filled with dried flowers, fresh fruit, yarn, or almost anything else. Don't pay more than NIS 30 to NIS 40 ($7.50–$10/£3.75–£5) for a basket with a handle, the kind used by country women to collect fresh grapes or figs. Bigger traylike baskets, the kind women in the markets carry on their heads, should cost NIS 45 to NIS 80 ($11–$20/£5.60–£10).

## BOOKSTORES

Most bookstores carrying a selection of books in English are within 2 blocks of Zion Square. Look for the following stores: The well-stocked **Steimatzky** chain, with its large main branch at 39 Jaffa Rd. and smaller branches at 9 King George St. and on the Ben-Yehuda Mall. Steimatzky's maintains very small branches in many major hotels and sells a good selection of new English- and foreign-language periodicals, books, and guidebooks to various regions of the country. Prices are high, but look for interesting remainder tables.

For used books, try **Sefer Ve Sefel Bookshop** (4 Yavetz St., upstairs; ℂ 02/624-8237), where you'll find the largest selection of English-language fiction in Israel and used but often current guidebooks. **Clal Center Bookstore** (97 Jaffa Rd.) has a good, interesting stock of quality used English books (ask directions to their affiliates, **Moffit,** also in the Clal Center, and **Yalkut Bookstore,** in the rear plaza of the Redjwan Building on King George St.). **Tmol Shilshom Bookstore Café** (in a rear courtyard off 5 Yoel Salomon St.; ℂ 02/623-2758), has a small eclectic collection of new and used books and magazines, and remains open until midnight Sunday through Thursday; it's mainly a cafe/restaurant with a wonderful program of readings and live music. The **Bookshelf** (2 Jewish Quarter Rd.; ℂ 02/627-3889), in the Jewish Quarter of the Old City, has especially helpful management and an influx of good reading material, often shipped in from Princeton, New Jersey. It also offers fax and Internet services and does photocopying; it's open Sunday through Thursday from 10am to 6pm, and on Friday 10am to 2:30pm. **Stein Books** (52 King George St.; ℂ 02/624-7877), is well-known for Jewish studies and rare books; the **Book Gallery/Books on Schatz** (6 Schatz St., off King George St., a block south of Hillel St.), is an extremely well-stocked place with vast subterranean browsing rooms; it even offers a few elderly armchairs to encourage

> **Tips**  **Tourist Shops in West Jerusalem**
>
> You'll find interesting items in Judaica and tourist shops all over the Ben-Yehuda Mall area and in Mea Shearim, the ultra-Orthodox part of West Jerusalem that begins about 1km (½ mile) north of Zion Square. Remember that bargaining (or politely asking for a discount) has become customary in most of these shops, and that prices for identical and nearly identical items can vary greatly from store to store. For this reason, many of Jerusalem's tourist/Judaica stores display signs that say in Hebrew, if not English: NO REFUNDS, RETURNS, OR EXCHANGES. So, comparison shop before making a purchase: Once you buy it, it's yours.

reading while you browse. The convenient little **Gur Arieh** bookshop (8 Yoel Salomon St.), is worth checking out, and is a good place to pick up the *Jerusalem Post* or *Herald Tribune/Ha'aretz;* owner Fredi Engelberg is often more savvy than the tourism office. The **SPINI** bookstore, with lots of detailed maps, is at 13 Heleni Ha-Malka St. (② 02/624-4605), inside the Russian Compound. Most maps are in Hebrew, but some are in English. The **American Colony Hotel Bookshop,** at the American Colony Hotel in East Jerusalem, stocks works by many Middle Eastern writers and hosts publishing parties and talks by Palestinian, Israeli, and international writers of fiction, poetry, and cultural and political issues.

## CHOCOLATE
**Har Zahav Belgian Chocolate**  Fitting in perfectly with the quaint, gentrified, multicultural German Colony, this cafe/ice-cream parlor is well stocked with luxurious, exotic kosher chocolates. 24 Emek Refaim St., German Colony. ② 02/563-5721.

**Sweet 'N Karem** 👁  For handmade chocolates (and ice cream), this little gem run by Ofer and Sima (who taught themselves) is reason enough to come out and explore the already charming western fringe neighborhood of Ein Kerem (p. 206). In addition to being rich and filled with exotic tastes, it's all certified kosher. Open daily 9am to 6pm. At the crossroads in the center of Ein Kerem. ② 050/202-4481. Bus: 17.

## CRAFTS
### Contemporary Crafts
**Cadim Gallery** 👁  This cooperative gallery displays the work of award-winning potters and a range of excellent functional pottery and inventive Judaica by some of the country's best ceramists. 4 Yoel Salomon Mall. ② 02/623-4869.

**8 Ceramists Altogether** 👁  For contemporary handmade ceramics, this pottery cooperative in West Jerusalem will give you a good idea of the current Israeli ceramics scene. Look for beautiful ceramic Chanukah menorahs and Passover Seder plates as well as functional and decorative pottery made by the cooperative's artists. 11 Yoel Salomon Mall. ② 02/624-7250.

**Guild of Ceramists**  Eleven ceramists are represented in this cooperative shop at the Hillel Street end of the Yoel Salomon Mall. Among other things, many of these artisans will custom design tiles. 27 Salomon St. ② 02/624-4065.

**House of Quality**  Across the street from and midway between the Mount Zion Hotel and the Cinémathèque, this conglomeration of craft workshops offers all sorts of delights. I especially admire the witty, unique ceramic Judaica of Gaia Smith, and the silver creations of Oded Davidson, whose studios are here, but all of the craftspeople at this center are of very high caliber. Craftspeople are in their workshops at varying times. Just around the corner, in Saint Andrew's Guest House, you can also visit **Sunbula,** which sells traditional Palestinian crafts and embroidery. 12 Hebron Rd. No phone. Bus: 4, 5, 6, 7, 8, 18, 21, or 48 and walk to Hebron Rd.

## Traditional Ceramics

The outer walls of the Dome of the Rock are covered with turquoise and cobalt-blue ceramic tiles in the Persian tradition. Two world-famous Armenian pottery workshops, the Karakashian family's **Jerusalem Pottery** and the Balian family's **Palestinian Armenian Pottery,** listed below, were brought to Jerusalem at the start of the British Mandate in order to maintain the Dome of the Rock's lavish facade. Their traditional Anatolian hand-painted ceramics have come to be regarded as a national treasure: They've had exhibitions in Israeli and world museums, and in 2004 the State of Israel honored them with a series of commemorative postage stamps. These two workshops also produce items for sale to the general public. After a quick survey of the showrooms here, you'll appreciate the difference between their hand-painted folk ceramics, tiles, and bowls, and the mass-produced work available in the bazaars; the rich colors are unmatched anywhere else. Prices are very reasonable. *Tip:* Fans of Jerusalem's Armenian ceramics tradition will want to check out a beautifully illustrated book, *The Armenian Ceramics of Jerusalem, Three Generations,* by Nurith Kenaan-Kedar. Published in 2003, it chronicles the work of both the Balian and Karakashian families, and is available at the **Eretz Israel Museum Bookstore** in Tel Aviv, or at the **Steimatzky bookstore** on Jaffa Road in Jerusalem. Be sure to specify the English-language edition if you order it.

**Darian Armenian Ceramics**   This workshop, a newcomer to the field of Armenian ceramics, is the creation of Arman Darian, a recent immigrant from the former Soviet Armenia, where he studied traditional calligraphy and design. Here you'll find wonderful soup tureens, cups and plates, tiles, and lamp bases, all hand-painted in the Armenian tradition, but with new color combinations and graceful designs that are uniquely Darian's. You'll find beautiful first-quality pieces, but also experimental pieces and bargain seconds that you'd never find on the shelves of the more venerable workshops. Darian will also design to your specifications. 12 Shlomzion Hamalka St. ✆ 02/623-4802.

**Jerusalem Pottery** ★★ *Finds*   Near the sixth Station of the Cross (p. 181) in the Old City, this shop, run by the renowned Karakashian family, is notable for individual plates and tiles decorated with lovely traditional bird, animal, and floral designs, as well as for its interpretations of ancient Jewish and Christian motifs, many taken from ancient manuscripts or mosaic floors. Standards of craftsmanship are the highest, with the most careful hand painting (tile designs are incised) and the richest colors. I've seen this shop's magnificent and varied tiles used to face a colonial fireplace in Massachusetts and also to ornament a poolside garden wall in South Florida. The designs were equally at home in each environment. There's also a selection of plates, cups, and even ceramic mezuzah cases for doorposts. Jerusalem Pottery is open Monday to Saturday from 9:30am until 5pm; always call to check. 15 Via Dolorosa. ✆ **02/626-1587.** www.jerusalempottery.biz.

**Palestinian Armenian Pottery** ★★ *Finds*   This workshop's chief artist, Marie Balian, is most famous for her multitile ceramic panels, which are richly hand-painted visions of Persian gardens, desert oases, and Middle Eastern motifs. In 1992, the Smithsonian Museum in Washington, D.C., mounted Views of Paradise, a special exhibit of 22 of Balian's creations; her panels also adorn the Succot Patio at the house of the president of Israel. Palestinian Pottery produces a steady stream of traditional plates, bowls, teapots, pitchers, name and address tiles, and smaller panel compositions in floral designs that can be used as tabletops or as stunning architectural details. Ask to see the special display of Palestinian Pottery's work spanning the past 70 years. The workshop is near the American consulate in East Jerusalem, and is usually open Monday to Saturday from 9am to 4pm; it is always a good idea to call ahead and check on hours. 14 Nablus Rd. ℂ 02/628-2826. www.armenianceramics.com.

## FASHION

Jerusalem is not a style-conscious town—too many centuries of railing prophets and holy wars have seen to *that*—but there are some Tel Aviv designers with downtown Jerusalem shops worth browsing. Check **Dorin Frankfurt** (36 Jaffa Rd.; ℂ **02/624-2138**), known for classic clothing with elegant, relaxed lines; **Naama Bezalel** (26 King George St.; ℂ **02/622-3479**), for a line dotted with romantic details and a bit of 1950s and 1960s nostalgia; or **Kedem Sasson** (21 King George St.; ℂ **02/625-2602**), where the style hallmark is a combination of boldness and comfort.

## GIFTS

**Brinn and Berohm**  Jerusalem has one old-fashioned European-style shop packed full of Romanian and Hungarian embroidery and plenty of bric-a-brac. Run by the charming Emma Berohm, who is still young at over 100, it's located just near the intersection of Jaffa Road and Shlomzion Hamalka Street, 2 blocks east of Zion Square. Like most good haunts for treasure hunters, it's hard to see the shop's sign, but you'll find an eclectic, intriguing, and unplanned show window. It's often open just for half a day. Call to confirm hours. 10 Shlomzion Hamalka St. ℂ 02/623-4617.

**Chaim Peretz**  In this little workshop, Chaim Peretz makes attractive, very reasonably priced stained-glass art and Judaica, sold for considerably higher prices at stores elsewhere in the city. The walk to his shop, in the quaint, labyrinthine Nachlaot neighborhood south of Agrippas Street near Machane Yehuda, is always interesting (you'll inevitably have to ask the locals for directions). Once there, you'll find an array of charming menorahs, mezuzzot, Hands of Fatima, candleholders, and mirrors. If your stay in town is long enough, you can order your selection in the colors and designs you prefer. The shop is on a pedestrian lane off one of Nachlaot's neighborhood commons. If no one is around, ask along the street. A phone call ahead of time can be useful. 2 Rabbi Ariye St. ℂ 02/625-0859.

**Charlotte**  Founded in 1938, this store, on the street just behind the Central Post Office on Jaffa Road, is the oldest gift shop in West Jerusalem. The secret of its longevity is a carefully chosen mix of modern Israeli jewelry and crafts, handmade Bedouin objects, old pieces of copper ware, and unusual antiquities, all at very reasonable prices. Jerusalemites have never ceased to be delighted with Charlotte's selections, and if you stop by, you'll see the difference between this place and many of the less personal tourist shops on the Ben-Yehuda Mall. 4 Koresh St. ℂ 02/625-1632.

**Lifeline for the Old** (Value)  This shop sells toys, needlework, clothing, jewelry, Judaica, and crafts handmade by Jerusalem's senior citizens, and is a source of pleasure for both craftspeople and customers. Sales and donations keep this remarkable institution afloat. The workshops, which help provide a meaningful creative outlet for Jerusalem's elderly, can be visited Sunday to Thursday from 8:30am to 11:30pm. Prices are very reasonable. The gift shop is open Sunday to Thursday from 9am to 4pm and Friday from 9 to 11am. 14 Shivtei Israel St. ℂ 02/628-7829.

## GLASS

**Nekker Glass Company** ⭐ *Value*    It was this store, near the Mirrer Yeshiva on the northern fringe of Mea Shearim, that revived the ancient glass-blowing traditions that began in this part of the world more than 2,000 years ago. The Nekker family arrived in Jerusalem from Baghdad in the early 1950s and quickly set up a small glass factory employing both Arab and Jewish glass blowers. Slowly the factory began to experiment with designs and techniques from ancient times, and has even developed ways to reproduce soft, ancient patinas in a variety of colors. At Nekker's tiny workshop, you are invited to watch the glass blowers at work. Yehuda Nekker, the patriarch and chief designer, virtually dreams in glass. The stock is on sale for a fraction of what it costs in retail shops. A special line of museum-style reproductions is higher in price. The Nekker staff will pack your purchases securely for travel. 6 Bet Israel St. ℂ 02/582-9683.

## JEWELRY

**Hedya Jewelers and the Sarah Einstein Collection** ⭐    For unusual antique jewelry, visit this near-legendary shop where you'll find Sarah Einstein's collection of jewelry, often made from exquisite component pieces of antique objects such as Yemenite wedding necklaces or tribal Persian headdresses. They have been taken apart and combined with rare beads into smaller compositions that modern women can wear with flair and elegance. Among the extraordinary creations made by Sarah Einstein, her staff, and by Hedya, you'll find one-of-a-kind necklaces and earrings that range from delicate to dramatic and encompass every tradition in the Middle East. Hedya, an Israeli jewelry design workshop, creates accessories such as earrings to coordinate with Einstein's unique pieces. Hedya's own custom-made jewelry, Hands of Fatima, and Judaica are exquisite. Special orders are welcome. 23 Hillel St. (in the passageway between Hillel and Shammai sts.). ℂ 02/622-1151.

**Ophir** ⭐ *Value*    For half a century, Jerusalemites and visitors have been fans of this shop's delicate jewelry designs that echo Victorian, Edwardian, Art Deco, and Middle Eastern styles, and are made by the owner, Avraham Lor, himself. Prices are extremely reasonable, and Lor's stock is augmented by many unusual antique and semiantique items. Although for decades Ophir held forth in a tiny closetlike workshop, it's now housed in new, beautiful surroundings; however, much of the jewelry collection and other treasures are still to be seen in the "backroom" workshop. Open Sunday, Monday, Wednesday, and Thursday from 9am to 1pm and 4 to 7pm and Tuesday and Friday from 9am to 1pm only. 38 Jaffa Rd. ℂ 02/624-9078. www.ophir-jewelry.com.

## JUDAICA

**Archie Granot, Papercuts** ⭐⭐    Traditional Jewish paper cuts began to develop as a folk art in Europe and North Africa. In many homes it was the custom to hang a delicately cut piece of paper (called a *mizrach,* from the Hebrew word for "east") on the eastern wall of a room, to indicate the direction of Jerusalem. There are a number of excellent practitioners of this craft in Israel, but Archie Granot has raised this folk tradition to new levels with his extraordinary contemporary designs. Working with multiple layers and colors, he creates works of amazing intricacy, ranging from *mizrachs* in traditional and contemporary styles to wedding contracts and mezuzzot. Prices can range from a few hundred dollars to several thousand dollars. Granot's works are in the collections of the Israel Museum, the Victoria and Albert Museum, the Jewish Museum of New York, and the Philadelphia Museum of Judaica. 1 Agron St. ✆ 02/625-2210. www.archiegranot.com.

**Avi Biran, Silversmith**   Award-winning Avi Biran specializes in his own brand of contemporary Judaica—the designs have elegance, but also a sense of humor and insight that that makes you think about the rituals and customs these objects are meant to accompany. Prices range from several hundred dollars for a mezuzah or dreidel to thousands for a major Chanukah menorah. House of Quality, 12 Hebron Rd. ✆ 02/672-6242. www.avi-biran.co.il.

**Danny Azoulay**   A highly skilled craftsperson who came to Israel from Morocco as a small child, Danny Azoulay specializes in porcelain and fine ceramic Judaica, and his tiny shop is filled with hand-painted Chanukah menorahs, charity boxes laced with brass or silver designs, mezuzzot, spice boxes, and dreidels. One of my favorite designs is a tiny porcelain Chanukah lamp (too small for the strictly observant) that sells for about NIS 600 ($150/£75). Azoulay's creations delicately blend Florentine, Islamic, central European, and contemporary motifs into a style that is unique. At times you may be able to purchase seconds at a discount, either at this shop or at his studio, not far from Machane Yehuda. A number of Danny Azoulay's pieces can be seen at the Sir Isaac and Lady Edith Wolfson Museum in Heichal Shlomo. The shop also sells illuminated manuscripts and *ketubbot* (marriage contracts) by some of **Israel's finest scribal** artists, such as **Amalya Nini** and **Aden Halter.** 5 Yoel Salomon St. ✆ 02/623-3918.

**Gaia Smith**   Gaia Smith takes the long tradition of using architectural motifs in the back plates of Chanukah menorahs and goes delightfully wild. Her extraordinary hand-built menorahs and items of Judaica are designed around cottages in the Galilee with vistas of the hills, apartments on Central Park West with views of the Manhattan skyline, a child's toy-strewn bedroom on a wintry Chanukah night—all filled with wit, charm, and a touch of mystery. You might even bring photographs of the interior and exterior of your house and commission a menorah, charity box, or mezuzzot based on it. Smith's reputation among collectors, as well as her pricing, is on the rise. House of Quality, 12 Hebron Rd. No phone.

**Oded Davidson**   One of the country's most interesting Judaica silversmiths, Oded Davidson combines skill and vision to create unique designs delicately engraved with personal whimsy and charm. Davidson's silver dreidels, menorahs, spice boxes, and other creations (ranging in price from several hundred dollars to more than a thousand) have been bought by many collectors and museums, including the Sir Isaac and Lady Edith Wolfson Museum at Heichal Shlomo. You may arrange to see Davidson's remarkable portfolio by visiting his workshop; Davidson's in-person explanations of his work are always fascinating. Open Sunday to Thursday from 9am to 4pm (to noon on Tues). House of Quality, 12 Hebron Rd. ✆ 02/679-1082.

**Shlomo Ohana**   Some of the best-loved, though sometimes kitschy objects of Judaica have been created over the centuries by neighborhood metalsmiths working with humble materials such as tin, copper, and brass. In Shlomo Ohana's workshop, this tradition lives on. You'll find amulets, hamsas (Hands of Fatima), and Shabbat candleholders, all modestly priced. Shlomo Ohana, who was born in Morocco, also makes the simple glass-enclosed Chanukah lamps traditionally mounted beside doorways in

## The Art of Bargaining

Under normal conditions, Middle Eastern shopping is supposed to take a good deal of time, with lots of theatrics and diplomacy. But these days many merchants are willing to get down to the nitty-gritty with fewer rituals. If you find something you like, however, you must bargain for it. The main rules are to be courteous and keep your cool. Appear politely unsure the object is something you really want. It often helps if you're with a friend who pretends you're late for a bus or an appointment—you might even pretend to walk away. If a merchant doesn't come down on his price, don't panic and pay full price. On the other hand, never back a merchant into a corner: Never argue: "$25? I saw the same thing on Ben-Yehuda Street for $5!" This leaves the merchant no honorable alternative but to say, "Okay, go to Ben-Yehuda Street!" The chance is that you'll find the same thing or something similar close by; if not, if you leave gracefully, you can always come back and try again. Much depends on how badly the merchant needs to convert some of his stock to cash on the day of your visit. If nothing else, after a few hours of browsing and bargaining, perhaps you'll have a new appreciation for the intricacies of the Middle East peace process.

Jerusalem's 19th-century neighborhoods. His *davvening* (praying) Hassidim are a popular tourist item, and his grander Chanukah menorahs are impressive. The experience of visiting this workshop, deep in Mea Shearim's Ein Yaacov market, is always fascinating; in deference to Mea Shearim's ultra-Orthodox community, women should dress modestly, and men should avoid shorts. If the shop is closed, ask one of the neighbors when it will reopen. 20 Ein Yaakov St., Mea Shearim. ✆ 02/582-9996.

**Shulamit Noy Dunievsky**   In her busy ceramic workshop, Shulamit Noy Dunievsky designs hand-built contemporary Chanukah menorahs glazed in pastel colors, with motifs of oasis gardens, birds, starry desert nights, flowers, and pastoral creatures that ornament the back plates. A few designs are done by mold and run under NIS 450 ($113/£56), but Dunievsky's beautiful one-of-a-kind menorahs are the real collectors' items. Interesting and very reasonably priced contemporary kiddush cups and other items of Judaica are on display in an always-changing array of inventive designs. 18 Shivtei Israel St. ✆ 02/628-1987.

### THE OLD CITY MARKETS

A major attraction for visitors, the Old City markets have many shops offering such local products as olive-wood chess and nativity sets, rosaries, carved camels, boxes, and olive-wood Christmas tree ornaments—a great buy at about three for NIS 12 ($3/£1.50). You'll also find heavy, handblown glassware from Hebron, inlaid wooden boxes from Egypt and Syria, mother-of-pearl objects from Jordan, new and inexpensive imitations of antique Bedouin, Yemenite, and Bedouin-style jewelry, and locally made leather goods. *Tip:* The markets are filled with all kinds of Arabic desserts, spices, and snacks, all of which should be part of the Old City experience.

**Old tribal Bedouin flat-weave rugs and weavings** can be found in a few shops in the Arab bazaar around the Christian Quarter Road. Made of wool, goat, or camel hair, these tribal pieces represent one of the world's great remaining national crafts. In older, more expensive pieces, look for bold diamond patterns and rich, subdued reds, browns, yellows, and oranges made from natural dyes of henna, pomegranate, saffron bark, and leaves from desert plants. Newer pieces often tend to bright reds and other hard colors, but are still very attractive. The shop of **Mr. Maazen Kaysi** (no sign), with a plate-glass show window and a recessed entrance on the right side of the Christian Quarter Road (just past the first pedestrian street turning on the right as you come from David St.), has the finest and largest selection of Bedouin weavings and rugs. He also often obtains interesting kilims bought from new Israeli immigrants from central Asia as well as hand-embroidered Romanian peasant blouses bought from Romanian pilgrims. Prices are high, but bargain. For genuine **primitive tools, antique rustic artifacts, caftans, woven and embroidered antique textiles, and Druze basketry,** check out the unique **Ghassan Abdeeh,** 25 Aqbat al Khanka Rd. (go to end of Christian Quarter Rd., turn right onto Al Khanka). It's on the left as you go downhill.

The shops dealing in ancient antiquities are fascinating, but unless you're an expert, judge any object you may want to purchase in terms of its decorative value rather than its alleged age or rarity.

In the Jewish Quarter of the Old City, one of my favorite shops for old objects and Judaica is **Mansour Saidian** (no sign), opposite the Mizrachi Bank on the corner of Tiferet Israel Street. There's always a selection of 19th-century European and Iranian kiddush cups and old menorahs stashed away among the cases of newer objects and jewelry. Bargain!

The **Old City Oil Press Art Gallery** (33 Jewish Quarter Rd.), is interesting for its large, unusual collection of jewelry and other objects that incorporate old pieces of Roman glass. There's also contemporary Judaica, paintings, sculpture, and prints.

## PALESTINIAN EMBROIDERY

You'll notice antique Palestinian embroidered robes hanging from the doors of many shops in the Old City bazaar. Red, rose, and scarlet on hand-woven black cloth are the preferred colors, stemming from a tradition that goes back almost 3,000 years to the centuries when the prophets warned against women who sewed with scarlet threads of vanity. Many of the current embroidery designs can be traced back to patterns introduced by the Crusaders almost 1,000 years ago. You can find interesting scraps of embroidery suitable for framing for anywhere from NIS 25 to NIS 180 ($6.25–$45/£3.10–£23). Complete caftans, especially those with long, pointed medieval sleeves, if not worn, can be hung or mounted as dramatic decorative focal points. The shop of **Maher Natsheh** (10 Christian Quarter Rd.), carries a good range of antique and old textiles.

In addition to the many shops in the Old City markets selling caftans and antique or semiantique embroidery, three church-supported nonprofit shops (two in the Old City and one in West Jerusalem) offer a dazzling array of freshly made, top-quality embroideries all done by specially trained women who are working to support their families. Quality is assured, and prices at these shops are extremely fair.

**Melia** ⟨★⟩ The newest of the nonprofit embroidery shops, Melia offers many beautiful traditional pieces, as well as some imaginative decorative items. In addition to the classic divan pillowcases, I especially like a dramatically embroidered mirror frame as well as designer-embroidered women's jackets and embroidered T-shirts. There is also a selection of Western-style tablecloths and embroideries. Here, as in the other shops, the pieces with naturally dyed thread are the richest and most beautiful. Arab Orthodox Society Art and Training Center, Frere's St., inside the New Gate, Old City. ✆ 02/628-1377.

**Sunbula** ⚑  This nonprofit shop sells a magnificent collection of densely embroidered divan pillowcases, wall hangings, and shawls, all alive with traditional motifs and colors. Many fabulous pieces are less than NIS 450 ($113/£56). There are also heavy woven Bedouin tent rugs, embroidered linen tablecloths and napkins, and a good selection of inexpensive handmade crafts and gift items. Custom-tailored jackets and other fashion items can be ordered. The shop is run with an excellent eye for beautiful things. It is open Monday to Saturday from 9am to 6pm as well as Sunday from 11am to 1pm. The shop is in the Saint Andrew's complex, on a hill between the train station and the Cinémathèque, and is close to the House of Quality (see House of Quality, earlier in this chapter), where a number of quality Israeli artists have their workshops. Saint Andrews Hospice, King David and Remez sts., West Jerusalem. ✆ 02/672-1707.

## PHOTOGRAPHS

One of Jerusalem's little-known shopping pleasures is **Reprints of Antique Photographs of Jerusalem.** A number of venerable, family-run photography studios on Al Khanka Street in the Old City have gone through their archives and are now selling fascinating, often very beautiful reprints of views of Jerusalem (and the entire region) from the first half of the 20th century. Photo buffs and those interested in Jerusalem's history can spend hours browsing these collections. Kevork Kahvedjian, of **Elia Photo Service** (14 Al Khanka St.), has published a striking book, *Jerusalem Through My Father's Eyes,* containing over a half century of his father's photographic work at the Elia Studio. You'll find other photography shops on Al Khanka Street also selling remarkable matted reproductions of Old Jerusalem scenes from their archives for about NIS 80 ($20/£10), and some are truly exceptional. Higher-quality prints can also be ordered. To get to Al Khanka Street, enter Jaffa Gate and continue straight on David Street into the bazaar. At Christian Quarter Road, turn left and continue to the end. Turn right (downhill) onto Al Khanka Street at the end of Christian Quarter Road. The shops with antique photo collections for sale are all on the right side of the street.

**Vision Gallery**  Neil Folberg, noted for his landscapes and photographs of the Jewish world, is the owner of this world-class gallery that handles the works of international contemporary photographers and represents artists including Micha Bar Am, David Harris, Tom Baril, and Marc Riboud. Vintage photographs of the Middle East and of Jewish subjects are also featured. Prices begin at NIS 400 ($100/£50) for Middle Eastern prints and continue to hundreds and thousands of dollars. Israel's other gallery of note specializing in photography is the **Silver Print Gallery** in Ein Hod (p. 309). 18 Rivlin St. ✆ 02/622-2253.

## WALKING SHOES & SANDALS

If your walking shoes wear out, or you want to take advantage of the local market in comfy footwear, there are good choices in both the Old and New cities.

**Khalifa Shoes**  This long-established shop is packed with Naot Teva footwear (the Birkenstock-like sandals and shoes of Israel), as well as with international brands known for comfort, such as Clarke's and Ecco. International brands may cost more than at home, but if you need great walking shoes this is the place. It's open Sunday through Thursday from 9am to 6pm and Friday 9am to 1pm. 44 Jaffa Rd., West Jerusalem (corner of Rav Kook St., opposite Zion Sq.). ✆ 02/625-7027.

**Sharabati Shops**  With two locations in the Old City bazaar near Jaffa Gate, the Sharabati family stocks the largest collection of very reasonably priced, stylish leather sandals (as well as walking and sport sandals) in the market and is known for fair, unexaggerated opening prices—other sandal shops borrow stock to sell from them. Of course, they sell other things, including suitcases and leather jackets. A second branch is on Christian Quarter Road, the third store on the left from the intersection with David Street. Both shops are open daily from 10am to 5:30pm. On the left side of David St. as you descend the steps into the bazaar, midway between the Petra Hotel and Christian Quarter Rd. No phone.

## 9 Jerusalem After Dark

Israel has long been known for the high quality of its musicians, and the recent wave of Russian immigrants has led to an even greater embarrassment of riches. Classical music lovers will discover new and remarkable artists performing everywhere, from concert halls and clubs to street corners and pedestrian malls. Be on the lookout for performances by the **Rishon-le-Zion Symphony Orchestra;** this group from a suburb of Tel Aviv is filled with many remarkable musicians recently arrived in the country. The **Israel Museum** (© 02/563-6321 for the box office) hosts a full program of music, dance, theater, and film performances. Its Ticho House branch holds a Friday morning series of recitals, readings, and other cultural events. The **Bible Lands Museum** has a Saturday evening series of classical, jazz, and folk music; wine and cheese are served before each performance. Also watch for **English Theater productions** listed in the Friday editions of the *Jerusalem Post* and *Ha'aretz* newspapers, with actors and audiences drawn mainly from Israel's English-speaking immigrant community. You'll sometimes find translations of topical Israeli plays and revues, which can be especially interesting to visitors. The jazz and blues scene is surprisingly excellent.

To find out what's going on in town, look in the Friday edition of the *Jerusalem Post, Ha'aretz,* and in the monthly *Calendar of Events,* which you can pick up free at Tourist Information Office. Lectures, readings, films, concerts, and English-language and Hebrew performances will be listed. If you have a student card, bring it; at times you may be given a discount.

*Note:* Jerusalem's two main **ticket agencies** are **Klaim** (© 02/622-2333) and **Bimot** (© 02/624-0896). Both agencies operate mostly by telephone and take major credit cards. Your hotel can also help you phone in a reservation.

## PERFORMANCE CENTERS

**Al Hakawati Palestinian National Theater** At this theater you'll find cabaret-style productions and plays that are usually strongly political. From time to time, a specific production may be censored or unexpectedly shut down by the authorities, but both Israeli and foreign visitors are welcome, and English synopses are usually available. For those interested in the Palestinian movement, a visit here can be interesting, regardless of what is being performed. Nuzha St. (off Saladin St. just to the south of the American Colony Hotel), East Jerusalem. © 02/628-0957. Tickets about NIS 22 ($5.50/£2.75). Bus: 27.

**Beit Shmuel/Center for Progressive Judaism** Performances here offer the best in contemporary and popular Israeli singers and musicians, ethnic music, readings and lectures, and dance and theater performances. In summer, concerts are held in the outdoor courtyard; always bring something warm because Jerusalem can get downright chilly at night. Shama'a St., off King David St. © 02/620-3455 or 02/620-3456. www.beitshmuel. com. Bus: 6, 18, or 21.

**Bible Lands Museum**    This place is famous for its wide range of Saturday evening concerts with wine and cheese included in the admission price. You'll need a taxi to get here before buses start running. Museum Row, 25 Granot St. ✆ **02/561-1066.** www.blmj. org. Bus: 9 or 17.

**Israel Museum**    This museum is host to a wide range of concerts, performances, films, and exotic cultural and international events. Museum Blvd. ✆ **02/670-8811.** www.imj. org.il.

**Jerusalem Performing Arts Center (Jerusalem Theater)**    Located near the corner of Chopin (in the Rechavia District near the president's house), this modern complex opened its doors in 1975 and houses the Jerusalem Theater (Sherover Theater), Henry Crown Auditorium, and the smaller, more intimate Rebecca Crown Hall. Original Israeli plays and Hebrew translations of foreign classics and modern works are performed in the theater's main hall; visiting troupes also use the main hall for performances in foreign languages. The theater also hosts performances of the **Jerusalem Symphony Orchestra** and the **Israel Chamber Ensemble;** the Israel Philharmonic also performs here. From October through early June, the Henry Crown Auditorium hosts the **Etnacha Concert Series,** produced by Israel Radio's classics station. The Etnacha performances are free. 20 David Marcus St. ✆ **02/560-5755.** www.jerusalem-theatre. co.il. Bus: 15.

**The Khan Theater**    Located across from the railway station, this Ottoman Turkish caravansary was refurbished and opened in 1968 as a nightclub, catering mostly to visitors. In the last few years, it has upgraded its program to include concerts of chamber music or jazz, Hebrew repertory theater, and occasional performances in English. Besides the theater, the building houses the inventive, kosher Limonim restaurant (p. 161) on the upper terrace. There are still tourist programs of Israeli folk singers, traditional dances, and audience singalongs. 2 Remez St. ✆ **02/671-8281.** Bus: 4, 7, 8, 14, 18, 21, or 48, anywhere along King George V Ave. going south, or eastbound on Jaffa Rd.

**The Lab (Ha-Ma'abada)**    Located in the disused railroad complex, the Lab is the venue for innovative and avant-garde performances in music, theater, dance, and video art. 28 Hebron Rd. ✆ **02/629-2001.**

**Mount Zion Cultural Center**    Many Saturday nights after Shabbat you'll find a busy evening of Klezmer and Hassidic-style dancing and music starting around 8pm in winter, 9pm in summer. This section of Mount Zion houses yeshivas and Jewish outreach programs; many of the participants are students, but all are welcome. Call for information; prices vary by event. Outside Zion Gate, near King David's Tomb. ✆ **02/671-6841.** Bus: 1 or 38.

**Targ Music Center**    Located in the rustic village of Ein Kerem, at the far western edge of Jerusalem, the Targ Music Center hosts a variety of Friday late-morning/early-afternoon concerts, as well as other events. Allow at least 1½ hours by public transportation from downtown Jerusalem. Ein Kerem. ✆ **02/641-4250.** Bus: 17.

**Ticho House**    A block away from Zion Square, Ticho House maintains a busy schedule of performances, including poetry readings, events for children, and Friday morning concerts. Harav Kook St. ✆ **02/624-5068.** Bus: any bus to Zion Sq.

**Train Puppet Theater** *(Kids*    Jerusalem has become a center for puppetry and delightful, inventive performances are held here throughout the year. In October,

Jerusalem hosts an International Puppet Theater Festival. Liberty Bell Park. ✆ 02/561-8514. www.traintheater.co.il. Bus: 4, 14, or 18.

**YMCA**    Concerts and performances of Israeli music and folk dancing are held here throughout the year, usually on Monday, Thursday, and Saturday evenings. As there are no reserved seats, come early to nail down a spot. Always call to verify schedules and performances. 26 King David St. ✆ 02/569-2692. Bus: 6, 18, or 21.

## MORE ENTERTAINMENT

**Son et Lumière**    During the warmer months, a sound-and-light show combined with slides about the history of Jerusalem is featured in the Citadel of David at Jaffa Gate. Performances are in English at 8:45pm, from April to October, but check on times and tickets in advance. Be prepared for the chill created by the stone fortress and the night breezes. A free twice-weekly outdoor concert series consisting of local music groups was begun at the citadel during the summer of 1995; if it continues, it's a pleasant opportunity to enjoy performances ranging from ethnic to classical. Check with the Tourist Information Office for details. Jaffa Gate. NIS 32 ($8/£4).

**Sultan's Pool**    This dramatic setting is great for major outdoor classical, rock, and jazz concerts in warm weather; a typical month might include concerts by Sting or Bob Dylan, and a performance of *Carmen*. Check with the Tourist Information Office for schedules. In a valley beneath the Old City walls between Jaffa Gate and Mount Zion.

## CLUBS & BARS

Israelis (especially Jerusalemites) are not really a drinking people—an evening at a cafe over a meal, or wine and snacks is more the local style. The cafes on **Ben-Yehuda Street** offer outside tables where patrons come to see and be seen. Saturday nights are teenage mob scenes. You can also try the more intimate **Rivlin Street** and the neighboring **Salomon Street Mall,** which form the heart of the cafe/pub scene in West Jerusalem.

Of the major hotels, the cavelike bar at the **American Colony Hotel** in East Jerusalem is by far the most atmospheric, visited by locals, international journalists, and travelers in the know. You can also have drinks, good food, and atmosphere at the American Colony's **Courtyard Cafe/Bar,** set in the hotel's inner garden. In West Jerusalem, the **King David Hotel's bar** offers the most style. All the large hotels have bars, but with the exception of the Khan Theater (see above), a nightclub scene barely exists.

**The Lab**    This is a popular new dance club set up in one of the renovated buildings on the grounds of the old Jerusalem Train Station. It's friendly, not especially druggy, and not an obsessively pushy pickup joint. Mostly rock, but sometimes there's something different. Both the bar and the food are interesting and reasonably priced. Check ahead for hours and programs. 28 Hebron Rd. ✆ 02/629-2000 or 1-700/700-920. Bus: 8, 49, or 21 before last bus at 11:30pm; taxi back.

**Mona**    This rustic, recently opened restaurant inside the Jerusalem Artists' House at the Old Bezalel Art School has a very well-stocked bar that has attracted some of the journalists, politicians, Jerusalem personalities, and sophisticated internationals who used to frequent the legendary Fink's Bar, which closed in 2005 after a 68-year run. Like Fink's, Mona serves top-quality meals very late into the night (including tapas and half-portions of main courses in case you want a bit of something solid to wash down your drinks), but the spirit of the place is younger, and there are no Fink's-style bartenders with ponderous charisma. Mona's is known for meats and seafood, and has

## Wineries in the Hill Country

West of Jerusalem are a number of interesting small wineries. The **Latrun Monastery** (© 08/922-0065) is a gardened enclave founded by Trappist monks in 1890 just where the Judean hills begin to rise from the coastal plain 20km (12 miles) west of Jerusalem. A shop at the entrance gate sells Domain de Latroun wines, liqueurs, and spirits as well as honey and olive oil produced at the monastery. Visitors are welcome to explore the gardens, vineyards, and orchards. It's open Monday to Saturday from 9am to 1pm and 2 to 5pm. From Hwy. 1, the Tel Aviv–Jerusalem Highway, get off at the Latrun interchange. Follow Hwy. 3 briefly in the direction of Ashkelon, and you'll come to the Latrun Monastery, opposite the large Armoured Forces Monument. There is no entrance fee.

The **Soreq Winery** (© 08/934-0542) is a new boutique winery located 40 minutes south of Tel Aviv at Kibbutz Tal Shahar. Opened in 1994, the Soreq Winery produces cabernet sauvignons, chardonnays, and merlots. Call ahead to arrange a private tour of the winery. You can buy wine and cheese at the winery shop, and there is a picnic area on the premises. Open Sunday to Thursday from 10am to 5pm. From Hwy. 1 exit at the Latrun interchange. Take Hwy. 3 south toward Ashkelon for approximately 9km (5½ miles). The winery is located 2km (1¼ miles) after the Nachshon interchange. There is no entrance fee.

The **Tzora Winery** (© 02/990-8261) is a boutique winery with a rising reputation for cabernet sauvignon, sauvignon blanc, and chardonnay wines. It is located on Kibbutz Tzora in the mountains between Beit Shemesh and Jerusalem, and will arrange private tours if you call ahead. There is a wine and cheese store and picnic area on the premises. Open Sunday to Thursday 9am to 5pm, Friday 9am to 2pm, and Saturday 10am to 5pm. From Hwy. 1 exit at the Beit Shemesh (Sha'ar Hagai) interchange and take Rte. 38 south toward Beit Shemesh. From Rte. 38 (about 8km/5 miles from Hwy. 1) take Rte. 3835 to Kibbutz Tzora. There is no entrance fee.

The **Cremesan Winery** is run by members of the Italian Salisian monastic order. The beautiful winery can be visited (when security is good) daily at Beit Jalla, near Bethlehem on the West Bank, but until the security situation improves, you can purchase the interesting, Italian-style wines produced at Beit Jalla at the **Bet Jimal Monastery** (© 02/991-7671), inside Israel, near the town of Beit Shemesh. It is open Monday to Saturday 8:30am to 5pm. There are picnic tables overlooking a fine view behind the monastery, where you may visit until dusk. Bet Jimal Monastery is located 2km (1¼ miles) south of Beit Shemesh (left turn off Rte. 38).

a fireplace, which on cold nights is sometimes used. Hours are Saturday to Thursday, 7pm to midnight; closed Fridays. 8 Shmuel Ha Naggid St. © 02/622-2283.

**Mike's Place**   The Ben-Yehuda/Yoel Salomon Street Mall area is filled with pubs and bars that come and go. Mike's Place is the most long-lived and friendly in the area, with great nightly programs featuring live blues, folk, and current musicians from the local rock scene. The crowd is an easy mix of Israelis, students, tourists, professionals, and occasionally Palestinians (ages 18–50); in good weather, tables move out to a courtyard. There's a free pool table, and affordable pizzas, focaccia, and simple dishes are served day and night. No decor, no one dresses up, no bouncers, and never a cover charge, but there is a two-drink minimum. Open daily 10am until at least 2am; music starts around 10pm. 37 Jaffa Rd. (entrance through courtyard accessible from alley beside the 8 Altogether Ceramics Gallery on Yoel Salomon St.). (© 052/267-0753 (mobile phone).

**Yellow Submarine** A bit less conveniently located way out in south Jerusalem's ugly Talpiot Industrial Park, this place has live music and performances almost every night, often with dancing. There's a bar and organized parties; the music is usually punk-rock, and the crowd is young, the atmosphere is fun, and not at all lowlife. At times you'll find a program of blues singers or a really great jazz trio, and these bring in an older crowd. Usually open 10pm until after 4am. You must call to check hours and programs. *Note:* It's best to come and go by taxi. Admission/cover charges vary according to event. 13 Rehov Ha-Rechevim, Talpiot Industrial Park. (© 02/679-4040. www.yellow submarine.org.il.

## FILMS

West Jerusalem shows the latest European and American films, almost always in the original language with Hebrew subtitles. In the eastern part of the city, the films come mostly from Arab countries and are in Arabic without subtitles. The Friday *Jerusalem Post* carries film listings and times, but seldom the address or phone number of the cinemas.

The most prominent theater is the world-famous **Cinémathèque** (© 02/672-4131), or Israel Film Archive, which is the scene of nightly screenings of classics, the best of the current international scene, rarely shown international films, and the experimental and arcane. Films are usually in the original language, with Hebrew and (often) English subtitles. Members of the Cinémathèque get the first seats, but a half-hour before screening time tickets go on sale to the public. *Tip:* Every July, the Jerusalem Cinémathèque is the venue for a fabulous **International Film Festival.** Besides the movie houses, there are other places that screen films, such as the Jerusalem Theater, Binyane Ha-Uma, and the Israel Museum.

The Cinémathèque is located near the railway station. Go to the traffic intersection between the railway station and Hebron Road. Walk down the slope to the northeast, toward the Old City, and soon you'll come to the Cinémathèque, built into the hillside below the Hebron Road. Bus no. 8, 21, 48, 4, or 18 will take you there.

Other well-known cinemas and venues for film are **G. G. Gil,** Jerusalem Mall, Malha (© 02/678-8448), and the **Jerusalem Theater** (20 Marcus St.; © 02/560-5755).

## 10 Side Trips Outside Jerusalem

**KENNEDY MEMORIAL** Eleven kilometers (7 miles) from downtown Jerusalem, in the same general direction of Hadassah Medical Center, Yad Kennedy is reached by following the winding mountain roads past the Aminadav Moshav. Opened in May 1966, the 18m-high (59-ft.) memorial to Pres. John F. Kennedy is designed in the shape of a cut tree trunk, symbolizing a life cut short. The mountaintop memorial is encircled by 51 columns, each bearing the emblem of a state of the Union, plus the

District of Columbia. City bus no. 20 stops quite a distance away. Be prepared to take a cab and have the driver wait.

To the west, just inside the West Bank, is the village of Batir, site of a final stronghold in the last Jewish revolt against the Romans, in A.D. 135, led by Bar Kokhba. The view from the parking lot is breathtaking—a never-ending succession of mountains and valleys. The monument and adjoining picnic grounds are part of the John F. Kennedy Peace Forest.

**ABU GHOSH**   In the Israeli-Arab town of Abu Ghosh (biblical Kiriath Jearim), 13km (8 miles) west of Jerusalem, are two sites that can be reached by Egged bus no. 185 or 186 from the Central Bus Station at a cost of NIS 10 ($2.50/£1.25). Confirm with the driver that you want to be let out at Merkaz Abu Ghosh/Abu Ghosh Center. Abu Ghosh is one of the few Arab villages that decided to side with Israel in the 1948 War of Independence. Israelis love to flock to Abu Ghosh on Saturday to enjoy hummus and other Arabic-style foods at the town's numerous restaurants. A number of hummus places call themselves "Abu Shukri"; most are good, but have no connection to the *real* Abu Shukri in Jerusalem's Old City. On the other hand, Abu Gosh's **Lebanese Restaurant** is the best of the wall-to-wall dining choices in town, and serves some of the most fabulous lamb in Israel.

Abu Ghosh's great treasure is the 12th-century **Crusader Church of the Resurrection** ✪, acquired by the French in the late 19th century and now under the guardianship of the Lazarist fathers. Like the Crusader Church of Saint Anne in Jerusalem's Old City, the Church of the Resurrection was designed to create marvelous acoustics for Gregorian chant, but it's less heavily restored and more atmospheric. It is built over an ancient cistern and well that was in use from early Canaanite times. It's open Monday to Wednesday and Friday and Saturday from 8:30 to 11:30am and 2:30 to 5:30pm. The 20th-century **Church of Notre Dame of the Ark,** built on the site of a Byzantine church, marks the last place the Ark of the Covenant rested before it was brought to Jerusalem by King David. It's open daily from 8:30 to 11:30am and 2:30 to 5:30pm.

**NEOT KEDUMIM BIBLICAL LANDSCAPE RESERVE**   The reserve is in the Lod District between Jerusalem and Tel Aviv on Rte. 443 (✆ **08/977-0770**). Neot Kedumim is a kind of living museum of the farming, harvesting, and shepherding techniques of ancient times laid out across 250 hectares (618 acres) of land carefully planted with flora of the biblical period. An explanatory text brings the landscape vividly to life and relates it to accounts in the Old and New Testaments and the Talmud. Guides are expert at explaining references to nature in Judeo-Christian scriptures; you'll find an olive press and a *succa* (harvesters' shelter), and see how ancient ink was made from a powder composed of resin, ground pomegranates, and oak gallnuts. With an advance reservation, you may be able to join a group of 15 or more for a vegetarian buffet of reconstructed ancient recipes (American food critic Mimi Sheraton found the food delicious). Admission is NIS 40 ($10/£5); last admission 2 hours before closing. Open Sunday to Thursday from 8:30am to sunset and Friday and holiday eves from 8:30am to 1pm. Telephone for driving or bus instructions. Guided tours in English are given Friday at 9:30am; reserve ahead to arrange other times. There are also self-guided tours; trails are wheelchair accessible, and electric carts and wheelchairs are available on advance reservation.

**SOREQ STALACTITE CAVE/AVSHALOM NATURE RESERVE**   Located 20km (12 miles) west of Jerusalem along the road out of Ein Kerem toward Bar Giora

(✆ 02/991-1117), this nature reserve, with its unusual, delicate, and varied stalactites, is a favorite excursion for tour groups. Set in the limestone region, the caves are full of incredible formations. The scenery along the road from Ein Kerem to the moshav of Nes Harim, 1.6km (1 mile) from the caves, is by itself worth the pleasant excursion. Admission is NIS 23 ($5.75/£2.90), half-price for children, and includes a lecture with slides and a tour. Hours are Sunday to Thursday from 8:30am to 3:30pm and Friday from 8:30am to noon; no slide show Friday. Direct service is by tour bus only. Egged will take you on a tour to the caves and nearby sights for about NIS 100 ($25/£13).

**MINI ISRAEL** 🖈   This 3-hectare (7½-acre) tourist park is amazing in its scope and detail. It re-creates many of the country's most important landmarks in the form of miniature models built to a scale of 1:25. It's very similar to Holland's famous Madurodam in both tone and technique, and it's just as enjoyable. The park separates Israel into geographic regions and features landmarks from all faiths and cultures. The models are impressive in their detail: The planes at the mock-up of Ben-Gurion Airport actually taxi on runways, and praying pilgrims at the Western Wall sway back and forth. It's a good idea to try to see Mini Israel toward the end of your trip, when you'll be more familiar with many of the sites and landmarks reproduced here. Because it's inadvisable to travel to a number of Israel's most notable sights right now, the park represents your best chance to encounter some of the country's best-known landmarks (though by no means a substitute for an actual visit). Notable re-creations include the Old City of Jerusalem (including the Western Wall and the Dome of the Rock), the Baha'i Terrace Gardens at Haifa, and the Cave of the Patriarchs in Hebron. The park is especially amazing at twilight, when the interiors of buildings are lit. The family-friendly park has a restaurant/cafe food court on the premises (you're a captive audience if you're hungry or thirsty, and have come from Jerusalem on Mini Israel's shuttle bus) and a little play area for children. It takes about 2 hours to see everything. Mini Israel is fully accessible to those with disabilities. Because the exhibits are outdoors, avoid coming on a cold, rainy winter day, or in midday summer heat. It's hard to get here without a car (it's about a 30-min. drive), unless you're coming via bus tour, though at press time Mini Israel was offering to arrange a taxi package or morning shuttle (call for current schedules and fees) from Jerusalem. Regular tours to Mini Israel and other nearby sites are operated by Egged Tours (✆ 1-700/70 75 77) on Tuesday and Thursday.

Latrun Junction, off Hwy. 1. ✆ 08/921-4121. Admission for adults and children 6 and over NIS 70 ($18/£8.75); children 2–5 NIS 15 ($3.75/£1.90). Coupons and discounted rates available for children, seniors, and families at Tourist Information and hotel desks. A taxi package is available. Nov–Mar Sun–Thurs and Sat 10am–6pm, Fri 10am–2pm; Apr and Sept–Oct Sun–Thurs 10am–8pm, Fri 10am–2pm; May–June Sun–Thurs 10am–9pm, Fri 9am–2pm; July–Aug 10am–10pm; Fri 10am–2pm.

**DRIVING TOUR**    THE MOUNTAINS WEST OF JERUSALEM

| | |
|---|---|
| **Start:** | Sderot Herzl in West Jerusalem. |
| **Finish:** | Beit Guvrin. |
| **Time:** | 2½ hours, with minimal stops. |
| **Best times:** | Late morning, year-round. |
| **Worst times:** | Midafternoon, year-round. Driving westward into the sun on narrow, winding roads after midafternoon will be blinding. |

When Hwy. 1 from Tel Aviv to Jerusalem ascends into the Judean Mountains at Sha'ar Ha Gai (the Gate of the Valley), you can catch a few glimpses of the true magnificence of the Judean landscape. Sadly, this is all of the Judean Mountains that most visitors to Israel ever see. Intensive construction of communities along the Hwy. 1 corridor to Jerusalem, the widening and straightening of the highway, and a forest fire in 1995 that destroyed 70 years of reforestation have all diminished the wonders of this once dramatic route. But "the secret places of the hills" (to quote the Song of Songs) still exist untouched in the countryside just to the south of Hwy. 1, filled with forested mountains, ancient terraced hillsides, and dramatic ravines and vistas. Most visitors who rent cars in Israel take off for the mountains of the Galilee and Golan, or the Negev Desert. This drive, starting just minutes from Jerusalem, will pass vistas as dramatic as any in Galilee, and introduce you to some of the simple pleasures of the hills.

---

**From Sderot Herzl in West Jerusalem, take the right turn to Ein Kerem, and follow the road downhill to:**

### ❶ Ein Kerem

The birthplace of John the Baptist is now a semirustic village that has been incorporated into the city of Jerusalem. Although this is not part of the hidden countryside route that lies ahead, you might want to explore the churches of the town and walk down some of the local streets, where old Arabic cottages and villas are being renovated and gentrified into one of Jerusalem's most sought-after communities (p. 206). No time to stop at the big restaurants at Ein Kerem's crossroads, but check out Sweet 'N Karem, right at the town center, for homemade ice cream or lavish homemade chocolates to take on the road (p. 216).

**Follow the main road through Ein Kerem, and around to the left out of town. At the beginning of Rte. 386, which is the main road we shall follow, take a right turn at the sign to Mevasseret and follow this side road (which becomes Rte. 395) for a brief detour to:**

### ❷ Sataf

This small nature reserve is busy on the weekends, when the cheese cave is open, but wonderfully tranquil the rest of the week. The Judean countryside is filled with springs that run through soft strata of limestone; these springs provide the basis for many of the communities in the region. Although Sataf is now a reserve,

for thousands of years the spring here supported the villages that arose with each wave of civilization. You can visit the spring in a cave created over the eons, and crawl through a short man-made tunnel to a water collection pool. Swimming in the pool is supposed to be prohibited, but on both quiet and busy days, I've seen people try out the water. From the pool, you can follow pathways downhill to where Jerusalemites are allowed to rent plots of land and plant organic gardens watered according to traditional irrigation techniques. There is no admission fee to Sataf. Next to the parking area is a cafe/restaurant, good for soups, salads, and light meals. The view from the deck is great.

From the parking area near the spring, it's a short drive or a 45-minute walk (look for signs with the symbol of a picnic table) to visit the cave of **Shai Selzer,** the most wonderful goatherd and cheese maker in Israel. Here you can buy a variety of excellent goats' milk cheeses produced by three families that have permission to live on this mountain. There are Italian-style Parmesans, Alpine-style cheeses, blue cheeses reminiscent of the south of France, local varieties such as avitia (made to be eaten with watermelon), or mild soft cheeses wrapped in grape leaves—great with fresh bread and fruit as you travel. It's open in summer on

Friday from 4 to 7pm and Saturday from 11am to 7pm; in winter, it's open Saturday only 11am to 4pm.

**After exploring Sataf, return to the Mevasseret turnoff, and turn right onto Rte. 386. You will pass the Monastery of St. John the Baptist of the Wilderness uphill on the left and continue along a road with dazzling vistas. Don't hesitate to pull off the road and enjoy the quiet and the views. Watch for an orange sign and a very small parking area on the right indicating the:**

### ❸ Nahal Katlav Nature Walk

This pathway takes you into a richly forested valley; in late winter/early spring the whole area is alive with rockrose, cyclamen, red buttercups, broom, wild licorice, and garlic. There are also Katlav Tulips, from which, according to local belief, all tulips throughout the world are descended. In the distance to the lower right, hidden amid the forest, look for a lone, domed building, the "tomb of the sheik." According to Muslim legend, hundreds of years ago a mysterious wanderer visited a nearby village. When he hung his clothes on a dead pomegranate tree before bathing in the local spring, the tree came to life and blossomed. His tomb was a pilgrimage destination until 1948, when the Muslim population was forced to leave the area. The Katlav nature walk can take 1 to 2 hours depending on your pace and how far you decide to go.

After the Katlav walk area, at a "T" in the road, turn right onto 3866 to Beit Shemesh. The road continues through a Jewish national forest named for the late U.S. vice president Hubert Humphrey, a strong supporter of the State of Israel. There are a number of picnic areas and vista points along the way.

**At a fork in the road, follow the sign to the left, eventually leading into the small city of Beit Shemesh. You will pass through an industrial part, and eventually come to a traffic light at a "T" intersection. Turn left onto Rte. 38 to Beit Guvrin. After about 4km (2½ miles), turn left, where an orange sign indicates the road to the:**

### ❹ Monastery of Bet Jimal

Founded, along with an agricultural school, by the Salesian order in the late 19th century, this monastery is surrounded by orchards that have an air of medieval otherworldliness. For years, the monks have pleaded with the city of Beit Shemesh not to develop areas adjacent to or in direct view of this beautiful enclave; in most directions they have succeeded. For many visitors, the highlight of a stop at Beit Jimal is a chance to purchase homemade wine and take in the exceptional view from the monastery roof. At the adjacent Convent of the Assumption of the Virgin (to the left), beautiful ceramics (among the best folk art in the country) are for sale, hand painted by the sisters (most of whom have taken a vow of silence). Walk to the right, around to the back of the monastery, and you will find pieces of a mosaic floor from the 5th- and 6th-century Byzantine Church of the Tomb of St. Stephen. Discovered in 1915, they are displayed alongside a small chapel. Further behind the complex are picnic tables with a view down to the coastal plain—a wonderful place from which to watch the twilight. This site is believed to have been called, in ancient times, Kfar Gamla, the village of the great Talmudic leader Rabbi Gamliel.

According to Christian tradition, Rabbi Gamliel, who headed the Sanhedrin in Yavneh after the destruction of Jerusalem in A.D. 70, was the teacher of Saul, who later became St. Paul. The Salesian school, closed for many years when it was cut off from its potential students on the West Bank, is again functioning. You may visit the monastery and its extensive countryside Monday to Saturday from 8:30am to dusk. The wine and ceramics shops and monastery buildings are open until 5pm.

**From Bet Jimal, you can turn left back onto Rte. 38 south, and visit:**

# Driving Tour: The Mountains West of Jerusalem

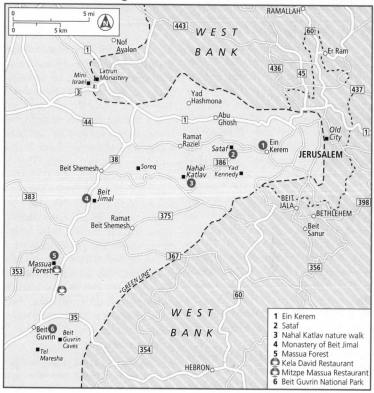

Legend:
1 Ein Kerem
2 Sataf
3 Nahal Katlav nature walk
4 Monastery of Beit Jimal
5 Massua Forest
☕ Kela David Restaurant
☕ Mitzpe Massua Restaurant
6 Beit Guvrin National Park

## ❺ The Massua Forest

The forest features an excellent restaurant and beautiful vistas overlooking the coastal plain; it's a right turn off Rte. 38.

**TAKE A BREAK**
**Mitzpe Massua Restaurant,** at the Ranger's Station, Massua Forest, Beit Shemesh–Beit Guvrin Highway (✆ 02/991-2464), a country-style restaurant with fabulous views, has kashrut certificates for both meat and dairy meals and an excellent and affordable cuisine. The Mitzpe Massua Restaurant is closed from late Friday afternoon until the end of Shabbat. The restaurant is open irregular hours. You must call ahead to reserve and discuss whether you want a light meal or a major feast and agree on a price. The restaurant is best during daylight, when you can enjoy the view. The appetizers and homemade breads are excellent. Farther south on the Beit Shemesh–Beit Guvrin Highway, as it passes through the Elah Valley, where the young David fought the Philistine Goliath with a slingshot, you'll find another good country dining choice, **Kela David** ✪, a vineyard, winery, and restaurant/cafe at Givat Yishiahu (✆ 02/999-4848). Traveling south on Hwy. 38, look for a pink house in the fields to the left; access is via a dirt road on the left just past what looks like a junkyard. Kela David is not kosher, and is open Monday to Saturday from 10am to 10pm. (See p. 163 for a review of Kela David restaurant.)

A good add-on to this drive would be to continue farther down Rte. 38 to the fascinating:

### ⑥ Beit Guvrin National Park

Now for some truly unusual archaeology. The park encompasses the Beit Guvrin caves, the ruins of Beit Guvrin, and the ruins of Maresha, a Judean town during the time of the First Temple. After the Babylonian destruction, Maresha was settled by Edomites, then Phoenicians. Eventually it evolved into a Hellenistic town that was conquered by the Hasmonean Jewish dynasty in the 1st century B.C. and forcibly converted to Judaism. Beit Guvrin was a strongly Jewish city from the late Second Temple period through the time of its destruction during the Bar Kochba Revolt of A.D. 132 to 135. Ruins of a 3rd-century synagogue have been found here, as well as artifacts from a 12th-century Crusader fortress destroyed by Saladin in 1191. Most of these finds are displayed in the collection of the Rockefeller Archaeological Museum in Jerusalem (p. 208).

The Arab village of Beit Jibrin stood here until the 1948 war; in 1949, the modern kibbutz of Beit Guvrin was built on the site. The ruins and vistas from the top of Tel Maresha (2km/1¼ miles from Kibbutz Beit Guvrin) are extremely beautiful. Some of the easiest caves to explore are the caves right at Tel Maresha. The 800 caves at Beit Guvrin are thought to be partly the product of natural erosion and largely the result of centuries of quarry activity by a number of different civilizations. Many are bell shaped, with light streaming in from quarrying holes on the ceilings, and have an odd, spiritual quality (one of the caves was used as a church in Crusader times). The caves have also been used as animal pens, water cisterns, and even as shelters for religious hermits; most recently they were a locale for Sylvester Stallone's movie *Rambo III*. In summer, the National Parks Authority has minibuses and guides to direct visitors to the best caves in this 500-hectare (1,236-acre) site. It's open Saturday to Thursday from 8am to 4pm (until 5pm Apr–Sept) and on Friday from 8am to 3pm. Admission is NIS 23 ($5.75/£2.90), with a small discount for students. The park has a snack bar.

From Beit Guvrin, take Rte. 38 back through Beit Shemesh and on to Hwy. 1, from which you can return to Jerusalem or drive northwest to Tel Aviv. Or, you can retrace the route back to Ein Kerem and Jerusalem.

# 7

# Tel Aviv

Tel Aviv is everything Jerusalem is not. The city began with a gorgeous strip of beach along the Mediterranean and went on from there to become the bold and busy city that never sleeps. Known locally as the Big Orange, Tel Aviv has no holy sites and until its founding in 1909, it had no history. It does have oyster bars, nightclubs, samba sessions at the beach on summer evenings, and miles and miles of massive medium-rise apartment buildings. In summer, the heat and humidity can put New York to shame, but a short walk or bus ride can always get you to the sparkling waters of the Mediterranean.

Tel Aviv is the country's commercial center and also the cultural capital; the nation's newspapers and most books are published here (except the *Jerusalem Post*), concerts are frequent, and the Hebrew-language theater thrives. Here you can find an art scene in the many galleries around the Gordon Street neighborhood, and there are top-flight fashion designers in Neve Zedek, Shenkin Street, and on upper Dizengoff and Ben-Yehuda streets. A look at the back of some of the free tourist magazines distributed throughout town, and you'll figure out that the city also hosts a thriving sex industry. To an idealistic kibbutznik, an Arab Israeli from Nazareth, or an observant Jew from Jerusalem's Mea Shearim district, the mere mention of Tel Aviv can conjure up an image of Gomorrah in its worst depravity.

Tel Aviv today is riding the wave of the country's high-tech economic boom, and it shows everywhere. In the past few years, the city's hotels and stock exchange have begun to buzz with the energy of high-powered business deals from all over the world. Glass skyscrapers dot the city's landscape; even more are under construction. The city is bustling with style and creativity. In 2008, *Vogue* filled an issue with articles on Tel Aviv's lively ambience and style. If peace is allowed to develop, many envision 21st-century Tel Aviv as the financial Singapore of a new Middle East.

As always, Tel Avivians love to play. In the 1980s, the city's beaches were beautifully renewed, and are now among the cleanest and most easily accessible urban beaches in the world. The Tel Aviv Museum of Art has an important collection of Impressionist and post-Impressionist art in its galleries; Beit Hatfutsot, the inventive Diaspora Museum of Jewish History draws visitors from all over the world. The 1990s saw the construction of an opera house, new performing-arts centers, and the development of a rarefied luxury restaurant scene.

Tel Avivians are also busy preserving, gentrifying, and recycling neglected landmarks and neighborhoods. The once virtually derelict Tel Aviv Port, at the northern end of the city, is now the hottest spot in town, wall-to-wall with inventive eateries, pubs, and shops overlooking the sea. Restored Old Jaffa is a must for evening dining and strolling, loved by visitors and Israelis alike.

Elsewhere in Tel Aviv, you'll notice exotic Arabesque/Art Deco structures from the 1918-to-1930 period, and wonderful 1930s and early 1940s International Style buildings that once defined the city's ultramodern image. In the 1930s, many refugee architects and designers from Germany sought shelter in Palestine. For them, the sands of Tel Aviv provided an opportunity to create a dazzling metropolis of the future based on clean, functional lines. By the beginning of World War II, Tel Aviv had burgeoned into an urban garden of ultramodern white concrete architectural wonders—the curvilinear balconies and rounded corners of Tel Aviv's building boom were featured in architectural journals throughout the world.

But despite its architectural pizazz, 1930s Tel Aviv close-up was not the sleek, perfectly planned utopia it appeared. Many of the dazzlingly photographed buildings admired by the outside world were filled with old-fashioned workshops. In summer, the broad, futuristic streets (designed by architects whose hearts were still in pre-1933 Berlin) sweltered under the sun, and blocked whatever evening breezes might blow in from the sea.

After Israeli independence, Tel Aviv mushroomed, first with refugee camps and temporary housing for the hundreds of thousands of Jewish survivors of the Holocaust who poured into the country; later with vast, drab housing projects. During

the austere 1950s, Tel Aviv, although a young city, became run-down, especially around its downtown center at Moghrabi Square. The beach, one of Tel Aviv's strong points, piled up with garbage and was neglected. The modern buildings of the 1930s and early 1940s, built of sand bricks, began to crumble. The city offered little in the way of museums, hotels, or restaurants, and word was out that Tel Aviv was a hot, humid, concrete heap, ungainly and uninteresting.

In the past 25 years, however, Tel Aviv has undergone a carefully nurtured revolution. The beach, only a few blocks from anywhere in the city center, has made a spectacular comeback. Performing groups, ranging from the Israel Philharmonic Orchestra and the Cameri Theater to the New Israel Opera, have put Tel Aviv on the cultural map.

Tel Aviv now incorporates the once-separate city of Jaffa, which does have a history going back thousands of years (the Prophet Jonah lived in this seaport before his encounter with the whale). If you climb the hill of Old Jaffa and look northward toward Tel Aviv's shoreline, you'll see a city that stands on the threshold of majesty—an amazing achievement for a metropolis that's merely 100 years old.

## 1 Orientation

### ARRIVING

**BY PLANE**    Flights arrive at Ben-Gurion International Airport at Lod, on the outskirts of the city. There is a fixed daytime **taxi fare** of approximately NIS 135 ($34/£17) from Ben-Gurion to central Tel Aviv. This fare includes one suitcase per passenger; additional suitcases are NIS 4 ($1/50p) each. After 9pm and on Shabbat, the fixed fare will be higher. **Trains** leave Ben-Gurion Airport for the Arlosoroff Train Station in Tel Aviv two times an hour from 3:30am to 11pm. Fare is NIS 16 ($4/£2). From there you'll need to take a local taxi. You're not too far to most Tel Aviv hotels, but with baggage, jet lag, and brutal summer heat, it's not walkable.

**BY TRAIN**    The **Central Railway Station** (sometimes called North Railway Station because it's in the northern reaches of the city) stands at the intersection of several major arteries—Petach Tikva Road, Haifa Road, and Arlosoroff Street. From here, municipal buses will take you throughout the city. For Israel Railways information call ℂ **03/611-7000.**

**BY BUS**    From the **Central Bus Station** into town, take bus no. 4, which runs along Allenby Road and then up Ben-Yehuda Street. As you ride along Ben-Yehuda, you'll be parallel to and a block away from Ha-Yarkon Street, where many hotels are located. Ask the driver for the stop closest to your hotel. Take the no. 5 bus to Dizengoff Square. For Dan Bus Lines information call ℂ **03/639-4444.**

**BY SHERUT**    Ten-passenger vans from Jerusalem and Haifa drop you off just outside the main door of the vast Tel Aviv Bus Station and leave for the return trip as soon as they're full. Much more convenient than wending your way through the six-story bus station, sheruts cost a shekel or so more than bus fares.

**BY CAR**    Major highways connect Jerusalem, Haifa, and Ashkelon with Tel Aviv.

## VISITOR INFORMATION

The **Israel Tourist Information Office** is located at 7 Mendele St. (ℂ **03/520-7600**), near Ben-Yehuda Street, right in the heart of Tel Aviv's main hotel district. It's open Sunday to Thursday from 9am to 5pm. This office will give you free information about sites in Tel Aviv and throughout Israel, as well as maps, useful brochures, and discount coupon books. You must come in person. A much less comprehensive Municipal Tourist Office is at 46 Herbert Samuel Promenade (ℂ **03/561-6188**). This one is open Sunday through Thursday 8am to 4:30pm.

On the Web, **Tel Aviv Guide** (www.telavivguide.net) offers lots of good information and visitor forums; **Tel Aviv 4 Fun** (www.telaviv4fun.com) has information about guided and independent tours, travel tips, and reviews of attractions, hotels, and dining. **Tel Aviv in Focus** (www.telavivinf.com) is a fabulous site, loaded with up-to-date information; its list of links is a treasure chest.

## CITY LAYOUT

Tel Aviv and Jaffa (Yafo in Hebrew) together form a large urban area. But the Tel Aviv–Jaffa you'll get to know is actually the downtown seafront section, extending east only to the thoroughfare of Ibn Givrol Street. This is a 6km (4-mile) strip at least 1km (½ mile) wide, but only certain sections are of interest to visitors—the rest of the turf is residential or industrial.

## MAIN ARTERIES & STREETS

Tel Aviv's big streets mainly run north and south, roughly parallel to the sea. **Herbert Samuel Boulevard** is right along the beach. It starts near the Dan Hotel and runs south to Jaffa, with a pedestrian promenade running alongside it—great for strolling and jogging. **Ha-Yarkon Street** is 1 block inland, and from the northern tip of Tel Aviv down to the border with Jaffa is dotted with hotels of all sizes and prices. At the northern tip of Ha-Yarkon, you'll find the **Old Tel Aviv Port,** filled with trendy cafes, pubs, and restaurants, many overlooking the sea. **Ben-Yehuda Street** is the next block inland. The streets between Ha-Yarkon and Ben-Yehuda from the Dan Hotel southward are thick with good restaurants and small hotels. Northern Ben-Yehuda is home to more exclusive design and clothing shops. At its southern end, Ben-Yehuda curves into **Allenby Street,** which continues southwest. Allenby is an old-fashioned low-budget shopping drag. Off Allenby you'll find the **Carmel Market,** Tel Aviv's roaring outdoor labyrinth where fabulous fruits and vegetables (as well as a million other things) are sold. The **Nahlat Binyamin** network of pedestrian streets, filled with shops, eateries, and a busy Tuesday and Friday crafts fair, is right off Allenby next to

## Getting Connected in Tel Aviv

Tel Aviv is one of the most Web-connected places on earth. You will never want for places to get online. Convenient to the hotel district, **Web Stop Internet Lounge,** 28 Bogroshov St. (© **03/620-2682**), is a home away from home for anyone who needs to feel connected. There's a coffee bar and a real bar (though limited) on the premises, as well as classy computer desks that seat two, log-on sites for laptop users, red velvet sofas, a computer with a minicam, and snacks that don't exactly say "tech-head" (such as sun-dried tomato and brie sandwiches). It's the kind of place with lots of regulars, where everybody knows your name. **Private Link,** 78 Ben-Yehuda St. (© **03/529-9889**), is convenient to the hotel district.

the Carmel Market, and farther south is the offbeat **Neve Zedek** neighborhood. Perpendicular to Allenby, inland from the Carmel Market, is **King George Street,** lined with bakeries, cafes, and small shops connecting to the next big north-south thoroughfare, **Dizengoff Street.** There's the big Dizengoff Tower Shopping Mall at Dizengoff and King George streets, lots of fast-food places up to and north of **Dizengoff Square,** and blocks of better shops at the northern end of Dizengoff Street. **Ibn Givrol** is the most inland of the major north-south streets. Its northern end is close to the Golda Meir/Tel Aviv Center for Performing Arts and the Tel Aviv Art Museum. Farther south, it's close to the Mann Auditorium and the Tel Aviv Cinémathèque, and is lined with lots of places to eat and dine. *Note:* The **no. 4 bus** and sherut line runs from the Central Bus Station northward along Allenby and then Ben-Yehuda streets. **Bus no. 5** runs from the Central Bus Station up to the main sector of Dizengoff Street. **Bus no. 10** runs down Ben-Yehuda and then Herbert Samuel Boulevard to Jaffa, with its restored quarter, many restaurants, and flea market.

## 2 Getting Around

**BY BUS**    From the new **Central Bus Station** to the center of Tel Aviv, bus no. 4 goes to Allenby Road and on to Ben-Yehuda Street; on Ben-Yehuda, you will be running parallel to and a block inland from Ha-Yarkon Street; take bus no. 5 to go to the Mann Auditorium, Dizengoff Square, Dizengoff Street, and the IYHA youth hostel B'nei Dan. *Note:* No. 4 and 5 sheruts run the 4 and 5 bus routes 7 days a week, and are slightly cheaper than the buses (see "By Taxi/Sherut Within Tel Aviv," below). From the Central Bus Station to Jaffa, take bus no. 46 and get off near the Clock Tower on Yefet Street.

Standard fare is NIS 5.60 ($1.40/70p), with an additional half shekel to and from peripheral areas.

To get to **Jaffa** from Tel Aviv, take bus no. 10, 25, or 26 heading southward. Bus no. 10 runs along Ben-Yehuda Street, a block inland from Ha-Yarkon Street, and takes you to Jaffa's Clock Tower on Yefet Street, close to Old Jaffa and the flea market. Bus no. 25, which you can pick up on King George Street near Dizengoff Street, runs through Jaffa on Jerusalem Street, a very long block parallel to and inland from Yefet Street. If you're walking (30–45 min.), simply head south along the waterfront promenade, which eventually runs into Jaffa. Bus no. 25 running northward will get you to the Diaspora Museum of Jewish History and Tel Aviv University. For **intercity Egged**

**bus information,** call ℂ **03/694-8888.** For information on **Dan Bus service,** which operates in the Tel Aviv/Sharon region, call ℂ **03/639-4444.**

**BY TAXI/SHERUT WITHIN TEL AVIV**   Ten-passenger vans run along the bus nos. 4 and 5 lines. They even run on a reduced schedule on Shabbat. If a van comes along, by all means take it rather than wait for the bus. Prices are a drop lower than bus fares on weekdays; on Shabbat there is a small surcharge.

When taxis are scarce, your best bet is to try at one of the major hotels. You have the right to demand that the meter (*ha-sha-*on) be used, but many drivers will negotiate a fixed nonmetered fare to your destination, which may or may not be to your advantage. There are legal surcharges above the metered fare on Shabbat and after 9pm. If you use the meter, ask for a receipt (ka-*ba-*lah).

**BY TRAIN**   For train schedules, call ℂ **03/577-4000.** The best train station for those staying in central Tel Aviv is the Arlosoroff Street Station, at the eastern end of Arlosoroff Street. There is train service up the coast to Nahariya; south to Beersheva; slow, infrequent service to the western edge of Jerusalem; and a rail link to Ben-Gurion Airport. Israel Railways is undergoing a period of revival and expansion. For the most current information on schedules and fares, go to **www.israrail.org.il**.

---

## *FAST FACTS:* Tel Aviv

*American Express*   American Express International is in the El Al Building at 32 Ben-Yehuda St. (ℂ **03/526-8888;** for lost traveler's checks, call ℂ 800/943-8694). Mail is held for American Express cardholders. Bookings can be made here, but this office does not deal in traveler's checks. Open Sunday to Thursday from 9am to 5pm and Friday 9am to 1pm.

*Currency Exchange*   There are a number of internationally connected ATMs in the hotel district along Ha-Yarkon and Ben-Yehuda streets. Check with your hotel desk about which is the closest. There are numerous currency exchange offices along Ha-Yarkon and Ben-Yehuda streets. They usually have exchange rates comparable to the banks, are open longer hours, and involve less waiting in line. Avoid shady people offering to change money on the streets no matter what rate they quote.

*Doctors & Dentists*   You can get a list of English-speaking doctors and dentists from your embassy, and often from your hotel's front desk. For First Aid SOS Doctors, call ℂ **800/225-5005.** There is an Emergency Dental Treatment Center at 18 Reines St. (ℂ 03/523-9241); or call **Dental First Aid** (ℂ 800/773-773), which operates 24 hours a day.

*Drugstores*   The *Jerusalem Post* lists under "General Assistance" the names and addresses of duty pharmacies that stay open nights and on Shabbat for the current week.

*Embassies & Consulates*   See appendix A for a list of embassies and consulates.

*Emergencies*   For police, dial ℂ **100.** In medical emergencies, dial ℂ **101** for Magen David Adom (Red Shield of David), Israel's emergency first-aid service and ambulance. For fire, dial ℂ **102.**

*Hospitals* For visitors with Blue Cross–Blue Shield insurance, call ✆ **03/ 579-0081,** or 755-3546 for information. Itchilov Hospital (✆ **03/691-4000**) has an emergency room, dental clinic, and Malam Traveler's Clinic for immunizations.

*Hot Lines* For the **Rape Crisis Center,** dial ✆ **03/523-4819;** drug counseling is available at ✆ **03/546-3587.** Dial the Crisis Counseling Hot Line (in English) at ✆ **800/654-1111** or 02/654-1111.

*Laundry & Dry Cleaning* Try 63 Ben-Yehuda St., near Bogroshov, which advertises "6 Hour Cleaning and Laundry." Hours are 7am to 1:30pm and 3:30 to 6pm. If you want to do it yourself, 51 Ben-Yehuda St. or 9 Mendele St., near Ben-Yehuda, have coin-operated machines. Figure NIS 24 ($6/£3) for washing, soap, and adequate drying.

*Newspapers & Magazines* See the special Tel Aviv events supplement published on Friday in the *Jerusalem Post* (available only in the Tel Aviv region). The English-language editions of *Time Out Tel Aviv* and *Time Out Israel* are available for free bimonthly at most major hotels. The emphasis in both editions is on Tel Aviv.

*Post Office* Tel Aviv's **Central Post Office** is at 132 Allenby Rd. General hours for all services are Sunday to Thursday from 7am to 7pm, though limited services (telephone and telegraph) are open nights and on Shabbat. **Telegrams** can be sent at all post offices or by phoning ✆ **171.** Check with your hotel for the closest neighborhood branch.

*Radio* Israel news can be heard at 576, 1170, and 1458 kHz at 7am, 1pm, 5pm, and 8pm. BBC World Service broadcasts at 1322 kHz.

*Safety* Israel's largest city has less crime than most cities its size, but there is still enough that you must observe the normal precautions. Don't walk in deserted areas, especially the beaches, after dark. Terrorism is always a concern. Get away from and report any unattended bags or packages.

*Television* There are often English-language programs and films (with Hebrew subtitles) on Israeli channels; one English-language channel from Lebanon specializes in very old American TV reruns and Christian religious programs. A selection of international cable and satellite channels is usually available at most hotels.

*Transportation Telephone Numbers* For all flight arrival and departure schedule information, including last-minute changes, call ✆ **03/972-3344;** for train schedules, call ✆ **03/577-4000;** for Egged Bus schedules, call ✆ **03/694-8888** or *2800 for all bus routes.

## 3 Where to Stay

Most of Tel Aviv's hotels are on Ha-Yarkon Street, which runs along the beach from Mograbi Square northward. The luxury hotels are on the sea side of Ha-Yarkon. Most of the mid- and lower-class choices are on the inland side of Ha-Yarkon, or on Ben-Yehuda Street. The Dizengoff Square area is another hotel area. Tel Aviv can be a very noisy city. If you're looking for a moderate or budget hotel, don't take a room facing a main street unless it has air-conditioning and soundproof windows. Get off the heavily trafficked streets or take a room in the back; Tel Aviv hoteliers charge the same rates for front and back rooms.

**PRIVATE ROOMS & APARTMENTS**    The Israel Tourist Information Office, 7 Mendele St. (© **03/520-7600**), compiles and prints a list of agencies and individuals who rent rooms and apartments. Though they will not make a contact or reservation for you, and they cannot guarantee the quality of service or accommodations, the tourist office staff will give you a copy of the list for free. The office is open Sunday through Thursday 8am to 4:30pm.

## ALONG HA-YARKON STREET

Ha-Yarkon Street runs along the Mediterranean. The deluxe hotels are all right off the sea and have either direct access to the beach or are across a small but busy road. The southern end of Ha-Yarkon is run-down, but new construction is upgrading this area. Just before the Dan Hotel, the street becomes more upscale; north of Atarim Square, Ha-Yarkon becomes a pleasant residential thoroughfare, but not as interesting for strolling. Near Gordon Street, Ha-Yarkon becomes a wider thoroughfare with divider barriers; guests staying in moderate hotels on the inland side of the street can't just dash across the road and down to the beach.

### VERY EXPENSIVE

**Carlton Hotel**    The entrance to this carefully run 1981-built hotel is through a covered highway section of Ha-Yarkon Street, so you feel as if you are at an airport, though once inside, the place is calm and comfortable. The clientele is a mix of business, leisure, and religious travelers. A large marina complex separates the building from the beaches, and although views from many guest rooms take in the sea, the Carlton feels more like a city hotel than most of its upscale neighbors. Guest rooms are fresh, insulated from traffic noise, and were totally redone in 2006; there are extra charges for rooms with sea view, and dazzling vistas from the small rooftop swimming pool.

10 Elizier Peri St., Tel Aviv. © **800/223-0888** in the U.S., or 03/520-1818. Fax 03/527-1043. www.carlton.co.il. 282 units. $320–$460 (£160–£230) double. AE, DC, MC, V. Parking (fee). Bus: 4. **Amenities:** 2 restaurants; rooftop pool; fitness center; sauna; business center; room service; massage; laundry service; dry cleaning; nonsmoking rooms; club-level rooms; synagogue. *In room:* A/C, satellite TV, dataport, minibar, coffeemaker, hair dryer, safe.

**Crowne Plaza**    The high-rise Crowne Plaza caters to business travelers but offers direct access to the beach. Decor is light, early '90s. There's a highly praised business center and better-than-average in-hotel restaurant services. At press time, guest rooms were in need of renovation. Most have balconies, and some are accessible to travelers with disabilities. The inventive, upper-bracket **Pacific Grill Bistro** 🕸 serves an unusual menu with interesting Pacific Rim/Asian touches; there's also an English-style pub. An indoor pool means year-round swimming. Deluxe rooms have Jacuzzis.

145 Ha-Yarkon St., Tel Aviv. © **03/593-0804.** Fax 03/760-0707. 239 units. www.crowneplaza.com. $320–$480 (£160–£240) double. Add 15% service. Rates include breakfast. AE, DC, MC, V. Valet parking (fee). Bus: 4 on Ben-Yehuda St.; ask for stop closest to Gordon St. **Amenities:** 3 restaurants; bar; pools (indoor, outdoor); health club; Jacuzzi; sauna; steam room; business center; massage; nonsmoking rooms; club-level floors; business-class rooms; rooms for those w/limited mobility. *In room:* A/C, TV, Wi-Fi, minibar, coffeemaker, hair dryer, safe.

**Dan Tel Aviv Hotel** 🕸    With an outstanding central location close to shops, restaurants, and right on Gordon Beach, the Dan started out as a small hotel in the 1950s, and in a series of expansions and renovations, was lovingly developed into today's

# Where to Stay & Dine in Tel Aviv

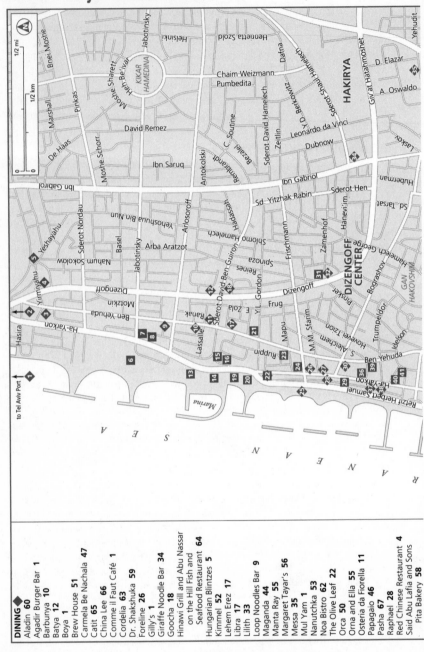

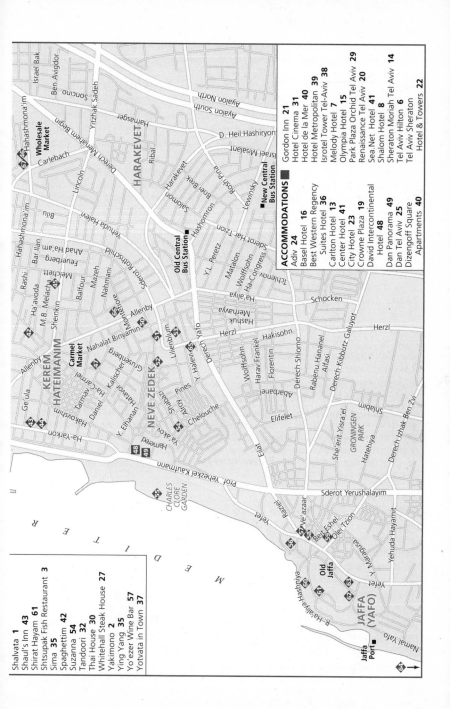

Shalvata **1**
Shaul's Inn **43**
Shirat Hayam **61**
Shtsupak Fish Restaurant **3**
Sima **35**
Spaghettim **42**
Suzanna **54**
Tandoori **32**
Thai House **30**
Whitehall Steak House **27**
Yakimono **2**
Ying Yang **35**
Yo'ezer Wine Bar **57**
Yotvata in Town **37**

## ACCOMMODATIONS

Adiv **24**
Basel Hotel **16**
Best Western Regency
  Suites Hotel **36**
Carlton Hotel **13**
Center Hotel **41**
City Hotel **23**
Crowne Plaza **19**
David Intercontinental
  Hotel **48**
Dan Panorama **49**
Dan Tel Aviv **25**
Dizengoff Square
  Apartments **40**

Gordon Inn **21**
Hotel Cinema **31**
Hotel de la Mer **40**
Hotel Metropolitan **39**
Isrotel Tower Tel-Aviv **38**
Melody Hotel **7**
Olympia Hotel **15**
Park Plaza Orchid Tel Aviv **29**
Renaissance Tel Aviv **20**
Sea.Net Hotel **41**
Shalom Hotel **8**
Sheraton Moriah Tel Aviv **14**
Tel Aviv Hilton **6**
Tel Aviv Sheraton
  Hotel & Towers **22**

### Map labels

Israel Bak
Ben Avigdor
Soncino
Hahashmona'im
Wholesale Market
Carlebach
Derech Menahem Begin
Yitzhak Sadeh
Ayalon South
Ayalon North
D. Heil Hashiryon
HARAKEVET
Hamasger
Ribal
Israel Mislant
Rosh Pina
Bnei Brak
Harakevet
Salomon
Lincoln
Bilu
Hahashmona'im
Bar Ilan
Yehuda Halevi
Ahad Ha'am
Feuerberg
Melchett
M.B. Melacha
Sheinkin
Allenby
Lewinsky
New Central Bus Station
Hashomron
Sderot Har Tzion
Y.L. Peretz
Matalon
Wolffsohn
Ha-Congress
Ha'aliya
Tchlenov
Schocken
Herzl
Old Central Bus Station
Rashi
Ha'avoda
Balfour
Mazeh
Nahmani
Store
Nahalat Binyamin
Gruzenberg
Lilienblum
Hashuk Merhavya
Herzl
Wolffsohn
Harav Frankel
Florentin
Derech Shlomo
Rabenu Hananel
Alfasi
KEREM HATEIMANIM
Carmel Market
Tarmav
Ha-Carmel
Daniel
Kalischer
Allenby
Ge'ula
Hakovshim
Ha-Yarkon
Pines
Y. Halevi
Derech Yafo
Derech Kibbutz Galuyot
Herzl
NEVE ZEDEK
Hatavor
Y. Elhanan
Ya'akov
Aroyi
Chelouche
Elifelet
Shabazi
Hamered
Abarbanel
Elifelet
Eilat
Derech Shlomo
Shabim
GRONINGEN PARK
She'erit Yisra'el
Hatehiya
Derech Izhak Ben Zvi
Prof. Yehezkel Kaufmann
CHARLES CLORE GARDEN
Sderot Yerushalayim
Yelet
Razi'el
Ve'azzar
Beit Eshel
Olei Tzion
Yehuda Hayamit
MEDITERRANEAN SEA
Old Jaffa
R-Ha'aliya Hashniya
Y. Margolis
Yelet
JAFFA (YAFO)
Jaffa Port
Namal Yafo

modern megacomplex. Because the hotel was built in many sections over 4 decades, the layout is a bit complicated—many of the lower-category rooms (superior) with older furniture face inner courtyards; upper-category rooms (deluxe) are divided into those facing busy Ha-Yarkon Street and those (extra charge) facing the sea; no balconies but some suites have terraces. Room decor is conservative, designed around darkish furniture and textiles. Service is very strong. The large indoor pool, overlooking the sea, offers the best winter swimming of any hotel in town. The Dan is not a high-rise, so traffic noise can be bothersome, but inner rooms are quiet. The Executive Lounge is especially attractive.

99 Ha-Yarkon St., Tel Aviv. ✆ 800/223-7773 in the U.S., or 03/520-2525. Fax 03/524-9755. www.danhotels.com. 286 units. $310–$500 (£155–£250) double. Rates include breakfast. Family plans available. AE, DC, MC, V. Bus: 4 on Ben-Yehuda St.; ask for stop near Dan Hotel. **Amenities:** 3 restaurants; bar; 2 pools (indoor, outdoor); health club; sauna; steam bath; children's activities in season; business center; 24-hr. room service; laundry service; dry cleaning; nonsmoking rooms; club-level rooms. *In room:* A/C, cable TV, Wi-Fi, minibar, hair dryer, safe.

**Tel Aviv Sheraton Hotel & Towers** ✰✰  Tel Aviv's most fun and stylish luxury hotel is right on Gordon Beach, just steps from the Ha-Yarkon Street restaurant and cafe district and the art galleries of Gordon Street. Most rooms were updated in 2005. They're bright with spring colors, and all contain fabulously comfortable new "Sweet Sleeper" beds. Club and tower rooms are beautifully decorated and come with pampering (separate) lounges and running light buffets—the tower lounge is superb. Of all the high-rise beachfront hotels, only this Sheraton has many rooms facing squarely onto the Mediterranean; try for these rooms—the views of the sunset, or of rolling waves on a stormy winter night, are wonderful. Personal attention in the Executive Towers is outstanding; the staff is helpful and knowledgeable without being intrusive. This Sheraton's dining facilities are the best of any hotel in the country, starting with its critically acclaimed **Olive Leaf** restaurant (p. 251).

115 Ha-Yarkon St., Tel Aviv. ✆ 800/325-3535 in the U.S. and Canada, or 03/521-1111. Fax 03/523-3322. 346 units. $280–$420 (£140–£210) double; add $80 (£40) for club rooms, $120 (£60) for tower rooms. Rates include breakfast. AE, DC, MC, V. Parking (fee). Bus: 4 to Ben-Yehuda and Gordon sts.; walk down Gordon St. to Ha-Yarkon. **Amenities:** 3 restaurants; lounge/bar; disco/nightclub; outdoor pools; health club; business center; 24-hr. room service; laundry service; dry cleaning; nonsmoking rooms; club lounge and tower lounge w/running light buffet. *In room:* A/C, TV, dataport (some rooms), minibar, hair dryer, safe.

## EXPENSIVE

**Isrotel Tower Tel-Aviv** ✰  Tel Aviv's newest (late 1990s) and by far most-luxurious all-suite hotel is located on the top 15 floors of a round, 30-story landmark skyscraper across the road from the beach. The hotel carefully caters to long-term business travelers; short-term leisure tourists sometimes get problem rooms and snubs from the staff. Suites are sleek, elegantly furnished, and include a salon with fully equipped kitchenette, separate bedroom with double bed, and a relatively roomy balcony. Pricier executive suites have slightly nicer decor, free access to a business lounge, breakfast, and other services and perks. The seasonal rooftop swimming pool and deck, reached by a spiral metal staircase, has an incredible view, but is not a place to bring children or anyone who suffers from even a touch of acrophobia. The sofa beds can be back wreckers. Minimum-stay requirements preclude booking for a night or two.

78 Ha-Yarkon St., Tel Aviv. ✆ 03/511-3636. Fax 03/511-3666. www.isrotel.co.il. 90 units. $300–$440 (£150–£220) suite. Executive suite rates include breakfast. Corporate and long-term rates available. AE, DC, MC, V. Free parking with executive suite. **Amenities:** Bar; pool; fitness center; business center; room service; laundry service. *In room:* A/C, TV w/pay movies, dataport, Wi-Fi (some), kitchenette, coffeemaker, hair dryer, safe.

---

**Tips  Hotel Dining**

All in-house hotel restaurants in Tel Aviv are kosher. Most are bland and over-priced, but in a city that's short on kosher restaurants, a few hotel restaurants really shine, and are good choices for kosher and nonkosher travelers alike: the elegant **Olive Leaf** at the Tel Aviv Sheraton Hotel & Towers (p. 251); the always interesting Asian-fusion **Pacific Grill Bistro** at the Crowne Plaza; and the rustic French **Aubergine** at the David Intercontinental. Except for these star choices, you'll do much better to step out and enjoy Tel Aviv's lively, wide-ranging restaurant scene.

---

**Ramada Continental Tel Aviv**    The Renaissance is the southernmost and best located of three beachfront tower hotels just north of Gordon Street. Pluses are direct beach access (no road to cross) and low rates that can often be found with a bit of searching. At press time, most rooms (except the more pricey executive rooms) were dated and worn; the club lounge and food services were less than top quality. There is a pleasant terrace cafe overlooking the sea in good weather; and an indoor heated pool ensures a chance to swim, even in winter. Rooms have balconies. *Note:* At press time, the hotel was still listed on the Marriott site, but will likely move to www.ramada.com.

121 Ha-Yarkon St., Tel Aviv. © **03/521-5555.** Fax 03/521-5588. www.marriott.com/tlvbr. 340 units. $180–$320 (£90–£160) double. Rates include breakfast. Check for special promotional rates. AE, DC, MC, V. Parking (fee). **Amenities:** Restaurant; cafe; bar; indoor pool; children's pool; fitness room; Jacuzzi; sauna; children's program in season; business center; laundry service; nonsmoking rooms; club-level rooms; rooms for those w/limited mobility. *In room:* A/C, TV, dataport, minibar, hair dryer, safe.

**Sheraton Moriah Tel Aviv**    Located directly on the beach, not far from the heart of the Ha-Yarkon Street restaurant district, the Sheraton Moriah is a step below the nearby Sheraton Hotel & Towers, but it's the best in the five-star hotel category. Public areas are stylish and sport a decor that makes use of natural textures—the result is a light, tasteful interior design that's not garish or overblown. All guest rooms now have new fabulously comfy "Sheraton Sweet Sleeper" beds with duvet covers enclosed by sheets; business-floor rooms are all completely renovated, and further guest room improvements should follow. Most rooms have balconies. Food services are excellent. The outdoor pool is accessed by a metal, spiral staircase—difficult for those with limited mobility.

155 Ha-Yarkon St., Tel Aviv. © **03/521-6666.** Fax 03/527-1065. www.sheraton.com. 346 units. $280–$340 (£140–£170) standard double. Rates include breakfast. AE, DC, MC, V. Parking (fee). Bus: 4 to Gordon St. **Amenities:** Restaurant; cafe; bar; outdoor pool; basketball and volleyball courts; sauna; children's programs in season; business center; salon; laundry service; nonsmoking rooms; club-level rooms; synagogue. *In room:* A/C, TV, minibar, hair dryer, safe.

**Park Plaza Orchid Tel Aviv** *Kids*    An option for families that want better-quality accommodations and more privacy, the Orchid Park was totally renovated in 1999 and partly redone in 2007. Updated rooms and suites in this beachfront (beach is across the road) high-rise are stylish and most attractive. Ongoing 2008 updating should get most rooms up to snuff. There are standard rooms; larger studio rooms; and one- and two-bedroom suites with kitchenettes (with fridges and microwaves). You can add up to two additional people in suites for $40 (£20) per person; breakfast, served in a room overlooking the sea, can be arranged for an additional charge. Service is not a strong point. The gym is large and well equipped. *Tip:* There is a wide range of neighboring restaurants (McDonald's; the great Yotvata; and Mike's Place) where you can breakfast or brunch better and much cheaper than in the hotel.

79 Ha-Yarkon St., Tel Aviv. © **03/519-7111.** Fax 03/517-4719. www.parkplaza.com/telavivil. 180 units. $170–$220 (£85–£110) standard double. AE, DC, MC, V. Bus: 4 to Ben-Yehuda St.; ask driver for closest stop. **Amenities:** Breakfast room; cafe; lobby bar; outdoor pool; fitness room; spa; Jacuzzi; sauna; business center; limited room service (8am–11pm); self-service laundry; nonsmoking rooms. *In room:* A/C, TV w/pay movies, dataport, Wi-Fi, minibar, coffeemaker, hair dryer, safe.

## MODERATE

**Adiv** (Value)    The Adiv, with gleaming, public areas faced with polished, rose-colored stone, is one of the most attractive moderately priced hotels in town. The location is excellent, on a side street half a block from Ha-Yarkon Street and the beach. Standard rooms are small and simple, but bright and modern—for a bit more money, a larger studio room with kitchenette might be worthwhile. Deluxe rooms were recently renovated. Most rooms are located toward the back of the building, where the blare of traffic is somewhat muffled. A nice perk is free coffee in the lobby. The staff is very attentive.

5 Mendele St., Tel Aviv. © **03/522-9141.** Fax 03/522-9144. www.adivhotel.com. 71 units. $130–$200 (£65–£100) standard double. Rates include breakfast. Internet discounts available. AE, DC, MC, V. Free parking. **Amenities:** Dining room; cafe; bar; room service; laundry service; free Wi-Fi. *In room:* A/C, TV, dataport, minibar, fridge, hair dryer, safe.

**Basel Hotel**    On the inland side of Ha-Yarkon Street, with a great, close-to-the-beach location, this convenient, well-run, Atlas-chain seven-story hotel looks smaller from the outside than it really is. The Basel offers a functional lobby larger than that of most hotels in its class, and comfortable guest rooms with medium-firm beds. Most rooms are in the depths of the building, away from street noise. Though the Basel is in the heart of the swanky beachfront hotel district, you have to detour a block around the divided Ha-Yarkon Street underpass if you're going to the beach on foot. Like most Israeli hotels, the Basel hasn't had a major renovation in a while, but it remains a comparative gem. Higher rates are in July and August; good discounts are often available.

156 Ha-Yarkon St. (btw. Gordon St. and Atarim Sq.), Tel Aviv. © **03/524-7711.** Fax 03/527-0005. www.atlas.co.il. 120 units. $170–$230 (£85–£115) double. Rates include breakfast. Discount packages available. AE, DC, MC, V. Limited free parking. **Amenities:** Restaurant; cafe/bar; outdoor pool; salon; limited room service; free Wi-Fi in lobby. *In room:* A/C, TV, dataport, Wi-Fi (some rooms), fridge, coffee/tea kettle, hair dryer, safe (fee).

**Best Western Regency Suites Hotel** (Kids)    Renovated in 2006, this seven-story Best Western affiliate is across from the beach and consists of one-bedroom suites with small living room areas and fully equipped kitchenettes. It offers discounts to long-term visitors and is ideal for families or business travelers who want to prepare some of their own meals. The living rooms have a sofa bed that can sleep two people; bedrooms have two twin beds. Higher floors are a bit quieter and higher in price; some upper-story suites offer glimpses of the sea. Breakfast is not included in the rates, but can be arranged at the small in-house coffee shop. It offers a big Israeli breakfast for NIS 48 ($12/£6) and a continental breakfast for NIS 24 ($6/£3). There are some provisions for those with disabilities.

80 Ha-Yarkon St., Tel Aviv. © **03/517-3939.** Fax 03/516-3610. www.telavivhotelsregency.com. 30 units. $200–$260 (£100–£130) suite, double occupancy. 1 child 11 and under stays free with 2 paying adults. Senior discounts are available. DC, MC, V. Free parking. **Amenities:** Dining room; cafe; bar; Jacuzzi; room service; laundry service; nonsmoking rooms. *In room:* A/C, TV, dataport, kitchenette, minibar (on request), coffeemaker.

**City Hotel**    Well located on a side street right off Ha-Yarkon, the City Hotel is part of the well-run Atlas chain and has pleasant, recently renovated public areas. Guest rooms are simple but comfortable, with 50-channel TV reception; at press time some were in the process of being redone—updated rooms have plasma TVs. Some rooms have balconies. Corner rooms, markedly roomier and only a bit more expensive, are a good deal here, especially if there's an extra person in the room. The buffet breakfast here is a cut above most in this category.

9 Mapu St., Tel Aviv. © 03/524-6253. Fax 03/524-6250. www.atlas.co.il. 96 units. $146–$210 (£73–£105) standard double. Rates include breakfast. AE, DC, MC, V. Free parking. **Amenities:** Dining room; cafe; bar; business center; room service; laundry service; nonsmoking rooms. *In room:* A/C, TV, Wi-Fi (some rooms), fridge (on request), coffee/tea kettle, hair dryer, safe (fee).

**Hotel de la Mer** ★★ Only an eighth of a block from the beach, this might be the prettiest boutique hotel in the country. Opened in 2001 (just when tourism took a dive), so it's not yet overly worn, the de la Mer has a variety of suites and standard rooms that are carefully designed and laid out according to the precepts of feng shui. Triple-glazed windows, air-conditioning, and a location just far enough in from Ha-Yarkon Street keep the blare of traffic at bay. Some rooms have sea views; bathrooms are modern but often tiny. The junior suites with terraces are among the most attractive accommodations at any price in Tel Aviv. There's no gargantuan Israeli breakfast buffet, but a very adequate morning meal is served in a cozy breakfast room, and tea and coffee are available gratis round-the-clock. Service is attentive. A small massage spa opened in 2006.

62 Ha-Yarkon St., Tel Aviv. © 03/510-0011. Fax 03516-7575. www.delamer.co.il. 27 units. $130–$210 (£65–£110) double; $230–$300 (£115–£150) suite. Rates include breakfast. AE, DC, MC, V. **Amenities:** Dining room; cafe; spa; room service; nonsmoking rooms. *In room:* A/C, TV, dataport, minibar or fridge, coffeemaker, hair dryer.

**Hotel Metropolitan** *Value* This modern 16-story hotel offers a good location close to the sea and many price bargains. There are two parts to the hotel: the Executive Wing (known as the Metropolitan Suites) and the main (standard) section. The Executive Wing contains one- and two-bedroom suites with somewhat upgraded decor, kitchenettes, and DSL Internet service, plus free use of the executive lounge, with its running light buffet and free Web access. The standard wing offers a variety of single and double rooms and junior suites that are spacious but less pleasantly appointed. Some rooms are accessible to those with disabilities. Most rooms have vistas of the cityscape or the sea; some have balconies. Decor throughout the hotel is functional, bland, generally worn, and ready for updating. The outdoor swimming pool with a sun terrace is a bright, welcome feature and was renovated in 2008.

9–15 Trumpeldor St., Tel Aviv. © 03/519-2727. Fax 03/517-2626. www.hotelmetropolitan.co.il. 245 units. $130–$200 (£65–£100) double. Rates include breakfast. Web discounts often available. AE, DC, MC, V. Parking (fee). **Amenities:** Dining room; bar; pool; fitness room; sauna; tour desk; car-rental desk; room service; laundry service; nonsmoking rooms; executive-level rooms; synagogue; rooms for those w/limited mobility. *In room:* A/C, TV, dataport, high-speed Internet (some), minibar or fridge.

**Olympia Hotel** Location, location, location! This modern midrange hotel, across the street from Atarim Square, was completely renovated in 1997. Guest rooms are bright but basic. Across the street and past Atarim Square, there's staircase access down to the beach beside the Sheraton Moriah Hotel. You won't find a pool or fitness center, but for a fee, hotel guests get access to these facilities at a nearby hotel. You can book (often with discounts) via the Internet.

164 Ha-Yarkon St., Tel Aviv. © 03/524-2184. Fax 03/524-7278. 64 units. $100–$180 (£50–£90) double. Rates include breakfast. AE, DC, MC, V. **Amenities:** Dining room; cafe; bar; limited room service (7am–11pm). *In room:* A/C, TV w/pay movies, fridge, hair dryer.

*Kids*  **Family-Friendly Hotels**

Two all-suite hotels right on the beachside on Ha-Yarkon Street are good bets for families with children: **Best Western Regency** (p. 246) and the **Park Plaza Orchid Tel Aviv** (p. 245). Both have kitchenette facilities. If you have a car, and are willing to drive 25 minutes north of Tel Aviv, **Kibbutz Shefayim Guest House** (p. 292), with its adjacent water park (including a swimming pool with waves), is fun for younger children and a very pleasant base for exploring the Tel Aviv/coastal region.

**Sea.Net Hotel** *Value*    Another of Tel Aviv's new moderately priced theme hotels, the Sea.Net is set up for the Internet-minded traveler. Brand-new rooms are designed to look like sleek, efficient offices; they're equipped with DSL Internet connections, interactive TVs, and a keyboard that enables surfing via the TV screen. Rooms are compact but contain a good-size work desk and a safe that's roomy enough to accommodate a laptop. Despite the ultramodern aura of planned obsolescence, there's a rooftop sun deck, a friendly bar/lounge, and the beckoning beach just half a block away, all of which make the Sea.Net a pleasant choice for tourists as well as business travelers.

6 Nes Ziona St., Tel Aviv. ✆ 03/517-1655. Fax 03/517-1655. www.seanethotel.co.il. 70 units. $100–$170 (£50–£85). Rates include breakfast. AE, MC, V. **Amenities:** Dining room; lounge; bar; room service; nonsmoking rooms; sun deck. *In room:* A/C, TV w/pay movies, high-speed Internet access, minibar, coffeemaker, hair dryer, safe.

## NORTHERN TEL AVIV
### VERY EXPENSIVE

**Tel Aviv Hilton**    This massive Hilton is set far back from Ha-Yarkon Street in a small park overlooking a quiet, sheltered lagoon. Built in the 1960s, it was completely redone from 1998 to 1999. The Hilton's state-of-the-art business center is unrivaled and always buzzing with international activity. The hotel also offers vacationers a full range of recreational facilities. Better-category rooms are stylish and among the best in Tel Aviv; a variety of suites are offered (one has a Jacuzzi beside a corner window with spectacular views). All rooms have balconies. Restaurant facilities (including a kosher sushi bar) are top quality and varied. The location is a bit of a hike from the major streets of interest. The fitness center is superb, and the sheltered Hilton beach is among the best in town; a large saltwater swimming pool, heated in winter, is unique among Tel Aviv hotels. The staff is efficient, but to some, a bit self-important.

Independence Park, Ha-Yarkon St., Tel Aviv. ✆ 03/520-2240. Fax 03/520-2195. www.hilton.com. 595 units. $335–$500 (£168–£250) standard double. AE, DC, MC, V. Parking (fee). **Amenities:** 5 restaurants; 2 bars; outdoor saltwater pool; 2 tennis courts; CYBEX fitness center; sauna; steam bath; business center; shopping arcade; massage; club-level rooms; executive lounge w/vast buffet; access to marina; medical clinic; airport shuttle. *In room:* A/C, TV, dataport, Wi-Fi, minibar, hair dryer.

### MODERATE

**Melody Hotel**    Located just across the road from the Hilton, the Melody is one of the gems of the Atlas Hotel chain. The hotel was totally renovated in 2007, with sleek, beautifully designed and furnished rooms equipped with soundproof windows; those facing the street have views of Independence Park and glimpses of the sea. Some rooms are equipped for those with limited mobility. The lobby is small and doubles as a coffee bar for breakfast; a rooftop deck is very pleasant. The staff is attentive, and a good beach is just across the street.

220 Ha-Yarkon St., Tel Aviv. ✆ **03/521-5300** or 03/542-5555 for reservations. Fax 03/521-5301. www.atlas.co.il. 53 units. $170–$250 (£85–£125) double. Rates include continental breakfast. AE, DC, MC, V. Free parking. **Amenities:** Cafe/bar; salon; room service; nonsmoking rooms. *In room:* A/C, TV/DVD, dataport, Wi-Fi, fridge, coffeemaker, hair dryer, safe.

**Shalom Hotel**   Now part of the Howard Johnson Chain, the Shalom Hotel is a modern, five-story structure with a bright lobby. All the front rooms have balconies with a glimpse of the Mediterranean and Independence Park. Guest rooms are functional but not special. In front of the hotel is the Stagecoach Restaurant and Pub, which has Wild West decor and live music every evening.

216 Ha-Yarkon St., Tel Aviv. ✆ **03/524-3277.** Fax 03/523-5895. www.shalom-hotel-ta.co.il. 48 units. $130–$160 (£65–£80) double. Off-season and student discounts available. Rates include breakfast. AE, DC, MC, V. Bus: 4 or 5. **Amenities:** Restaurant; bar; tour desk; limited room service; babysitting; laundry service; dry cleaning. *In room:* A/C, TV, dataport, fridge.

## DIZENGOFF SQUARE & BEN-YEHUDA STREETS
### MODERATE

**Center Hotel** *(Value)*   In the Atlas Hotels' spirit, the Center Hotel boosts Tel Aviv with lively decor, displays, and a video, all designed show to off the city's Bauhaus architectural treasures. It's right on Dizengoff Square (back rooms are quieter) with a helpful staff and compact, bright rooms totally renovated in 2005. The hotel offers free bicycles so you can better explore Tel Aviv, and the staff will advise on where to go. There's a tiny reception/lobby and a place for breakfast, but the Center puts all of Tel Aviv at your feet; it's a cut above other cookie-cutter moderately priced hotels.

2 Zamdnhoff St. ✆ **03/526-6100.** Fax 03/526-6101. www.atlas.co.il. 56 units. $160–$200 (£80–£100) double. Rates include breakfast. AE, DC, MC, V. **Amenities:** Breakfast served next door in Hotel Cinema; free use of hotel bicycles; laundry service. *In room:* A/C, cable TV, Wi-Fi, fridge (some rooms), coffeemaker, safe.

**Hotel Cinema** *(★)*   This beautiful Art Deco hotel, opened in 2001 and part of the well-run Atlas chain, is Israel's most enticingly designed midrange hotel. Once a landmark Bauhaus-style 1930s cinema, the hotel's up-to-the-minute, very comfortable rooms are decorated with specially re-created carpeting, textiles, and furnishings that recall the sets from a Fred Astaire–Ginger Rogers classic. You check in at the Cinema's former candy counter, beneath an ultramodern staircase to the mezzanine, and are given a bag of popcorn with your key. A drawback for some is the blare of traffic and music around Dizengoff Square. Quieter rooms at the back are in great demand, but for light sleepers, even a back room with double-glazed windows may not be enough to keep out the Dizengoff din. There are connecting rooms, good for families. A number of rooms have balconies, and there's a rooftop terrace and Jacuzzi overlooking Dizengoff Square.

1 Zamenhoff St., at Dizengoff Sq. ✆ **03/520-7100** or 542-5555. Fax 03/520-7101. www.atlas.co.il. 82 units. $166–$230 (£83–£115) double. Rates include breakfast. Long-term and Internet discounts available. AE, DC, MC, V. Call ahead to arrange parking. **Amenities:** Dining room; cafe; Jacuzzi; sauna; car-rental desk; business center; room service; laundry service; rooms for those w/limited mobility. *In room:* A/C, TV, kitchenette (some rooms), minibar, fridge, coffeemaker, hair dryer, safe (fee).

### INEXPENSIVE

**Dizengoff Square Apartments** *(Value)*   This is a very central, modern apartment hotel with rooms and suites of varying sizes. All have kitchenettes with microwave ovens. Rooms are utilitarian; those at the back are best to get away from the 24-hour roar from Dizengoff. Long-term discounts are available; the management is helpful, and there's an Internet desk for guests. Rooms are cleaned daily and coffee and tea are on the house beside the reception desk.

89 Dizengoff St., at Dizengoff Sq. ℂ **03/524-1151.** www.hotel-apt.com. 22 units. $70–$100 (£35–£50) double. Long-term discounts available. AE, DC, MC, V. **Amenities:** Internet desk; complimentary coffee and tea daily. *In room:* A/C, satellite TV, Wi-Fi, kitchenette, hair dryer, safe.

**Gordon Inn** *(Value)*    Opened in 1995, this well-managed guesthouse bridges the gap between hostel and hotel. The small private rooms are spartan, with metal-frame beds and thin mattresses; only half have private bathrooms. There are also larger group or family rooms, each equipped with wardrobes and bedside reading lamps; most have private bathrooms. Clientele is young and international. Continental breakfast is served in a pleasant dining room. The location, on Gordon Street with its many art galleries, adds a touch of class, but its spot on the corner of Ben-Yehuda Street means heavy bus and traffic noise. Lockers are $2 (£1) a day extra. The Gordon's got no charm, but is by far the best choice in its price category.

17 Gordon St., Tel Aviv. ℂ **03/523-8239.** Fax 03/523-7419. sleepin@inter.net.il. 31 units, 18 with private bathroom. $64 (£32) double, no private bathroom; $84 (£42) double, with private bathroom. Rates include continental breakfast. AE, DC, MC, V. Bus: 4 on Ben-Yehuda St. to Gordon St. **Amenities:** Dining room; bar; nonsmoking rooms. *In room:* A/C.

## SOUTH TEL AVIV

Across a divided thoroughfare from the sea (but a 2-block walk to a guarded swimming beach), two high-rise hotels, the Dan Panorama and the massive David Inter-Continental, hold forth alone as a tourist island in a relatively isolated, empty stretch between Tel Aviv and Jaffa, approximately 2.4km (1½ miles) south of the main Ha-Yarkon Street hotel district. There are no adjacent, interesting streets for strolling that surround these hotels, and the beach in this area is not great for swimming. But Old Jaffa is a 15-minute walk along the Seaside Promenade, and a 5-minute walk across a not-well-tended park takes you to the bustling Carmel Market (from which you can reach the restaurants and cafes of the trendy Nahlat Binyamin and Rothschild St. areas). Note that walking through the empty Carmel Market at night is not advisable. Across the highway is the excellent beachfront Manta Ray restaurant (p. 266). Rates here are lower than for a comparable hotel on Ha-Yarkon Street.

### EXPENSIVE

**Dan Panorama**    Down a notch both in price and ambience from the Dan Tel Aviv on Ha-Yarkon Street, but still pleasant, this upscale high-rise was built in the 1980s and is next door to a convention center and the Textile Industry Center. Guest rooms all have balconies with fabulous vistas of the sea and the city, and there is an ongoing process of redecorating. The spectacular breakfast buffet outdoes many of those in the most expensive hotels in town, and the pool complex, located on a lower-level rooftop, is surprisingly spacious. Executive-floor rooms have recently been refurbished, and the executive lounge, with a free Internet desk and a good buffet of light snacks, is well run and pleasant. I especially like the free Jacuzzi in the fitness center.

10 Kaufman St., Tel Aviv. ℂ **03/519-0190.** Fax 03/517-1777. www.danhotels.com. 500 units. $200–$280 (£100–£140) double. Rates include breakfast. AE, DC, MC, V. Parking (fee). Bus: 10. **Amenities:** 2 restaurants; bar; outdoor pool; fitness center; Jacuzzi; business center; shops; 24-hr. room service; synagogue. *In room:* A/C, TV, Wi-Fi, minibar, hair dryer, safe.

**David Intercontinental Hotel** *(★★)*    Opened in 1999, this 24-story tower is by far the newest megahotel in Tel Aviv. Public areas are enclosed by a soaring, balcony-lined atrium that dwarfs the lobbies of all other hotels in Tel Aviv, but don't catch vistas of the Mediterranean; the hotel doesn't have the feel of an urban beachfront resort offered by other top Tel Aviv hotels. Guest rooms do have views of the sea; the higher your room, the more dazzling vistas of Tel Aviv you get. Rooms are spacious, very comfortable, and up-to-date, though the flowered textiles in the decor are surprisingly passé. There are nice touches throughout the hotel: duvet covers over the blankets and eco-friendly toiletries in bathrooms. The inventive Aubergine Restaurant, an excellent choice for fine kosher dining, is on the premises. The pool is small for a hotel this size.

12 Kaufman St., Tel Aviv. © 03/795-1111. Fax 03/795-1112. www.intercontinental.com/telaviv. 600 units. $320–$440 (£160–£220) double. Rates include breakfast. AE, DC, MC, V. Parking (fee). Bus: 10 from Ben-Yehuda St. **Amenities:** 2 restaurants; 2 cafes; outdoor pool; lap pool; children's pool; fitness room; business center; salon; 24-hr. room service; laundry service; dry cleaning; synagogue. *In room:* A/C, TV, minibar, hair dryer, safe.

## JAFFA
### INEXPENSIVE

**Beit Immanuel Hostel**  This is a lovely, atmospheric church hospice with clean rooms located in a commercial/industrial neighborhood on the Tel Aviv/Jaffa border. It's beautifully maintained in a garden enclave and within walking distance of Old Jaffa. Each of the private rooms has its own bathroom; some rooms have balconies. There's no lockout, an 11pm curfew, no smoking anywhere in the building, and dinner is offered for $10 (£5) Sunday to Thursday and for $12 (£6) on Friday. If you need to leave very early in the morning, alert staff the night before to unlock the building's door.

8 Auerbach St. © 03/682-1459. Fax 03/682-9817. $18 (£9) per person in single-sex dorms; $60–$70 (£30–£35) double. Cash only. Bus: 46, ask for the Beit Immanuel Auerbach St. stop. **Amenities:** Dining room; laundry service. *In room:* A/C, coffeemaker (some rooms).

## 4 Where to Dine

### OFF & ON HA-YARKON, BEN-YEHUDA & DIZENGOFF STREETS

*Tip:* Ha-Yarkon Street, Ben-Yehuda Street, and the side streets between them are loaded with restaurants and within walking distance of most Tel Aviv hotels, but don't miss dining in romantic Old Jaffa and other parts of Tel Aviv, where the city's spectacular restaurant scene (among the best in the world) truly rides high.

### EXPENSIVE

**The Olive Leaf** ✸✸ MODERN FRENCH  This hotel restaurant overlooks the Mediterranean and is the most stylish kosher eatery in Israel. Elegantly simple, calmly innovative, and without a drop of tacky glitz in its decor or menu, the Olive Leaf is a great opportunity for kosher (and nonkosher) visitors to experience good contemporary French cuisine. The menu constantly changes, but is always more innovative and light than those at the more predictable kosher French restaurants of the neighboring Dan and Hilton hotels. Look for sweetmeats smoked on citrus fires with mushrooms and veal brain ragout; Mediterranean fish soup scented with anise; Cornish hen wrapped in smoked goose breast, served on an eggplant/pesto pastry; and a hefty rib-eye steak with hyssop in wine sauce. A dessert cart is lavish and worthwhile. Service is included in the prices; guests of the Sheraton who pay in foreign currency are exempt from the additional 15.5% VAT. Great lunch specials allow you also to enjoy the daylight view. Reserve a table by the window.

In the Sheraton Hotel, 115 Ha-Yarkon St. © 03/521-9300 or 521-1111. Reservations recommended. Main courses (priced in dollars only) $22–$35 (£11–£18). Fixed-price lunches from NIS 80 ($20/£10). AE, DC, MC, V. Sun–Thurs noon–3pm and 7:30pm–midnight.

**Raphael** ✪ RUSTIC FRENCH   This is another very top-drawer restaurant in the hotel district—good if you don't want to taxi to more interesting special-night-out choices elsewhere. It's sleekly designed, with dim lighting, a stylish bar in the dining room, and it overlooks the Mediterranean (but at night all you see of the Med is blackness and a neon gas station sign). Chef Rafi Cohen is among Israel's best, and his ever-changing menu reflects a feel for French/Mediterranean cuisine heavily touched with the flavors of Israel. Everything is presented beautifully, often chopped and sliced into robust country textures. You might find lamb meatballs and Jerusalem artichoke cooked with turmeric and garlic and served with whole chickpeas or a more fusion-type dish such as potato gnocchi and tiny, scalloplike Brittany periwinkles in a sauce of butter, olive oil, and roasted tomatoes. The cold calamari salads and the risottos are excellent, as is the wine and dessert list. Best to dine early here: By 9pm, Raphael is usually crowded and noisy.

87 Ha-Yarkon St. ✆ 03/522-6464. Reservations necessary. Main courses NIS 100–NIS 150 ($25–$38/£13–£19); fixed-price lunch from NIS 95 ($24/£12). AE, DC, MC, V. Daily noon–3pm and 7pm until last customer; last order taken at 10:30pm. On lower floor of high-rise attached to the south side of the Dan Hotel. Accessible to those with disabilities.

## MODERATE

**Forelin** ✪✪ CONTINENTAL   Very convenient to the hotel district, Forelin is known for seafood and meat in elegant, international styles at reasonable prices. For starters, try the excellent fish soup served with seafood rouille and toasted house bread; eggplant stuffed with calamari and dried tomato with yogurt and coriander; or rustic chicken liver pâté. Second courses, available in small or big portions, include shrimp tempura in piquant Asian sauce; spiced lamb kabobs in *techina;* or delicate sautéed soft-shell blue crab in garlic cream. Big main courses are served with potato or vegetables and salad and include steaks, fresh oven-baked fish, great seafood pasta, and a combination seafood "feast." There's a special dessert chef turning out wonderful creations.

10 Frishman St. ✆ 03/522-2664. Reservations recommended. Main courses NIS 60–NIS 100 ($15–$25/£7.50–£13). AE, DC, MC, V. Daily noon–midnight.

**Whitehall Steakhouse** STEAKS   A modern, air-conditioned retreat just off Ha-Yarkon Street near the Dan Hotel, Whitehall offers luncheon specials, which include french fries, hash potato, or sautéed vegetables. Steaks, burgers, kabobs, and chicken livers head the menu here, but there are also a few pasta, fish, and seafood choices on the luncheon and dinner menus.

6 Mendele St. ✆ 03/524-9282. Reservations useful. Main courses NIS 48–NIS 108 ($12–$27/£6–£14); luncheon specials NIS 48–NIS 80 ($12–$20/£6–£10). AE, DC, MC, V. Daily noon–midnight.

## INEXPENSIVE

**Yotvata in Town** ✪ Kids DAIRY/VEGETARIAN   The kind of restaurant Israelis loved best 30 years ago was a little place turning out simple, freshly made salads and good-quality dairy dishes. Popular Yotvata has carried this concept into the 21st century and turned it into a bustling, high-powered, multistory emporium on the beachfront. Everything is made from the best-quality produce bought directly from kibbutzim and from the famous dairy kibbutz at Yotvata. For around NIS 50 ($13/£6.25) there are salads, cheese platters served with fresh herbs and vegetables, blintzes, pancakes, vegetable pies, pastas, and pizzas. At the upper end of the price range, the menu has expanded to include a selection of fish, chicken, pasta, and hamburgers, as well as bagels and lox. The mixtures of natural fruit juices are famous, as are Yotvata's many ice-cream parlor desserts.

76 Herbert Samuel Promenade. ✆ 03/510-4667. Main courses and light meals NIS 36–NIS 80 ($9–$20/£4.50–£10). AE, DC, MC, V. Daily 7am–4am.

## ALONG BEN-YEHUDA STREET
### MODERATE

**Barbunya** 🌟 *Value* *Kids*  FISH   Up near the Hilton hotel, this no-frills restaurant serves very fresh fish. At lunch and dinnertime, you can often spot the place by the line of dedicated customers that extends out to the street. Once inside, you'll find paper tablecloths and a choice of fish and shrimp, depending on the day's catch. There's a slightly higher price for red snapper, shrimp, and grouper. Fish is either grilled or fried in garlic and lemon or butter, and comes with an all-you-can-eat array of Middle Eastern salads and iced club soda. Substitutions are not possible, but you do have the option of ordering dessert for an extra charge. Quick service is great for kids; come early or late to avoid lines. Half a block north, across the street at 192 Ben-Yehuda St., Barbunya has a second busy location.

163 Ben-Yehuda St. ✆ 03/527-6965. Reservations not accepted. Fixed-price meals NIS 70–NIS 80 ($18–$20/£8.75–£10). AE, DC, MC, V. Sat–Thurs noon–midnight; Fri noon–6pm.

**Libra** 🌟🌟 BISTRO/CAFE   With a quintessentially Tel Aviv Bauhaus setting, this stylish, easygoing, and reasonably priced place offers a mildly fusion menu created by famed chef Mika Sharon. Dishes are not dogmatically fusion—everything is hearty, but also done with Mika's unique touch. At dinnertime, you can get an entrecôte steak with truffles and mashed potato, or a fabulous dish of shrimp and calamari stuffed with lemon grass, chili, ginger, and peanuts. Before 5pm there are beautiful brunches, sandwiches, and light meals. I like the poached seafood salad and the crispy calamari, all with Mika's signature elegance and inventiveness, but you'll also find a great burger with Heinz ketchup. Ask about daily special dishes. Desserts and chocolates are fabulous, and there are amazing teas. The front terrace offers the chance to dine in Bauhaus splendor when the weather is right.

120 Ben-Yehuda St. ✆ 03/528-8734. Reservations useful. Main courses NIS 50–NIS 100 ($13–$25/£6.25–£13). AE, MC, V. Sun–Fri 8am–midnight; Sat 9am–midnight. Breakfast and light meals 8am–5pm; dinner after 5pm.

**Osteria da Fiorella** ITALIAN   This excellent nonkosher restaurant serves "vera cucina italiana" (authentic Italian cuisine) prepared by a family that immigrated to Israel from Rome in the early 1980s. There are two sparkling floors divided into cozy dining areas. The menu has most of the traditional Italian dishes, plus special Roman-Jewish home-style treats such as *straccotto* (veal slowly cooked for Shabbat). The house Fiorella sauce, made with four cheeses, tomato, and vodka, is a wonderful creation. Ask about daily fish specials. For dessert, look into the Roman-Jewish–style cheesecake.

148 Ben-Yehuda. ✆ 03/527-4750. Main courses NIS 45–NIS 90 ($11–$23/£5.60–£11); complete lunch specials from NIS 60 ($15/£7.50). AE, DC, MC, V. Sun–Thurs noon–11pm; Fri noon–3pm; Sat 7–11pm.

### INEXPENSIVE

**Lehem Erez** 🌟 *Value* SANDWICHES/SALADS   I could eat here every day. Erez Komarovsky's breads are fabulous, and the cheeses, vegetables, and dressings that make up his sandwiches are near gourmet. Heftier choices include the rich smoked salmon with aioli, avocado and egg on Russian bread, and the lamb kabobs on Lebanese focaccia. Erez's cakes are famous throughout Israel, and the brownies should be eaten *very* slowly. Both sidewalk and indoor seating are available. Lehem Erez branches are popping up all over Israel, and takeout is great to pack for the road (see Ibn Givrol St. location, p. 261). Tons of places make sandwiches to order, but Erez is beyond compare.

120 Ben-Yehuda St. ✆ 03/529-1793. Sandwiches NIS 30–NIS 45 ($7.50–$11/£3.75–£5.60). AE, DC, MC, V. Sat–Thurs 8am–8pm; Fri 8am–8pm.

**Loop Noodles Bar** *(Value)* ASIAN   Everything in this small, stylish place is delicious and very fairly priced, from the many noodle, rice, and soup dishes to the Asian chicken salad with cucumber and sesame seeds and the soba noodles with chicken and sweet and hot peppers. It's convenient to the Ha-Yarkon Street hotel area, and the lightness of the menu is especially good during Tel Aviv's hot, humid summers.

177 Ben-Yehuda St. (℃) 03/544-9833. Main courses NIS 38–NIS 64 ($9.50–$16/£4.75–£8). MC, V. Sun–Thurs noon–11pm; Fri noon–4pm.

**Thai House** *(Finds)* AUTHENTIC THAI   This unassuming place is the brain-child of an Israeli who spent many years living (and cooking) in villages in different areas of Thailand, fell in love and married there, and has relocated his family to Israel. The restaurant will please Thai food aficionados and amaze those not familiar with the cuisine. There are pad Thai noodles and other standard Thai dishes found in Western restaurants (all done beautifully), but are also many authentic village and regional dishes: dumplings, fish, seafood, and wonderful salads laden with diced fresh vegeta-bles, chili peppers, mangoes, and other fresh fruits in season. All are alive with flavor and breathtaking in their purity. The soups are meals in themselves; the staff is well-informed and enthusiastic, and will direct you to good things. Ask questions and take some chances here.

8 Bogroshov St. (corner of Ben-Yehuda St.). (℃) 03/517-8568. Main courses NIS 36–NIS 85 ($9–$21/£4.50–£11). AE, DC, MC, V. Daily noon–11pm.

## ON & AROUND DIZENGOFF STREET
### MODERATE

**Goocha** *(Value)* SEAFOOD   The menu at this very popular place near the hotel district is fun and has real style, yet prices are quite reasonable. A fast turnover guar-antees very fresh fish and seafood prepared in crispy mode or in great sauces such as butter and garlic; coconut milk, curry, and coriander; ginger and honey; cream, gar-lic, and chives; or tomato, basil, and thyme. Mussels, shrimp, and calamari are my favorites here, but starters are also scrumptious. There's steak, chicken, and veal avail-able, and for NIS 25 ($6.25/£3.10), you can take away a paper cone filled with fresh crispy shrimp and calamari to munch as you window-shop trendy upper Dizengoff. A second branch is at 14 Ibn Givrol St.

Corner of Dizengoff and Ben-Gurion boulevards. (℃) 03/522-2886. Reservations recommended. Main courses NIS 42–NIS 100 ($11–$25/£5.25–£13). AE, DC, MC, V. Daily noon–around midnight.

---

*Kids* **Family-Friendly Restaurants**

**Spaghettim** (p. 258), with its 60 spaghettis (including, yes, chocolate), heads the list of good family choices, followed by the trendy **Yotvata** (p. 252), a favorite of Tel Aviv teenagers and students, with its menu of delicious dishes and fruit shakes made from farm-fresh products. No-frills **Barbunya** *(Kids)* (p. 253), near the hotel district, offers good fresh fish and extremely speedy service, with appetizers and seltzer included—get there early at dinnertime. **Said el Abu Lafia and Sons Pita Bakery** (p. 268) in Jaffa sells wonderful Ara-bic pizzas and stuffed breads—bring lots of napkins and have a picnic in the nearby gardens of Old Jaffa.

**Tandoori** ★★ INDIAN   Why visit an Indian restaurant in Israel? Only for some of the best food, ambience (relaxing, but elegant), and pleasant service in Tel Aviv. Tandoori is serenely presided over by Vinod Pushkarna and his wife, Reena, whose Jewish-Bombay heritage helped to create the restaurant's special atmosphere. Try the ever-changing all-you-can-eat daily luncheon buffet, one of the best values in town, or share a succulent plate of boneless tandoori chicken with rice and side dishes. Two can dine for around NIS 70 ($18/£8.75) per person. You can also have an extensive multicourse feast. I especially like the chicken dishes served in skewered chunks, such as the boneless breast of chicken marinated in mint and herbs; the fabulous chicken *tikka masala;* and a dry sautéed vegetable dish so light and elegant it almost seems to herald Indian nouvelle cuisine. The homemade dessert dumplings and Indian ice creams made of thickened milk and dried fruits and nuts are very interesting. There's a beautiful menu that carefully explains the exotic dishes and many regional cuisines on the menu. Ask about *lassi,* a refreshing chilled yogurt-and-fruit drink.

In the Dizengoff Square Hotel, 2 Zamenhoff St. ✆ 03/629-6185. Reservations recommended. Main courses NIS 36–NIS 75 ($9–$19/£4.50–£9.40); all-you-can-eat lunch buffet NIS 60 ($15/£7.50). AE, DC, MC, V. Daily 12:30–3:30pm and 7pm–1am.

## INEXPENSIVE

**Batya** *Finds* EUROPEAN/JEWISH   Strangely enough, trendy Tel Aviv remains Israel's center for East European Jewish cooking, and Batya, presided over by the wonderful Batya Yom Tov, is one of the oldest restaurants specializing in this traditional cuisine. You'll step into a delicious, pre-cholesterol-conscious world of kreplach, golden chicken soup, chopped liver, stew, duck with Polish mustard sauce, baked Shabbat pudding, and brisket with potatoes. Decor is no-frills, and a good part of Batya's clientele has probably been patronizing the restaurant since it was established in 1941.

197 Dizengoff St. ✆ 03/527-3888. Main courses NIS 36–NIS 46 ($9–$12/£4.50–£5.75). V. Daily 11am–10pm.

## ALONG ALLENBY STREET & SOUTHWARD

This area, stretching from the beginning of Allenby Street south to the Tel Aviv–Jaffa border, is away from most tourist hotels but contains some of the best restaurants in the country. Some fine upper-bracket restaurants are located near the booming Tel Aviv stock exchange in the area between Ahad Ha-Am Street and Rothschild Boulevard. These places can be very busy at lunchtime, but in the evening, the mood is more relaxed.

## EXPENSIVE

**Carmela Be Nachala** ★★★ FUSION/FRENCH   You couldn't want a more charming place for lunch or dinner—a graceful veranda-circled building that's almost 100 years old. Chef Daniel Zissenbach's menu is sometimes classic, sometimes inventive, and praised by critics and the public alike. You're encouraged to order half portions and to try a number of Carmela's specialties at one meal. Dishes here are inventive without being forced. On the seasonally changing menu, look for appetizers that include incredible roasted eggplant with pickled lemon, *techina,* and olive oil; fresh herb salad with roasted cashews; crab bisque filled with assorted seafood; and a wonderful grilled pear in olive oil, black pepper, and blue cheese. Main courses include prawns and scallops in ouzo, olive oil, tomato, and olives; grilled fresh fish with lentils, cumin, onion, lemon, and green *techina;* and choice beef filet *a la plancha* with creamed Gorgonzola sauce. There is a very large list of boutique Israeli wines, and a dessert plate with assorted minisamples to linger over. A seven-dish tasting meal for two is served daily at lunch only for NIS 135 ($34/£17). There are also superb brunches. The staff is informed and attentive, yet very easygoing and not at all pompous; a wine specialist explains the wine list. The restaurant is nonsmoking.

46 Ha Tavor St., Nahlat Binyamin. ☎ 03/516-1417. Reservations necessary. Main courses NIS 90–NIS 130 ($23–$33/£11–£16); half-courses are half-price; fixed-price weekday (Sun–Thurs) lunch specials vary. Add 10% service. AE, DC, MC, V. Sun–Thurs 10am–11pm; Fri 9am–11pm; Sat noon–11pm.

**Orca** ★★ CONTEMPORARY FRENCH   With a chic, contemporary setting and an exciting menu by Chef Eric Stroitman, whose resume includes the Cordon Bleu and training in prestigious French and Israeli restaurants, Orca is one of the most popular and highly praised luxury dining spots in Tel Aviv. There are small tapas served at the bar until very late hours and an ever-changing menu that's heavy on seafood and fish. Everything is original and filled with beautiful flavor and texture combinations. Most famous is Stroitman's fabulously rich appetizer of a large ravioli filled with goat cheese and crab meat, served with a whole egg yolk; other signature appetizers include fried mussel salad; foie gras brûlée; and squid stuffed with bulgur wheat with a hyssop wrapping. Among main courses, look for seafood fettuccini in a fisherman sauce with poppy seeds; entrecôte with truffle gnocchi; and fresh sea fish filet on a delicately roasted eggplant with tarragon yogurt. The house bread is terrific, and the homemade truffle spread with crostini is a wonderful late-night tapa. Desserts are always surprising and rewarding. There's a well-stocked bar. Late-night bar offerings include such treats as oxtail and bone marrow salad, fresh oysters on ice (in season), and spareribs.

57 Nahalat Binyamin. ☎ 03/566-5505. Reservations necessary. Main courses NIS 100–NIS 125 ($25–$31/£13–£16); fixed-price weekday lunch from NIS 95 ($24/£12). AE, DC, MC, V. Mon–Fri 12:30–3:30pm and 7:30pm–1:30am; Sat 12:30–5pm and 7pm–1am. Closed Sun.

## MODERATE

**China Lee** GLATT KOSHER CHINESE   This enduring, busy establishment—decorated in the typical style of a 1950s American Chinese restaurant—serves a good range of noodle, vegetarian, beef, chicken, duck, and fish dishes. The soups are rich and filling. Dim sum and lemon chicken are good selections, as are the duck and veal choices at the top end of the price list, but dishes tend to be rather sweet. The Asian staff (adorned with yarmulkes) is very helpful.

7 Montefiore St. ☎ 03/510-3140. Main courses NIS 48–NIS 100 ($12–$25/£6–£13); fixed-price lunch NIS 60–NIS 90 ($15–$23/£7.50–£11). AE, DC, MC, V. Sun–Thurs noon–midnight; Fri noon–3pm; Sat after Shabbat–midnight.

**Kimmel** ★ COUNTRY MEDITERRANEAN   An old Tel Aviv building in the shadow of the Shalom Tower skyscraper houses this delightful place. At lunch, it's fast-paced and filled with business people, but in the evenings, it becomes a cozy rustic retreat. The inventive menu starts with earthy house bread and is flavored with lots of *zataar* (local spices) as well as dill, garlic, lemon, and olive oil, and interesting sauces of wild berry/pepper, lemon/honey, fig, pistachio, or raisins. Appetizers include mushrooms stuffed with gooseliver in plum-and-fig sauce; bouillabaisse; and calamari stuffed with risotto and seafood. Main courses range from lamb chops in spicy barbecue sauce to ostrich filet in curry, lemon, and garlic.

6 HaShahar St. ☎ 03/510-5204 or 510-1596. Reservations necessary. Main courses NIS 65–NIS 110 ($16–$28/£8.10–£14). AE, DC, MC, V. Daily noon–after midnight (kitchen closes at 11pm).

**Nanutchka** ★ GEORGIAN/RUSSIAN   This ethnic restaurant has taken off with Tel Avivians and tourists because it provides a lively mix of old and new plus very tasty,

## An Ethnic Dining Experience

If you want to sample Tel Aviv's most authentic Middle Eastern food at bargain prices and are willing to take a 15-minute bus ride, **Etzel Street** in the **Hatikvah District of South Tel Aviv** is the place to explore. Pick up southbound bus no. 16 on Allenby Street near Moghrabi Square, and ask the driver to let you off at Rehov Etzel in Hatikvah. Probably Tel Aviv's best-kept restaurant secret, Hatikvah is a vast area inhabited by Israeli families from such countries as Yemen and Iraq, and lengthy Etzel Street is virtually wall-to-wall with restaurants serving skewered meats, Oriental salads, and delicious Iraqi pita breads that the waiters obtain straight from the ovens of the many bakeries that dot the street—one of Etzel Street's mottoes is that Iraqi pita more than 3 minutes old is stale.

Here you can purchase your meals by the skewer, which means you can put together a skewer of beef and a skewer of turkey breast (about NIS 20/$5/£2.50 each in most places) plus a salad and french fries, and come up with a tasty, filling meal for around NIS 60 ($15/£7.50). Or you can be more daring and order breast of goose and chicken hearts and livers plus the *pièce de résistance* of Etzel Street restaurants—the enormously rich but delicate gooseliver skewer, barbecued to perfection and going for about NIS 39 ($9.75/£4.90). The street is like a food festival; just pick out a place that looks busy and interesting (preferably next door to a bread bakery), and grab yourself a table.

interesting food. Come at lunchtime, and you can watch elderly Georgian ladies from the former Soviet Union preparing the deep-fried and poached dumplings and dough pockets stuffed with beef and goose—or with cheeses, mushrooms, and vegetables—that are the heart of Nanutchka's popular appetizer and tapas menu. Main courses include hearty stews of lamb and casseroles of meat cooked in sauces laced with dried fruits, but there are also lighter dishes of exotically flavored fish and chicken stewed with onion, tamarind, and pomegranate. You'll also find Georgian/fusion dishes such as "Black Sea egg rolls" stuffed with crab and shrimp—everything is scrumptious and worth trying. From noon through early dinner, Russian and Caucasian Mountain music plays softly in the background. By late evening, the dumpling ladies have vanished, and Nanutchka becomes a bar-bistro with a splendid mix of Russian and Western rock, plus traditional music, and people often dancing in the aisles.

2 Lilenblum St. ☎ 03/516-2254. Reservations recommended. Main courses NIS 50–NIS 80 ($13–$20/£6.25–£10); lunch (Sun–Thurs noon–5pm) NIS 45–NIS 60 ($11–$15/£5.60–£7.50). AE, DC, MC, V. Daily noon–2am.

## INEXPENSIVE

**Brew House** INTERNATIONAL    Set in a microbrewery on a trendy section of Rothschild Boulevard, this bustling, snazzy place has live jazz, swing, and blues on Friday afternoons and Sunday evenings. Glistening brewery paraphernalia winds its way like a sculptural installation through the multilevel space and provides dark, alelike designer beers with a low alcohol content. Beer runs NIS 14 to NIS 28 ($3.50–$7/£1.75–£3.50). Along with your drink, you can have a hot dog with mustard, a hefty NIS 54 ($14/£6.75) hamburger, assorted pub snacks, sausages with sauerkraut, or a pile of spicy Buffalo wings (two sizes), among other items.

11 Rothschild Blvd. ☎ 03/516-8666. Main courses NIS 54–NIS 100 ($14–$25/£6.75–£13); light meals NIS 25–NIS 60 ($6.25–$15/£3.10–£7.50). AE, DC, MC, V. Daily noon–1 or 2am.

**Spaghettim** _Value_ _Kids_ ITALIAN   This is a restaurant that can make you fall in love with spaghetti. It has more than 50 kinds of interesting sauces, including classic carbonara and unusual creations such as an olive oil–based sauce filled with breast of tender, fresh sautéed chicken, dill, garlic, and lemon; or a salmon-and-asparagus sauce with white wine and nutmeg. Soups and salads, like the spaghetti dishes, are filled with fresh herbs and vegetables and are hefty in size. For dessert, there's a choice of _pannecotta_, Italian ice creams, and al dente spaghetti with dark chocolate, ice cream, and brandy sauce. The food is delicious, filling, and imaginative; even the restaurant's charge of NIS 9 ($2.25/£1.10) for home-style bread doesn't seem unfair. Israeli and imported wines are offered.

48 King George St. ☎ 03/620-7666. Reservations recommended. Main courses NIS 35–NIS 60 ($8.75–$15/£4.40–£7.50). AE, DC, MC, V. Daily noon–1am.

## YEMENITE QUARTER & CARMEL MARKET

Walk along Allenby Street from Moghrabi Square. At 54 Allenby St., turn right and walk to the grid of little streets at its far end. This is the Yemenite Quarter (Karem Ha-Teimanim), a favorite of Tel Avivians and visitors alike. Don't let the neighborhood's appearance rattle you—the people here are honest and respectable, and it's a perfectly safe area to traverse. Built in 1909, this is one of the oldest parts of the city. Its tangled streets harbor many restaurants; they are not especially Yemenite, but do serve some of the tastiest Middle Eastern food in Tel Aviv. Some restaurants in the quarter have become pricey and tourist oriented; below are some of the best.

### MODERATE

**Maganda Restaurant** YEMENITE/MIDDLE EASTERN   The Maganda is airy, modern, and very attractive. The cuisine is Yemenite Middle Eastern, strictly kosher, and includes grilled meats such as lamb shashlik, kabob, and skewered duck. You can also come for a light meal of spicy oxtail soup, hummus on amazing Yemenite breads, and baked vegetables stuffed with rice and meat. The menu is in English and Hebrew. In summer, the restaurant offers rooftop dining. To get here, enter the Yemenite Quarter, turn right at the end of the alley, then left onto Najara Street.

26 Rabbi Meir St. ☎ 03/517-9990. Reservations recommended. Main courses NIS 36–NIS 90 ($9–$23/£4.50–£11). Cash only. Sun–Thurs noon–midnight; Sat after Shabbat.

**Shaul's Inn** MIDDLE EASTERN   The blockbuster of this neighborhood, with heavy wooden chairs, flagstone floors, and a large photomural of a Yemenite wedding on one wall, this kosher restaurant at the corner of Eliashiv can get packed out to the street on Saturday nights. Stick to the main room on the ground floor; downstairs, where there is an intimate restaurant and bar, the prices are more than double. English is spoken here, and the waiters will help you choose from the Middle Eastern menu. The specialty is the deliciously tasty lamb's breast stuffed with rice and pine nuts. Have a Turkish or Greek salad or a gorgeous stuffed eggplant, cabbage, or pepper.

11 Eliashiv St. ☎ 03/517-7619. Reservations recommended. Main courses NIS 36–NIS 90 ($9–$23/£4.50–£11). AE, DC, V. Sun–Thurs noon–midnight; Fri noon–3pm; Sat after Shabbat. Go west and half a block down Ge'ulah St. off Allenby. Make a diagonal left turn onto Ha-Ari St., turn right onto Rabbi Meir St., and then left onto Kehilat Aden St.

## SHEINKIN STREET

Beginning on the west side of Allenby Street, across from the Carmel Market, Sheinkin Street is sometimes called Tel Aviv's Greenwich Village. It's a mix of cafes, unusual shops, and family stores—a stroll and a meal here lets you sample a slice of Tel Aviv life away from the hotel district and the beaches. King George Street, which makes a "V" with Sheinkin Street at Allenby, is home to a number of excellent and reasonably priced bakeries if you'd like a snack to take back to your hotel room.

**Orna and Ella** VEGETARIAN/CAFE The most famous of the cafe/restaurants on Sheinkin Street, Orna and Ella offers a homey sense of intimacy and perhaps reminds yuppies from North Tel Aviv of their grandparents' British Mandate–era apartments. It's got great pastries, brioche, and espresso, but there is also a short menu of choice sandwiches, salads, pastas, and the signature sweet-potato pancakes and goose breast hamburger. The lines are often out the door, and not just because customers tend to linger over conversation—the cafe would not be so successful without food that's a cut above the rest. The waiters are young and very Israeli.

33 Sheinkin St. ✆ **03/620-4753.** Light meals, snacks, and pastries NIS 24–NIS 66 ($6–$17/£3–£8.25). AE, DC, MC, V. Sun–Fri 10am–midnight; Sat 11am–midnight.

## NEVE TZEDEK

This neighborhood, the oldest in the city, is coming alive with galleries, boutiques, cafes, and a major performance and theater center after decades of neglect. The Suzanne Dellal Center for Dance and Theater is the centerpiece for the revival of the area.

### EXPENSIVE

**Catit** ★★★ MEDITERRANEAN/FRENCH No menu in the country is as rich, complex, and expertly prepared as Meir Adoni's at Catit, combining Adoni's special gifts as a chef with traditions from around the Mediterranean. Think grilled calamari, filled with lamb meat and mozzarella, in grilled eggplant, goat yogurt, *techina,* roasted bean, and olive oil; sea fish seviche with red beet carpaccio and sheep yogurt ravioli in basil and green oil; foie gras on grilled semolina with vanilla pastry and caramelized bananas in a sauce of veal stock and coffee; grilled eel wrapped in watermelon jelly; and grilled snapper with garlic purée, calamari, roasted almonds, and eggplant crème. The wine list is perfect, and desserts, led by a version of *kadaif* (a traditional local dessert) fit for the gods, are dynamite. The setting is pleasant, but no match for the food. You come here to *experience* the rich dishes. Prices are among the highest in Israel, but two luncheon prix-fixe specials make a gourmand's lunch possible for about NIS 400 ($100/£50) per couple (less-expensive special prix-fixe deals are also offered).

4 Hechal Ha Talmud St. ✆ **03/510-7001.** Reservations required. Main courses NIS 120–NIS 220 ($30–$55/£15–£28). AE, DC, MC, V. Daily noon–midnight.

**Suzanna** CAFE/BISTRO Very central to Neve Tzedek and catching the spirit of the neighborhood, this charming spot is filled with people from nearby theater and dance groups, boutique shoppers, and locals. You can stop here for coffee and brioche, soup and a hefty salad, focaccia, cheese, and wine, or a full meal of pasta or fresh grilled sea bream. Everything is good and served with style. There's a roof terrace that turns into an interesting bar after dinnertime.

9 Shabazzi St. ✆ **03/517-7580.** Main courses and light meals NIS 25–NIS 80 ($6.25–$20/£3.10–£10). AE, DC, V. Daily 10am–2am.

## NEAR IBN GIVROL STREET, HA-BIMAH & MANN AUDITORIUM

Ibn Givrol Street runs through Tel Aviv's center of culture, from the Cinémathèque at the corner of Ibn Givrol Street and Rehov Ha'Arba'a northward to Shderot Shaul Ha Melech where you'll find the Tel Aviv Museum of Art and the Golda Meir/Tel Aviv Center for the Performing Arts. This area is lined with restaurants, including choices for fine dining as well as places for quick meals and post-theater coffee and cake. Rehov Ha'Arba'a, at the southern edge of the area, is lined with wall-to-wall top-choice restaurants.

### EXPENSIVE

**Lilith** ⍟ KOSHER MEAT    An excellent special-night-out choice for kosher diners, Lilith combines quality ingredients with a kitchen that's always interesting but not overblown with forced inventiveness. Located near the Tel Aviv Museum of Art and the Center for Performing Arts, Lilith's ambience is suitably sophisticated, though not quite luxurious. The menu varies according to season, but the gnocchi and ravioli dishes in truffle-oil dressing are scrumptious and the main-course steak and fish dishes are excellent. There are specials every day, and it's a good idea to try to choose at least one of them. Desserts are worthwhile. Business lunch specials run from noon to 6pm.

4 Weizmann St. ⓒ 03/609-1331. Reservations recommended. Main courses NIS 59–NIS 150 ($15–$38/£7.40–£19). AE, DC, MC, V. Sun–Thurs noon–midnight. Closed Fri–Sat.

**Messa** ⍟ NOUVELLE FRENCH    The daring, much-talked-about, 21st-century design of this restaurant is sumptuous: white on white, with polished white marble floors, drapes, and a long white communal table with a polished burl-wood top running down the center of the dining room, lined with facing columns of white upholstered arm chairs. The basic effect is Roman banquet hall meets *Vogue* and *Architectural Digest.* The decor and long tables draw the crowds, and you might not be comfortable with the scene at Messa unless you are designed as professionally as the restaurant itself. This is talented Chef Aviv Moshe's personal restaurant, so it won't have a turnover of chefs, but the gourmet menu choices (some touched with the chef's Kurdish family traditions) constantly change. Among appetizers, look for a dish of calamari served with lemon cream eel and gooseliver; main-course hits include the seafood toast—grilled coquilles St. Jacques and shrimp served on thickly sliced toast with anchovy butter, and a good vinaigrette salad on the side; and the seafood couscous in crab and lemon thyme broth. Rich meat dishes round out the menu. The wine list is carefully planned, and there's a dramatic black-on-black designer bar to see and be seen in.

19 Ha'arba'a St. ⓒ 03/685-6859. Reserve at least 2 days in advance. Main courses NIS 110–NIS 160 ($28–$40/£14–£20); fixed-price lunches from NIS 100 ($25/£13). AE, DC, MC, V. Daily noon–3:30pm and 7–11:30pm.

### MODERATE

**Papagaio** SOUTH AMERICAN GRILL    Israelis love this all-you-can-eat grill where you pay a fixed price and take whatever you like from skewer-carrying waiters, or roasts and steaks fresh off the fire. The meats are cut and done in Argentine style, seasoned with salt, pepper, and served with chimichanga sauces as well as with a table full of interesting salads, tapas, and vegetables. At dinner, the choices include 10 to 12 kinds of meats as well as fish, chicken, and chorizo; the lunch menu is limited to seven choices. For noncarnivores, a grilled salmon option is available only at dinner. Drinks and dessert are extra, and there is a 10% service charge. On Wednesday, Thursday, and Friday evenings there is live entertainment starting around 9:30pm.

14 Ha'arba'a St. ⓒ 03/562-6888. Reservations recommended. All-you-can-eat dinner NIS 130 ($33/£16); lunch NIS 90 ($23/£11). AE, DC, MC, V. Sun–Fri noon–4pm and 7pm–midnight; Sat 12:30pm–midnight.

**Pasha** *Value* MIDDLE EASTERN   In this stylish but reasonably priced kosher restaurant you can sample the seasonings and tastes of home-style dishes that are the heart of both Jewish and Arab family kitchens and eateries throughout the region. The menu includes worthwhile appetizers of meat pies; Middle Eastern salads; stuffed vegetables in tasty sauces; and traditional, mildly exotic main courses of grilled meats, *pargiot maklouba* (seasoned rice casserole of deboned chicken thighs); or lamb *moussakhan* (served on sumac bread). For dessert, try Arabic-style desserts and a variety of coffees. Not gourmet, but hearty, fun, and so popular that branches of Pasha are popping up all over the country. The house bread is great.

8 Ha'arba'a St. © 03/561-7778. Reservations recommended. Main courses NIS 34–NIS 86 ($8.50–$22/£4.25–£11). AE, DC, MC, V. Sun–Thurs noon–midnight; Fri noon–4pm; Sat after Shabbat–midnight.

**Yin Yang** *⚜⚜* PAN ASIAN/FUSION   This excellent, sophisticated Chinese restaurant, also offering a range of Vietnamese-influenced dishes, could compete with the best of them in New York or San Francisco. Chef/owner Israel Aharoni, high priest of Israel's restaurant revolution, has designed a menu that's both more authentic and inventive than you'd find in a Chinese restaurant for Westerners. Vietnamese salads are good choices for starters: I like the shrimp and papaya (in season); the black mushroom salad; and the spicy calamari. Vine leaves stuffed with meat cooked in lemon grass are an example of Aharoni's cross-cultural daring. For main courses, try smoked goose breast in tea leaves; an elegant chicken and mushroom dish served with quail eggs; or exotic goose breast cooked with plums. Special dishes, such as smoked duck, must be ordered in advance and are in a higher price range. Interesting but less-expensive veggie dishes round out the menu. Very reasonably priced luncheon specials are offered Sunday to Friday from noon to 5pm starting at NIS 48 ($12/£6).

17 Ha'arba'a St. © 03/686-9888. Reservations recommended. Main courses NIS 45–NIS 120 ($11–$30/£5.60–£15). AE, DC, MC, V. Mon–Sat noon–11pm.

### INEXPENSIVE

**Lehem Erez** *⚜ Value* SANDWICHES/SALADS   Erez Komarovsky's wonderful gourmet bread bakery/restaurant in upscale Herzlia has become a local legend, and although you have to go up to Herzlia to try the complete Erez restaurant, a number of Lehem Erez (Erez Bread) bakery cafes have opened throughout the Tel Aviv area. There are constantly changing lists of sandwiches designed by Erez, all made with top-quality ingredients, richly herbed and drizzled with olive oil (a salami, fig, arugula, and buffalo-milk cheese sandwich was delicious). There are also platters and salads, but who could pass up Erez's bread? The dessert list is legendary, with chocolate fondant, ice cream, muffins, cheesecakes, lemon tarts, and decadent brownies among the rich creations. A business lunch, served from 11am to 5pm, includes a sandwich, salad, hot or cold drink, and dessert. The menu is in Hebrew, but the staff will patiently translate. Great for an after-theater coffee and dessert.

52 Ibn Givrol St. © 03/696-9381. Sandwiches NIS 20–NIS 30 ($5–$7.50/£2.50–£3.75). AE, DC, MC, V. Daily 8am–1am.

**Giraffe Noodle Bar** ASIAN   Stylish but casual, with sidewalk tables in good weather, Giraffe serves up a variety of delicate, quality *gyoza* (dumplings), Asian salads, dim sum, and sushi. The spicy egg noodles with chopped shrimp, pork, and goose breast is the house specialty, but you'll also find a range of Japanese, Thai, and Chinese noodle dishes. French-style desserts here are extremely good and add a touch of elegance, especially if you're combining a meal here with a concert or performance.

49 Ibn Givrol St. © 03/691-6294. Main courses NIS 35–NIS 60 ($8.75–$15/£4.40–£7.50). AE, DC, MC, V. Daily noon–1am.

**Sima's** *(Finds)* MIDDLE EASTERN/MIXED GRILL   Sima's is an old-fashioned kosher Jerusalem institution (p. 158) that's ventured to open a location on Tel Aviv's trendiest restaurant street. The reason? Sima's famous, fabulously seasoned "Jerusalem Mixed Grill" (lamb, chicken, livers, hearts, and other secret ingredients) that's won raves from gourmets the world over. There's a good choice of other Middle Eastern dishes, but the star of the show is the mixed-grill sandwich in pita bread (to which I love to add a sliced tomato) for NIS 40 ($10/£5). Decor is sleek, but in the surly tradition of the original Sima's as a market-worker's eatery, if the place is busy, they may announce that you can only order the mixed-grill sandwich as a takeout item—to be served the mixed grill at a table, you have to order it as a more expensive platter. If you're at a table with others ordering main courses, they'll let you stay. A great source of iron and vitamin B.

24 Ha'arba'a St. © 03/624-6644. Reservations useful. Main courses NIS 54–NIS 100 ($14–$25/£6.75–£13). AE, MC, V. Sun–Thurs noon–midnight; Fri noon–3pm; Sat after Shabbat.

## NORTH BY THE YARKON RIVER

The neighborhood, just south of the Yarkon River, sometimes called Little Tel Aviv, is centered on Yirmiyahu Street, a short street near the point where Ben-Yehuda and Dizengoff streets meet, a block from the bend in the Yarkon. Take a bus or a cab north on Ha-Yarkon, Ben-Yehuda, or Dizengoff streets all the way to Yirmiyahu.

### MODERATE

**Red Chinese Restaurant** CHINESE   With the exception of the world-class Yin Yang in South Tel Aviv (p. 261), this is the best Chinese restaurant in town and has thrived for years in one of the city's most sophisticated, affluent neighborhoods. It's a bit more affordable than Yin Yang, with the kind of menu familiar to those who frequent Chinese restaurants in England or America. Not kosher, it offers shrimp and calamari dishes as well as a wide range of duck, fish, pork, chicken, and vegetarian choices. There is also a small Thai-style menu. Wine and beer are served.

326 Dizengoff. © 03/546-6347. Reservations recommended evenings. Main courses NIS 36–NIS 85 ($9–$21/£4.50–£11). AE, DC, MC, V. Daily 1pm–midnight. Bus: 4 or 5 to end of Dizengoff or Ben-Yehuda.

**Yakimono** *(Finds)* JAPANESE/SUSHI   With a 3-decade-long run, Yakimono is the oldest sushi restaurant in Tel Aviv—other places come and go, but no one else has mastered the long-term logistics of obtaining and serving the freshest fish possible for sushi and sashimi. You'll always find a changing selection of fresh sushi and sashimi of the day, as well as shrimp, cuttlefish, octopus, and eel, along with tempuras and ramen noodle soups. The restaurant is justly proud of its seaweed, cucumber-skin, and salmon-skin hand rolls. There is an authentic sushi counter as well as tables in a large enclosed sidewalk veranda. *Tip:* A kosher version of Yakimono has been set up at the Hilton hotel, which has a demanding Japanese clientele.

5 Yodei Ha'sira St. © 03/544-3864. Reservations useful. Main sushi dishes NIS 40–NIS 70 ($10–$18/£5–£8.75). AE, DC, MC, V. Daily noon–1:30am.

### INEXPENSIVE

**Hungarian Blintzes** BLINTZES   Blintzes, doughy crepes filled with either sweet or savory ingredients, are a well-loved East and central European tradition. At this long-running blintz paradise, the dozens of choices are all vegetarian, and run from mushroom goulash in paprika blintzes to sweet cheese or apple and cinnamon—all served with a dollop of sour cream if you choose. There are good soups and salads to

## For Chocolate Lovers

The **Chocolate Bar**, 45 Rothschild Blvd. (℃ **03/560-4570**), is a shop/cafe that has the best chocolate confections, handmade chocolates, and pastries in the city. It's a Shangri-la for chocolate soufflés, pies, croissants, coffees, liquors, cakes, soups, and ice cream. Located on trendy Rothschild Boulevard, this is a good place for dessert after a meal in the area (or to pick up chocolates for later in your hotel room). It's open daily 10am to after midnight. **Roy Chocolate**, 15 Yad Harutzim St. (℃ **03/687-4411**), is Tel Aviv's wonderful kosher *chocolaterie*. Trained in Belgium, Roy Gershon creates masterpiece chocolates of heavenly flavors and textures; interactive activities such as candy making and chocolate sculpting can be arranged. Call for details. It's open Sunday to Thursday from 8am to midnight, and Friday from 8am to 1pm. Both Roy Chocolate and the Chocolate Bar make stuff so rich that a little goes a long way, especially if you're on a diet or a budget.

round out a meal. At the holiday of Shavuot, when dairy dishes are traditionally eaten, you'll need a reservation just to get near the place.

35 Yirmyahu St. ℃ **03/605-0674**. Reservations accepted. Main courses NIS 36–NIS 45 ($9–$11/£4.50–£5.60). AE, DC, MC, V. Sun–Thurs 12:30pm–1am; Sat after Shabbat. Bus: 4.

**Shtsupak Fish Restaurant** FISH/SEAFOOD   Well worth a trek or taxi ride from the hotel district, the bustling Shtsupak serves wonderful fresh fish and is a bit better and more atmospheric than its rival, Barbunya (p. 253). Both places are functional and no-frills, and serve excellent, fresh grilled or fried fish and shrimp that comes with a big meze of Middle Eastern salads (included in the price). Shtsupak, however, has a sidewalk dining terrace; a somewhat more leisurely pace; and usually comes out ahead of Barbunya when it comes to salads, sauces, and the size of its portions.

256 Ben-Yehuda St. ℃ **03/544-1973**. Reservations recommended evenings. Complete meals NIS 55–NIS 75 ($14–$19/£6.90–£9.40). AE, DC. Mon–Sat noon–midnight.

## IN THE TEL AVIV PORT

The old Tel Aviv Port, which used to be a derelict stretch of warehouses and garages along the northern stretch of Tel Aviv's beachfront, is now booming with some of the city's most stylish restaurants, shops, and bars, all linked by a boardwalk promenade. There are interesting "fusion" establishments such as designer clothing stores/cafes or spa/bar/restaurants. It's a great place to stroll on a summer or early fall evening, grab a bite, party-hop, or dine elegantly on a terrace that overlooks the sea. Cars and taxis must stay outside the perimeter of the vast, fenced-in port, which is an added plus— pedestrians entering the entire enclave are checked by security guards at each of the port's gates. Things are busy through the wee hours, but the port is also a favorite spot for a relaxing beachfront breakfast or lunch. In addition to the restaurants below, there are snack and bakery counters, and restaurant bars for every need, ranging from the **Speedo Bar** (adorned with posters of models in Speedo bathing suits and a Speedo clothing boutique to attract a similarly attired clientele looking for speedy connections) to **Galina** (a more elegant pickup bar/restaurant) with a terrace and a horseshoe-shaped bar to facilitate eye contact); and **Seabreeze Spa/Bar/Restaurant** (offering a nonsmoking bar and delicious, heath-conscious meals with a massage).

To get here, take bus no. 4 or 5, or sherut no. 4. Taxis will let you off at the closest gate to the restaurant of your choice. Most people just browse and find a restaurant they'd like to try, but after 8pm or on weekends, you'll need a reservation. After dinner, you can stroll out to the old Redding Electric Plant, which is now used as a venue for exhibitions, on a distant point at the northern end of the complex.

## EXPENSIVE

**Gilly's** *✿* GRILL   In summer, Gilly's means fine-grilled meats served on a spacious deck overlooking the sea. In colder weather, there's a vast, high-ceiling dining room. The menu, like the setting, is very roomy: There are more than 20 appetizers each day, ranging from a great spicy fish soup loaded with seafood to cured salmon in tequila and orange-peel marmalade. A lavish green salad tossed with blue cheese and fresh seasonal fruit can be ordered as a meal in itself. But people come here for the meat: beef filet wrapped in puff pastry, rich veal *cordon bleu,* beef stew with root vegetables in red wine with tomatoes, veal in white-wine and mushroom sauce, and much more. There's also a main course menu of pasta, fish, seafood, and hamburgers prepared in ways you'll rarely see: beef filet burgers with foie gras; with basil, roasted peppers, and feta cheese; or just American-style. Entrees are served with potato au gratin and salad; meats come with a choice of sauces. On the long dessert menu, the apple puff pastry with ice cream and pear sauce is great. There are prix-fixe luncheon specials.

Hangar 15, Tel Aviv Port. ✆ **03/605-7777.** Reservations necessary. Main courses NIS 66–NIS 130 ($17–$33/ £8.25–£16). AE, DC, MC, V. Daily 10am–last customer.

**Mul Yam** *✿✿* SEAFOOD   Lionized by local food critics (and the *New York Times*) and with prices that cover the airfare for the ingredients in many of its dishes, this cutting-edge seafood restaurant/oyster bar has a name that's a Franco-Hebrew pun: "Mul Yam" in Hebrew means "facing the sea," and also (if you're a Hebrew speaker who knows French) "sea mussels." The *moules* (mussels) from the pun are rarely on the menu, but a variety of top-quality crustaceans and mollusks are flown in several times a week from distant, chilly seas. Here Tel Aviv's nonkosher elite consume fresh-off-the-plane oysters in an informal place that looks like a small seafood restaurant in Maine or Cape Cod (the decor may be upgraded soon). The kitchen is fantastic and inventive. The appetizers are heavenly: Look for filet of sea bass with crispy gnocchi and pumpkin cream; or crab soup velouté with herbes de Provence, served with peeled shrimp. Main courses on the constantly changing menu might include a dynamite cold lobster salad; pumpkin and ricotta ravioli with shrimp and clams in lobster sauce; or a medley of scallop, scampi, shrimp, and lobster in white wine. Main courses are served with a side dish and brioche. Whole grilled Nova Scotia lobster in herbed butter starts at NIS 220 ($55/£28). A special dessert chef produces light, elegant items to top off your meal. This is Xanadu for those coming to Israel for gourmet seafood.

Tel Aviv Port. ✆ **03/546-9920.** Reservations necessary. Main courses NIS 100–NIS 220 ($25–$55/£13–£28); lunch special NIS 140 ($35/£18). AE, DC, MC, V. Daily 12:30–3:30pm and 7:30–10:30pm.

## MODERATE

**Boya** MEDITERRANEAN   This very busy place, with a deck overlooking the sea, serves everything from tapas, pizzas, salads, and focaccia to grilled rib-eye steak, seafood linguine, and fine sautéed shrimp in white wine. There are also a dozen beers, good espresso, and a dessert list that includes homemade Arabic sweet-cheese *kanafeh* (made on the spot), passion-fruit pie, and (also made on the spot) a chocolate volcano and banana tarte tatin. The waist-high sea wall that separates the promenade from the beach serves as an impromptu counter-seating area for those having tapas and drinks—on a windy night the spray from the waves just dusts your food. Tapas, ranging from hummus to grilled shrimp, are in the NIS 20-to-NIS 40 ($5–$10/£2.50–£5) range. Leisurely breakfast/brunches are also served. Everything is good; this is an excellent choice if you want to people-watch and experience the eclectic feel of dining at the Tel Aviv Port.

Tel Aviv Port. © 03/544-6166. Reservations suggested (specify indoor or terrace seating). Main courses NIS 64–NIS 105 ($16–$26/£8–£13). AE, DC, MC, V. Sat–Thurs 9am–midnight; Fri 8:30am–1am.

**Comme il Faut Café** ✹ MEDITERRANEAN   Another quintessential Tel Aviv Port eatery with a terrace by the sea, Comme il Faut maintains a somewhat calm air, even on frenzied weekend summer nights, and a delicious but healthy menu. It's the concept of the owners of a Tel Aviv fashion-design house of the same name (a showroom is in the spacious, adjacent section of the cafe's wooden pavilion). There are small, medium, and large dishes; each menu size is completely different. Small includes open sandwiches such as goat cheese with antipasti and *zataar* pesto, or chicken breast with avocado and roquette leaves. The changing medium menu might include seafood skewer on a chickpea crepe with parsley, green *techina,* and tomato salad; or grilled prawns with black lentils and yogurt sauce. The large menu might feature an oven-baked catch of the day with couscous salad, or curried vegetable casserole with wild rice. There are also enormous courses for two, such as a grilled seafood banquet, or a pot of *moules* marinière (mussels) with fresh-baked potato chips. Desserts are healthy and exquisite; there are 11 fresh-squeezed designer-fruit creations, including carrot with coconut milk and coriander; and a zingy apple, fennel, and ginger.

Tel Aviv Port. © 03/544-9211. Reservations suggested at night. Small and medium menus NIS 32–NIS 60 ($8–$15/£4–£7.50); large menu (per person) NIS 60–NIS 170 ($15–$43/£7.50–£21). AE, DC, MC, V. Sun–Thurs 8am–11pm; Fri 8am–5pm; Sat 11am–11pm.

## INEXPENSIVE

**Agadir Burger Bar** ✹ *(Value)* BURGERS/CAFE   A new, very expanded version of downtown Tel Aviv's little Agadir Burger Bar/Restaurant on the Nahlat Binyamin Pedestrian Mall, which is famous for the best burgers and the most inventive toppings in town, this location has groupings of eclectic sofas and easy chairs as well as more standard tables, which in good weather spread into an outdoor deck. If you eat here during the day, or before the place morphs into its bar incarnation at night, the menu includes tempura shrimp, spicy North African merguez sausages, salads, and chicken soup with veal dumplings. The hamburgers, in varying sizes, can be topped with additions such as portobello mushrooms; spiced goose breast; assorted herbs, spices, and chili butter; goat cheese; or guacamole. The nightly bar scene is young and busy.

Tel Aviv Port. © 03/605-7777. Main courses NIS 40–NIS 60 ($10–$15/£5–£7.50). AE, DC, MC, V. Daily noon–midnight.

**Shalvata** ✹ *(Finds)* *(Kids)* SALADS/SANDWICHES   By day, Shalvata ("asylum" in Hebrew), is a whimsical, laid-back outdoor restaurant where you can unwind with your toes in the cool sand and where kids can make sand castles in between mouthfuls of sweet-potato quiche or hot dogs and chips with lots of ketchup. Tables, couches, and lawn chairs are set in the sand overlooking the water, shaded by thatch *palapas* and umbrellas. At night the restaurant becomes a breezy, easygoing dance bar that makes you think you've been transported to a beach in the Caribbean. A friendly pickup spot for people of all backgrounds and persuasions, Shalvata offers tapas, salads, and desserts that are tasty and can be gracefully eaten while talking to a stranger, as well as a full bar that features a well-chosen list of Israeli wines. The frozen margarita is a house favorite. The music is always right; different nights feature jazz, Latin/salsa, hip-hop (with DJ), or '60s chill-out music. Shalvata is a fun, affordable place to dance, talk, and eat—even with someone you already know well.

Tel Aviv Port. ✆ 03/455-1279. Reservations suggested. Main courses NIS 24–NIS 48 ($6–$12/£3–£6). AE, DC, MC, V. Sun–Thurs 10am–after 2am; Fri–Sat 9am–after 3am. Closed mid-Nov to May.

## ON ALMAH BEACH NORTH OF JAFFA
### MODERATE

**Manta Ray** ★★ *Finds* SEAFOOD    The quintessential beach restaurant, Manta Ray is an open-air pavilion that looks out on the rolling surf of an empty stretch of Tel Aviv's coast, and is perfectly positioned to catch the sun setting over the Mediterranean. The food is simply prepared, but full of flavor and ingenuity. Manta Ray is famous for its plate of 12 ever-changing small appetizers; it's always an interesting combination of traditional Middle Eastern, contemporary, or exotic dishes and comes with wonderful bread. The platter can easily be shared, and allows you to sample the kitchen while enjoying the view (discuss the selections with your waiter). Main courses come with green salad and a pile of delicious, sliced, and grilled sweet potatoes. Among my favorites are the grilled shrimp, the sage-scented sea bass filet, and the fried calamari, but it's virtually impossible to go wrong with any of the main courses. The atmosphere here is informal, and you will feel just as comfortable ordering a light meal as a major feast.

Almah Beach, near Dan Panorama Hotel. ✆ 03/517-4774. Reservations recommended; necessary summer evenings. Main courses NIS 75–NIS 100 ($19–$25/£9.40–£13). DC, MC, V. Daily 9am–midnight. Bus: 10 from Tel Aviv to Jaffa; get out at the Intercontinental Hotel stop.

## JAFFA
### EXPENSIVE

**Cordelia** ★★★ MODERN FRENCH    Chef Nir Zook, who created every detail of Cordelia's unique design and menu, is a master of taking risks. At night, the darkened dining room is lit by candelabras and chandeliers whose lights reflect and re-reflect in mirrors, windows, and wine goblets. The decor balances between romantic and Gothic without quite going off the edge, and fits perfectly with the restaurant's 1,000-year-old Crusader-era building. The ever-changing menu is food as theater, designed to surprise and amaze. A beautiful, creamy pâté of liver comes to the table in the shape of a stick of butter encrusted with black sesame seeds so that it looks like a bar of chocolate halvah covered with chocolate sprinkles. Even an innocent cream of eggplant and dill soup is so filled with flavor it will stop normal conversation. Main courses might range from the luxurious textures of shrimp and "St. Jacques porcini" and an interesting ostrich pavé in crunchy cocoa to tender chestnut and pumpkin ravioli and smoked salmon in grape sauce. Highly praised is a fusion dish with slices of rare beef filet and steamed grape leaves on jasmine rice or warm wheat flavored with coarse salt and sumac. Desserts spin out into charming fantasies (one choice was a "fig orgy" guaranteed to leave diners breathless), or are variations on classics; there's even a sugar-free chocolate mousse. There are fine intermediate courses of sorbets and soft goat cheeses made by the chef's brother. Add a star if you're up for adventure.

30 Yefet St. ✆ 03/518-4668. Reservations necessary. Main courses NIS 80–NIS 130 ($20–$33/£10–£16); tasting menus from NIS 180 ($45/£23). AE, DC, MC, V. Mon–Sat noon–3pm and 7pm–midnight. Turn right at 30 Yefet St. into a wide, arched alley on the right as you walk up Yefet St. from the clock tower.

**Margaret Tayar's** ☆☆☆ *(Finds)* FISH   This fish restaurant, a landmark for Jaffa and Tel Aviv locals, has regularly made the top of the Ten Best Restaurants in Israel list put out each year by *Ma'ariv,* one of the country's largest newspapers. It's also won raves from *Gourmet* and other international press. In the worst of winter, it's a four-table affair with a seafaring interior, but as soon as the warmer weather arrives, the restaurant expands its easygoing spirit into a large covered terrace overlooking the sea, with a sweeping vista of the Tel Aviv shoreline. Whatever the season, you know you are in the presence of an inspired cook who loves to see people enjoying her creations. Portions are enormous, and everything is delicious, whether you choose Margaret's signature deep-fried filet of fish stuffed with "caviar"; rolled grape leaves filled with rice, nuts, and raisins served in yogurt and herbed olive oil; superb couscous; or masterfully seasoned whole grilled fish. Margaret Tayar makes everything herself each day, from the marinated North African salads and spicy fish sauces (which you might want served on the side) to the strudel filled with Middle Eastern fruits (order the strudel at the start of your meal, so it will be fresh from the oven in time for dessert). She is always whipping up masterpiece tidbits, and she'll be happy to help you put together a dinner that shows off the wonders of her kitchen for NIS 130 to NIS 160 ($33–$40/£16–£20) per person (although portions here are so large that two can easily share this kind of feast).

4 Retsif Ha-Aliyah Shenei St. 🕜 03/682-4741. Reservations recommended. Main courses NIS 60–NIS 100 ($15–$25/£7.50–£13). Cash only. Oct–May Mon–Sat 1–7pm; June–Sept Mon–Fri noon–4pm and 7pm–midnight, Sat noon–7pm. Closed Sun. Always call to confirm opening hours. Bus: 10 to Jaffa Clock Tower.

**Yoe'ezer Wine Bar** ☆☆☆ CONTINENTAL   The creation of Shaul Evron, an Israeli journalist and food writer, Yoe'ezer Wine Bar is a gourmand's dream tucked under the cavernous arches of a building that dates from Crusader times. Here you can sit for hours talking and sampling excellent wines and brandies as well as fine breads and cheeses, a rich pâté de Champagne, a confit de foie gras, antipasti as beautiful as a still life; exquisite veal liver (usually fresh on Mon) with truffles; and oysters flown in from Brittany at the week's end. You can keep things simple, or go on to main courses that include shoulder of lamb slow cooked for 7 hours; a memorable beef bourguignon; or a fine, thick heart of entrecôte steak. Quality and skill show in all dishes, and prices are reasonable enough that you can put together a virtual banquet. A plate of fine Israeli cheese and bread is NIS 70 ($18/£8.75), and the wine list runs from expensive imports to well-chosen and very reasonably priced Israeli wines (Yoe'ezer has one of the most amazing collections of rare Burgundy wines outside of France). Desserts, which include Belgian chocolate cake, are splendid.

Yefet St. opposite the clock tower. 🕜 03/683-9115. Reservations advisable. Main courses NIS 60–NIS 120 ($15–$30/£7.50–£15). AE, DC, MC, V. Daily 1pm–1am. The wine bar is on the inland (east) side of Yefet St., a few feet down an alley opposite the clock tower.

## MODERATE

**Noa Bistro** ☆☆ LEVANTINE FUSION   Atmosphere, plus the amazing, inventive food of Nir Zook (chef/owner of the luxury Cordelia restaurant; see above), make this a wonderful choice for a leisurely, gourmet meal that won't break the bank. The menu is tasty and ever changing, including unusual salads, goat cheeses from Zook's own farm, a great house liver pâté, and many of Nir Zook's signature creations, such as *shakshuka* (a Middle Eastern spicy pan-fried egg and tomato casserole)—made here with shrimp. Look for fresh sea fish filet in tomatoes and vine leaves; chicken breast in eggplant; fabulous homemade pastas; and spicy North African sausages. On the meat side of the menu, you'll find entrecôte lavishly covered with mushrooms, and Zook's own interpretation of traditional Middle Eastern meat-and-hummus casserole. There's a six-dish tasting menu for NIS 130 ($33/£16); a good bar and wine list, and a big menu of luxurious brunches. The setting, in a complex of Crusader-era buildings, is delightfully personal and exotic.

14 Hatzorfim St. © 03/518-9720. Reservations advisable. Main courses NIS 35–NIS 100 ($8.75–$25/£4.40–£13). AE, MC, V. Sun–Thurs 9:30am–last customer; Fri–Sat 8:30am–last customer. Turn right at 30 Yefet St. into a wide, arched alley on the right as you walk up Yefet St. from the clock tower, then a left.

**Shirat Hayam** GLATT KOSHER FISH/MEAT   Set in an evocative, restored building in the gardens at the top of the hill of Old Jaffa (near the Hammam), this restaurant offers wonderful views, and fish and meat dishes all done with a special touch. Among the appetizers you'll find kosher "shrimp" in sesame, and salmon pâté. Excellent fresh fish that can be ordered in a number of different ways is a major attraction here, but the Shirat Hayam baked duck is also quite famous. Most main courses come with a big meze of 14 salads and side dishes. There is a large selection of interesting desserts and kosher ice creams. For those who are exploring Jaffa and need a glatt kosher choice, this is one of the few available.

33 Hatzorfim St. © 03/681-3271. Reservations recommended. Main courses NIS 80–NIS 100 ($20–$25/£10–£13). MC, V. Sun–Thurs noon–midnight; Sat 1½ hr. after Shabbat–midnight. Closed Fri. Bus: 10 to Jaffa Clock Tower.

### INEXPENSIVE

**Aladin** MIDDLE EASTERN   The food here is average, but you couldn't ask for a more wonderful setting in which to dine: a 600-year-old building with covered terraces overlooking the sea and a spectacular view of the Tel Aviv coastline. The building's interior (at one point in its long history a Turkish bath) is decorated with exotic metalwork. This is the place to order a selection of Middle Eastern salads with pita bread, or have a slow unhurried meal of grilled fish or meat while watching the sunset. The atmosphere is informal and congenial and there's a good selection of wines, teas, and coffees.

5 Mifratz Shlomo St. © 03/682-6766. Reservations not accepted. Main courses NIS 44–NIS 90 ($11–$23/£5.50–£11). AE, MC, V. Daily 11am–1am.

**Dr. Shakshuka** ★ (Value) KOSHER NORTH AFRICAN   With its long, shared tables; great food and prices; happy customers; and helpful staff, this is one of the best ethnic restaurants in the country. *Shakshuka* is a pan-fried casserole of poached eggs and spicy tomato sauce; Dr. Shakshuka's many versions of this dish come from Libya and have been the best in Jaffa for two and a half generations. But there's much more here: Tripoli-style couscous with *mafrum* (potato stuffed with ground meat, served with stewed beef and vegetable soup); stuffed vegetables; kishke (North African–style intestine stuffed with meat and rice); grilled lamb patties; and fresh grilled or fried fish. Main courses come with a meze of fresh pita and eight Middle Eastern salads. Lemonade is the drink of choice; a la carte, the meze is NIS 15 ($3.75/£1.90).

4 Beit Eshel St. © 03/518-6560. Main courses NIS 32–NIS 44 ($8–$11/£4–£5.50). MC, V. Sun–Thurs 8am–midnight; Fri 8am–2pm; Sat after Shabbat.

**Said el Abu Lafia and Sons Pita Bakery** ★ (Value) (Kids) BAKERY   Near the clock tower, this bakery is a Tel Aviv institution and offers fresh-from-the-oven breads; delicious one-person Palestinian pita-bread pizzas; peasant-style cheese, potato, and vegetable *burekas;* and stuffed breads—any one of which is a meal in itself. Everything is takeout, sold across display cases open to the sidewalk. The parks and vista points of Old Jaffa across the street and up the hill are ideal for picnics. Don't confuse Abu Lafia's with neighboring imitations. Bring lots of napkins.

7 Yefet St. © 03/683-4958. Baked goods NIS 8–NIS 16 ($2–$4/£1–£2). Cash only. Mon–Sat 8am–10pm. Bus: 10 to clock tower.

## JABALYA BEACH

About 2.4km (1½ miles) south of Old Jaffa and the port area is Jabalya (in Hebrew sometimes "Givat Aliya") Beach. You need a car or a taxi to get to this out-of-the-way area. Tel Avivians in the know patronize the excellent seafood restaurants here, enjoying the unobstructed views of the sunset. Long neglected, this neighborhood has become a piece of prime residential real estate. There's a public beach with safe swimming, and changing rooms at the foot of the hill.

### MODERATE

**Hinawi Grill and Abu Nassar On The Hill Fish and Seafood Restaurant** ★ *Value*
MEAT/FISH    The venerable Abu Nassar Seafood Restaurant has now joined forces with the Hinawis, a family famous for procuring the best meats in Jaffa. Together, they hold forth in a large modern-glass pavilion with a thatch-roofed terrace for dining and taking in the view of the sea and sunset. Here you can be sure of fresh fish and tender, aged meats in good portions for a fair price. Early in the evening, you'll find both Israeli Arab and Jewish families enjoying everything on their plates. Later, the atmosphere is more leisurely. To start the meal there's a traditional meze of excellent Arabic salads at NIS 20 ($5/£2.50) per person for six selections, served with a basket of toasted garlic pita. As an appetizer, or as a larger main course, the fresh calamari stuffed with shrimp, pine nuts, and parsley in garlic and butter sauce is exquisitely rich and succulent. Grilled sea bass usually tops the list of fresh fish selections, all of which are served with french fries and vegetables. Grilled shrimp is also a popular choice. Simply grilled sirloin and filet mignon top a long list of fine meat choices. The location, overlooking Jabalya Beach, 2.4km (1½ miles) south of Old Jaffa, is in an interesting residential part of the city with restaurants only locals know of. Taxi is best to get there.

130 Kedem St., Donolo area, Jabalya (Givat Aliya) Beach, Jaffa. © 03/507-5539 or 506-7132. Reservations necessary Thurs–Sat. Main courses NIS 70–NIS 120 ($18–$30/£8.75–£15). AE, DC, MC, V. Daily noon–midnight.

## 5 What to See & Do

### THE TOP ATTRACTIONS
#### MUSEUMS

**Bet Hatfutzot/Diaspora Museum** ★★★ *Kids*    This extraordinary museum in Ramat Aviv was the brainchild of Dr. Nahum Goldmann, founder and first president of the World Jewish Congress. There's no other exhibit about Jewish communities throughout the world quite like this. In the huge, strikingly modern building are countless artful exhibits that chronicle the 2,500-year history of the Jewish Diaspora. The collection contains no objects from the past, but is rather a multimedia history lesson: Here is what happened to the Jewish people, and what they accomplished, between the time when they were driven from Israel and the time when they returned. Photographs, documents, replicas of artifacts, films, music, maps, and scale models vividly bring to life the communities, synagogues, households, and workshops of Jews living in dozens of countries. There is an introductory Chronosphere (slide projection

# Tel Aviv Attractions

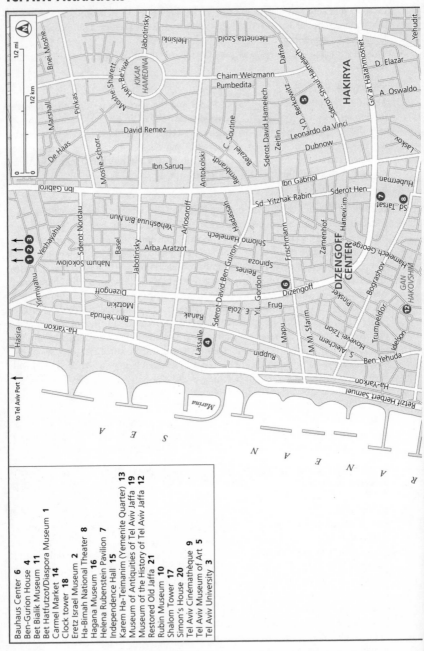

Bauhaus Center **6**
Ben-Gurion House **4**
Bet Bialik Museum **11**
Bet Hatfutzot/Diaspora Museum **1**
Carmel Market **14**
Clock tower **18**
Eretz Israel Museum **2**
Ha-Bimah National Theater **8**
Hagana Museum **16**
Helena Rubenstein Pavilion **7**
Independence Hall **15**
Karem Ha-Teimanim (Yemenite Quarter) **13**
Museum of Antiquities of Tel Aviv Jaffa **19**
Museum of the History of Tel Aviv Jaffa **12**
Restored Old Jaffa **21**
Rubin Museum **10**
Shalom Tower **17**
Simon's House **20**
Tel Aviv Cinémathèque **9**
Tel Aviv Museum of Art **5**
Tel Aviv University **3**

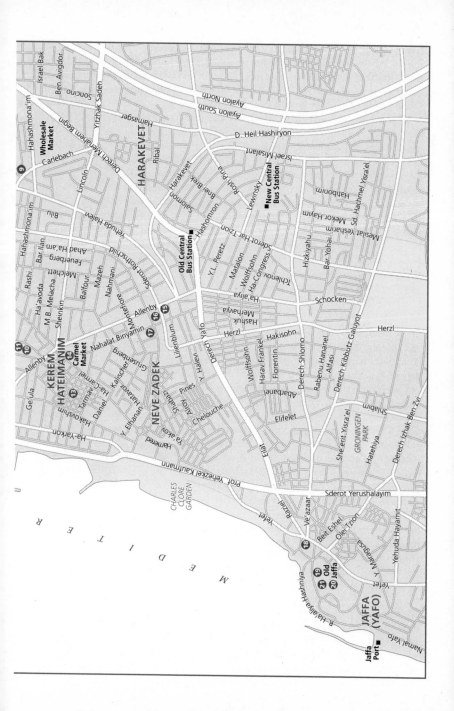

lecture) about the Diaspora for an extra fee (if you already know the basics of Jewish history, skip it). Among the highlights are a model of a 13th-century Jewish community with more than 100 tiny figurines clad in period dress and engaged in various occupations and fascinating scale models of famous synagogues, including one in China built in 1653. The ground floor hosts special, well-chosen visiting exhibitions.

Most rewarding, especially for those who have time for a return visit, is the archival film collection of dozens of Jewish communities throughout the world, and the extraordinary collection of Jewish music. If you're ancestor hunting, for a small fee you can get a computer printout on any of 3,000 Jewish communities, and look for information on record in the museum's genealogy research center. Jewish visitors can also record information about their families. (The research center can be time-consuming, as the office is understaffed, and the archives, which depend totally on material given to them by visitors, are by no means complete.) There's a dairy cafeteria on the premises, or you can lunch at any of the many university campus cafeterias. The small museum bookshop is a worthwhile stop. *Note:* At press time, the museum was operating on curtailed hours, but this may change as tourism returns.

Tel Aviv University campus, off Klausner St. inside the Matatia Gate (University Gate 2). ✆ 03/640-8000. www.bh.org.il. Admission including audio guide NIS 36 ($9/£4.50). AE, DC, MC, V. Discounts for students and seniors. Sun–Tues and Thurs 10am–4pm; Wed 10am–6pm. Check for hours during Jewish holidays; call ahead for special tour reservations. Bus: 7, 24, 25, 45, 49, 74, 86, or 274.

**Eretz Israel Museum** ★★★ *Kids*   This museum complex lies within a large enclosure that also encompasses **Tel Qasile** ★, an ancient mound in which 12 strata of past civilizations have been discovered. Selected artifacts from Tel Qasile are displayed in the museums, but especially fascinating is the archaeological site, where you can enter and explore a rebuilt typical house from the pre-Israelite Canaanite period.

Besides Tel Qasile, Eretz Israel has eight attractions. The **Kadman Numismatic Pavilion** has exhibits chronicling the history of coinage and monetary systems. The **Glass Pavilion** ★ has a fine, rare collection of glass vessels spanning 3,000 years of civilization, from 1500 B.C. to A.D. 1500, the largest collection of ancient glass in Israel. The **Ceramics Pavilion** shows how pottery was made, decorated, and used throughout the ages, and has a reconstructed dwelling from biblical times complete with pots. The small **Ethnography and Folklore Pavilion** holds a wealth of Jewish ethnic art and handicrafts—household and religious items, jewelry, and costumes, set in scenes from daily life. A special feature is a wall of antique Chanukah menorahs from all over the world. The **Nechushtan Pavilion** is devoted to mining and metallurgy as practiced during biblical times in the Timna Valley, Arava, and Sinai. The **"Man and His Work" Center** holds truly fascinating displays showing how men and women have earned their daily bread in Israel since ancient times. In the **Mosaic Square,** you can see the mosaic floor of a Samaritan synagogue (discovered *in situ* on the grounds of the museum) as well as mosaic floors brought from a Roman villa in Bet Guvrin, a synagogue from Tiberias, and a mosque from Ramla. For astronomy shows, the **Lasky Planetarium** also displays its collection of moon rocks. An especially pleasant addition to the complex is a park called **Landscapes of the Holy Land.** The museum shop is well stocked with reproductions, jewelry, crafts, and other great gift choices. A kosher cafeteria is open from 11am to 2pm. *Tip:* The Museum Gift Shop is one of the best places in Israel for interesting souvenirs and gifts.

2 Chaim Levanon St., Ramat Aviv. ✆ 03/641-5244. www.eretzmuseum.org.il. Admission NIS 38 ($9.50/£4.75). AE, MC, V. Discount for students and seniors. Sun–Wed 10am–4pm; Fri 10am–2pm. Bus: 24, 25, 27, 45, 74, 86, or 274.

## Frommer's Favorite Tel Aviv Experiences

**Restored Old Jaffa**   Wandering on a summer evening in this seaside Old City, and dining at one of the nearby restaurants overlooking the water.

**The Beaches**   My favorite is Gordon Beach, a quick dash from the many galleries in the Gordon Street area, handy to many dining spots.

**Jaffa Flea Market**   Magnet for some, too scuzzy for others, the market is now swamped with used jeans and Indian cotton blouses. You can still find objects from British Mandate and early state periods, plus reproductions of antique Moroccan menorahs. Bargain mercilessly.

**Helena Rubinstein Pavilion**   Here you'll find ever-changing exhibitions of works by Israeli and foreign artists. It's open the same hours as the Tel Aviv Museum of Art (see below), with which it is affiliated.

6 Tarsat Blvd. (**©** 03/528-7196. Admission NIS 45 ($11/£5.60); includes admission to Tel Aviv Museum of Art. Mon, Wed, and Sat 10am–4pm; Tues and Thurs 10am–10pm; Fri 10am–2pm and 7–10pm. Bus: 5, 18, or 25.

**Tel Aviv Museum of Art** ✪   This energetic museum houses temporary as well as permanent exhibitions consisting of paintings, drawings, prints, sculpture, and photography of both Israeli and international artists from the 16th century to the present, with the overwhelming emphasis on 20th century and current art. The collections of modern and Impressionist art, as well as 20th-century Russian painting, are especially good; the Jaglom Collection of Impressionist and post-Impressionist art includes works by Pissarro, Matisse, Modigliani, and Chagall. Check out the mural by Roy Lichtenstein in the entrance lobby. Gallery talks in English are offered Wednesday at 11:30am.

The Friday *Jerusalem Post* lists the museum's lively and well-attended films, concerts, and lectures. Call for information about the museum's shuttle bus, which sometimes gives an interesting historical and architectural tour of Tel Aviv, and is included in the price of your admission ticket. **Giacometti,** a stylish "modern Italian" restaurant, is set in the museum's sculpture garden and offers fixed-price meals starting at NIS 75 ($19/£9.40); it's open daily from noon until the last customer.

27 Shaul Ha-Melekh Blvd. (**©** 03/696-1297 or 696-1297 box office. www.tamuseum.com/museum. Admission NIS 45 ($11/£5.60); includes admission to Helena Rubinstein Pavilion. Discounts for students. Mon, Wed, and Sat 10am–4pm; Tues and Thurs 10am–10pm; Fri 10am–2pm and 7–10pm. Bus: 9, 18, 28, 70, 90, or 111.

## MORE ATTRACTIONS

**Bauhaus Center**   Tel Avivians now understand the rich Bauhaus/International Style heritage of their city, and this gallery/boutique is dedicated to the architectural design and decor of these movements. The center is famous for its tours of Tel Aviv's Bauhaus treasures. Call for tour information.

99 Dizengoff St. (**©** 03/522-0249. www.bauhaus-center.com. Free admission. Sun–Thurs 10am–7pm; Fri 10am–2pm.

**Ben-Gurion House** ✪   The house and personal items remain as they were when Paula and David Ben-Gurion lived here. Ben-Gurion's impressive personal library, comprising some 20,000 books, bears witness to his knowledge and scholarship. The building itself is an interesting example of Bauhaus/International design. Most of the signs in the museum are in Hebrew only, but this will not detract much from your visit. In the bedroom, note a blocked-in window that was used as a bomb shelter.

17 Ben-Gurion Blvd. ℂ **03/522-1010.** www.ben-gurion-house.org.il/eindex.html. Free admission. Sun and Tues–Thurs 8am–3pm; Mon 8am–5pm; Fri 8am–noon; 1st Sat each month 11am–2pm. Bus: 4 or 5.

**Bet Bialik Museum**    From 1925 to 1933, this was the home of the first great modern Hebrew poet, Haim Nachman Bialik. The 94 books he wrote, with translations in 28 languages, are here, as are articles, correspondence, paintings, photographs, and an archive of hundreds of his manuscripts. If you understand Hebrew or Yiddish, the guides can tell you many interesting stories about the famous writer; there is a brief English brochure on the house, though display descriptions are not yet in English. Despite the lack of English explanation, the decor and atmosphere of the house gives you a feel for the world of the cultured, European-oriented Tel Aviv community of the 1920s. A wonderful collection of paintings by Jewish artists from the pre–State of Israel era, filled with visions of the life and landscape of British Mandate Palestine, is an additional pleasure at this gem of a museum. Combine this stop with a visit to the neighboring Rubin Museum (see below).

22 Bialik St. ℂ **03/525-4530.** Free admission. Sun–Thurs 9am–4:30pm; Sat 11am–2pm. Closed Sat in Aug and Fri year-round. Bus: 4.

**Hagana Museum**    Established beside the home of Eliyahu Golomb, a former Hagana general, this is a fascinating place, well worth a visit if you're an Israeli history buff. The museum records the history of the Israeli military from the time of the farm-field watchmen at the beginning of the century down through the War of Independence. On the third floor, you see the various ways the Israelis hid arms inside farm machinery to escape British detection, and how they stealthily manufactured hand grenades and Sten guns in clandestine kibbutz workshops. There's one homemade grenade with the letters USA stamped on it, so that had a Hagana soldier been caught with the bomb, the British wouldn't have suspected that it had been made locally. But the joke here was that "USA" are the first letters of three Yiddish words meaning "our piece of work."

  Almost all of the explanatory captions in this four-story museum are in Hebrew, but never fear—the museum has a group of English-speaking interpreters.

23 Rothschild Blvd. ℂ **03/560-8624.** Admission NIS 10 ($2.50/£1.25). Sun–Thurs 8am–4pm. Bus: 4 or 5.

**Independence Hall**    Meir Dizengoff, the first mayor of Tel Aviv, lived here, and it was in this historic house that the independence of Israel was declared on May 14, 1948. Exhibits here detail Israel's declaration of independence.

16 Rothschild Blvd. ℂ **03/517-3942.** Admission NIS 12 ($3/£1.50). Sun–Thurs 9am–2pm.

**Museum of Antiquities of Tel Aviv Jaffa (Jaffa Museum)**    This beautiful building was actually a Turkish administrative and detention center during the 19th century. Displays in the five halls are of objects excavated from 30 sites within the city, covering a time span beginning in the 5th millennium B.C. and ending with the Arab period.

10 Mifratz Shlomo St. ℂ **03/682-5375.** Admission NIS 15 ($3.75/£1.90); half-price for seniors, students, and children. Sun–Thurs 9am–1pm. To get here, at the top of the hill in Old Jaffa, walk from Kikar downhill on Mifratz Shlomo St. The museum will be on your right.

**Museum of the History of Tel Aviv Jaffa**    This museum, housed in Tel Aviv's former City Hall, uses photographs, models, a film (in English), and documents to tell the story of the city's founding and early history.

27 Bialik St. ℂ **03/517-3052.** Free admission. Sun–Thurs 9am–2pm. Bus: 4.

**Rubin Museum (Reuven House)**   Israel's great painter, Reuven Rubin (1893–1974), captured on canvas the spirit and landscape of Mandate Palestine. Though the holy cities of Jerusalem and Safed were among his favorite subjects, he also painted scenes of sun-dappled Jaffa and Tel Aviv, his home city. There a documentary film about Rubin's life and work, and the Rubin Museum hosts temporary exhibits, usually of modern Israeli artists. Combine this with a stop at the 1920s period house of Israel's first great Hebrew writer, Haim Nachman Bialik (see above).

14 Bialik St. (**C** **03/525-5961**. Admission NIS 20 ($5/£2.50), free for children. Mon and Wed–Thurs 10am–3pm; Tues 10am–10pm; Sat 11am–2pm. Closed Sat July–Aug.

**Safari Park (Zoological Center)** ★ *Kids*   This park is a wide-open plain (100 hectares/247 acres) where African animals roam free. So successful has the park been with its breeding herds of hippos, elephants, giraffes, and other animals, that it exports creatures all over the world. For obvious reasons, visitors must remain in closed vehicles while traversing the 8km (5-mile) trail, but there is a shorter walking trail as well. You will have the opportunity to see lions, elephants, rhinos, giraffes, gazelles, impalas, zebra, ostriches, storks, and much more. There is also a monkey enclosure, as well as an aviary and reptile area. Add a star to the current rating if you have children with you, or if you've never seen this kind of park. The lion area closes an hour before the rest of the park. Across the street is the Ramat Gan National Park (free admission), with more animals.

Ramat Gan. (**C** **03/631-3531**. Admission NIS 48 ($12/£6); additional charge for Safari Bus if you don't have a car. Sat–Thurs and holidays 9am–4pm Sept–June; until 5pm July–Aug; Fri 9am–1pm year-round. Visitors may remain in the park for 1 hr. after the last entrance hour. Closed only on Holocaust Memorial Day, Israel Memorial Day, Yom Kippur Eve, and Yom Kippur. Bus: 30 (Yona Ha-Navi St.), 35 (Central Bus Station), or 67 (Central Ramat Gan).

**Simon's House**   Christian tradition places the house of Simon the Tanner (venerated by Christian pilgrims for centuries) next to the lighthouse of the port, at the site of a small mosque. Acts 10 recalls Saint Peter's visit to Simon's house in "Joppa."

8 Shimon Ha-Burski St. (**C** **03/683-6792**. Free admission. Daily 8–11:45am and 2–4pm; until 6:30pm in summer. To get here, walk south through Kikar Kedumim, the main square of restored Old Jaffa. At the end of the square, turn right to the steps.

**Tel Aviv University**   The university's handsome, multifaceted campus has contemporary architecture and Mediterranean subtropical landscaping reminiscent of a branch of the California State University system. More than 35 buildings house the widest spectrum of studies of any university in Israel, and its enrollment of 18,000 students is the largest. Courses for English-speaking students are given here. You can combine a stroll around the campus with a visit to Bet Hatfutzot (see above), which is on the university's grounds.

Ramat Aviv. Bus: 24 or 25. Get off at gate 2.

## MONUMENTS

At the center of the plaza suspended above the roadway in Dizengoff Square is a huge sculpture-fountain by Yaacov Agam named *Water and Fire.* Five large concentric metal rings are painted so that when the rings turn, the painted surfaces produce differing effects of light and color. At the same time (when everything is functioning), jets of water shoot upward from the rings, and at the top of the sculpture, in the midst of the shooting water, rises a jet of flame. Music accompanies the whole display in a show that lasts for 20 minutes. Agam's computerized sculpture begins to play at the beginning of each hour starting at 11am and continuing until 10pm. If you arrive a few minutes early, you may be able to get a seat on one of the benches surrounding the sculpture.

To the south, along Rothschild Boulevard, in the center of the island at Nahalat Benyamin Street, is the impressive **Founder's Monument,** depicting the three phases of Tel Aviv's history. The bottom shows the workers of 1909 digging and planting, while snakes and animals form a lower border. The middle level shows the Herzlia Gymnasium, in Levantine Fantasy style (the building was demolished in 1959); the uppermost section is modern Tel Aviv, showing the Ha-Bimah Theater, Bialik's home, and many ultramodern Tel Aviv landmarks.

## ESPECIALLY FOR KIDS

The **Eretz Israel Museum** (p. 272) is great for kids: It has demonstrations of traditional crafts, a planetarium, a reconstructed Canaanite period house, and a nature exhibit. The **Bet Hatfutzot/Diaspora Museum** (p. 269) is a real learning experience for all ages. Many exhibits are especially geared to the young.

**Safari Park** (p. 275) is especially good for older children, who will enjoy watching wild animals of all kinds roam free.

## JAFFA ★★★

Now an integrated component in the sprawling Tel Aviv–Jaffa complex, Jaffa has a long and colorful history, dating from biblical times. This is the port, the Bible tells us, where King Solomon's ally, the Phoenician king Hiram of Tyre, landed cedars of Lebanon for the construction of Solomon's Temple; from here Jonah embarked for his fabulous adventure with the whale. The Greeks were here too, and they fostered the legend that a poor maiden named Andromeda, chained to a rock and on the verge of being sacrificed to a sea monster, was rescued by Perseus on his winged white horse. Today, visitors are shown this rock, a tourist attraction since ancient times.

The Crusaders also came this way. Richard the Lion-Hearted built a citadel here that was promptly snatched away by Saladin's brother, who slaughtered 20,000 Christians in the process. Napoleon passed through 600 years or so later; a few Jewish settlers came in the 1890s; and Allenby routed the Turks from the port in 1917.

One Jewish legend has it that all the sunken treasure in the world flows toward Jaffa, and that in King Solomon's day the sea offered a rich bounty, accounting for the king's wealth. According to the legend, since Solomon's time, the treasure has once again been accumulating—to be distributed by the Messiah on the Day of the Coming "to each man according to his merits."

Today, Jaffa still shows traces of its romantic and mysterious past. The city is built into a kind of amphitheater on the side of a hill. The old section of the city has become the starlit patio of Tel Aviv, providing an exceptional view, fine restaurants, and the most beautifully restored Old City in Israel. The flea market district, near the clock tower, is ramshackle but has real personality.

The streets from Tel Aviv run into Jaffa's Jerusalem Avenue and Tarshish Street where a great stone tower and the Turkish mosque, Mahmudiye (1812), reminds you of the city's continuing Arab community.

## A STROLL AROUND OLD JAFFA

The reclamation of Old Jaffa—only a short time ago a slumlike area of war ruins and crumbling Turkish palaces—has proven to be one of the most imaginative of such projects in all Israel. Atop the hill and running down in a maze of descending streets to the sea are artists' studios and galleries, outdoor cafes, fairly expensive restaurants, and gift shops, all artfully arranged among the reconstructed ruins. Climb to the top of the hill and wander through the lanes (named for the Hebrew signs of the zodiac). At the summit is **Kikar Kedumim,** the central plaza, and at one side of it, the **Franciscan Monastery of Saint Peter,** which was built above a medieval citadel. You can visit the church for prayers on Sunday. Opposite the church is an excavation area, surrounded by a fence, where you can inspect remnants of a **3rd-century-B.C. catacomb.** Facing the catacomb is a hilltop garden, **Gan Ha-Pisgah,** atop which, surrounded by trees, is a white monument depicting scenes from the Bible: the conquest of Jericho, the near-sacrifice of Isaac, and Jacob's dream.

Past the church gardens, on the sea side of the hill, is a small and charming cafe. Wander through the elaborately decorated dome-roofed room and out onto the deck, for a superb all-encompassing view of Tel Aviv and the Mediterranean coastline. Incidentally, **Andromeda's Rock** is traditionally the most prominent of those blackened stones jutting up from the floor of the bay. The view is brilliant in the morning sunlight. At night, it takes on more of a fairy-tale aura.

Returning to Kikar Kedumim, near the Muscat Restaurant, you enter the restored maze of Old Jaffa's market streets, filled with interesting antiques and souvenir shops to explore. For those interested in art and interior design, the **Ilana Goor Museum,** the beautifully renovated mansion of one of Israel's successful sculptors, is a delightful stop. Over the centuries this building has been put to many uses, including a long stint as a caravansary for 19th-century Jewish pilgrims. Now each room is like a page out of *Architectural Digest,* filled with Ilana Goor's own works, and her private collection of art. There's a rooftop cafe with good food and sweeping views as well as a small one-of-a-kind museum shop. The admission fee is rather exorbitant for what is essentially a gallery, but the building is interesting on many levels. It's open Monday to Thursday and Saturday from 10am to 10pm and Friday 10am to 4pm; admission is NIS 28 ($7/£3.50).

A short (.5km/¼-mile) stroll south of Old Jaffa brings you to the disused port of **Jaffa Harbor,** now a fenced-in area of dockside restaurants.

## 6 Organized Tours & Special Events

**ORGANIZED TOURS** The **Association for Tourism of Tel Aviv–Jaffa** leads a free walking tour of Old Jaffa starting at the clock tower on Yefet Street (bus no. 10 from Tel Aviv) on Wednesday mornings at 9:30am. Call the **Tel Aviv Tourist Information Office** (© 03/516-6188) for current information. The association also arranges (for a fee) excellent English-language guided tours of Neve Tzedek and of the Bauhaus areas of the city; advance booking is required. The new **Jaffa Visitor Center** (© 03/682-6796) in Kikar Kedumim, right at the center of the restored section of Old Jaffa, gives out free detailed maps of Old Jaffa accompanied by historical information that makes it easy to do a self-guided tour of the area. The Jaffa Visitor Center also rents a **self-guided audio tour** for NIS 45 ($11/£5.60). The helpful center is open Sunday to Thursday from 9am to 6pm. The **Israel Tourist Information Office** at 7 Mendele St. (© 03/520-7600) gives out free municipal maps with four **"Orange" self-guided walking tour routes** ✹✹✹ of Tel Aviv, marked on the map. Signs along the routes mark the way as you go. Some of the routes are too long to undertake on a sweltering summer day, but if you break them up into smaller units, they are a good basic itinerary of what to see in different neighborhoods. The **Bauhaus Center** (p. 273) offers architecture-oriented tours of Tel Aviv at 11am on Saturday—you must call ahead for reservations and tour details.

Another good source of guided tours is the **Society for the Protection of Nature in Israel (SPNI),** 85 Nahalat Binyamin St. (© **03/566-0960;** teleteva@spni.org.il). Call © **03/638-8625** for information on the society's English-language walking tours in the Tel Aviv area. These are highly recommended group tours that individuals can join; day tours cost NIS 80 to NIS 300 ($20–$75/£10–£38) per person; there are longer tours and occasionally free Saturday walking tours. Go to the American Friends of SPNI website (www.aspni.org) and reserve as far in advance as possible. Most tours are given in Hebrew, but in many cases, the guide can give you a brief English translation.

**Boat Tours** from Jaffa Port to the Tel Aviv Marina and back run on Saturday and cost NIS 24 ($6/£3). Call **Kef** (© **03/682-9070**) or **Sababa** (© **03/681-6739**) in Jaffa Port for schedules and reservations.

**SPECIAL/FREE EVENTS**    Many summer evenings after 8pm there is free samba dancing on the Herbert Samuel Esplanade, beside the beach in South Tel Aviv. There is also music and dancing at other points along the beach on evenings throughout the week. Check in person with the Israel Tourist Information Office, 7 Mendele St. (© **03/520-7600**), for current information.

There are free evening outdoor concerts in Yarkon Park and in Old Jaffa during the summer. Check the newspapers or the Israel Tourist Office for dates.

Nahalat Benyamin Pedestrian Mall has an outdoor craft bazaar and street performers every Tuesday and Friday from 10am to 5pm. Take bus no. 4.

## 7 Outdoor Pursuits & Sports

**BEACHES**    Tel Aviv's seashore is within walking distance of Dizengoff Square. A promenade runs the entire length of the beach. Most beaches have free showers and facilities for changing. The cleanest beaches are behind the Dan and Sheraton hotels (Frishman to Gordon sts.) and at the Hilton hotel.

In a slightly more remote location, the **Bat Yam Beach,** 4.8km (3 miles) south of Jaffa, is wide and sandy, and gets crowded only on hot Saturdays in summer; the sea here is usually a bit cleaner than in downtown Tel Aviv. From Ben-Yehuda Street, you can take bus no. 10, which begins its run at City Hall. June to September there is an admission fee of NIS 16 ($4/£2).

*A word of caution:* Swimming at Israeli beaches can be dangerous. The problem is a totally unpredictable undertow that can be hazardous even for a strong swimmer. It's safe, however, to swim at beaches where guards are stationed. Pay attention to the safety symbols along the beaches in the form of small flags. The color of the flag tells the story: Black means absolutely no swimming in the area; red warns you to be especially cautious; and white indicates that the water's fine. Tel Aviv's city beaches are protected in many places by a system of breakwaters and are the safest in the area.

**CYCLING**    Tel Aviv is relatively flat and, in that respect, more bicycle-friendly than the mountainous cities of Jerusalem and Haifa. Drivers, however, are not bicycle-friendly. Serious cyclers should check ahead with the **Israeli Cycling Federation,** 6 Shitrit St., Tel Aviv (© **03/649-0459;** www.ofanaim.org.il). For bike rentals, try **Shuli and Mike's Bikes,** 280 Dizengoff St. (© **03/544-2292**); and **O-Fun,** 245 Dizengoff St. (© **03/544-2292**); rates run approximately NIS 45 ($11/£5.60) per day from the time you rent until the day's closing time for the shop.

**JOGGING**   The long beachfront promenade, running several miles from the northern end of Jaffa to the Hilton hotel, provides an excellent stretch for urban jogging, without the inconvenience of cross streets and traffic lights. It's busy, which adds an element of safety, and you can stop for a dip in the sea or cool off at the public showers that dot the beaches at various intervals. There is a jogging track at **Sportek** on Rokach Boulevard (© **03/699-0307**), at the northern entrance of Tel Aviv. Admission to the track is free.

**BOATS**   Small motorboats, pedal boats, and rowboats are available to rent by the hour on the lake at **Yarkon Park,** near Yehoshua Gardens (© **03/642-0541**) at the northern end of the city, daily from 9am to 6pm. Motorboats are NIS 100 ($25/£13) per half-hour; pedal and rowboats are NIS 65 ($16/£8.10) per full hour. **Danit Tours** (© **052/340-0128**) does party and group boat tours from the Tel Aviv Marina. Call for information and see if you can join a group ride into the sea.

**SWIMMING**   Aviv Beach, midway between Mogravi Square and Jaffa, is designated for surfboarding, kayaking, wind sailing and kite boarding. Contact **Surf Point** (© **03/517-0099;** www.surf-point.co.il) for equipment rental and lessons. Surfboard rental starts at NIS 120 ($30/£15); the website is mostly in Hebrew.

## 8 Shopping

### SHOPPING STREETS & MALLS

Allenby Street, a typical bustling Tel Avivian street, is full of furniture stores, lower-price clothing shops, bakeries, bookstores, and kiosks. The **Opera Tower** is an upscale mall, right where Allenby Street meets the sea and a short walk from the Ha-Yarkon Street hotel district (it takes its name from the municipal opera house that was located near here during British Mandate times). Well stocked with cafes, galleries, and shops of interest to visitors, the mall is developing into something of a center for fashionable clothing, and is the centerpiece for the revival of a neighborhood, once an architectural and social dazzle in the 1930s and 1940s. It's open standard business hours, with some cafes remaining open later in the evening.

Two blocks south of Dizengoff Square, toward King George Street, you'll find the enormous indoor **Dizengoff Center Shopping Mall,** located on the lower floors of a megaoffice complex. This modern, jampacked, multilevel shopping center is filled with houseware shops, a large array of clothing shops and boutiques, and specialty shops. You'll find branches of American stores popular with teenagers here. There are many fast-food counters, including a Pizza Hut. It is open Sunday to Thursday from 9:30am to 9pm and Friday from 9:30am to 2pm. You can take a pleasant dip in the Mediterranean at one of the city's best beaches when you finish making your rounds.

### SHOPPING A TO Z
#### ART

Tel Aviv's Gordon Street district is the center for the sale of serious art in Israel. Gordon Street and the cross streets, from Ha-Yarkon to Dizengoff streets, are almost wall-to-wall galleries and unusual shops. The shady, once-grand Rothschild Boulevard, with its superb restaurants, is also becoming a bit of an art district. Most galleries are open Sunday to Thursday from 10am to 1pm and 5 to 8pm.

Heading the list of places to check out is the new **Sotheby's Auction Gallery,** 46 Rothschild Blvd. (© **03/560-1666;** fax 03/560-8111), with exhibitions of important

Israeli and international art as well as Judaica. The **Stern Gallery,** 30 Gordon St. (℃ **03/524-6303**), specializes in Israeli and foreign Jewish artists of international renown, ranging from Kadishman, Lea Nickel, and Reuvin Rubin to works by Marc Chagall. They also have special exhibitions of younger artists and occasional block-busters such as Four Generations of Pisarros. Other notable galleries include the **Givon Gallery** (contemporary works), 35 Gordon St. (℃ **03/522-5427**); the Mabat Gallery, 37 Gordon St. (℃ **03/532-6863**), with the newest art; **Noga Gallery of Contemporary Art,** 60 Ahad Ha'am St. (℃ **03/566-0123**), contemporary, with many special exhibits; and the contemporary **Julie M.,** 10 Bezalel Yefe St., corner of Ahad Ha'am St. (℃ **03/560-7005**). In Old Jaffa, look for the **Horace Richter Gallery,** 24 Simhat Mazal Arie St. (℃ **03/682-5842**), with beautifully mounted, carefully chosen exhibitions.

## BOOKSTORES
There are many Steimatzky branches in Tel Aviv, including those at 107 Allenby Rd. (℃ **03/566-4973**), 109 Dizengoff St. (℃ **03/523-3415**), and 4 Tarsat Ave., near Ha-Bimah Theater (℃ **03/528-0806**). For antiquarian, rare, and used books, try **Pollack's,** 36 and 42 King George St. (℃ **03/523-8613**), with its sidewalk-browsing terrace and unusual selection inside; it's open Sunday to Friday from 9am to 1:30pm and Tuesday only from 4 to 7pm. If you're desperate for English reading material, especially fiction, **Halper's Quality Used Books,** 87 Allenby St. (℃ **03/629-9710**), is the mother lode, with at least a quarter of a mile of packed bookshelves winding through its premises.

## CRAFTS
**Almaz Ethiopian Crafts** *Finds*    On sale here are embroidered cloth amulets and hangings; clothing touched with traditional Ethiopian designs; *kipot* (yarmulkes), colorful mezuzzot, and other Judaica items; and traditional ceramics, all made by recent Jewish immigrants from Ethiopia. This store is the main outlet for a project that preserves the craft traditions of Ethiopian women, and helps build self-confidence and incomes of new immigrant families. The staff can advise on other places where you can find special Ethiopian crafts. The store is open Sunday to Thursday 10am to 7pm. 71 Ibn Givrol St., Gan Ha'Ir Shopping Center, lower level. ℃ **03/539-0353.**

**Chomer Tov Ceramic Co-op**    You'll find decorative and functional items in this lively contemporary ceramics gallery showing the work of 14 artists. It's in the heart of quaint, eccentric Neve Tzedek, not far from the Suzanne Dallal Dance Center. It's open Sunday to Thursday from 10am to 7pm and Friday from 10am to 2pm. 27 Shabazzi St. ℃ **03/516-6229.**

**Contemporary Crafts Market**    This outdoor craft market, held every Tuesday and Friday, is filled with ceramics, jewelry, Hands of Fatima, menorahs, and interesting gift items. This is one of the best weekly craft markets I've encountered, and prices are both fair and affordable. At the edge of the market, you'll often find a group of Druze women from the Galilee making delicious, freshly baked Druze-style bread. Nahlat Binyamin Pedestrian Mall.

**Dervish**    Two legendary world-traveling sisters from South Africa founded this craft shop filled with a constantly changing array of one-of-a-kind folk and tribal craft items the owners personally collect on their expeditions. Their eye for beautiful objects is excellent, and their bargaining abilities must be extraordinary. You never know what the stock will be like. There are special receptions with delightful snacks whenever a new caravan load of goods comes in; ask if any of these gatherings will be coming up and if you can have an invitation. The receptions are a good opportunity to buy collector items and to mingle with Israelis who share an interest in ethnic art and exotic travels. The shop makes museum-quality reproductions of ethnic jewelry and serves free exotic coffee and Yemenite tea while you browse. Prices range from under NIS 30 ($7.50/£3.75) to more than NIS 4,000 ($1,000/£500). It's open Sunday to Thursday from 9am to 1pm and 4 to 7pm; call about Friday hours. 21 Dov Hoz St., Tel Aviv (Dov Hoz St. runs off the section of Gordon St. that's btw. Ben-Yehuda and Dizengoff sts.). (C) 03/524-8852.

**Shlush Shloshim Ceramics Co-op**    Eleven women artists sell their work here at studio prices. The co-op is in Neve Tzedek, in an interesting neighborhood of eccentric boutiques and shops. It's open Sunday to Thursday from 10am to 7pm; Friday 10am to 3pm; and Saturday 11am to 6pm. 30 Shlush (Chelouche) St., Neve Tzedek. (C) 03/510-6067.

## DEPARTMENT STORES
**Hamashbir Lazarchan**    This is Israel's department store chain—serviceable, but not top-drawer or exciting. It's a good place to pick up basics you might not have brought with you. Open Sunday to Thursday from 10am to 9pm, Friday until 2pm. Dizengoff Center, Dizengoff and King George sts. (C) 03/528-5136.

## FASHION
North Tel Aviv is the country's center for quality women's clothing and custom-designed fashion. Considering that style was almost considered sinful in the early Zionist movement, there has been a revolution in Israeli attitudes, especially in the past few years. **Kikar Ha Medina** in the northern part of Tel Aviv is a large, sometimes poorly kept square, but it's the heart of the city's high-rent neighborhood, and the retail shops around the square are filled with expensive international chains, but also top-of-the-line Israeli stores. The northern stretch of Dizengoff Street, starting around Gordon Street, is wall-to-wall high-style clothing shops. Among the many and varied places to explore elsewhere in the northern part of town are **Gideon Oberson's** stylish designer showroom at 36 Gordon St. ((C) 03/524-3822)—Oberson has moved from bathing suits to custom fashion; **Dorin Frankfurt,** 40 Ben-Gurion St., near 164 Dizengoff ((C) 03/527-0379; www.dorinF.com), an acclaimed Israeli whose designs tend toward natural textiles and easy, elegant lines; and **Gottex** with an outlet shop at 148 Dizengoff. A stroll through the upper reaches of Dizengoff and Ben-Yehuda streets will reveal many additional shops and designer showrooms. **Naama Bezalel,** 212 Dizengoff St. ((C) 03/523-2964), is famous for touches of nostalgia, heavy on the 1950s and 1960s.

The Sheinkin Street area and the Neve Tzedek neighborhood are filled with little personal places and boutiques showing the lines of younger local Israeli designers—the best in Israeli fashion is sometimes elegant, sometimes brash, often slightly insane, and made with an eye to hot, hot weather. *Tip:* Friday mornings there is often a **young designer's bazaar** on the lower level of the Dizengoff Center Shopping Mall. Check with Dizengoff Center Information ((C) 03/621-2400) to see if it's on.

## JEWELRY & JUDAICA
### Yemenite Jewelry & Judaica
**Ben Zion David Yemenite Silver Art**    You can see Yemenite-style silver jewelry, with its intricate filigree patterns, at shops throughout Israel; at Ben Zion David's workshop and showroom, in the heart of the beautifully restored Old Jaffa bazaar, you'll find some of the best examples of craftsmanship and design in this tradition

created by more than 1,000 years of Yemenite Jewish silversmiths. The many branches of the David family have been skilled silver workers for generations; perhaps because of the family's long reputation for quality and fairness, prices here are quite reasonable, despite the upscale tourist location. There's an enormous selection of earrings, bracelets, rings, and necklaces, as well as delicate mezuzzot, candlesticks, and Chanukah dreidels—all ornamented with fine filigree designs. The showroom is generally open Sunday to Thursday from noon until late in the evening, Friday from 11am to 3pm, and on Saturday evenings after Shabbat. Credit cards are accepted. 3 Mazal Dagim St. Old Jaffa. ℭ 03/683-5336.

## MARKETS

**Carmel Market (Shuk Ha-Carmel)**    At the six-sided intersection of Allenby, Nahalat Binyamin, King George, and Sheinkin streets, you enter this gigantic, throbbing, open-air food-plus-everything-else market where vendors hawk everything from pistachios and guavas to sun hats and memorial candles on open tables lining the many shopping streets. Many vendors have their own songs, which tell you all about the price and quality of what is being sold. Sometimes one vendor sings against another in a competitive duet. The market runs into side streets, large and small, one side favoring dry goods and the other dried beans, fruit, nuts, and spices in all colors and fragrances, sold from sacks. The market is open Sunday to Thursday from 8am until dark and on Friday from 8am to 2pm.

**Jaffa Flea Market (Shuk Ha Pishpishim)** ⭐    Tradition has it that you can get the best buys here early Sunday morning. If you are the first customer on the first day of the week, the seller hopes a quick sale will bring him luck through the week. You can weave your way through a mixed array of treasures and junk. Merchandise varies, but copper, brass, old Persian tiles, and jewelry are always to be found, as well as Judaica items, old family-photo albums, and tons of used jeans and mildewed clothing from India. Bargaining is the order of the day; feel free to indulge in lengthy haggling. Language may be a problem, but you can get a lot understood with your hands. It's great fun even if you don't buy anything. Combine the market with an exploration of Old Jaffa and a leisurely, interesting lunch.

The flea market is open Sunday to Thursday from 10am to 6pm and on Friday from 10am to 2pm. Take bus no. 10 from Ben-Yehuda Street in Tel Aviv. East of the clock tower at foot of Old Jaffa.

**Nahalat Binyamin Arts and Crafts Market** ⭐    This large outdoor fair takes over the streets of the Nahalat Binyamin Pedestrian Mall (btw. Allenby St. and the Carmel Market), Tuesday and Friday, often with street performers and Druze ladies making freshly baked, delicious Druze bread in various corners. The crafts are uneven, but prices are fair, and there's always interesting Judaica and jewelry that make good gifts and keepsakes. Nahalat Binyamin is lined with good eateries (some of the best in the city) in all price ranges, as well as some amazing 1920s Tel Aviv architecture—all of which makes it more than just another street fair. One of Tel Aviv's real pleasures. It's open Tuesday and Friday from 10am to 5pm. Magen David Sq. (Allenby St., across from start of King George St., at the edge of the Carmel Market). Bus: 4.

**Tel Aviv Port Antiques Fair and Organic Market**    This new but growing antiques fair in the enormously popular Tel Aviv Port is filled with books, old records, furniture, toys, and all sorts of treasures. It's open Friday from 10am to 8pm. The interesting organic foods market (where you can buy anything from whole-grain cookies and cakes to a fabulous mango to store in your hotel room for Shabbat) is open Friday from 10am to 6pm. Tel Aviv Port, at northern edge of Tel Aviv. Bus: 4 or 5; sherut: 4 (which runs on Sat).

## MUSEUM SHOPS

**Eretz Israel Museum Shop** ⭐  Without a doubt the best museum shop in the country, with well-chosen Judaica, crafts, toys, and children's books, jewelry, replicas, and gift ideas. It's open Sunday to Thursday 10am to 6pm and Friday 10am to 2pm. Eretz Israel Museum, 2 Haim Levanon St., Ramat Aviv, Tel Aviv. ✆ 03/641-5244.

## 9 Tel Aviv & Jaffa After Dark

No matter what season, Tel Aviv throbs with activity after sundown. Strollers are out on the boulevards, people-watchers crowd the cafes, clubs and discos throb and crash, and restaurants are packed.

The most popular form of nighttime entertainment in Tel Aviv is to stroll around and people-watch. Two areas that are traditionally devoted to this pastime are Dizengoff Street and the Herbert Samuel Esplanade–Ha-Tayelet—which runs along the sandy beach. Outdoor cafe life on Dizengoff Street starts near Dizengoff Square and works northward. The scene is pretty packed most nights, but its real crescendo is reached on Saturday nights after the cinemas let out. Pick out a seat at one of the sidewalk cafes and order a coffee, or, if it's hot, cool off with a coffee ice-cream soda (one of the most popular Israeli drinks) or tasty apple cider.

To find out what's going on in the city, buy the *Jerusalem Post* Friday-morning edition, which contains the weekend magazine that lists everything there is to do and see and an additional, informative "In Tel Aviv" section. Also pick up *Events in the Tel Aviv Region* and other free tourist publications from the travel desk of your hotel (or check out the Sheraton's well-stocked information shelves just to the left of the main entrance).

In addition to the listings below, **Hayarkon Park** (✆ 03/642-2828), at the northern edge of Tel Aviv, hosts large outdoor concerts; there are also concerts in Hayarkon Park's Wohl Amphitheater (✆ 03/521-8210).

## THE PERFORMING ARTS

While Jerusalem has many cultural offerings, Tel Aviv is the true cultural center of Israel. Mann Auditorium is the home of the Israel Philharmonic, and there are many other musical groups. The Israel Ballet is also centered in Tel Aviv. Major ticket outlets are **Le'an,** 101 Dizengoff St. (✆ 03/524-7373); **Hadran,** 90 Ibn Givrol St. (✆ 03/527-9955); and **Castel,** 153 Ibn Givrol St. (✆ 03/604-4725).

## CONCERTS, OPERA & DANCE

**Bet Lessin**  This theater hosts contemporary plays in Hebrew, jazz groups, and contemporary and folk musicians. If your Hebrew is snappy, there are also stand-up comedy nights. 101 Dizengoff St. ✆ 03/725-5333.

**Israel Philharmonic Orchestra**  The **Mann Auditorium,** which can seat 3,000 concertgoers, is the home of this prestigious orchestra, founded in 1936 by Bronislaw Huberman. Zubin Mehta is music director. Even now that its magnificent concert hall has been built, the orchestra continues to give performances in other towns, carrying on a tradition that began during the War of Independence, when it played just behind the lines for the troops near Jerusalem and Beersheva. The orchestra is on vacation during August, September, and October until after the Jewish holidays. Huberman St. ✆ 1-700/703-703. www.ipo.co.il.

**New Israeli Opera**     Housed in the architecturally interesting and controversial **Golda Meir/Tel Aviv Center for the Performing Arts,** the New Israeli Opera is the country's newest cultural gem, performing a lively program of classic and modern opera. The company draws heavily on the talent of immigrants from the former Soviet Union. The Tel Aviv Center for the Performing Arts hosts classical, jazz, and popular concerts. 19 Shaul Ha Melekh St. Box office for all events ✆ 03/692-7777. www.israel-opera.co.il. Tickets NIS 120–NIS 300 ($30–$75/£15–£38).

**Suzanne Dellal Center for Dance and Theater**     This complex, built in post-modern style, is the venue for visiting dance groups as well as for Israel's contemporary Bat Sheva Dance Company and the Inbal Dance Theater, which often draws upon Israel's ethnic traditions for its style. The Dellal Center hosts interesting modern and experimental productions, as well as a wide range of concerts and music events, and has become the heart of the effort to revive and restore the old, potentially quaint Neve Tzedek neighborhood of Tel Aviv. Bus nos. 10 and 25 pass nearby. 6 Yehieli St. www.suzannedellal.org.il. Box office ✆ 03/510-5656.

**Tel Aviv Museum of Art/Recanati Hall**     The museum hosts a wide range of afternoon and evening events, including music recitals, performances of chamber orchestras and ensembles, visiting choirs, theater and dance performances, and film screenings. There is a cafe on the premises. Box office: 27 Shaul Ha-Melekh Blvd. ✆ 03/607-7020.

**Tzavta**     This club specializes in Israeli music, both folk and popular as well as theater productions. 30 Ibn Givrol St. ✆ 03/695-0156.

## THEATER

**Ha-Bimah National Theater**     Founded in Moscow in 1918 by the renowned Stanislavsky and moved to British Mandate Palestine in 1928, the Ha-Bimah National Theater is the nation's first and best-known repertory theater. While performances are in Hebrew, some productions offer simultaneous translations. This theater was the first to present Hebrew translations of plays by Shakespeare, Molière, Shaw, and O'Neill. Kikar Ha-Bimah. ✆ 03/629-5555. Ticket prices vary, depending on the company performing.

**New Cameri Theater**     This theater presents both repertory classics and new Israeli plays in Hebrew. Tuesday evenings there are simultaneous translations in English. 30 Leonardo Da Vinci St. ✆ 03/606-0960. Orchestra and mezzanine seats about NIS 125 ($31/£16); balcony seats NIS 100 ($25/£13); earphone rental is additional.

## THE CLUB SCENE

Tel Aviv and Jaffa are the nightlife centers of Israel. Their clubs have been the breeding ground for almost all Israeli singers who have gone on to international careers. The scene, especially the disco scene, changes so frequently, that only the few long-term landmarks are listed here. Some discos are on rather tacky-looking streets, but that's no indication they'll be cheap; the atmosphere can be very different inside. Nothing starts before midnight; most places are open daily.

## CLUBS & DANCE BARS

**Dome**     Dome has the largest dance floor in the city, with chill-out areas, voyeur terrace, and student parties on Friday after midnight. Hatzefira St. ✆ 03/561-1022. Admission NIS 70–NIS 120 ($18–$30/£8.75–£15).

**Fifth Dimension**     This is a very popular place in the Tel Aviv Port, with a large dance floor. Friday is usually alternative party night. Many places to browse in the port en route. Tel Aviv Port. ✆ 052/242-5891. Admission varies.

**HaOman 17**   This is Israel's great megaclub, with top Israeli and international DJs and major parties Thursday, Friday, and Saturday nights after 1am. 88 Abarbanel St. ℭ 03/681-3636. Admission NIS 70–NIS 120 ($18–$30/£8.75–£15).

**Maxim**   This place has small, dark, intimate rooms, and is next to a spaghetti bar in case hunger strikes. 48 King George St. ℭ 03/528-1333. Admission NIS 70–NIS 100 ($18–$25/ £8.75–£13).

**Move**   Move is the hit of the moment and packed with young Israelis. Tuesday is gay night. It's open Monday to Saturday after 11pm. Tel Aviv Port. ℭ 03/602-0426. Admission NIS 70 ($18/£8.75).

**Shesek**   A shadowy pickup place in an upscale restaurant-and-bar neighborhood, Shesek has dueling DJs on Sunday. 17 Lilenblum St. ℭ 03/516-9520. Cover varies depending on performance.

## BARS, PUBS & WINE BARS

Singers and pianists appear nightly at the bars in the major five-star hotels such as the Dan, Hilton, Ramada, Sheraton, and Sheraton Moriah.

**Chamara**   As beautiful upscale a bar as you'll find in Israel, Chamara serves dynamite food by high-profile chef Rafi Cohen, as the bar is attached to the adjacent deluxe Raphael restaurant. 87 HaYarkon St., beside Dan Hotel. ℭ 03/522-6464.

**East**   An Asian fusion resto-bar with soft music at dinner, but by 10pm, East switches to exotic tapas, and the decibel level rises. The location, in the derelict neighborhood of the disused Old (outdoor) Tel Aviv Bus Station, is very "in," but not for wandering in. A taxi is essential coming and going. Open daily 7:30pm until the last customer leaves. 12A HaSharon St. ℭ 03/687-7000.

**Jaffa Bar** ♠   Jaffa Bar is an easygoing, sprawling place with eccentric couches and armchairs scattered both in and outside an atmospheric Crusader-era building. The sleek bar is long and well stocked, and there's a good, reasonably priced food and tapas menu designed by Nir Zook, whose gourmet restaurant, Cordelia (p. 266), is right across the way. It's open daily from 6pm until late. Simchat HaZchuchit, off 30 Yefet St., Jaffa. ℭ 03/ 518-4668. Turn right into the covered alleyway 2 blocks south of the clock tower as you come from Tel Aviv.

**Joey's Bar**   An American-style bar run by Americans, Joey's well-stocked place is a haven for yuppie travelers. Music is American rock from the '60s, '70s, and '80s; beer starts at NIS 15 ($3.75/£1.90). It's open daily from 5pm to 8am. 42 Allenby St. ℭ 03/517-9277.

**Mike's Place** ♠♠   This American-style pub, facing the sea and offering live blues, jazz, and folk music every night, is an Israeli-American institution. Students, backpackers, locals, diplomats, families, and tourists come here day and night for the friendly, laid-back atmosphere, and also for the burgers (ground on the spot and grilled on open fires) and the good pub menu. Sports events are shown on wall screens. Happy hour is 4 to 9pm daily except Saturday, when it's all day until 9pm; it's open daily from noon until the last customer leaves. 86 Herbert Samuel Promenade. ℭ 052/267-0965. www.MikesPlaceBars.com.

**Nanutchka**   The bar at this ethnic Georgian (Caucasus Mountains, not Atlanta) restaurant with dynamite food goes from mild to totally crazy after dining hours. There's occasional dancing and live music, a friendly feel, and Georgian tapas with which to down your drinks. It's open daily from noon to after midnight. 28 Lilenblum St. ℭ 03/516-2254.

**Sea Breeze Spa & Bar**    Right on the beach at the Tel Aviv Port, with decks, palm trees, and banquets in the sand, this is a place where you can have a body wrap, aromatherapy, and Thai or Shiatsu massage, and then watch the sun set over the Mediterranean. Inventive cocktails and light meals are served. It can become less laid-back as the night goes on. Hangar 24, Tel Aviv Port. ℂ **03/524-4214.**

**Shalvata**    You can hear the sound of the wind in the thatch and palm trees on breezy nights at this fun place, set on the sands of the Tel Aviv Port. It's great for meeting people. There's dancing, with different nightly themes; DJs; and good, inexpensive food. It's open daily, starting at 5pm. Tel Aviv Port. ℂ **03/602-5008.**

**Terminal**    On the ground floor of a Bauhaus building, facing the sea, this is one of Tel Aviv's busiest pubs, crowded and filled with conversation by late afternoon; throbbing with music and overflowing onto the street with activity on summer nights. The crowd is part Tel Avivian, part international, and part backpacker. Corner of Gordon and Ha-Yarkon sts. ℂ **03/544-0585.**

**Yoe'ezer Wine Bar** ★★    This is a connoisseur's wine bar, with an extraordinary collection of Burgundian wines, run by one of Israel's great gourmets. Here your wine can be accompanied by exquisite food (p. 267). It's set in a Crusader-era building, hidden a few steps down a little alley on the inland side of Yefet Street, just opposite the clock tower. The crowd is a comfortable mix of youngish yuppies and over-40-somethings. It's open daily from 1pm to 1am. 2 Yoe'ezer Ish Habira St., Jaffa. ℂ **03/683-9115.**

## GAY & LESBIAN BARS/MEETING PLACES

Independence Park, in front of and beside the Tel Aviv Hilton (p. 248) on Ha-Yarkon Street, is a major cruising and gay pickup place, nicely landscaped and relatively safe. Hilton Beach, behind the Hilton hotel, is a mixed place with families, tourists, surfers and some amount of beachfront cruising as well. Avoid the very seedy and dangerous (now disused) Old Tel Aviv Bus Station area. The English-language edition of *Time Out Tel Aviv*, available in many hotels, will have a current list of the ever-changing party scene. Each year, Tel Aviv hosts the most famous Gay Pride Parade in the Middle East. Check websites, such as Aguda (www.aguda-ta.org.il/tourism.php), for scheduled times.

**Dix**    Dix is a gay bar with an upstairs area for cruising and meeting. It's open Monday to Saturday from 10pm. 6 Dizengoff Sq. ℂ **03/525-2633.**

**Evita**    This is a cafe/restaurant with good food that turns into a gay lounge/bar after the postdinner witching hour. Daily; call for hours and theme nights. 31 Yavne St. ℂ **03/566-9559.**

**Minerva Bar Gallery**    This always-interesting basement art gallery with an adjacent bar is an easygoing meeting place for the lesbian community. Both the bar and gallery are open daily from 8pm until late. Increasingly pan-gender-friendly. 98 Allenby St. ℂ **03/566-6051.** Bar cover NIS 50 ($13/£6.25).

## FILM

Tel Aviv has at least two dozen cinema houses; the international film scene is lively and popular. English and American films aren't dubbed, as they are in Europe, so you can sit back and enjoy the English soundtrack; otherwise check to see if foreign-language films include English subtitles. Tickets run from NIS 40 to NIS 50 ($10–$13/£5–£6.25). The commercial shorts that accompany many films are fascinating.

**Tel Aviv Cinémathèque**   Located not far from the Mann Auditorium, the Ciné-mathèque, with an ever-changing daily program, screens three or four films each day, ranging from international classics to rarely seen and experimental films. The Cinémath-èque also hosts an annual International Film Festival at the end of March/early April, as well as special festivals of Israeli films throughout the year. 2 Sprinzak St. © 03/691-7181.

## 10 Side Trips from Tel Aviv

### REHOVOT

**Rehovot** (22km/14 miles southeast of Tel Aviv; pop. 90,000) is easily reached by train or bus from Tel Aviv. Both train and bus fares are NIS 15 ($3.75/£1.90), and the trip takes 30 minutes. The town is a pleasant, rather ordinary small city, but its star attrac-tion, the **Weizmann Institute of Science** ✶✶ (© 08/934-4500 for the visitor cen-ter; www.weizmann.ac.il) makes an excursion very worthwhile.

An easy 5-minute walk from the train station down Herzl Street, Rehovot's main thoroughfare (or a 20-min. walk from the bus station, but the driver *may* consent to let you off at a closer stop), takes you to the **Weizmann Institute,** Israel's foremost sci-entific establishment and think tank. You enter through a gateway on Rehovot's main street, and as soon as you're inside the grounds you'll feel as if you've stepped into another world. This is a beautiful compound of futuristic buildings, lawns of the deepest golf-course green, lily ponds, and colorful gardens—all apparently, for the spiritual satisfaction of the hundreds of scientists from all over the world at work here.

Dedicated in 1949 in honor of Israel's first president (himself a world-renowned chemist), the institute grew out of the Daniel Sieff Research Institute, established in 1934. Conducting both fundamental and applied research, the Weizmann Institute also has a graduate school where about 700 students work for their master's degrees and doctorates.

The **visitor center** offers a 17-minute film about the institute and provides you with self-guided walking tours that will help you to understand what's going on in this dynamic, world-famous institution. For a small additional fee and with advance reser-vation, you can also tour Weizmann House, the home of Dr. and Mrs. Weizmann on the grounds of the institute.

The **Weizmann House** ✶✶ was built by Dr. and Mrs. Weizmann as their residence in the 1930s, and is a wonderful example of International Style architecture. It's a daz-zling, streamlined interpretation of a Roman/Mediterranean atrium house, the master-piece of the German refugee architect, Erich Mendelssohn, who also designed the original Hadassah Hospital and Hebrew University on Mount Scopus in Jerusalem. The interior of the house is marked by an airy, sinuous staircase set in a stair tower lit with narrow vertical windows; private living and reception wings with French doors lead to a central pool patio. Another 1930s element, round porthole windows, brings light into the house from exterior walls. The furnishings were carefully designed by Mendelssohn, who involved Dr. and Mrs. Weizmann personally in the project. The house itself (like Washington's Mount Vernon and Jefferson's Monticello) reveals much about the personality of Dr. Weizmann, the world in which he lived, and the interna-tional visitors he entertained. A film about Dr. Weizmann's amazing life is shown in the house. The Weizmann House is open Sunday through Thursday from 10am to 3pm, but only as part of a prearranged guided tour. To inquire about a house tour, call the visitor center at the Weizmann Institute (© **08/934-4500** or 934-4499) before your planned visit. Be sure to specify your English-language requirement. Near the residence is a simple tomb marking the Weizmanns' resting place and a Memorial Plaza dominated by a Holocaust memorial depicting the Torah being snatched from flames.

The **Clore Science Gardens** ☆, also on the campus of the institute, is an interactive exhibit that examines natural phenomena with the spirit of verve, humor, and inventiveness that marked Dr. Weizmann's approach to scientific inquiry. The additional entrance fee to the science gardens is a very worthwhile investment, especially for students and children.

Admission fee for the visitor center is NIS 15 ($3.75/£1.90) for adults, NIS 10 ($2.50/£1.25) for children. Combined admission to the visitor center and Clore Science Gardens is NIS 40 ($10/£5) for adults and NIS 30 ($7.50/£3.75) for children. The campus is open Sunday to Thursday from 10am to 4:45pm and Friday to 2pm. Tours of the Weizmann House must be reserved in advance by calling ℭ **08/943-4500.**

## ASHDOD

If you're traveling directly along the coast between Tel Aviv and Ashkelon, you'll pass Ashdod, now surpassing Haifa as Israel's largest and busiest port. Ashdod was one of the main Philistine coastal cities, and it was to Ashdod that the Philistines carried off the Ark of the Covenant in the period of the Judges, before the time of King Saul (1 Sam. 5:1–6). The Ark of the Covenant turned out to be a hot potato for its Philistine captors: Its mere presence in Ashdod caused the idol of the Philistine god, Dagon, to fall on its face and smash to bits inside its temple during the night. Disease broke out in the city; in panic, the people of Ashdod sent the ark to the inland Philistine town of Gath (modern Gat), and after misfortunes struck that community, the ark was sent back to the Israelites.

Present-day Ashdod is about 3.2km (2 miles) north of the ancient site. It's a planned, sprawling city of 140,000 (and growing by leaps and bounds with housing projects for recent immigrants), filled with factories and apartment blocks. Located as it is, along a glorious strip of coastline, Ashdod is scheduled to develop a tourist infrastructure sometime in the future, but for now the main tourist attraction is Idi, one of the most famous seafood restaurants in Israel.

### Where to Dine

**Idi** ☆☆ SEAFOOD   People come to Idi (David Israelovits is chef and proprietor) from as far away as Jerusalem and Herzlia for the fabulous fixed-price tasting menu of fresh fish and seafood. Travelers in this area who love seafood, or have a car, will find Idi a very worthwhile excursion. You'll have many choices, but it is best to go with Idi's recommendation of the day. The famous meze (appetizers), accompanied by home-baked Georgian bread, is a wonderful collection of creations, including crisp, deep-fried phyllo rolls stuffed with seafood; tartar of fresh fish; and a dynamite taramasalata. The fish-and-seafood bouillabaisse is famous, as are the mussels in wine and the deep-fried calamari rings and sautéed shrimp served in a pan of chunky chopped garlic sauce. For a main course you'll be offered a selection of grilled or broiled fish and also be served additional treats from the kitchen, such as calamari stuffed with mushrooms and shrimp in a rich butter, garlic, and dill sauce or steamed crab. Chocolate sorbet, halvah parfait, hot walnut pie, and a heavenly black-and-white chocolate mousse are some of the possible desserts. Decor is nautical; dress is informal. Thursday nights feature live Greek music and more than a usual number of house specialties. You can order a la carte, but Idi *is* the menu, and few people trek out here just for something light.

6 Bosem St., Light Industrial Area, Ashdod Port. ℭ **08/852-4313.** Reservations necessary 3 weeks in advance for Thurs evening; 1 week in advance for Fri–Sat. Complete tasting dinner NIS 160 ($40/£20); complete lunch NIS 140 ($35/£18). Cash only. Daily noon–midnight.

# 8

# The Golden Coast

Like the rest of the country, the Golden Coast combines the old and the new in a uniquely Israeli juxtaposition. Neon and chrome exist side by side with biblical and even prebiblical ruins. And there's much to see and do on the beaches of sand, pebbles, or rocks; sports enthusiasts can swim, fish, dive, boat, ski, or surf.

Today, the narrow coastal strip (only 16km/10 miles wide from the sea to the West Bank in some places) is the heart of the State of Israel, and most of its people live there. In biblical times, the ancestral heartland of the Jewish people was in the Judean mountains and farther north, in the Galilee and the hills of Samaria. The coast was almost always foreign territory. The southern part of the coastal strip, including Gaza, Ashkelon, and Ashdod, was inhabited by the Philistines, a people originating in the Aegean, who by 700 B.C. had largely assimilated into the local Semitic population. To the north, the worldly port cities of Jaffa, Dor, and Akko were bastions of the Phoenicians—coastal Canaanites who spoke a language similar to Hebrew, and who were renowned for their prowess as seafarers and traders (in the 8th c. B.C., Phoenician ships, sailing from Eilat, on the Red Sea, were circumnavigating Africa). Phoenician hegemony continued northward along the coast to include Sidon, Tyre, and Byblos, in present-day Lebanon; Hyram of Tyre was an ally of King Solomon and provided architects, craftsmen, and material for the building of the First Temple.

Over the centuries, the coast became more central to the mosaic of the Holy Land's history. The construction of the Port of Caesarea (20 B.C.–5 B.C.) was the greatest building achievement of King Herod. It quickly developed into an outpost of Roman civilization that counterbalanced the charismatic Jewish capital at Jerusalem, and was soon counted among the most elegant and important cities in the Mediterranean. St. Paul was imprisoned in Caesarea, and it was there that many early Christians were martyred. A thousand years later, cities such as Akko and Caesarea were conquered and fortified by the Crusaders—the impressive Crusader ruins at Akko and Caesarea attest to the power of the clash between Islam and Christendom that took place here. The 20th century brought lush kibbutzim, vineyards, wineries, and fish farms to the coastal plain. The 21st century is bringing wonderful beachside and country restaurants (both el cheapo and gourmet), as well as shopping malls and traffic jams.

**SEEING THE AREA** It's best to see the Golden Coast in sections: The southern and central coasts are convenient to Tel Aviv and can also be visited from Jerusalem; the north-central and northern coasts are easily accessible from Haifa and the Galilee. The water can be almost bathtub-warm in summer and swimming is possible from April until November. In fact, in a February heat wave, some visitors from northern climes find the Mediterranean near Tel Aviv is as warm as the North Atlantic ever gets in August.

*Warning:* On many days undertows lifeguards. Be extremely wary about and whirlpools develop that not even the swimming in unguarded areas if there is strongest swimmer can fight. Obey the any wave activity.

## 1 Herzlia

15km (9 miles) N of Tel Aviv

Herzlia is one of Israel's most famous beach resorts. It was founded in 1924 as an agricultural center, but has changed dramatically with the unexpected growth of Tel Aviv. As that large Israeli metropolis grew northward, the beaches of Herzlia suddenly became much more accessible and desirable.

Today, when you're talking about Herzlia, you're talking about luxury. The waterfront area is studded with fine hotels and some of the country's most expensive villas; very good restaurants abound (mostly inland, in a bleak industrial zone). A disproportionate number of foreign diplomats and business people reside in Herzlia; their neighbors are airline captains and other high-income earners. Swimming here is better than in Tel Aviv, and many Tel Avivians and visitors come up for a day of beachcombing beside the often clearer waters, as well as a pleasant meal.

### ESSENTIALS

**GETTING THERE    By Bus**    An Egged bus from Allenby Street in Tel Aviv to Herzlia takes about 45 minutes; fare is NIS 9 ($2.25/£1.10). From Herzlia you take Herzlia Municipal Bus no. 29 to the beach; the fare is NIS 5.60 ($1.40/70p). If you tell the Tel Aviv bus driver that you want to go to the beach, he'll let you out at the connecting bus stop near the highway, saving you a trip into town.

**By Car**    Herzlia is on a main highway, 20 minutes north of Tel Aviv.

**VISITOR INFORMATION**    Herzlia's sprawling layout is confusing for the first-time visitor. The luxury Sharon Hotel, right on the beach, is a major landmark. Inland just a block is De Shalit Square (Kikar De Shalit), around which you'll find a moderately priced hotel and affordable restaurants. Many fine (and more expensive) restaurant choices are located inland at the New Industrial Center.

### THE BEACHES

This whole beachfront section of town is known as Herzlia Petuah, to differentiate it from the inland city, on a hill to the east. The Herzlia beach is lovely, but expensive by Israeli standards. The best beaches are the **Zebulun;** the **Sharon,** next to the Sharon Hotel; and the **Accadia,** between the Dan Accadia and Daniel hotels. These beaches have changing facilities. Entrance fees are NIS 20 ($5/£2.50) for adults and NIS 12 ($3/£1.50) for children. Remember that a dangerous undertow exists, and swimming is strictly prohibited when a lifeguard is not on duty.

### WHERE TO STAY

#### EXPENSIVE

**Dan Accadia Hotel** ⭐ *Kids*    Located right on the beach in the far southern part of town, this low-rise resort hotel—built in 1956, last renovated in 1999, and continually being updated—is set among lawns and gardens that center on the pool area. Standard rooms are a bit small, but all have balconies, and the room decor is pleasant. There are also deluxe "chalet" rooms in the pool garden, as well as very comfortable suites. There are activities for children on weekends and during the summer, and poolside barbecues

# The Golden Coast

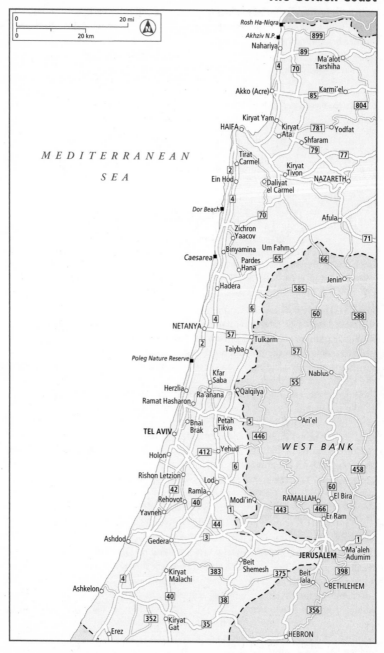

and dancing. The staff here can arrange horseback riding and access to the golf course of the Dan Caesarea Hotel (one of the few in Israel), a half-hour drive to the north. Reader feedback on the staff has been mixed.

Herzlia on the Sea 46851. © **09/959-7070.** Fax 09/959-7090. www.danhotels.com. 207 units. $400–$500 (£200–£250) double. Rates include breakfast. Family plan, children's rates, and package discounts available; rates lower in winter. AE, DC, MC, V. Free parking. **Amenities:** Restaurant; bar; outdoor pool (seasonal); children's pool; 6 tennis courts; health club; business services; shopping arcade; salon; 24-hr. room service; massage; laundry service; non-smoking rooms; synagogue; beach. *In room:* A/C, TV, Wi-Fi, minibar.

## MODERATE
**Tadmor Hotel**  The Tadmor Hotel, a 5-minute walk from the beach, is an Israeli institution. Hotel staffs from all over the country train here, and chefs are cultivated and launched from the Tadmor. To this end, the hotel has two in-house restaurants and a good lunch buffet. The four-story building has character; it looks a bit like a desert fortress from a 1940s movie. Rooms are well maintained and comfortable, but bathrooms are small. Large gardens, an outdoor swimming pool, and a fine park with a children's playground are additional highlights.

38 Basel St., Herzlia 46660. © **09/952-5000.** Fax 09/957-5124. www.tadmor.co.il. 58 units. $110–$140 (£55–£70) double. Rates include breakfast. Family plans and 7-day discounts available. AE, DC, MC, V. Free parking. From Mena-hem Begin Blvd., Herzilia's main east-west thoroughfare, which changes into Hama'apilim St. and becomes Keren Hayesod St., turn left at Ben Zvi St. and right after Shalit Sq. at Basel St. **Amenities:** 3 restaurants; dining room; out-door seasonal pool; room service; laundry service. *In room:* A/C, TV, safe.

## OUTSIDE HERZLIA
**Kibbutz Shefayim Guest House** *(Kids)*  This low-rise, modern, extremely popular kibbutz guesthouse is right on the sea, a 10-minute drive north of Herzlia. A children's playground and a busy (often mobbed) public water park with a swimming pool with waves and slides is a big attraction, open mid-April to mid-October. The grounds of the kibbutz are enormous, and include wild, sandy paths along the top of cliffs over-looking the sea, and a beach that's good for bathing on calm days; when the sea is even mildly rough, the presence of rocks in the water makes for hazardous swimming—swim only when lifeguards are on duty. There's a kibbutz ambience: At times, a kib-butz tractor brings guests up and down the cliff to the beach, and you're welcome to explore kibbutz life, but one sign of the kibbutz movement's evolution is the major shopping mall on the grounds. Rooms are simple but comfortable enough.

Kibbutz Shefayim. © **09/959-5577.** Fax 09/959-5555. www.h-shefayim.co.il. 166 units, some with shower; some with tub. $136–$200 (£68–£100) double. Rates include breakfast. Discounts on Kibbutz Hotel Plan. AE, MC, V. From Hwy. 2, the main Tel Aviv–Haifa coastal road, look for Shefayim exit sign. **Amenities:** Pool; beach; water park; rooms for those w/limited mobility. *In room:* A/C, TV.

## WHERE TO DINE
The best place to look for inexpensive meals is in **De Shalit Square (Kikar De Shalit),** a pleasant little plaza surrounded by snack shops, ice-cream parlors, and small restaurants catering to locals and the beach crowd alike. You'll find more expensive, inventive restaurants in the building complexes of Herzlia's New Industrial Center, inland from the beach, near Hwy. 2, the main Tel Aviv–Haifa coastal road. In fact, people from all over Israel come here for some of the best dining experiences in the country. All the restaurant choices below, with the exception of Tandoori and Picasso (which have locations in Tel Aviv), are worth a trip from Tel Aviv.

## EXPENSIVE

**Terassa** ☆ CONTINENTAL   Right on the beach, with an outdoor dining terrace and a beautiful view of the sunset, this is an easygoing restaurant with ceiling fans and sea breezes, and a wide selection of seafood, fish, and meat. For appetizers, try the interesting Greek/Mediterranean array of small salads *(mezedes)*. You can also have light courses such as goat cheese mousse, a plate of little fried fishes, or foie gras in onions and raisins—all run under NIS 64 ($16/£8). Among the main courses, you'll find a changing daily menu that includes items such as fried mullet in chili and lemon sauce, salmon trout in coriander and cream, and fried mussels. There's also a selection of lamb, beef, and chicken, and at times Terassa does brick-oven pizza. With its fine view, this is a good place to come off-hours just for coffee and dessert or evening drinks.

Dan Accadia Hotel Beach Promenade. ☎ 09/959-7107. Reservations recommended. Main courses NIS 60–NIS 110 ($15–$28/£7.50–£14). AE, DC, MC, V. Sun–Thurs 6pm–midnight; Fri–Sat noon–midnight.

## MODERATE

**Black Steer Grill House** ☆ SOUTH AFRICAN STEAKHOUSE   The best steak restaurant in the Tel Aviv area, the Black Steer is part of a famous South African chain with locations in Zimbabwe, Indonesia, and Australia. Choose from a variety of grilled steaks, great barbecue ribs, and chicken—all served with tasty South African–style marinades. The complete business lunches, served from noon to 5pm, are unbeatable deals, starting at NIS 100 ($25/£13), but whenever you dine, you'll have excellent value and a filling meal. If you're not a carnivore, you'll find vegetarian choices, too.

3 Yohanan Ha Sandlar St., New Industrial Center. ☎ 09/955-7464. www.blacksteer.co.il/english.cfm. Reservations necessary. Main courses NIS 60–NIS 160 ($15–$40/£7.50–£20). AE, DC, MC, V. Daily noon–midnight.

**Erez** ☆☆ MODERN ISRAELI/MEDITERRANEAN   Erez has developed from a gourmet bread bakery into a restaurant serving the most interesting modern Israeli cuisine in the country. Owner/chef Erez Komarovsky (though not in the restaurant as much as before) is endlessly inventive and brash in creating his menu, which changes almost daily. Some dishes are virtually free-verse poems in their components and presentation: lamb shish kabobs on skewers of rosemary stalks served with couscous tabbouleh dotted with ruby pomegranate seeds; saltwater fish with tomatoes and *zataar* (local spices) baked on olive-wood fires in a stone oven; shrimp and calamari with coconut milk, mango, and local Israeli herbs. Everything is not only cosmopolitan, but also filled with the flavors of Israel. House bread, salads, and wonderful roasted eggplant are must-try first courses, though any dish wrapped in Erez's pastry crusts will be wonderful. There are also lighter courses of unusual pastas, salads, stuffed breads, and country cheeses. Prices are moderate, the wine list good, and desserts are wonderful (the chocolate marquise is divine). Lunch (when you'll find great value specials), is from noon to 5pm, but the dinner menu (after 5pm) offers the most variety. A very worthwhile tasting menu can be arranged in advance. The atmosphere is casual and fun. Decor is functional; there's no view, but it's informal enough to bring kids, who love checking out the parakeets in the garden.

52 Berekit St. ☎ 09/955-9892. Reservations suggested. Main courses NIS 55–NIS 80 ($14–$20/£6.90–£10); tasting menu NIS 160–NIS 180 ($40–$45/£20–£23). AE, DC, MC, V. Sun–Thurs 11:30am–midnight; Fri–Sat 1:30pm–midnight.

**Tandoori** ☆☆ INDIAN   This is the most opulent of the fine restaurants in the Israeli Tandoori chain, with twin curved marble staircases leading to the upper dining area, and decorative silver and enamel work imported from Jaipur. A dining experience here is one of tranquillity and elegance, yet prices are reasonable. As in all the Tandoori restaurants, the traditional Indian dishes you'll find here are prepared with a special light touch. I especially like the *sabzi jalfrezi,* a very modestly priced dish of vegetables lightly steamed and then quickly dry-sautéed with ginger, garlic, cumin seeds, and fresh mustard. The boneless tandoori chicken dishes are my favorites, especially chicken *tikka masala,* but the whole range of lamb and fish choices is superb. It's worthwhile to try the traditional Indian home-style desserts. The chain is also famous for its cocktails. An all-you-can-eat luncheon buffet Sunday to Thursday is excellent and a great bargain.

Mercazim Building, 32 Maskit St., New Industrial Center. ℂ **09/954-6702.** Reservations recommended. Main courses NIS 35–NIS 80 ($8.75–$20/£4.40–£10). AE, DC, MC, V. Daily 12:30–3:30pm and 7pm–1am.

### INEXPENSIVE

**Agadir Burger Bar** ⓐ BURGERS/PUB FOOD    Fabulous burgers with exotic toppings plus many eclectic menu offerings and a young, eccentric ambience make this a real winner and a link-up spot until way after midnight (see p. 265 in chapter 7).

9 Hamenofim St., New Industrial Center. ℂ **09/951-6551.** Reservations at times accepted. Main courses and tapas NIS 36–NIS 50 ($9–$13/£4.50–£6.25). AE, DC, MC, V. Daily 11am–after midnight.

## 2 Netanya

34km (21 miles) N of Tel Aviv

Netanya is regarded as the capital of the Sharon Plain, the rich and fertile citrus-grove area stretching from the outskirts of Tel Aviv to Caesarea. Perched on verdant cliffs overlooking the Mediterranean, it is also the center of Israel's diamond industry.

Founded in 1929 as a citrus center, the seaside town has for many years been a popular holiday place for Israelis. Over the years visitors (especially long-term visitors and seniors) have been joining them, for they've discovered that Netanya is quiet and convenient, geared to service, and within easy reach of several areas, including Tel Aviv and Caesarea. It's a sizable city, with all sorts of cafes, hotels, and shops—but the real appeal remains the sunny beach and easygoing pace. (*Note:* Those with walking problems may find the stairs up and down the cliff to Netanya's beaches something of an obstacle. Elevators now go up and down the cliffs at strategic locations.) Those who decide to rent an apartment and stay in Netanya for a month or more will find the local English-speaking community extremely well organized. Many Israelis from France have also settled here. The population of Netanya has grown by more than a fifth in recent years with an influx of new immigrants from Eastern Europe and the former Soviet Union, so Netanya has more of a European flavor than other Israeli cities.

A handsome park parallels the beach—and the coast itself has become popular with Scandinavian visitors who take dips in December and January. Most everybody else waits until April or May, when the weather is almost perfect.

### ESSENTIALS

**GETTING THERE    By Bus**    Several express buses operate between Netanya and Jerusalem. Connections are available from Haifa, and there is regular bus service from Tel Aviv. Netanya buses (no. 601 or 605) leave Tel Aviv about every 15 minutes during the day until 7pm. The last bus to Tel Aviv departs at 11pm. Fare is NIS 16 ($4/£2).

**By Car**    There is a main coastal highway, Hwy. 2, that connects Tel Aviv and Haifa; the wider Hwy. 4 parallels it slightly inland. Netanya can be reached from both Hwy. 3 and 4.

**VISITOR INFORMATION** The **Tourist Information Office** (☎ 09/882-7286) is in a little modern kiosk at the southeastern corner of Independence Square. Hours are 8:30am to 4pm Sunday to Thursday and from 9am to noon on Friday. Winter hours may be shorter. This office is especially helpful and will answer questions about Netanya or other places in Israel. Be sure to pick up a copy of the monthly booklet listing special events, entertainment, and services in Netanya. If you're traveling by bus, you might also want to pick up their bus timetable, which you might find clearer than the information you'll get at the station.

*Tip:* Netanya closes down between 1 and 4pm every day, so plan to shop or go to the bank before or after the afternoon siesta.

**SOCIAL CLUBS** Many international social clubs hold regular meetings in Netanya, including Rotary, Lions, Hadassah, Freemasons, Pioneer Women, B'nai B'rith, and the British **Olim Society.** Ask at the Tourist Information Office for information about making contact. The **Association of Americans and Canadians in Israel (AACI),** 28 Shmuel Ha-Naziv St. (☎ 09/833-0950; www.netanyaaaci.org.il), offers a good schedule of lectures, excursions, and other social activities ranging from volunteer English tutoring to bridge, amateur theater, and bingo.

*Tip:* If you'd like to meet an Israeli citizen, apply 3 days in advance at the Tourist Information Office, and you'll soon find yourself invited to a home for a friendly chat and a cup of coffee.

**SPECIAL EVENTS** The city sponsors free evening concerts and events throughout the summer. A **chess tournament** is held in Netanya yearly during May and June; every 2 years there's an international match. Games start at 3:30pm and last until 10pm. For further information, contact the Tourist Information Office.

**CITY LAYOUT** Netanya is a big town, but it's not really difficult to find your way around. From Hwy. 2, you will see the exit for Netanya, which will get you onto **Herzl Street,** Netanya's main east-west boulevard. At the beginning of Herzl Boulevard, not far from Hwy. 2, you'll pass the large **Kanion** (indoor shopping mall). Farther down, on the left, where Herzl crosses Dizengoff, is the bus station. Another 6 blocks, and Herzl ends at the great expanse of **Ha-Atzma'ut Square,** by the sea in the very heart of Netanya. Most of the hotels and restaurants recommended below are within a few blocks of the square.

The square, the town's pedestrian promenade, has been enlarged in recent years, and now extends up Herzl Street all the way to Dizengoff Street.

Around Ha-Aztma'ut Square you'll find everything you need, including the Tourist Information Office, banks, ATMs, places to change money, a post office, and eateries of many kinds as well as pubs, discos, a movie theater, hotels, and more. Be warned that since the center of Netanya was not designed for a population of almost 200,000, parking is a serious problem and many streets are RESIDENT PARKING ONLY. Towing, rather than ticketing, is common, and parking regulations are enforced with draconian rigor.

## BEACHES, SPORTS & OTHER OUTDOOR PURSUITS

**BEACHES & WATERSPORTS** The main attraction in Netanya is, of course, the lovely beach, and you'll have perfect beach weather here more than 75% of the year. Elevators now take you up and down the cliffs that line the beach. The water is great for swimming—you can go out pretty far before it starts to get deep. There's a lifeguard on duty; do swim in the approved area, whose boundaries are clearly posted. In addition to sand, swimming, and sun, you can enjoy the attractions in the beach complex,

## The Anglo-Saxon Connection

Visitors to Israel from English-speaking countries are often amazed at how easy it is to get around using their native language, especially in light of the fact that Israel's two official languages, Hebrew and Arabic, don't even share alphabets that remotely resemble our own. In major cities, signs, traffic instructions, and restaurant menus are almost always in both English and Hebrew. Israeli entrepreneurs have become adept at designing shop signs and logos that blend English and Hebrew lettering (which are written in opposite directions) into interesting compositions, and the chance is good that your 20-something waitperson, the sales clerk where you take your film to be developed, or the elderly Palestinian owner of a grocery shop will be able to shift into fluent English at a moment's notice. And unlike many European countries, which dub English-language films and television programs, in Israel you won't have to watch Tom Hanks or Jerry Seinfeld (or more ludicrously, Katherine Hepburn and Spencer Tracy in a revival classic) bantering away in Hebrew.

Of course, the British were here from 1918 to 1948, but 30 years of the British Mandate are only one part of the formula that has made Israel so user-friendly to the English-speaking world. Immigrants to Israel from English-speaking countries, though only 1% of the general population, have had an impact far beyond their numbers. Known locally (and to their own bemusement) as Anglo-Saxons, these Israelis have provided two of the nation's eight presidents: **Chaim Weizmann,** a British subject whose scientific discoveries were crucial to the Allied victory in World War I; and Dublin-born

which include restaurants and snack shops, beach chairs, large public umbrellas, a basketball court, and a gymnastics field. You'll see people **fishing** up on the rocky breakwater. **Surfing** and **sail boarding** can be arranged at the Kontiki Club down on the Netanya beach—lessons, too—open daily from 8:30am until sunset.

Of course it's beautiful to see the sun set over the Mediterranean, and in the high tourist season, student patrols keep watch to make sure everything is okay. The lifeguards leave the beach in the late afternoon. Still, be cautious at night here; stay where you see other people, especially if you're a woman alone. During the winter when the student patrols are not around, it's not a good idea to hang around the beach or the parks on the cliffs at night.

*Tip:* If you have a car, you might want to drive to sheltered **Mikmoret Beach,** about 11 to 13km (7–8 miles) north toward Caesarea. It goes on for miles, and is a great place for walking. There are lifeguards and other facilities; parking in summer is NIS 24 ($6/£3) per car, but the fee is deducted from your bill if you eat a meal at the beach's restaurant.

**HORSEBACK RIDING & OTHER SPORTS**   Riding is available at two locations. The **Ranch** (© **09/866-3525**), in northern Netanya, has horseback riding daily from 8am until sunset; take bus no. 17 or 29 from the Central Bus Station. There's also the

Chaim Herzog, whose father served as Chief Rabbi of Ireland. **Golda Meir,** a former schoolteacher from Milwaukee, held many important positions in Labor Party governments, including that of prime minister from 1969 to 1974. Former prime minister **Benjamin Netanyahu** was raised and educated in America. Israel's most famous and eloquent diplomat, South African–born and Cambridge-educated **Abba Eban,** served as ambassador to the United Nations and was foreign minister for many years. The legendary **Henrietta Szold,** Baltimore-born first president of Hadassah, held the social welfare portfolio of the National Council of Palestine Jewry in the 1930s and was responsible for developing many elements of the emerging nation's system of health, education, and social services. South Africans, Britons, and Americans were heavily involved in creating the Association for Civil Rights in Israel, and are at the forefront of the women's rights, religious rights, and ecology and peace movements. Americans are also strongly represented in the West Bank settlement movements. Despite their extraordinary contributions, Anglo-Israelis are regarded by many of their fellow countrymen as something of a people apart.

The **Association of Americans and Canadians in Israel (AACI)** and the **British Olim Society,** with branches in most main cities, offer busy schedules of lectures, get-togethers, activities, tours, and legal advice for seniors, singles, and families. They are a terrific resource for English-speaking visitors who plan to stay in Israel for an extended period of time.

**Cactus Ranch** (✆ **09/865-1239**), open daily from 8am until sunset. Rates are approximately NIS 110 ($28/£14) per hour. It's always wise to reserve ahead.

**Bicycle rentals** can be arranged at the Hotel Promenade (✆ **09/862-6450**). Rates start at NIS 35 ($8.75/£4.40) for half a day

Paragliding off the sandy bluffs along the Israeli coast has become a major sport in Netanya. Lessons and equipment can be arranged at NIS 125 ($31/£16) per hour through **Dvir Paragliding** (✆ **09/899-0277** or 050/833-3103; fax 09/899-1705). For other Israeli paragliding sites, contact **AGUR,** the Israel Hang-gliding and Paragliding Club, Sea Palace Beach, PO Box 1035, Bat Yam 59110 Israel; or **Sky Paragliding LTD.,** 4 Hacharuv St., Rishpan 46915, Israel (sky-pg@inter.net.il).

**NATURE WALKS & HIKING**   The **Poleg Nature Reserve,** 8km (5 miles) south of Netanya, offers an interesting hike along the Poleg River, upstream from the point where it meets the sea. The riverbanks are lined with giant eucalyptus trees, planted almost a century ago to help drain the swamps that had developed throughout the plain of Sharon (eucalyptus seedlings were imported from Australia by early Jewish settlers, who valued their ability to withstand drought). In winter and early spring, the wildflowers along the route have made the Poleg Reserve a favorite destination for botanists. Unfortunately, the Poleg River has become dangerously polluted, a situation not unusual in the intensively developed coastal plain. Recently, the Mediterranean

## Impressions

*We [from English-speaking countries] have experienced democracy at first hand. We know what democracy is and should be. That can be, perhaps has been, our greatest contribution.*

—Alice Shalvi, Israeli educator and founding
chairwoman, Israel Women's Network

beach near the Poleg Reserve has been closed to swimming, and the river water itself is absolutely off-limits.

The **Iris Nature Reserve** ✿, at the southern edge of Netanya, is a sanctuary for wild and cultivated irises. There is an adjacent pond that attracts seaside birds and water-fowl. In February and March, the reserve is carpeted with wild, dark-blue irises—pathways let you immerse yourself in this paradise that few travelers know about. There is a parking lot on Ben-Gurion Boulevard, and you are asked to stay on the pathways. There is no admission fee. Check with the Netanya Tourist Information Office to see if the irises are blooming.

**SPORTS CENTERS**   **Elitzur Sports Center** (© 09/865-2931) has a heated swimming pool and also has squash and tennis facilities. The center is at the end of Radak Street (take bus no. 8 from the Central Bus Station). It's open daily from 6 or 8am until 5 to 10pm (call to check which hours are on what days). The **Orde Wingate Institute** (© 09/863-9523; www.jewishsports.net/wingate_institute.htm), named for a British officer who was extremely sympathetic to the Zionist cause during the British Mandate, is the national center for sports and physical education, with every program and sports facility imaginable. It's 8km (5 miles) south of Netanya, off the main Haifa–Tel Aviv coastal road. It has a swimming pool, as do many Netanya hotels.

## VISITING A DIAMOND FACTORY

Israel is the number-one spot in the world for cutting and polishing diamonds, and Netanya is Israel's number-one diamond center, with two large factories. If you're in the market to buy, you can probably save about 20% by buying here. Even if you're not interested in buying, a visit to the **National Diamond Center**, 90 Herzl St. (© 09/862-0436), could still be an unusual experience. Telephone for information about the center's interesting and pressure-free tours. The Tourist Information Office can direct you to additional diamond industry tours in Netanya.

## WHERE TO STAY

In most cases, you needn't go far out of Ha-Atzma'ut Square to find a hotel. Netanya is oriented toward warm-weather vacationers, and prices are seasonal. Even inexpensive hotels can charge moderate to expensive rates during high season. Generally speaking, high season is from early July to the end of August, plus Jewish holidays, and low season is November to February; between these times prices will be somewhere between the high- and low-season rates.

In winter, be sure to check for heating—days can be balmy, but nights can get chilly. *Note:* All of Netanya's hotel kitchens are kosher.

### NORTH OF HA-ATZMA'UT SQUARE

Rechov Ha-Melech David is the main street going north out of Ha-Atzma'ut Square, close to the beach.

## Moderate

**Blue Bay Hotel**   The most northern of the town's hotels (and one of the largest), the Blue Bay is set on a cliff overlooking the sea and offers hourly shuttle service into the center of Netanya. Much renovation has been done over the past few years; avoid those rooms that have not been upgraded. There's a resort atmosphere, with a new fitness center, and you can arrange bicycle rentals and in-room massage.

37 Hamelachim St., Netanya. ✆ **09/860-0100.** Fax 09/833-7475. www.blue-bay.co.il. 196 units. $125–$250 (£63–£125) double. Rates include breakfast. AE, DC, MC, V. Free parking. Bus: 29. **Amenities:** Restaurant; bar; disco; outdoor heated seasonal pool; lit tennis court; health club; spa; sports equipment rental; massage. *In room:* A/C, TV, fridge, coffeemaker, microwave, safe.

**Seasons Hotel**   Until the advent of the Carmel Hotel at the southern edge of Netanya, the 35-year-old Seasons was the city's top hotel. Guest rooms are large, with balconies and sea views; suites are very comfortable. The hotel was last renovated in from 1994 to 1995, but there has been recent room freshening. Facilities include a heated outdoor swimming pool, fitness room, and a night-lit tennis court.

Nice Blvd., Netanya. ✆ **09/860-1555.** Fax 09/862-3005. www.haonot.co.il. 100 units. $140–$270 (£70–£135) standard double; $340–$470 (£170–£235) deluxe double and suite. Rates include breakfast. AE, DC, MC, V. Free parking. **Amenities:** 3 restaurants; dining room; cafe; bar; pool; children's pool; lit tennis court; spa; Jacuzzi; sauna; children's activities; business services; salon; room service; synagogue. *In room:* A/C, TV, Wi-Fi, minibar, hair dryer, safe.

## SOUTH OF HA-ATZMA'UT SQUARE

On the south side of Ha-Atzma'ut Square, several main streets and side streets will lead you to hotel choices that are only a short walk from the beach and the busy square.

## Moderate

**Residence Hotel**   Billing itself as "Netanya's most luxurious three-star hotel," the eight-story Residence is building its clientele by offering cut-rate prices for people staying a minimum of 1 week. Location is right in the center of town, overlooking the beach. Most rooms were renovated in 2005, so this choice is better than what is available in much of Netanya. Special reduced rates are offered in June, September, and November 1 to November 15. The Residence Hotel is part of the Zyvotel chain, with a number of properties in Netanya; guests can use the Jacuzzi and sauna at the nearby Hotel Galil. The clientele is heavily French, and a visit here will help you brush up on the language.

18 Gad Machnes St., Netanya. ✆ **09/830-1111.** Fax 09/862-3711. www.zyvotel.com. 96 units. $120–$200 (£60–£100) double. Rates include breakfast. AE, DC, MC, V. *In room:* A/C, TV.

## Inexpensive

**Margoa**   Just a short distance from the information kiosk and the beach is the Margoa—actually there are two hotels, the Margoa "A" on your left and the Margoa "B" on your right, by the sea. The reception desk, as well as the dining, for both hotels is at the Margoa A. Rooms come with heat, air-conditioning, and wall-to-wall carpeting. Some of the rooms in Margoa A have balconies. There's a Jacuzzi, but no swimming pool. Rooms have nice extras such as hair dryers and refrigerators that you won't find at many hotels for this price.

9 Gad Machnes St., Netanya 42279. ✆ **09/862-4434.** Fax 09/862-3430. www.hotelmargoa.co.il. 75 units. $100 (£50) double Oct–June; $200 (£100) double July–Sept. Rates include breakfast. Long-term stay discounts available. AE, MC, V. **Amenities:** Dining room; Jacuzzi; nonsmoking rooms; synagogue. *In room:* A/C, cable TV, fridge, hair dryer.

## SOUTH NETANYA

### Expensive

**Carmel Hotel** ✿★ Built in 1994, this high-rise hotel on a now-quiet stretch of beach (slated eventually to become a luxury resort center) 3.2km (2 miles) south of downtown Netanya is by far the city's best hotel and sets a new standard for luxury in Netanya. Half of the hotel's 200 rooms are timeshares or condominiums, and the clientele is largely from France and Belgium. Public areas are busy, and rooms are attractive, but some are becoming a bit worn. There are rooms for travelers with disabilities. Like much of Netanya, the hotel is located on a cliff above the beach—getting down to the beach can be a problem, although an elevator service is planned. There are ample parking facilities (always at a premium in Netanya).

Jabotinsky St., Netanya. ℭ **09/860-1111** or 860-1175 for reservations. Fax 09/860-1171. www.carmel-hotel.co.il. 96 units. $200–$300 (£100–£150) double; $270–$370 (£135–£185) deluxe double. Rates include breakfast. Add 15% service charge. AE, DC, MC, V. Free parking. **Amenities:** Glatt kosher certification; 2 restaurants; dining room; large seasonal outdoor pool; health club; Jacuzzi; children's activities (in season); massage; rooms for those w/limited mobility. *In room:* A/C, TV, fridge (on request).

## PRIVATE ROOMS & APARTMENTS

One of the best ways to save money on accommodations, particularly if you plan to stay in Netanya for some time, is to rent a private room or apartment. Actual rental arrangements are generally handled by local agents, and you'll have to pay an agent's fee, which is a flat 10% of the total rental (no extra charge if meal arrangements are made).

Room rentals are available for at least 3 to 4 days, apartments for a week or more. Most of them are within walking distance of the sea. Rooms in private homes come with sheets and blankets; no meals are served, though guests may use the refrigerator and stove. The cost is about $50 to $70 (£25–£35) per person in summer; prices go up on weekends and holidays, and are lower off season.

Apartments have basic furniture. The place is clean when you arrive, but upkeep is left to you for the length of your stay. A studio or what is known as a two-room flat (living room, one bedroom, kitchen, bathroom, balcony) starts at about $1,000 (£500) per couple per month and goes up from there.

Consult the **Tourist Information Office** desk at Ha-Atzma'ut Square (ℭ **09/882-7286**) for listings of private room and apartment rental agents.

## WHERE TO DINE

Most of the town's cafes and restaurants line Ha-Atzma'ut Square.

### EXPENSIVE

**Lucullus** ✿★ FRENCH This is a very French restaurant, both in its decor and in its traditional menu; for many decades, and through various location changes and incarnations from nonkosher to kosher, it has been the best restaurant in Netanya. There's nothing revolutionary here—just classic dishes done within the bounds of kashrut in Chef Bernard Gabai's personal way. Appetizers include a smooth pâté of gooseliver served with crispy fried onions and toast, home-smoked salmon, an array of excellent salads, and foie gras. Main courses are very generous and served with vegetables, a potato, and hefty salad. Everything is beautifully prepared, including the simplest breaded schnitzel. Choices include crispy bass, duckling a l'orange, entrecôte steak, and grilled gooseliver served with balsamic vinegar. A special roast beef for four people must be ordered in advance. There's a dining terrace in good weather. Kosher *lemehedrin*.

8 Nitza Blvd. ✆ **09/861-7831.** Reservations necessary. Main courses NIS 60–NIS 90 ($15–$23/£7.50–£11); fixed-price menu NIS 90–NIS 150 ($23–$38/£11–£19). MC, V. Sun–Thurs noon–3pm and 6–11pm.

## MODERATE

**Marrakesh** ✦ MOROCCAN    The best Moroccan restaurant in town is spacious and touched with many charming elements of Moroccan decor. The wide-ranging menu begins with a medley of traditional Moroccan starters, but main courses are served in generous portions, so save room. There's a house *tagine* of lamb slow cooked in plums, apricots, and almonds; traditional chicken with olives; spicy Moroccan meatballs; a choice of many grilled meats and fish; homemade sausages, and such authentic dishes as beef tongue cooked with mushrooms, brains in hot chili sauce, and artichoke stuffed with ground lamb. There's also excellent couscous and a gourmet house specialty of lamb cooked with truffles that must be ordered in advance. Lots of traditional desserts and gracious service round out an absolute feast. If you don't go overboard, you can eat well here for a very moderate price. There are fixed-price lunch specials.

5 King David St. ✆ **09/833-4797.** Reservations recommended. Main courses NIS 50–NIS 150 ($13–$38/£6.25–£19). MC, V. Sun–Thurs noon–midnight; Fri noon–3pm; Sat after Shabbat.

**Tulip** INTERNATIONAL    Set in a modern, glass pavilion on a cliff overlooking the sea at the far end of Ha-Atzma'ut Square, this restaurant serves the most cosmopolitan menu in town. Choices range from salads and stylish pastas to omelets and sandwiches; there's even a great Thai mushroom soup. More expensive items include herbed fish; there are business lunch specials from noon to 4pm and a romantic dinner for two prix fixe with fish, side dishes, and wine for NIS 200 ($50/£25). A selection of lavish pastries and cakes makes this a good stop for coffee and dessert.

Gan Ha Melech. ✆ **1-700/504350.** Reservations recommended for summer and holiday evenings. Main courses NIS 44–NIS 120 ($11–$30/£5.50–£15). AE, DC, MC, V. Sun–Thurs 9am–midnight; Fri 9am–2pm; Sat after Shabbat–midnight.

## INEXPENSIVE

**Pundak Ha-Yam Grill** GRILL    Just off Ha-Atzma'ut Square, you'll find a plain, no-nonsense grill filled with sizzling meats, hardworking waiters, and minimal decor—but this restaurant is nonetheless a top favorite with locals. Why? The grilled meats are prepared to order, right before your eyes; service is quick; portions are good; and prices are moderate. Order shashlik, steak, heart, or liver, and you'll get a salad, french fries, a plate of spaghetti, and several rounds of flat bread, too. For noncarnivores, there are interesting salads.

1 Ha-Rav Kook St. ✆ **09/861-5780.** Reservations not accepted. Main courses NIS 36–NIS 70 ($9–$18/£4.50–£8.75). MC, V. Sat–Thurs noon–midnight; Fri noon–3:30pm.

**Yotvata** CAFE/VEGETARIAN    One of the best-quality dairy and vegetarian restaurants in the country, Yotvata has everything brought in fresh from the famous Yotvata Kibbutz down in the Negev. Giant servings of natural juices made from your choice of 15 different kinds of fruits are available as well as blintzes, vegetable pies, pasta dishes in cream sauces, cheesecakes, farm-fresh omelets, fabulous salads, and great ice cream. Saint Peter's fish rounds out the top end of the menu's price range. Everything is prepared with style.

Ha-Atzma'ut Sq. ✆ **09/862-9141.** Main courses NIS 40–NIS 80 ($10–$20/£5–£10); light meals NIS 22–NIS 32 ($5.50–$8/£2.75–£4). AE, DC, MC, V. Daily 8am–1am.

## NETANYA AFTER DARK

There's no problem finding plenty of things to do around Netanya after a day at the beach. Everything in Ha-Atzma'ut Square is open until around midnight or later, and the square is alive with strollers, sippers, diners, and people-watching cafe-sitters on a warm evening.

Be sure to check with the Tourist Information Office and the weekly calendar in the Tel Aviv section of Friday's *Jerusalem Post* for special events, performances, and activities of all kinds, including the weekly activities at the AACI, the Women's International Zionist Organization (WIZO), and the British Olim Society. There's quite a lot going on, especially during the summer months. Each week, in the amphitheater in **Gan Ha-Melekh Park,** which runs along the beachside cliffs just north of the square, there are screenings of free full-length feature films, and classical and light music (performed Sun–Thurs 5:45pm–sunset). There's also entertainment in **Ha-Atzma'ut Square** by top Israeli singers and folklore groups as well as community folk dancing every Saturday, beginning at 8pm. Weekly programs for children start at 6:30pm, with magicians, clowns, and so on.

Because Netanya is a resort town, with a seasonal turnover in clubs and discos, it's best to check about current choices with the well-informed Tourist Information Office at Ha-Atzma'ut Square. **Bridge** is often sponsored by WIZO on alternate Wednesday evenings; **bingo evenings** at the Association of Americans and Canadians in Israel, 28 Shmuel Ha-Naziv St. (✆ **09/833-0950**), are Sunday at 8pm.

## 3 Caesarea

40km (25 miles) N of Tel Aviv; 49km (30 miles) S of Haifa; 16km (10 miles) N of Netanya

This is one of my favorite places in Israel. It's relatively quiet and has beautiful beaches, dramatic ruins beside the sea, a luxury hotel, and an 18-hole golf course.

Caesarea's beautiful excavations give you a real feeling for the tide of history that has washed Israel's shores. Located about a third of the way from Tel Aviv to Haifa, behind a cluster of banana groves, Caesarea is the spectacular city of Herod the Great (37 B.C.–4 B.C.), who set out to construct a port to rival Alexandria. It was Herod who built and beautified the town, adding a spectacular harbor and naming the city in honor of his Roman suzerain and benefactor, Augustus Caesar. By the time of Herod's death, Caesarea was one of the grandest port cities of the eastern Mediterranean. The city had a mixed population of Greeks, Syrians, Romans, Phoenicians, Egyptians, and some Jews.

Caesarea was the headquarters of Roman rule in Israel, and figures prominently in the story of the apostle Paul: He was warned not to go to Jerusalem; he went anyway, returning to Caesarea in chains to stand trial for heresy. The Jews increasingly resented the Roman domination of their land, and tensions came to a head from A.D. 60 to A.D. 70 when pogroms against the Jewish population began, culminating in the brutal massacre of 2,000 Jews in the Caesarea amphitheater. All Judea subsequently rose in revolt, and the Romans retaliated by destroying Jerusalem in A.D. 70 and conquering Masada in A.D. 73. In A.D. 132, the rebellion of Bar Kochba brought another massacre, and the greatest sages of the time, including Rabbi Akiva, were brought to the amphitheater of Caesarea, tortured in public, then flayed and burned alive. In the next century, Roman Caesarea saw the execution of many early Christians.

Under the Byzantines, the city's history was less grisly. Caesarea was home to a succession of important church scholars, who codified the church laws, and was the seat of a metropolitan bishop responsible for all the Christian communities of the eastern Mediterranean. A small but significant Jewish community thrived throughout this time. The Arab conquest, in A.D. 640, put an end to this period.

In 1101, Baldwin I and his Crusader army landed in Caesarea and slaughtered the entire Arab population. Among the treasures Baldwin's troops discovered after this conquest was a green crystal vessel reputed to be the famous Holy Grail. It was taken to Italy, where it is preserved today, known as the Sacro Catino, in the Cathedral of San Lorenzo in Genoa. Caesarea changed hands several times during the following century, even though Saint Louis of France had fortified its walls in 1252 (even joining in the physical labor). Most of the Crusader ruins we see today date from Saint Louis's 13th-century fortress. When Muslim armies took the town (1265 and 1291), they did their best to pull down the defenses, remembering that this had been Baldwin's beachhead, and for the next 500 years Caesarea's impressive structures slowly became covered by sand.

In the 1700s, Ahmed al Jezzar Pasha, Ottoman governor of the province, sent his workmen to Caesarea to reclaim its Carrara marble, columns of decorative stone, and finely carved capitals for use in the reconstruction and beautification of his provincial capital at Akko (Acre). The vast, beautiful city that Herod had created seemed virtually lost.

An Arab village survived here, but it was abandoned by its inhabitants during the 1948 war. Caesarea's modern history really begins in 1940, when nearby Kibbutz Sedot Yam was founded. Its members discovered the unexpected richness of Caesarea's archaeological remains, and a full campaign of restoration followed. Today, the city is one of Israel's most impressive archaeological sites.

## ESSENTIALS

**GETTING THERE    By Bus**    Public transportation to Caesarea is poor and very time-consuming (which makes an organized tour a good option). To get to Caesarea by bus, you must first take a bus to Hadera from Tel Aviv, Netanya, or Haifa. Buses to Hadera from all these towns run roughly every 30 to 45 minutes. From Hadera, buses leave six times a day for Caesarea, departing Sunday to Thursday. Check with Egged information in Haifa for current timetables both ways. On Friday, the last bus leaves Hadera at 12:40pm, and no buses run on Saturday. Return buses to Hadera leave Caesarea about 20 minutes after each inbound arrival. You can also take one of the intercity Egged buses between Tel Aviv and Haifa, and ask to be let off on the main highway near the road to Caesarea, but from there, it's a desolate hike of about an hour to the national park.

**By Car**    There are exits to Caesarea clearly marked from Hwy. 2 and 4, the two parallel highways that run along the coast between Tel Aviv and Haifa.

**VISITOR INFORMATION**    Just inland from the Crusader city entrance is a small restaurant and a shady parking lot. Be sure to wander behind the restaurant for a look at the ruins of a Byzantine street (described below). Finally, about a kilometer (½ mile) north of the city, a 10- or 15-minute walk along the beach, is the impressive Roman aqueduct.

## EXPLORING CAESAREA
### CAESAREA NATIONAL PARK ⚔

The remains of Caesarea (Qesarya, in Hebrew) are spread along a 3km (2-mile) stretch of Mediterranean beach. There are two separate entrances: You'll arrive at either the Roman theater or the Crusader city, which are in fact right next to each other, though the entrance gates are .5km (¼ mile) apart. Admission to Caesarea National Park is good for both the Crusader city and for the theater. You can enter the city for free after the 5pm closing time to visit restaurants that have sprung up inside the park or stroll the ruins, but special exhibits are closed at night.

You can get a map showing the details of the succession of cities that have risen at this site, both on land and in the water—the cities and harbors of Straton's Tower (the earliest settlement at the site of Caesarea), as well as the Herodian, Roman, Byzantine, and Crusader incarnations of Caesarea. I recommend that you do this, as it will give you a much better idea of the scope of the place. There is also an excellent **Audio-visual Presentation** (✆ 04/617-4444) that brings the site to life, with interesting information about historical figures and re-creations of what Caesarea would have looked like at different times in its history. Call ahead for information, presentation schedules, and to reserve a place.

The excavations you see today are only a very small part of what's actually here, waiting to be discovered; new finds are constantly being unearthed. In recent years, ruins of a massive temple dedicated to Roman gods was uncovered and attributed to the great builder King Herod; it may be open for public viewing during the time span of this edition. I'll assume you're going to see the ruins from south to north, starting with the theater.

The **Roman Theater,** capable of seating 5,000 spectators, was constructed in the time of Jesus and Pontius Pilate, and has been restored. You may be lucky enough to visit when a summer concert or other performance is planned, and sit on the warm, pale limestone seats with the Mediterranean as a backdrop. Test the acoustics by sitting in the stands and listening to someone speak on stage or clap hands.

You enter the **Crusader city** on a bridge across the deep moat, then through a gatehouse with Gothic vaulting. Emerging from the gatehouse, you'll find yourself in the large fortified town, which covered a mere fraction of the great Herodian/Roman city. Sites within the fortified town are marked by signs in Hebrew and English. Especially noteworthy are the foundations of the Crusader Church of Saint Paul (1100s), down toward the sea, near the little Turkish minaret (1800s). The citadel, next to the group of shops and restaurants, was badly damaged by an earthquake in 1837, as was most of the Crusader city.

The **Port of Sebastos,** a quay part of the Crusader port, extends from the Crusader city into the sea, but King Herod's harbor at Caesarea, completed in 10 B.C. and also named Sebastos, extended at least three times as far as what you see today. It curved around to the right, where a separate northern breakwater extended to meet it, roughly where the northern Crusader fortification walls meet the sea.

The breakwater was also a wide platform, with room for large quantities of cargo, housing for sailors, a lighthouse, colossi (gigantic statues), and two large towers guarding the entrance gates to the harbor. The harbor could be closed off by a chain stretched between the two towers, preventing ships from entering; it was big enough and protected enough to permit ships to winter over, allowing the departure of ships laden with cargo from the East just as soon as winter ended.

Herod's harbor was one of the largest harbors of the Roman world, mentioned by historian Flavius Josephus as an especially amazing feat of engineering because it was a total creation—built without the usual benefit of a topographical feature such as a bay or cove. Historians did not find the harbor until 1960, when a combination of aerial photography and underwater archaeological explorations revealed the ruins sunken offshore.

We don't see more evidence of this fantastic port structure because two geological fault lines are just off the coast running below the Herodian port. Historians and archaeologists believe that the harbor structure probably sank vertically downward after its construction as a result of an earthquake.

The excavation of the underwater ruins is an important international project, one of the major endeavors of the Center for Maritime Studies at Haifa University. At the **Caesarea Diving Center/Gal Mor Diving Center,** Old City 38900, Caesarea (© **04/ 636-1787;** fax 06/636-0311), at the site of the ancient harbor, you can join a guided dive with equipment supplied for NIS 250 ($63/£31) for 1 hour. The dive explores ruins of the ancient harbor, and passes by ancient shipwrecks, classical statues, and fragments of a once-great lighthouse. Usually the center requires a minimum of three people for a tour, but for a surcharge, one- or two-person tours can be arranged. All major credit cards are accepted; reserve ahead, although dives cannot be guaranteed if sea conditions are not good. An abbreviated version of the tour is available for snorkelers.

Admission (including the Roman Theater and Crusader city) is NIS 28 ($7/£3.50) for adults, and half-price for children; the interactive tour is NIS 40 ($10/£5) for adults and NIS 35 ($8.75/£4.40) for students and children. Hours are Saturday to Thursday 8am to 4pm (until 5pm Apr–Sept), and Friday from 8am to 3pm. Call © **04/636-7080** or 636-1358 for information.

## THE BYZANTINE STREET

Fifty meters (164 ft.) east of the Crusader city entrance, behind the little snack shop, is the Byzantine Street, or Street of Statues, which is actually part of a forum. The statues depict an emperor and other dignitaries. Much of the stone for construction of the forum was taken from earlier buildings, as was the custom at the time.

## THE HIPPODROME

Head east from either the Byzantine Street or the Roman Theater to reach the ruined hippodrome, in the fields between the two access roads. Measuring 72×288m (236×945 ft.), the hippodrome could seat some 20,000 people. Some of the monuments in the hippodrome may have been brought from Aswan in Egypt—expense was no object when Herod built for Caesar.

## THE JEWISH QUARTER & ROMAN AQUEDUCT

Caesarea's Jewish Quarter is outside the walls of the Crusader city, near the beach directly north of the city. The community that flourished here during Roman times was well within the boundaries, and the walls, of Herod's city.

The great aqueduct north of the Jewish Quarter is almost 9km (6 miles) in length, though most of it has been buried by shifting sands. There was an earlier aqueduct here, but the present construction dates from the 2nd century A.D. The southern part of the aqueduct is exposed to view, and you can see it.

## THE AQUEDUCT BEACH

Swim at the white, sandy lagoons beside the romantic Roman aqueduct. Even in off season (late spring, early autumn) the sea is warmer than the North Atlantic and the

Pacific ever get in the States. Some days the sea is lake-calm, but at other times, as everywhere on the coast, beware of rocks and severe undertows. Currently the beach is free, with an impromptu parking area. Stow all bags in the trunk and keep your eye on the car.

## THE NEW CITY

Largely residential, the modern city of Caesarea is notable for its very worthwhile museum of Spanish and Latin American art, the **Ralli Museum,** located on Roth-schild Boulevard (© **04/626-1013**). The museum contains a large collection of works by Latin American and Spanish artists (including artists of Sephardic origin); is housed in a spacious, beautifully designed new building; and is one of Israel's unexpected and little publicized surprises. The gems of the collection include sculptures by Dalí and Rodin, but the works of Latin American surrealists, representing artists from Mexico to Uruguay, are powerful and impressive. The museum is open daily 10:30am to 3pm and closed on Sunday and Wednesday. Admission is free. Children 5 and under are not allowed to enter.

## WHERE TO STAY

**Dan Caesarea** 🍀🍀 *Kids*   One of the most unusual and beautiful places to stay in Israel, the Dan Caesarea is set amid acres of lush gardens, with a vast swimming pool and restful birdsong in the exotic trees and plantings. The building is 1980s modern, but rooms are spacious and comfy, with terraces that take in wonderful views. It's a great place to relax (the staff are attentive) but also an excellent base for exploring the area at leisure by car—it's next to Israel's best golf course, which guests can use for a fee, and horseback riding, fishing, diving, bicycling, and other local activities can be arranged. There is a full program of in-hotel sports including kids' basketball. Restaurant choices in Zichron Yaacov and among the romantic nearby ruins of Caesarea are fabulous.

Old Caesarea Park. © **04/626-9111.** Fax 04/626-9122. www.danhotels.com. 114 units. $220–$340 (£110–£170) double; add $78 (£39) per room surcharge Thurs–Sat. Rates include breakfast. Family plan and children's rates available. AE, DC, MC, V. Free parking. **Amenities:** Restaurant; cafe; outdoor pool; access to golf club; 2 lit tennis courts; health club; Jacuzzi; sauna; children's activities (in season; holidays); babysitting; laundry service. *In room:* A/C, TV, dataport, hair dryer, safe (some rooms).

## WHERE TO DINE

While there are few overnight facilities in Caesarea itself, there are some pleasant restaurants, especially among the ancient ruins. Few visitors realize that these places stay open after the archaeological park has officially closed; you can enjoy extensive or light meals on their waterfront terraces as well as fabulous sunsets and starry nights.

**Aresto** 🍀 CONTINENTAL   This is the kosher choice in Caesarea, and a very good one it is. There are breakfasts, light meals (like a stylish salad of red tuna and sweet potato in balsamic dressing), focaccia and *taboon*-oven pizzas; and fish and pasta main courses. You can come just for coffee and dessert. Indoor and outdoor seating have views over the ruins but no direct sea view.

Old Caesarea Park. © **04/636-3473.** Reservations recommended. Main courses NIS 40–NIS 100 ($10–$25/£5–£13). AE, DC, MC, V. Sun–Thurs 9am–midnight; Fri 9am–2pm.

**Crusaders** 🍀 SEAFOOD   Good, fresh grilled and fried fish and seafood in hearty portions, and a smattering of meat dishes, keep this busy restaurant filled with Israelis and foreigners. There's indoor and terrace seating; some outdoor tables overlook the sea—in good weather try to nail one down. There's a full bar; Crusaders often stays open until the wee hours.

Old Caesarea Park. ☎ 04/636-1931. Reservations recommended. Main courses NIS 80–NIS 100 ($20–$25/£10–£13). AE, DC, MC, V. Daily noon–1am or later.

**Helena** ★★★ MEDITERRANEAN    This beautiful restaurant is set around an elegant, bay-window wall and deck terrace overlooking the sea. Here, Amos Sion, one of the best young chefs in Israel, designs a contemporary menu that shines and is truly rooted in Mediterranean cooking traditions. The menu changes daily, but is dotted with dishes filled with local cheese, yogurts, herbs, breads, and spices. You might find sautéed scallops in blue-cheese sauce with seaweed and Egyptian spices; a rustic Middle Eastern fish *siniya* (casserole) with red mullet, spinach, and Swiss chard in warm *techina* (sesame) sauce with pine nuts; chicken in date syrup on mustard pasta drops; or a simple salmon filet in hyssop butter sauce. Exotic elements such as Galilee lamb sausages on parsley salad with chickpea stew or seafood casserole in coconut milk, Thai curry, and ginger appear throughout the menu, but everything is light, elegant, and unforced. The excellent wines are all Israeli boutique labels; desserts are fabulous. With a sunset over the sea, and waves brushing the ruins of Caesarea, you couldn't find a more perfect place for a romantic repast.

Old Caesarea Park. ☎ 04/610-1018. Reservations recommended. Main courses NIS 60–NIS 120 ($15–$30/£7.50–£15). AE, DC, MC, V. Daily noon–11pm.

**The Port Café** *Kids* INTERNATIONAL    Overlooking the beach, this restaurant offers great views of the sea from both indoors and its outdoor terrace. It's an informal spot that's notable for its brunch; midday sandwiches, pizzas, focaccia, and salads; and a variety of slightly unusual pasta choices (spaghetti in cream and sweet-potato sauce) that could make a hefty lunch or dinner. There's a winter menu of warming soups in addition to a wide range of coffees and teas. In summer the milkshakes and the house specialty, a frozen mint lemon drink, are especially welcome. Or you can just come for the view and dessert. The wine list is extensive. Everything is dairy or vegetarian.

Old Caesarea Park. ☎ 04/610-0221. Main courses NIS 40–NIS 60 ($10–$15/£5–£7.50); 10% discount with admission ticket to Caesarea National Park. MC, V. Daily 9:30am–midnight.

## 4 Israel's Wine Country

The hills northeast of Caesarea contain a pretty area that could be called Israel's "wine country." **Zichron Yaacov,** the main town in this region, was founded in 1882 under the special patronage of Baron Edmond de Rothschild, and has the distinction of being one of the first agricultural towns to be developed in Israel in modern times. With sweeping vistas of the Mediterranean from its vantage point on the Carmel mountain range, Zichron Yaacov has undergone major restoration in the past few years. Its main street, the quaintest in Israel, is dotted with cafes, craft shops, and restaurants—some have begun comparing the ambience here to a fragment of Carmel, California, or the Hamptons, on Long Island.

Zichron Yaacov means "memorial of Jacob," and was named for the baron's father, James de Rothschild (in Hebrew, Jacob); these days, many just call it "Zichron." Of interest here are the Carmel Mizrachi Winery in Zichron Yaacov and the Baron and Binyamina Wineries in nearby Binyamina (see below).

**Hameyasdim Street,** old Zichron's main thoroughfare, is lined with the town's original houses, some of which have been restored. Stop in to see the **Aaronson**

**House,** 40 Hameyasdim St. (© **04/637-7666**), where a small museum commemorates the heroic and tragic Aaronson family. The Aaronsons' story is a national legend
that has grown more romantic and poetic with time. Aaron Aaronson (1876–1919)
was an agronomist of international repute who received his training in France under
the aegis of the Rothschilds. He discovered and studied an ancestor of modern wheat
that grows in the vicinity. He and his sisters, Sara and Rebecca, and his assistant,
Absolom Feinberg, with whom he had set up an experimental farm at Athlit, were at
the center of NILI, an anti-Turkish spy ring that supplied the British with intelligence
during World War I (Palestine at that time was part of the Ottoman Empire, an
enemy of Britain, France, and America). Feinberg was killed while traveling through
Gaza on a desperate mission to contact the British army in Sinai. After the Six-Day
War, 50 years later, when a search was made so Feinberg could be reburied in
Jerusalem, the site of his grave in Gaza was identified by a palm tree that sprouted
from dates he had been carrying in his pocket when he was ambushed. Both Sara and
Rebecca had been in love with Feinberg; Sara was arrested and committed suicide after
being tortured by the Turks. Aaron Aaronson himself, one of the most promising and
admired members of the Jewish community in Palestine, died in a plane crash on his
way to the Paris Peace Conference at the end of World War I. The house, with its
period ambience and display of historical mementos, is open Sunday to Thursday
from 8:30am to 1pm, Tuesday from 3:30 to 5:30pm, and Friday from 9am until
noon. Admission is NIS 16 ($4/£2).

The **First Aliyah Museum,** 2 Ha-Nadiv St. (© **04/621-2333**), is a multimedia
exhibit of life in the 19th-century Jewish agricultural centers, especially those such as
Zichron Yaacov, founded under the patronage of the Rothschild family. The attempts
to reenact elements of 19th-century life are sometimes didactic or heavy-handed, but
the methods of presentation are interesting. The museum is wheelchair accessible. It's
open Sunday, Monday, Wednesday, and Thursday 9am to 2pm; Tuesday 9am to 7pm;
Friday 9am to 1pm; and Saturday 10am to 2pm. Admission is NIS 20 ($5/£2.50).

You can also visit **Ramat Ha-Nadiv,** or the Heights of the Benefactor, containing
the tomb of the Baron Edmond de Rothschild (1845–1934) and his wife, Baroness
Adelaide de Rothschild, set in handsome gardens filled with all the varieties of plantings the Rothschilds helped to develop in Israel. Near Ramat Ha-Nadiv's vista point,
overlooking Caesarea and the Mediterranean, you'll see a stone map marking the
many towns and agricultural settlements developed under Rothschild sponsorship.
The Rothschilds were reinterred here, according to their wishes, after the establishment of the State of Israel.

Opposite Zichron Yaacov, on the coast, is **Kibbutz Maagan Michael,** whose beautiful carp ponds at the edge of the sea also serve as a **bird sanctuary.** Depending on
the season, bird-watchers can find herons, cranes, storks, and exotic birds, including
(at rare times) flamingos.

The **Hof Ha-Carmel Field School at Maagan Michael** (© **04/639-9655;** fax 04/
639-1618) is an important bird-watching center. November through February, during
migrations between Europe and Africa, is an especially rich time for sightings at this
station. You can arrange a private guided tour of the sanctuary through the Field
School; the rate is approximately NIS 585 ($146/£73) for the day. If you want to visit
on your own, the Field School can supply you with advice and printed material in
English. Kibbutz Maagan Michael produces plastic products and also has a livestock
center featuring in-residence Israeli cowboys and herds of Brahman-type cows.

The lovely **artists' village of Ein Hod** is located inland from Hwy. 2. Road signs point the way for drivers, and from 10am to 5:30pm there is intermittent Egged bus service from Haifa all the way up the mountainside to this famous colony. You can also take bus no. 921 to the Ein Hod roadway that intersects with Hwy. 4, and hitch-hike up the mountainside from there. (True hikers will find the half-hour uphill trek a simple one, but for others, it can be hard, especially in the heat of summer.)

**Ein Hod (Well of Beauty)** was built over an abandoned Arab village in 1953 by Israeli sculptors, painters, and potters, under the guidance of Marcel Janco.

The village now includes a museum of surrealist art, several workshops, and an out-door theater. It's a picturesque place, tranquil and rugged looking, with a view of slop-ing olive groves and the distant Mediterranean that can inspire even the nonartistic. Crumbling archways and Moorish vaults are relics of the past that have been incorpo-rated into the homes of the village. Most of Ein Hod's full-time residents are artists or craftspeople who sell their work in a large, cooperative gallery. But many also sell things from their own houses and workshops, so it's worthwhile to take time and stroll through the lanes of the village (some of the best artisans' houses are in outlying areas) and enjoy the gardens and eccentric homes of this charming enclave.

Cooperation is emphasized: The village members have their own council of elders. The gallery takes a much smaller percentage on sales than do other galleries. Many workshops are shared, and the proceeds from the **Ein Hod Amphitheater's** shows and concerts, which range from folk and classical to hard rock (summer weekends only), are used for the welfare of the village. Call ℂ **04/984-3152** or 984-2029 for informa-tion. There's a snack bar and a more pricey Argentine meat restaurant in Ein Hod if you want to stay for a meal.

The **Janco-Dada Museum of Surreal Art** (ℂ **04/984-2350**) is open Saturday through Thursday 9:30am to 5pm and Friday 9:30am to 2pm. Admission is NIS 20 ($5/£2.50). The village has a modest but pleasant snack bar/cafe and a good Argen-tine restaurant for visitors.

The **Ein Hod Gallery** (ℂ **04/984-2548**) carries a good selection of the village's work—silver jewelry, lots of ceramics, lithographs, etchings, oil paintings, watercolors, tapestries and shawls, sculpture, and woodwork. The gallery staff will box your pur-chases and mail them to you wherever you live. The main gallery, displaying work by 95 different artists and craftspeople, is open Tuesday to Thursday and Sunday 10am to 5pm, Friday 10am to 2pm, and Saturday 11am to 4pm; closed Monday. All major credit cards are accepted. Among Ein Hod's many artisans' shops, check out the **Sil-ver Print Gallery** ꞗ (ℂ **04/984-1067**), near the Ein Hod Square and entrance to the village. It's one of the best places in the country for photographs of pre-1948 Israel, as well as photographs from the early years of Israel's existence and works by Israel's fore-most photographers. Artisans' homes and personal workshops exhibit a wide range of artwork and quality, including custom-designed furniture, clothing, ceramics, silk-screenings, clothing, and jewelry. Admission to the galleries and workshops is often by a small donation for adults. Many individual artists workshops can be visited through-out the year except for Yom Kippur.

Among the **local wineries,** consider visiting one or more of the following:

**Baron Wine Cellars**   This midsize winery produces wine under the Tishbi, Tishbi's Cellar, and Baron labels. Its reputation for white wines (sauvignon blanc, chardonnay, and emerald Riesling) is very good; it also produces champenoise, a sparkling wine. Signs throughout Binyamina will direct you to the winery.

Binyamina, south of Zichron Yaacov. © **04/638-0434** or 629-0280. Tours by appointment only. NIS 20 ($5/£2.50). Sun–Thurs 9am–4pm; Fri 9am–2pm.

**Binyamina Winery**    Another midsize winery, Binyamina offers the visitor a tour of its production center and vineyards. There is wine tasting and a shop on the premises. Investment in new staff and equipment here in the early 1990s make this a very interesting though less prestigious stop. Signs throughout Binyamina will direct you to the winery.

Binyamina, south of Zichron Yaacov. © **04/638-8643**. Tours by appointment only. NIS 16 ($4/£2). Sun–Thurs 8am–4pm; Fri 8am–1pm.

**Carmel Mizrachi Winery**    The sister winery of Carmel Mizrachi in Rishon LeZion, south of Tel Aviv, this is the largest winery in Israel; founded in 1906, it produces 60% of all the country's wine exports. There are organized tours, wine tastings, and a shop on the premises with a complete selection of Carmel Mizrachi products sold at about 15% below standard retail price. Among notable choices are the cabernet sauvignon 1985 from the Rothschild series and the merlots from the Estate series. Also look for a fruity red wine called hilulim, the first wine produced after the grape harvest. Check to see if there will be any of the winery's occasional evening parties, with all-you-can-eat buffets and live music, while you're in town.

Zichron Yaacov, Ha-Nadiv St. © **04/639-0997**. Reservations necessary for tours. NIS 20 ($5/£2.50). Sun–Thurs 9am–3pm; Fri 9am–12:30pm.

## WHERE TO DINE
### EXPENSIVE
**Hanishika (The Kiss)** 🌟🌟 CONTEMPORARY FRENCH    One of Zichron's two fabulous gourmet restaurants (the other is Picciotto, below), this restaurant, with its roots in rustic Provençal cooking, is charming, serving a rich and excellent French menu. With its own signature dishes, different from Picciotto's but equally fine, Hanishika turns this stretch of Zichron's main street into a gourmet's dream. Look for casseroles of lamb or pork, and chef's specials of the day. Special luncheon deals are also offered.

37 Hameyasdim St. © **04/639-0133**. Reservations necessary. Main courses NIS 66–NIS 130 ($17–$33/£8.25–£16). AE, DC, MC, V. Mon 7pm–1:30am; Tues–Sat 12:30–3:30pm and 7pm–1:30am.

**Picciotto** 🌟🌟 CONTEMPORARY FRENCH    Set in a renovated 19th-century cottage on the main street of Zichron, Picciotto is one of the best new restaurants in the country and offers an ever-changing menu that is delightful and satisfying. A meal starts with bread served with an olive tapenade. Foie gras heads the list of admired appetizers, and you can also try one of the skillfully prepared soups (the orange sweet-potato soup is a special pleasure). Main courses might include a hearty beef or pork filet grilled with olive oil and balsamic vinegar; seafood and fish dishes that are original and delicious; and interesting poultry or fowl, such as mullard (a duck-goose hybrid). Desserts, whether somewhat restrained or exotically lavish, are phenomenal. *Tip:* Fixed-price luncheon specials are offered; especially for weekday lunch, drop-ins are possible.

41 Hameyasdim St. © **04/629-0646**. Reservations necessary. Main courses NIS 66–NIS 130 ($17–$33/£8.25–£16). AE, DC, MC, V. Mon–Sat noon–4pm and 7–11pm.

### INEXPENSIVE
**Ha Temanyia Shel Santo** YEMENITE    You may have to search a bit to find this longtime mainstay from the days before Zichron became gentrified—it's in a rear garden

courtyard behind no. 52—but it's worth the search for the superb home-style food. Start with hummus, salad, and bread, followed by grilled chicken or stuffed vegetables. It's the ethnic side dishes, such as the soups, kabobs of meat flavored with cilantro, or Yemenite potato cakes that make this restaurant stand out. Plus, it's kosher.

52 Hameyasdim St. ✆ **04/639-8762.** Main courses NIS 30–NIS 60 ($7.50–$15/£3.75–£7.50). AE, DC, MC, V. Sun–Thurs 11:30am–10pm; Fri 11:30am–2pm.

## A SIDE TRIP TO DOR

On Hwy. 2, the highway that skirts the beach, signs announce Nasholim, a kibbutz located on one of Israel's most beautiful bathing beaches, **Dor Beach** ⋆. A wide expanse of sandy beach, it's touched by the gentle waves of natural lagoons. Looming nearby is **Tel Dor,** a mound containing the remains of an ancient city that was inhabited since Bronze Age times by Phoenicians, Israelites, Greeks, and Romans. The ruins of a massive Greco-Roman temple dedicated to Zeus on a hill at the southern edge of the beach add drama to the site. Entrance is free. Farther to the north at modern Dor is a picturesque area of caves eroded by the sea to form a natural tunnel at the water's edge. Unfortunately, tides sometimes fill the sheltered lagoons with a soup of garbage, and weekends can be dreadfully crowded. There are changing facilities and a simple place for snacks. Admission in season is NIS 20 ($5/£2.50) for adults and NIS 10 ($2.50/£1.25) for children. It's open Saturday to Thursday from 7am to 5pm and Friday 7am to 4pm. Visitors swim at their own risk out of season and after hours.

## WHERE TO STAY

Kibbutz Nasholim. **Note:** There is no exit from Hwy. 2 to Nasholim. To reach Nasholim, leave Hwy. 2 and use the parallel inland road between Binyamina and Faradis.

**Nasholim Kibbutz Holiday Village**    This kibbutz-operated vacation village is about an hour's drive from Tel Aviv, and easily accessible from Caesarea and Haifa. It's a great place to spend the day, or several days. Islets around the fine beach make for sheltered, warm swimming, even out of season, but at times garbage gets swept in. Rooms are very simple, lined up like rows of cabanas with small terraces in front; all have shower-only bathrooms. There are antiquities around this recreation village, and it's a good base for sightseeing and coastal bird-watching. Meals are among the best in the kibbutz guesthouse system; the dinner buffet is very worthwhile. The place is mobbed with Israeli families and kids during the summer school vacation and on Jewish holidays.

Carmel Beach 20815. ✆ **888/669-5700** or 201/556-9669 for reservations in the U.S. and Canada, or 04/639-9533. Fax 04/639-7614. www.nahsholim.co.il. 80 units. $170–$230 (£85–£115) double. Rates include breakfast. Discounts available if booked on Kibbutz Hotel Plan. MC, V. **Amenities:** Restaurant; dining room; cafe; tennis courts; playground; disco. *In room:* A/C, TV, kitchenette (some), fridge, coffeemaker.

## 5 Akko (Acre)

23km (14 miles) N of Haifa; 56km (35 miles) W of Tiberias

Akko, with its romantic minarets, massive city seawalls, and palm trees framed against the sky, has had a long, eventful history. It was first mentioned in the chronicles of Pharaoh Thutmose III, about 3,500 years ago, but is perhaps 2,000 years older. It was a leading Phoenician port, and although it was allotted to the tribe of Asher, the tribe was never able to conquer it. The town is mentioned as part of David's kingdom, and was given by Solomon to Hiram, king of Tyre, in return for his help in building The Temple.

Alexander the Great conquered Acre in 332 B.C., and later, in 280 B.C., it was captured by the Ptolemies, and renamed Ptolemais. Under this name it is mentioned in the New Testament as a stopping place of Saint Paul. Julius Caesar stayed here in 48 B.C.

From the time of Acre's allocation to the tribe of Asher, a Jewish minority lived here in relative peace with the other local inhabitants, but during the Bar Kochba revolt many Jews were killed by the Romans. Even so, remnants of the Jewish population continued to live here.

When the Arabs conquered Ptolemais in A.D. 636, the town reverted to the name of Akka (the Arabic version of the name "Akko"); but when the Crusaders took the town in 1104, they renamed it Saint Jean d'Acre. The town became the regional seat of Crusader government, and it expanded to include an entire underground city, which you still can visit today. Except for one 4-year period, the Crusaders held Acre until the 13th century, when they were defeated by the Mamlukes, who sacked the town. The fall of Acre ensured the doom of Crusader dominion in the Holy Land.

It was not until 1749, when Bedouin sheik Daher el-Omar conquered the town, that Akko experienced a resurgence, but his plans for a serious rebuilding program came to a sudden end when he was murdered in 1775 by the notoriously cruel Ahmed al Jezzar Pasha. Under the impetus of Al-Jezzar Pasha, the town's most important rebuilding took place, including the Jezzar Pasha Mosque, the Khan El-Umdan, the Turkish bathhouse now housing the Municipal Museum, the massive stone walls, and the aqueduct to the north. These structures still stand today.

Akko's decline as a major port was sealed by the advent of the steamship and modern naval technology, with shipping activities gradually transferred to the larger port at Haifa across the bay. On May 4, 1947, Akko was the scene of the largest prison break in history when 251 prisoners escaped from Akko Fortress with the help of Jewish underground fighters.

## ESSENTIALS

**GETTING THERE    By Bus**    Bus nos. 262 and 272 (express) and 271 (local) leave the Haifa bus station every 10 minutes, bound for Akko; the schedule is less frequent on Saturday. Bus or train fare is NIS 16 ($4/£2). Trains leave Haifa for Akko and avoid the often terrible road traffic.

**By Car**    Independence Road in Haifa port runs north out of the city past a heavily industrial area. At a crossroads called the "checkpost," bear left, following the signs, over the railroad tracks, and you'll be on the northern coastal road to Akko and Nahariya.

**VISITOR INFORMATION**    Directly across from the Jezzar Pasha Mosque is the **Tourist Information Office** (ⓒ **04/995-6707** or 1-700/708-8020; www.akko.org.il), open Sunday to Thursday from 8:30am to 5pm. Here—or next door, at the entrance to the Subterranean Crusader City—you can buy a large, wonderfully detailed map of the entire city of Akko, and a combined admission ticket to all sites and museums in the city may also be purchased here. Operating in conjunction with this office is the **Western Galilee Tourist Society,** 1 Weitzman St., Old Akko (ⓒ **04/981-7419;** fax 04/981-7423), which distributes information on touring, local festivals, and lodging throughout the entire Western Galilee.

*A note for women:* Medieval Akko is fascinating, but women unaccompanied by men, even in pairs or in groups, attract a lot of attention around the labyrinthine Old City, especially after dark.

# Akko (Acre)

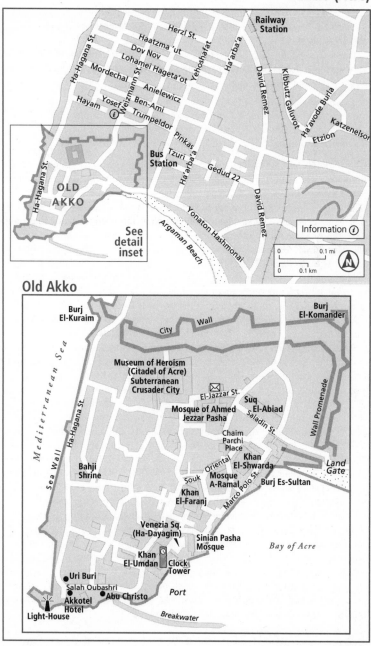

## Old Akko

**GETTING AROUND**   Coming into town by car, you can simply follow the signs for the Old City. There is a small parking lot on the left (NIS 16/$4/£2), just inside the city walls.

If you arrive from Haifa by bus, city bus nos. 1, 2, 61, 62, 63, and 65 all make stops at the entrance to the Old City. A taxi should run around NIS 20 ($5/£2.50) at most.

**CITY LAYOUT**   Today, Akko comprises two distinct parts. There's the modern city of Akko, with about 40,000 residents, and a number of large industrial plants (including Steel City) and immigrant housing projects. Then there's the Old City, still surrounded by high, thick stone walls on all sides, situated on the tip of land jutting out into the sea, forming the protected Bay of Akko.

## EXPLORING OLD AKKO

Allow yourself a half-day to wander through Old Akko's medieval streets. Unlike the restored Old City of Jaffa, which is filled with tourist galleries, Old Akko is both charming *and* genuine, and its streets teem with real life. The best place to start your tour is at the **Jezzar Pasha Mosque.** Right across the street from Al-Jezzar Pasha's mosque is the marvelous **Subterranean Crusader City,** and just a few steps farther is the **Municipal Museum** (exhibits sometimes closed for renovations) housed in Ahmed al Jezzar Pasha's Turkish bath.

Next you'll wander through the pleasant and colorful streets of the **bazaar.** Be sure to see the most picturesque shop in the bazaar, **Kurdy and Berit's Coffee and Spices,** at no. 13/261 (ask around, it's deep in the market). If you make a purchase at Kurdy and Berit's, the very hospitable owner may invite you to try a cup of thick Arabic coffee. Akko's "formal" market is **Suq El-Abiad,** but numerous streets within Old Akko serve as shopping areas. You'll pass the **El-Zeituneh Mosque** to the **Khan El-Umdan** caravansary, marked by a tall, segmented tower. A **caravansary,** or khan, was a combination travelers' inn, warehouse, banking center, stable, and factory traditionally built around a lightly fortified courtyard to house caravans, pilgrims, and other visitors.

The market streets, filled with delicious Arabic bakeries and hummus restaurants, are an excellent area to find snacks. Just beyond is the port, a good place to stop for lunch (see "Where to Dine," below). At the port, you can also hire a boat to take you on a **sea tour** of the city walls (about NIS 36/$9/£4.50 per person). Don't be afraid to bargain. Many boat operators will be glad to take you on a motor- or fishing-boat cruise around Old Akko. Settle on a price in advance (about NIS 80/$20/£10 for an hour is the average), and get a boat that looks comfortable. A large tourist boat, the *Princess,* takes visitors on a 20-minute ride around the Old City walls, but only when enough people are waiting to make the run profitable. The fare is NIS 20 ($5/£2.50) per person.

In Venezia Square (Ha-Dayagim in Hebrew), facing the port, is the **Sinian Pasha Mosque,** and behind it the **Khan El-Faranj** caravansary. Yet another khan, named **El-Shwarda,** is a short distance to the northeast. A few steps back is the Jezzar Pasha Mosque. You'll also want to visit the dreaded **Al-Jezzar Wall,** where barbaric punishments were meted out, and the outer wall of the Akko prison, scene of a massive prisoner escape in 1947 (during the British Mandate) engineered by the Jewish underground. The escape was reproduced in the film *Exodus.*

### THE TOP ATTRACTIONS

**Jezza Pasha Mosque**   Ahmed al Jezzar ("the Butcher") Pasha was the Ottoman-Turkish governor of Akko during the late 1700s, and notorious for his habit of mutilating both those in his government and those he governed. According to legend, on

Al Jezzar Pasha's whim, faithful chamberlains and retainers were ordered to slay their own children as signs of loyalty to the Pasha, and the Pasha rewarded government officials and loyal subjects with amputations of hands, arms, eyes, and legs to test their willingness to submit to his whims. If this was how he treated his friends, you can imagine the fate of his enemies. When Napoleon invaded Egypt, the English joined the Ottomans in trying to drive him out. Al Jezzar Pasha marshaled the defenses of Akko, and the city withstood Napoleon's assault in 1799. Napoleon's forces never recovered from this impasse, and Napoleon's dream of conquering Egypt died outside the walls of Akko. The Pasha died in Akko in 1804, to the great relief of the city's inhabitants.

Ahmed al Jezzar Pasha's contributions to Akko included building fountains, a covered market, a Turkish bath, and the harmonious mosque complex that bears his name. Begun in 1781, it is an excellent example of classic Ottoman-Turkish architecture and stands among the Pasha's most ambitious projects. Every great man in the empire wanted to endow a mosque in his own name, an act that not only added to his glory on earth but also gained points for him in heaven. A number of charitable institutions were usually constructed around the mosque, and shops were built into the walls, the rent from the shops paying for the mosque's maintenance. Though the greatest of these complexes were in Constantinople, the Ottoman capital, the one in Akko is a graceful provincial example of the exotic style of Ottoman architecture (rooted in both Byzantine and Persian traditions); it also illustrates how the traditional mosque complex worked.

As you approach the mosque area, Al-Jezzar Street turns right off Weizmann Street. The mosque entrance is a few steps along Al-Jezzar Street on the left. Before you mount the stairs to the mosque courtyard, notice the ornate little building to the right of the stairs. It's a *sabil,* or cold-drinks stand, from which pure, refreshing drinking water, sometimes mixed with fruit syrups, was distributed—a part of the mosque complex's services. Note especially the fine tile fragments mounted above the little grilled windows just beneath the *sabil's* dome. Tile making was an Ottoman specialty.

Up the stairs, you enter the mosque courtyard. Your ticket will enable you to explore the complex of Crusader buildings, including a church (now flooded and used as cisterns) over which the mosque was built. Just inside the entry, mounted on a pedestal, is a marble disc bearing the *tughra,* or monogram, of the Ottoman sultan. It spells out the sultan's name, his father's name, and the legend "ever-victorious."

The arcaded courtyard around the mosque can be used for prayers during hot days of summer, as can the arcaded porch at the front of the mosque. The *shadirvan,* or ablutions fountain, opposite the mosque entry, is used for the ritual cleansing of face, neck, hands, and feet five times a day before prayers. You must slip off your shoes before entering the mosque proper. This is not merely a religious rule, but a hygienic one: Worshipers kneel on the carpets during prayer, and want to keep them clean.

Inside you'll notice the mihrab, or prayer niche, which indicates the direction of Mecca, toward which worshipers must face when they pray. The galleries to the right and left of the entrance are reserved for women, the main area of the floor for men. The *minbar,* a sort of pulpit, is that separate structure with a curtained entry, stairs, and a little steeple. Around to the right are a mausoleum and a small graveyard that hold the tombs of Ahmed al Jezzar Pasha and his successor, Suleiman Pasha, and members of their families. The mosque is still used by Akko's Muslim population, so when it's in service for prayer (five times a day), you must wait until the prayers are over to enter the mosque (about 20 min.).

Al-Jezzar St. Admission to mosque complex and subterranean Crusader vaults NIS 5 ($1.25/60p). Daily 8am–noon, 1:15–4pm, and 4:45–6pm. Modest dress required. No entrance during prayers (exact times vary according to time of the year; check with the tourist office).

**Municipal Museum (Turkish Bath)**    Down at the end of Al-Jezzar Street, just around the corner, is the Municipal Museum, originally the hammam, or Turkish bath, built by Ahmed al Jezzar Pasha as part of his mosque complex in the 1780s. The museum's collections, including antiquities, an exhibit on Napoleon's attack, the Museum of Heroism, and a folklore exhibit are often closed as the building undergoes repairs, but the building itself is fantastic. Visiting art exhibitions are also displayed here.

Turkish baths were modeled after the Roman plan, with three distinct rooms. The first was the entry and dressing room, the next was the tepidarium (its Roman name), with warm steam, and the last was the caldarium, with hot steam. The hot room was always the most ornate.

As you walk through the first two rooms, note the tiny glass skylights in the domes. The third room, the one for hot steam, is rich in marble and mosaic work. In the center is a circular platform for steam bathing. The heat source was beneath it. Some Turkish baths have a small swimming pool here instead. Four private steam cubicles occupy the four points of the compass.

Al-Jezzar St. Admission NIS 12 ($3/£1.50) for adults; discounts available for students and children. Includes admission to Crusader City. Sun–Thurs 8:30am–6pm; Fri 8:30am–2pm; Sat 9am–5pm. Closings are 1 hr. earlier in winter.

**Museum of Underground Prisoners**    The museum is in the Citadel of Akko. This complex of buildings was used as a prison in Ottoman and British Mandate times. Part of the prison has been set aside in honor of the Jewish underground fighters imprisoned here by the British. With the help of Irgun forces, 251 prisoners staged a mass escape in May 1947. If you saw the movie *Exodus,* that was the breakout featured in the film and this was the prison. The prison is also revered by Arab Israelis and by Palestinians, whose own national fighters were detained and, in many cases, executed here during the British Mandate.

Among the exhibits are the entrance to the escape tunnel and displays of materials showing the British repression of Zionist activity during the mandate. Not all prisoners were lucky enough to escape, however. Eight Irgun fighters were hanged here in the 10 years before Israel's independence. You can visit the death chamber, called the Hanging Room, complete with noose.

Inmates here included Zeev Jabotinsky and Dov Gruner, among other leaders of Zionism and Israel's independence movement. Before the mandate, the prison's most famous inmate was Baha' Allah (1817–92), founder of the Baha'i faith (see "Bahji," below).

Just north of Crusader City. ✆ **04/991-8264.** Admission NIS 12 ($3/£1.50) adults; discounts available for students and children. Sun–Thurs 9am–5pm.

**New Akko Ethnographic and Folklore Museum**    Scheduled to open in late 2008, this new museum, set in a dramatically restored market building located near the northeast entrance to the Old City, will contain a reproduction of a 19th-century market, including blacksmith, jewelry, pharmacy, tailor, money-changing, letter-writing, and leather-work shops. A second section of the museum will display collections of antique furniture (including pieces inlaid with mother of pearl in the old Damascus tradition), old coins, mirrors, game tables, copper ware, boxes, and other decorative items. Check with the Tourist Information Office for further details; a combined admission ticket for the new Ethnographic museum and other museums and historic sites in Akko may be offered during the time span of this edition.

**Subterranean Crusader City**    Virtually across the street from the Mosque of Ahmed al Jezzar Pasha is the Subterranean Crusader City. In the entrance is a tourism information kiosk, where you can buy a city map and an entrance ticket.

The Crusaders built their fortified city atop what was left of the Roman city. The Ottomans, and especially Ahmed al Jezzar Pasha, built their city on top of the largely intact buildings of the Crusaders. In Ottoman times, the cavernous chambers were used as a caravansary until Napoleon's attack. In preparation for the defense of his city, Al-Jezzar Pasha ordered the walls heightened, and the Crusader rooms partially filled with sand and dirt, to better support the walls. Today, you get a good look at how the Crusaders lived and worked in the late 1100s.

The bottom of the hall was built by the Crusaders, the top by the Ottomans. The next hall you enter once held an illegal (in Muslim times) wine press. Next comes the courtyard, with the 38m-high (125-ft.) walls of **Akko Citadel,** which was used by the British as a prison during the mandate and now houses the Museum of Heroism (see above).

Beyond the courtyard, through a huge Ottoman gate, are the **Knights' Halls,** once occupied by the Knights Hospitalers of Saint John. In the ceiling of the hall, a patch of concrete marks the spot where Jewish underground members, imprisoned by the British in the citadel (directly above the hall), attempted to break out.

Back through the courtyard, you now head for the **Grand Maneir,** or center of government, in the Crusader City. Past it, through a narrow passage, is the **Crypt,** so named only because of its present depth; it was actually the knights' refectory, or dining hall. Beyond the refectory is a longer tunnel leading to the **Post (El-Posta),** a series of rooms and a courtyard similar to a caravansary, the precise use of which is not known.

Across from Jezzar Pasha Mosque. Admission NIS 28 ($7/£3.50) adults; discounts available for students and children. Admission includes entrance to Municipal Museum. Sun–Thurs 8:30am–6pm; Fri 8:30am–2pm; Sat 9am–5pm. Closings are 1 hr. earlier in winter.

## AL-JEZZAR'S WALL

To appreciate the elaborate system of defenses built by Ahmed al Jezzar Pasha to protect against Napoleon's fleet and forces, turn right as you come out of the Municipal Museum/Museum of Heroism onto Ha-Hagana Street and walk a few steps north. You'll see the double system of walls with a moat in between. Jutting into the sea is an Ottoman defensive tower called the Burj El-Kuraim. You're now standing at the northwestern corner of the walled city. Walk east (inland) along the walls and you'll pass the citadel, the Burj El-Hazineh (Treasury Tower), and cross Weizmann Street to the Burj El-Komander, the strongest point in the walls. The land wall system continues south from here all the way to the beach.

At the entrance to the Old City on Weizmann Street, near the Walls of Al-Jezzar, is a sunken children's playground bordered by the Dahar El-Omer Walls. Dahar El-Omer (or Daher El-Amar) was the sheik who rebuilt the city walls after capturing Akko from the Mamlukes.

## THE KHANS & THE PORT

Make your way south through the city, toward the port, and if you need a point of reference, ask a local to point you toward the **Khan El-Umdan.** The khan, a market and inn complex for visiting merchants and caravans (dating from 1785), is much older than its tower, which was built as a clock tower in 1906 to celebrate the 30th year of the reign of the Ottoman sultan Abdul Hamid II. El-Umdan means "The Pillars," and when you enter this vast colonnaded court you'll know how it got its name. Another of Ahmed al Jezzar Pasha's harmonious works in the public service, this caravansary served commerce. It was built on the site of a Crusader monastery of the Dominican order.

Just to the east of Khan El-Umdan is Venezia Square (Ha-Dayagim) and the **Sinian Pasha Mosque.** The port is to the southeast and industrious fishers are still at work here. Behind the port are two more caravansaries. The **Khan El-Faranj** (Afranj), or the Inn of the Franks, is a few steps north of the Sinian Pasha Mosque. This complex originated in 1729 as a Franciscan convent, but some of the building was apparently rented to French and Italian merchants.

Northeast of the Khan El-Faranj is the **Khan El-Shwarda,** right next to a tower in the city walls called **Burj Es-Sultan.** The Burj is famous because it is the only structure erected by the Crusaders that remains intact. At the tower's base is one of Napoleon's cannons, cast in Liège and captured by the Ottoman and English forces.

Walk up Marco Polo Street to your next stop. Marco Polo, by the way, was one of several famous visitors to Akko in medieval times; another was King Richard the Lion-Hearted. The **Khan El-Shwarda,** at the northern end of Marco Polo Street, occupies the site of a convent of the nuns of Saint Clare that closed in 1291 when Akko fell. There's not a lot to look at today.

The **Mosque A-Ramal** (or El-Ramel), the former "Sand Mosque," on Marco Polo Street, was built from 1704 to 1705. A Crusader inscription was found on the southeast wall of this mosque, which today forms part of the back wall of the fourth shop on the left from the mosque entrance. The Latin inscription reads, "Oh, men who pass along this street, in charity I beg you to pray for my soul—Master Ebuli Fazli, builder of the church." The mosque is open daily from 4 to 6pm (admission is free).

An old **lighthouse,** still in use, stands atop the Crusader fortification of Burj Es-Sanjak, on the extreme southwest point of land at Akko. From here you get a marvelous view, both north and south. Just north of the lighthouse, you'll notice a large space in the seawall. This stretch of the wall was destroyed during the heavy earthquake of 1837, the same earthquake that leveled several cities in the mountains.

## BAHJI

To Baha'is, this shrine to their prophet Baha' Allah is the holiest place on earth. Baha'i followers believe that God is manifested to men and women through prophets such as Abraham, Moses, Jesus, and Muhammad, as well as the Bab (Baha' Allah's predecessor) and Baha' Allah himself. The Baha'i faith proclaims that all religions are one, that men and women are equal, that the world should be at peace, and that education should be universal. Baha'i followers are encouraged to live simply and to dedicate themselves to helping their fellow men and women. They look forward to a day when there will be a single world government and one world language.

The Baha'i faith grew out of the revelation of the Bab, a Persian Shiite Muslim teacher and mystic who flourished from 1844 to 1850, and was executed by the Persian shah for insurrection and radical teachings. In 1863, Mirza Husein Ali Nuri, one of the Bab's disciples, proclaimed himself Baha' Allah, the Promised One, whose coming had been foretold by the Bab. Baha' Allah was exiled by the Persian government in cooperation with the Ottoman leaders to Baghdad, Constantinople, Adrianople, and finally to Akko, where he arrived in August 1868. He and several of his followers were imprisoned for 2½ years at the Akko Citadel. The authorities later put him under house arrest, and he was eventually brought to Bahji, where he remained until his death in 1892. He is buried here in a peaceful tomb surrounded by magnificent gardens. Baha'is are still persecuted, especially in Iran where the faith was born; the Shiite Muslims in authority today look upon them as blasphemers and heretics.

You can visit the shrine at **Bahji (Delight),** where Baha' Allah lived, died, and is buried, on Friday, Saturday, and Sunday only, from 9am to noon. The house's beautiful gardens are open to visitors every day, from 9am to 4pm. Catch a no. 271 bus heading north toward Nahariya, and make sure it stops at Bahji.

Going north from Akko, you'll see an impressive gilded gate on the right-hand side of the road after about 2km (1 mile). This gate is not open to the public. Go past it until you are almost 3km (about 2 miles) from Akko, and you'll see a sign, SHAMERAT. Get off the bus, turn right here, and go another short distance to the visitors' gate. The Ottoman–Victorian house holds some memorabilia of Baha' Allah, and the lush gardens are a real treat.

## ARGAMAN BEACH

Argaman Beach, just south of the Old City, is one of Israel's most beautiful Mediterranean beaches, with a view of Haifa in one direction and the exotic skyline of Akko on the other. The beach is good for sunning, but unfortunately the water near Akko suffers from serious pollution. If you're staying at the Palm Beach Hotel (see below), stick to the swimming pool.

Off season, visitors are usually welcome for a day-use fee to enjoy the facilities at the **Palm Beach Hotel and Country Club** (*©* **04/981-5815**) on Argaman Beach. These include an outdoor Olympic-size swimming pool plus a heated indoor pool; tennis, volleyball, basketball, and squash courts; Ping-Pong tables; a health club; a Finnish sauna; and a private beach with lounge chairs and shades. Call ahead to make a reservation and inquire about the current day-use fee.

## WHERE TO STAY

Outside of el cheapo private hostels, there are only two choices: a new hotel in the Old City and a high-rise on the beach south of town.

**Akkotel** *(Finds)*   Opened in 2007, this charming 16-room boutique hotel, set in a lovingly restored building right against the walls of the Old City, offers a great chance to overnight in Old Akko and enjoy the city's atmosphere. It's not a luxury hotel, but everything is fresh, atmospheric, and carefully designed, with traditional arches and exposed stone walls. Large, one-of-a-kind guest rooms are equipped with modern amenities and comfortable beds. Larger rooms can fit families; bathrooms have either a tub or a shower. Owner Ilya Morani and his family are most welcoming and helpful about explaining the intricate Old City; a rooftop terrace and restaurant offers spectacular views. Dining facilities are not kosher.

1153 Salah-Al-Din St., Akko Old City. *©* **04/987-7100.** Fax 04/981-0626. www.akkotel.com. 16 units. NIS 700 ($175/ £88) double. Rate includes breakfast. AE, MC, V. Free street parking. **Amenities:** Restaurant; dining room; roof terrace. *In room:* A/C, satellite TV, minibar/fridge, hair dryer.

**Palm Beach Hotel and Country Club**   A high-rise with sweeping views, the Palm Beach is the best place to stay in Akko. The greatest benefit of staying here, in addition to the wonderful beach and view, is the free use of the country club and other facilities—the outdoor pool is gigantic. While nonguests may be able to use the club when it's not too busy, staying at the hotel guarantees the privilege. All rooms have sea views and have been recently spruced up, but they're small, with 1980s decor; most double beds are full-size rather than the usual larger queen-size. All the hotel's restaurant facilities are kosher. There is a bus into town; the Old City is a 15-minute walk away.

Akko Beach, 24101 (1.6km/1 mile south of the Old City on the coastal road [Hwy. 2] to Haifa). © 04/987-7777. Fax 04/991-0434. www.palmbeach.co.il. 127 units. $130–$160 (£65–£80) double. Add 20% on weekends. Rates include breakfast. AE, MC, V. Free self-parking. **Amenities:** Restaurant; cafe; bar; 2 pools (indoor, outdoor); lighted tennis courts; fitness center; squash and basketball courts; Jacuzzi; wet and dry sauna; children's playground; room service; massage; laundry service; beach; disco; synagogue. *In room:* A/C, TV, dataport (most rooms), minibar, hair dryer, safe.

## WHERE TO DINE

**Abu Christo** ★ *Finds* SEAFOOD    This well-known restaurant is particularly nice in good weather, when you can sit out on the shaded terrace beside the sea and enjoy the delightful vista, which includes a view of Haifa across the bay, waves almost at your feet, and, at times, local daredevils diving from the ancient ruins. It's a wonderful place for a leisurely, Greek Island–style meal. For appetizers, a generous and especially good round of Middle Eastern salads and pita is included in the price of every main course. Most main courses are straightforward dishes such as steak and grilled skewers of lamb. The best choice is the very fresh grilled catch of the day (the grouper is delectable), served with french fries; there's also interesting seafood such as skewered shrimp in sesame garlic sauce cooked on an open fire. Abu Christo often features special low-price treats, such as tiny fresh fish fried in garlic, which you eat, bones, heads, and all. There's a full bar and very attentive, friendly service. Be sure to reserve a table alongside the sea.

Near the Lighthouse, Old City. © 04/991-0065. Reservations recommended weekends. Main courses NIS 44–NIS 100 ($11–$25/£5.50–£13). AE, DC, MC, V. Daily 10am–midnight.

**Oudeh Brothers Restaurant** SEAFOOD/MIDDLE EASTERN    This traditional, pleasant restaurant has four large, airy dining rooms (alas, no waterfront view) and a large patio dining area beside the courtyard of the Khan El-Faranj. There's no sea view, but it offers a wonderful 25-salad meze, lamb shashlik with rice and salad; meat with hummus, pickles, and pita; and lots of seafood, including lobster and shrimp. Turkish coffee is on the house if you've ordered a meal.

Old City market area. © 04/991-2013. Reservations recommended weekends. Main courses NIS 44–NIS 100 ($11–$25/£5.50–£13). Higher prices for lobster. MC, V. Daily 9am–midnight.

**Uri Buri** ★★ SEAFOOD    Set in an old Turkish house facing the open sea, with small, informal, intimate rooms decorated with Arabic touches, this restaurant's secret ingredient is owner/chef Uri Yirmias, who has an exceptional talent for preparing seafood and fish to perfection. Ask what's freshest and best to order. Uri's Coquilles St. Jacques, pan-seared according to his special recipe, are amazingly rich and tender, like a filet mignon from the sea. Among the daily specialties you might encounter are tiny, tender calamari with kumquats and pink grapefruit; fresh fish with marvelous mustard/honey or rosemary and balsamic vinegar sauce; and wonderful bisques and chowders. Also look for a fabulous "terrine" of grilled red pepper filled with feta cheese, cashews, and local black olives; Uri's fun deep-fried calamari rings with three dipping sauces; and his Creole shrimp in a five-spice cream sauce with mango (in season). Dishes here are so wonderful that Uri encourages half-portions so you can sample the menu. There's also a major tasting menu that's a good idea—the menu for one can easily be shared, and you can order an additional half-portion of what you liked best. When the weather's good, there's dining on an open terrace with sea views.

93 Haganah St., near the lighthouse (Midal Or) in the Old City. ✆ 04/955-2212. Reservations necessary. Main courses NIS 80–NIS 140 ($20–$35/£10–£18). AE, MC, V. Wed–Mon noon–11pm.

## AKKO AFTER DARK

One of Akko's most enjoyable evening activities is strolling around through the tiny Arabian Nights streets, past the old khans and the towering minarets framed by moonlight and stars, gazing from the old port out across the bay toward the sparkling lights of Haifa. On a quiet moonlit night, you can stand in the courtyard of Khan El-Umdan and imagine all the people, animals, activities, and human dramas that have passed through here. Another atmospheric moonlight walk is around the city's seawalls.

Exotic Arabic music fills the air day and night all around Old Akko. Light and music pour out into the streets from the open doors of billiard parlors, and you're welcome to come in and shoot a few games. Beer or wine at a seaside cafe or restaurant and interesting talks with fellow travelers is another option.

## SIDE TRIPS FROM AKKO

The main highway between Akko and Nahariya parallels fragments of a stone **aqueduct** built by Ahmed al Jezzar Pasha in 1780 over the ruins of a Roman aqueduct. The aqueduct originally supplied Akko with water from the Galilee's springs. Its picturesque ruins include many archways framing sabra plants. Before you reach Nahariya, you will pass two communities that are well worth a visit: Kibbutz Lohammei HaGetaot and the beautiful horticultural community of Nes Amim, populated by Christians from many nations. In the countryside farther inland (east), there's also a chance to visit traditional Ethiopian Jewish potters and to purchase examples of their craft.

**Kibbutz Lohammei HaGetaot** ✦✦    The Ghetto Defenders' Kibbutz, 3.2km (2 miles) north of Akko, was founded in 1949 by a small group of survivors of Jewish ghettos in Poland and Lithuania. Initially scattered in towns and refugee camps throughout Israel, they felt they could best rebuild their lives among others who had similar tragic memories as former partisans and participants in ghetto uprisings. The kibbutz flourished, and today their children and grandchildren manage the schools, factories, and beautiful orchards of this very symbolic community.

The **Ghetto Fighters' House** at Kibbutz Lohammei HaGetaot, the **Museum of the Holocaust and Resistance,** and **Yad La Yeled,** the Memorial and Museum of Children, together form Israel's second-largest memorial and museum of the Holocaust after Yad VaShem in Jerusalem. This complex, with its own archives and study programs, documents Jewish life in communities throughout Europe before and during the Holocaust. The complex contains a museum of writings, diaries, and artwork from the ghettos and concentration camps, and these detailed, very personal exhibits vividly inform about the ghetto uprisings and the destruction of Jewish communities, including those in Holland, Saloniki, Vilna, and Hungary. Among the many models and installations is a replica of the Anne Frank House in Amsterdam. Especially moving are the paintings and drawings done by children. The museum is the center for an international education program designed to teach about the Holocaust, in the hope that such knowledge will help prevent such cruelties from being permitted in the future.

Akko-Nahariyah Rd. ✆ 04/995-8080. Free admission; contributions accepted for the guided tours. Sun–Thurs 9am–4pm; Fri 9am–1pm; Sat and minor Jewish holidays 10am–5pm. Bus: 271 (midday frequency: every 30 min.) from Haifa to Nahariya will make requested stops at the kibbutz.

## (Finds) Ethiopian Pottery: The Jewish Women Ceramists of Beta Israel

Ethiopian women in the Wollaka region were responsible for cooking and other work having to do with fire, including the making of clay pots, and the Jewish women (Beta Israel) of the villages in this area were famous for their low-fire pottery ware, which they sold in markets. It was folk wisdom of the region that if your mother was good at pottery making, you must be Beta Israel. As tourists began to visit the area in the 1950s, Beta Israel women began making native clay figurines and models of village houses and village life for sale to travelers. Although not a previously known Jewish folk-art tradition, many of these works have real charm, and the works of the best artists have become collector's items. Arriving in Israel, Ethiopian Jews were culturally disoriented and removed from their traditions, but some of the women potters have been encouraged to continue to work at their craft. Judaica is one of the new directions they are exploring, and although Chanukah was unknown to Ethiopian Jews (they were separated from other Jewish communities before the Maccabean restoration of The Temple of Jerusalem in 167 B.C., which the holiday commemorates), their vibrant clay Chanukah menorahs are exotically African in style.

In a one-person crusade to save this craft, veteran Israeli Dorit Katzir has set up a kiln and cooperative workshop for these ceramists in her beautiful organic farming village of Klil, located about 10km (6 miles) inland from the sea, in the countryside between Akko and Nahariya. For those interested in purchasing examples of this low-fire, rough-black unglazed folk art, a visit to the studio can be arranged by contacting Dorit Katzir (© **04/996-7045;** mobile phone 05/465-4385; fax 04/996-5145). Prices range from NIS 80 ($20/ £10) for simple items to thousands of shekels.

You can best visit Klil by private car, or if you have a private guide, ask to include the workshop in your itinerary. Katzir will give you directions to Klil by phone; she asks that only those seriously interested in seeing the craft and making a purchase come. Examples of Beta Israel pottery can sometimes be found at craft shops in Israel (try Yad B'homer at 9 Massada St. in Haifa, or various museum shops).

## WHERE TO STAY

**Nes Ammim Guest House**    Another short drive from Akko, to the north and through an enchanting avocado forest, is a 200-member Christian village organized in 1963 for the purpose of bringing Jews and Christians into closer contact. This community is famous for growing flowers. While here, you can enjoy the wonderful greenhouse creations and the botanical gardens, and get a free tour of the community. Guest rooms were last redone in 1997; they are compact and simple, with narrow single beds, but bright and cheerful. There are 13 family-size rooms; rooms for travelers with disabilities are also available. There is a large, refreshing swimming pool. Although not a kibbutz, the hotel is part of the Kibbutz Guest House Association, and can be booked through their packages. Food services are glatt kosher. Study tours on the subject of Jewish-Christian relations can be arranged through Nes Ammim.

**For visitors on day tours:** If you're not staying here, but are interested in the community, call ahead and arrange for a tour. The Nes Ammim community is especially interested in making the land alive again, and you will be amazed by its efforts and dedication. Coming by bus is a bit more of a challenge, but it can be arranged; call ahead and they'll tell you the best way to do it.

Mobile Post, Ashrat 25225. 🕾 **04/995-0000.** Fax 04/995-0098. reservations@nesammim.com. 58 units. $144 (£72) double on Kibbutz Hotel Choice Package. Rate includes breakfast. AE, DC, MC, V. From Akko drive north along the main highway (Hwy. 2) past Kibbutz Lohammei Hagetaot; then look for signs pointing east to Nes Ammim and Regba; turn right onto the Nes Ammim-Regba road and go 4km (2 miles) inland. **Amenities:** Dining room; bar; playground; rooms for those w/limited mobility. *In room:* A/C, TV, kitchenette (family-size room).

## 6 Nahariya & North to the Border

33km (21 miles) N of Haifa

Founded by German Jews in the mid-1930s, Nahariya is a quiet summer resort, popular with older tourists and retired, European-born Israelis. It used to be popular with Israeli honeymooners, but most have moved on to more exotic places. Maybe there's a connection between Nahariya as a honeymoon site and the fact that archaeologists dug up a Canaanite fertility goddess on its beach.

The town has a pretty main street, Ha-Ga'aton Boulevard, with a stream (in winter) running down its median, shaded by breezy eucalyptus trees. With its eucalyptus-shaded shops running down to a sparkling sea, Nahariya has real potential, but so far it remains sleepy and low-key; there are a few rather ordinary shops, cafes, and restaurants in the downtown area.

Lifeguards go home and lock the fences around the public beaches at 5pm, so if you want to hit the beach without courting skin cancer, this is not the ideal place. The sparkling sea is sometimes a soup of garbage washed down from chaotic Lebanon; to make matters worse, the city has no sewage treatment plant. But Nahariya has many fans, and it's a pleasant base for exploring the northern coast and Western Galilee.

## ESSENTIALS

**GETTING THERE    By Bus** From Akko, take the no. 271 or 272 Haifa-Akko-Nahariya bus. The ride is less than 25 minutes when traffic is good; train or bus fare is NIS 10 ($2.50/£1.25).

**By Car** From Akko, Nahariya is a 15-minute drive north on Rte. 2 or 4.

**VISITOR INFORMATION** When you leave the Central Bus Station, turn left and walk south about half a block on Ha-Ga'aton. On the left you'll see a small square, and at the far end of the square a seven-story edifice with flags waving in front. This is the Municipal Building, where you'll find the **Tourist Information Desk** (🕾 **04/ 987-9800**), open Sunday to Thursday from 9am to 1pm and 4 to 7pm, Friday from 9am to noon, and closed Saturday. The train station is just next door.

If you're interested in meeting the locals, the staff at the Tourist Information Desk can arrange it. Local chapters of Rotary, Lions, Soroptimists, and Freemasons also extend a warm welcome to international members; contact the Tourist Information Desk for meeting times and places.

**CITY LAYOUT**    It's pretty easy to find your way around this small city. The Central Bus Station and the railway station are just off Rte. 2 on Ha-Ga'aton Boulevard, Nahariya's main road. Head down Ha-Ga'aton and you'll be going due west, to the sea.

## BEACHES & OUTDOOR PURSUITS

The beaches of Nahariya, the town's raison d'être from a visitor's point of view, suffer, like other places on the northern Israeli coast, from the region's lack of a sewage treatment plant and the proximity of Lebanon, where decades of chaos have led to garbage dumping into the sea. The junk often swirls into Nahariya's waters, and at times in recent years, coliform bacteria counts per 100 milliliters of seawater at Nahariya were four times the Israeli Health Ministry's acceptable level (although within the more lenient standards of other Mediterranean countries).

The main beach, **Galei-Galil,** just to the north of Ha-Ga'aton Boulevard, has won prizes in the past for cleanliness and safety. Today, the fenced Galei-Galil area also offers an Olympic-size outdoor pool; a heated, glass-enclosed indoor pool that's open year-round; a children's pool; dressing rooms; playgrounds for children; and restaurants. It is open June through September daily from 8am to 5:30pm and October through May daily from 8am to 5pm. Admission is NIS 16 ($4/£2); discounts are available for children.

At the marina breakwater you'll see people **fishing** off the rocks, and you can rent a sailboat or go snorkeling. **Tennis, basketball,** and **volleyball** courts are other attractions, as is the big water slide just on the north side of the beach.

If you just want to take a dip in the Mediterranean, the free **Municipal Beach** is 2 blocks south. The view from both beaches is lovely. On a clear day—and most of them are—you can see all the way from Rosh Ha-Niqra at the Lebanese border to the north to Haifa in the south.

For a hike with the **Friends of Nature (Hovevei Hateva),** check with the Tourist Information Office desk (© **04/987-9800**). Hikes are often scheduled for Saturday.

## MUSEUMS & ANCIENT SITES

Nahariya's **Municipal Museum** is in the seven-story Municipal Building, on Ha-Iriya Square. The fifth floor houses an art exhibit. The sixth floor, in addition to an interesting malacology (shell) collection, displays many artifacts from the area around Nahariya, whose fascinating history dates all the way from the Stone Age. On the seventh floor you can learn about the history of the town. The museum is open Sunday to Friday from 10am to noon, plus Sunday and Wednesday afternoons from 4 to 6pm. Admission is free.

The ruins of a **Canaanite temple** were accidentally discovered on Ha-Ma'apilim Street, a few yards up from the Municipal Beach, in 1947. Experts believe it to be a temple dedicated to the Canaanite goddess of the sea, Asherath (or Astarte), dating from about 1500 B.C. The ruins can be seen from the beach, and you can arrange with the Municipal Museum to be taken inside the site. There's no admission fee.

The **beautiful mosaic floor of a 4th- to 7th-century Byzantine church** can be seen on Bielefeld Street, near the Katznelson School. The floor—one of the finest yet discovered—depicts hunting and working scenes, as well as the flora and fauna designs typical of mosaic floors found in Byzantine churches. Check with Tourist Information Office (© **04/987-9800**) to arrange a visit. There may be an admission fee of under NIS 5 ($1.25/60p).

## WHERE TO STAY

Most of Nahariya's hotels are located, quite logically, at the western end of Ha-Ga'a-ton Boulevard near Galei-Galil Beach. Deals and bargains abound outside of summer and Jewish holidays. You can also check with the Tourist Information Office (*(C)* **04/ 987-9800**) for lists of rooms to rent in private houses. Prices are around $40 to $60 (£20–£30) per person, including breakfast, depending on season and facilities.

**Carlton Hotel**    Located on the main street in the center of town, this six-story hotel once had a reputation as the best hotel in Nahariya, but fell into a long decline until heavy renovations were made in 2006. It's neat and fresh now; especially pleasant (and a step above standard rooms) are garden rooms with terraces overlooking the pool. There isn't a real beach atmosphere at this main street location, but the heated out-door pool, which is covered in winter, provides the chance for off-season swimming. In summer and on weekends, the hotel is filled with activities that, together with late-night main street action, can be very noisy. There are also family rooms and suites. The beach is a 10-minute walk away; it's 2 minutes to the train station.

23 Ha-Ga'aton St., Nahariya. *(C)* **04/900-5555**. Fax 04/982-3771. 200 units. $160–$240 (£80–£120) double; $100 surcharge per room during Passover and the Jewish New Year. Rates include breakfast. AE, MC, V. Free parking. **Amenities:** Restaurant; bar; large outdoor pool; children's pool and activities room; Jacuzzi; sauna; concierge; tour desk; business services; salon; room service; laundry service; synagogue; rooms for those w/limited mobility. *In room:* A/C, cable TV, minibar, coffeemaker, hair dryer, safe.

**Frank Hotel**    Owned for more than 50 years by a Nahariya family originally from Germany, this is an efficiently run hotel with a long-established clientele of Israelis and Europeans. Located 2 blocks north of Ha-Ga'aton Boulevard, this 1960s-style hotel is in a quieter neighborhood, just across from the beach. It offers lots of German-language TV channels and free Wi-Fi. As in many hotels close to the beach, some of the rooms may be a bit musty, but things are kept very clean. There are many regular European guests.

4 Ha-Aliyah St. (PO Box 58), Nahariya 22381. *(C)* **04/992-0278**. Fax 04/992-5535. www.hotel-frank.co.il. 50 units. $110–$160 (£55–£80) double. MC, V. **Amenities:** 2 restaurants; 2 bars; Wi-Fi; rooms for those w/limited mobility. *In room:* A/C, cable TV.

**Park Plaza**    For me, this is the best hotel in town. It's a relatively new, six-story structure on the beach, with bright, airy, light-filled public areas and guest rooms, many of which face the sea. Guests have free use of the facilities of a country club right across the road, including a large swimming pool, tennis courts, sports facilities, a sauna, Jacuzzi, and fitness club. You also get access to the country club's private beach. All rooms have fully equipped kitchenettes with microwaves and fridges.

17 HaAliya St. *(C)* **800/814-7000** for reservations in the U.S. or 04/900-0248. Fax 04/992-3983. www.parkplaza nahariya.co.il. 90 units. $150–$180 (£75–£90) double. Rates include breakfast. Winter discount available. AE, MC, V. **Amenities:** Restaurant; bar; hairdresser; use of country club facilities across the road. *In room:* A/C, TV, dataport, kitchenette, hair dryer, safe.

## WHERE TO DINE

Nahariya is not exactly what you'd call a gourmet's mecca. It's small and many vaca-tioners take meals in their hotels. If you decide to go out, the first place to try is Ha-Ga'aton Boulevard, with its bistros, sidewalk cafes, and two commercial plazas: Ha-Banim Square (Kikar Ha-Banim) and Ha-Iriya Square (Kikar Ha-Iriya). The plazas are across Ha-Ga'aton from one another, at its intersection with Herzl Street, half a block west of the bus station. Each square has a cinema, lots of shops and services, and some indoor-outdoor eateries.

**El Gaucho** ARGENTINE   This restaurant specializes in Argentine-style grilled meat, and lots of it, cooked over the coals set behind the many cuts of fresh meat on display for all to see. The decor here is ranch: cowhide chairs, a South American pan flute, and wall-mounted cow horns. You can dine inside or on the *palapa*-covered patio. The chefs are from South America, and much of the meat served here is veal. Menu items range from an inexpensive half-chicken dinner to the house specialty, a 750-gram (about 1½-lb.) mixed grill, a giant repast for two (or even more). Dinners are served with bread and butter, baked potato with butter and sour cream, vegetables, salad, dessert, and the special *chimichurra* meat sauce that's so scrumptious you'll be sopping it up with the bread.

Ha-Ga'aton Blvd. ℂ **04/992-8635.** Most main courses NIS 55–NIS 110 ($14–$28/£6.90–£14). MC, V. Daily noon–midnight.

**Penguin Cafe** ICE CREAM/SNACKS   Located outside the big Penguin Restaurant complex (see below), Penguin Cafe offers such hot-weather favorites as banana splits, milkshakes, and fruit cocktails, as well as blintzes, pancakes, pastries, and beverages. You can even order pizza with kosher "shrimp" for a change of pace. There are also low-calorie frozen yogurts mixed on the spot with fresh fruits of your choice.

33 Ha Ga'aton Blvd. ℂ **04/992-4241.** NIS 10–NIS 50 ($2.50–$13/£1.25–£6.25). MC, V. Daily 8am–midnight.

**Penguin Restaurant** ECLECTIC   The Penguin is the nearest thing Nahariya has to a minimall, with a bookstore and many trendy shops surrounding the dining space. The menu runs from pasta, schnitzel, and Chinese food to fish, salads, and hamburgers. Photos on the walls remind you of the original tin-roofed Penguin and the bleak, empty landscape that was Nahariya in the 1940s.

21 Ha-Ga'aton Blvd. ℂ **04/992-8855.** Main courses NIS 36–NIS 80 ($9–$20/£4.50–£10). V. Daily 8am–11pm.

**Singapore Chinese Restaurant** CHINESE   Two blocks north of Ha-Ga'aton and across from the Yarden and Eden hotels, you'll find this roomy place done up pleasantly in Chinese decor. The menu contains 110 items; as you'd expect, there are a number of Singapore specialties, including lemon chicken, a Singapore Sling cocktail, and Singapore ice cream with Chinese fruits for dessert. There are bargain set-price meals available, too.

Ha-Meyasdim and Jabotinsky. ℂ **04/992-4952.** Reservations recommended summer weekends. Main courses NIS 40–NIS 70 ($10–$18/£5–£8.75). DC, MC, V. Lunch daily noon–3pm; dinner daily 7pm–midnight. Closed Chinese New Year and major Jewish holidays.

## COUNTRY ACCOMMODATIONS & DINING OUTSIDE OF NAHARIYA

**Pivko Village at Kibbutz Kabri** *Finds*   These tasteful, contemporary, airy wooden cabins in the countryside east of Nahariya, each with its own large outdoor Jacuzzi, can be a restful place to base yourself while exploring the area. Every two cabins share a spacious living room, which means unless you've got two couples to fill two cabins, or come midweek off season (when there may not be full occupancy), you might find an Israeli family with kids and friends in your living area. Pay double, you get the whole cabin to yourself; despite complications, it's a lovely spot with gorgeous vistas. Local hiking, meals in the kibbutz dining room, and a gourmet meal at nearby

Adelina (see below) can be arranged. Gourmet breakfast plans are additional, or you can cook meals on the grill or in the kitchenette. An interesting choice for families or small groups; each cabin has an Internet-connected computer.

Kibbutz Kabri. ℂ 04/995-2711 or 050/724-7086. www.pivko-village.co.il/indexe.html. 6 units. NIS 600 ($150/£75) double; additional child NIS 100 ($25/£13). AE, DC, MC, V. Free parking. **Amenities:** Kibbutz dining room; barbecue grill. *In room:* A/C, cable TV, Internet-connected computer, kitchenette, Jacuzzi for 6.

**Adelina at Kibbutz Kabri** 🦌   When even an out-of-the-way kibbutz comes up with a sophisticated restaurant such as Adelina, you know that Israel has been conquered by the wave of contemporary Mediterranean cuisine. The restaurant is set in a simple building of stone and wood, beside a dining terrace with vistas of the countryside and, in the distance, a glimpse of the sea. The menu constantly changes, but flavor abounds: Look for a generous meze or a medley of first courses consisting of rich, rustic variations of traditional dishes, local cheeses, and thick robust soups—all filled with freshly chopped herbs and served with herbed, crusty fresh bread. Meats are top quality, served with well-prepared sauces; at times, among the fish and seafood selections, you may find a gourmet Spanish zarzuela of mussels, shrimp, and calamari in a picante sauce of tomatoes, fish stock, wine, and brandy. There's a variety of homemade desserts and a good wine list, though you can bring your own. The fixed-price meals come with dessert and coffee and make for a lovely gourmet country repast in a wonderful setting.

Kibbutz Kabri, east of Nahariya. ℂ 04/995-2707. Reservations required. Fixed-price dinner NIS 150–NIS 210 ($38–$53/£19–£26); fixed-price lunch NIS 100–NIS 140 ($25–$35/£13–£18). MC, V. Mon–Sat noon–3pm and 7–10pm.

## SIDE TRIPS NORTH OF NAHARIYA
### AKHZIV

Heading north along Hwy. 2, after 4km (2½ miles) you'll see the road to **Akhziv Beach,** a private beach on the left (west). It's another kilometer (½ mile) to the beach proper, where you'll find a parking lot, changing rooms, shelters, and snack stands, as well as freshwater showers. It's open daily from 8am to 7pm in July and August. There's a charge of NIS 25 ($6.25/£3.10) per person for admission during the summer swimming season.

Heading north again, 1km (½ mile) past the Akhziv Beach road, you'll pass the parking lot and entrance to **Akhziv National Park** (ℂ 04/982-3263), with its sheltered beach, restaurant, picnic area, and changing facilities amid the ruins of a seaside Arab village. Admission is NIS 36 ($9/£4.50) for adults and NIS 28 ($7/£3.50) for children. It's a beautiful spot for a picnic, and there's a guarded but somewhat rocky beach for swimming. The park is open daily from 8am to 7pm in July and August; until 5pm the rest of the year. *Tip:* Off season, at sunset, you can sometimes just wander through the gates for free and head up the hill through the lovely gardens.

Akhziv existed when Joshua assigned the tribes of Israel to their various territories, and is mentioned in the Bible as a Canaanite town that the tribe of Asher, to whom it was allotted, was never able to conquer. At the Nahariya Municipal Museum, you can learn about the varied history of the town through the wealth of archaeological artifacts on view.

In more recent times, Akhziv was an Arab village, but the inhabitants fled in 1948 and the village remained deserted for a number of years. In 1952, Eli Avivi, one of Israel's legendary eccentrics, received government permission to settle in Akhziv, and promptly declared the "independence" of **Akhzivland,** which is just north of the park boundary. The ramshackle building that is Akhzivland's main structure houses Mr. Avivi's living quarters and his personal museum of artifacts found on and near Akhzivland. You can visit the museum for a small admission charge.

## GESHER HAZIV & THE AKHZIV BRIDGE
While the town of Akhziv has a history dating from biblical times, the name is most often remembered in connection with a tragic, heroic event that took place here on the night of June 17, 1946. Attempting to cut British rail communications with neighboring Arab states, a Hagana demolition team was destroying railroad bridges along this line. At the Akhziv Bridge, however, they were spotted by a British sentry, who fired a flare in order to get a better look. The flare ignited the team's explosives. The bridge was blown, but no one survived. The 14 who perished are commemorated by a large black metal monument across the road from the local youth hostel.

## ROSH HA-NIQRA
This dramatic site borders Lebanon, astride a tall cliff overlooking the sea. On a clear day, standing atop the cliff, you can see the coastline as far as Haifa. Beneath the cliffs are **grottoes** carved out by the sea, reachable via cable car; the cable-car schedule is subject to seasonal, security, and holiday changes. April to June and September Saturday through Thursday 8:30am to 6pm, Friday 8:30am to 4pm; July and August Saturday to Thursday 8:30am to 11pm, Friday 8:30am to 4pm; October to March daily 8:30am to 4pm. The cable-car ride and admission to the grottoes costs NIS 45 ($11/£6) for adults, with a discount for children and students. You can walk into the caves and passages and see the pools of luminescent water lapping the rocks. To see the artifacts that have been recovered from these caves, visit the **Municipal Museum** in Nahariya.

To reach Rosh Ha-Niqra, take the bus from Nahariya, which runs several times a day; sherut service is also available in front of the Nahariya Central Bus Station on Ha-Ga'aton Boulevard, though you may have to fight to have them take you all the way to the cable car. You can grab a bite at a reasonably priced self-service restaurant on top of the cliff called Mitzpe Rosh Ha-Niqra. The view is breathtaking. It's open the same hours as the cable car.

# 9

# Haifa

Some compare Haifa, beautifully situated on a hill overlooking a broad bay, to San Francisco or Naples. Israel's third-largest metropolitan area (pop. 300,000) and the capital of the north, Haifa is like a triple-decker sandwich—the industrial area that comprises Israel's most important port is the lowest tier; the business district (Hadar), higher up, is the second; and the Carmel district, with its panoramic vistas, nestled even higher on the upper pine slopes, constitutes the third. Just to the south of Haifa are magnificent beaches that locals flock to but few tourists know about. Plans are now in progress to convert these unspoiled beach areas into Haifa's own "Riviera"; you'll see a great deal of hotel, apartment, and marina construction underway along the shoreline during the next few years. Like much of the intensive development going on along Israel's Mediterranean coast, this project is controversial, with environmentalists and beach lovers who had wanted to turn the area into a national park opposing the loss of Israel's most accessible stretch of natural shoreline.

**HAIFA TODAY**  Very different from either Jerusalem or Tel Aviv, the city is a pleasure to visit just to get a sense of its beauty and lifestyle. In a society unlike any other in the Middle East, Jews and Arabs live and work side by side; 25% of Haifa's population is either Muslim or Christian. In 1898, Theodore Herzl, the father of modern Zionism, wrote his prophecy of the Jewish homeland that would one day be reborn: "Next to our temples, you find

Christian, Mohammedan, Buddhist, and Brahmin houses of divine worship . . . my comrades and I make no distinction between people. We ask for no one's religion or race but let him be a Man, that is enough." With its Baha'i Center, churches, synagogues, and mosques, as well as its politically progressive, hardworking Jewish and Arabic population, Haifa, more than any other city in Israel, has come to fit that vision.

Haifa is a good base for exploring the northwestern part of Israel. You won't need to rent a car if you base yourself here; many organized day tours originate in Haifa or, because Haifa is a major transportation hub, you can just use public transportation to explore cities such as Akko or even Safed on your own. In the evening, after a day of touring the area, Haifa offers a good choice of restaurants, films, concerts, and urban strolling to keep you busy.

**A LOOK AT HAIFA'S PAST**  Almost every square foot of Israel has been populated since earliest ages, and Haifa is no exception. The prophet Elijah knew this territory well—from the top of Mount Carmel he won a major victory over 450 priests of Baal during the reign of King Ahab and his notorious Phoenician wife, Jezebel. In late biblical times, the Phoenician port of Zalemona thrived here, with predominantly Greek settlers, and the Jewish agricultural village of Sycaminos (sometimes called Shikmona) clung to the northwestern peak of Mount Carmel

(3rd-c. Talmudic literature mentions both towns).

The Crusaders called the area Caife, Cayphe, and sometimes Caiphas. Once a center of glass and cochineal-purple industries, Haifa was destroyed when the Arabs reconquered the area, and it virtually slept until the late 19th century, when Jewish immigration helped bring about a revival.

Haifa got its first shot in the arm in 1905, when the Haifa–Damascus Railway was built. The Balfour Declaration and British occupation boosted it some more, as did a 1919 railway link to Egypt. But the real kickoff came when the British built its modern harbor—an arduous enterprise begun in 1929 and completed in 1934. Thereupon Haifa began its transformation into the vital trading and communications center it is today, taking on major importance as a shipping base, naval center, and terminal point for oil pipelines.

In 1898, when he visited Palestine and sailed past the spot that was to become modern Haifa, Theodor Herzl had a prophetic vision about the place: "Huge liners rode at anchor . . . at the top of the mountain there were thousands of white homes and the mountain itself was crowned with imposing villas. . . . A beautiful city had been built close to the deep blue sea." Herzl recorded this experience in his book *Altneuland* (Old New Land), and miraculously, Haifa developed precisely along the lines he predicted. Herzl's dream came alive for hundreds of thousands of homeless, scarred refugees who arrived here after the Nazi Holocaust. As they crowded the decks for their first glimpse of the Promised Land, the hills of Haifa must have seemed like a vision of heaven.

On April 21, 1948, Haifa became the first major city controlled by Jews after the end of the British Mandate and the UN Partition decision in 1947. Although Haifa's previous growth had already spurred development of residential areas such as Bat Galim, Hadar Ha-Carmel, and Neve-Shaanan, the new wave of immigration (more than 100,000) gave rise to others: Ramat Ramez, Kiryat Elizer, Neveh Yosef, and Kiryat Shprinzak. Haifa Bay, east of the port, became the backbone of the country's heavy industries, with oil refineries and associated industries, foundries, glass factories, fertilizer and chemical industries, cement works, textile manufacturing, and yards for shipbuilding and repair. Israelis are fond of saying that "Tel Aviv plays while Jerusalem prays. But Haifa works!" A visit here is filled with pleasures and new insights into what Israel is all about.

## 1 Orientation

### ARRIVING

Haifa's intercity bus and train transportation center is at its northernmost tip, in the district called Bat Galim, about 2km (1½ miles) northwest of the downtown port area.

**BY PLANE**   Unless you have a specific reason for going there, Haifa is not generally the first destination travelers head for on arriving at Ben-Gurion Airport. **Trains** leave Ben-Gurion Airport Station for Haifa approximately once or twice an hour from 4:50am to 11:15pm on weekdays, depending on the day of the week. Friday and Saturday schedules are limited to before and after Shabbat. To check train schedules that will coordinate with your plane's arrival, go to www.israrail.org.il/english/index.html. The trip is approximately 1½ hours, and the fare is approximately NIS 40 ($10/£5). Check with your hotel as to which station in Haifa is best for your destination.

**For sheruts or taxis from Ben-Gurion Airport to Haifa,** contact the Haifa Tourist Information Desk. The trip is approximately 1½ hours. The fare for a sherut (shared taxi or van) should be about NIS 70 ($18/£8.75) per person; however, sherut service to Haifa and the north depends on how many travelers happen to want it, and is not as frequent as service to Tel Aviv and Jerusalem. If no one else is going on to Haifa when you arrive, shared service may not be available. The plus is that a sherut will deliver you right to the door of your destination in Haifa, so there will be no local taxi fare. Private taxi to Haifa will run at least NIS 260 ($65/£33) with a surcharge for Shabbat and nighttime service.

Sherut service from Haifa to Ben-Gurion Airport can be arranged through **Amal Taxi** (© 04/866-2324). Fare is approximately NIS 65 ($16/£8.10) one-way per person. Another sherut service to Ben-Gurion is **Kavei Ha-Galil,** 11 Berwarld St. (© 04/866-4444, -4445, -4446).

**BY TRAIN** The New Central Railway Station is in Bat Galim, near the Central Bus Station. In the station you'll find a simple air-conditioned restaurant with set-price breakfasts and lunches, open Sunday through Thursday from 5am to 7pm, closing early on Friday and all day Saturday.

**From Tel Aviv:** Trains along the coast to Netanya and Haifa leave approximately every hour from 5:45am to 7pm, Sunday through Thursday; the last Friday train leaves at 2pm; there's no Saturday service. The trip on the express train to Haifa takes 1 hour; the local train takes 20 minutes longer. The fare is NIS 28 ($7/£3.50). Less frequent service from Haifa to Akko and Nahariya is available. Train information can be obtained by calling © 04/856-4564, or going to www.israrail.org.il/english/index.html.

**BY BUS** The Egged Bus Terminal, with intercity buses to and from all points in Israel, is next to the Central Railway Station in Bat Galim. From here, you'll have to take a city bus to either of my recommended hotel districts, in Hadar or Central Carmel. For Hadar, catch bus no. 10 or 12; for Central Carmel and the top of the mountain, you want bus no. 3, 22, or 24. Interurban bus information can be obtained by calling © 04/854-9555. For buses within Haifa, call © 04/854-9131.

**BY CAR** Major highway networks connect Haifa with Tel Aviv, Jerusalem, and the Galilee. The main routes are Hwy. 2 and Hwy. 4 along the coast from Tel Aviv.

**BY FERRY** At press time, passenger ferry service from Cyprus and other ports in Europe had been suspended due to security concerns. When passenger service to Haifa resumes, ships will dock right in the port at the Maritime Passenger Terminal. It's only a short walk to the Paris Square (Kikar Paris) station of the Carmelit subway that climbs the mountain to Hadar and Central Carmel.

**VISITOR INFORMATION** The **Haifa Information and Visitors Center,** 48 Ben-Gurion Blvd. (© 04/853-5606; www.tour-haifa.co.il), is open Sunday to Thursday 9am to 5pm, Friday 9am to 1pm, and Saturday 10am to 3pm. It's located on the main street of the German Colony neighborhood far from most hotels, but it's well organized and worth visiting. From the hotel district in Central Carmel, you can catch a taxi, take the Carmelit down to Paris Square, and then walk over to the German Colony; or check with the desk at your hotel about the best bus route to the center.

## CITY LAYOUT

Of all its graces, Haifa is richest in panoramic views. For purposes of orientation, you might think of Haifa as a city built on three levels. Whether you come by ship, bus, or train, you will arrive on the lower, or **port,** level of the city. The second level, **Hadar**

**Ha-Carmel,** meaning "Glory of the Carmel," is referred to simply as Hadar. This is the downtown business section as well as the home of the contemporary art section of the Haifa Museum and some restaurants and budget hotels. At the top of the hills is the **Carmel District,** a patchwork of verdant residential neighborhoods with its own small but busy commercial center called **Central Carmel,** numerous hotels and pensions, restaurants, small museums, and two of Haifa's brightest cultural beacons: Haifa Auditorium and Bet Rothschild (the James de Rothschild Cultural Center).

Because Haifa is built all the way up the side of a mountain, many of its main streets are sinuous switchbacks, curving and recurving like spaghetti to accommodate the steep slopes of Mount Carmel. If you're driving, the streets are always bewildering, and you will find it hard to orient yourself: Just remember, in Haifa, don't think in terms of north, south, east, or west. The two directions are up or down. About the only straight road in Haifa is the one that climbs the slopes of Carmel's underground: the Carmelit subway.

## 2 Getting Around

**BY SUBWAY**   The **Carmelit** is a fast, efficient, and amazing means of getting up and down Haifa's various levels. Its lower terminal station is located on Jaffa Road, a few blocks north of the port entrance and not far from the old (Merkaz) railway station. The Carmelit's upper terminal is at the Carmel Center.

Pulled on a long cable up and down the steep hill, the Carmelit resembles a sort of scale-model Métro. From bottom to the top, the stops are: (1) Paris Square (Kikar Paris, lower terminus, port area); (2) Solel Boneh (Hassan Shukri St.); (3) Ha-Nevi'im (Hadar business district, tourist center); (4) Masada (Masada St.); (5) Eliezer Golomb (Eliezer Golomb St.); (6) Gan Ha-Em (Central Carmel business district, upper terminus). When you take the Carmelit, don't panic—the incline is so great that the floors of the cars break into escalator-like steps.

Trains run every 10 minutes. The Carmelit operates Sunday through Thursday from 6:30am to midnight, Friday from 6:30am to 3pm, and resumes service on Saturday from 30 minutes after the end of Shabbat until midnight; it is closed during Shabbat. Ticket machines have English as well as Hebrew instructions. The fare is NIS 5.50 ($1.40/70p).

**BY BUS**   Bus fares are charged according to your destination, so you must tell the driver where you're going. Most fares to places inside Haifa itself are NIS 5.60 ($1.40/70p). Haifa's municipal buses operate from 5am to 11:30pm Sunday through Thursday; on Friday, bus service halts around 4:30pm; there is limited Saturday service from 9am to midnight on some lines. For information on buses inside Haifa, check with your hotel, the Haifa Information and Visitors Center, or call ✆ **04/854-9131.** For interurban lines, call ✆ **04/854-9555.**

---

*FAST FACTS:* **Haifa**

*Bookstores*  There are **Steimatzky** bookstores at 82 Ha-Atzma'ut St., 16 Herzl St. in Bet Ha-Kranot, and 130 Ha-Nassi Blvd.; for a selection of used English books, try **Beverly's Books,** 18 Herzl St., second floor (usually closed Wed).

*Currency Exchange*  Banking hours are Sunday through Friday from 8:30am to 2:30pm. Afternoon hours are Sunday, Tuesday, and Thursday from 4 to 6pm. **Change Spot,** 5 Nordau St., Hadar (✆ **04/864-4111**), is open Sunday to Thursday

9am to 5pm, Friday 9am to noon. ATMs connected to Cirrus and PLUS can be found at banks on HaNassi Boulevard, in the Carmel Center.

*Doctors* Call the **Rambam Hospital** in Bat Galim (✆ 04/854-3111).

*Drugstores* Standard hours are Sunday through Thursday from 8am to 1pm and 4 to 7pm; Friday from 8am to 2pm. According to a rotating schedule, one or two pharmacies remain on duty nights and on Shabbat; their names will be posted in any pharmacy window.

*Embassies & Consulates* For emergencies, call the U.S. Embassy in Tel Aviv (✆ 03/519-7575).

*Emergencies* Dial ✆ **101** for Magen David Adom first-aid services; ✆ **100** police; ✆ **102** for fire.

*Hospitals* Call the **Rambam Hospital** in Bat Galim (✆ 04/856-7878).

*Hot Lines* Call the English **Crisis Counseling Hot Line** (✆ **1-800/654-1111** or 02/654-1111) or the **Rape Crisis Center** (✆ **1202** or 04/853-0533).

*Laundry & Dry Cleaning* Laundromats in Haifa are not easily accessible from tourist areas; ask at your hotel.

*Libraries* The main library is at 50 Pevsner St. (✆ **04/866-7766**). Hours are Sunday through Thursday from 9am to 8pm, Friday 9am to 1pm.

*Newspapers & Magazines* The *Jerusalem Post, International Herald Tribune* (including the English edition of the top Israeli newspaper, *Ha'aretz*), *Jerusalem Report Magazine*, and *Eretz* (a magazine of history, nature, and travel) are readily available.

*Police* See "Emergencies," above.

*Post Office* Haifa's most accessible post office with the longest hours is in Hadar, at the corner of Shabtai Levi and Ha-Nevi'im streets (✆ **04/864-0917**). It is open Sunday through Thursday from 8am to 7pm; Friday 8am to 1:30pm; closed Saturday.

*Radio* English broadcasts are on Israeli radio 576 kHz and 1458 kHz at 7am, 1, 5, and 8pm.

*Religious Services Events in Haifa,* available at Municipal Tourist Information Offices, lists all major church, mosque, and synagogue services.

*Safety* Haifa is generally a low-crime city. Extra care should be exercised near the port after dark.

*Taxis* For special taxis to destinations outside Haifa, call **Kavei Ha-Galil** (✆ **04/866-4444** or 866-4445) or **Amahl's Sheruts** (✆ **04/866-2324**).

*Television* Most hotels have English-language cable channels, including CNN and Sky News.

*Useful Telephone Numbers* The **Association of Americans and Canadians in Israel (AACI),** 131 Sderot Hameginim, Haifa (✆ **04/856-7638**), is a good resource for those thinking about immigrating or spending a period of time in residence in the Haifa area. It offers help for absorption of North American immigrants, social and cultural programs, tours, lectures, and activities.

## 3 Where to Stay

With one exception, Haifa's recommended hotels are all up in the Central Carmel area, with its fabulous vistas. Despite the fact that you're way up on the top tier of Haifa, thanks to the Carmelit you're only minutes away from the other parts of the city.

## CENTRAL CARMEL
### EXPENSIVE
**Crowne Plaza Haifa** ✿  Built in 1999, and upgraded in price in 2007 from a Holiday Inn to a Crowne Plaza, this is Haifa's newest hotel and first international chain property. It provides excellent value in every way. It's a five-story modern structure with well-designed public areas and newer guest rooms than you'll find in other Haifa hotels. The location, one street downhill and parallel to the main Carmel area thoroughfare Ha-Nassi Street, offers great vistas and is close to the Carmelit station, but you need to be good at uphill climbing to stay here. Business services are strong: Special executive rooms come equipped for business travelers, and there's a business lounge with snacks and refreshments. Junior suites and standard rooms with connecting doors are good for families.

111 Yefe Nof St. ✆ **04/835-0835.** Fax 04/835-0836. www.h-i.co.il. 100 units, all with bathtubs. $220–$270 (£110–£135) double. Rates include breakfast. AE, DC, MC, V. Underground parking (fee). Carmelit: Gan Ha-Em/Central Carmel. **Amenities:** Restaurant; dining room; indoor pool; health/fitness center; Jacuzzi; sauna; concierge; business services; laundry service; dry cleaning; nonsmoking rooms. *In room:* A/C, TV, minibar, coffeemaker, hair dryer, safe.

**Dan Carmel Hotel** ✿✿  For 40 years, the Dan Carmel has reigned as Haifa's most important and luxurious hotel. The lobby is a wonderful example of 1950s decor—a style just now reaching the age to be appreciated for nostalgic as well as interesting aesthetic value. There are spacious public areas overlooking beautiful gardens, marvelous vistas from virtually all guest rooms, and a large country club–style outdoor swimming pool that gets temptingly warm in late summer. Most rooms need updating (standard rooms especially), and there are extra charges for better views, but the staff is one of the most helpful in Israel, food services are good, and a stay here is always pleasant. For suites or executive rooms, there's a rooftop business lounge with a fireplace, dazzling views from its terrace, and a running light buffet; the in-house **Rondo Restaurant,** when open, is the most elegant kosher choice in Haifa. Children's activities are good.

85–87 Ha-Nassi Blvd., Haifa 34642. ✆ **04/830-3010.** Fax 04/830-3030. www.danhotels.com. 219 units. $250–$330 (£125–£165) double. Rates include breakfast. AE, DC, MC, V. Parking (fee). Carmelit: Gan Ha–Em. **Amenities:** 2 restaurants; dining room; cafe; bar; pool; children's pool; health club; sauna; business center; salon; 24-hr. room service; laundry service; dry cleaning; nonsmoking rooms. *In room:* A/C, TV, minibar, hair dryer, safe.

### MODERATE
**Dan Gardens**  This partially renovated, moderately priced choice is a small, well-run bed-and-breakfast hotel. The 10 front rooms have beautiful views of the city, the harbor, across Haifa Bay to Acre, and the mountains beyond. Each of these rooms has an entire wall made of glass (get one of these if you can); back rooms (including the one single) are quite ordinary. A plus is that you get use of the nearby Dan Panorama hotel swimming pool in season. The long, long flight of stairs from the street to the hotel's front door is a drawback for many visitors (call ahead if you need assistance carrying bags). The neighborhood is lovely and very central, just around the block from the Carmel Center, with its cafes and restaurants, and the Carmelit stop.

124 Yefe Nof St., Haifa 34454. ☎ **04/838-3666**. Fax 04/838-2121. www.danhotels.com. 31 units. $120–$140 (£60–£70) double. Rates include breakfast. AE, DC, MC, V. Parking (fee). Bus: 21, 28, or 37. Carmelit: Gan Ha–Em. **Amenities:** Dining room; pool nearby; nonsmoking rooms. *In room:* A/C, TV, dataport, minibar, coffeemaker.

**Dan Panorama**   With an incredibly convenient location, this hotel, set in a high-rise built in 1986, is less expensive and usually busier than its sister hotel, the Dan Carmel, down the street. It's just steps away from the Carmelit station on the main shopping/restaurant street of the Carmel District, and actually part of the upmarket Panorama shopping mall complex. Rooms are 1980s-modern design, a bit worn but efficient (even lower-category rooms have hair dryers), and classified in price according to their views (windows in many rooms are not really big enough to make the most of their vistas). The pool has been fitted onto the roof of one of the building's lower wings, and catches breezes on hot days. Lots of pleasant Dan Hotel chain touches here, such as the especially good spread at the breakfast buffet. Look for bargain Internet and Dan Hotel 7-Day Package deals.

107 Ha-Nassi Blvd., Haifa 34632. ☎ **04/835-2222**. Fax 04/835-2235. www.danhotels.com. 267 units. $170–$200 (£85–£100) double. Rates include breakfast. AE, DC, MC, V. Parking (fee). Carmelite: Gan Ha–Em. **Amenities:** 2 restaurants; cafe; bar; outdoor swimming pool; children's pool; fitness center; sauna; business services; concierge; 24-hr. room service; laundry service; dry cleaning. *In room:* A/C, TV, dataport, Wi-Fi, kitchenette (some), minibar, hair dryer.

**Nof Hotel**   The Nof Hotel has a great location at the top of the Carmel Center, near the Carmelit station and between the two Dan hotels, yet it's less expensive than its neighbors. "Nof" means "view," and every guest room at the Nof has especially large windows to take in absolutely breathtaking vistas. The hotel looks impressive in size from the outside, but it actually has a small, personal feeling to it. Room refurbishing and a new wing are planned, but at press time, the Nof had been hard hit by the tourism slump, and decor in guest rooms was wearing thin. The hotel dining room is good, and the in-house kosher Chinese restaurant (see "Where to Dine," below) is excellent. A drawback in summer is the lack of a swimming pool. Check your room to see if it's sufficiently updated and in order—some rooms are in better condition than others.

101 Ha-Nassi Blvd., Haifa 31063. ☎ **04/835-4311**. Fax 04/838-8810. www.inisrael.com/nof. 90 units. $140–$160 (£70–£80) double. Rates include breakfast. Discounts for more than 3 nights and for Baha'i groups. MC, V. Free parking. **Amenities:** Restaurant; cafe; bar; room service; laundry service; nonsmoking rooms. *In room:* A/C, TV, fridge (on request), hair dryer.

## INEXPENSIVE

**Hotel Beth Shalom Carmel**   This modern, efficient German Protestant guesthouse is open to all travelers, with clean, updated, and airy rooms equipped with heating. Minimum stay of 3 nights is sometimes in effect. The location, just across the street from the Carmel's three luxury hotels, is great; extra amenities include use of a small garden and a library. Wi-Fi is $5 (£2.50) per day.

110 Ha-Nassi Blvd. (PO Box 6208), Haifa 31060. ☎ **04/837-3480**. Fax 04/837-2443. www.beth-shalom.co.il. 30 units, all with bathtub. $88 (£44) double. Rate includes breakfast. AE, DC, MC, V. Carmelit: Gan Ha–Em. **Amenities:** Dining room; nonsmoking rooms. *In room:* A/C, TV, high-speed Internet, fridge, coffeemaker, hair dryer.

## NEAR THE PORT
### INEXPENSIVE

**Port Inn Guest House** *Value*   This congenial guesthouse located in an old, atmospheric building is just what Haifa needed in the budget price range. It's in the port area (with its authentic market and Arabic eateries), close to the Carmelit and bus stops so you can get around the city quickly, and not far from the newly restored and

# Haifa

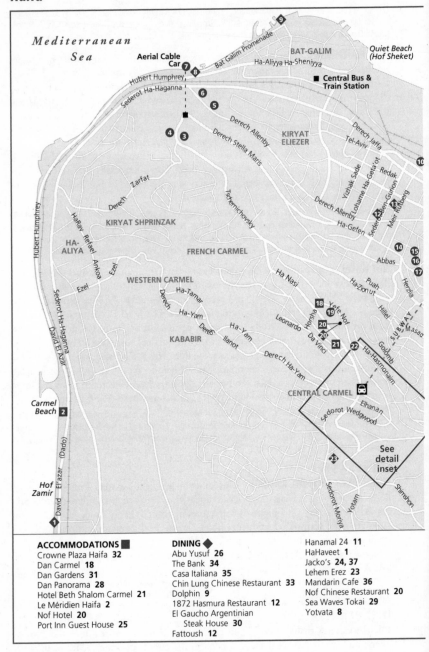

*Mediterranean Sea*

BAT-GALIM

Quiet Beach (Hof Sheket)

Aerial Cable Car

Bat Galim Promenade

Ha-Aliyya Ha-Sheniyya

Hubert Humphrey

Central Bus & Train Station

Sederot Ha-Haganna

Derech Allenby

KIRYAT ELIEZER

Derech Jaffa

Derech Stella Maris

Tel-Aviv

Redak

Derech Zarfat

Tschernichovsky

Yizhak Sade

Yohanne Ha-Gefaiot

Sederot Ben-Gurion

Meir Rutberg

KIRYAT SHPRINZAK

Derech Allenby

Ha-Gefen

HaRav Refael

Ankoa

HA-ALIYA

Ezel

FRENCH CARMEL

Abbas

Puah

Herzlia

Hubert Humphrey

Ezel

WESTERN CARMEL

Ha-Tamar

Ha-Nasi

Ha-Zion ut

Hillel

Sederot Ha-Haganna

David El Azar

Derech

Ha-Yam

Derech Ilanot

KABABIR

Ha-Yam

Leonardo

Horsha

Yefe Nof

Da Vinci

Masaa

SUBWAY

Derech Ha-Yam

Ha-Hasmonaim

Golomb

Carmel Beach

CENTRAL CARMEL

Elhanan

Sederot Wedgwood

See detail inset

Hof Zamir

David El'azar (Opea)

Sederot Morya

Yotam

Shimshon

ACCOMMODATIONS ■
Crowne Plaza Haifa **32**
Dan Carmel **18**
Dan Gardens **31**
Dan Panorama **28**
Hotel Beth Shalom Carmel **21**
Le Méridien Haifa **2**
Nof Hotel **20**
Port Inn Guest House **25**

DINING ◆
Abu Yusuf **26**
The Bank **34**
Casa Italiana **35**
Chin Lung Chinese Restaurant **33**
Dolphin **9**
1872 Hasmura Restaurant **12**
El Gaucho Argentinian Steak House **30**
Fattoush **12**

Hanamal 24 **11**
HaHaveet **1**
Jacko's **24, 37**
Lehem Erez **23**
Mandarin Cafe **36**
Nof Chinese Restaurant **20**
Sea Waves Tokai **29**
Yotvata **8**

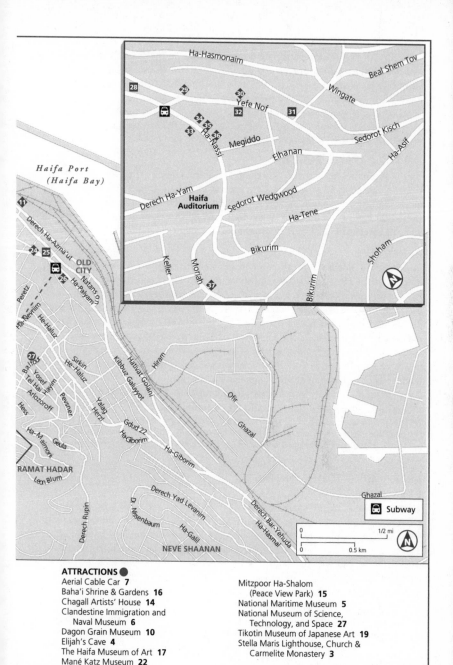

## ATTRACTIONS ●

Aerial Cable Car **7**
Baha'i Shrine & Gardens **16**
Chagall Artists' House **14**
Clandestine Immigration and
  Naval Museum **6**
Dagon Grain Museum **10**
Elijah's Cave **4**
The Haifa Museum of Art **17**
Mané Katz Museum **22**

Mitzpoor Ha-Shalom
  (Peace View Park) **15**
National Maritime Museum **5**
National Museum of Science,
  Technology, and Space **27**
Tikotin Museum of Japanese Art **19**
Stella Maris Lighthouse, Church &
  Carmelite Monastery **3**

gentrified German Colony, with its many cafes and restaurants. Rooms are simple but touched with lively colors; there are dorm beds, and private singles and doubles all with shared (shower) bathrooms. There's a lovely garden terrace, friendly lounge/TV room, and breakfast room; you get free use of the kitchen. There's also an Internet terminal (fee). Most important is the super-helpful management.

34 Jaffa Rd., Haifa. ✆ 04/852-4401. Fax 04/852-1003. www.portinn.co.il. 10 units, some with shared bathroom (3 dormitories with shared bathrooms). $80 (£40) double with shared bathroom; $25 (£13) dormitory bed. Rates include breakfast. Cash only. **Amenities:** Breakfast room; lounge; use of kitchen; laundry service.

## ON THE CARMEL BEACH

This beautiful beachfront area, just being developed at the edge of the city, is served by buses during the day, but can seem somewhat isolated from the rest of Haifa at night. The area offers a beach-resort atmosphere but is also close to the hi-tech **Matam Industrial Park,** at the heart of Israel's own version of California's Silicon Valley. It is also convenient to Haifa's new **International Convention Center.** Parking is free.

### EXPENSIVE
**Le Méridien Haifa**    Set on one of Haifa's best bathing beaches, this semiluxury hotel (built in 1997) offers standard guest rooms (they're called "superior" by the hotel) with sea views, as well as a variety of one- and two-bedroom suites with kitchenette facilities. Two hundred of the 300 rooms and suites in this high-rise are set aside for hotel purposes; the rest of the units are residential and long-term rentals. Guest rooms are modern and sleekly furnished. The variety of suites makes this a good choice for vacationing families as well as long-term business travelers working at the nearby Matam Industrial Park. Kitchenettes in some rooms compensate for the fact that the hotel is not near shops or restaurants. Bus service up into town is not frequent, so unless you have a car, the location, though nice for beach lovers, is isolating.

10 David Elazar St., Carmel Beach, Haifa. ✆ 04/850-8888. Fax 04/850-1170. www.sheraton.com. 200 units. $250–$300 (£125–£150) double; $300–$350 (£150–£175) 1-bedroom suite. Rates include breakfast. AE, DC, MC, V. **Amenities:** 3 restaurants; dining room; cafe; bar; pool (indoor, outdoor); children's pool; beach; tennis court; health club; spa; business center; shops; 24-hr. room service; synagogue. *In room:* A/C, TV w/pay movies, dataport, kitchenette (some), fridge, hair dryer, safe.

## IN THE HILLS SOUTH OF HAIFA
### EXPENSIVE
**Isrotel Carmel Forest Spa Resort** ★★★    Opened in 1997, this luxury spa offers a green, tranquil alternative to the many massive spa hotels in the desert near The Dead Sea. The setting contributes to making this the most beautiful spa hotel in Israel. The tastefully, freshly decorated public areas and guest rooms overlook the distant Mediterranean and acres of woods. The big windows of some rooms look out directly onto public footpaths and lack privacy unless you close the curtains—try for a room that overlooks the forest or the gardens. There are aromatherapy, seaweed wraps, water aerobics, horseback riding, tai chi, mountain biking, Shiatsu, Reiki, reflexology, Thai or Swedish massage, and weight-loss programs, all top quality. The vegetarian buffets are near gourmet and filled with natural, wholesome ingredients. You won't need a car once here, so consider that the meter on a rental car would just be ticking away while you luxuriate or chill out.

Carmel Forest, PO Box 90000, Haifa 31900. ✆ 888/ISROTEL (411-6835) or 201/816-0830 in the U.S. and Canada or 04/830-7888. Fax 04/830-7886. www.isrotel.co.il/English. 126 units. $400–$700 (£200–£350) double. Rates include full board. Treatment programs extra. AE, DC, MC, V. Free parking. **Amenities:** Restaurant; dining room; pools (indoor, outdoor); spa; Jacuzzi; sauna; basketball; tennis; volleyball; hairdresser; massage; laundry service; nonsmoking rooms; synagogue. *In room:* A/C, TV, minibar, coffeemaker, hair dryer, safe.

## BED & BREAKFAST ACCOMMODATIONS

The **Haifa Tourist Board,** 106 Ha-Nassi Blvd. (© **04/853-5606;** www.tour-haifa. co.il), can arrange for a variety of accommodations. A double room in an apartment runs in the $70 to $90 (£35–£45) range. A double room in an apartment with a private bathroom or with a self-catering setup with private bathroom and separate entrance would be more. The reservations service is open Sunday to Thursday from 9am to 3pm. Expect to pay host families in cash; breakfast is usually extra.

## 4 Where to Dine

Haifa caters to every culinary taste and pocketbook. The city's **Falafel Row,** at the corner of Haneviim and Hechalutz streets, in Hadar, not far downhill from the Nordau Pedestrian Mall, is one of the best spots in Israel for falafel; even an average Haifa falafel stand usually can hold its own with the best places in other towns. Haifa is also home to very authentic, popular Arabic restaurants, as well as excellent Continental and international-style dining spots.

## HADAR/NORDAU STREET MALL

After observing the success of Jerusalem's lively Ben-Yehuda Mall, Haifa decided to take the plunge and turn Nordau Street, a block above Herzl Street, into a tree-lined pedestrian area. The result has brightened the whole Hadar District, but the cafes and light meal spots here basically cater to those people who work in the downtown center, and at press time massive street renovation makes this a difficult area to visit.

## CENTRAL CARMEL

*Note:* The Carmelit stop for all the restaurants in this section, unless otherwise noted, is Central Carmel.

### MODERATE

**El Gaucho Argentinian Steak House** MEAT    This is a kosher dining choice for those looking for a hefty meal. The Gaucho chain specializes in Argentine-style grilled meat, cooked over the coals behind the many cuts of fresh meat on display for all to see. The decor here is ranch style, and many of the chefs are from South America. This is one place in Israel where you can find lower-cholesterol veal. Menu items range from an inexpensive half-chicken dinner to the house specialty, a 750-gram (about 1½-lb.) mixed grill, a giant repast for two (or even more) diners. Meals are served with bread and margarine, baked potato, vegetables, salad, dessert, and a special *chimichurra* meat sauce that's so scrumptious you'll be sopping it up with the bread. There are also one or two nonmeat choices on the menu.

120 Yefe Nof St. (across from the Holiday Inn). © **04/837-0997.** Reservations suggested. Main courses NIS 55–NIS 135 ($14–$34/£6.90–£17). AE, DC, MC, V. Sun–Thurs 12:30pm–midnight; Fri 12:30–3pm; Sat after Shabbat.

**Nof Chinese Restaurant** CHINESE    A comfortable and well-known kosher Chinese restaurant, the Nof Chinese specializes in hot-pot creations and a variety of regional styles of preparation. The dining room is stylish and comfortable, and the panorama of the city and the bay in the daytime is dramatic. For the budget-minded, there are fixed-price luncheon specials.

101 Ha-Nassi Blvd., inside the Nof Hotel. ℭ 04/835-4311. Reservations recommended. Main courses NIS 55–NIS 90 ($14–$23/£6.90–£11). AE, DC, MC, V. Sun–Thurs noon–3pm and 7pm–midnight; Sat after Shabbat. Closed Fri–Sat until after Shabbat.

**Sea Waves Tokai** ⚸ ASIAN   This is one of Haifa's more exotic choices, with an interesting menu that combines Chinese- and Japanese-style specialties. The Chinese menu's highlights include hot-pot and sizzling iron-plate dishes, as well as crispy duck with honey sauce and meaty spareribs. The ambience is attractive: The *pièce de résistance* Peking duck must be ordered a day in advance. There are lunch and dinner special deals.

108 Yefe Nof St. ℭ 04/838-3800. Reservations recommended evenings and weekends. Main courses NIS 55–NIS 110 ($14–$28/£6.90–£14). AE, DC, MC, V. Daily noon–3:30pm and 7–11:30pm.

## INEXPENSIVE

**The Bank** CAFE   This is a bright, stylish place with summery furnishings where you can enjoy sitting at sidewalk tables and watching the activity around Central Carmel. The Bank is good for light meals: pancakes, blintzes, sandwiches, salads, crepes, cakes, and cappuccino, or many kinds of ice-cream confections. The hefty salad is especially recommended.

119 Ha-Nassi Blvd. ℭ 04/838-9623. Light meals NIS 30–NIS 60 ($7.50–$15/£3.75–£7.50). MC, V. Daily 10am–11pm or midnight. Carmelit: Gan Ha-Em.

**Casa Italiana** (Value) EUROPEAN/ITALIAN   A real favorite with Americans, this is a small, family-run restaurant where you can have a filling meal of spaghetti, cannelloni, or a truly hefty pizza with fresh toppings for less than NIS 41 ($10/£5.10). Breads and focaccia are served straight out of the oven with heaping salads and wonderful main courses such as goulash, just like my grandmother made; steaks; American home-style hamburgers; trout; and Saint Peter's fish. A rich bowl of vegetable soup and garlic bread makes a fine inexpensive lunch. The management here is very friendly and takes good care of returning customers.

119 Ha-Nassi Blvd. ℭ 04/838-1336. Main courses NIS 40–NIS 65 ($10–$16/£5–£8.10). AE, MC, V. Sat–Thurs 5:30–11pm; closed Fri.

**Chin Lung Chinese Restaurant** CHINESE   At first there seems to be no restaurant at all behind the sign and posted menu near the corner of Sea Road (Derech Ha-Yam). But go down the adjoining steps, and you'll discover a nice cellar dining room with a small-town American-style folksy Chinese decor, done in gold and crimson, with gold tablecloths and fresh flowers. The food is mostly Szechuan-style, which can be spicy but needn't be if you don't like hot food. There are 50 items to choose from here; shrimp and calamari dishes are at the high end of the price range. Beer, wine, and cocktails are served.

126 Ha-Nassi Blvd. ℭ 04/838-1308. Main courses NIS 45–NIS 90 ($11–$23/£5.60–£11); business lunch NIS 55 ($14/£6.90). MC, V. Daily noon–3pm and 6:30pm–midnight. Carmelit: Gan Ha-Em.

**Mandarin Cafe** CONTINENTAL   This popular cafe makes its own home blend of coffee and serves a wide-ranging, delicious, and very reasonably priced menu that includes goulash, pastas, calzones, and hefty sandwiches and salads. The desserts, too, are good and won't break your budget. If you're tired of going through the production of a major restaurant meal, this is a good choice. There are two kinds of seating: bar stools at high tables to encourage a fast meal and normal tables and chairs in case you want to eat slowly and relax. The Moriah location, 117 Moriah Blvd. (ℭ 04/834-4112), is roomier, with a garden and live jazz on certain nights.

129 Ha-Nassi Blvd. ✆ **04/836-3554**. Main courses NIS 30–NIS 60 ($7.50–$15/£3.75–£7.50). MC, V. Sat–Wed 9am–1am; Thurs–Fri 9am–2am.

**Lehem Erez** ✦ BAKERY/CAFE   This is the new Haifa branch of a great Israeli cafe/bakery chain, serving wonderful sandwiches laden with herbs, the freshest vegetables, and local cheeses or rustic meats. Sandwiches are all served on fabulous breads lightly drizzled with olive oil or touched with herbed, homemade dressings. The selection changes with the season: A summer sandwich of buffalo-milk cheese, arugula, salami, and fresh figs will not be around in January, but the combinations will always please. The dessert list is legendary; look for chocolate fondant, lemon tarts, cheesecakes, and brownies so quietly rich it could take half an hour to slowly devour one. You'll also find salads and platters, but who would pass up Erez's breads? Takeout is available.

33 Moriah St. ✆ **04/810-1690**. Lunch specials NIS 30–NIS 55 ($7.50–$14/£3.75–£6.90). AE, DC, MC, V. Daily 8am–midnight. Follow Ha-Nassi out past the Haifa Auditorium, where it forks into Moriah St.

## MODERATE

**Jacko's** ✦ FISH   This new Carmel Mountain branch of the famous Jacko's near the port (see below) is more stylish, as befits its upmarket location, but like the original Jacko's, it serves the best fish and seafood in town. The Aegean meze of ikra, feta cheese, Arabic salads, roasted eggplant, and other treats is a great way to start the meal. Honey-soaked Sephardic-Aegean semolina cake is the dessert of choice.

11 Moriah St. ✆ **04/810-2355**. Reservations necessary. Main courses NIS 70–NIS 100 ($18–$25/£8.75–£13). AE, DC, MC, V. Sun–Thurs noon–11pm; Fri noon–5pm; Sat noon–6pm.

## NEAR THE PORT
### EXPENSIVE

**Hanamal 24** ✦✦ MEDITERRANEAN   Haifa's one real gourmet restaurant is located in what was a warehouse in a grungy, dark part of the port area, near the railroad tracks, but once you get inside and climb the stairs, you find yourself in an absolutely beautiful dining space divided into smaller zones that create an intimate feel. The menu is constantly changing, but dishes at this dual-chef restaurant are all special signature creations that are carefully planned. For starters, try fresh shrimp served on a bed of earthy hummus infused with lime; or forest mushrooms stuffed with goat cheese, garlic, and pistachios. Main courses change daily, but always include a choice of interestingly presented lamb, poultry, meat, fish, and seafood. Desserts are splendid, and the wine list is good. You'll need a taxi to get here, but for fans of fine restaurants, this one is worth exploring.

24 Hanamal St. ✆ **04/862-8899**. Reservations necessary. Main courses NIS 90–NIS 130 ($23–$33/£11–£16). Prix-fixe luncheon and dinner specials offered. AE, DC, MC, V. Mon–Sat noon–midnight.

## MODERATE

**Jacko's** ✦ Finds FISH   This little no-frills restaurant in the market is run by Jacko, a retired fisherman, and his entire family. Now, outsiders also wait on you and the decor has improved, but the fish is still good, prepared without pretense, the prices reasonable, and the friendly spirit of Jacko's family still reigns. As Jacko originally came from Izmir, on the coast of Turkey, you'll also find a Sephardic-Aegean touch in first courses such as the Turkish-style "paella" or in the meze of little salads that comes with your main course. The sesame shrimp and the shrimp sautéed in wine and garlic are fresh and tasty. Always ask the waiter about specials and the catch of the day. From the Carmelit stop at Paris Square, walk 2 blocks down South Nathanson Street and turn right into the market. From there, anyone will point out the place to you—it's a Haifa institution.

12 Ha-Dekekim St. ℂ **04/866-8813**. Reservations generally necessary. Main courses NIS 70–NIS 100 ($18–$25/ £8.75–£13). AE, DC, MC, V. Sun–Thurs noon–11pm; Fri noon–5pm; Sat noon–6pm. Carmelit: Paris Sq.

### INEXPENSIVE
**Abu Yusuf** ✦ ARABIC    The sign is in Hebrew, English, and Arabic, and this award-winning restaurant has been loved by speakers of all three languages for decades. Newly redecorated but still basically no-frills, Abu Yusuf's food tends toward the Lebanese, featuring *kubbe,* hummus with meat, grilled heart (delicious), and roast chicken. One trip to the wonderful salad bar of 20 Middle Eastern dishes comes with a main course, or you can order the salad bar alone and have a fine meal with fresh pita bread and a shot ("jot") of anise-flavored arrak brandy. Abu Yusuf offers fresh fish and grilled lamb dishes. Very good value.

1 Ha-Meginim St. ℂ **04/866-3723**. Main courses NIS 40–NIS 100 ($10–$25/£5–£13). MC, V. Sat–Thurs 9am–mid-night; Fri 7am–4pm. Carmelit: Paris Sq.

## GERMAN COLONY
This neighborhood, filled with stone cottages and mansions built by German Christians in the late 19th century, has great potential for charm and gentrification. The Haifa municipality is helping things along with the construction of a pedestrian promenade on the neighborhood's main street, Ben-Gurion Boulevard, which is perfectly aligned with the dramatic Baha'i Shrine farther up the slopes of Mount Carmel. At twilight, the view of the illuminated Baha'i gardens and shrine is very dramatic.

### EXPENSIVE
**1872 Hashmura Restaurant** ✦ RUSTIC FRENCH    Occupying a restored German Colony mansion built in 1872 (hence the date in the name), this restaurant offers charm and good, hearty French-style meals that arrive at your table in generous portions. The house has been beautifully restored and turned into a restaurant with beamed ceilings, whitewashed walls, and dark, polished wooden floors and furnishings; there are four smaller, intimate dining areas on the ground floor, and upstairs, a spacious room often used for parties. The menu changes both daily and seasonally: Very early in summer, you might find a creamy pâté de foie gras served with tart, diced early figs or apricots. Appetizers include shrimp, either grilled or steamed in garlic butter, and a house puff pastry with goat cheese and pesto sauce. You'll find main courses of pasta, fish, and seafood, but the pride of the menu is the meat. Choose from lamb ribs with baked potatoes in a heavy, rich lamb stock; beef filet Rossini topped with melt-in-your-mouth gooseliver and portobello mushroom, served with creamy potato rissoles; or breast of mullard in cardamom sauce. Dishes are substantial but artistically presented, and come with salad, potato, and vegetable. In addition to the standard classics, you'll often find something inventive on the dessert list.

15 Ben-Gurion Blvd. ℂ **04/855-1872**. www.hashmura.co.il. Reservations necessary. Main courses NIS 65–NIS 115 ($16–$29/£8.10–£14). Fixed-price lunch (weekdays noon–5pm) from NIS 75 ($19/£9.40). AE, DC, MC, V. Daily noon–midnight.

### INEXPENSIVE
**Fattoush** MODERN MIDDLE EASTERN    This restaurant's terrace overlooks the Pedestrian Walk and is great for people-watching. It's famous for its fresh house salad, filled with mint, green onion, and other surprises, but there's also a menu of interesting

dishes such as sliced chicken breast and green pepper prepared in a wok with Middle Eastern seasonings and served with a small side dish of yogurtlike *leben*. Lots of good salads, grilled meats, coffees, teas, and desserts round off the menu—the best dessert is an elegant, homemade *kanafeh* (traditional ancient dessert of baked sweet cheese, grain, pistachio, and watered honey). In winter, when the terrace is too chilly, Fattoush retreats inside its stone house, where there's an old-fashioned dining room, plus a downstairs Bedouin room with tribal rugs and low divans on which you can stretch out. The music is soft and always right, whether folk, jazz, classical, or Middle Eastern. There's a short wine list.

38 Ben-Gurion Blvd. 📞 04/852-4930. Main courses and salads NIS 40–NIS 80 ($10–$20/£5–£10). AE, DC, MC, V. Daily 9am–2am.

## BAT GALIM

Bat Galim means "Daughter of the Waves" in Hebrew, and you'll know how it got its name when you stroll along its beachfront promenade. If you take a ride on the aerial cable car between the beach and Mount Carmel, at the lower terminal you'll be right at the end of Bat Galim. The restaurants I mention below are all within a 5-minute walk of the terminal.

If you're not coming via cable car, you can easily walk over from the main bus or train stations—Bat Galim is located behind the stations. If you're at the Central Station, go through the underground tunnel that connects it to the train station; when you come out of the train station, you'll be in Bat Galim. You can also take bus no. 40, 41, 42, or 44, which go from the bus station to the cable car terminal; or if you're driving, come across at Hel Ha-Yam, the main boulevard running just east of the bus station.

### MODERATE

**Dolphin** SEAFOOD   A la carte prices here are higher than in other neighborhood restaurants, but the reputation of the restaurant is very good. A typical dinner might include the excellent house fish soup, tomato based and richly herbed; followed by shrimp cocktail, an excellent grouper seviche, or fried calamari; and concluded with by a main course of fresh fish or jumbo shrimp tempura. The warm apple pie is famous, but the traditional Aegean-Sephardic semolina cake is also interesting. It's 1 block inland from the Bat Galim Promenade.

13 Bat Galim Ave. 📞 04/852-3837. Reservations recommended evenings. Main courses NIS 70–NIS 120 ($18–$30/£8.75–£15). AE, DC, MC, V. Daily noon–4pm and 7pm–midnight. Bus: 40, 41, or 42.

### INEXPENSIVE

**Yotvata** 🕏 DAIRY/VEGETARIAN   Right on the beach, at the lower terminus of Haifa's famous aerial cable car, this is an extremely popular emporium for dairy and vegetarian food. Everything is made from the best-quality produce, bought directly from kibbutzim and the famous dairy kibbutz at Yotvata. For under NIS 50 ($13/£6.25), you can get salads, cheese platters served with fresh herbs and vegetables, blintzes, pancakes, vegetable pies, pastas, and pizzas. At the upper end of the price range, you'll find a selection of fish, chicken, pasta, and hamburgers, as well as bagels and lox. The mixtures of natural fruit juices are famous, as are Yotvata's many ice-cream desserts.

End of Bat Galim Promenade. 📞 04/852-6835. Main courses NIS 35–NIS 80 ($8.75–$20/£4.40–£10). AE, DC, MC, V. Daily 7am–4am.

## DADO BEACH

Haifa is blessed with fabulous beaches within its municipal boundaries, but few tourists get to see them. Dado Beach (Hof Dado), just south of the Le Méridien

Hotel, is one of the most accessible, with white sands, open waves, and a number of clubs, pubs, and restaurants.

**HaHaveet (The Barrel)** ☆ SEAFOOD   Serving delicious heaps of excellent fried calamari, sautéed shrimp, and fresh fish, this is a little beachfront place with a big covered terrace and wooden picnic tables open to views of the water, the sound of the waves, and sea breezes. You can come here for a major no-frills seafood meal; a sandwich; or grilled meat, pasta, a big fresh salad, or a Middle Eastern appetizer. For dessert, there's ice cream, apple pie, hot chocolate cake, or watermelon *(avateeach)* served with a special cheese that goes perfectly with it and the sunset over the sea. Twenty different beers are on the menu; at night the restaurant becomes a beachfront pub with house-designed cocktails (of both the ice-cream variety and not), in addition to wines, liqueurs, juices, and hot drinks. In the daytime, you might want to dine here after a swim—there are showers and changing rooms nearby.

Dado Beach (Hof Dado) Promenade. ℂ 04/852-2215. Main courses NIS 40–NIS 85 ($10–$21/£5–£11). AE, DC, MC, V. Daily noon–after midnight. Bus: 43. By car, get off Hwy. 2 at Le Méridien Hotel and follow road south under bridge to Dado Beach parking. From the 1st public parking lot at Dado Beach, HaHaveet faces the beach at the northern end of the Dado Promenade.

## CAFES
### CENTRAL CARMEL
On the loft balcony above the dairy self-service Cafe Carmel in the vast Panorama Center is the **Viennese Gallery** (ℂ **04/835-2222**). The view is incredible from up here, and the distinctive architecture does everything to maximize the view, with a curved, two-story wall. The Viennese Gallery serves mostly desserts and coffees, but there is also a selection of quiches, salads, omelets, soups, and cold platters. Although the surroundings are fancy, prices are really quite reasonable. You can get a gorgeous Viennese pastry with a whole pot of freshly brewed tea or coffee for NIS 32 ($8/£4), but there are also more lavish Viennese fantasy concoctions with rich ice creams. You'll find it open from 10am to 11pm daily (until midnight Fri–Sat). If you're not a guest at the Panorama Hotel and therefore unable to put the tab on your VAT-free bill, you will pay an extra 15.5%.

You'll also find **Kapulski's Café,** in the Panorama Shopping Mall, facing Ha-Nassi Blvd., just under the Panorama Towers. Kapulski's is less fancy, but is also a good place for tea or coffee and very good pastries, as well as salads, quiches, and other nicely prepared lighter meals. Prices range from NIS 20 to NIS 50 ($5–$13/£2.50–£6.25). Kapulski's closes for Shabbat. **Greg Café** is Haifa's answer to Starbucks, Aroma, and every other dispenser of caffeine. With branches at the Cinémathèque/Auditorium on Ha-Nassi Street and at Haifa University, it serves fabulous coffee and is good for breakfast and for takeout.

## 5 Attractions

Before setting out, check with the Haifa Tourist Information Office's ***What's on in Haifa*** and the **Tourist Information Telephone Hot Line** (ℂ **04/837-4253**), both of which will tell you what's happening while you're in town.

## SUGGESTED ITINERARY

**Day 1** Visit the Baha'i Gardens, enjoy the panorama, and take in a wing or two at the Haifa Museum while checking out central Haifa.

**Day 2** Spend at least half the day at one of Haifa's fine municipal beaches if the weather's good. Dado Beach, south of the city, is accessible by bus. Choose from among Haifa's other fine museums, such as Clandestine Immigration, Mané Katz, or the Japanese Tikotin Museum for the rest of your day.

**Day 3** Excursions. Take one to Mount Carmel; the Carmelite monastery at Mukraqa (with its sweeping view of northern Israel; the site of Elijah's contest with the prophets of Baal); and the Druze villages (p. 416), the artists' village at Ein Hod (p. 309), or to Old Akko (p. 314).

## THE TOP ATTRACTIONS
### IN HADAR

**Baha'i Shrine & Gardens** ★★    Haifa's most impressive sightseeing attraction is the splendid Baha'i Shrine and Gardens, reached from Zionism (Ha-Zionut) Avenue. The immaculate, majestic Baha'i gardens—with their stone peacocks and eagles and delicately manicured cypress trees—are a restful, aesthetic memorial to the founders of the Baha'i faith. Haifa is the international headquarters for the gentle Baha'i faith, which began in Persia in the mid–19th century in a bloodbath of persecution.

Baha'is believe in the unity of all religions and see all religious leaders—Christ, Buddha, Muhammad, Moses—as messengers of God sent at different times in history with doctrines varying to fit changing social needs but bringing substantially the same message. The most recent of these heavenly teachers, according to Baha'is, was Baha' Allah. He was exiled by the Turkish authorities to Acre, wrote his doctrines there, and died a peaceful death in Bahji House just north of Acre. See "Akko (Acre)," in chapter 8, for more information.

In the Haifa gardens, the huge domed **shrine** entombs the remains of the Bab, the Baha' Allah's herald. The tomb is a sight to see, with ornamental gold work and flowers in almost every nook and cranny. The Bab's remains, incidentally, were hidden for years after he died a martyr's death in front of a firing squad. Eventually, however, his followers secretly carried his remains to the Holy Land.

On a higher hilltop stands the Corinthian-style **Baha'i International Archives** building, modeled after the Parthenon, and the **Universal House of Justice,** with 58 marble columns and hanging gardens behind. These are business buildings, not open to tourists. They, and the shrine of the tomb of the Bab, all face toward Acre, the burial place of Baha' Allah.

The beautiful grounds were originally planned by Shoghi Effendi, the late Guardian of the Faith. The Baha'i gardens have recently undergone a massive redesign aimed at putting them on the world's horticultural map. They are now a geometric cascade of hanging gardens and terraces down to Ben-Gurion Boulevard—a gift of visual pleasure to the city that gave the Baha'i religion its home and headquarters. In addition to tourists, you'll see pilgrims who have come from all parts of the world to pay homage to the first leaders of this universal faith. At the entrance to the shrine, where you must remove your shoes, you will be given a pamphlet providing further details on Baha'i history and doctrine.

Off Ha-Tzionut Ave. ✆ 04/831-3131. Reservations for admission required. Free admission. Guided tours given every hour, on the hour. Modest dress required. Shrine daily 9am–noon; gardens daily 9am–5pm. Bus: 22 from the port; 23, 25, or 26 from Hadar.

**The Haifa Museum of Art**   The first branch of the Haifa Museum (the other two are the Tikotin Museum of Japanese Art and the National Maritime Museum) is home to a strong collection of contemporary painting, sculpture, and prints by Israeli and foreign artists, but with a strong emphasis on Israeli art. The museum is divided into five areas, each containing a different category of art or type of exhibit: emerging Israeli art, centering on artists who have never shown in a museum before; new mediums; a special presentation of installation art; "personal choice," containing an Israeli cultural figure's selection from the museum's collection with commentary; and a special visiting exhibition or headline exhibit from the museum's collection.

26 Shabtai Levi St. ✆ 04/852-3255. Joint admission to Haifa Museum of Art, Tikotin Museum of Japanese Art, and National Maritime Museum NIS 35 ($8.75/£4.40). Sun–Mon and Wed 11am–5pm; Tues and Thurs 4–8pm; Fri 10am–1pm; Sat 10am–4pm. Bus: 12, 22, or 41. Carmelit: Ha-Nevi'im station.

**Tikotin Museum of Japanese Art**   The exceptional Tikotin, a gem by any standards and the second branch of the Haifa Museum, has examples of almost all kinds of Japanese art and crafts, along with a library of approximately 3,000 books. The Tikotin's beautiful contemporary building hosts 10 to 12 special exhibits of Japanese arts and crafts, which are changed to reflect the current season. The museum is located near the Dan Carmel Hotel in Central Carmel.

89 Ha-Nassi Blvd. ✆ 04/838-3554. Joint admission to Haifa Museum of Art, Tikotin Museum of Japanese Art, and National Maritime Museum NIS 35 ($8.75/£4.40). Sun–Mon and Wed 11am–5pm; Tues and Thurs 4–8pm; Fri 10am–1pm; Sat 10am–4pm. Bus: 22 or 23. Carmelit: Gan Ha-Em station.

**National Maritime Museum**   This third branch of the Haifa Museum, near Bat Galim, encompasses 5,000 years of seafaring history in the Mediterranean and the Red Sea. The **Museum of Ancient Art,** recently relocated here from the central Haifa Museum Complex, displays archaeological collections of Mediterranean cultures from the beginning of history until the Islamic conquest in the 7th century. There are outstanding collections of Greco-Roman culture, Coptic art, painted portraits from Fayum, coins from Caesarea and Acre, terra cottas of all periods, and finds from the Haifa area. The artifacts obtained through underwater archaeology are particularly impressive. The marvelous ethnology section of the Haifa Museum is also located here, but due to limited space, little of it is on display.

198 Allenby Rd. ✆ 04/853-6622. Joint admission to Haifa Museum of Art, Tikotin Museum of Japanese Art, and National Maritime Museum NIS 35 ($8.75/£4.40). Sun–Mon and Wed 11am–5pm; Tues and Thurs 4–8pm; Fri 10am–1pm; Sat 10am–4pm. Bus: 3, 5, or 43.

**Mané Katz Museum**   This building, near the Dan Panorama hotel in Central Carmel, was once a rustic mountaintop villa in which the French artist Mané Katz lived (the neighborhood has certainly changed). The museum now houses a collection of Mané Katz's own work and personal collection—drawings, aquarelles, gouaches, oil paintings, sculpture, and Judaica—as well as interesting, well-planned visiting exhibits of contemporary art.

89 Yefe Nof (Panorama Rd.). ✆ 04/838-3482. Admission visiting exhibits NIS 20 ($5/£2.50); Mané Katz collection free admission. Sun–Mon and Wed–Thurs 10am–4pm; Tues 2–6pm; Fri 10am–1pm; Sat 10am–2pm. Bus: 22, 23, or 31. Carmelit: Central Carmel.

**Mitzpoor Ha-Shalom (Peace View Park)**   The grounds of the Baha'i gardens are split by Zionism Avenue. Farther up the hill is the lovely Mitzpoor Ha-Shalom (Peace View Park), also called the Ursula Malbin Sculpture Garden. Amid trees, flowers, and sloping lawns are 18 bronze sculptures by Ursula Malbin of men, women, children, and animals at play. The view from here is magnificent—you can see all of Haifa's port area, Haifa Bay, Acre, Nahariya, and up to Rosh Ha-Niqra at the Lebanese border, plus all the surrounding mountains.

Zionism Ave., at the corner of Shnayim Be-November St. Free admission. Bus: 22 from the port; 23, 25, or 26 from Hadar.

## IN CARMEL

**Mount Carmel National Park**   Israel's largest national park has 10,000 hectares (24,711 acres) of pine, eucalyptus, and cypress forest. It encompasses a large area of the Carmel mountain range and has many points of interest that are well marked and easily reachable. Within the park are the caves of the Carmel ridge; 250 sites inhabited by prehistoric humans beginning 100,000 years ago have been discovered. Elsewhere, special nature-reserve areas dedicated to studying and maintaining the original Mediterranean habitat of the area have been set up. And, of course, the park also has picnic areas, playgrounds, a restaurant, and restrooms. There are bicycle and walking paths and also a Druze hospitality center, serving tea and Druze breads. Admission to the nature reserve in the park is NIS 20 ($5/£2.50).

Carmel mountain range. ✆ 04/823-1452. www.parks.org.il. Admission NIS 38 ($9.50/£4.75) per car. Bus: 37. By car, take Rte. 4 (the old Tel Aviv–Haifa hwy.) to Oren junction and turn east. From Rte. 70 (Faradis-Yokne'am), turn west to the Eliakim interchange and at the town of Nesher, head toward the University of Haifa.

**Technion**   The Technion, the Israel Institute of Technology, is Israel's version of MIT. Founded in 1912, its 120-hectare (297-acre) campus is a most impressive university complex, offering views of the city, the bay, the coastline clear to Lebanon, and the snow-topped Syrian mountains.

Because so many people come to see the Technion, the **Coler-California Visitor Center** (✆ **04/832-0664**) has been established to introduce the campus to visitors. You'll be greeted by a real working robot when you come in. There's also a free 20-minute video about the school, and there are high-tech multimedia touch-screen videos, Internet kiosks, and laser disc productions that offer additional information. You'll also receive a pamphlet and map of the campus, which you can use to take your own **self-guided tour.** The student-priced **cafeteria** downstairs is recommended for a good budget lunch.

Many **entertainment activities** are held every evening (except Mon) at Bet Student, the Technion's Student House (✆ **04/832-0664**). Call during the daytime for info on folk, disco, and '60s dancing, films, and other activities. You can also stop in at Bet Student's pub, cafeteria, or restaurant for a meal at student prices.

Technion City. ✆ 04/829-3863. www.technion.ac.il. Free admission. Visitor center Sun–Thurs 8am–3pm; closed Fri–Sat. Bus: 17 from Central Bus Station; 31 from Central Carmel; 19 from Hadar at Daniel St., next to the Armon Cinema on Ha-Nevi'im St., just down from Masaryk Sq.

**Haifa University**   On the Mount Carmel road from Haifa to the nearby Druze village of Daliat-el-Carmel, you'll see the buildings and tower of Haifa University. The campus was originally designed by Oscar Niemeyer, the designer of Brazil's superfuturistic capital city of Brasilia; new sections, planned by other architects, were added later. The university began operation in 1963, under the joint auspices of the City of Haifa and the Hebrew University. At that time, the students numbered 650; now 13,000 full-time degree students attend the university.

The campus offers a magnificent view. From the 30th-floor (top-floor) observatory of the **Eshkol Tower,** which you can visit on your own Sunday through Thursday from 8am to 3:30pm (free admission), you get an incredible view of practically the entire north of Israel. Throughout the university's public spaces you'll find a surprising number of paintings and sculpture. The large murals located in the university lobby are especially notable.

The campus has several impressive art galleries. The **Oscar Ghez Gallery,** on the Eshkol Tower's 30th floor, houses a moving memorial collection of works by artists who perished in the Holocaust, compiled by Oscar Ghez over a 30-year period. The **University Art Gallery** in the main building displays important works by Israeli and foreign artists. The **Reuben and Edith Hecht Museum** contains a compact but impressive Israeli archaeology collection with rotating exhibitions; there is also a wing devoted to art—paintings by Impressionists and the Jewish School of Paris. The museum is open Sunday, Monday, Wednesday, and Thursday from 10am to 4pm; Tuesday from 10am to 7pm; Friday from 10am to 1pm; and Saturday from 10am to 2pm (free admission). Adjoining the **Hecht Museum** is the **Maagan Michael Ship Museum** (open Mon, Wed, and Thurs 10am–2pm; Tues 10am–7pm; free admission), slated to hold the world's oldest vessel, a 2,400-year-old Phoenician-era merchant ship salvaged by university archaeologists off the coast just south of Haifa. To take a free **guided tour** of the campus; you must call in advance to reserve a spot (© **04/824-0097**).

The Haifa University Students Association sponsors many activities throughout the academic year. Call the **Students Association** (© **04/824-0544**) for information. There is also a Hillel House (© **04/824-0762**) with a full schedule of activities.

Mount Carmel. © **04/824-0093**, 824-0007, or 824-0097 for tour reservations. http://research.haifa.ac.il/~hecht/eng.htm. Campus tours Sun–Thurs 10am–3:30pm. Bus: 24, 36, 37, or 37A.

### Stella Maris Lighthouse, Church and Carmelite Monastery ☆

In the 12th century, during the Crusader occupation of the region, groups of religious hermits began to inhabit the caves of the Carmel District in emulation of Elijah the Prophet, whose life was strongly identified with this mountain. Within a century, these monastic hermits were organized into the Carmelite order; although the Carmelite order spread throughout Europe, its founders on the Carmel range were exiled at the time of the Mamluke conquest in 1291 and did not return until the 18th century. Construction of the present monastery and basilica was begun in 1836. Situated across the street from the Old Lighthouse, with a magnificent view of the sea, the entire ensemble of buildings, including the lighthouse, is known as "Stella Maris." An earlier monastery complex on this site served as a hospital for Napoleon's soldiers during his unsuccessful siege of Acre in 1799. The pyramid in front of the church entryway stands as a memorial to the many abandoned French soldiers who were slaughtered by the Turks after Napoleon retreated from his toehold on the coast near Akko. It bears the inscription "How are the mighty fallen in battle," from King David's lamentation over Saul and Jonathan.

The **church** is a beautiful structure, with Italian marble so brightly and vividly patterned that visitors sometimes mistakenly think the walls have been painted. Colorful paintings on the dome, done by Brother Luigi Poggi (1924–28), depict episodes from the Old Testament, the most dramatic being the scene of Elijah swept up in a chariot of fire; but the statue of the Virgin Mary, carved from cedar of Lebanon, is also notable. The **cave** situated below the altar, which you can walk down into, is believed to have been inhabited by Elijah.

Be sure to visit the rooms to the right of the entryway, where you'll find a charming nativity scene, a museum with artifacts from the Byzantine church occupying this same spot before the Carmelites built here, and a small souvenir shop. One of the monks will gladly give you a free pamphlet with information about the history of this site, and the Carmelite order, dating back to the arrival of the Crusaders on this

## Frommer's Favorite Haifa Experiences

**Promenading**   The view of Haifa from the promenade in Central Carmel makes you keep coming back for more. Day or night, it's always lovely. For the best experience, combine the Elysian vista with a meal at a restaurant right on the edge of the promenade.

**Beachcombing**   Haifa's great beaches are to the south of the city, reachable by municipal bus, sherut, or, in summer, special shuttle from the big Central Carmel hotels. At the easy-to-reach Dado Beach, just to the south of the Le Méridien Hotel, you can combine a dip in the warm gentle waves with shish kabob or falafel, or a very fresh fish from one of the many beachside stands. Stay late and you'll see the sunset over the Mediterranean. For Haifans, such paradisiacal luxuries are routine.

**A Day Trip to Old Akko**   It's amazing to think that two such different cities could be located on opposite ends of Haifa's sweeping bay: modern Haifa with its panoramas, and medieval Akko, with its labyrinth of bazaars, caravansaries, and mosques. A short drive or bus ride gets you 23km (14 miles) up the coast where you can explore this largely unrestored architectural treasure, have lunch or dinner in true Mediterranean style at an outdoor harborside cafe, and even take a boat ride around the Old City's wave-battered walls.

mountain in the late 12th century. They will answer any questions you may have and guide you to the various interesting details of the church, such as the many little votive candles burning on the altar above the cave, each representing a Carmelite community in another country (the United States has its candle up on the left). The views are wonderful. From Stella Maris, Haifa's little aerial cable car can take you down to the Bat Galim Beach Promenade, where you can walk in the Mediterranean or dine at eateries along the waterfront.

Stella Maris Rd. ⓒ 04/833-7758. Daily 6:30am–1:30pm and 3–6pm. English Mass Mon–Sat 6:30am; Sun 7 and 9am. Modest dress required. Bus: 25, 26, or 31.

### IN THE PORT
**Clandestine Immigration and Naval Museum**   The clandestine immigration movement of Jews into Palestine during and after World War II—called "Aliya Bet"—is one of the most harrowing phases of Israeli history. Throughout the time of the Holocaust, when Jews so desperately needed a haven, admission to British Mandate Palestine was largely denied to them by the British government. Nevertheless, Jews fleeing from the Nazis during World War II and, after the war, Jewish escapees from displaced persons camps constantly attempted to enter Palestine on rusty, unsafe illegal vessels. Some succeeded in making it undetected past British ships guarding Palestine's Mediterranean coastline; others were not so fortunate. The **Struma,** from 1941 to 1942, waited for months at sea for some country to accept the 765 refugees aboard until it was torpedoed by the Russian navy and sank off Turkey. All but one on board perished. Others, like the **Patria,** went down in Haifa harbor, with hundreds killed in sight of safety; still others, like the **Exodus 1947** (made famous by the Leon Uris book *Exodus* and the 1960 film of the same name), ran the British blockade only to have its

passengers shipped to a Cyprus detention camp, or, pathetically enough, returned to a detention camp in Germany. The blockade-running vessel *Af-Al-Pi Chen* (**Nevertheless**) is now a part of the Clandestine Immigration and Naval Museum, a memorial commemorating all the ships that defied the British blockade to smuggle immigrants into Palestine.

204 Allenby Rd. ℂ 04/853-6249. Admission NIS 15 ($3.75/£1.90) adults; half-price for students and children. Sun–Thurs 9am–4pm. Closed Fri–Sat. Bus: 3, 5, 43, or 44.

## MORE ATTRACTIONS

The **Rothschild Community House (Bet Rothschild),** in Central Carmel near Haifa Auditorium at 142 Ha-Nassi Blvd. (ℂ **04/838-2749**), often has something of interest for tourists. Call to see what's up. Interesting, too, are the changing art exhibits and folklore programs at **Bet Ha-Gefen** (ℂ **04/852-5251**), the Arab-Jewish Community Center, on Ha-Gefen Street opposite the Chagall Artists' House, which also sponsors music and art programs for Jewish and Arab children, as well as joint exhibitions of their work.

**Aerial Cable Car**    Directly across the road from the *Af-Al-Pi Chen* is the lower terminal of the Haifa Aerial Cable Car. The ride is not as dramatic as it looks from a distance, but it is a fast way to get up or down the side of the mountain. The popular Yotvata restaurant (p. 343), famous for its salads and ice cream, is at the lower terminal. The cable car rides through the air from the beach at the western end of Bat Galim up to the tip of Mount Carmel, the site of the Old Lighthouse and Stella Maris. The top terminal has a place where you can get refreshments; the bottom terminal's downstairs hall contains an exhibit of a different featured artist's work each week. *Note:* At press time the cable car was closed for repairs.

ℂ 04/833-5970. Round-trip NIS 22 ($5.50/£2.75); one-way NIS 15 ($3.75/£1.90). Sat–Thurs 10am–5:30pm; Fri 10am–1:45pm. Bus: 26, 28, or 31 to the top terminal; 40, 41, or 42 to the bottom terminal.

**Chagall Artists' House**    Established in 1954, this gallery exhibits the works of contemporary Israeli artists.

24 Ha-Zionut Ave. ℂ 04/852-2355. Free admission. Sun–Thurs 9am–1pm and 4–7pm; Sat 10am–1pm. Bus: 10, 12, 22, 23, 25, 26, 32, or 41.

**Dagon Grain Museum**    On display are earthen storage jars, striking mosaic murals, and various exhibits showing the development of one of humankind's oldest industries—the cultivation, handling, storage, and distribution of grain from ancient to modern times. There are even some grains of wheat here that are more than 4,000 years old, as well as fertility statues and flint grain sickles.

Kikar Plumer. ℂ 04/866-4221. Free admission. Tours Sun–Fri 10:30am; call for reservations. The museum is only open to the public for guided tours. Bus: 10, 12, or 22. Carmelit: Plummer Sq.

**Elijah's Cave**    From the *Af-Al-Pi Chen*, it's just a short walk up to Elijah's Cave, nestled at the base of steep Cape Carmel, below the Stella Maris lighthouse and the Carmelite Monastery. Tradition has it that Elijah hid here when fleeing the wrath of King Ahab and his wife, Jezebel. It's also the site where Elijah established his school upon his return from exile, thus earning the name "School of the Prophets," where Elijah, among others, studied. The cave is also said to be a place where the Holy Family found shelter for a night on their return from Egypt.

The cave is sacred to Jews, Christians, Muslims, and Druze, all of whom venerate the prophet Elijah. Pilgrimages and huge dramatic ceremonies are held at this cave many times each year. Head coverings are available at the entrance to the cave.

230 Allenby Rd. (℃) 04/852-7430. Free admission; donations accepted. Summer Sun–Thurs 8am–6pm, Fri 8am–1pm; winter Sun–Thurs 8am–5pm, Fri 8am–1pm. Closed Sat and holidays. Bus: 3, 5, 44, or 45 will let you off at the highway nearby.

**National Museum of Science, Technology, and Space** *(Kids)* This museum showcases the latest discoveries in Israeli science and offers hands-on interactive science displays, ranging in subject from puzzles to chemistry to astronomy. For an extra fee, you can visit the multisensory theater, which kids will find fun and interesting. To get here, walk up the hill from Herzl Street; the museum is in the Technion's architecturally stunning original building on the Old Technion campus, on your right. Hours may change according to season and academic holidays. Always call ahead to reserve a tour in English.

Old Technion Campus, 12 Balfour St. (℃) 04/862-8111. www.madatech.org.il. Admission NIS 35 ($8.75/£4.40) adults; discounts for students. AE, DC, MC, V. July–Aug Sun–Mon and Wed–Thurs 10am–6pm, Tues 10am–7:30pm, Fri 10am–2pm, Sat 10am–6pm; school year Sun–Wed 9am–4pm, Thurs 9am–8pm, Fri 10am–2pm, Sat 10am–6pm. Bus: 18, 19, 21, 28, 37, 42, or 50 stops nearby. Carmelit: Haneviim.

## 6 Organized Tours

The **Haifa Tourism Development Association,** 84 Ben-Gurion Blvd. (℃ **04/853-5606**), offers a free 2½-hour **guided walking tour** of Central Carmel (atop the mountain) at 10am every Saturday. The meeting point, marked by a sign, is on Panorama Road (Yefe Nof) at the intersection with Shar Ha-Levanon, right behind the Gan Ha-Em Carmelit station (it's also behind the Nof Hotel, which faces Ha-Nassi Blvd.). To reach the meeting point, take bus no. 23 from Ha-Nevi'im Street, or bus no. 21 from Herzl Street, both in Hadar; they run on Saturday (note that the Carmelit does not). Modest dress is required. The Haifa Tourism Development Association also offers maps for a variety of self-guided tours throughout the city. For nature hike routes and walks through the vast, wild Park Ha-Carmel, contact the Haifa Hiking Club (℃ **04/838-4867**) or the Carmel Field School (℃ **04/866-4159**).

The following companies offer all sorts of tour plans of the Haifa region: **Egged Tours,** 4 Nordau St. (℃ **04/862-3131**), and **Mitzpa Tours,** 1 Nordau St. (℃ **04/867-4341**).

The **Society for Protection of Nature in Israel (SPNI),** 18 Hillel St. (℃ **04/866-4135;** fax 04/866-5825), offers excellent urban and nature-trail tours of the Carmel mountains.

## 7 Outdoor Activities, Sports & Other Pursuits

**BEACHES**    Haifa's great secret is its beaches. Starting with **Bat Galim** and moving south to the broader, more beautiful **Dado** and **Zamir beaches,** the miles of golden sands are dotted with changing facilities and simple beach cafes. Admission is free; take bus no. 41, 42, 43, 45, 3a, or 99. In winter, at least one restaurant pavilion remains open until 7pm; in summer until 8:30pm. A meal costs around NIS 60 ($15/£7.50). Dinner at a simple stand at the beach in summer, watching the sunset over the Mediterranean at the end of an afternoon of swimming in the warm turquoise sea, is an experience Haifans love.

**CYCLING**   Look into **Mountain Bike Haifa** (www.geocities.com/Pipeline/5850), a local cycling club. The Haifa Tourism Development Association office will provide you with current biking information.

**FOLK DANCING**   Israeli **folk dancing sessions** meet at Haifa University and at Bet Ha-Student at the Technion. **International Folk Dancers** meet Thursday at Bet Rothschild, to the side of the Haifa Auditorium on Ha-Nassi Boulevard. Check with the Haifa Tourism Development Association for current schedules.

**SWIMMING**   In the Central Carmel section you'll find the **Maccabi swimming pool** on Bikkurim Street (✆ **04/838-8341**), heated in winter and serviced by bus no. 21, 22, or 23 and by the Carmelit. Admission is NIS 25 ($6.25/£3.10), but the fee doubles in winter. Don't forget the pleasant gardened **pool at the Dan Carmel Hotel,** where an outsider can buy a whole day's worth of pool privileges, as well as the use of shaded swings and slides for kids, for NIS 80 ($20/£10).

**TENNIS & SQUASH**   At the **Haifa Tennis Center** (✆ **04/852-2721** or 04/853-2014) you can rent a court (for two people or more) at NIS 40 ($10/£5) per hour in the evenings; NIS 30 ($7.50/£3.75) per hour during the day. The **Haifa Squash Center** (✆ **04/853-9160**) is generally for members, but for a one-time payment of NIS 60 ($15/£7.50), you can purchase a multiple-entry, short-term pass. Both centers are a 15-minute ride south of downtown Haifa, in the Kefar Zamir suburb; take bus no. 43 or 3A. Call in advance to reserve a court.

## 8 Shopping

Haifa has a number of modern indoor shopping malls, including the **Panorama Center** in Central Carmel, **Migdal Haneve'im** in the Hadar District, and the **Horev Center** on Horev Street at the intersection of Pica Street. The **Panorama Center,** 1 block from the Central Carmel Carmelit stop, is most easily accessible to visitors staying in the Carmel Center, and offers branches of a number of the country's best women's clothing stores, including Dorin Frankfort.

**Steimatzky bookstores** has a branch at the **Auditorium Mall,** just beside the Haifa Auditorium, 142 Ha-Nassi Blvd., and handy to the hotels in the Carmel Center.

**Massada Street,** with its own Carmelit stop halfway up the mountain between Hadar and the Carmel Center, has become home to a number of small, offbeat antiques and curiosity shops. My favorite stop here is **Yad B'homer Contemporary Crafts Gallery** at 9A Massada St. (✆ **04/862-9239**). Here you can see the work of eight artisans, as well as special exhibits of guest craftspeople. There is also a shelf of very reasonably priced Ethiopian figurines and Judaica. It's open Sunday, Monday, Wednesday, and Thursday from 10am to 1pm and 4 to 7pm and Tuesday and Friday from 10am to 2pm. Most shops on the street keep similar hours. A walk down Massada Street gives you a feel for the architectural structure of Haifa's residential neighborhoods, with 1930s and 1940s apartment buildings virtually climbing up and down the mountain on either side of the street.

If you take an excursion to the artists' village of **Ein Hod** (p. 309), south of Haifa, you can shop for silver, enamel, and gold jewelry; handblown glass; pottery; and other contemporary crafts at the village's official gallery.

## 9 Haifa After Dark

Haifa does not have as much nightlife as Tel Aviv, or even Jerusalem, but there are some nighttime activities. Check in the *International Herald Tribune,* which includes the English edition of *Ha'aretz,* Israel's preeminent newspaper, or the *Jerusalem Post,* which despite its name lists events, cultural offerings, and movies throughout Israel. The Friday-morning editions of both *Ha'aretz* and the *Jerusalem Post* include the indispensable weekly calendar of happenings, some of which are in Haifa.

The student associations at the Technion and at the University of Haifa have entertainment of one kind or another going on almost every night. Check with the universities for details.

### THE PERFORMING ARTS

**Haifa Auditorium**    This is Haifa's largest concert hall, where you can find symphony, opera, the Israel Philharmonic, dance concerts, and many other cultural events and big happenings; there's also usually an interesting art display in the lobby, which you can see anytime for free, from 4 to 7pm (except Fri). Haifa Auditorium is just a short distance south of the Central Carmel commercial district, where Ha-Nassi Boulevard becomes Moriah Avenue. Ticket prices vary according to performance. 138 Ha-Nassi Blvd. (*C*) **04/835-3555.**

**Haifa Municipal Theater**    Lots of shows are offered at this theater where the play performances are sometimes in Hebrew, sometimes in English, and sometimes both in simultaneous translation. Ticket prices vary according to the performance. 50 Yefe Nof St. (*C*) **04/860-0500** box office.

**James de Rothschild Cultural and Community Center**    Next to Haifa Auditorium, this community center always has something going on: a dance, an exhibit, or a concert. Also inside the community center is the Haifa Cinémathèque (see below). Bet Rothschild, 142 Ha-Nassi Blvd. (*C*) **04/838-2749.**

### THE CLUB & MUSIC SCENE

Looking for a club, a place to hang out, listen to music, have a drink, and dance? The **Haifa Tourism Development Association,** 84 Ben-Gurion Blvd., in the German Colony, has compiled a list of recommendable spots; stop by for information.

**Fever**    This disco is a favorite of teenagers. Summer weekend evenings are busiest. The schedule is constantly changing, but it is open after 11pm. Thursday is over-25 night. Gan Ha-Em Promenade. No phone.

**Martef Esser (Cellar Ten)**    This is now a nightspot run by and for students, with live music of many kinds (jazz, classical, and more), and a nice coffeehouse/bar atmosphere. There are discounts if you have a student ID card, and no smoking inside. Hours vary, but during the school year it is generally open after 10pm Wednesday to Friday and Sunday to Monday; closed Tuesday and Saturday. In the summer it's open after 10pm and closed Monday and Saturday. 23 Jerusalem St., Hadar. (*C*) **04/824-0762.** www.martef10.com. Cover charge (varies depending on performance) Thurs–Sat.

### THE BAR SCENE

Many of Haifa's restaurants have bars with entertainment. Both the upper and lower terminals of the Aerial Cable Car, too, are enjoyable places to stop on an evening out, with restaurants, bars, and dancing; you can ride the cable car most of the year until midnight.

**Bear Pub**    Bear Pub offers indoor and outdoor spaces, and hefty sandwiches, pub food, and a nice atmosphere. Sunday to Friday 11am to 4am; Saturday 6pm to 4am. 135 Ha-Nassi Blvd. ✆ **04/838-6563.**

**Irish House**    This is a very Hibernian place serving Guinness and meat pies, and with TV screens tuned to international sports. Daily 9pm to 3am. 120 Yefe Nof St. ✆ **04/830-3376.**

**Wine Bar at 1872 Hashmura Restaurant**    Located in the charming 1872 Hashmura Restaurant (p. 342), this hideaway is an elegant spot for sampling wine, cheese, and gourmet snacks. Thursday to Saturday evening only; reservations recommended. 15 Ben-Gurion St. ✆ **04/855-1872.**

## FILMS

**Haifa Cinémathèque**    Housed in the James de Rothschild Cultural and Community Center, this film repertory theater shows a wide variety of international films (up to three different movies every day, many in English, and most with English subtitles), including experimental, foreign, classic, and art film screenings. The Cinémathèque hosts the **Haifa Film Festival** each fall at the time of Succot. Call for up-to-date information on what's playing. 142 Ha-Nassi Blvd. ✆ **04/810-4299.** www.ethos.co.il/cinema. Tickets NIS 30 ($7.50/£3.75).

## 10  Day Trips from Haifa

### DALIAT-EL-CARMEL & ISFIYA

These Druze villages are located 15 minutes from the Ahuza section of Carmel. If you're driving, just ask for the road to Daliat-el-Carmel. Isfiya is the first village you'll reach from Haifa; Daliat-el-Carmel is a very short ride farther. The trip takes about half an hour, and it's a splendid drive along the uppermost rim of Carmel. The Mediterranean is way down below you, as are the entire city, the port, and the industrial area. Bring your camera.

Architecturally, the villages are no longer the quaint enclaves of 30 or 40 years ago; instead, they've become part of the urban sprawl at the outer edge of the city. Israelis visit the villages for the many home-style Middle Eastern restaurants that have sprung up, and for bargain-basement shopping, especially on Saturday (see below).

The Druze are Arabic-speaking people who are, however, not Muslims. Theirs is a rather secretive religion; they draw heavily on the Bible and venerate such personages as Jethro (a Midianite priest and the non-Israelite father-in-law of Moses). The Druze were loyal to Israel during the 1948 war, and several of their brigades are highly respected detachments in the Israeli army.

They are an industrious people; you'll see their terraced hillsides meticulously cared for and, as a result, very fertile. Many houses are new, and also square and boxlike in the Arabic style. Outside their own villages, Druze find employment on kibbutzim as electricians, builders, carpenters, and mechanics. Their hospitality is legendary.

In both villages, you can buy quite unusual souvenirs and handcrafted items, such as new or antique baskets and trays in the Druze style at moderate prices, but bargaining is necessary. (**Note:** Markets are closed on Fri, the Druze Sabbath day.) There are several pleasant cafes in both villages. You'll see older men in flowing gowns and headdresses, often with big mustaches, while the younger men wear Western-style clothes.

You can reach the villages on **bus no. 192,** which leaves infrequently from the Central Bus Station, but bus service back to Haifa seems to vanish by 3pm. Various tours also go to these villages (check with the Haifa Tourism Development Association for details). There's a sherut service that leaves Haifa during the evening from 6pm to

6am, departing from Hadar at the corner of Shemaryahu Levin and Herzl streets. Between 6am and 6pm, the sherut service from the port area is at the corner of Ha-Atzma'ut Road and Eliyahu Ha-Navi Street, near Paris Square. The sherut takes 25 minutes to reach Daliat-el-Carmel and the fare is the same as by bus.

## WHERE TO DINE
The Druze villages are lined with eating establishments geared to the weekend crowd. Every place is good. Try what catches your eye. *Tip:* A good Druze restaurant will make the delicious giant napkin-size, flat Druze bread for you on the spot—by the time Druze bread cools, it's considered stale.

**Ganei Daliyah** MIDDLE EASTERN   This place has a pleasant garden; a covered dining terrace; and a colorful proprietor, Toufik Halaby. Standard Middle Eastern dishes are a cut above the norm, and there are a few well-prepared unusual offerings. The pigeon stuffed with onion, pine nuts, and sumac, grilled on an open fire, is earthy and excellent, as are the homemade Druze bread and the oven-baked sweetbreads. On weekends, there may be oven-roasted lamb. This is a good choice for a leisurely road-side repast. If you come late at night and have had too much arrak, Halaby rents rooms in a simple hotel above the restaurant. Arabic and Hebrew are spoken. Coming from Haifa, look for the restaurant with its front garden and sign on the right as you leave Isfiya and before you enter Daliat-el-Carmel.

Isfiya–Daliat-el-Carmel Rd. (C) 04/839-5367. Reservations recommended weekends. Main courses NIS 50–NIS 90 ($13–$23/£6.25–£11). AE, V. Daily 10am–11pm (sometimes until midnight).

## MUHRAKA
Half a mile south of Daliat-el-Carmel, the road to Muhraka forks off to the left side of the main road. Its destination is not posted, but it meanders and climbs through scrub oak and pine woods to the monastery at Muhraka, the place where Elijah defeated the prophets of Baal. You'll see a dramatic stone **statue of Elijah,** sword raised to heaven, and a lovely **Carmelite monastery,** open Monday through Saturday from 8am to 1pm and again from 2:30 to 5pm (on Fri until noon only). The view from the roof of the monastery (admission is NIS 2/50¢/25p) is unsurpassed; you can see halfway across Israel to Migdal Ha-Emek and the mountains near Nazareth. There are tables for picnics on the grounds outside the monastery. The name "Muhraka," or "place of burning," hints at a time when this extraordinary vista point was a sacred high place for burned offerings and sacrifices in Canaanite and early Israelite times. From here, you can look across almost the whole of Israel to see the other sacred Canaanite high place in the region, Mount Tabor, near Nazareth, which was also the site of the Transfiguration of Jesus. There is no public transportation here. The Druze-Muhraka area is most easily visited by car, as a daylong bicycle excursion from Haifa, or on a tour or with a private guide who has a vehicle.

## ORGANIZED TOURS
A 3-hour tour to **Ein Hod** leaves Haifa most weekdays at 9:30am. It includes a drive through the Carmel mountain range, visits to the University of Haifa and the Druze market of Daliat-el-Carmel, and stops at art galleries, artists' studios, and other points of interest. (See p. 309 for more about this fascinating artists colony.) Check with the Haifa Tourism Development Association, Egged Tours, and United Tours for current schedules. The **Society for Protection of Nature (SPNI),** 18 Hillel St. ((C) **04/866-4135**), sells excellent hiking and walking maps of the Carmel range.

# 10

# Galilee

In Herodian times, according to Josephus, 204 towns in these hills supported about 15,000 residents each, giving Galilee a population of three million. This estimate is regarded by most historians as high, but there is no doubt that the ancient Galilee supported a population unsurpassed until modern times. Today, this fertile countryside is the site of most of Israel's collective farms (kibbutzim), and it is also home to most of Israel's one million Arab citizens, who maintain a traditional way of life and close ties to the land.

Roughly speaking, everything to the north and east of Haifa is known as "the Galilee" (Ha Galil)—Israel's lushest region. In February and March, the residents of Israel pour into the Galilee to enjoy the ocean of wildflowers and blossoming trees that cover the valleys and slopes, and to recall the perseverance of the original late-19th- and early-20th-century settlers of the Galilee's Jewish agricultural communities who lived in tents, risked malaria, and performed backbreaking labor to cultivate land that had been neglected for centuries. Today, the landscape is a carefully designed texture of fields, olive groves, vineyards, orchards, kibbutzim, and traditional Arab villages with minarets and ancient churches.

It was only natural that this once fertile region should have been the first area to be redeveloped in the early 20th century, when the region began to reawaken. Initially it was to the shores of the Sea of Galilee, in the Jordan Valley and around the Emek Yizreel (Valley of Jezreel), that the early Zionist pioneers came with their dreams of a socialist utopia, founded on principles of agricultural toil. Then, in the 1920s and 1930s, they brought their communal settlements to the western plains and to the mountains of the north of Galilee. Babies born in these settlements grew into hardy young farmers, their playgrounds not the ghettos of Russia and Poland that their parents had known, but rather the meadows and fruit orchards of their settlements. During the War of Independence in 1948, several Galilee settlements fought and farmed at the same time. War memorials throughout the region are a testament to these times.

**TOURING THE REGION**  You can approach the Galilee from the southeast on the road that runs northward up the Jordan Valley, or there are two good central routes for entering Galilee from the west: One is from Haifa to Akko and east to Safed, then down to the Sea of Galilee. The other is due east from Haifa to Nazareth and straight across to Tiberias. An offshoot of the Haifa-Nazareth road is a route that detours down through the Jordan Valley, south of the Sea of Galilee; at the Jordan Valley, turn north. In summer, the Jordan Valley, which is far below sea level, can be oppressively hot. Give yourself time to enjoy the beaches of the Sea of Galilee, which can be paradisiacal.

The Galilee is filled with so many places of natural and historical beauty that it's worth it to rent a car, at least for a few days of travel.

# 1 Nazareth ✶ & the Yizreel Valley

Nazareth: 40km (25 miles) SE of Haifa

The largest and most fertile valley in Israel, the Yizreel Valley, often called simply Ha-Emek ("the valley"), lies between the Galilee mountains to the north and the Samaria range to the south. Nazareth, the town where Jesus grew up, was only a tiny hamlet in biblical times, scarcely recorded on maps or mentioned in historical works. Today, Nazareth is a bustling city, filled with industry and new construction. Nazareth is the major cultural and commercial center for Israel's Arab community, and the first language of most inhabitants of Nazareth is Arabic.

## ESSENTIALS

**GETTING THERE    By Bus**    Bus service is available to Nazareth from all major cities.

**By Car**    Nazareth is in the center of the lower Galilee, almost midway between Haifa and Tiberias. From Tiberias, take Rte. 77, and turn south onto Rte. 754 near Kana, which will take you into Nazareth. From Haifa, take Rte. 75.

**VISITOR INFORMATION**    The **Tourist Information Office** (℃ **04/657-0555**) is on Casa Nova Street (also called El Bishara St. or Annunciation St.) near the intersection with Pope Paul VI Street, open Monday through Friday from 8:30am to 5pm, Saturday from 9am to 1pm. A Nazareth website—with excellent information on places of interest, walks, shopping, and food—is www.nazarethinfo.org.

**Currency Exchange**    Use the centrally located **Bank Ha-Poalim** on Pope Paul VI Street beside the Hamashbir Department Store, open Monday, Tuesday, and Thursday from 8:30am to 12:30pm and 4 to 6pm; Wednesday and Friday 8:30am to noon. **Change Spot Nazareth** (℃ **04/657-7288**), a money-changer, is located on the second floor of the Jumbo Center on Pope Paul VI Street near Casa Nova Street. It's open Monday to Saturday from 8:30am to 8pm. It's usually faster than the bank and charges no commission.

**Bus Station**    There is no actual bus station: Intercity buses stop on busy Pope Paul VI Street near Bank Ha-Poalim. **Egged Information** is just across from the bank (℃ **04/656-9956**), open daily 6am to 6pm. Buses to Haifa or to Tiberias leave approximately every 30 minutes. It is best to ask at the information counter for the number of the most convenient bus next departing for your destination.

**Police**    For **Police,** phone ℃ **100;** for first aid ℃ **101;** for fire ℃ **102.**

**Pharmacy**    Farah Pharmacy (℃ **04/655-4018**), Pope Paul VI Street, beside Egged Information, is open Monday, Tuesday, Thursday, and Friday 9am to 1pm and 4 to 6:30pm and Wednesday and Saturday 8am to 2pm.

## NAZARETH

This ancient part of town clings to the inside of a vast bowl, its stone houses tiered like the seats of an amphitheater. Today, the city houses Israel's largest Arab community outside Jerusalem—more than 80,000—approximately 35% to 40% Christian and 60% to 65% Muslim. With Jerusalem, it is also the headquarters of the Christian mission movement in Israel, with more than 40 churches, convents, monasteries, orphanages, and private parochial schools. Nazareth's very name is used by Arabs and Israelis to designate Christians, just as Jesus was also known as the Nazarene. In Arabic, Christians are called *Nasara,* and in Hebrew *Notzrim.* Because it has a more cosmopolitan population,

Nazareth has become the cultural and political center for the more moderate Arabic-speaking community in northern Israel. Um al Fahm, the other major Arab Israeli city in the north, is more traditionally Muslim, and a center for Islamic religious and political movements.

To get a feel for old Nazareth, turn into the narrow alleys that wind up and back into the terraced limestone ridges, and wander through the narrow cobbled streets of the Arab Market. Keep in mind that Nazareth is completely closed on Sunday and in full swing on Saturday. Like every city in Israel, Nazareth faces its own special problems. In 2000, Christians and Muslims clashed over whether to build a church or an Islamic shrine on a plot of land near the Basilica of the Annunciation. There is both despair and anger over the continuing Intifada and the lack of prospects for peace. But the city is also undergoing a cultural renaissance—interesting cafes, venues for small concerts, readings, and theatrical performances are opening in the beautiful, freshly restored old mansions off the main streets of the town center. The town is filled with poets, novelists, and playwrights; the works of Nazareth's preeminent modern poet, Tahar Mohammed Ali (who has a tourist shop in the old market), have been translated from Arabic into English and Hebrew to critical acclaim. There is also a community of innovative filmmakers, mostly working on a shoestring, but some, like the hometown favorite, Elias Suleiman, who chronicles the condition of Nazareth (and Israeli-Arab) society with a wry eye, have received international attention and awards.

## ORIENTATION

**ARRIVING**   Nazareth has a "bypass," a road that circles the town, which explains the confusing signs that point in opposite directions for the same destination. One of these destinations is **Nazareth Elit** (or Nazorat Ilit—meaning Upper Nazareth), the new, modern, mostly Jewish suburb to the north, planned by the government to create a Jewish community beside the city of Nazareth, which is actually a separate municipality. Housing is so tight in Nazareth that Nazareth Elit is starting to become a mixed Jewish, Christian, and Muslim town. You'll pass by it on your way to Tiberias.

**CITY LAYOUT**   Down Paul VI Street and into the center of Nazareth, you follow the signs to the Basilica of the Annunciation, Nazareth's principal religious monument off Paul VI Street on Casa Nova Street (also known as Bishara or Annunciation St.). Use the basilica's huge cupola, topped by a beacon, as your landmark—everything you'll need is within sight of the basilica. There are very few street signs, and building numbers are often in Arabic. Remember that it's downhill to the basilica and the center of town from most points in the city. The main roadway downhill into Nazareth (and uphill out of it) is separated into a right-hand roadway, clogged with cars parking, unloading, and waiting; and a central, less-gridlocked roadway for (we hope) moving traffic.

Casa Nova Street is the approach to the basilica, and on it you'll find restaurants, cafes, hotels, hospices, and the Tourist Information Office.

The bus station in Nazareth is a stretch of Paul VI Street just east of Casa Nova Street, a few steps from the Basilica of the Annunciation.

## WHAT TO SEE & DO

There are four major things for tourists to do in Nazareth: Shop in the market, visit the holy Christian shrines, enjoy the many Arabic restaurants and sweet shops in the city, and visit the fascinating "Nazareth Village," a recreation of what life was like in the tiny hamlet of Nazareth at the time of Jesus.

CHRISTIAN SHRINES   The **Basilica of the Annunciation** ✶✶ is located on Casa Nova Street, on the spot where, according to Christian tradition, the angel Gabriel appeared before Mary, saying: "Behold, thou shalt conceive in thy womb, and bring forth a son, and shall call his name Jesus." The present Basilica of the Annunciation, a beautiful monument completed in 1966, was built over earlier structures dating from 1730 to 1877.

The earliest church was built over the grotto in which Mary sat when Gabriel spoke to her. As you enter the basilica, you'll be on the ground (or grotto) level, which is in fact the church's crypt. After you've toured the crypt, walk back to the entrance and you'll see steps up to the nave.

Unlike most Christian shrines in Israel, this basilica has a bold, modern design. Around the nave, on the walls, are murals that were created by artists from around the world. Note the Japanese mural of the Madonna and Child on the left (north) wall— Mary's robe is made entirely of Japanese seed pearls. The mural from the United States, on the right (south) wall, at first seems discordant and excessive, but it works when viewed from the basilica's north-side door.

Summer hours are daily from 8 to 11:45am and from 2 to 5:45pm; in winter it's open daily from 9 to 11:45am and from 2 to 4:45pm. (Many of the churches in Nazareth observe these same hours, closing for the "noontime siesta" during the middle of the day.) Walk out the north-side door to reach the other religious sites.

The **Church of Saint Joseph** is 90m (295 ft.) away, constructed on the site believed to have been occupied by Joseph's carpentry workshop. From the sanctuary, stairways on either side go down to another floor below, where you can see old stone construction, an ancient water cistern, and a mosaic floor dating from the Byzantine period. Hours are the same as at the Basilica of the Annunciation, above.

On the main street in the bazaar is the **Greek Catholic "Synagogue" Church,** believed to be the site of the ancient Nazareth synagogue that Jesus frequented: "And He came to Nazareth, where He had been brought up; and, as His custom was, He went into the synagogue on the Sabbath day, and stood up to read" (Luke 4:16). Farther along the road is the **Franciscan Mensa Christi Church,** believed to occupy the spot where Jesus ate with his disciples after the resurrection.

**Mary's Well,** with its source inside the **Greek Orthodox Church of the Annunciation,** is another Christian holy site. The church was built at the end of the 17th century over the remains of three former churches. At the church entrance, on the archway above the stone staircase leading down to the well, there is a colorful mural showing the angel Gabriel coming to Mary and announcing in six languages, "Hail, thou that are highly favored, the Lord is with thee: blessed art thou among women." The ceiling is covered with brightly colored murals depicting scenes from the Bible. Proceed through the archway before you and you'll come to the well—a small spring and a round stone well.

The **Basilica of Jesus the Adolescent,** maintained by the French Salesian order, is one of the most beautiful churches in Nazareth. Built in 1918, the Gothic church contains pillars composed of clusters of slender columns that support the vaulted roof. There's a lovely marble statue of *Jesus the Adolescent* by the sculptor Bognio. It is a climb to get to the top of the hill north of the center of town, but it is worth the effort. Go down Casa Nova Street to Paul VI Street, turn left, go up 2 blocks, and go down the street to the left of the public fountain; the church is 1 short block up this street, straight ahead. It's open year-round daily from 8am to 5pm.

## Walking the Jesus Trail

For millions of modern travelers, walking in the footsteps of Jesus has come to mean a few feet from a tour bus to the Church of the Annunciation or to the banks of the Jordan River. But in ancient times, people walked everywhere. Now a group of local Israelis has mapped out the routes Jesus would have taken as he crisscrossed the Galilee from Nazareth to Zippori, Kana, and down to the Sea of Galilee, passing olive groves, ancient springs, and historic sites and ruined places. A careful, 65km (40-mile) itinerary (mainly downhill from Nazareth) has been constructed, which can be hiked by independent walkers or done through tour operators and organized tours; included are places to camp, overnight lodgings, places to eat and buy supplies, always with an eye to authenticity and a close feeling for the land. An optional return route to Nazareth includes the ethereal Mount Tabor. For more information, go to www.jesustrail.com.

**Our Lady of Fright Chapel,** sometimes called the Tremore, is built on a wooded hill south of the center opposite the Galilee Hotel. It is on the spot where Mary watched while the people of Nazareth attempted to throw Jesus over a cliff—the Precipice, or Lord's Leap rock, .5km (¼ mile) away.

Although the majority of Nazareth's population was Christian before the 1950s, the city now has a Muslim majority, and is home to some lovely Islamic structures that are local landmarks (interiors are open only for Muslim prayer). Built between 1960 and 1965, the beautiful and modern **Al-Salam Mosque** is in the eastern quarter of town, a block away from Paul VI Street. In the southern part of the city is the new **Al-Huda Mosque.**

**SHOPPING IN THE MARKET**    The market streets, entered via Casa Nova, are narrow, crowded, and highly exotic. Remember that the deeper you get into the market, the smaller the shops become and the lower the prices. One of the first things to note is the trench running dead center of the street, and one of the first precautions is to stay out of it as much as possible—it's the donkey trail. Snaking upward, the narrow roadway is lined with tin-roofed shops in which you'll see everything from plows and ram's horns to cakes, leather goods, chandeliers, plastic buckets, and fine jewelry. Daily necessities are displayed side by side with antiques from Turkish times that sell for thousands of shekels. You can buy a finjan coffee set here or a *kefiya* (the Arab headdress). One shop, deep in the market, carries *narghilis* (water pipes). If you're a coin collector, try the tiny shops where you'll find a variety of coins and prices. Whatever you buy, be sure to shop around, and whatever you do, bargain over everything. The old part of town is filled with fabulous stone mansions, many of which are now used as cafes and cultural centers. Check with the tourism office about walking tours being offered of this area.

**Nazareth Village** 🎯 *Kids*    This nonprofit institution, located on an area of undeveloped land in downtown, contains a wonderful re-creation of houses, farms, workshops, oil and wine presses, and terraced fields as they existed in the time of Jesus. Everything is based on knowledge gleaned from archaeological digs in the area, and the fascinating structures have been built with the same materials and techniques used 2,000 years ago. Inhabitants of the village, garbed in ancient costume, perform traditional labors, such as plowing, wine and olive oil pressing, cooking, and weaving. The re-created architecture, work, and social traditions are designed to help visitors understand the environment in which Jesus lived and found material for his teachings and parables. Clearly designed for Christian tourists, the tours include readings from the New Testament at various points along the way, but the village should be of interest to visitors of all faiths and it carefully delineates the nature and customs of the Jewish environment that existed in Nazareth 2,000 years ago. The re-creation of a very modest 1st-century-A.D. synagogue that would have existed in a Galilean village while The Temple at Jerusalem was still standing is especially interesting; together with the re-created *mikvah* (ritual bath) for purification, it helps you to envision what made Jewish communities of the time unusual. You can also explore the details of a carpenter's house, a landlord's house, and the house of a weaver. There are a number of tours offered—some with a special emphasis on the life of Jesus and on illustrating daily life and conditions described in New Testament parables; others more centered simply on the nature of rural Galilee life in ancient times. For an additional charge, it may be possible to arrange for a 1st-century vegetarian meal, served in a Bedouin tent. Meals are normally available only to groups of 20 by prearrangement; however, if you reserve in advance, you might be able to be added to such a group. There are also traditional bread-baking activities. The men, women, and children inhabiting the village are both Christian and Muslim residents of modern-day Nazareth.

Beside the YMCA in downtown Nazareth. ⓒ **04/645-6042.** www.nazarethvillage.com. NIS 50 ($13/£6.25) adults; NIS 25 ($6.25/£3.10) children. Additional charge for meals. Sat and Mon–Thurs 9am–5pm. Hours are flexible and you must call ahead to schedule a tour. Additional evening tours offered Christmas, Easter, and in summer.

## WHERE TO STAY

**Fauzi Azar Inn** *Finds*    This is an unusual guesthouse set in a beautifully converted old stone Nazareth mansion, with high ceilings, lots of atmosphere, and an energetic Jewish-Israeli manager, Maoz Yimon, who is very savvy and helpful about making Nazareth and the surrounding countryside accessible and understandable to travelers. There are few amenities, but rooms are freshly decorated and each is different, ranging from large family-size rooms to cozy, compact singles that could be shared by two people if they're thin and intensely in love. The spirit is friendly and personal, and the many secrets and pleasures of Israel's largest and most important Arabic community will be yours for the asking if you stay here. The website offers detailed instructions on how to find the inn, which is in Nazareth's Old City.

Old City, Nazareth Center. ⓒ **04/602-0469** or 054/432-2328. www.fauziazarinn.com. 10 units, with shared bathrooms. $60–$100 (£30–£50) double; $20 (£10) dormitory bed. Cash only. **Amenities:** Salon; patio; tour advising center.

**Hotel Galilee**    This modern, pleasant four-story establishment is a 5-minute walk south of the Church of the Annunciation. The entire hotel was renovated in 1999 for the millennium, and although rooms are simple, they are bright, relatively fresh, and comfortable. Most rooms have shower-only bathrooms. The hotel has a bar and coffee shop, as well as rooms that are heated in winter.

Paul VI St., Nazareth. ⓒ **04/657-1311.** Fax 04/655-6627. www.b-and-b.co.il/galilee. 93 units. $75–$120 (£38–£60) double. Rates include continental breakfast. Cash only. *In room:* A/C.

**Rimonim Nazareth**    Built in 1999 and located on the main road in the center of town, just 1km (½ mile) from the Church of the Annunciation, this is the largest, most luxurious, and newest hotel in town. It was designed to service prosperous pilgrims and groups, but also offers amenities for business travelers. Rooms have standard comforts; there are two suites that are suitable for family groups. The hotel's underground, relatively secure parking is especially important in downtown Nazareth, where narrow streets can result in the occasional scratch or dent on a rental car. Look for Internet deals on the website for Rimonim Hotels, especially if you plan to stay more than 2 nights.

Paul VI St., Nazareth. ©️ **04/650-0000**. Fax 04/650-0055. www.rimonim.com. 226 units. $140–$170 (£70–£85) double. Rates include breakfast. Website discounts available. MC, V. Free parking. **Amenities:** Cafe; bar; business lounge; room service; laundry service; nonsmoking rooms. *In room:* A/C, TV, dataport, minibar, hair dryer, safe.

**St. Gabriel Hotel**   Built in the 1950s to serve as a monastery, this beautiful, atmospheric building was converted into a hotel in the 1990s. The lobby is decorated with traditional crafts; guest rooms have exposed stone walls and offer fine vistas of the city. Bathrooms (most have a shower only) and furnishings are new, but this was a monastery, so expect simple, rather small accommodations in exchange for the ambience. The location, in an upper neighborhood of central Nazareth, means a certain amount of difficult climbing; a car can be very useful if you stay here. The hotel offers Saturday-morning walking tours of Nazareth, including the basilica, some of the mansions of the Old Town, and a bus ride back up the steep hill to the hotel, where you have lunch. Breakfasts are adequate, but not the lavish buffet presentations found in most Israeli hotels. Views are spectacular.

Salesian St. (PO Box 2318), Nazareth. ©️ **04/657-2133**. Fax 04/655-4071. 65 units. $90–$125 (£45–£63) double. Rates include breakfast. MC, V. *In room:* TV.

## Near Nazareth: Zippori

Two thousand years ago, Zippori (Sepphoris) was a thriving city and Nazareth a humble village less than 6km (4 miles) away. Now those roles are reversed: Nazareth is the bustling city, and Zippori is a cooperative agricultural village as well as the site of a vast and fascinating archaeological park. If you have a car, this is a placid and convenient place from which to explore the area.

**Zippori Village Guesthouses** ★ *Kids* *Finds*   These rustic cottages, built by Mitch and Suzy Pilcer (formerly from the U.S.) in 1997, are set in a garden and sport front porches, a bedroom, a small living room with fireplace, sofa bed, Jacuzzi, and a fully equipped kitchenette that is kosher *halavi* (for nonmeat only). A ladder leads to a loft area with beds and a sofa. With extra floor mattresses supplied by Mitch, a large family can be accommodated. The management is personal and very well informed (Mitch is a tour guide), offering brochures and regional advice. A country breakfast (kosher) with organic bread, vegetables, cheeses, goat-milk yogurt, and other local products is left each morning at 7:30am beside your door. (Fresh eggs come directly from the guesthouse chicken coop). You need a rental car in order to consider a stay here. Nearby are wonderful hikes and tours, farms, and even donkey rides for children.

Moshav Zippori. ©️ **04/646-2647** or 057/782-9568 cellphone. Fax 04/646-4749. www.zipori.com. 5 cottages, all with bathroom. Sun–Wed $100 (£50) per couple; Thurs–Sat $115 (£58) per couple; $25 (£13) per child. Rates include kosher breakfast. Discounts for large families and long-term stays. AE, DC, MC, V. **Amenities:** Barbecue/picnic area; touring advice. *In room:* A/C, TV/VCR, Wi-Fi, kitchenette, microwave.

## WHERE TO DINE

There are lots of places on Paul VI Street and Casa Nova Street near the basilica where you can grab a falafel, a *shwarma,* or a meze of Arabic salads and pita bread. There are also many spots for tea, coffee, and a piece of baklava. All have been around forever, and all serve good food, though few have much style. The best restaurant for a really good meal, Fahoum's, is also centrally located near the basilica.

**Al Rida** ★ *Finds* TRADITIONAL NAZARETH   Set in a restored mansion, with wonderful views of the basilica from its roof terrace and with a piano that occasionally gets played to the delight of customers (no regular program), this restaurant is a great addition to the Nazareth renaissance. The brainchild of veteran Jerusalem restaurateur Daher Zedani, who is famous for creating places where guests can connect and talk amid candles and exotic atmosphere, Al Rida serves traditional Nazareth cooking. The menu changes, but look for dishes such as lamb neck oven-baked with garlic and greens; artichoke hearts filled with meat; and spicy veal sausages marinated in wine and fried with lemon and garlic. Aged, tender meat is used for filet, kabobs, and shashlik; there are inventive salads, such as rocket, strawberries, and poppy seeds, and traditional teas, coffees, and desserts.

21 Bishara St. ⓒ/fax **04/608-4408.** Main courses NIS 50–NIS 100 ($13–$25/£6.25–£13). AE, MC, V. Mon–Sat 1pm–2am; Sun 7pm–2am. Call for directions.

**Diana** MIDDLE EASTERN   This longtime established restaurant in town, with the fanciest decor and the widest menu, serves all kinds of unusual Arabic specialties. Although the full range of the menu is not always on hand, in addition to the standard dishes, you'll always find something special featuring the chef's unique twists and touches. In addition to the oven-baked lamb, kabobs, shashliks, and traditional dishes such as chicken *musakhan,* prepared with sumac and thick country yogurt, you can order a range of continental-style dishes, including shrimp in garlic and butter sauce.

Paul VI St. ⓒ **04/657-2919.** Reservations recommended. Main courses NIS 50–NIS 120 ($13–$30/£6.25–£15). AE, MC, V. Daily noon–midnight.

**Fahoum Restaurant** *Value* MIDDLE EASTERN   Located a block from the Basilica of the Annunciation, this bright, spotlessly clean restaurant serves delicious food and outshines its neighboring competitors. You can have a fine light meal by selecting some of the traditional Arabic salads (the tasty *hatselem,* or eggplant purée salad, is laced with lemon and garlic), but the restaurant is best known for meats cooked over a wood fire and for its authentic lamb ribs. Try the fine lamb or beef shashlik (cubes of meat on the skewer); the boneless fried chicken in lemon garlic; or the nicely seasoned kabobs (skewered ground meat). The oldest restaurant in town, Fahoum is spacious but no-frills in style and presided over by a gracious, English-speaking owner, Naief Fahoum.

303 Casa Nova St. (at intersection of Paul VI St.). ⓒ **04/655-3332.** Reservations recommended Sat. Main courses NIS 44–NIS 65 ($11–$16/£5.50–£8.10). AE, DC, MC, V. Daily 8:30am–9pm.

## Middle Eastern Desserts

On the left-hand side of Casa Nova Street, just before it meets the basilica, is **Abu-Diab Mahroum's Sweets** (ⓒ **04/656-4470**). There are several stores named Mahroum's Sweets—make sure you go to the original near the Basilica of the Annunciation. The shop windows are filled with baklava, Turkish delight *(maajoun)* with nuts, *Esh el-Bulbul* ("Hummingbird's Nest," a nest of shredded wheat filled with nuts and laced with honey), and *burma* (a roll of shredded wheat stuffed with pistachios and soaked in honey or syrup). Dessert and Turkish coffee costs about NIS 16 ($4/£2) or less. Mahroum's is open daily from 7am to 9pm.

## AN ATTRACTION NEAR NAZARETH

**Mount Tabor** (or Tavor) ★, at 540m (1,772 ft.) above sea level, is the tallest of the Lower Galilee Mountains. It stands a little more than 9.6km (6 miles) southeast of Nazareth and must have been a dominant feature of the landscape Jesus knew in his childhood. At the summit stands the **Basilica of the Transfiguration,** which marks where Jesus was transfigured as he spoke to Moses and Elijah in the presence of three of his disciples (Luke 9:28–36). It was built in the 1920s over the ruins of long-destroyed Crusader and Byzantine churches. Also on the mount is the **Church of Elias** (Elijah), built in 1911 by the Greek Orthodox community. From here on a clear day you can see the Sea of Galilee, Mount Hermon, the Mediterranean Sea, and the Emek. At this dramatic mountain, in the period of the Judges (ca. 1150 B.C.), the Prophet Deborah and her general, Barak, led the Israelite tribes to victory over the Canaanite general Sisera of Hazor (Judg. 4:12–16). Like the summit of Mount Carmel, near Haifa, where the Prophet Elijah challenged the Canaanite prophets of Baal, the summit of Mount Tabor is believed to have been a Canaanite "high place" or altar from at least the 2nd millennium B.C. The defeat of the Canaanites at such a prominent sanctuary may have had a stunning psychological effect on the populace of that time.

Mount Tabor is accessible from Nazareth by Egged bus or taxi. Although it looks close, the way is circuitous. If you're driving from the northern part of Nazareth, take Rte. 754 to Rte. 77; from Rte. 77 at the Golani Junction, turn south onto Rte. 65 to Mount Tabor. From southern Nazareth, take Rte. 60 to Afula; at Afula take Rte. 65 to Mount Tabor. At the base of the mountain, in the Arabic village of Shibli, you'll find a very modest but charming **Center of Bedouin Heritage** (© 04/676-7875). It's open Saturday to Thursday from 9am to 5pm; admission is NIS 12 ($3/£1.50). If you are driving or walking, the road becomes increasingly steep the higher you ascend, with absolutely hair-raising hairpin turns. Beware of vehicles in front of you conking out and rolling downhill. The descent can seem even more horrific, but the view from the summit is magnificent.

## THE YIZREEL VALLEY

The Yizreel Valley houses some of Israel's oldest and best-known settlements—**Mishmar Ha-Emek, Hazorea, Givat Oz, Ginegar,** and the giant moshav, **Nahalal.** The rich, dark soil is crisscrossed in checkerboard patterns of fruit trees, vineyards, and green vegetable fields. It is a breathtaking quilt of colors, some blocks golden with wheat, some black with heavy cultivation, others orange with brilliant flowers.

About 70 years ago, however, this lush area was a breeding swamp of malaria. In the early 1920s, the Keren Kayemet (Jewish National Fund) launched its biggest land reclamation project; over a period of time, the swampland was drained and every mosquito was killed. Russian, German, and Polish settlers filled the new settlements. The cultivation of the Emek became legendary, rhapsodized in dozens of romantic songs in which the tilling of soil and the smell of roses are common lyrics.

As you look at this splendid fertility, remember also that this has been one of the bloodiest fields of war in history. Here the Egyptians shed blood 4,000 years ago, as did the Canaanites, the Mongols, the Greeks, the Romans, and the Crusaders in later centuries. From Mount Tabor, overlooking the Emek's northeast corner, the Prophet Deborah launched her famous attack against the Canaanite armies. And several years later, Gideon's forces came from Mount Gilboa on the Midianites and slaughtered the plundering Bedouin tribe.

But it was also on this fertile plain that the ancient Israelite nation suffered one of its most calamitous national defeats—when King Saul (the first king of Israel) and his sons, including Jonathan (the closest friend of David, second of Israel's kings), died during a clash with the Philistines. It is with regard to this battle that the Second Book of Samuel records David's immortal lament.

*How the mighty are fallen!*
*Tell it not in Gath,*
*Publish it not in the streets of Ashkelon*
*Lest the daughters of the Philistines rejoice . . .*
*Saul and Jonathan were lovely and pleasant in their lives,*
*And in their deaths they were not divided . . .*
*Lo, how the mighty are fallen,*
*And the weapons of war perished.*

Later, the Turks fought here, as did Napoleon. In 1918, General Allenby defeated the Turkish forces on the Emek, and Israel's armies in 1948 overwhelmed the Arabs. It is ironic that the Emek region, which has been so ravaged, today flourishes in such splendor.

## WHAT TO SEE & DO

As you travel from Haifa to Nazareth, you pass farm settlements, the most important of which are **Yagur** and **Allonim.** Yagur is one of the country's oldest kibbutzim, founded in 1922. About 30 or 40 minutes out of Haifa, be sure to stop at the observation signpost on your right, after climbing into the foothills of Lower Galilee—the view of the Yizreel Valley spread out below is one of the loveliest in Israel.

**Zippori (Sepphoris) National Park** 𝄞   Now a small agricultural community, the ancient city of Sepphoris dates from the era of the Maccabees in the 2nd century B.C. An enormous period of expansion and building that started in the 1st century A.D. turned the city into "the ornament of the Galilee," according to Flavius Josephus. With its worldly, mixed population of Hellenistic pagans and Jews, it is interesting to speculate about the influence of Zippori on Jesus, who grew up in what was then the small village of Nazareth, a mere 6.4km (4 miles) away. According to some traditions, Zippori was **the birthplace of Mary,** and as a city requiring the services of many skilled carpenters and builders, cosmopolitan Zippori may have been a place often visited by Jesus; the landscapes and vistas around Zippori, unlike those of modern, urbanized Nazareth, may still resemble the countryside Jesus knew. The Crusaders built a church, in Zippori, the ruins of which can still be seen, dedicated to St. Anne and St. Joachim, the parents of Mary. Another tradition, however, holds that although the home of Mary's family was in Zippori, Mary was born in Jerusalem close to what is now the Lion's Gate.

The Jewish community in Zippori grew rapidly after the Bar Kochba revolt of A.D. 135, when thousands of refugees from Judea migrated into the Galilee. By the late 2nd century, Zippori was the seat of the Sanhedrin and the home of many great rabbinical sages, including Yehuda Ha-Nassi, who codified the Mishnah. During the Talmudic era, the city contained numerous synagogues; in 1993, archaeologists uncovered a **mosaic synagogue floor** 𝄞 from the 5th century A.D., decorated with an elaborate zodiac design and inscriptions in Hebrew, Aramaic, and Greek. Other impressive finds in Zippori are the ruins of a 4,000-seat Roman amphitheater and a vast, late Roman–era Dionysian mosaic floor of a villa that includes the **"Mona Lisa of the Galilee"** 𝄞, a hauntingly beautiful depiction of a young woman that is one of the greatest examples of ancient mosaic portraiture ever discovered. There is also an intricate mosaic depiction of Nile landscapes, including the famous Nilometer. In other parts of the excavations, you'll find a Crusader fortress and church. A computer/multimedia program has been set up to help bring the site to life for visitors.

6.5km (4 miles) northwest of Nazareth, on Rte. 79. ☎ **04/656-8272.** Admission NIS 23 ($5.75/£2.90) adults; NIS 12 ($3/£1.50) children. Sat–Thurs 8am–5pm (in winter to 4pm); Fri 8am–3pm. No public transportation.

## Archaeology Update: Ancient Church at Megiddo

In November 2005, archaeologists working beside the present-day Megiddo Prison, not far from Tel Megiddo, uncovered the mosaic floor of what may be the oldest church building (early 4th c. A.D.) yet to be discovered in Israel. The mosaic floor is ornamented with geometric designs as well as a central medallion of two fish (a traditional early Christian symbol). Most important, the design of the floor includes a windfall of mosaic inscriptions in Greek that shed light on the nature of the Christian world in the Holy Land just before or during the period when Roman emperor Constantine ended persecution of Christians (A.D. 313) and made Christianity the official religion of the empire (A.D. 324). One inscription mentions a Roman army officer who donated the money to build the floor; another commemorates four women apparently important in the church. An inscription on the western side of the floor refers to a woman by the name of Ekeptos, who "donated this table to the God Jesus Christ in commemoration." Thrillingly, this mosaic inscription tells us exactly where the "table" (most likely the altar) of this very early (prebasilica-style) church would have stood, and even enables us to envision something of the composition of the congregation and the theological beliefs of the people who prayed here. Although the church was not open to the public at press time, the Ministry of Tourism hopes to arrange visitor access to the site, with its clues to the most ancient traditions of Christian ceremony and belief. Check with the Megiddo Visitor's Center.

**Beit She'arim Burial Caves National Park**   Somewhat reminiscent of the Sanhedrin Tombs in Jerusalem, these catacombs filled with burial caves are located on the main road from Haifa that heads toward Afula (the principal town of the Jordan Valley).

In the late 2nd and early 3rd centuries, the town of Bet She'arim[0] was the home of the Supreme Religious Council, the Sanhedrin, as well as headquarters of the famous Rabbi Yehuda Ha-Nassi (Yehuda the Prince), the compiler of the Mishnah. Many learned and famous Jews were laid to rest in the town's cemetery, a network of caves beneath a tranquil grove of cypress and olive trees. Over the centuries, however, the tombs were destroyed and the caves looted. The town was abandoned, and earth and rock covered the entrances to the catacombs as if they had never existed. But finally they were unearthed, first in 1926 and then fully explored after the War of Independence.

Enter the burial chambers through an opening in the rock or a stone door. Inside are sarcophagi carved with rams' horns and lions' heads, menorahs, and other examples of Roman-era Jewish folk art. So far, catacomb 20 is the most interesting, with its legible inscriptions, carvings, and interesting relics. Archaeologists claim that only a fraction of the original effects remain, that robbers have looted the almost 200 sarcophagi.

The entire site here is well tended, with a parking lot, visitor facilities, and an outdoor cafe. Check out the introductory film.

Off Rte. 75 and Rte. 722, near HaTishbi Junction. ✆ **04/983-1643**. www.parks.org.il. Admission NIS 18 ($4.50/£2.25) adults; NIS 8 ($2/£1) children. Sat–Thurs 8am–5pm (to 4pm in winter); Fri 8am–3pm.

**Megiddo (Armageddon) National Park** ✯ You'll pass Hazorea and Mishmar Ha-Emek, two old and large kibbutzim, before you come to **Megiddo (Armageddon),** located about 20km (12 miles) southeast of Haifa. This has always been the primary fortress overlooking the Emek, which, due to its strategic position on the major route leading from Egypt to Syria and Mesopotamia, has always been coveted and attacked. Archaeologists have uncovered the remains of cities of more than 20 distinct historical periods here on this *tel* (Hebrew for an archaeological mound or hill), dating from 4000 B.C. to after A.D. 500. It is mentioned frequently in biblical and other ancient texts. There is evidence that Megiddo was a fortified, walled town in the early 3rd millennium B.C.

In the Old Testament, the name Megiddo appears in a number of places, mostly in relation to war. In the New Testament, the book of Revelation names Armageddon (a corruption of the Hebrew Har Megiddo—Mount Megiddo) as the place where the last great battle will be fought when the forces of good triumph over the forces of evil.

Megiddo has been a place of battle continuing right down into the 20th century. General Allenby launched his attack against the Turks from the Megiddo Pass in 1917, and in 1948 the Israeli forces used the fortress site as a base of operations against entrenched Arab armies. As you enter the Megiddo National Park there is a **museum** with detailed information about the excavations, the artifacts found there, the biblical and historical references relating to its past, and a model of the site as it now exists. Many more artifacts discovered here have been removed, and may now be found in Jerusalem's Israel and the Rockefeller museums.

You can walk among the ruins, including what may be a **palace** from the time of King Solomon, **King Ahab's "Chariot City,"** and what some archaeologists call **stables** with a capacity for almost 500 horses (other archaeologists claim that the structures are not stables, though exactly what they were is a matter of controversy). There is also a large **grain silo** from the reign of Jeroboam Ben Joash, king of Israel in the 8th century B.C., and a building some attribute to the time of King David (1006 B.C.–970 B.C.). On strata way down below the later buildings, you can see excavated ruins of temples 5,000 and 6,000 years old, constructed during the Chalcolithic period.

Most amazing of all is the **water tunnel** ✯ dating from the reign of King Ahab in the 9th century B.C. You enter it by walking 183 steps 36m (118 ft.) down into a large pit in the earth (the collection pool inside the city walls), from which you can walk along the tunnel extending 65m (213 ft.) to a spring located outside the city, which was camouflaged by a wall covered with earth, designed to assure a constant supply of fresh water to the city even when it was under siege. (Read "The Psalm of the Hoopoe," in James Michener's *The Source,* to learn how tunnelers digging from both ends of a tunnel such as Megiddo's managed to meet underground using simple engineering techniques.) *Note:* The water tunnel closes half an hour before the rest of the park.

You can see remnants from Megiddo's imposing city walls, gates, and entryways, some of which were built during the time of King Solomon. The observation points offer a spectacular view of the huge valley below.

20km (12 miles) from Haifa. ✆ **04/983-1643.** Admission NIS 23 ($5.75/£2.90) adults; NIS 12 ($3/£1.50) children. Apr–Sept Sat–Thurs 8am–5pm, Fri 8am–3pm; Oct–Mar Sat–Thurs 8am–4pm, Fri 8am–3pm. Located just north of junction of Rte. 65 and Rte. 66.

## 2 Tiberias ⟨★⟩

330km (205 miles) N of Jerusalem; 116km (72 miles) E of Haifa

From Haifa, the favorite road to Tiberias (Teverya in Hebrew) is the one from Nazareth, if only for that dip in the road and that sudden unfolding of the mountains when the Kinneret (the Sea of Galilee) is suddenly spread down below you—an incredibly beautiful azure lake set like a jewel in a pastoral valley.

The ancient city of Tiberias, built in A.D. 18 by Herod Antipas (son of Herod the Great), was named in honor of the Roman emperor Tiberias. With its hot springs and mild, far-below-sea-level climate (warm in winter; brutally hot in summer), it became one of the most elegant winter resorts in this part of the ancient world. Classical writers describe a city adorned with colonnaded streets, impressive Roman baths and temples made of imported white marble, and broad marble steps leading into the waters of the lake. For more than a century, rabbis condemned Tiberias as a place of pagan cults and immoral activities; worse yet, it was built on a cemetery, making it forbidden to Jews as a place to live. But the healing powers of the hot springs caused the rabbinical prohibition to be rescinded, and by the late Roman era, many of the rabbinical leaders themselves were enjoying the restorative powers of the baths and hot springs.

A century and a half after The Temple of Jerusalem was destroyed, Tiberias became the great center for Jewish learning. It was here that the Mishnah was completed in the 2nd and 3rd centuries A.D., at the direction of Rabbi Yehuda Ha-Nassi, "Judah the Prince." Here the Jerusalem Talmud was compiled in the 4th century A.D, and the standardized rules for vowel and punctuation grammar were introduced into the Hebrew language by the scribes of Tiberias. Mystics, academicians, and men believed to have magic powers have been drawn to Tiberias throughout its history.

Both the town and the towering scholarship declined after the 5th century A.D., due to the many wars fought here by the Persians, Arabs, Crusaders, and Turks. A medieval Arab historian named Al MuQadassi recorded that the residents of the town led a life of decadence—dancing, feasting, playing the flute, running around naked in the summer heat, and swatting green flies, the eternal plague of the region until modern times.

Tiberias today is a mildly honky-tonk tourist town, packed during school holidays and rather dead during the winter, but it's the liveliest place to spend the night in the area, and the main tourist base for the Galilee and Golan regions. Although the waterfront at Tiberias has large, modern hotels, Tiberias also offers a scattering of old, charming houses and the arabesque domes of Ottoman-Turkish mineral water bathhouses as well as a scattering of archaeological digs and the tombs of the great rabbinical sages. There's also a gem of an Ottoman-era mosque, near the waterfront promenade, in a state of semi-ruin, but there are plans to restore it. The beaches in town are mostly small and ugly, but welcome on a hot summer day. Two blocks inland from the lakefront, Ha Galil Street, with its black native basalt buildings, is filled with shops and brings to mind an old-fashioned, small-town American main street. For centuries, what little industry existed in Tiberias was built around pilgrimage and veneration of ancient tombs, some with very dubious traditions. All this has been overwhelmed by Tiberias's new incarnation as a center for discos, party boats, fish restaurants, and international tour groups. The pubs and restaurants along the Waterfront Promenade pound with disco and heavy metal on summer evenings. Little of the town's splendid history is immediately visible.

Because Tiberias is so far below sea level, the climate is mild in the fall, winter, and spring, but torrid when Tiberias is busiest in July and August. In winter, visitors may

# Tiberias

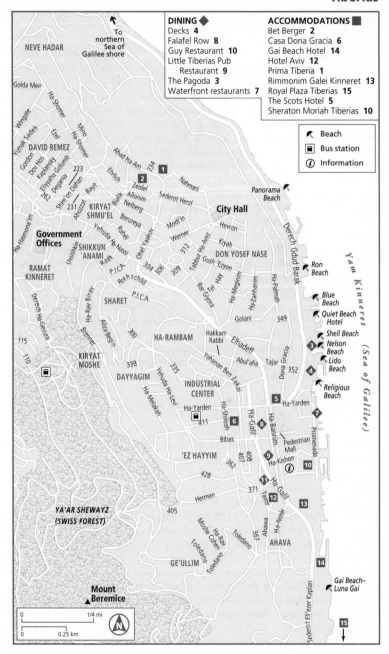

**DINING ◆**
Decks **4**
Falafel Row **8**
Guy Restaurant **10**
Little Tiberias Pub
  Restaurant **9**
The Pagoda **3**
Waterfront restaurants **7**

**ACCOMMODATIONS ■**
Bet Berger **2**
Casa Dona Gracia **6**
Gai Beach Hotel **14**
Hotel Aviv **12**
Prima Tiberia **1**
Rimmonim Galei Kinneret **13**
Royal Plaza Tiberias **15**
The Scots Hotel **5**
Sheraton Moriah Tiberias **10**

↖ Beach
🚏 Bus station
ⓘ Information

NEVE HADAR

To
northern
Sea of
Galilee shore

Golda Meir

Ha-Shomer
Wingate
Yizhak Sadeh
Gordon
Dov Hos
Kaplansky
Ezel
Mina
Ha-Shomer
DAVID REMEZ
Eliyahu Golumb
Degania
Shim'on Dahan
Ahad Ha-Am
234
Ehrlich
Zeidel
Allonim
Neiberg
Bialik
Berureya
Rahel
Ohel Yaakov
Nahmani
Sederot Herzl
223
231
263
Ahuzzat
Bayit
KIRYAT
SHMU'EL
Yehuda Ha-Nassi
Rash
Modi'in
Werner
312

**City Hall**

Panorama
Beach

Hevron
Kiyah
DON YOSEF NASE

Ha-Hasmona'im
Ussishkin
SHIKKUN
'ANAMI
**Government
Offices**
RAMAT
KINNERET
Ha-Rav Bi'ray
Bremer
Aliza Begin
P.I.C.A.
Roth schild
P.I.C.A.
SHARET
300
304 306 309
Tabbur Ha-Arez
Gush 'Ezyon
Hay
Ha-Meginim
Ha-Zahevanu
Ha-Zahevanu
Ron
Beach
Blue
Beach
Quiet Beach
Hotel
Shell Beach
Nelson
Beach
Lido
Beach

Derech Gdud Barak
Ha-Palmah

*Y a m   K i n n e r e t*
*(Sea of Galilee)*

Derech Ha-Gevura
115
110
KIRYAT
MOSHE
338
DAYYAGIM
Yehuda Ha-Levi
Ha-Melakah
HA-RAMBAM
335
Hakkam
Rabbi
Yohanan Ben Zakai
Elhadeff
Abul'afia
Bar Giyora
Golani
349
Tajar
Dona Gracia
352
Religious
Beach

INDUSTRIAL
CENTER
Ha-Yarden
411
Ha-Shiloah
Bibas
'EZ HAYYIM
428
Hermon
405
Ha-Yarden
Ha-Galil
Ha-Banim
Pedestrian
Mall
Ha-Kishon
362
407 408
371
Ha-Galil
Tavor
Ahava
367
Ha-Hotel
AHAVA

Promenade

YA'AR SHEWAYZ
(SWISS FOREST)
Moshe Cohen
Ha-Rav
Toledano
Toledano
Toledano
GE'ULLIM

**Mount
Beremice** ▲

Sederot Eli'ezer Kaplan

Gai Beach–
Luna Gai

0        1/4 mi
0    0.25 km

Ⓝ

**369**

## Tiberias Archaeology Update

For more than 1,000 years, most of the treasures of Tiberias's past have been lost to history to the modern world. Lately, however, Tiberias has been the site of some of the most dramatic archaeological finds in Israel. Uncovered from 2005 to 2006 is a portion of a mosaic floor and apse belonging to a large 4th-century-A.D. basilica complex that may have contained as many as 25 rooms. As there are no historical references to other large structures or basilicas in the area, many believe this may be the actual building that housed the ancient rabbinical academy of Yehuda Ha-Nassi, in which the Jerusalem Talmud was compiled. (Much compilation of the Jerusalem Talmud was done in Sepphoris/Zippori, but the Sanhedrin, or assembly of rabbis, moved to Tiberias in the 3rd c. A.D. and worked there for more than a century.) Other finds include a 5th-century-A.D. seal containing a representation of the face of Jesus—one of the oldest representations of Jesus known to exist—and a horde of gold coins from the Arabic period just before the Crusades. Perhaps this treasure was hidden before the onslaught of the Crusaders or other marauders: Whatever the circumstances, the owner apparently did not survive to reclaim it.

To visit the ongoing excavations at Tiberias, check with the Tiberias Tourism Office, or go to the excavation website (**www.tiberiasexcavation.com**). You can even volunteer to work on this exciting dig while making Tiberias your vacation headquarters—unlike other more rugged, remote excavations, the pleasures of swimming in the Sea of Galilee and dining in Tiberias's restaurants are close at hand. *Note:* The discovery of the seal with the representation of Jesus was made by volunteers from the staffs of the American and British embassies.

be able to ski on Mount Hermon (1½-hr. drive, 2,700m/8,858 ft. above sea level) in the morning and (on warm days) do an afternoon water-ski on the Sea of Galilee (210m/689 ft. below sea level). In the evening, you can eat a NIS 16 ($4/£2) falafel packed with every salad or condiment imaginable at the pedestrian mall, or a NIS 160 ($40/£20) supper at one of Israel's most acclaimed restaurants and go dancing on one of the Sea of Galilee's evening party boats afterward. In less than an hour you can drive from Tiberias to the Golan Heights, the Lebanese border, Safed, Nazareth, the Yizreel Valley, or down through the Jordan Valley to the south, as well as to any place on the Sea of Galilee.

Tiberias lies on one of the earth's major geological fault lines, the Syrian/African Rift, and in 1837 the city was virtually destroyed by an earthquake. A few portions of the city's black basalt medieval walls survived that catastrophe, but almost nothing else of medieval or ancient Tiberias can be seen today outside of the archaeological sites open to the public.

The entire area, geologically speaking, is known as the "Great Rift." The fault line begins in southern Turkey and northern Syria, extends southward through Israel down to Eilat, goes under the Red Sea, and all the way to Lake Victoria in Malawi, Africa.

It is this rift that has given shape to the mountains and valleys, and it is the reason why you can stand at the Sea of Galilee, 210m (689 ft.) below sea level, and look up toward the north and see Mount Hermon towering 2,700m (8,858 ft.) above sea level. It's also the reason for the earthquakes and volcanic eruptions over the eons, as well as the mineral hot springs around the shores of Lake Kinneret and The Dead Sea. The town's older buildings, and Tiberias's Old City Wall, are composed of volcanic rock, called black basalt.

Another interesting feature of the low-lying Syrian/African Rift is that it forms an incredible highway for bird migration between Europe and Africa. Two of Israel's major wildlife reserves—Hula Valley in the north, Hai Bar in the south—serve as stopping-off points for the birds on their long journey, and are popular with bird-watchers and nature lovers.

## ESSENTIALS

**GETTING THERE    By Bus**    There is direct service from all major cities.

**By Car**    From Jerusalem via the Jordan Valley, it's a 2½-hour drive; from Haifa, 1 hour and 20 minutes. Four main roads lead to Tiberias and the Sea of Galilee: from Safed, from the Jordan Valley, via Mount Tabor, and from Nazareth.

**VISITOR INFORMATION**    The area code is **04.** The **Tiberias Tourist Information Office** is in the archaeological park in front of the Sheraton Moriah Hotel (✆ **04/672-5666;** open Sun–Thurs 9am–4pm, Fri 9am–12:30pm). If Katherine is on duty, you'll get great information. There are often extended hours in July and August. The office gives out free maps and information and can direct you to lists of bed-and-breakfast accommodations. A **free walking tour** of Tiberias is offered Saturday at 10:30am starting in front of the Sheraton hotel.

**SPECIAL EVENTS**    The **Ein Gev Music Festival** takes place at Kibbutz Ein Gev in spring during Passover week. Israeli folk dance and song festivals are organized along the waterfront in summer; ask the Tiberias Tourist Information Office for details. The **Succot Swimathon** is across the Kinneret (4.8km/3 miles). Everyone is welcome to join, but bring a medical certificate stating that you are in good health. For information, contact the Tiberias Tourism Information Office, Ha-Banim Street, Tiberias (✆ **04/672-5666**).

**ORIENTATION**    Tiberias (pop. 45,000) spreads out along the Kinneret shore and climbs the hillside to the west. The very center of Tiberias is **Kikar Ha-Atzma'ut,** or Independence Square, in the Old City. Surrounding Ha-Atzma'ut Square is what little is left of historic Tiberias.

The **Central Bus Station** (✆ **04/672-9222**), on Ha-Yarden Street, is 2 blocks inland from Ha-Atzma'ut Square. Tiberias's main street changes names as it winds through the city. As it descends from the mountains to the lake it's called Ha-Nitzahon Road; in the residential district of Kiryat Shmuel up on the hillside it becomes Yehuda Ha-Nassi Street, and as it descends to approach the Old City its name changes to Elhadeff (or El-Hadeff or Alhadif) Street. After passing Ha-Atzma'ut Square, it becomes Ha-Banim Street, and this name serves it all the way to the southern limits of the city.

Northwest of the Old City, up on the hill that overlooks downtown, is the large residential district of **Kiryat Shmuel,** which has many moderately priced hotels, but is a rather dull, out-of-the-way area to stay in. South of the Old City about 1.5km (1 mile) is the section called **Hammat,** or **Tiberias Hot Springs.** Ruins of an ancient synagogue and town, a national park, a museum, and the Tomb of Rabbi Meir Baal Haness are located near the springs.

North of the Old City, Gdud Barak Road skirts past several beaches on its way to Magdala (where Mary Magdalene came from), Tabgha (where the miracle of the loaves and fishes took place), the Mount of Beatitudes (where Jesus preached the Sermon on the Mount), and Capernaum (Kefar Nahum), a fishing community that was the hometown of Peter and a center for Jesus' ministry.

---

### FAST FACTS: Tiberias

*Banks*  Bank Mizrachi at the corner of the Pedestrian Mall and Ha-Banim Street has an outdoor ATM that is connected to Visa, MasterCard, and Cirrus and NYCE systems.

*Bookstores*  Steimatzky is located at 3 Ha Galil St. (© **04/679-1288**), open Sunday, Monday, Wednesday, and Thursday from 8am to 1pm and 4:30 to 7pm; Tuesday 8am to 1pm; Friday 8am to 2pm; and closed Saturday. You can get area maps and English-language newspapers here, such as the *Jerusalem Post* and the *Herald Tribune* (which includes the English edition of *Ha'aretz*). Come early if you want a weekend paper on Friday morning.

*Emergencies*  Magen David Adom (© **100** or 04/679-0111), at the corner of Ha-Banim and Ha-Kishon streets across from the Jordan River Hotel, is open 24 hours.

*Maps*  Steimatzky bookstore and the Tiberia Tourist Information Office sell a selection of regional road maps. In addition to standard road maps, look for Corazin Publishing's fold-out *Go Galilee* and *Map of the Galilee, Golan and the Northern Valleys*. It costs about NIS 22 ($5.50/£2.75); Corazin also publishes the map *The Northern Coast and Western Galilee*. **Corazin maps** are filled with details and explanations about historical and natural sites throughout Israel.

*Police*  Telephone © **100** or 04/679-2444.

---

## GETTING AROUND

You can rent a **bicycle** at Hotel Aviv (© **04/672-0007** or 672-3510), at the southern end of Ha Galil Street, starting at NIS 40 ($10/£5) for standard bikes and NIS 50 ($13/£6.25) for mountain bikes for a full day, with hourly and half-day rates available. It's open daily. For an additional fee, you can have pickup service at points around the lake if you don't feel up to biking back to Tiberias. You can rent a car at any of five different major rent-a-car companies with offices in Tiberias, many of them found in the block of Elhadeff Street north of Ha-Yarden Street. They include **Avis** (© **04/672-2766**), **Budget** (© **04/672-0864**), **Eldan** (© **04/679-1822**), **Hertz** (© **04/672-1804**), and **Reliable/Sixt** (© **04/672-4112**).

## WHAT TO SEE & DO

The main city on the Sea of Galilee, Tiberias has an interesting split personality. **Ha Galil Street** (which is one-way heading south) is reminiscent of a tree-shaded main street in any small American town—it's lined with small shops serving the population from the surrounding countryside. If the old basalt rock buildings with their second-story balconies were renovated, the street could be charming. A block to the east is the other main street of Tiberias, **Ha-Banim Street** (running one-way heading north), passing high-rises, megahotels, and the Midrehov, or Pedestrian Mall, leading to the Waterfront Promenade, packed with Israeli and foreign tourists during the summer and Jewish holidays, throbbing at night with wall-to-wall discos, pubs, cafes, and restaurants. Ancient and Byzantine/Talmudic-era Tiberias was larger and more spread out than the modern city; many archaeological sites are outside its present boundaries.

**Ha Galil Street** runs just outside the most recent of the town's old defensive walls, destroyed over the past few centuries by a number of earthquakes that have struck the region. Here you can see the ruins of the **rampart** that enclosed the city; you can also see the **remains of mosques** and old buildings from the densely packed Arab town that once existed here. Most of Tiberias's Arab population fled at the time of the 1948 war.

The **Waterfront Promenade** has a magnificent view across the lake. Ninety meters (295 ft.) to the left are the remains of a **Crusader fort** (now the Castle Inn Hostel), jutting up in black basalt stone from the water. Directly across the lake is Kibbutz Ein Gev and other settlements. To the left is Mount Hermon. It is from this mountain that the sources of the Jordan River are formed. The mountains in the distance, opposite you, are part of the Golan Heights (see p. 414 for a description of a Golan trip). On busy nights, the restaurants along the promenade sell thousands of tasty, but nearly identical, St. Peter's fish meals.

The **Galilee Experience** (© 04/672-3620) is an overrated multimedia exhibition depicting the history and heritage of the region. The entrance fee is NIS 28 ($7/£3.50), and what you get is a 30-minute state-of-the-art multislide show centered around Jesus and the rise of Christianity, and also around 20th-century Zionism. (Some visitors to the Galilee Experience are not prepared for the exhibit's focus on the area's most famous inhabitant, Jesus.) Little mention is made of the ancient Jewish history of the area, or of Israel's large Arabic community, which makes up half the population of the Galilee. Located on the Waterfront Promenade, the Galilee Experience is open Saturday through Thursday, from 8am to 10pm, and Friday from 8am to 4pm.

Located off Yochanon Ben-Zakkai Street is **Rambam's (Maimonides's) Tomb.** Rabbi Moses Ben-Maimon, known both as Maimonides and the Rambam, was the greatest Jewish theologian of the Middle Ages. A Sephardic Jew, born in Cordova, Spain, but who lived most of his life in Morocco and Egypt, he was an Aristotelian philosopher, a physician (who served as personal physician to the famous Saladin, at his royal court in Egypt), and a leading scientist and astronomer. His principal work was *The Guide for the Perplexed.* Although he didn't live in Tiberias, according to one legend, as he was dying, the great Maimonides had himself strapped to a donkey and was carried northward from Egypt, toward the Holy Land, where he hoped to be buried. The inhabitants of Tiberias found his body and buried him in their city. The famous philosopher, who died in 1204, is now honored by a newly restored mausoleum and gardens. Nearby is the **tomb of Rabbi Yochanon Ben-Zakkai,** founder of the Yavne Academy in the years following the destruction of Jerusalem in A.D. 70 (the Yavneh Academy was central to keeping Judaism alive in the decades after Jerusalem's destruction); and on a hillside just west of town is the **memorial to Rabbi Akiva,** a cave in which according to tradition he was buried. This great sage compiled the commentaries of the Mishnah before the Romans tortured him to death at Caesarea around A.D. 135 for his role in supporting the Bar Kochba revolt.

The tomb of the 2nd-century-A.D. **Rabbi Meir Baal Haness** (Meir, Master of Miracles), located on the hill above the hot springs, is considered one of Israel's holiest sites; pilgrims visit in search of medical cures and help with personal problems. Rabbi Meir is remembered in a white building that has two tombs. The Sephardic tomb, with the shallow dome, was built around 1873 and is believed to contain the actual grave, close to the interior western wall of the synagogue; the building with the steeper dome is the Ashkenazi synagogue, erected in about 1900. Huge bonfires are lit at his tomb by the Orthodox 4 days before the Lag b'Omer holiday in the spring. All the tombs are open Sunday through Thursday between 8am and 4pm and Friday from 8am to 2pm. Tiberias is home to other tombs in varying states of neglect, and strong pilgrimage traditions have developed over the centuries. A marble structure beside a modern apartment building, the **Tomb of the Matriarchs,** is believed, according to some traditions, to be the final resting place of a number of biblical women, including Jacob's third and fourth wives, Bilhah and Zilpah; Yocheved (the mother of Moses); Zipporah (Moses' wife); Elisheva (wife of Aaron); and Avigail (one of the wives of King David).

Down on Tiberias's lakeside promenade, squeezed in among the fish restaurants and inconspicuously set back from the shore, stands **Terra Sancta,** a church and monastery run by the Franciscans. Another name for the church is Saint Peter's Parish Church. The first church was constructed here by the Crusaders around A.D. 1100. After the Muslims conquered Tiberias in 1187, the church was converted to a mosque; around the middle of the 17th century, the Franciscans began coming each year from Nazareth to celebrate the Feast of Saint Peter, paying the Muslims for the use of the site. Later on the Franciscans obtained the site for themselves.

The present church still contains part of the original Crusader church—the part of the apse (altar), which, on the outside, is shaped like the bow of a boat. The rest was built by the Franciscans in the 19th century. The church's facade, with red stone imported from Assisi, is reminiscent of the Franciscan church in Assisi where the order began. In the courtyard facing the church is a white stone monument built by the Polish in 1945, dedicated to Our Lady of Czestochowa, and a bronze statue of Saint Peter, a copy of the statue in Saint Peter's Basilica in Rome. You can visit the church daily from 8 to 11:45am and from 3 to 5:30pm. Mass is held Monday to Saturday at 7am, and on Sunday and holidays at 8:30 and 11am.

While you're here, you can also visit the historic **Greek Orthodox Church** located along the waterfront, a block or two south of Terra Sancta, or the **Church of Scotland,** which is a block or two to the north.

The **art gallery district** is located between Elhadeff and Dona Gracia streets, extending northward from Ha-Yarden Street. You'll find one gallery in the medieval castle on Dona Gracia Street and many others nearby.

## ORGANIZED TOURS

Every Sunday and Monday at 9am and Thursday at 6pm, a free 2-hour walking tour of Old Tiberias leaves from the **Tiberias Tourist Information Center** (© 04/672-5666), across from the Sheraton Moriah Hotel. Saturday at 10:30am, a free walking tour leaves from the lobby of the **Sheraton Moriah Hotel,** under the hotel's sponsorship. These walks are a real pleasure, led by interesting guides; reconfirm all times with the tourist office. With Tiberias as a starting point, you can take guided tours of both the Golan Heights and the Sea of Galilee. Check the sections on those areas, later in this chapter, for details.

In addition to the large tour companies, you may want to hire **private tour guides** to take you by sherut or taxi. Inquire at your hotel or youth hostel, at the major hotels, or at the tourist office. These tours can be reasonably priced and a welcome change of

*Moments* **Dancing on the Waters**

In good weather, the Lido Cruises Sailing Company sends out evening party boats to cruise the Sea of Galilee in the moonlight or under the stars. From the shore, you'll hear pulsating disco music blaring into the night as the ferries ply the lake (the bane of those trying to get an early night's sleep). But on board the boats are filled with Israeli Arabs, Jews, and a smattering of tourists dancing in the wind to traditional Arabic tunes, pop Israeli music, international hits, and even a waltz or two. It's a happy pandemonium: Everyone dances with everyone—Galilee Arabs with Jews from Jerusalem and Tel Aviv; men with men for traditional Arabic *debkas;* women with women for the macarena; everyone together for golden oldies or the latest on the Israeli hit parade. There's always a chance you'll share the boat with a quiet crowd that just wants to contemplate, but that's also memorable. It's NIS 50 ($13/£6.25) to join in this vision of a deliriously happy, peaceful Middle East for an hour; and it's free with a voucher you get when you dine at Decks, the best restaurant in Tiberias.

pace from the bus tours. The Society for Protection of Nature (SPNI) includes walks and hikes in the tours it offers in the Galilee Region. Check with the society's English website (www.aspni.org) or offices in Tel Aviv (© **03/638-8677**) or Jerusalem (© **02/ 624-4605**). SPNI's Alon-Tavor Field Study Center, M.P. Lower Galilee 14101 (© **04/ 676-7798**), organizes hikes in the Jordan and Jezreel valleys as well as elsewhere in the region; they offer information on trails and hotel accommodations in local field schools.

## CRUISES & FERRIES

**Lido Cruises Sailing Company** (© **04/672-1538**) at times offers ferry runs between Lido Beach in the northern part of town and Kibbutz Ginnosar, toward the northeastern corner of the lake, for NIS 28 ($7/£3.50); bicycles are free and there is no discount if you only travel one-way. Departures often depend on a minimum number of passengers. Lido Cruises Sailing Company also offers water-ski and sail-board rental.

The **Kinneret Sailing Company,** on the Waterfront Promenade (© **050/554-6446**), runs ferry service between Tiberias on the west side of the Kinneret and Kibbutz Ein Gev on the east side, departing daily from the Tiberias Waterfront Promenade and arriving at Ein Gev 45 minutes later. After spending an hour at Ein Gev, it departs for Tiberias. Schedules vary according to season, with three or four lake crossings in summer. The round-trip costs NIS 50 ($13/£6.25). Many people take the Kinneret Sailing Company ferry to try out the excellent restaurant at Kibbutz Ein Gev or just to stroll around the kibbutz. You can also plan to take the ferry one-way and take bus no. 18 or 21 back to Tiberias. Buses go between Tiberias and Ein Gev about every 2 hours.

## SPORTS & OUTDOOR ACTIVITIES

Watersports are offered on and around the lake, including water-skiing, water parachuting, sail boarding, giant water slides, kayak trips, and more. Call the Tiberia Tourist Information Office for information.

**BEACHES**   The **Blue Beach** charges NIS 28 ($7/£3.50) for the use of its lake facilities and a beach-chair rental.

The **Quiet Beach's** NIS 26 ($6.50/£3.25) fee includes all the swimming facilities and is open daily (in season) from 8am to 6 or 7pm. The **Ganei Hammat Swimming**

**Beach,** opposite the Ganei Hammat Hotel, near the Tiberias Hot Springs, is open daily from 9am to 5pm. It offers deck chairs, showers, and a snack kiosk. Admission is NIS 24 ($6/£3). The **Gai Beach,** 1km (½ mile) south of town, beyond the Galei Kinneret Hotel, has a water park with incredible slides and a fine beach with all the requisite facilities; it charges a NIS 50 to NIS 60 ($13–$15/£6.25–£7.50) admission fee. **Sironit Beach,** also south of town, is open daily (in season) from 8am to 5pm, April through October. There's also a **municipal beach** (NIS 18/$4.50/£2.25 fee) south of Sironit Beach, open daily (in season) from 9am to 5pm.

**HORSEBACK RIDING**    In the countryside around the lake, you can join groups for trail riding in the Galilee; call **Vered HaGalil Guest Farm** (© **04/693-5785;** www.veredhagalil.co.il; p. 393). Vered HaGalil offers beautiful (and beautifully tended) horses for everything from well-planed range riding to 15-minute rides for kids.

## WHERE TO STAY

Tiberias has everything from youth hostels to five-star hotels, with a few religious guesthouses as well. You should note that most hotels in Tiberias have kosher kitchens and that several cater to the Orthodox and have glatt kosher certification (see p. 41 for an explanation of kashrut). The Tiberia Tourism Information Office gives out lists of rooms to rent in private homes.

### DOWNTOWN TIBERIAS
#### Expensive

**Rimmonim Galei Kinneret** *(Overrated)*    The Galei Kinneret, hidden from the main road by gardens, is the oldest of the quality hotels in town (it was a favorite of Ben-Gurion) and is a place for Israelis to see and be seen. It was heavily renovated in 1997, but the old standards and personality of the hotel still continue. The original building from the early 1940s is of severe white International-Style design, to which newer wings have been added. The general atmosphere is relaxing; unlike other downtown hotels, the Galei Kinneret has shaded lawns and its own beach directly on the lake. Public areas and guest rooms are comfortable but not spectacular. The pool is heated and covered in winter. *Gemultlich* as a semi-Bauhaus Israeli resort can be, this is a cultural and historic oddity, but unless you are from the Israeli Establishment, it could fall flat. Full or half board is often required.

1 Kaplan St., Tiberias. © 04/672-8888. Fax 04/679-0260. www.rimonim.com. 120 units. $347–$410 (£174–£205) double; $200 (£100) higher during Jewish holidays. Rates include breakfast. Add 15% service charge. AE, V. **Amenities:** Dining room; cafe; bar; heated swimming pool; floodlit tennis court; fitness center; sauna; hot tub; watersports rentals; children's activities; business lounge; business services; room service; nonsmoking rooms; synagogue. *In room:* A/C, TV, minibar, coffeemaker, hair dryer, safe.

**Sheraton Moriah Tiberias** *((((((★*    The best of all the giant downtown hotels along the waterfront, this modern 14-story high-rise offers a convenient location at the southern end of the Waterfront Promenade. In 2006, guest rooms were heavily renovated and a state-of-the-art spa, with a full range of massage programs, was installed. Ask for a room with a view of the lake (many have balconies). The pool area is pleasantly sheltered from the promenade and open all year; dining facilities are above average, with theme buffets at the main in-house restaurant; service is attentive; and in season and on weekends there's live entertainment and activities for children. The roomy junior suites are a good choice for families.

Ha-Banim St., Tiberias. © 04/671-3333. Fax 04/679-2320. www.sheraton.com. 258 units. $280–$430 (£140–£215) double. Rates include breakfast. AE, DC, MC, V. Parking (fee). **Amenities:** Restaurant; dining room; cafe; bar; heated outdoor pool; health club; spa; Jacuzzi; sauna; children's activities; business services; business lounge; arcade; shops; hairdresser; room service; massage; laundry service. In room: A/C, TV, minibar, coffeemaker, hair dryer, safe.

**The Scots Hotel** ★★ *(Finds*  These 19th-century stone buildings in the heart of downtown Tiberias have been hidden behind high walls and overgrown gardens for more than a century, serving originally as a hospital run by the Church of Scotland and later as an atmospheric but very simple hostel and guesthouse. In 2004, the management renovated the entire romantic enclave. The result is a charming hotel with lots of character and sparkling new guest rooms, carefully planned and offering all the modern conveniences. There are two categories of rooms: standard and the slightly more expensive "antique" rooms that make dramatic use of arched ceilings, exposed basalt walls, and other original architectural details. Other pluses are beautiful, secluded gardens with sweeping vistas of the lake and Tiberias; a pool; a private beach; and a friendly staff. Booked by both tour groups and individual travelers of all faiths, this is a real gem, and the prettiest hotel in Tiberias. Dining facilities are not kosher.

1 Gdud Barak St., Tiberias. ℂ 04/671-0710. Fax 04/671-0711. www.scotshotels.co.il. 69 units. From $320 (£160) standard double half board; additional charge for lake view and antique rooms; additional charge Thurs–Sat. Minimum 2-night stay required at times. AE, DC, MC, V. Amenities: Restaurant; dining room; bar; pool; laundry service; nonsmoking rooms; garden; beach. In room: A/C, TV, minibar, coffeemaker, hair dryer, safe.

### Inexpensive
**Casa Dona Gracia**  This hotel, set in a modern building that has been renovated into a Sephardic cultural center and museum, is named for Tiberias's legendary patroness, Dona Gracia, who was herself a refugee from the Spanish Inquisition. It's a few blocks inland from the lake, near the bus station, and a good choice for travelers on a budget. Though it's a bit institutional in terms of service, rooms are fresh, modern, and simple but bright and cheerful. As rooms differ in size, view, and shape, ask to see more than one before you make your choice. In summer, during the Jewish holidays, and whenever there are special reunions or meetings of Sephardic groups or families, Casa Dona Gracia may be booked solid. At other times, especially for those who don't want a swimming pool, it can offer a slightly offbeat, interesting window into Tiberias's large Sephardic community.

3 Haprahim St., Tiberias. ℂ 04/671-7176. Fax 04/671-7175. www.donagracia.com. 68 units. $110–$140 (£55–£70) double. Rates include breakfast. MC, V. Parking. Amenities: Restaurant; dining room; cafe; bar; laundry service; nonsmoking rooms; synagogue. In room: A/C, TV, kettle.

**Hotel Aviv** *(Value*  A good budget choice, built in 1998, and located on a quiet street in downtown Tiberias, the Aviv offers large, no-frills rooms with kitchenettes. The layouts of the rooms (called holiday flats) vary, so check a few if possible. Some contain completely separate kitchenettes; others are more like suites, with a living area, separate bedroom, and kitchen—especially good for families. All have balconies, and some have whirlpool tubs. The management rents bikes and organizes tours of the area. There are pleasant public areas, and street parking is permitted here. Do not confuse this with the nearby Hostel Aviv.

Achva St., PO Box 1751, Tiberias. ℂ 04/671-2272. www.aviv-hotel.co.il (in Hebrew). 30 units. $80–$120 (£40–£60); higher rates during Jewish holidays. Rates include breakfast. AE, DC, MC, V. Free street parking. In room: A/C, TV, kitchenette, fridge.

## SOUTH OF DOWNTOWN TIBERIAS
### Expensive
**Gai Beach Hotel** *(Kids*  Great for families with children, the Gai Beach is a sprawling low-rise set right on the beach with an adjacent water park filled with giant slides,

a vast wading pool, and a pool with artificial waves. The hotel is a bright, sparkling place with large windows in the comfy, 1980s modern guest rooms (those on ground floors have terraces) and public areas that bring in dazzling sunshine and offer vistas of the lake. The water park is open from Passover to October, and the hotel has a private beach. The hotel offers rooms for travelers with disabilities. High season includes July and August, Christmas, and the Jewish holidays. Relatively quiet when school is in session.

Hamerchatzaot St., Tiberias. ℂ 04/670-0700. Fax 04/679-2776. www.gaibeachhotel.com. 198 units. $240–$330 (£120–£165) double. Rates include breakfast. AE, DC, MC, V. Free parking. Located on the main road leading into downtown Tiberias from the south. **Amenities:** Dining room; bar; water park w/indoor and outdoor pools; children's pool; spa; Jacuzzi; sauna; seasonal sports and fitness activities; children's activities; room service; massage; synagogue; rooms for those w/limited mobility. *In room:* A/C, TV, minibar/fridge, safe.

## Moderate
**Royal Plaza Tiberias** (Value    Composed of two renovated hotels that have been joined together, the Royal Plaza doesn't offer architectural pizazz, but it does have comfortable, roomy, rather formally decorated rooms and prices that don't skyrocket as much as those at other Tiberias hotels during the summer. There are so many sections to the hotel, and so many different styles of rooms, that it could be worthwhile to look around before checking in. The hotel is located 3.2km (2 miles) south of Tiberias center, on the main lakefront road not far past the hot springs. Pluses include a pleasant British-style pub/bar, business facilities, and a spa with massage treatment rooms. Suites are spacious, contain Jacuzzis, and are a good option for families. There's also a family deal for a double plus two children in a separate room ranging from $320 to $480 (£160–£240).

Ganei Menorah Blvd., Tiberias. ℂ 800/538-4683 or 718/338-6537 in North America or 04/670-0000. Fax 04/670-0001. www.royal-plaza.co.il. 160 units. $180–$270 (£90–£135) double. Rates include breakfast. AE, DC, MC, V. Free parking. **Amenities:** Dining room; cafe; bar; pool; children's pool; sauna; massage; rooms for those w/limited mobility. *In room:* A/C, TV, dataport, coffeemaker, hair dryer, safe.

## KIRYAT SHMUEL
Kiryat Shmuel is both a residential and hotel district on the mountain overlooking Tiberias and the Sea of Galilee. All of the many hotels and smaller, pensionlike places in this area have kosher dining rooms. Most have good views. But this is not an exciting neighborhood to be in—you don't get a feel for Tiberias or the Galilee staying in this urban residential area. Most tourists who choose this part of town are older Israelis or European tourists.

You'll want to take a taxi to get up to Kiryat Shmuel if you're arriving in Tiberias by bus—it begins .5km (¼ mile) away from downtown, and that is all uphill. Many of the hotels here are even farther uphill.

## Moderate
**Prima Tiberia**    This large, good-value establishment is part of a respected, moderately priced national chain, which guarantees a certain level of standards and service. It offers magnificent views and a large, seasonal outdoor swimming pool set in a garden. Some rooms contain a sofa bed and can be set up for three adults or a family with two children. In winter or at slow times, lower rates can be obtained.

14 Ahad Ha-Am St. (PO Box 555), Tiberias. ℂ 04/679-1166. Fax 04/672-2994. www.prima.co.il. 173 units. $120–$170 (£60–£85) double. AE, DC, MC, V. Parking. **Amenities:** Restaurant; cafe; bar; outdoor seasonal pool; Jacuzzi; playground; laundry service; synagogue. *In room:* A/C, cable TV, fridge.

## Inexpensive
**Bet Berger**    This place has an excellent reputation in the budget category—Israeli families and older couples return to it year after year. Rooms are simple but clean, and

have kitchenettes with refrigerators, which helps cut down on your restaurant expenses. Some of the rooms have balconies; most bathrooms have showers only. It's located on a residential street, and is the most professional of Kiryat Shmuel's low-budget hotels—a good choice for those who are looking for affordable accommodations.

25 Neiberg St., Tiberias. © 04/671-5151. Fax 04/679-1514. 45 units. $90–$140 (£45–£70) double. Discounts for long-term stays; surcharges for Jewish holidays. MC, V. **Amenities:** Dining room; room service. *In room:* A/C, TV, kitchenette.

## WHERE TO DINE

In addition to the choices in Tiberias, many travelers who have use of a car will enjoy dining at some of the delightful restaurants in the countryside and on the shore around Kinneret; see "Country Dining Around the Sea of Galilee," below.

### ON THE WATERFRONT

The specialty in Tiberias is Saint Peter's fish, so-called because it is the very fish that swam in the Sea of Galilee when Jesus called Peter away from his nets to become a "fisher of men." It's a white fish that is indigenous to the Sea of Galilee, and its taste resembles that of bass.

The best place to search out a good portion of Saint Peter's fish, or even shish kabob for that matter, is along the **Waterfront Promenade** in the Old City.

Three of the large, attractive waterfront restaurants have the same management, the same menu, the same prices, and the same delicious food. These are the **Nof Kinneret** (© 04/672-0310), the **Galei Gil** (© 04/672-0699), and the **Roast on Fire** (© 04/672-0310). The indoor decor is different in each restaurant, although outdoor dining on the boardwalk is virtually the same, so stroll along and see which you like the best; if the weather is good, you'll likely want to eat by the water. All three restaurants offer their fish fried, charcoal grilled, or in a special sauce. The **Karamba** restaurant (on the waterfront in between the above choices), with the same prices, offers interesting sauces with your fish, and a slightly wider menu, but no tables right on the water. Plan to spend about NIS 60 to NIS 120 ($15–$30/£7.50–£15) for something simple, or for a large (more than a pound) serving of Saint Peter's fish, french fries, salad, and pita bread; if you add wine or coffee and dessert, your total could come to about NIS 135 ($34/£17). Karamba is open daily from 8:30am to midnight; in summer, it may be open 24 hours.

### NEAR THE MOSQUE

This historic, Ottoman-era mosque is now in a state of near ruin, incongruously surrounded by a supermarket and fast-food eateries. However, there is a movement to restore the building for use as a place of worship. The Midrehov, or pedestrian street, a block from the mosque, leads down to the Waterfront Promenade. Both places are lined with restaurants, cafes, and pubs, almost all with outdoor tables.

For espresso, cappuccino, and excellent baked goods and pastries, try the **Contidoria Yatsek** and **Kapulsky's,** which are right next to each other. At either place, a pastry and cappuccino at a sidewalk table will cost from NIS 28 to NIS 36 ($7–$9/£3.50–£4.50). Both also sell baked goods to go. They're open daily from 8am to 10 or 11pm.

### DOWNTOWN

A bit away from the crush of the Waterfront Promenade, around Ha Galil and Ha-Banim streets, you'll find restaurants that are less tourist-oriented, although you must remember that tourism is Tiberias's major industry. The north end of Ha Galil Street and Ha-Yarden Street next to Shimon Park is **"Falafel Row."** The lineup starts right outside Ha-Atzma'ut Square and stretches up toward the bus station. Quality and fixings can vary, but the cost should be about NIS 16 to NIS 20 ($4–$5/£2–£2.50). The best falafel and *shwarma* stands offer a big selection of salads to tuck inside your pita. Many say the falafel here is the best in Israel. The Pedestrian Mall leading to the Waterfront Promenade is filled with places where you can pick up a slice of pizza, a falafel, or a *shwarma.*

## Moderate

**Little Tiberias Pub Restaurant** CONTINENTAL   This nonkosher spot is the best of the downtown restaurants that are not on the waterfront. It's relaxed (perhaps too relaxed, as service can be very slow) and unpretentious. Everything comes out of the kitchen a bit more special than at neighboring restaurants—even that Israeli standby, chicken schnitzel, is a pleasant surprise here. There are hefty salads that are meals in themselves, and good spaghetti and lasagna at the lower end of the main-course menu. In the upper price range, I strongly recommend the steaks and fresh fish; shrimp and calamari are also available. You can have a very good meal here, away from the hustle of the Waterfront Promenade.

Ha-Kishon St. ✆ **04/679-2806**. Reservations suggested. Main courses NIS 50–NIS 100 ($13–$25/£6.25–£13). AE, DC, MC, V. Daily noon–1am.

## Inexpensive

**Guy Restaurant** *(Value)* SEPHARDIC HOME-STYLE   This friendly kosher, family-style restaurant specializes in home-style Sephardic and Middle Eastern Jewish cooking. It is 1 block south of Ha-Yarden at the southern end of Ha Galil Street, in a small white building on the right as you head south, set back from the road. Delicious house specialties include eggplant, artichokes, tomatoes, or other vegetables stuffed with rice or rice with meat; as well as (in season) plums, dates, figs, and apricots stuffed with meat, rice, and nuts. Main meat courses are served with french fries, salad, pita bread, and pickles. Prices are very reasonable.

Ha Galil St. ✆ **04/672-3036**. Main courses NIS 45–NIS 80 ($11–$20/£5.60–£10). Cash only. Sun–Thurs noon–midnight; Fri noon–1 hr. before Shabbat; Sat after Shabbat.

## NORTH OF DOWNTOWN—THE LIDO COMPLEX

Tiberias has three wonderful restaurants that are about a 5-minute walk up Gdud Barak Street from the downtown promenade. They have great atmosphere (two are on the water), romantic settings, and delicious food, and are well worth the stroll. They also have free parking, if you're coming from out of Tiberias.

## Moderate

**Decks** *(★★ (Finds)* KOSHER BARBECUE   One of the most beautiful restaurants I've encountered in Israel, set on a long deck jutting out over the Sea of Galilee, Decks serves wonderful meats, poultry, and fish barbecued over fires of citrus wood, olive wood, and American hickory imported from Georgia. Pass the outdoor cooking fires, and through a sweeping open-air bar, to reach the dining area, a long, moonlit wooden deck stretching to the lake, with wonderful vistas and refreshing breezes (it's covered with a transparent tent in winter). Waiters are well-informed and helpful. Most main courses are served at your table on specially designed plates that keep your meal warm but not dried out during a leisurely dinner. Absolutely heavenly is the very reasonably priced breast of mullard, a local duck-goose hybrid as rich and tender as filet mignon and cooked to perfection. The lamb is remarkable; most cuts are from delicate local female baby lamb. A specialty, not usually written on the menu, is boneless shoulder of lamb, priced according to weight and of gourmet quality—it's worth requesting. The specially prepared salmon and tuna are moist and juicy, cooked in a traditional charcoal oven found on the coast of Dalmatia. When available, Decks also makes carpaccio from Mediterranean tuna so freshly caught it sings. Regular menu choices include herbed breast of chicken, prime rib, and filet mignon. All main courses are served with bountiful portions of grilled vegetables and fire-baked potatoes. There are good salads and focaccias for first courses, and flambé crepes and nondairy ice cream touched with homemade berry sauces for dessert. The house drink of lemon and mint on crushed ice is a nice touch. Decks is often heavily booked by groups, creating something of a party atmosphere; reserve early. Be aware that a meal here can easily run into the expensive price category but is still very worthwhile. *Note:* Dinner comes with a voucher for one of the Lido Sailing Company's evening party boats.

Gdud Barak St. (✆) **04/672-1538.** Reservations necessary. Main courses NIS 70–NIS 135 ($18–$34/£8.75–£17). AE, DC, MC, V. Sun–Thurs 7pm–after midnight; Sat after Shabbat. Call for possible lunch hours.

**The Pagoda** KOSHER CHINESE/THAI ✿   The Pagoda gives you the chance to dine right on the water, with spectacular views of the lake. The building is an airy pavilion extending over the water, designed by Chinese architects to take advantage of the site. The pagoda-style roof, with its genuine Chinese beaming and joinery, is indicative of the management's attention to detail. The noodle soup overflows with chunks of tender stir-fried chicken, doughy homemade noodles, and crisp slices of fresh cucumber—but make sure to ask specifically for the homemade noodle version; the spicy Thai chicken coconut soup is an exotic light meal in itself. For light, healthful food, the Thai-style steamed dishes, including fresh fish, are good choices. There are Chinese choices, but the Thai side of the menu is the most interesting. Avoid the goose-leg faux "spareribs" that have been imposed upon the restaurant in the name of kashrut, replacing Pagoda's once-famous lamb-spareribs. During the Sabbath, the Pagoda opens its nonkosher affiliate, the charming **House Restaurant,** just across the road on Gdud Barak Street (Fri 1pm–midnight, Sat 1–4:30pm). The menu, prices, and phone number are the same as the Pagoda's—the one difference is that it operates on the Sabbath (and is the best choice in town for Fri night and Sat dining).

Gdud Barak St. (✆) **04/672-5513.** Reservations recommended. Main courses NIS 45–NIS 90 ($11–$23/£5.60–£11); sushi fixed menu for 2 NIS 85–NIS 95 ($21–$24/£11–£12). AE, DC, MC, V. Sun–Thurs 12:30–3pm and 6pm–midnight.

## COUNTRY DINING AROUND THE SEA OF GALILEE

Tiberias can become very hectic in the evening, especially during the summer. If you have a car, a drive out into the countryside for dinner can be very pleasant.

**A Good Spot in the Middle** GRILL/PUB   Away from the rush of downtown Tiberias restaurants, this is a roadhouse restaurant/bar with a broad picnic table–covered porch overlooking the road and the lake across the street. Its always friendly spirit shifts in style according to the hour—it's a good choice for a hefty or light meal as you drive around the lake, but after dinner A Good Spot in the Middle slowly builds into a nightlong party as regulars and visitors filter in from the countryside. The restaurant is proud of its fried cheese, salads, and oven-smoked grilled pork steaks, pork filet, and filet mignon. The traditional stuffed vegetables, especially the eggplant, are the best I've had in this part of the country. The home-style couscous dish is great—grab it on the days it's available. The restaurant is located 6.4km (4 miles) south of Tiberias on the right side of the road.

The Tiberias-Degania road. (✆) **04/675-2074.** Main courses NIS 50–NIS 100 ($13–$25/£6.25–£13). AE, DC, MC, V. Summer daily 11am–4am; winter daily 11am–1am.

**Kibbutz Ein Gev Fish Restaurant** ✦ FISH   For great, freshly caught Saint Peter's fish served indoors or on porches and terraces overlooking the lake, this is the place to come. The fame of the fish here has spread around the world, and even though the restaurant is the largest in Israel, it is often filled to the brim. But if you avoid the midday tour groups, this can be a pleasant place for a meal. You can order your fish in two sizes: medium and slightly larger (the larger size is the better deal)—it will come with french fries or oven-baked potatoes and a side salad, as well as a choice of good side sauces. The best time to come here is *early* evening; reserve a table on the terrace by the waterfront in good weather and watch the sunset and soft twilight over the Sea of Galilee as you dine. *Tip:* Stick to the local Saint Peter's fish—the other choices are not why you dine here.

Kibbutz Ein Gev. ✆ **04/665-8035** or 665-8036. Reservations recommended. Main courses NIS 75–NIS 95 ($19–$24/£9.40–£12). Add 10% service charge. AE, DC, MC, V. Daily 10am–10pm.

**Vered HaGalil Restaurant** ✦ AMERICAN   This famous country lodge offers a small menu of hearty American-style food in a lovely garden setting in the hills above the Sea of Galilee. You can choose hamburgers, grilled steaks, fish and ostrich, chicken in a basket with all the fixings, and smoked trout fresh from the Dan River, as well as original house specialties such as trout in an orange and Cointreau sauce. There's a selection of less-expensive light meals, and many locals stop by just for coffee and homemade pie (apple, pecan, or Golan boysenberry) or to talk over a bottle of wine. The scene is mellow and the clientele is largely into nature.

Vered HaGalil Guest Farm, Korazim Rd. ✆ **04/693-5785.** Reservations recommended Fri–Sat. Main courses NIS 45–NIS 110 ($11–$28/£5.60–£14). AE, MC, V. Daily 8am–9:30pm for meals; 8am–11pm for dessert. Follow Korazim Rd. a few miles north of the Sea of Galilee.

## TIBERIAS AFTER DARK

There are summer shows and performances by local and foreign entertainers at the **Bet Gavriel Amphitheater and the majestic Sherover Promenade** ✦, on the southern tip of the Sea of Galilee (across from the Tsemach Junction). With parklike grounds, a snack bar/restaurant, and stunning vistas of the lake, it's a memorable venue for concerts—and also for a light meal in the cafe/snack bar during daytime, when you can make the most of the panorama. Check with the Tiberia Tourist Information Office for a schedule of performances.

Folklore events are often scheduled at the hotels, where everyone is welcome to attend. For full details, contact the tourist office at the end of the Ha-Banim Street Pedestrian Mall.

There are also many late-night pubs, cafes, bars, and restaurants. Good places for a quiet drink with live music include the **Sheraton Moriah Plaza** and the **Jordan River** hotels at the southern end of the Old City.

There are plenty of opportunities to go dancing, as well. The most unusual is the summer **disco dancing** on the boat operated by the Kinneret Sailing Company on the Sea of Galilee; call ✆ **04/665-8007,** or stop by its office at the Waterfront Promenade, for information. An evening **disco cruise** also leaves from the Lido Kinneret Beach (Lido Kinneret Cruises; ✆ **04/672-0330**) at varying times, depending on demand. Be there before 8pm.

For a lively, tropical ambience bar with a small dance floor, there's **Papaya,** at the intersection of the Waterfront Promenade and the Pedestrian Mall; it's open nightly

5pm to 4am. **Big Ben,** on the Pedestrian Mall, has a more traditional indoor pub as well as a terrace; the crowd at times is a bit older and less rowdy.

Many, in fact most, of the hotels (and even the youth hostels) around town have nice bars and pubs where you can relax in the evening and enjoy a drink and conversation with fellow travelers.

## EASY EXCURSIONS

**Hot Springs of Tiberias**    Located 1.6km (1 mile) south of Tiberias, the thermal baths have been famous for their curative powers for more than 3,000 years and have continued to have a following to this day. Pharmacies in Israel keep well-stocked supplies of mineral salts from these Tiberias springs.

The hot waters contain high amounts of sulfuric, hydrochloric acid, and calcium salts, and over the centuries they've reportedly cured skin problems and such ailments as rheumatism, arthritis, and gynecological disorders. They are probably among the earliest-known thermal baths in the world, noted by Josephus, Pliny, church historians, and many Arabic writers. Some biblical commentators have surmised that Jesus cured the sick here. There's a local legend that Solomon entered into a conspiracy with demons to heal his kingdom's ailing people at this site, tricking them into perpetually stoking the fires in the earth below to heat up the water.

Several treatments are available, including the mineral bubble bath, physiotherapy, therapeutic massage, inhalation, mud baths, and so on. *Note:* Bring a bathing suit and towel. There's an inexpensive restaurant on the premises.

To gain a better understanding of the waters, check out the **museum** next to the springs. While visiting the springs, you can also spend some time exploring the ancient ruins of Hammat. See also another hot spring at "Hammat Gader" in the next section.

ℂ **04/672-8500.** Admission to the mineral pools NIS 70 ($18/£8.75) Sun–Thurs; NIS 80 ($20/£10) Fri–Sat for adults; discounts for children. Sun–Mon and Wed 8am–11pm; Tues and Thurs 8:30am–8pm; Fri 8am–4pm; Sat 8:30am–8pm. Free shuttle bus to hotels in downtown Tiberias Sun–Fri 8am–2pm.

**Hammat Tiberias National Park** ⚲    **Hammat Tiberias** (or Hammat), a spa and city 3.2km (2 miles) south of Tiberias, existed well before the founding of Tiberias in the 1st century A.D. Hammat and Tiberias existed side by side for hundreds of years as "twin cities." In Roman and Byzantine times, Hammat developed into a spa resort visited by travelers from all over the known world. The ruins of Hammat are now a national park.

Hammat contains the ruins of one of Israel's most magnificent ancient synagogues, as befits a town that would have hosted wealthy visitors from distant Jewish communities. Most spectacular is the Hammat Tiberias synagogue's well-preserved **mosaic calendar floor** ⚲⚲ (4th c. A.D.), which depicts the zodiac cycle and, in its outer corners, four women representing the seasons of the year. At the center of the zodiac, the sun god Helios rides on a chariot through the heavens; beyond the zodiac, a separate mosaic panel depicts traditional Jewish symbols, including the Ark of the Covenant flanked by two ceremonial menorahs. The famous native zodiac floor of the Bet Alpha synagogue (which served a Byzantine-era farming village in the Jordan Valley) may have drawn on this very sophisticated mosaic for inspiration.

Entrance to the ruins is through the **Ernest Lehman/Haman Suleiman Museum,** which inventories information on regional history and the curative powers of the hot springs. *Warning:* Be aware that the open water flowing through the gardens around the ruins comes directly from the hot springs and will scald you should you decide to do something foolish, like test it with your toe. Up the hill from the baths is the **Tomb of Rabbi Meir Baal Haness** (Rabbi Meir, Master of Miracles), a disciple of Rabbi Akiva, and one of the great sages who helped to compile the Mishnah in the 2nd century A.D.

© 04/672-5287. www.parks.org.il. Admission NIS 12 ($3/£1.50) adults, half-price children. Winter daily 8am–4pm; Apr–Sept 8am–5pm. Egged bus: 2 or 5. Parts of the park and museum are wheelchair accessible.

## 3 The Sea of Galilee ★★★

The Arabic and Aramaic poets called it "the Bride," "the Handmaiden of the Hills," and "the Silver Woman." The ancient Hebrews called it "the Harp," in honor of the soothing harplike sounds of its waves, and because it roughly resembles the shape of an ancient harp. Today, Israelis still call the Sea of Galilee "harp"—in Hebrew Kinnor, or Kinneret, as it is popularly known. According to one lexicographer, an ancient sage wrote: "God created the seven seas, but the Kinneret is His pride and joy." It's a marvelous lake, its surface constantly changing during the day. In summer the Sea of Galilee's waters are sparkling and almost bathtub warm; if you find a tranquil, beautiful beach for a swim, you'll emerge from the lake feeling refreshed, soothed, and cleansed.

Some 210m (689 ft.) below sea level, the Sea of Galilee is 21km (13 miles) long, from the place where the Jordan flows in at the north to where it empties out in the south.

It was here that Jesus preached to the crowds and fed them by multiplying the bread and fishes; it is also where he restored the sick and maimed. Today, parts of the sea are filled with speedboats and water-skiers; other parts are as serene and mysterious as in ancient times.

Kinneret's waters are a vast reservoir of sardine, mullet, catfish, and the unusual combfish. They are the same fish once caught by the disciples, and they are caught in the same manner today, though some of the kibbutzim have developed careful methods of farming fish.

### TOURING THE AREA

To tour the Sea of Galilee, we'll head north, starting a circle that will bring us back to Tiberias before heading into the Upper Galilee region. As of this writing there is no regular bus route that completely circles the lake, so you'll have to depend on a tour bus, rental car, bicycle, or boat.

### MAGDALA & MIGDAL

Just over 3km (2 miles) north of Tiberias along the lakeside road, you'll come to the old village of Magdala, the birthplace of Mary Magdalene. There's not much to see, except for lovely scenery. The town was right down by the water's edge. On the hill just to the south of old Magdala, along the far (west) side of the highway, you can still see the sarcophagi (stone coffins) carved out of the rocks, in the place that was Magdala's cemetery. The modern town of Migdal, founded in the 20th century, is about 1.6km (1 mile) to the north of the site of ancient Magdala.

### THE GINOSSAR VALLEY

A little farther on, about 10km (6 miles) north of Tiberias, you'll find yourself in a lush valley with many banana trees. These are part of the agriculture of **Kibbutz Nof Ginossar,** one of the larger kibbutzim, with a vast and busy kibbutz hotel. In the kibbutz, you'll find the multimedia **Yigal Alon Museum of the Galilee** (© 04/672-7700; www.jesusboat.com). More a learning experience about the area than a museum,

it offers only one genuine antiquity, **a Galilee fishing boat, from approximately the 1st century A.D.,** preserved in the muddy sediment of the lake floor and revealed in the 1980s when, because of drought, the lake receded to record low levels. The boat is touted by some guides as "the Jesus boat." Although it may be typical of fishing boats from the time of Jesus, there is, of course, no evidence that ties it to any specific persons. Still, it's an amazing discovery, and of special interest to pilgrim groups. The wooden frame of the boat is preserved in a climate-controlled boathouse structure. The museum is open Sunday to Thursday 8:30am to 5pm, Friday from 8am to 1pm, and on Saturday from 9am to 5pm.

## TABGHA 🐦🐦

14km (9 miles) north of Tiberias

To reach Tabgha, where Jesus miraculously multiplied the loaves and fishes, proceed northward along the shoreline from Migdal, passing Minya, a 7th-century Arabian palace that is one of the most ancient and holy Muslim prayer sites. It's open daily from 8am to 4pm.

At Tabgha, you'll find the beautifully restored **Benedictine monastery** and the **Church of the Multiplication of the Loaves and Fishes** 🐦🐦 (✆ 04/672-1061). When the ancient church ruins, hidden for 1,300 years, were excavated, the **mosaic basilica floor** of a Byzantine-era church that once stood on this site was found. The floor is one of the most lyrical and skillfully made ever discovered in Israel. The section of the floor in front of the ancient altar is starkly unadorned, rather primitive, and interesting mainly for what it depicts: two fish and a humble basket filled with loaves of bread. In contrast, the main section of mosaic is a skillfully executed, colorful tapestry of all the birds that once thrived in this area: swans, cranes, ducks, wild geese, and storks. The mosaic artist has captured the liveliness, humor, and grace of these creatures with a style rarely seen in this art form. The Nilometer, used to measure the flood levels of the Nile and famous throughout the ancient world, is also represented, leading some to speculate that the talented mosaic designer might have been Egyptian.

Be sure to read the history of this church posted just inside the entrance, in the church's courtyard. The early Judeo-Christians of nearby Capernaum (Kefar Nahum) venerated a large rock, upon which Jesus is said to have placed the bread and fish when he fed the 5,000. The rock, a natural **dolmen,** is believed by historians to have been a sacred place since prehistoric times, and was used as the altar in a Byzantine church erected over the spot in about A.D. 350.

The church is open Monday to Saturday from 8:30am to 5pm and Sunday 10am to 5pm; modest dress is required. Admission is free, but donations are accepted. There's also a good bookstore and souvenir shop on the premises.

Just east of the Multiplication Church is the **Heptapegon** ("Seven Springs" in Greek), also called the Church of the Primacy of Saint Peter, or Mensa Christi. To reach it, you must leave the Multiplication Church, return to the highway, turn right, and climb the hill to a separate entrance. This Greek Orthodox church is open daily from 8:30am to 1pm and 2 to 5pm; modest dress is required, and admission is free.

It was here on the shores of Galilee that Jesus is believed to have appeared to his disciples after his crucifixion and resurrection. Peter and the others were in a boat on the lake, fishing, but with no luck. When Jesus appeared, he told them to cast their nets again. They did, and couldn't haul in the nets because they were so full of fish. As the disciples sat with their master having dinner, Jesus is said to have conferred the leadership of the movement on Peter, as first among the disciples. The theory of Peter's primacy, and the tradition of that primacy's being passed from one generation of disciples to the next, is the basis for the legitimacy of the Roman pontiff as leader of Christendom.

The black basalt church rests on the foundations of earlier churches. Within is a flat rock called **Mensa Christi,** or "Christ's Table," where Jesus dined that evening with his disciples. Outside the church, you can still see the stone steps said to be the place where Jesus stood when he appeared, calling out to the disciples; on the beach are seven large stones, which may once have supported a little fishing wharf. If it's not too hot, you can easily walk to nearby Capernaum (3km/2 miles) and even to the Mount of Beatitudes.

## MOUNT OF THE BEATITUDES 🐾🐾
8km (5 miles) north of Ginossar; 3km (2 miles) north of Capernaum

Just beyond Tabgha, on a high hill, is the famous Mount of the Beatitudes, now the site of an Italian convent. Here Jesus preached the Sermon on the Mount—the site, though beautiful in itself, bears a special feeling of spirituality. There are many good views of the Sea of Galilee and its surroundings, but the vista from this place is among the most magnificent. One odd fact about this church is the inscription on the sanctuary, which informs you that the entire project was built by Mussolini in 1937. The church is open daily from 8:30am to noon and 2:30 to 5pm. Admission is free, but the fee per car is NIS 5 ($1.25/60p). Take bus no. 459, 541, or 963 from Tiberias. Ask the driver to let you off at the closest stop, which is 1km (½ mile) from the church.

## CAPERNAUM (KEFAR NAHUM) 🐾
This site marks the site of Kfar Nahum (the village of Nahum), a lakeside town where Jesus preached and his disciples, Peter and Andrew, made their homes. During the lifetime of Jesus, in the 1st century A.D., Kfar Nahum was a prosperous fishing community, port, and way station on the main trade route from Israel's Mediterranean coast to Damascus. It even had its own Customs House and was probably the most cosmopolitan of the lakeside towns until the building of the Roman resort of Tiberias, in the mid–1st century. The town was abandoned around A.D. 700 and never reconstituted. Today, you'll find a modern Franciscan monastery, which was built on the abandoned site in 1894, as well as ancient excavations spanning 6 centuries. Among the most impressive are the ruins of **a 3rd- or 4th-century synagogue** built on the site of an even earlier synagogue—perhaps one that Jesus would have prayed in. Nearby are several houses of the period and the excavated remains of **a 5th-century octagonal church built over the ruins of the traditional site of Saint Peter's house,** in which Jesus would have stayed. Byzantine architects frequently built domed octagonal structures over places of special veneration (the octagonal Dome of the Rock in Jerusalem, built by early Muslim rulers in A.D. 691, but designed by Byzantine architects, is an example of this type of structure). Other finds include an ancient olive press and a 2nd-century marble milestone on the Via Maris (Coastal Rd.), the Roman route that stretched from Egypt to Lebanon (an inland fork of the Via Maris passed through this district en route to Damascus). It was in Kfar Nahum that Jesus began to gather his disciples around him, saying, "Follow me, and I will make you fishers of men."

Capernaum's splendid 3rd- to 4th-century synagogue was built of imported white limestone rather than native black basalt. The ruins include tall columns, marble steps, shattered statuary, a doorway facing south to Jerusalem, and many ancient Jewish symbols: carved seven-branched menorahs, palm branches, and rams' horns. Again, this structure is not the actual synagogue in which Jesus taught, since it dates from several centuries after his time, but it may stand on the same site. It is interesting to speculate on what the proximity of Saint Peter's house to the synagogue might tell us about the position of his family in Capernaum's Jewish community. The excavations of basalt stone in the garden lead toward the sea, where you can still glimpse the remains of a small-boat basin with steps leading to the water. Admission is NIS 5 ($1.25/60p); the site is open daily from 8:30am to 4:15pm.

### Where to Dine
**Caper Naum Restaurant** MIDDLE EASTERN   Virtually the only place to eat on the northern shore of the Sea of Galilee, this restaurant caters to pilgrim bus groups

that visit the nearby Christian sites at Tabgha and at Capernaum. If you're an independent traveler exploring this corner of the shoreline, the restaurant can provide a convenient breaking point between the area's churches and ruins, especially if you arrive during a lull in the bus arrivals. You can stop by just for a light meal of hummus and salads or a soup, or you can have the house special meal of Saint Peter's fish, salad bar, and dessert. Though a mass-production place, the fish is tasty and the location is superb.

Near Kfar Nahum. ⓒ 04/672-4805. Reservations recommended. Complete meals NIS 70–NIS 80 ($18–$20/£8.75–£10); add 15% service. AE, DC, MC, V. Daily 9am–8pm.

## KORAZIM ★★

Four kilometers (2½ miles) north of the lake, on a rise of land, with sweeping views of the lake, are the ruins of **Korazim (Chorazin),** a flourishing Jewish town in Roman times. According to the New Testament, Korazim was one of the towns chastised by Jesus. For a thousand years the ruins of this village lay hidden under an ocean of impassable thistles until the land was cleared in the late 20th century. The centerpiece of this village is a large 4th- to 5th-century-A.D. synagogue made of local black basalt, heavily ornamented with carved grapevines, birds, animals, and images of people harvesting the bounty of the land. You can also visit lightly reconstructed streets, houses, and a ritual bath attached to the synagogue, which was apparently destroyed either by earthquake or during civil unrest in the 7th century. A ceremonial chair carved from basalt, which served as the seat of honor for the synagogue, is especially interesting. This is a hauntingly evocative site that gives the visitor a feeling for what a Jewish community in the Galilee was like 1,500 years ago. The national park office here (ⓒ 04/693-4982) is open from 5am to 4pm; in summer to 5pm. Admission to the site is NIS 18 ($4.50/£2.25) for adults and NIS 8 ($2/£1) for children.

At the Korazim-Almagor crossroad between Tiberias and Rosh Pinna is the beautiful guest farm and dude ranch, Vered HaGalil Guest Farm (see "Where to Stay Around the Sea of Galilee," below).

## LUNA GAL WATER AMUSEMENT PARK

Coming around the northern end of the lake, you reach a junction from which Hwy. 87 heads into the new capital of the Golan Heights, the town of Qasrin (p. 417). Farther down the eastern side of the lake, we come to Luna Gal-Hof Golan (Golan Beach; ⓒ 04/673-1750), the largest water park in Israel. It offers a variety of activities including water-skiing, pedal boats, kayak tours of the Jordan River, sail boarding, water parachuting, and more. There is an entrance fee of NIS 100 ($25/£13) for adults and NIS 80 ($20/£10) for children. Many activities cost extra, but the price is worth it, especially for kids. Luna Gal is open April to October Saturday through Thursday from 9:30am to midnight and Friday 9:30am to 5pm. From Tiberias, you can take bus no. 22.

## KURSI

17km (11 miles) from Tiberias; 7km (4 miles) north of Ein Gev

Kursi is on the eastern shore; according to the gospels, it is the "country of the Gergesenes" (or Gadarenes), where Jesus cast the demons out of a man who was possessed and into a herd of swine, which then plunged into the lake and drowned.

For many years, speculation existed about the exact location of Kursi (also called Gergasa) and about what kind of religious structure might have been built here in commemoration of the casting out of the demons. After the Six-Day War, a bulldozer clearing the way for a new road happened to uncover the ruins of a Byzantine church complex, complete with a monastery (perhaps the largest ever built in the Holy Land), dating from the 5th to the 7th century. The monastery apparently contained hostel facilities for the thousands of pilgrims who came to the Galilee during Byzantine times. Over the decades since 1967, a large basilica with an intricate mosaic floor has been uncovered, as well as a cave chapel that may have marked the place (according to the Gospel of Mark, a tomb) where Jesus encountered the possessed man. Most remarkable among the discoveries is the underground crypt where more than 30 skeletons were found, all of middle-aged men, except for one child. There is a place to buy votive candles and a snack counter. The national park at Kursi (© 04/673-1983) is open daily from 8am to 4pm (until 5pm in summer); admission is NIS 12 ($3/£1.50) for adults and NIS 6 ($1.50/75p) for children.

## EIN GEV ⟨⟩
12km (7½ miles) north of Tzemach Junction; 7km (4½ miles) south of Kursi

About two-thirds of the way south along the lake's eastern shore brings you to **Kibbutz Ein Gev,** one of the loveliest places in Israel. You can stop by and take a free minitrain tour of the kibbutz (ask at the office next to the Ein Gev restaurant). Nestled between the hills of Golan and the lakefront, Ein Gev was founded in 1937 by German, Austrian, and Czechoslovakian refugees. (It was former Jerusalem mayor Teddy Kollek's kibbutz.) These days Ein Gev has a 5,000-seat auditorium, which has presented some of the world's greatest musicians at its annual music festival. On the hillsides are tiers of vineyards, and elsewhere on the grounds are a banana plantation and date groves. Fishing is another big industry here; Ein Gev is home to the country's largest restaurant, serving Saint Peter's fish straight from the Sea of Galilee. The kibbutz also offers accommodations at Ein Gev Resort Village (see "Where to Stay Around the Sea of Galilee," below).

Not far from the auditorium, in a garden, is a bronze statue by the Israeli sculptress Hanna Orloff, depicting a woman holding a child aloft, in memory of a young mother-to-be from the kibbutz who was killed in the 1948 battle for Ein Gev. This settlement bore the brunt of heavy attacks in the 1948 war, and its position at the foot of the Golan Heights, below heavy Syrian military emplacements, made it a perennial target. From 1949 to 1967, Ein Gev kibbutz members depended on an endless maze of slit trenches throughout the grounds, as well as concrete underground shelters.

It's easy to get to Ein Gev from Tiberias by bus no. 22 or via ferry. Farther south along the lake is a campsite, at **Kibbutz Ha-On,** with its **ostrich farm** and moderately priced Holiday Village and Bed & Breakfast accommodations; continue south along the shoreline and you'll come to **Ma'agan,** with its **Holiday Village.** Ma'agan is very near the junction for the road to the hot-spring resort of Hammat Gader. (Ask at the Tiberias Tourist Information Office or at the Tzemach Junction for information on other campsites around the lake and in the vicinity.)

## HAMMAT GADER ⟨⟩
The **hot springs of Hammat Gader** (© 04/675-1039), east of the southern tip of the Sea of Galilee, are a favorite Israeli spa and vacation spot. Nestled in the valley of the Yarmuk River, this dramatic site has been inhabited for almost 4,500 years.

The springs can be reached by bus from Tiberias. Bus schedules vary according to season, so check with the bus station for a morning departure and afternoon returns. Hammat Gader is 22km (14 miles) southeast of Tiberias. If you're driving, it's about 8.5km (5 miles) east of the junction with Rte. 92 that skirts the eastern side of the

## The Grand Old Man of the Lake

Ein Gev's patriarch fisherman, **Mendl Nun,** an expert on Lake Kinneret's nature, archaeology, and fishing traditions, is the founder of the **Anchor Museum,** a museum of the lake's nautical history, at Ein Gev. Those interested in the ethereal Sea of Galilee, both in modern and ancient times, should pick up his book, *The Sea of Galilee and Its Fisherman in New Testament Times,* which is especially informative for anyone who would like to understand the setting for the events in the gospels that occurred around the Kinneret. Nun's writing is filled with real feeling for the place he has made his home for more than half a century. This and his other books about the Sea of Galilee are available at Kibbutz Ein Gev's gift shop beside the Ein Gev Restaurant in Kibbutz Ein Gev.

lake. As you wind down the steep road into the Yarmuk Valley, you'll pass several sentry and guard posts. The steep hillside on the other side of the valley is Jordan; you are also very close to the Syrian border.

The Roman city here was first constructed in the 3rd century A.D., restored and beautified in the 7th century, and destroyed by an earthquake around 900. The **ruins of the Roman spa city** are extensive and significant, and several important parts (the baths, the theater) have been excavated and beautifully restored. The still-apparent elegance of the Oval Hall, the Hall of Fountains, and the Hall of Pillars in the Spring Area point to the magnificence of this rustic Roman resort in ancient times. Don't miss the wonderful lions on the mosaic synagogue floor (5th c. A.D.). The ruins are set up as a **self-guiding tour** (ask at the park office about guided tours of the park).

The spa was known as El-Hamma to the Arabs and Turks, and the site is dominated by the minaret of a mosque that has fallen into disuse and been disfigured by graffiti.

**For present-day hot springs fans,** there are modern swimming pools, hot pools, hot sulfur springs, and baths for medical therapy and beauty treatments; there is also an **alligator farm in a jungle setting** with elevated walkways. For the kids, the park has trampolines and water slides. You will also find showers, changing rooms, a bar, and a restaurant. Admission Sunday to Thursday costs NIS 75 ($19/£9.40); on Friday, Saturday, and holidays, it is NIS 80 ($20/£10) and NIS 45 ($11/£5.60) after 6pm. Bring your own towel and bathing suit. Sit in the far end of the warm-water pool and feel the mineral water crash down onto your back from the waterfall. Residents of the area as well as visitors come in droves (especially after work), often bringing picnics. The many clay oil lamps found here may indicate the ancient inhabitants of the area enjoyed night bathing after a long day of work.

You'll find Hammat Gader's pools open Sunday to Tuesday 7am to 4pm; Wednesday to Friday 7am to 9pm; and Saturday 7am to 9pm. Hours constantly subject to change. Antiquities and children's activities close at 4pm. As if the ruins, hot springs, and alligator farm were not enough, a good **Thai restaurant,** the Siam (② **04/665-9922**), housed in a Thai-style building, has also been set up on the premises (if you dine at the restaurant, your admission to Hammat Gader is free). In 1993, there were rumors that alligators, either accidentally or as a result of a deliberate act of sabotage, had escaped into the Sea of Galilee; no sightings or hunting parties led to anything more concrete than the Loch Ness monster.

## KIBBUTZ DEGANIA

Located at the very southern tip of the Sea of Galilee, Degania is the country's very first kibbutz, founded in 1909 by young Russian Jewish pioneers. Without any real experience in farming, this handful of self-made peasants left city jobs to fight malarial swamps and Bedouin and local marauders. Much of the philosophical basis of kibbutz life was first formulated in this Jordan Valley settlement by its leader, A. D. Gordon. Gordon believed that a return to the soil and the honesty of manual work were the necessary ingredients for creating a new spirit in people. Although never a member of the kibbutz, he farmed until his death at age 74. On Degania's grounds a natural history museum, **Bet Gordon** (© **04/675-0040**), contains a library and exhibition of the area's archaeology, flora, and fauna.

Degania grew so quickly that its citizens soon branched out to other settlements. The father of Moshe Dayan, the famous commander (with the eye patch) of the Sinai Campaign, left Degania to help establish Nahalal, Israel's largest moshav (cooperative settlement). Eventually, some of the Degania members split with the original Degania over political and philosophical issues (especially about the nature of the Stalinist-era USSR). They broke away from Degania, establishing their own kibbutz right next door, and called it simply Degania B. The older Degania is now called Degania A.

Outside the entrance to Degania, there's a small tank—a reminder of the battle the inhabitants of Degania waged against Syrian tanks in 1948 (the members fought them off with Molotov cocktails). Today, both Degania A and B are thriving.

## HOF ZEMACH WATER AMUSEMENT PARK

Near Kibbutz Degania, there's another water amusement park called Hof Zemach (© **04/675-2440**). The carnival atmosphere includes a beach, sunbathing areas, grassy picnic grounds, a buffet, and watersports equipment rentals. Like Luna Gal, Hof Zemach is open only in season; check with the tourist office in Tiberias for current information.

## RIVER JORDAN BAPTISMAL SPOT

Kibbutz Kinneret, just west of Degania, has established a spot where Christian pilgrims can immerse themselves in the waters of Jordan in safety and tranquillity. The baptismal spot, called **Yardenit** (© **04/675-9111**), is 180m (591 ft.) west of the lakeshore highway (follow the signs). The river seems to flow peacefully, but its currents can be dangerous, so no swimming is allowed. The area set aside for baptisms is sheltered and there are guide railings leading into the water. Snack and souvenir stands provide refreshment and sustenance (no charge for the baptismal dip). A special lift has been installed to enable visitors with disabilities to enter the water with a minimum amount of difficulty. It's open Saturday to Thursday 8am to 6pm and Friday 8am to 5pm; the last baptismal is 1 hour before closing.

## WHERE TO STAY AROUND THE SEA OF GALILEE

**Ein Gev Resort Village** ⭐ *Finds*   Staying at this beautiful, historic kibbutz, founded in the 1930s (former Jerusalem mayor Teddy Kollek and his wife were among Kibbutz Ein Gev's first members) is a special pleasure. Both the kibbutz itself and the guest facilities are in so paradisiacal a setting that it's hard to believe this was a barren, stony stretch of shoreline only 65 years ago.

Partly set in a date-palm grove and a eucalyptus grove beside the lake, the Resort Village offers basic, modern family or group accommodations in five-person bungalows that include a bedroom-kitchenette with dining nook and a small bunk-bed room off the main room. The bungalows also sport picnic tables and a place to barbecue. There are also newer, standard double rooms in one- and two-story motel-style buildings overlooking the lake but a bit away from the beach; these are also equipped with fridges or small kitchenettes. Newer, more upscale units were built in 2000, and these are in the higher price category. There is a minimarket for groceries in the resort; Kibbutz Ein Gev, 1km (½ mile) down the road, has an excellent lakeside fish restaurant (p. 382) that offers free transportation and discounts for Resort Village guests. The Ein Gev Resort Village beach is the loveliest on the lake, but there are no special activities for children. Off season or midweek, see if it's possible to get a four-person bungalow for the price of a double: The bungalows are in the area right beside the beach, under the date palms.

Kibbutz En Gev, Galilee. © **04/665-9800.** Fax 04/665-9818. www.eingev.com (in Hebrew). 166 units. $144–$180 (£72–£90) double; higher on Fri–Sat, Jewish holidays, and July 15–Aug 31. Rates include breakfast. Discounts on Kibbutz Hotel 7-Day Package or in North America through ITC (© 888/669-5700). MC, V. The Holiday Village is 1.6km (1 mile) south of Ein Gev Kibbutz. **Amenities:** Restaurant; dining room, beach. *In room:* A/C, TV, kitchenette (some), fridge (some).

**Kibbutz Lavi Hotel**   This beautifully gardened religious kibbutz has a heated indoor swimming pool and offers comfortable and simple (and recently renovated) accommodations set in a garden. Buses travel to Lavi direct from Tiberias, and the ride takes only 15 minutes. There is a minimum weekend rate of one full board plus one half-board night, and holiday prices are considerably higher. Meal facilities are glatt kosher and there is a beautiful kibbutz synagogue with an adjacent religious study house/library, plus lectures on kibbutz life for visitors. Because the kibbutz is Sabbath observant, more-religious Jewish travelers feel comfortable here.

Kibbutz Lavi, Lower Galilee Post 15267. © **04/679-9450.** Fax 04/679-9399. 188 units. $144–$180 (£72–£90); add 70% for Jewish holidays and 50% July 15–Aug 31. Rates include breakfast. Discounts are available under Kibbutz Hotel Chain 7-Day Package. MC, V. Free parking. **Amenities:** Dining room; heated indoor pool; tennis courts; nonsmoking rooms; synagogue. *In room:* A/C, TV, hair dryer.

**Kibbutz Ma'agan Holiday Village** *(Kids)*   Located on the southeastern shore of the Sea of Galilee, with a guarded beach and vistas across the lake, Ma'agan sports 36 double rooms completed in 1999 (ask for these) as well as recently built minisuite units for four people, arranged in subtle tiers so that each suite has a water view. The suites contain a living room/kitchenette with a couch that converts into a bed and a separate bedroom in most units. Many guests here do their own cooking. This holiday village is geared toward families, with an outdoor swimming pool, children's pool, and a children's playground. It's lively, but not as pretty as neighboring Ein Gev (see above), which is less family oriented.

Kibbutz Ma'agan, Sea of Galilee. © **04/665-4400.** Fax 04/665-4455. maaganhv@netvision.net.il. 148 units. $166 (£83) double; add 30% weekends, July 15–Sept 1, and Jewish holidays; add $50 (£25) for suite, plus per-person charge. Rates include breakfast. Discounts available on Kibbutz Hotel Chain 7-Day Package. AE, V. **Amenities:** Pool; children's pool; minimarket; beach. *In room:* A/C, TV, kitchenette (some), fridge.

**Kibbutz Nof Ginossar Hotel**   This rather busy kibbutz hotel, heavily booked with tour groups, is located on the kibbutz nearest to Tiberias—only a 10-minute ride from downtown. There is regular bus service, but it's a better choice for someone with a rental car. The kibbutz is next to the lake and offers comfortable rooms; it has its own museum, outdoor swimming pool, tennis court, gardens, and beach, with kayaks, sail boards, sailboats, and fishing poles for rent. The second-floor dining room (kosher) has a great view of the Sea of Galilee. The guesthouse conducts a regular series of kibbutz tours and lectures with slides of kibbutz life. The **Yigal Alon Museum of the**

Galilee (p. 384), a media and educational exhibit, is on the grounds of the kibbutz, as is the locally famous 2,000-year-old Galilee fishing boat uncovered during a drought in the 1980s.

Kibbutz Ginossar 14980. © 04/670-0300. Fax 04/679-2170. ginosar@netvision.net.co. 170 units. $166 (£83) double. Add 30% July 15–Aug 31 and for Jewish holidays. Rates include breakfast. Discounts available on the Kibbutz Hotel Chain 7-Day Package. MC, V. Amenities: Dining room; outdoor pool; tennis court; watersports rental; beach. In room: A/C, TV.

**Poria Taiber Youth Hostel** Located at Poria, on the western side of the Sea of Galilee in the hills overlooking the lake 4km (2½ miles) to the southwest of Tiberias, this rustic, small Israeli Youth Hostel Association hostel in a beautiful setting can arrange for family or private rooms when the hostel is not full. It has kitchen facilities, clean sheets, and hot water, and is open all day long. Because it is so high above the lake, it's a bit cooler on summer nights than Tiberias itself, which is below sea level. This is a delightful inexpensive base for travelers with cars; there is no public bus, and it's often reserved for large groups who come with their own bus. Call for current information.

PO Box 232, Tiberias. © 04/675-0050 or 1-599/510-510 nationwide reservations. Fax 04/675-1638. poria@iyha. org.il. 44 units. $50 (£25) per person double with private bathroom. Rate includes breakfast. Cash only. Free parking. Amenities: Dining room. In room: A/C, TV, fridge, coffee/kettle.

**Vered HaGalil Guest Farm** ★★ Finds Kids This very personal place is the creation of Yehuda Avni, originally from Chicago (he immigrated to Israel in the late 1940s) and his Israeli-born wife, Yonah, who created a paradisiacal enclave with gardens, a pool, and buildings that fit in with nature where there had once only been acres of impassable thistles. Now their children and grandchildren, as well as a carefully chosen young staff, contribute to the attentive but informal spirit of Vered HaGalil. The guest farm and its facilities are ideal for those who want to ride and to intimately explore the Galilee countryside. It is also a beautiful retreat and a fine base for travelers who want to explore the region by car. A well-informed tour desk will advise you about all kinds of special places in the area.

There are three kinds of accommodations: 1960s Northern California–style **one-room cabins,** each with private bathroom, double beds, and shaded porches overlooking the countryside (some have Jacuzzis); **cottages,** with roomy living areas, Jacuzzis, and terraces overlooking the Sea of Galilee; and **garden apartments,** with 1½ bathrooms, a spacious living room, separate bedroom, and private garden. A family or group of four or five can easily share these accommodations. Backpackers are welcome (in limited numbers) to sleep on the lawn or in the barn for free, so long as they pick up their litter. Vered HaGalil makes special effort to adapt to the needs of visitors with disabilities for both accommodations and riding.

Yehuda Avni has designed trail rides by the hour, day, or week, into the hills or down toward the Sea of Galilee. Other planned tours last several days, exploring places such as Nazareth, and combining Arab meals with camping or hotel overnights to Gilboa, Mount Tabor, around the Sea of Galilee, and into the Golan Heights. The horses are beautiful and very well cared for. There are ponies for small children, and horses with extragentle dispositions for inexperienced riders.

Riding lessons begin at $30 (£15) for 30 minutes. Horseback rides cost $30 (£15) for an hour, $60 (£30) for 2 hours, $125 (£63) for half a day on the trail, and $300 (£150) for an overnight "Bonanza." There are also 2- to 5-day all-inclusive trips. All rides are accompanied by guides. Tours include the Mount of Beatitudes, Mount Tabor, the Gilboa, the Golan, Nazareth, and the Sea of Galilee. There is a 10% discount for overnight guests at Vered HaGalil, and if guests pay for riding in foreign currency as part of their hotel bill, the 15.5% VAT is also deducted.

M.P. Darom HaGolan 12385. © 04/693-5785. Fax 04/693-4964. www.veredhagalil.co.il. Sat–Wed $138 (£69) double cabin; Thurs–Sat $190 (£95) double cabin; Sat–Wed $164 (£82) double cottage; Thurs–Sat $225 (£113) double cottage; extra charge for apts; add $40 (£20) per child; add $57 (£28) per additional adult. Discounts for stays of 2 nights or more. Higher rates for Jewish holidays and July–Aug. Rates include breakfast and service charge. AE, MC, V. The farm is at the Korazim-Almagor crossroad, 3.5km (2 miles) past the turnoff to the Mount of Beatitudes. **Amenities:** Restaurant; bar and grill; outdoor pool; picnic area; equestrian stables; table tennis; horseshoes. *In room:* A/C, TV, kitchenette (some), fridge (some), hair dryer (on request).

## ROSH PINA

This small town, 26km (16 miles) up the winding road from Tiberias to Safed, was founded by Jewish pioneers in 1882 as a cooperative farming settlement. The name "Rosh Pina" means "cornerstone," and indeed this settlement, the first new Jewish community to be founded in the Galilee in modern times, became the cornerstone for Jewish resettlement of the region. A group of restored original **19th-century cottages** gives this sleepy community a bit of architectural charm, and in recent years Rosh Pina has blossomed with charming bed-and-breakfasts and restaurants. If you're staying in restaurant-impoverished Safed and have a car, you may want to head this way for a good meal. A number of spots in the community, such as Auberge Shulamit, offer fine vistas, and the town itself is a crossroad on the routes between Safed, Tiberias, the Hula Valley, and the extreme upper Galilee.

### WHERE TO STAY
**Expensive**
**Auberge Shulamit** ⚐   In the style of a French country restaurant with a few rooms for overnight guests, the Auberge Shulamit offers a romantic overnight hideaway for travelers, be they from Tel Aviv or Toronto. You can have a long evening of wine and fine food without worrying about driving home on the dark, hairpin-turn roads of the area. Guest rooms are country cottage in style, with four-poster beds, satin sheets, and down comforters; one room priced at $260 (£130) has a Jacuzzi. The rates include a wonderful breakfast set on the panoramic terrace in good weather.

David Shuv Rd., Rosh Pina. © 04/693-1485 or -1494. Fax 04/693-1495. www.shulamit.co.il. 4 units. $210–$260 (£105–£130) double; extra charge and 2-night minimum Thurs–Sat. Rates include breakfast. AE, DC, MC, V. **Amenities:** Restaurant. *In room:* A/C, TV.

**Mitzpe Hayamim Health Farm**   The name of this health resort/spa means "view of the seas," and from here you can see the Kinneret and, on a clear day, the Mediterranean. This is not a place to lay your head after a hard day of touring the Galilee. Instead, it is a peaceful environment in which you pamper yourself with Chinese, Thai, Indian, and Shiatsu massage, aromatherapy, herbal baths, health and weight-loss programs, and manicures and pedicures. Vegetarian buffet meals are delicious, featuring organically grown vegetables from Mitzpe Hayamim's own gardens, as well as fish and local cheeses and yogurt. Rooms are varied and come in a number of sizes; decor is simple but tasteful, stylish, and very personal. The heated indoor swimming pool is open year-round, and a small Jacuzzi is open until the wee hours. Treatment programs vary in price; the clientele comes in all shapes and ages. The location is outside of Rosh Pina itself, away from things, and the idea is to withdraw to a self-contained retreat. There are deals, even for weekends, advertised for Israelis, and if you work on it, you can get these somewhat lower rates, too. Children 9 and under are not permitted.

The Rosh Pina–Safed road, between Rosh Pina and Safed. ℃ **04/699-9455**. Fax 04/699-9555. www.mizpe-hayamim.com. 88 units. $356–$570 (£178–£285) double; add $70 (£35) Thurs–Fri and July–Aug. Rates include half board. Higher rates Jewish holidays. MC, V. Free parking. **Amenities:** Restaurant; dining room; cafe; bar; heated indoor pool; basketball and tennis courts; spa; business services; room service; massage; laundry service; nonsmoking rooms. *In room:* A/C, TV, minibar, coffeemaker, hair dryer, safe.

## WHERE TO DINE
### Expensive

**Auberge Shulamit** ✦ FRENCH   This romantic restaurant is the creation of an amazing couple much loved throughout the area. With wonderful views, it occupies the upper floor of a building that was a country inn during the 1930s and 1940s. The view eastward toward the Sea of Galilee and the Golan Heights is so good that the inn was used as the monitoring center for the Israeli-Syrian Cease Fire Commission from 1948 to 1967 (since 1967, the Israelis have occupied the Golan Heights). The menu here is excellent, rich, slightly old-world, and originally designed by Chef Gadi Berkuz, who is famous for his own style of smoked goose breast and spareribs and his list of smoked meats ranging from trout and filet of salmon to Cornish game hen. Beyond the smoked meat list, you might try filet mignon Rossini. In autumn and winter, look for an incredible Turkish chestnut soup or hot Russian borscht. Other first courses include grilled portobello mushrooms with a special barbecue sauce and a very rich Hungarian gooseliver on a bed of fried apples and onions. For dessert, look for candied chestnuts with vanilla ice cream. There is a full wine list, and house wine is served by the glass or half-carafe. If you care to stay the night, there are adjacent rooms that by Israeli standards are quite romantic (see "Where to Stay," above).

David Shuv Rd. ℃ **04/693-1485**. Reservations necessary. Main courses NIS 75–NIS 135 ($19–$34/£9.40–£17). AE, DC, MC, V. Daily 12:30pm–midnight.

**Babayit Shel Rafa (The Doctor's House)** ITALIAN/ARGENTINE   This is one of the quaint Rosh Pina eateries that truly serves up memorable meals—hearty, but verging on gourmet cuisine. The onion and beef empanadas are excellent, as are the South American–style cannelloni filled with veal sweetbreads and spinach, the chorizo sausages, rich stews, and veal and steak filets that form the heart of the menu. The setting is rustic, with lovely vistas of the countryside.

Old Rosh Pina. ℃ **04/693-6192**. Reservations necessary. Main courses NIS 75–NIS 135 ($19–$34/£9.40–£17). AE, DC, MC, V. Daily 12:30–11:30pm.

### Moderate

**Am-burger** ✦ AMERICAN/CONTINENTAL   The name of this restaurant is a pun—in Hebrew, Am-burger means "people burger," and it's definitely a people's restaurant: The food is top quality, nicely prepared but without the pretensions you usually find in so many quality restaurants throughout Israel. It's famous for hamburgers—quarter-pounders to three-quarters of a pound, made from freshly ground steak or lamb, and served with a variety of toppings—but there's much, much more. Look for fried and grilled calamari; gooseliver pâté; crabs in butter, garlic, wine, and ginger; delicious goulash and French onion soup; grilled giant shrimps; veal kabobs in *techina;* spicy chicken wings; and pastas, schnitzel, good salads, and vegetarian dishes. Everything is tasty and reasonably priced, and main courses are served with vegetables, rice, or potatoes. The location, in the Rosh Pina Shopping Mall isn't atmospheric or quaint, but locals who know the many atmospheric tourist traps of Rosh Pina come here for excellent food, served in hefty portions, and easy style. Steak plates for two may run around $40 (£20), but most dishes, including fish and seafood, are under $25 (£13).

In the New Ha Galil Shopping Center, Rosh Pina. (✆ **04/680-1592**. Reservations recommended. Main courses NIS 45–NIS 110 ($11–$28/£5.60–£14). AE, DC, MC, V. Daily noon–10:30pm.

## INEXPENSIVE

**Chocolata** *(Finds* *(Kids* CHOCOLATE/LIGHT MEALS   You come to this little place, legendary throughout Israel, for the chocolate soup and homemade chocolates, but there's also a range of good salads, pastas, and sandwiches. Just the aroma of the place can be enough to take care of your daily chocolate allowance. It's beside Old Rosh Pina's restored synagogue building.

Restored Old Rosh Pina. (✆ **04/686-0219**. Main courses NIS 30–NIS 60 ($7.50–$15/£3.75–£7.50). MC, V. Daily 9am–late at night.

## BED & BREAKFASTS IN THE GALILEE

There is a good range of bed-and-breakfast establishments in the region, including accommodations in private homes and in moshav and kibbutz facilities that are somewhat less expensive than those in the official Kibbutz Hotel and Guest House chain. Most tourist information offices in major cities (including those in Tiberias, Haifa, and Safed/Rosh Pina) now are equipped with computers that let you access the current lists of bed-and-breakfast facilities available throughout the Galilee. You can telephone for reservations ahead of time, or play things by ear when you arrive.

The **Kibbutz Country Lodgings** is the less-expensive list of kibbutz accommodations listed by the **Kibbutz Hotel Chain office** (www.kibbutz.co.il). Rooms on the country lodgings list are a bit less fancy than those in the more upmarket Kibbutz hotels, but they're adequate, often in beautiful locations, and give you a closer look at kibbutz life than the more insulated Kibbutz hotels. At some kibbutzim, the rooms are in special guest buildings; in others, you get an empty kibbutz member's room or apartment that has been especially set up for visitors. Rates are from $120 to $150 (£60–£75) for a double most of the year. In North America, you can book a 1-week or more itinerary of Kibbutz Country Lodgings bed-and-breakfasts as well as a package with a rental car through the **Israel Tourism Center** (✆ **888/669-5700** in the U.S. and Canada, or 201/556-9669; Israelhotels@worldnet.att.net). There is a booking fee, but it could be worth the hassle of doing things yourself. Check the Kibbutz Hotel Chain website so that you can select the kibbutzim you'd prefer. Once you get to Israel, you can book kibbutz bed-and-breakfast accommodations through the **Kibbutz Hotel Chain office** in Tel Aviv (www.kibbutz.co.il); however, the American Israel Tourism Center's office is better equipped to deal with your questions about accommodations and itineraries. *Tip:* There are all sorts of special deals such as stay 4 nights at one kibbutz and get a fifth at the same kibbutz free.

Another network filled with interesting B&B accommodations (known as zimmers) in the Galilee and throughout Israel is **Accommodations in Israel—B&B's, Country Lodging, Rural & Agro Tourism** (www.zimmeril.com). Another group of unusual, interesting budget options can be found at **Hostels in Israel** (www.hostels-israel.com/dynamic.asp?cid=9836), a network of 20 very good, unusual hostels and budget lodgings throughout Israel, including the Galilee and the Golan. Prices for a private double room in these establishments range from $75 to $120 (£38–£60) per night.

At the beautiful, centrally located, completely vegetarian **Moshav Amirim** (p. 403), you can arrange for bed-and-breakfast with a number of moshav families. All families in Amirim's B&B program can prepare superb meals for you with advance notice; there is also a wonderful vegetarian restaurant **(Dahlia's)** on the moshav. Bed-and-breakfast arrangements in private homes are not generally recommended for families traveling with children.

## 4 Safed (Zefat) ⊕

36km (22 miles) NW of Tiberias; 74km (46 miles) E of Haifa

From Tiberias and the Sea of Galilee, our next destination is the ancient and mystical city of Safed (Zefat, Zfat, Tsfat, Tzfat), about 45 minutes northeast of Tiberias and less than 2 hours due east of Nahariya. Once Israel's major mountain resort, Safed is now more religiously oriented.

Skirting the Yermak mountain range (900m/2,953 ft.), you finally climb up into Safed (pronounced with one syllable, *Tsfaht*, in Hebrew), which, at 837m (2,746 ft.), is Israel's highest town. This quiet city is built on three slopes and looks down onto a beautiful panorama of villages and tiered hillsides. Safed's name comes from a Hebrew root word, *tsafeh*, meaning to scan, or look—in other words, a lookout.

Safed's known history began in A.D. 66, during the time of the Second Temple, when Flavius Josephus started building a citadel on the mountaintop in the center of Safed. In 1140, the Crusaders again built a fortress on this peak, the ruins of which can be seen today. But whatever community existed here in those centuries was small and unimportant.

During the 16th century, the Ottoman Turks chose Safed for the provincial capital, and it became the primary government, economic, and spiritual center for the entire Galilee region. It was during this period that Sephardic Jews from Spain came here. Having escaped the horrors of Spain under the Inquisition, many of these Jewish intellectuals launched into a complex and mystical interpretation of the Hebrew scriptures called cabala (cabbala, kabala, kabbalah). The town became a great center of learning, with a score of synagogues and religious schools. The first printing press in the East was introduced during this period of intellectual mysticism, and in 1578 the first Hebrew book—a commentary on the scroll of Esther—was printed. During this golden age of Safed, Ashkenazi Jews were also attracted to Safed, and the entire community and its rabbinical scholars became renowned and revered throughout the Jewish world. At its height, the Jewish community numbered about 10,000, but by the 18th century, Safed was in serious decline.

In 1837, the entire town was leveled by a powerful earthquake after which both the Jewish and Muslim communities of Safed struggled on in increasing poverty. The wave of anti-Jewish rioting that swept British Mandate Palestine in 1929 was particularly severe in Safed, where the Jewish population was mainly elderly and religious. During the 1948 war, control of the strategic heights of Safed was crucial to control of the Galilee. Although outnumbered, Israeli forces held the town, and the large Arab population of Safed fled amid panic and rumors. Since then, the center of Safed (pop. 24,000) has had three parts to its personality—a resort town, an artists' colony in the abandoned Arab neighborhoods of the city, and the long-established religious community. Until the 1960s, Safed, with its cool nights, was Israel's favorite summer resort, but as Israelis became more international in their vacation habits, Safed's tourism industry withered; the once-vibrant Artists' Quarter is now relatively quiet, all the better for those who decide to explore the town. Although large apartment complexes have been built on the periphery, and Jerusalem Street is an architectural hodgepodge, the back streets of Safed, winding, cobbled, and resounding with the chant of prayers, are still medieval. July and August are the most popular months because of

Safed's cool climate. In the winter, it can be windy and as much as 20° cooler than Tiberias. Year-round, especially at night, Safed is usually the coldest city in the country.

## ESSENTIALS

**GETTING THERE** **By Bus** Buses run between Safed and Tiberias, Tel Aviv, and Jerusalem.

**By Car** Follow the main but winding roads from Tiberias, Haifa, and Akko.

**GETTING AROUND** Most city buses, such as no. 1, 13, 14, or 3, go from the center to the hotels on Mount Canaan.

**VISITOR INFORMATION** The **Safed/Hazor/Rosh Pina Tourism Association Office** is unfortunately not in Safed, but in the Galilee Mall at the entrance to Rosh Pina (© **1-800/323-223** or 04/680-1465; www.zhr.org.il, in Hebrew), open Sunday through Thursday from 8am to 4pm. Also, at the Safed Municipality Office, 50 Jerusalem St., there's often a shelf with maps and brochures, but no one in attendance.

**CITY LAYOUT** Safed is built on hilltops. The main part of town is compactly clustered atop one hill, while South Safed occupies another hilltop to the south, and Canaan perches on a hillside across the valley to the east. Although you may find occasion to go to Mount Canaan (a few hotels are there), you'll spend most of your time in the center of Safed. Jerusalem Street (Rechov Yerushalayim) is a circular street that girdles the hill, passing through the commercial street, the Artists' Quarter, and residential sections before beginning its circle again. Walking the circle should take only 15 minutes, and it is a good way to see most of Safed.

The **Egged Bus Station** (© **04/692-1122**) is at the lowest point on Jerusalem Street's circle through town, where it intersects with Derech Jabotinsky. Walk up to Jerusalem Street from the bus station and go right, and after 360m (1,881 ft.) you will come to the tourism office. But if you come up from the bus station and go left, you'll be headed toward the commercial district. In any case, once you find Jerusalem Street you can't get lost in Safed.

## WHAT TO SEE & DO

While there is much to see in Safed, a traveler unfamiliar with the city's crooked streets and unimpressive doorways may pass some of the city's best sites. I'll do my best to help you uncover the secrets of Safed, starting with its fascinating synagogues. But first, consider getting some local help by taking a **guided tour.** You can arrange for an informative walking tour of Old Safed with **Aviva Minoff,** an excellent licensed tour guide. The 2½-hour tours generally leave from the Rimon Inn, Monday through Thursday at 10am and Friday at 10:30am. For information, call © **04/692-0901,** preferably before your arrival. Note that modest dress is required when touring the religious quarter of Safed. Alternatively, look for the locally published book, *Six Self Guided Tours to Tzfat,* by Yisrael Shalem (approx. NIS 25/$6.25/£3.10); it's sold at Greenbaum's bookstore on the pedestrian mall in the center of Safed.

### THE SYNAGOGUES

During Safed's golden age in the 16th century, some of the synagogues here were devoted to the study of the cabala, a mystical interpretation of the Bible and other sacred writings in which every single symbol in holy writ has deep, hidden significance: Each letter, number, and even accent in the holy books has meaning beyond its face value. In cabala, an offshoot of mainstream Judaism, Hebrew words, numbers, and the names of God have mystical powers in themselves, and can be used to ward off evil and to perform miracles.

Cabalists believed that the system originated with Abraham and was handed down by word of mouth from ancient times. Historians of religion dispute this, however, saying that cabalism arose only in the 600s; it continued to be a thriving belief until the 1700s. Cabalism was, in a way, a reaction to the heavy formalism of rabbinical Judaism. It allowed for more latitude in the interpretation of holy writ and gained great popularity in the 1100s. The most significant cabalist text is the Zohar, a mystical commentary on the Pentateuch (the first five books of the Hebrew scriptures). For an interesting fictionalized interpretation of what Safed was like at the height of its glory as a Jewish religious center, I recommend the chapter, **"The Saintly Men of Safed," in James Michener's novel The Source.**

It's not easy to describe exactly where the various synagogues are—the religious quarter has few street names and is really a collection of alleyways and courtyards. Ask for "kiryat batei knesset," the synagogue section.

Among the most famous old synagogues here is the one named for the scholarly 16th-century **Rabbi Joseph Caro,** author of the *Shulchan Aruch* (the Set Table), which is the standard codification of practical Jewish law. Nearby is another named in honor of **Rabbi Moshe (Moses) Alsheich** (a renowned biblical commentator) and the only fully intact synagogue to survive the 1837 earthquake. Just a few steps away is the synagogue of **Rabbi Isaac Abuhav,** a sage of the 1400s; it contains an ancient Torah scroll said to have been written by the rabbi himself. Nearby is another, dedicated to **Rabbi Yosef Bena'a,** a famous 12th-century liturgical poet also called Ha-Lavan (the White).

The synagogue quarter has two houses of worship dedicated to the greatest of the cabalist scholars, **Rabbi Isaac Luria** (known as Ha'Ari, or "the Lion," an acronym for Adoneinu Rabbeinu Yitzchak, "Our Master Teacher Isaac"). Although Luria lived, studied, and taught in Safed for only 2½ years at the end of his life (he died here at the age of 38), his work changed the face of Judaism forever. The fortresslike Sephardic synagogue, graced by fine carved-wood doors, is built where the rabbi studied and prayed, at the edge of the cemetery. The **Ashkenazi Ha'Ari Synagogue** is closer to Jerusalem Street, at a spot where the rabbi is said to have come to welcome the Sabbath with his followers. Rabbi Luria was the author of the *Kabbalat Shabbat* (Receiving the Sabbath), the liturgical arrangement of prayers recited at the start of the Sabbath in normative Judaism.

The original building, constructed after Rabbi Luria's death, was destroyed by an earthquake in 1852 and later restored. Its ark, done in the 1800s, is especially notable. If you come with an official guide, you will get a better sense of how every nook and cranny has a story and sometimes a supernatural occurrence connected with it.

At the end of the synagogue area is a **cemetery** containing the sky-blue tombs of many famous religious leaders; they're the ones with rocks placed upon them as symbols of love, respect, and remembrance. There is also a military cemetery containing the resting places of soldiers who fell in all the wars, and nearby is a third cemetery containing the graves of Israelis who served with the underground Stern Gang and Irgun groups at the time of the British Mandate. Buried here are those executed by the British in Acre prison, including Dov Gruner, who is one of the best known of the outlawed fighters.

Another holy site is the **Cave of Shem and Eber** (or Ever), the son and grandson of Noah. This cave, located just off Ha-Palmach Street near where the Ha-Palmach stone overpass crosses Jerusalem Street, is said to be the place where Shem and Eber lived, studied, and were buried. Legend also has it that Jacob spent 14 years here studying before he went to the house of Laban, and that here he immersed himself in a ritual purifying bath before he wrestled with the angel. Today, there is a synagogue opposite the cave; if the cave is locked, you can ask the caretaker of the synagogue to open it for you.

## 20TH-CENTURY MEMORIALS

Going down the hill from Jerusalem Street, in the area between the synagogues and the Artists' Quarter, is a straight stairway: **Oleh Ha-Gardom.** Stand at the top of this stairway, where it intersects with Jerusalem Street, and you're within sight of a lot of Safed's 20th-century historical landmarks.

Oleh Ha-Gardom was the dividing line between Safed's Jewish and Arab quarters until 1948; that's why all the synagogues are clustered on the right-hand side, as you're facing down the stairway. The present Artists' Quarter is in what used to be the Arab section. Look up toward the citadel and you'll see a small opening in the fortress from which a direct line of machine-gun fire could be sent straight down the stairway, a British attempt to keep an uneasy peace between the two communities. The same day the British withdrew, the Arab and Jewish factions went to war. Look at the walls of the old police station, and you'll see it's pocked with bullet holes from the fighting.

Down Jerusalem Street from this intersection you can also see a war memorial, with a tablet describing how the fighting favored first the Arabs, then the Jews. Poised on a stone mount is a Davidka (little David), one of those homemade Jewish mortars that, though not too accurate or damaging, made a terrific noise and gave the impression of being much more dangerous than it actually was.

At the top of the hill, in the beautiful hilltop park, are the ruins of a Crusader fortress (unfortunately not well maintained at present) from which you can enjoy a fine view of Mount Meiron, Mount Tabor, the Sea of Galilee, and a smattering of tiny hill villages and settlements. This site, the highest in Safed, was once the scene of a 1st-century Galilean stronghold and later a 12th-century Crusaders' lookout post. A war memorial commemorates the Israelis who were killed pushing the Arabs back from the heights.

## MUSEUMS, EXHIBITIONS, SITES & LEARNING CENTERS

The **Artists' Quarter** is the area down the hill from Jerusalem Street between the Oleh Ha-Gardom stairway facing the police station and the stone overpass that crosses Jerusalem Street. Here you will find picturesque houses, tiny streets, manicured gardens, and outdoor art displays. Many artists have galleries in their homes, and the homes themselves are often so charming and atmospheric that some owners charge a small admission. This is a good place to think about acquiring good, inexpensive gifts and souvenirs. Many of the exhibitions sell reproductions of the artists' work. Prices vary, but many are fairly inexpensive.

**Ascent Institute of Safed**   An outreach organization for Jews who are interested in studying Jewish tradition, law, Jewish spirituality, and mysticism, the Ascent Institute offers a wide range of courses, lectures, activities, and events, and will help direct you to hospitality with local families for Shabbat and holidays—all the more unusual because of the mystical Safed ambience and history. You can stay in dormitory facilities at the institute for $20 (£10) per person per night, or $50 (£25) in a double room, with small room rate discounts for each course you take. This can be a rather intense place and is specifically designed for Jewish travelers who want to renew and expand their attachment to Judaism. But even if you don't sign up for a course or stay here, it's worth checking out Ascent's program of events, many of which are open to all travelers.

2 Ha'Ari St., Old Safed. ℂ 04/692-1364. www.ascentofsafed.com.

**General Exhibition**    While many of the houses in the artists' colony may be closed in winter, the General Exhibition, which shows a wide range of work by many Safed artists, is open year-round. The galleries display everything from paintings to ceramics to silk. You can purchase objects here, or get in touch with artists whose work you find interesting. Next door is the New Immigrant Artists Exhibition.

Old Mosque, Artists' Quarter. ℂ 04/692-0087. Sun–Thurs 9am–6pm; Fri 9am–2pm; Sat 10am–2pm. Head downhill from the intersection of Jerusalem and Arlosoroff sts.

**Habad (or Chabad) House**    Located on Ha-Maginim Street between Maginim Square (Kikar Maginim) and the Oleh Ha-Gardom steps, this is a Jewish history museum, with special exhibitions for children. The museum is part of an outreach program of the Lubavitch Hassidic movement.

Ha-Maginim St. ℂ 04/992-1414. Free admission. Sun–Thurs 9am–4pm.

**Hameiri House**    Located down the hill, in south Safed, Hameiri House is the **Museum and Institute for the Heritage of Safed.** It's housed in a historic 16th-century edifice, the restoration of which was done over a 27-year period, completed in 1985. Artifacts and documents portray the history of Safed's Jewish community; photographs and videos of elderly residents are interesting, especially if a translator is available.

Old City. ℂ 04/697-1307. Admission NIS 12 ($3/£1.50). Sun–Thurs 9am–2pm; Fri 9am–1pm.

**Israel Bible Museum**    Dedicated in 1985, this museum (previously the home of the Turkish governor in Safed) is full of inspirational, dramatic art pieces by contemporary artist Phillip Ratner. The building is lovely, with dramatic vistas, and well worth the climb up the staircase at the north end of the town park. Or you can enter from the other side, walking down from Derech Hativat Yiftah, which is the road that circles the citadel.

Hativat Yifta St., across from the staircase into the park. ℂ 04/699-9972. Free admission. Oct–May Sun–Thurs 10am–2pm, Fri 10am–1pm; June–Sept Sun–Thurs 10am–4pm, Fri 10am–1pm.

**Museum of Hungarian-Speaking Jewry**    Chava and Yosef Lustig, who survived the Holocaust, have created this museum and memorial to the world of Hungarian Jewry that existed before World War II. The exhibit includes artifacts, crafts, items of Judaica, letters, books, diaries, clothing, and other items that hint at both the spiritual and material world of this community.

Ha'atzmaut Sq. ℂ 04/692-3880. www.hungjewmus.org.il. Free admission. Sun–Fri 9am–1pm.

**Museum of Printing Art**    Safed was the site of the first Hebrew press in Israel, which was set up in 1576 and published Israel's first Hebrew book a year later. Here you can see a copy of the first newspaper printed in Israel (1863); a copy of the *Palestine Post* of May 16, 1948, announcing the birth of the State of Israel; a centuries-old cabalistic text printed in Safed; examples of modern Israeli graphics; and many other things.

Corner of Arieh Merzer and Arieh Alwail sts. ℂ 04/692-0947. Free admission. Sun–Thurs 10am–noon and 4–6pm; Fri–Sat 10am–noon.

### Plant a Tree

Just outside the highway entrance to Safed is a **Keren Kayemet Le-Israel (Jewish National Fund) Tree Planting Center.** At this site, Joseph Caro wrote in the 16th century, and here during the British Mandate, Palmach soldiers built a fortress, which the British destroyed, only to have it built again. The **restored fortress** was opened to the public in 1971, with an exhibition of documents, press cuttings, and photographs relating to the site.

Here the Jewish National Fund has established the **Biriya Forest,** where you are welcome to plant a tree with your own hands. It costs about $18 (£9). Hours are Sunday through Thursday from 8am to 2pm and on Friday until 12:30pm. For further information, contact the tourist information office.

## SPORTS & OUTDOOR ACTIVITIES

**SWIMMING**    As you turn into town, in a hollow to the right of the road, near the Central Bus Station, is **Emek Hatchelet Swimming Pool (⟨²⟩ 04/692-0217)**, which has been around since 1959. The area is beautifully landscaped, and has lounge chairs, tables, and big umbrellas. Admission is NIS 30 ($7.50/£3.75) for adults and half-price for children. There are two pools (one for children), game tables, a playground, and a minigolf course. Aside from showers and dressing rooms, facilities include a restaurant serving everything from ice cream to a full steak-and-fries meal. It's open daily from June through part of September, 9am to 5pm. Several days a week the afternoon hours are reserved for men-only or women-only swims.

## WHERE TO STAY

**Bar-El B&B**    This B&B, set in an old stone Arabic house with traditional architectural details, gives you a chance to experience life in Safed's charming artist's quarter. The B&B is two rooms with a kitchenette and bathroom, a view, and can sleep up to five people. Breakfasts are excellent—Genine and Rony Bar El are great cooks, have a catering business (vegetarian and fish dishes), and they're also very helpful with information about Safed and can plug you into interesting tours of the city and the area.

23 Yod Zayin St., Artists' Quarter. ⟨²⟩/fax **04/692-3661** or 050/786-8277. www.bar-el.com. 1 unit. $165 (£83) double; $30 (£15) extra person. Rate includes breakfast. Cash only. **Amenities:** Roof terrace. *In room:* A/C, TV, Wi-Fi, kitchenette w/hot plate for Sabbath.

**Ruth Rimon Inn** ⋆    This charming place in the Artists' Quarter, just a 5-minute walk from the center of town, is my favorite hotel in Safed. Part of the main building derives from the 17th-century Turkish period, when it served as a khan (inn) and a post office. The dining room was originally the stable, and you still can see where the horses were tied. In addition to the usual luxuries, you'll find acres of gardens, a swimming pool, more than half the rooms with large balconies, beautiful views, extra touches such as a guitarist in the bar on weekends, and some interesting history as well. A relatively recent addition has more than doubled the size of the Rimon Inn; the newer rooms are comfortable and freshly furnished, but not as atmospheric as the rooms in the older section. A variety of deluxe rooms are $60 (£30) extra per room. Special deals abound.

Artists' Quarter (PO Box 1011), Safed 13110. ⟨²⟩ **04/699-4666.** Fax 04/692-0456. www.rimonim.com. 82 units. $175–$260 (£88–£130) double; add $80 (£40) for Jewish holidays. AE, V. Free parking. **Amenities:** Restaurant; cafe; bar; outdoor pool; gym; spa; sauna; children's pool; massage; laundry service. *In room:* A/C, TV, minibar, hair dryer, safe.

## OUTSIDE OF SAFED

**Amirim Holiday Village** *Finds*    Amirim is a vegetarian moshav (cooperative village) set in a forested area with beautiful views of the countryside; it is famous throughout Israel for its relaxed ambience and good vegetarian food. Most of the moshav families rent out comfy guest rooms and there are also a number of private, rustic wooden cabins that are in great demand (cabin Nof 10 [www.nof10.com] costs extra, but offers a fabulous view). There are many dining choices in the moshav at veggie cafes and in a central restaurant, or arrangements can be made for a special dinner prepared by some of Amirim's most popular cooks. The moshav's swimming pool, open in season, is available to guests at the moshav. Contact Phillip or Yoram for reservations and advice about the kinds of cabins and rooms that might best suit your needs.

Rte. 886, 4km (2½ miles) north of junction with Rte. 89. ℂ 04/698-9170 or 698-0434. amirim.com/village/en. For reservations e-mail Yoram (hagalil@netvision.net.il) or Phillip (alitamirim@hotmail.com). Cabins $160–$220 (£80–£110). Rates include breakfast. Higher rates for certain cabins and on Thurs–Sat and Jewish holidays. AE, DC, MC, V. **Amenities:** Vegetarian restaurants and cafes; swimming pool; massage and beauty treatments; rooms for those w/limited mobility. *In room:* A/C (some), TV, kitchenette.

**Motke and Mazel's B&B**    Located 6km (4 miles) northwest of Safed, this B&B is located in a pretty, rustic location facing the mountains. Decent accommodations in Safed are so scarce that this place might be a pleasant alternative for visitors with cars. There are nicely decorated rooms with bedrooms, a living room, and kitchen areas. Delicious breakfasts include great omelets and homemade jams.

Moshav Kerem Ben Zimra. ℂ 04/698-0603. 2 units. $120–$160 (£60–£80) double. Rates include breakfast. Cash only. **Amenities:** Breakfast room. *In room:* A/C, TV, kitchen.

## WHERE TO DINE

The first thing you'll notice about Safed is its multitude of sandwich, snack, and falafel shops along Jerusalem Street (the main downtown road), open day and night, except for the Sabbath, when the whole town is closed up tight.

Safed is not a great place for fine dining, but if you have a car there are good choices in nearby Rosh Pina and in the surrounding countryside.

## COUNTRY DINING IN THE GALILEE MOUNTAINS
### NEAR SAFED

These choices are possible lunch or dinner excursions from Safed, but can also be reached from such places as Rosh Pina, Vered HaGalil, or even Akko, Nahariya, Maalot, Tiberias, or Haifa. Besides the opportunity to enjoy unusual meals, these restaurants offer a chance to explore remote parts of the countryside.

**Bat Ya'ar Ranch Steak House** *🐾* STEAKS    You'll need a good map or careful instructions from the tourist office to get here, but once you've arrived, you could swear you're in Wyoming. A series of rough wooden buildings house a horseback riding farm; up the path, past a beautiful vista point, is the restaurant. Grilled hamburgers, steaks, and chicken are served with fries or baked potato and salad in a rugged, ranch-style room. The quality is good, and the fresh air and views demand a pre- or postdinner stroll, if not a full-scale hike. It's out of character for Safed, but Israel is filled with such unexpected contrasts.

Birya Forest 5km (3 miles) northwest of Safed. ℂ 04/692-1788. Reservations necessary. Main courses NIS 60–NIS 120 ($15–$30/£7.50–£15). MC, V. Daily 11am–10:30pm.

**Ein Camonim** CHEESE/WINE    This dairy, specializing in goat cheeses, has set up an informal restaurant with picnic tables and benches so patrons can enjoy their products. You get a fixed-price platter of assorted cheeses, fresh-baked bread, a carafe of wine, a basket of raw vegetables, and dessert (go for the cheesecakes). Everything is fresh and delicious, and the pace of your meal is leisurely. One order can be shared; children eat for half-price.

Rte. 85, 5km (3 miles) west of the Kadarim Junction; 20km (12 miles) from Safed. © 04/698-9894. Fixed-price meal NIS 90 ($23/£11). AE, DC, MC, V. Sun–Fri 11am–8pm.

## SAFED AFTER DARK

Summer is the time for most of Safed's musical events. About eight chamber music concerts are held throughout the year, mostly in the summer, as well as a summer musical workshop. The **Klezmer Festival of East European Jewish Music** is the highlight of the summer programs. Check with the tourist office for the weekly scene. For piano concerts, check out **Hemdat Yamim** (© 04/698-9085) on the Acre-Safed highway, which usually has concerts every Monday and Saturday evening during the summer.

The **Yigal Alon Cultural Center and Theatre** on Jerusalem Street (© 04/697-1990) has everything from Shakespeare to ballet and popular folk dancing. It's named for the man who led the forces that liberated Safed in the 1948 war.

## EASY EXCURSIONS
### MEIRON

Eight kilometers (5 miles) west of Safed is the town of Meiron, a holy place for religious Jews for 1,700 years. Meiron has had a continuously Jewish population for nearly 18 centuries. When Judea fell to the Romans after the Second Revolt against Rome in A.D. 135, the mountainous northern Galilee took on many refugees. One early Meiron inhabitant, a 2nd-century Talmudist named Shimon Bar Yochai, was ultimately forced to hide in a cave in Peqiin, outside Meiron. There, according to legend, he wrote the mystical *Zohar,* or Book of Splendor, which is central to the cabalist belief.

Meiron is the scene of considerable pageantry during the holiday of **Lag b'Omer,** which occurs in the spring just 3½ weeks after Passover. Thousands of Orthodox Jews pour into Safed and there follows a torchlight parade to Meiron, with singing and dancing. Here they burn candles on top of Rabbi Shimon's tomb and light a great bonfire into which some, overcome by emotion, throw their clothes. In the morning, after the all-night festivities, 3-year-old boys are given their first haircuts, and the cut hair is thrown into the fire.

There still exists a **ruined ancient synagogue** from the 3rd century A.D., as well as **Rabbi Shimon's tomb** and a rock called the **Messiah's Chair.** Reputedly, on the day the Messiah arrives, he will sit right here while Elijah blows the trumpet to announce his coming. **Mount Meiron,** the highest peak in the Galilee at 878m (2,881 ft.), dominates the rugged countryside, with vistas that sweep virtually across northern Israel. The local **SPNI Field School** (© 04/698-0023) offers trail maps and information about a number of hikes through the beautiful, wooded Meiron Nature Reserve.

## BETWEEN THE COAST & SAFED
### MA'ALOT TARSHISHA & NORTHWESTERN GALILEE

Nineteen kilometers (12 miles) east of Nahariya, Ma'alot Tarshisha, with a population of 8,000, is at the center of the forested Northwestern Galilee (Crusader Castle Country), and sits astride the main road from the coast to the Upper Galilee. Its location makes it an ideal base for those who want to rent a car and freewheel for a few days around the region. The 1997 opening of the Hacienda Plaza Resort, formerly a private retreat on the outskirts of the city, made it possible to stay here in comfort.

Ma'alot is a development town founded in 1957; the municipality is united with the contiguous Arab-Israeli town of Tarshisha, whose history dates from Talmudic times. It's a pleasant, busy community, the center of the region's carefully planned checkerboard of agricultural, industrial, and natural districts. The town made history in 1974 when terrorists who had infiltrated into Israel from Lebanon took a school filled with Israeli children hostage; 14 children were killed in the attack. To this day security around every town and city in the northern Galilee is very tight.

## Where to Stay

**Hacienda Shalom Plaza Resort**    Another of the network of country club–style retreats originally built in the 1970s for the federation of unions and now turned into a hotel, the Hacienda is surrounded by 6.8 hectares (17 acres) of beautifully tended woods and gardens. With its heated indoor/outdoor swimming pool and crisp, clear mountain location, it's a tranquil, well-run base for exploring the whole of the northern Galilee, from Bar'am Synagogue in the east to the Crusader castles at Yechiam and Montfort in the west. It's also so convenient to the coast that it provides a good alternative to the rather undistinguished hotel choices in Akko and Nahariya. Rooms that have been renovated cost 10% more. Meals here are healthful but rather institutional. Weekend nights are $50 (£25) more per room.

Yefe Nof, Ma'alot. © 04/957-2255. © *6556 reservations from inside Israel. Fax 04/957-3735. www.shalom plaza.co.il. 115 units. $200–$250 (£100–£125) double. Rates include breakfast. Add 15% for Jewish holidays. AE, DC, MC, V. Parking. **Amenities:** Dining room; bar; pool; spa; sauna; basketball and volleyball courts; children's activities; room service; massage; laundry service; synagogue. *In room:* A/C, TV, minibar, coffeemaker, hair dryer.

## Where to Dine

**Kurdish Restaurant and Guesthouse at Shtula** *Finds* HOME-STYLE KURDISH    Sara Hatan came to Israel from Kurdistan as a young wife and mother in 1951 and raised a large family in the moshav of Shtula in the rugged Galilee mountains near the Lebanese border. Over the years, she became known as a fabulous cook, turning out Kurdish specialties according to the recipes she had learned from her mother, grandmothers, and aunts. In the mid-1990s, the front of her house was turned into a small restaurant where you'll find dynamite *kubbe* (cracked wheat meat or vegetable dumplings) soups, *shuftas* (Kurdish meat patties), stuffed vegetables, Kurdish breads, salads, pickles, and festive dishes such as special chicken and rice. A tasting menu of everything in Hatan's repertoire (call ahead) is NIS 160 ($40/£20); a less-extravagant complete dinner goes for NIS 100 ($25/£13). To talk to Hatan through an interpreter as she calmly makes her famous *kubbe* on a summer afternoon in the shade of her backyard fig tree is a special experience. Hatan never abandoned her house in times of shelling from Lebanon ("Who would tend my goats and sheep?" she asks). In 1996, trusting in God and the goodness of strangers, she made a dangerous (and illegal) trip to her childhood town amid the warring factions of Kurdistan (northern Iraq) to see the friends and neighbors she left behind as a young woman ("It was my dream to go back. If not then, when?"). She went in loaded with miracle medicines to distribute among old friends, and came back laden with the kinds of pots and pans she was unable to bring when she immigrated to Israel. Now her dishes finally taste "the way they're supposed to." Meals like Hatan's are made with more than just skill and traditional recipes. Her daughter, Ora, now runs the business. It's off the beaten track, but a worthwhile trip.

Moshav Shtula, Western Galilee. ✆ **04/980-6068** or 0050/269-406 mobile phone. Main courses NIS 40–NIS 55 ($10–$14/£5–£6.90); fixed-price dinner NIS 80–NIS 100 ($20–$25/£10–£13). AE, DC, MC, V. Sun–Thurs noon–8:30pm; Fri noon–3pm. Call to check hours and discuss the kind of meal you want. From Rte. 899, the road that parallels the northern border, take the turnoff to Even Menachem. In Even Menachem, you'll have to ask for the way to Shtula. The Kurdish Restaurant is on the main road of Shtula, on the left, not far from the entrance to the town. Look for a Coca-Cola sign.

## What to See & Do

**Montfort Castle** (R)   Perched on a mountaintop in the wild, densely forested northern tier of the Western Galilee, Montfort was originally built by French Crusaders; it was conquered by Saladin's armies in 1187 but recaptured by Crusaders in 1192. In the 13th century it was bought by the German Knights of the Teutonic Order who renamed it Starkenberg Castle and greatly added to its defenses. Despite its impregnable defenses, the castle was finally overrun by Sultan Baybars in 1271, who allowed its defenders safe passage to Akko. Goren Park offers a wonderful observation point, with a great sunset view of the castle; there is an uphill trail from the parking lot to the castle that could take from 30 minutes to an hour to hike, depending on your pace and fitness. SPNI can supply you with maps that will detail 4- and 5-hour hikes through the majestic countryside that lead to the castle.

South of Rte. 899, accessible by trail from Goren Park. Free admission. Open daily, 24 hr.

**Tefen Industrial Park Open Museum**   A castle of modern industry and technology, Tefen's attractions are its art gallery, the wonderful permanent collection of art that adorns the interiors of its building, and the beautiful contemporary sculptures that are part of the landscape of the complex. Among the very accessible Israeli sculptures in Tefen's permanent collection are Nubian sandstone pieces by Itzak Danziger, an op-art portrait of Theodore Herzl by Uri Lipshitz, and a large ensemble called *The Walkers,* in which Ofra Zimbalista created lifelike statues by casting plaster of Paris directly on human models. The casts obtained by this process were then removed, reassembled, and covered with a mixture of cement and sand. The Israeli sculptor Achiam's granite head of King David is especially fine. The pleasures offered by Tefen continue with a **Gallery of Modern Art,** offering well-mounted temporary exhibits, the **Museum of German Jewry,** documenting the history of that community, with special emphasis on German Jewry's contributions to the State of Israel, and a **Museum of Vintage and Classic Cars** displaying a collection of 40 vehicles, ranging from turn-of-the-20th-century motorcars to a reproduction of a Bugatti and an actual 1946 Chevrolet. After visiting Tefen, you might drive though the planned residential community of Kefar Vradim, the dream suburb for local professionals, and from there to the Israeli Arab town of Me'ona and on to Yechiam Castle via the scenic Rte. 8833.

Off Rte. 89, 1km (½ mile) east of Ma'alot Tarshisha. ✆ **04/978-2977.** Admission NIS 25 ($6.25/£3.10). Sun–Thurs 9am–5pm; Sat 10am–5pm.

**Yechiam (Judin) Castle**   The most easily accessible of all the country's Crusader ruins, Yechiam is an atmospheric, romantic place with windows and doorways framing vistas of the coastal plain it was designed to dominate. Probably built by the Templars in the late 12th century, Yechiam was destroyed by the Mamluke Sultan Baybars in the late 1200s. Its massive, strategic ruins were rebuilt in the 18th century by the local Bedouin warlord, Sheik Dahr El-Omar. Kibbutz Yechiam has renovated part of the castle and installed a series of restaurants, all quite pleasant, that have come and gone. At press time the restaurant was closed, but you should call to see if it's reopened before you visit. Yechiam Castle is one of the most romantic places to dine in Israel, and restaurant guests can wander through the ruins of the castle until 11pm. Crusader castles were made for twilight; watching nightfall framed by the stones of Yechiam is a memorable experience.

Kibbutz Yechiam. © **04/985-6004.** Admission NIS 18 ($4.50/£2.25) adults; half-price children. Summer daily 8am–5pm; winter daily 8am–4pm. 12km (7½ miles) east of Nahariya. Off Rte. 8833, which runs south of and parallel to Rte. 89.

## BETWEEN SAFED & THE UPPER GALILEE
### SASA & THE BAR'AM SYNAGOGUE

Kibbutz Sasa is on the northern foothills of Mount Meiron 16km (10 miles) northwest of Safed. In 1949, American and Canadian settlers built atop a 900m-high (2,953-ft.) hill and persevered despite many problems, including a polio epidemic. The thriving kibbutz is now the center of an area of forest reservations.

Just 5km (3 miles) to the north, the 3rd- to 4th-century-A.D. **Bar'am Synagogue** ★★ is probably the best preserved and most beautiful of all the ancient synagogues in Israel. Its location, in the wild mountains near the Lebanese border, is breathtaking. According to some scholars, the synagogue may have been in use through early medieval times. In the style of early Galilee synagogues, the building faces south, toward Jerusalem. Beautifully carved clusters of grapes ornamenting the main entrance testify to the town's abundant vineyards and orchards. At some point the design of the synagogue was changed and the main entrance walled over with large ashlars that can be seen in a 19th-century engraving of the ruined site, made from an early photograph. Archaeologists theorize that over the centuries, it became customary for worshipers to face both the Ark of the Torah and Jerusalem while praying, and the central doorway, on the southern wall of the synagogue, was walled over in order to build a Torah shrine. By the late 19th century, the ashlars walling the entrance, as well as other chunks of the synagogue, had been carried off by locals for reuse in other buildings.

Medieval through 19th-century travelers record the existence of a second, smaller ruined synagogue at Bar'am, now totally obliterated. According to one visitor, an inscription on the lintel of one of its doorways reads: "Do not be surprised by snow in Nisan [Mar–Apr]. We have seen it in Sivan [May–June]." Although this lintel stone has vanished, the inscription over the main doorway was preserved and carted off to the Louvre in 1861. Its message: "May there be peace in this place and in all the places of Israel." The **National Park at Bar'am** (© **04/698-9301;** www.parks.org.il) is open daily from 8am to 4pm (until 5pm in summer); admission is NIS 18 ($4.50/£2.25). The park is wheelchair accessible.

The ruins of the Maronite (Christian) Arab village of **Birim** surround the cleared areas around the synagogue. As noncombatants during the 1948 War of Independence, the residents of Birim had quartered Israeli troops in their homes. Late in the war, the people of Birim were told by the Israeli army to evacuate their town for what was promised would be a short time during a possible enemy offensive. They were never allowed to return, despite a ruling by the Israeli Supreme Court in the early 1950s upholding the villagers' rights to their homes. Since then, the former inhabitants of Birim, who all possess Israeli citizenship and are now scattered throughout the Galilee, have maintained an unending legal struggle to reclaim their village.

Past the synagogue, you can follow a path to the left and uphill to the **Church of Birim,** still maintained by the people of the village for weddings and funerals. If you climb the rather difficult stairs onto the roof of the church, you will be rewarded with a dramatic panorama of countryside so intensely loved by two peoples. Arabic graffiti on the church walls promise that the members of the congregation will return.

## 5 Upper Galilee & the Golan Heights

### TOURING THE REGION

From Tiberias or Rosh Pina, Hwy. 90 heads north toward Kiryat Shmona and Metulla. North of Kiryat Shmona, roads head west and south along the Lebanese border back toward Safed, and east to Hurshat Tal National Park, Baniyas Waterfall, and the Mount Hermon Ski Center in the Golan Heights.

**GUIDED TOURS**   I highly recommend a 1-day guided bus or group tour. Several are available from Tiberias. A 1-day tour of the Golan Heights will cost you NIS 140 to NIS 190 ($35–$48/£18–£24), depending on which tour you choose. **Egged Tours** (© **04/672-9220**) does full-day tours from Tiberias to the Galilee and the Golan for the same prices, going to about the same places. The Egged tours leave at 8:30am on Tuesday, Thursday, and Saturday from the Tiberias Central Bus Station; you can also arrange to be picked up at your hotel for no extra charge. The **Society for Protection of Nature in Israel** (p. 375) also offers quality tours and hikes of the region.

Yet another option is to check with Tiberias's major hotels, many of which will have information about private guided tours. If you want to start out from somewhere other than Tiberias, Egged and Galilee offer tours leaving from Haifa, Tel Aviv, and Jerusalem; check their information booklets or call for details.

### UPPER GALILEE

North of the Sea of Galilee are Israel's northern panhandle and a small area along the Golan border dense with natural beauty and tranquillity—at least off season when it is not flooded with Israelis on vacation. The region connects naturally into the Golan. If you're overnighting, try to make arrangements in advance. If you don't phone ahead, travel early from Tiberias or Safed and pin down a place to stay as soon as possible. Hwy. 90 will take you right into the heart of this area, passing by the outskirts of Rosh Pina (see earlier in this chapter).

#### FROM MISHMAR HA-YARDEN TO AYELET HA-SHAHAR

Along the main road is the turnoff to Mishmar Ha-Yarden, Galilee's oldest moshav, established around the turn of the 20th century and one of the few Jewish communities overrun and destroyed during the 1948 war. Beyond the moshav, crossing the Jordan into Golan, is the bridge called **Benot Yaakov (Daughters of Jacob),** believed to be the place where Jacob crossed the river on his return from Mesopotamia. The bridge is also on the ancient caravan route from Damascus to Egypt, which is part of the Via Maris.

On the left (west) side of the road is **Tel Hazor,** a prehistoric mound that serves as yet another reminder of this land's history. Canaanite Hazor was perhaps the region's most important city by far eclipsing smaller Canaanite towns such as Jerusalem; but after the Israelite conquest (around 1200 B.C.) the city's power declined. As a major city in the northern Kingdom of Israel in the centuries after the death of King Solomon, when Judah and Israel separated, Hazor was fortified in the time of King Ahab and a water system was built to divert the Hazor's water supply inside the walls of the city. After Hazor was destroyed by the Assyrians in 732 B.C., it never became a sizable community again, and fell into oblivion. Hazor is one of the most continuously and intensely excavated sites in the country. Yigal Yadin, one of Israel's greatest archae-ologists, felt certain the vast archives of Hazor (potentially rich with extra-biblical material) must lie buried somewhere in the enormous site, but so far, years of digging have not uncovered them. Artifacts from the area are exhibited at the **Hazor Museum** (© **04/6934-855**), near the entrance to Kibbutz Ayelet Ha-Shahar. Displays are from 21 different archaeological strata spanning 2,500 years, from the early Bronze Age to the Hellenistic period in the 2nd century B.C. The excavation of Hazor is recorded in the extensively photographed book, *Hazor,* by Yigael Yadin, whose writing makes archaeology truly accessible and exciting for all readers. Admission to **Tel Hazor National Park** (© **04/693-7290**), including the Hazor Museum, is NIS 18 ($4.50/ £2.25). It is open daily from 8am to 4pm and until 5pm in summer.

## Where to Stay
**Kibbutz Ayelet Ha-Shahar**    A short distance past Tel Hazor, on the east side of the road, this kibbutz hotel is a romantic, slightly historical choice, set close to the ruins and next to the Hazor Museum. This is not one of the more luxurious kibbutz hotels. There are two kinds of accommodations set among gardens: The better-grade 144 rooms of the kibbutz hotel (with tubs in the bathrooms) and the 62 rougher, some-what less-expensive rooms of the kibbutz's country lodgings (shower-only bathrooms, but rooms have great views). Hiking, rafting, and bird-watching expeditions can be arranged through the kibbutz.

Upper Galilee 12200. © **04/686-8611.** Fax 04/693-4777. www.zimmer.co.il/hashachar/english.html. 206 units. Hotel $135–$200 (£68–£100) double, country lodging about $30 (£15) less; higher rates for July–Aug and Jewish holidays. AE, DC, MC, V. **Amenities:** Dining room; outdoor pool; tennis courts; children's play area; synagogue; ani-mal sanctuary. *In room:* A/C, TV (hotel only), fridge (country lodgings only), coffeemaker.

## THE HULA VALLEY
The best view of this beautiful reclaimed swampland is from the **Nebi Yusha fortress** just off the main road, on the "Hill of the 28." A memorial in front of the British Tag-gart Fort recalls the time when these Hagana soldiers climbed the hill from Hula in the dead of night and fought to gain this strategic point. The odds were against them as they weathered a rain of machine-gun fire and grenades from the windows of the fort. When efforts to dynamite the building failed, the group's commander strapped the dynamite to his back, ignited it, and threw himself at a weak point in the wall. In all, 28 fighters died in taking this hilltop strong point, and today birds make nests in the many shell holes on the walls of the fort.

Beyond the memorial plaques is an observation point with a magnificent view of the valley below. This breathtaking area, which stretches in both directions as far as the eye can see, was once a vast marshland teeming with wildlife. It was the smallest of the three lakes fed by the Jordan—the Sea of Galilee and The Dead Sea are the other two. To Israelis who remember the marshland, the Hula was a lovely place—a home for water buffalo, wild boar, exotic birds, and wildflowers. Species of cranes and storks would migrate here, coming and going from as far away as Russia, Scandinavia, and India. To those who knew its thickets of papyrus, its dragonflies and kingfishers, and its tropical water lilies (some claim it looked a little like the shores of the Nile), the Hula was a bit of paradise. The Arabs had legends about the Hula's charms, where spirits walked in the evening mist luring young people into the mysterious marsh.

After years of wrangling with neighboring governments—as well as with the French and British—the Israelis finally drained the marshes after they achieved independence. Because the country needed every drop of water and every square foot of fertile land, only one small section of the valley was left as a wildlife preserve. Control over the Hula's waters was also a necessary phase of the Lowdermilk and other Jordan River diversion plans, which bring water to the barren southern reaches of Israel.

However, the project upset the ecosystem and harmed the region's natural aquifer. The draining of Hula Lake and the marshes also deprived millions of migrating birds of a strategic watering hole on the migration route from Europe and Western Asia down the Jordan Valley to Africa. In 1970, a reconstruction project to re-create the marshes was launched, and the Hula Nature Reserve was created.

**Hula Valley Nature Reserve** ⚐   The reserve today is once again alive with gray herons, cormorants, ducks, pelicans, wild boar, water buffalo, and other former species of the area that had died off or gone elsewhere when the swamps were drained. The best hours for a visit are early in the morning, especially in summer, when the birds and animals of the Hula are active. A new path has been constructed, suitable for wheelchairs. At the visitor center, free films about the reserve are shown. A combined ticket with the nature reserves at Baniyas, Dan, Gamla, and Ayun costs NIS 40 ($10/£5).

Right in the center of the Hula Valley, at Yesud Hama'ala (but still on the reserve), is the picturesque, restored **Dubrovin Farm,** housing an agricultural museum (entrance fee of NIS 12/$3/£1.50) and a moderately expensive rustic restaurant that specializes in smoked meats. The Dubrovin Farm, a series of stone houses built at the turn of the 20th century, was the homestead of a family of Russian Christians who converted to Judaism and turned this section of the Hula swamp into a model farm. In 1986, the farm was donated to the Jewish National Fund and opened to the public. If you decide to dine here, show your entrance ticket to the museum, and your admission fee will be deducted from the price of your main course. The reserve also has a snack bar and picnic area.

15km (9 miles) south of Kiryat Shmona and 3km (1½ miles) east of the highway. ☏ **04/693-7069.** Admission NIS 23 ($5.75/£2.90) adults, NIS 12 ($3/£1.50) children. Sat–Thurs 8am–5pm (until 4pm in winter); Fri 8am–3pm. Wheelchair-accessible pathways.

## Where to Stay
**Kibbutz Kfar Blum Hotel** ⚐   Set amid flowering gardens, with rushing streams on its grounds, this country hotel is one of the most beautiful of any of the country's kibbutz properties. In 2000, a new wing of deluxe suites was completed, but for nature lovers, the older rooms with their more established gardens are very enticing. There are rustic "deluxe rooms," larger studio rooms with balconies, and luxurious two-room suites equipped with Jacuzzi bathtubs. The office will give advice on fishing, birdwatching, and jogging, which are prime kibbutz activities, and will also arrange Jordan River kayaking as well as local tours and hikes. There's free access to the spa, with a rain cave, Turkish bath, and sauna. A full range of massage and beauty treatments can be arranged. The spacious lobby offers free Wi-Fi. *Tip:* In summer, there is a short, prestigious **Chamber Music Festival** hosted by the kibbutz.

Kibbutz Kfar Blum, Upper Galilee 12150. ☏ **04/683-6611.** Fax 04/683-6600. www.kfarblum-hotel.co.il. 130 units. $150–$280 (£75–£140) double. Add 15% for Jewish holidays. Rates include breakfast. AE, MC, V. Free parking. From Rte. 90 north of the Hula Nature Reserve, the turnoff to the hotel is to the right (east) toward Kefar Blum. **Amenities:** Dining room; bar; outdoor heated pool; children's pool; tennis courts (2 lit); basketball and volleyball courts; fitness room; sauna; children's activities; beauty treatments; massage; laundry service; nonsmoking rooms; synagogue; free Wi-Fi in lobby. *In room:* A/C, TV, minibar, coffeemaker, hair dryer, safe.

## Outdoor Activities

Kayaking in one- and two-person kayaks can be arranged at Kibbutz Kfar Blum ((C) **04/683-6611**). The cost for 1 hour is NIS 115 ($29/£14) per couple and includes transportation back to Kibbutz Kfar Blum at the end of the run. March to October is kayaking season. White water it is not, but a wet suit could come in handy. **Abu Kayak,** at Ha-Yarden Park ((C) **04/692-0622**), where the Jordan River runs into the northern end of the Sea of Galilee, rents kayaks and tubes at similar prices. Look for its 10% discount ad in area tourist magazines.

## KIRYAT SHMONA

Kiryat Shmona ("The Town of the Eight") is an especially attractive Israeli town, named for eight early Jewish pioneers who were killed in 1920 defending the area against Arab marauders. The town contains carefully laid-out residential districts, a busy bus station, and a fascinating monument to the turbulent past: three old army tanks, painted in bright basic colors, next to a gas station on the left side of the road as you enter from the south. It's largely populated by Israelis of Middle Eastern descent, with a smattering of new immigrants from the former Soviet Union. The surrounding countryside may be beautiful, but the area has sometimes come under attack by katushya rockets launched from Lebanon.

This is the "big town" in Upper Galilee (pop. 18,000), with a wide main boulevard: You'll find lots of fast, inexpensive falafel and *shwarma* places here if you're looking for a quick meal. At the junction of Hwy. 90 and Rte. 99 (to Banias and Nimrod's Castle), you'll find a small shopping center with a Burger Ranch (a useful navigation landmark and a place to get a quick bite).

## Where to Stay

**Kibbutz Kfar Giladi**    Halfway between Kiryat Shmona and Metulla, this kibbutz hotel is set on a wooded hilltop offering pleasant walks and great views. The kibbutz offers tidy rooms (some equipped for travelers with disabilities), good recreational facilities, and kosher dining facilities.

Upper Galilee 12210. (C) **04/690-0000.** Fax 04/690-0069. www.kfar-giladi.co.il. 175 units. $144–$186 (£72–£93) double. Rates include breakfast. Higher rates July–Aug and Jewish holidays. AE, MC, V. **Amenities:** Dining room; bar; heated pool; 2 lit tennis courts; basketball and volleyball courts; health club; spa; playground; synagogue; rooms for those w/limited mobility. *In room:* A/C, TV, minibar, coffeemaker, hair dryer.

## EN ROUTE TO METULLA

From Kiryat Shmona, you can head north past Kefar Giladi and Tel Hai to Metulla, then backtrack to Kiryat Shmona before heading east to Golan.

Situated along the Lebanese border, Metulla is as far north as you can go in Israel proper. Founded in 1896 by a Rothschild grant, Metulla is a pretty, pine-scented orderly little community where residents farm and cultivate bees. During the rainy season you can see a waterfall cascading from the Tanur Pass into the Iyon River. Because of its proximity to the border, the town has many soldiers and has experienced a considerable amount of military action.

Metulla became a bustling place during the Israeli invasion of Lebanon, but now that the troops are withdrawn it has settled back into picturesque serenity. With its limestone buildings accented by dark wood, cypress, and evergreen trees, Metulla is reminiscent of a Swiss mountain village, tidy and tranquil.

Metulla has a tiny museum, and the Nahal Ayoun Picnic Ground is by the Lebanese border, shaded by tall eucalyptus trees and furnished with picnic tables and campgrounds. Past the picnic ground, a rough road skirts the Lebanese border, heading east and south to the **Nahal Ayoun (or Ha-Tanur) Nature Reserve** (© **04/695-1519**) that runs along the entire east side of Metulla, along the Ayoun Stream, between Metulla and the Lebanese border. You can drive or walk into the reserve from this road; admission is NIS 18 ($4.50/£2.25) for adults and half-price for children. It's open Sunday to Thursday from 8am to 4pm (until 5pm in summer) and Friday 8am to 3pm.

The 27m-high (89-ft.) **Ha-Tanur (Oven Waterfall),** one of the loveliest spots in Israel, is the nature reserve's big draw. In all but the driest months, the falls tumble into tempting, shaded pools. There are two pathways to the waterfall: The long trail, originating in the upper parking lot, runs downstream and takes about 1½ hours (if you have no transport waiting for you at the lower parking lot, it's an uphill walk back to your car). The short trail begins and ends at the lower parking lot and makes a half-hour walking circuit that takes in some of the nicest parts of the reserve, including the falls.

If you have a car, or if you don't mind a bit of a hike, go to **Lookout Mountain,** the peak about 1km (½ mile) west of Metulla, for a bird's-eye view of the area.

## Where to Stay

Guests at Metulla hotels receive discount admission to the sports facilities at the Canada Sports Center, a large sports center in the heart of town that offers lots of arcades and activities for children, as well as an ice-skating rink and places for a quick snack.

**Alaska Inn**   Comfortable guest rooms, all equipped with Jacuzzi tubs, plus an outdoor swimming pool, sauna, and health club make this a pleasant place in which to pamper yourself a bit. Deluxe rooms in a separate wing cost 20% extra. The buildings look a bit Swiss, and the vistas are splendid. The desk will arrange tours of the area.

PO Box 13, Metulla. © **04/699-7111.** Fax 04/699-7118. www.alaskainn.co.il. 49 units. $150–$200 (£75–£100) double. Add 20% for deluxe double. Rates higher July–Aug and Jewish holidays. Rates include breakfast. AE, DC, MC, V. Parking. **Amenities:** Dining room; bar; tour desk; room service; laundry service; nonsmoking rooms. *In room:* A/C, cable TV, minibar, coffeemaker, hair dryer, Jacuzzi.

**Hotel-Pension Arazim**   This comfortable hotel in the center of town pays old-world attention to service and quality. It often serves as a communications center for journalists when things get hot on this portion of the Lebanese border. All rooms have central heating and four suites have Jacuzzi tubs.

Metulla 10292. © **04/699-7144.** Fax 04/699-7666. www.arazim-hotels.co.il. 34 units. $140–$190 (£70–£95) double. Rates higher July–Aug and Jewish holidays. Rates include breakfast. AE, MC, V. Parking. **Amenities:** Dining room (kosher); bar; outdoor pool; children's pool; tennis courts; business services. *In room:* A/C, cable TV, fridge, coffeemaker.

## EN ROUTE TO MOUNT HERMON & THE GOLAN HEIGHTS

East of Kiryat Shmona, along Rte. 99 to Mount Hermon—that snowcapped peak you've probably already noticed—is a beautiful national park, hot springs, a Crusader fortress, and a ski center.

**Hurshat Tal National Park**   This national park, located just 5km (3 miles) from Kiryat Shmona, is famous for its ancient Tabor oak trees, set among lawns filled with picnicking families on Saturday and in summer. Some of the trees may date from the time of Jesus and the Second Temple. According to Muslim legend, 10 soldiers of the Prophet Muhammad camped here at the time of the Muslim conquest in A.D. 638. Finding no place to tie their horses, they thrust their staffs into the ground and used them as hitching posts. When they awoke the next morning, the staffs had become enormous trees shading a paradise of wildflowers. The Dan River, a tributary of the

Jordan, passes down this valley, collecting in a series of artificial lakes and ponds. The freezing (or refreshing) swimming pool (with water slides) in the park is also fed by these streams. Over the years, this tranquil, poetic spot has been turned into a summer playground, packed with Israeli families who come here to swim, picnic, and camp. But in winter and early spring, Horshat Tal remains a lush green, magical place. You can fish in the fishponds and keep your catch.

Off Rte. 99. (C) 04/694-2440. Admission NIS 35 ($8.75/£4.40) adults; NIS 20 ($5/£2.50) children. Daily 8am–4pm (until 5pm in summer). Bus: 26, 27, or 36 from Kiryat Shmona stop close to the park entrance.

## Where to Stay

**Kibbutz Ha-Goshrim Hotel**    Located next door to the beautiful Hurshat Tal National Park, this very popular kibbutz guesthouse is another good base for exploring Upper Galilee and the Golan. Founded by Turkish Jews in 1948, it has numerous recreational options and offers a watersports program that includes kayak rentals and trips. Rooms are scattered in several buildings; ask to see the superior rooms, which are newer and a bit higher in price, and decide if you feel they're worth the difference. Some rooms can accommodate up to two children; there are also rooms for travelers with disabilities. The nearby Pub Gosh (below) is a good dining choice in an area with few options.

Kibbutz Ha-Goshrim. (C) **04/681-6000.** Fax 04/681-6002. www.hagoshrim-hotel.co.il. 180 units. $112–$170 (£56–£85) double. Add 15% for Jewish holidays. Rates include breakfast. AE, MC, V. **Amenities:** Dining room; pool; tennis courts; fitness room (fee); Jacuzzi; sauna; children's playground; seasonal children's activities; laundry service; synagogue; rooms for those w/limited mobility. *In room:* A/C, TV, minibar, coffeemaker, hair dryer.

## Where to Dine

**Pub Gosh** VEGETARIAN/FISH    For those seeking a good restaurant in this part of the countryside, Pub Gosh, run by Kibbutz Hagoshrim, is a worthy choice. **Note:** It's kosher, but open 7 days a week—food is brought from the kibbutz hotel, which has a kashrut certificate and operates on Shabbat. The pub is a rustic wooden building (blessedly heated and air-conditioned in season) set in a forest beside a stream. The menu includes hefty portions of soups, salads, pasta dishes, pizzas, and the restaurant's star attraction, excellent local trout prepared in a number of ways. The soups, meals in themselves, are served inside a small loaf of country bread (quite a stylish presentation for a kibbutz-run place), but as at many restaurants, the stock seems powder-based. In good weather, there are outdoor tables set alongside the stream.

Kibbutz Hagoshrim, Upper Galilee. (C) **04/695-6753.** Main courses NIS 45–NIS 70 ($11–$18/£5.60–£8.75). AE, MC, V. May–Oct daily noon–10pm or later; call to verify schedule.

## TEL DAN

The prehistoric settlement at Tel Dan, 9km (5½ miles) east of Kiryat Shmona and then 3km (1½ miles) north, was a thriving Canaanite community when Joshua led the conquering Israelites here more than 3,000 years ago. In fact, Dan was the northern limit of the Promised Land (the southern limit was Beersheva).

**Tel Dan Nature Reserve**    Cold-water springs gush right up from the ground here, forming the Dan River, which is one of the three principal sources of the Jordan River. The dense vegetation around the site is lovely. Swimming is not permitted. Excavations in the reserve, which include a pre-Israelite cult center, are ongoing. In 1993, an inscription bearing what may be a reference to the "House of David" was found here, an exciting discovery, as it would be the first extra-biblical mention of King David's royal family to be discovered. You can also see a very impressive, heavily reconstructed **City Gate** from the Israelite period (9th c. B.C.), as well as an earlier, arched, Canaanite-era gate, which may be the earliest evidence of the use of an arch ever uncovered by archaeologists.

There is also a 700-year-old Arabic stone flour mill. Reconstructed by the National Parks Authority, it is run by water power, and is near a 2,000-year-old pistachio tree, walking trails, and picnic areas. The nature reserve has wheelchair-accessible paths.

If you come by bus, it's a 30-minute walk from Kibbutz Dan bus stop. Buses run between Kibbutz Dan and Kiryat Shmona about every 2 hours. You can buy a combination ticket for all nature reserves in the area for NIS 40 ($10/£5).

In nearby Kibbutz Dan is a small nature museum, **Bet Ussishkin** (✆ **04/694-1704**), with exhibits covering the flora, fauna, geology, topography, and history of the region. Bet Ussishkin also contains a Society for the Protection of Nature in Israel (SPNI) station where you can get excellent maps and information about hiking safely in the Golan. *Important:* You must check in at an SPNI station before hiking independently through the Golan Heights. You can also pick up information about seasonal bird-watching in the area here. Hours are Sunday through Thursday from 8:30am to 4:30pm, Friday 8:30am to 3pm, and Saturday 9:30am to 4:30pm. Admission is NIS 20 ($5/£2.50). Keep your receipt: The admission fee at Bet Ussishkin gets you a discount at the Tel Dan Nature Reserve.

Rte. 99, near Kibbutz Dan. ✆ **04/695-1579**. www.parks.org.il. Admission NIS 23 ($5.75/£2.90) adults; half-price children. Sat–Thurs 8am–4pm; Fri 8am–3pm.

### Where to Dine

**Dag Al HaDan Trout Restaurant** ✿ *Kids* FISH  Set amid the streams of the Dan River's headwaters, this is a delightful spot for a meal, except on weekends, when it often gets frantically busy. You can eat outside, on tables beside willow trees and brooks, or on picnic tables inside the rough stone and wood pavilion. A quick walk around the trout pools and tanks will assure you that the trout is spectacularly fresh—you can have yours grilled with garlic butter sauce, smoked with mustard sauce, baked with herbs and a lemon or mushroom sauce, or fried with almond sauce. You can also order salmon filet or steak, but with trout so fresh and so famous, why order anything else? You can start your meal with an assortment of small Middle Eastern salads (included with homemade bread in the dinner price), or you can just stop for something lighter, such as a salad and delicious fish soup. There is a grilled shish kabob children's plate for NIS 45 ($11/£5.60), and a good assortment of beers, nonalcoholic drinks, and desserts. Friday and Saturday until noon, Dag Al HaDan serves a great breakfast/brunch with salads, eggs, local cheeses, and a choice of smoked fish.

Off Kiryat Shmona-Banias Rd. ✆ **04/695-0225**. Reservations necessary weekends. Main courses NIS 75–NIS 90 ($19–$23/£9.40–£11). AE, DC, MC, V. Sun–Thurs noon–11pm; Fri–Sat 8:30am–11pm.

## THE GOLAN HEIGHTS

This wild plateau, with its vistas of the Galilee below, is especially worthy of a visit. Occupied since 1967 by Israel, which captured the Golan from Syria during the Six-Day War, and annexed it for security reasons in 1981, the Golan Heights are lightly populated with Druze villages and Jewish towns constructed by the Israeli government specifically for security purposes. Unlike in Gaza and the West Bank, the period of Israeli control in the Golan has been marked by economic development, prosperity, and relatively tranquil relations between the Druze and the Israeli settlers. The Israeli infrastructure on the Golan now includes a network of orchards, cattle ranches, wineries, nature reserves, and country B&Bs that Israelis and visitors have come to treasure. The future of the Golan is not entirely clear. Prime Ministers Rabin, Barak, and Olmert have been quoted as stating that in exchange for a genuine peace with Syria, most of the Golan may be returned to that country, with the Golan overlooking the Sea of Galilee demilitarized to prevent possible sniping or other attacks on the Galilee. Syrian leaders insist on the return of every inch of land and access to the eastern shore of the Sea of Galilee. Meanwhile, the Golan affords visitors the pleasure of flowing winter springs and waterfalls, and a variety of ancient sites ranging from **prehistoric dolmens** to the ruins of 1,900-year-old synagogues, as well as Israel's only ski resort and a number of its best **wineries.** The region's most spectacular ancient site is the **ruin of Gamla,** a Jewish town destroyed in A.D. 67 during the First Revolt against Rome, located on an especially beautiful and dramatic mountain ridge. The Golan is one of the areas where a rental car is most useful, although with luck, you might find a well-informed cabdriver in Tiberias to take you around the Golan for a special full or half-day deal. In summer, the plateau is blazing hot; in winter it can be bitterly cold and windy.

## VISITOR INFORMATION & TOURING THE REGION

The **Golan Tourist Association** has set up a fabulous website (www.etour.golan. org.il) that includes detailed information on everything in the Golan, from accommodations, hiking in nature reserves, visiting ancient sites, biking, wineries, restaurants, festivals, special events, history, and politics to kite surfing in the Kinneret and observing the Griffon Vulture nesting season in the Golan's interior. When you get to the Golan's "capital," the village of Qasrin, be sure to visit the state-of-the-art exhibit, *Golan Magic,* which will give you an incredible preview of what to see and do in the Golan (p. 417).

Hiking in the Golan Heights must be arranged in advance through an SPNI field school or information station. The SPNI Field School in Qasrin (© **04/696-1234**) is on Zavitan Street, off Daliyot Street; in the Upper Galilee SPNI is at the Beit Ussishkin Museum at Kibbutz Dan (© **04/694-1704**).

**Banias (Hermon River) Nature Reserve** ⚘    For thousands of years, Banias, with its cold, flowing waters, has been a holy place to a dozen peoples and half a dozen religions. Banias figures in the New Testament as the place where Jesus designated Peter as "the rock" on which the church would be built. In ancient times the Canaanites, and later the Greeks, built shrines and temples here. The Greek name Paneas (after Pan, the god of pastures, flocks, and shepherds) was modified in Arabic to Banias, as Arabic has no "p" sound. Though an earthquake collapsed the impressive grotto of the Greeks, you can still see little shrines, most of which date from the Hellenistic period. Under the Romans, the settlement was named Caesarea Philippi after Philip, son of Herod, who followed in the ancients' ways and also built a temple.

Christians built a chapel to Saint George on the hillside, which Muslims later converted into a shrine dedicated to El-Khader (the prophet Elijah). A steep path still leads up to the shrine. While the shrine is usually closed, you should still go up for the view.

Off Rte. 99. © **04/690-2577.** Admission NIS 23 ($5.75/£2.90); combined admission to Nimrod's Castle and Banias NIS 31 ($7.75/£3.90) adults; half-price children. Sat–Thurs 8am–4pm (until 5pm in summer); Fri 8am–4pm.

## WHAT TO SEE & DO
### Banias Waterfall

The beautiful and legendary **Banias Waterfall** ⚘⚘ is less than a mile inside the Golan, some 15km (9 miles) from Kiryat Shmona and less than 1km (½ mile) off the main road. Banias is one of the principal sources of the Jordan River. Head down to the stream for a look at the waters, which begin several hundred feet higher on the Hermon slopes. From here the destination, after dropping into the Jordan River, is the Sea of Galilee. Jordan (from "Yared-Dan") means "descending from Dan," and the river, whose origins are right here, picks up again south of the Sea of Galilee for a twisting, turning run of 113km (70 miles) before emptying into The Dead Sea and becoming a stagnant, oily mixture.

This ancient site has been landscaped by the Nature Reserves Authority. You can take a fast dip, if you can stand the icy waters. The Crusaders fortified a nearby hilltop with what is now called **Nimrod's Castle** (see below). Buying the combined Banias/Nimrod's Castle admission ticket and hiking or driving over to explore the castle is recommended.

You can buy a combination ticket to the Banias, Hula Tel Dan, Nahal Ayoun, and Gamla nature reserves for NIS 40 ($10/£5); combined entrance to Nimrod Castle and Banias NIS 31 ($7.75/£3.90) for adults, half-price for children.

**Nimrod's Castle (Kalat Nimrod)** ⚔   Nimrod's Castle, now a national park, is one of the biggest and best-preserved Crusader ruins in the area and has a spectacular view. You can visit by car, but in cooler weather the 1½- to 2-hour hike from Banias is well worth the effort.

As you come under the wall of the castle (built in the 13th c. to stop invading Crusaders) you'll see the narrow vertical slits where archers were once stationed. Inside, see many deep water-filled cisterns, some 9m (30 ft.) deep.

As you can see from up here, whoever controlled Nimrod in bygone days controlled the traffic from Lebanon to Tiberias and the Jordan Valley. To the left is the zigzagging cleft of Banias rift. In a lush, green pocket farther on, you see Tel Dan kibbutz, then a series of carp ponds, Kiryat Shmona on the hills beyond, and the rectangles of brown and green of the Hula Valley extending southward for miles and miles. Behind the castle to the north sits Mount Hermon, rising to 1,950m (6,398 ft.).

Rte. 989, .5km (1 mile) northeast and uphill from Banias Nature Reserve (follow signs to Kallat Namrud). ℂ 04/698-4316 mobile phone. Combined admission to Nimrod's Castle and Banias NIS 31 ($7.75/£3.90); half-price children. Sat–Thurs 8am–4pm; Fri 8am–2pm; closing 1 hr. later in summer.

## The Druze Villages

The Druze villages on the slopes of Mount Hermon are inhabited by the fiercely independent people whose religion is something of a mystery to outsiders. They are farmers for the most part, and don't mind tilling the steep, rocky ground as long as they are left in peace. For the past 1,000 years, the Druze have had considerable autonomy. It just wasn't worth the time and expense to conquer them.

The Druze religion is an offshoot of Islam, but very different from either of the major branches, Sunni and Shiite. The beliefs of the Druze religion are kept secret from outsiders, but the sect reveres the Fatimid caliph Al Hakim (996–1021), the sixth of the Fatimid line, who in the year 1020 proclaimed himself to be an incarnation of God. The Druze also revere Jethro, the Midianite father-in-law of Moses.

In public life the Druze believe in loyalty to the countries in which they reside, and Israeli Druze have served with distinction in the Israeli army. The Druze of the Golan, however, though they have had a tranquil and prosperous existence since the Israeli occupation began in 1967, also feel they must uphold their commitment to Syria, and most publicly support a return of the Golan Heights to Syrian control.

Between the Druze villages of Majdal Shams and Mas'ada is the small lake of **Birkhet Ram,** now used as a reservoir. Although its round shape hints at a volcanic origin, Birkhet Ram was actually formed by the action of underground springs. Visit the **Birkhet Ram Restaurant** if you're hungry, because you won't find many restaurants in Golan, and it offers the best view of the lake from its balcony. It's open from 8am to 6pm. There's a good falafel stand and snack shop here as well—any of the little restaurants in the Druze towns is guaranteed to be good.

## En Route to Qasrin

After the slow, bouncing ride back from Hermon to the main road, the road becomes well paved. Fifteen kilometers (9 miles) south of Mas'ada is an observation point from which you can see across the Israeli-Syrian border, which is patrolled by a UN peacekeeping force. In the distance is the abandoned Syrian border city of Kuneitra; beyond is the wide, barren plain that leads to Damascus.

**Kuneitra** (or Quneitra, now in Syria) was the chief Syrian city in Golan before the war. It was occupied by Israel from 1967 to 1974. Under terms of a disengagement withdrawal brokered by the United States, Kuneitra was returned to Syria. Israel had hoped that a repopulated Kuneitra would be incentive for Syria to defuse tension on the border, but the city has remained largely deserted, one of many ghost towns created by politics and war.

Nearby, on the Israeli side of the border, is **Kibbutz Merom Ha-Golan,** a commune of settlers from all over the world initially set up by the Israeli government to help secure the Golan border.

## QASRIN

Qasrin is 20km (12 miles) from Merom Ha-Golan; 38km (24 miles) from Tiberias. Situated in the center of Golan, the new (1977) Israeli "capital" of Golan, Qasrin (Kazrin, Katzirin), with a present population of about 3,000, was founded on the site of a 2nd- to 3rd-century Jewish town of the same name. Qasrin is the region's administrative hub, with new apartments, offices, schools, factories, and a few shops. It is a good place to stop for groceries or snacks (there are a few falafel stands and snack bars on the main street) and emergency services. And there are many interesting sights nearby. Bus service is from Kiryat Shmona (bus no. 55).

A few unlikely contrasts serve as strong reminders of the town's strategic locale: a pleasant suburban town surrounded by barbed wire; bomb shelters encircled by rose gardens; and bomb shelters that house recreation centers, clubhouses, and music halls. Qasrin is known for its sweet, **natural mineral water,** which is bottled and exported to the rest of the country.

### What to See & Do

*Golan Magic* ⚡  Located in a new mall at the eastern entrance of Qasrin, this is the **Golan Tourist Association's** dynamic, high-tech exposition of what to see and do in the Golan and a must for visitors before venturing farther into the area. There's a 180-degree panoramic screen film presentation of the Golan's highlights, plus a humungous three-dimensional topographical map of the Golan that helps you to understand the area you'll be traversing. It's right next to the Golan Heights winery, the Eden mineral water bottling factory, and an olive oil factory, all of which offer tours, so you can plunge into the Golan's industrial magic as soon as you step outside the exhibit.

In the eastern shopping mall. ☎ **04/696-3625** or 052/388-2882. www.etour.golan.org.il. Free admission. Sun–Thurs 9am–6pm; Fri 9am–3pm.

**Golan Archaeological Museum and Ancient Qasrin Park** 𝕴    A small museum of regional history that is modern, light, and well planned is the heart of this complex. Here you can also see an exhibit and short film about the Golan stronghold of Gamla, destroyed by the Romans in A.D. 67 during the First Revolt against Rome. The museum is open Sunday through Thursday from 8am to 5pm, Friday from 8am to 3pm, and Saturday from 10am to 4pm.

The **Ancient Qasrin Archaeological Park** 𝕴 (✆ **04/696-2412**) is just outside Qasrin to the southeast along the main road. Here you'll find the partially restored ancient synagogue of Qasrin, dating from the Byzantine and early Arab periods. You'll also find two reconstructed houses from the Talmudic era, complete with reproductions of furnishings and implements from those times. This reconstruction helps give a revealing picture of what daily life in the early Jewish communities of the Golan and Galilee would have been like. Hours are irregular, so call ahead.

PO Box 30, Qasrin, Golan Heights 12900. ✆ **04/696-9636**. Admission museum NIS 18 ($4.50/£2.25); park NIS 18 ($4.50/£2.25); museum and park NIS 24 ($6/£3). AE, DC, MC, V. Sun–Fri 8am–5pm; Sat 10am–4pm. Call ahead to confirm opening hours.

**Golan Heights Winery** 𝕴    Producing wines in the Golan, Yarden, and Gamla series, this winery is generally agreed to be the best of the larger Israeli wine producers and one of the great business success stories in Israel. A skilled staff, state-of-the-art equipment, and the Golan's cold winters and cool summer nights have combined with the unusual volcanic soil of the winery's vineyards to produce wines that have changed the international reputation of Israel's wine industry. The Yarden series is the most prestigious, but you'll find notable choices in each series. Look for Blanc de Blanc (a sparkling wine); Golan Sion Creek White (a semidry white wine); Gamla Sanglovese (dry red wine); and Yarden Muscat (dessert wine). Instructive tours and very enjoyable tasting visits can be made; advance reservations are requested. The winery accepts most major credit cards.

Rte. 87, 2km (1 mile) east of central Qasrin. ✆ **04/696-8409** or 696-8435. www.golanwines.co.il. Tour NIS 20 ($5/ £2.50) per person; tasting NIS 15 ($3.75/£1.90). Sun–Thurs 8am–4pm; Fri 8am–1pm.

**Ya'ar Yehudiya Nature Reserve** 𝕴𝕴    One of the most rewarding landscapes for hiking, this 6,600-hectare (16,309-acre) reserve stretches from Qasrin to the shores of the Sea of Galilee, and is famous for its ancient Tabor oaks (a type of evergreen), forested valleys, and **waterfalls.** Within the reserve you'll find amazing variety: streams, waterfalls (especially near Gamala), rivers, marshes, pools, and canyons carved from basalt rock. There are detailed, color-coded hiking trails that range from easy to very challenging routes that require rappelling and scaling ladders (for these you must be accompanied by a professional guide). There is also a camping area and snack bar. You must check in with the visitor center for guidelines, trail maps, and trail condition updates. Fauna includes wild boars, hyraxes, foxes, and jackals, and also a range of songbirds, eagles, and vultures. One of the top attractions of the park is the **The-Meshushim Pool,** set amid natural hexagonally shaped columns. The columns were formed when mineral-rich molten rock cooled slowly, taking on this crystalline structure. Also in Ya'ar Yehudiya are several **ancient dolmens,** the use and provenance of which is still something of a mystery. The dolmens are not far from Gamla National Park (see below).

Rte. 87, 7km (4¼ miles) east of the Yehudiya Junction, or 5.5km (3½ miles) south of Katzrin. ✆ **04/696-2817**. www. parks.org.il. Admission NIS 20 ($5/£2.50). Apr–Sept daily 8am–5pm (to 4pm in winter).

## Where to Dine

**Meat Shos** *(Finds)* STEAK   This very simple but pleasant place, with an open kitchen, is all about meat—don't even think about coming if you want anything else. All meats here originate on the farms of the Golan; they're filled with flavor and prepared with expertise. The house bread, a rustic sourdough, comes with homemade condiments, including a black olive tapenade, a dynamite *chimichurra,* pickled garlic cloves, and other treats. They're all wonderful when combined with such first courses as exquisitely seasoned beef carpaccio, a rich liver pâté, or spicy lamb kabobs in green *techina* sauce (you could have a country luncheon of bread and first courses alone). The delicious steaks head up the menu and come in a number of cuts, including T-bones (unusual in Israel), but the flavorful Golan lamb chops and ribs are the most special choices. Main courses come with such extras as deep-fried onion rings, good fried potatoes, and garden salads. A well-chosen selection of wines from the Golan Heights Winery as well as from local boutique wineries is also on hand. Meat Shos serves food, made from ingredients that are kosher, but there is no kashrut certificate because it's open on Shabbat.

Qasrin Industrial Park, Qasrin. © **04/696-3334.** Reservations suggested. Main courses NIS 70–NIS 120 ($18–$30/ £8.75–£15). MC, V. Daily noon–11pm.

**Qasrin Bakery** BAKERY   The Golan is not thick with restaurants, but the town bakery has baguettes and *burekas,* and also sells sandwiches on freshly baked breads. It's a great spot to pick up the makings of a picnic; there are also a few tables in case you want to eat in.

Downtown Shopping Center, Qasrin. No phone. Cash only. Sun–Thurs 7am–11pm; Fri 7am–3pm.

## GAMLA

**Gamla National Park** *(Kids)*   Gamla, where Jewish residents battled Roman legionnaires in A.D. 67, is a dramatic historical as well as nature site, 12km (7 miles) southeast near Zomet Daliyot. Gamla was one of the early Jewish strongholds recaptured by Rome during the First Revolt against Rome (A.D. 66–70). At the end of this war, Jerusalem and the Second Temple were destroyed (A.D. 70), and the Zealots of Masada committed mass suicide rather than fall into Roman hands (A.D. 73). The story of the battle at Gamla is chillingly similar to that of Masada, but the number of dead was many times higher.

The well-fortified town of Gamla was first conquered by Jewish forces under Alexander Yannai in 90 B.C. Its name came from the shape of the site: a hill that looks like the hump of a camel *(gamal).* Shortly after the revolt against Rome broke out in A.D. 66, Gamla filled with Jewish refugees fleeing Roman control. The inhabitants at first held out against a Roman siege army, but in the end (according to the Roman Jewish historian, Josephus), when the Romans breached Gamla's defenses, 9,000 people flung themselves from the cliff—choosing death before subjugation. If this indeed happened, the resistance to the death at Gamla in A.D. 67 was different in strategy and spirit from the mass suicide at Masada 6 years later, when all hope of Jewish victory had long been lost. In Gamla, at the start of the revolt against Rome, the Jews wanted to demonstrate that they would pay any price to stop Rome from regaining control of the Galilee and Judea. There was hope that their sacrifice would result in victory, or at least a compromise with Rome.

There is a shorter trail to the ruins as well as a longer nature hike. Both routes are marked; the longer hike from the road to the site of Gamla, though an arduous 1 to

1½ hours, is especially beautiful amid the waterfalls and wildflowers of late winter and the spring. Bring drinking water in warm weather. The ruined, dramatically located synagogue, marked by the tiered stone benches around its periphery, is one of the very few synagogues that can be dated from the time of the Second Temple and is especially memorable, overlooking the forested valley and countryside. *Tip:* Early mornings and late afternoons, the majestic Griffon vultures of the area can be seen wafting in the skies over this hauntingly beautiful site. *Note:* On weekdays, Gamla National Park may be closed due to army maneuvers in the area. Always call to confirm hours.

Off Rte. 808. (C) 04/682-2282. Admission NIS 23 ($5.75/£2.90). Sat–Thurs 8am–4pm (until 5pm in summer); Fri 8am–3pm.

## MOUNT HERMON SKI CENTER

The moshav of Neve Ativ has developed the Mount Hermon Ski Center ((C) **04/698-1337**), high on the slopes of Mount Hermon. The ski center caters to skiers and nonskiers alike. There's even a lift that is exclusively for nonskiers that goes 1 mile to the 1,989m (6,526-ft.) summit, where there's an observation point and cafeteria. The snow season usually begins in December or January and lasts until about mid-April. There are times when there's real snow cover, but often there's just about nothing. Despite Israeli enthusiasm for a ski resort of their own, this is not a must-stop for serious skiers.

Roads up to the site are subject to blockage by heavy snow, so check on conditions in advance by telephone, radio report, or newspaper. On Saturday in ski season, the hotels in this region, the roads, and the parking lot fill up early. Also, on Saturday and holidays a special traffic pattern is in effect for the narrow roads in this region: You must approach the resort via Ma'sada and Majdal Shams only; you exit via Neve Ativ. Those driving should just follow the flow of Saturday traffic. Or take the bus from Kiryat Shmona.

The parking lot is below the ski center. You'll be stopped on the road to pay an entrance fee of NIS 40 ($10/£5) to the site. From the parking lot, shuttle buses run you up to the base station.

As for the slopes, there are four runs from the upper station, the longest of which is about 2.4km (1½ miles), for average to good skiers. Beginners can use the short chairlift, which is a 390m (1,280-ft.) trip to a height of 266m (873 ft.) above the base station. Gentle slopes at the bottom of the hill are good for first runs and for children.

Other facilities include picnic tables and a snack bar at the base, a ski school, and an equipment rental shop. Most Israelis rent equipment, which is yet another reason why you should arrive early if you plan to ski on Saturday. Plan on spending about NIS 480 ($120/£60) per person for a day on the slopes: admission and lift fees, equipment rental, and a snack for lunch.

The ski center is open daily from 8:30am to 3:30pm, weather and security conditions permitting.

## 6 South of Galilee: The Jordan Valley

Although the River Jordan is at times little more than a desert stream, its waters, which come from the Sea of Galilee, are crucial to the agriculture of the area. It has brought fertile silt down from the Sea of Galilee for so many centuries that its valley is one of the most bounteous farming regions in the country.

## ALONG THE JORDAN RIVER

From the Tzemach Junction at the southern tip of the Sea of Galilee, you approach the Jordan Valley **from the north** on Hwy. 90, following the route of the Jordan River, beginning at its source at the southern shore of the lake.

## A CRUSADER CASTLE

**Belvoir (Kochav Ha-Yarden) National Park** ♺    This park is home to the most spectacular ruined Crusader castle in the region. Constructed by the Knights Hospitalers in 1140, this fortress, with incredible views of the Jordan Valley, was designed to dominate the entire region. It was conquered by Saladin after a number of determined assaults in 1189 to 1191, and dismantled in 1218 to prevent a Crusader reoccupation. Especially interesting are carved basalt stones that can be seen in secondary use at various places in the Crusader ruins. Some of this stonework, bearing the menorah and other Jewish motifs, has been identified as having originally been part of a synagogue, and testifies to the ravaging of the area by the Crusaders. A car is necessary if you wish to visit the site on your own. Parts of the site are wheelchair accessible.

Rte. 717, 19km (12 miles) south of the Zemach Junction. © **04/658-1766.** Admission NIS 18 ($4.50/£2.25). Daily 8am–4pm (until 5pm in summer).

## BET SHEAN

As you approach the pass at Bet Shean, the temperature increases as the altitude plummets to 90m (295 ft.) below sea level. Despite the burnt-orange rocky hillsides and the low annual rainfall of 30 centimeters (12 in.), this is a highly fertile area. Springs and streams from Mount Gilboa have been directed toward the Jordan Valley's fields, and the fertile soil here supports thousands of acres of wheat, vegetables, banana groves, and cotton fields.

Bet Shean, now an agricultural center and a quiet development town, is another ancient city that, due to its position on the great caravan route from Damascus to Egypt, has had a long succession of foreign rulers.

At **Tel Bet Shean** ♺♺ (a *tel* is a hill created by successive layers of ruined cities), which is part of **Bet Shean National Park,** archaeologists have cut into layer upon layer of civilization. Five separate strata of Canaanite and Egyptian civilizations have been uncovered, including altars and ruins of the Ramses II period and early Israelite ceramics dating from the time when King Saul's body was hung by the Philistines on the Bet Shean wall. Later strata revealed a Scythian period (the Greeks named the town Scythopolis), and in a higher stratum the layers of dirt and rock revealed fragments from Roman times. Closer to the top of the *tel,* archaeologists have uncovered the remains of Crusader fortifications from the Middle Ages, and still higher up, the jugs and farm tools of the Arab and Turkish settlers of the last 5 centuries.

The most dramatic part of the Bet Shean Archaeological Park, however, is the vast Roman/Byzantine era city, which once stretched in an orderly fashion across the flatter countryside, starting from the foot of Tel Bet Shean. Roman Bet Shean was a mixed city of pagans, Jews, and their Israelite/monotheistic neighbors, the Samaritans (in the vicinity, mosaic synagogue floors of Samaritan communities have been found that are strikingly similar to those of neighboring Jewish synagogues of that era). You'll see the best-preserved **Roman theater** in Israel. This 8,000-person structure has 15 tiers of white limestone in nearly perfect condition and several more tiers of crumbling black basalt. Broken columns and statue fragments are scattered on the floor. There's also an impressive Cardo, or colonnaded main street typical of Roman-designed cities.

Outside the archaeological park to the north, in a factory district at the edge of modern-day Bet Shean, is the late-Byzantine **Monastery of the Noble Lady Mary** ☆. This complex contains an extremely beautiful and complicated series of mosaic floors (you may have to make special arrangements with the visitor center to see them). Information about the many sites in the vast archaeological area, which is still in the process of being developed for the public, is best obtained at **Bet Shean National Park Visitors Center** (© **04/658-7189**) or the **Guidance Center** (© **04/658-1913**). Admission is NIS 23 ($5.75/£2.90); half-price for children. The park is open daily from 8am to 4pm, to 5pm in summer. Much of the park is wheelchair accessible.

## THE JORDAN VALLEY

Once you head south from Bet Shean, you are in the abundantly fertile Jordan Valley. You'll see emerald-green splashes of farm settlements in the distance, and soon you'll come to straight rows of beautiful fruit trees. The vegetation is particularly apparent in the Bet Shean Valley, at the entrance to the Jordan Valley. One ancient sage wrote: "If Paradise is in the land of Israel, its gate is Bet Shean."

You are now in subtropical country—notice the profusion of date-palm trees, banana groves, pomegranate and grapefruit orchards, and mango trees as well as the neat blue rectangles of carp-breeding ponds. It's hard to imagine the heavy toll this land took on the lives of early settlers.

Note that the river Jordan often dwindles to a mere trickling stream and rarely looks like it's supposed to—lush and green, with myrtle and reeds.

## THE WESTERN APPROACH TO THE JORDAN VALLEY: FROM AFULA TO BET ALPHA

The road from Afula follows a historic route, although road signs announce only communal settlements. Throughout history, pilgrims have traveled along this path to reach the waters of the River Jordan.

Southeast of Afula, you'll pass **Kibbutz Yizreel.** The road then skirts the slopes of **Mount Gilboa,** where the tragedy of Saul occurred. There is a farm collective and a road running right to the top of the mountain, where there is a view of everything—the Galilee mountains, the Emek, the Mediterranean, and Jordan.

On the left is a string of communal settlements—**Ein Harod, Tel Yosef, Bet Ha-Shita.** A large, well-developed settlement, founded in 1921, Ein Harod has a population of nearly 2,000 settlers. It has a hostel, an amphitheater, a culture hall, an archaeological and natural history museum, and an art gallery that has exhibited works by Chagall, Hanna Orloff, Milich, and the American artist Selma Gubin.

Just after Ein Harod, the road sign points to Kibbutz Heftziba and Kibbutz Bet Alpha, both communal settlements. **Kibbutz Bet Alpha** was one of the early Jordan Valley settlements, founded in 1922 by pioneers from Poland and Galicia who cleared the swamps. In 1928, during regional swamp-draining operations, a remnant of a 6th-century rural synagogue, called the Bet Alpha Synagogue, was uncovered in what is now Kibbutz Heftziba. An excavation financed by Temple Emmanu-El of New York City revealed what has become one of the most beloved examples of ancient Jewish art in Israel.

**Bet Alpha Synagogue** ☆☆    The ruins of the Bet Alpha Synagogue, uncovered just after World War I, contain a charmingly naive 6th-century-A.D. mosaic floor that was probably the pride of a small farming community and is now one of Israel's great artistic treasures. Beit Alpha was one of the first ancient mosaic synagogue floors discovered in the Holy Land in modern times. Other synagogue floors found after Beit Alpha's may be more sophisticated in their execution, but none is so filled with feeling and so packed with information for scholars to study. It revolutionized ideas about ancient Jewish attitudes toward representational art, which many previously believed had been nonexistent. Through examination of this and other mosaic floors, we have new clues about how Jews of this era lived and what they may have believed. The floor is divided into three panels: a depiction of Abraham's near sacrifice of Isaac; a representation of the sun pulled by a star chariot surrounded by the constellations and signs of the zodiac; and a tableau representing The Temple of Jerusalem and religious objects associated with the Jewish religion. This representation of The Temple and its ritual objects would have been made 5 centuries after the destruction of the actual building in Jerusalem. We now know that the combination of a depiction of a scene from the Bible, a zodiac, and a representation of The Temple seem to have adorned other synagogue floors throughout Israel in Byzantine times.

Among the many mysteries of the Beit Alpha floor is the fact that the signs of the zodiac move counterclockwise and do not correspond to the surrounding representations of the four seasons. According to one theory, this indicates that the mosaicists and the Bet Alpha community did not understand the astronomical and astrological relationships of the zodiac, and merely used the design for decorative purposes. Another theory holds that the artisans deliberately rearranged the zodiac to negate its pagan implications. Other scholars theorize that Cancer, the sign of Judaism, was deliberately placed at the top of the wheel, ascendant to Leo, the sign of Rome in order to depict an astrological belief in the eventual victory of Judaism over its oppressor. Some scholars believe that the zodiac motif discovered here (as well as at synagogues uncovered at Na'aran, near Jericho, Hammat Tiberias, and Zippori) was used to symbolize the orderly rhythms of God's universe, or perhaps even the concept of God. It has also been suggested that the geometric mosaic designs to the side of the main floor were boards for games similar to backgammon and chess, and that this may indicate the synagogue was a Jewish community center in every sense of the word. Childlike though the representation of the sacrifice of Isaac may be, look at the terror in the eyes and face of Isaac and the artistic power of the flames. A Greek inscription commemorates Marianos and his son Hanina, two (probably) Jewish artisans who created the floor. It is interesting to note that an inscription on the mosaic floor of the Samaritan synagogue found in Bet Shean attributes part of that floor, so similar in style, to the same father-and-son team, indicating friendly contact between the two monotheistic sects that had formerly been bitter rivals at the time of Jesus. One also wonders if other floors by Marianos and Hanina lie waiting to be discovered elsewhere in the area. When you're there, check out the new explanatory video presentation for the site.

Kibbutz Heftziba, Rte. 669. ☏ **04/653-2004.** Admission NIS 18 ($4.50/£2.25) adults; half-price children. Daily 8am–4pm (to 5pm in summer).

## Gan Garoo Australia Israel Park *(Kids* Our sophisticated 6-year-old consultant to *Frommer's Israel* (and a major zoo *mayvin*) feels this is a rather odd place, but for those kids who may never make it to Australia itself, this Middle Eastern penal colony of transported Australian kangaroos, koalas, and cassowaries should be included as a stop in the otherwise hot and boring Jordan Valley. It's a loosely organized place, where kids are free to mingle with the animals and adults are free to worry about how to care for a child who gets punched or bitten by a kangaroo while touring the Holy Land, but

it's a refreshing change of pace for a kid who can't face another ruined city or biblical site. Gan Garoo is strategically located near the entrance to another screamfest for kids, Gan Ha-Shlosha (see below).

Entrance to Gan Ha-Shlosha. ℂ **04/648-8080.** Admission NIS 40 ($10/£5). Mon–Fri 9am–4pm; Sat 9am–5pm.

**Gan Ha-Shlosha (Sachne) National Park** *Kids*    Fed by aquifers, **Sachne,** Israel's large and unique natural swimming pool, is remarkably clear of solvents and silt, and miraculously warm year-round. With a natural Jacuzzi beneath its waterfall, tall trees, and distant mountains, Gan Ha-Shlosha/Sachne is a favorite Israeli picnic and swimming site. Although the site is a national landmark, it's also a water park, often filled with screaming tour groups of schoolchildren. Active kids will love it; adults looking for a quiet place to swim might well give it a miss. The park is wheelchair accessible. It has busy refreshment and snack cafes.

Nearby in Gan Ha-Shlosha Park is the **Museum of Regional and Mediterranean Archaeology** (admission is included in the entrance fee to the park), an interesting exhibition that attempts to place ancient Palestine within the framework of Mediterranean civilization. There are displays of locally collected statuary, pottery, metalwork, jewelry, and coins dating from the Neolithic to the Mamluke eras. Nearby Bet Shean is represented, but there are objects from more distant places, such as Iran. It's open Sunday through Friday from 8am to 2pm.

On Rte. 669 3km (2 miles) southeast of the Bet Alpha Synagogue. ℂ **04/658-6219.** Admission NIS 35 ($8.75/£4.40) for adults; half-price children. Winter daily 8am–4pm; summer Sat–Thurs 8am–6pm, Fri 8am–4pm.

# 11

# The Dead Sea & the Negev

Ben-Gurion believed the Negev was the key to Israel's future, but it's also the key to understanding the desert origins of Israel's most distant past. Flying over the area on the way to Eilat will give you a general appreciation of the region, but if you actually walk the Negev's sands and watch the stars falling from the Negev sky, you'll have a chance to connect with the primordial nomadic landscapes in which western monotheism was formed.

If you have the usual preconception of what a desert is like—nothing but sand—you're in for a surprise. The Negev is not a desert in that sense at all. In fact, the Hebrew word for this southern region is *midbar,* meaning wilderness. There are stretches of sand in the Arava region just north of Eilat, but for the most part, the Negev is a vast world of boulders and rocks; dramatic, wind-sculpted mountains; and amazing erosion craters punctuated by Bedouin encampments, kibbutzim,

and lonely Israeli development towns originally built to house Jewish immigrants from Morocco, Yemen, and other lands in the Middle East. For decades, the Negev was regarded as a sort of Israeli Siberia, but lately, a wave of idealism and energy has begun to sweep the region. New accommodations, desert eco-tour programs, and upgrading of national parks have all combined to make the wonders of the area accessible to travelers.

**TOURING THE REGION** Because of the sometimes extraordinary desert heat, it's best to see the Negev by rented car, if at all possible. If you are traveling by bus, choose one or two places to see intensively, rather than scurrying from site to site in the heat. Dehydration occurs very quickly. Keep emergency water with you at all times. In summer, it's a good idea to bring along salt pills and insect repellent. Winter can be chilly to downright cold.

## 1 South to Beersheva

83km (52 miles) S of Jerusalem; 113km (70 miles) SE of Tel Aviv

For thousands of years, Beersheva was a trading post and desert watering hole; its modern history as a settled town dates only from its founding as a small outpost of the Ottoman-Turkish Empire in 1907. The book of Genesis contains two versions of the story of the town's origin. The first tells of a covenant made between Abraham and Abimelech over a well that Abraham had dug in the desert here. The second story also involves a well (in Hebrew, *be'er*) dug by the servants of Isaac, who gave the well and the town its name: "And he called it Shebah: therefore the name of the city is Beersheba unto this day." The phrase "from Dan to Beersheva" appears repeatedly throughout the Bible. Dan was at the northern boundary of traditional Israelite territory; Beersheva at the southern end.

Today, Beersheva is the capital of the northern Negev, and a sprawling city of 250,000 inhabitants, with housing projects, shopping malls, and newer districts of detached and semidetached homes surrounded by increasingly lush gardens. The ever-expanding Ben-Gurion University rivals the universities at Jerusalem, Tel Aviv, and Haifa, and is the pride of the city. Immigrants from more than 70 nations have settled here, and tucked away throughout the city you'll find unusual synagogues, cultural centers, and shops serving these diverse communities. But the region still doesn't have enough jobs for its people, and Beersheva, like other towns in the Negev, faces serious economic problems.

Tourism-wise? Beersheva's Sinfonietta is so good that world capitals would kill to have it, and a bit of community atmosphere can be found in the old downtown district, where there are a few authentic, long-running family eateries, plus some cafes with occasional live entertainment. The "Well of Abraham" site has been excavated, but in the crush of the city, you don't get much feel for the exotic, tribal oasis described in the Bible. A much-touted Thursday-at-dawn Bedouin market is now mostly ultracheap junk (excellent Bedouin crafts can be found at the Lakiya Bedouin/ Negev Weaving project [p. 429]). But the city offers little atmosphere, ancient or modern, and only one decent hotel (which at press time was busy housing Israelis evacuated from Gaza in 2005). Unless you're visiting the university, you'll find Arad, The Dead Sea, and Mitzpe Ramon are better bases for overnighting if you want to explore the beauty of the Negev landscape.

## ESSENTIALS

**GETTING THERE** **By Bus** From Jerusalem or Tel Aviv, several buses make the 1½-hour ride every hour. There is no bus service on Shabbat.

**By Car** From Jerusalem and Tel Aviv, I strongly advise the long route via Kiryat Gat, which circumvents the West Bank. Take Hwy. 1 to Hwy. 40 South to Beersheva.

**VISITOR INFORMATION** The **Tourist Information Office** (© **08/623-4613**) is at 1 Derech Hevron (Abraham's Well), at the southern end of Keren Kayemet Yis-rael Street (KKL St.), the *midrehov,* or pedestrian street in the heart of the Old City downtown center of town. It's open Sunday through Thursday from 8am to 4pm. The fabulous My Negev website (www.my-negev.co.il) is filled with great information for long- and short-term visitors. Just click on "My Beersheva."

Most shops and businesses in Beersheva close between 1 and 4pm, reopening from 4 to 7pm.

**ORIENTATION** Beersheva's **Central Bus Station** is located on Eilat Street, across from the modern Canion Ha-Negev Shopping Center. To the left of the entrance to the bus station are stops for local buses to the Old City, where the restaurants listed below are located. A new railway station has been constructed nearby, but at present there is limited rail service to Beersheva. Other trains may be added, however, if a planned railway to Eilat is put into operation.

West of the bus station you'll find the original Turkish and British Mandate–era **Old Town,** laid out as a grid. It is this commercial "downtown" of Beersheva where you will find teashops, cafes, and restaurants.

**Herzl Street** is the major downtown north-south thoroughfare. Main streets east and west are **Ha-Atzma'ut (Independence) Street** and **Keren Kayemet Le-Israel,** which has been made into a pedestrian-only street to compete with the modern indoor malls elsewhere in town. Right where Herzl and Ha-Atzma'ut intersect is the old Turkish city hall, the Allenby Garden, and behind the Turkish city hall, the Great Mosque and the small Negev Museum.

# The Negev

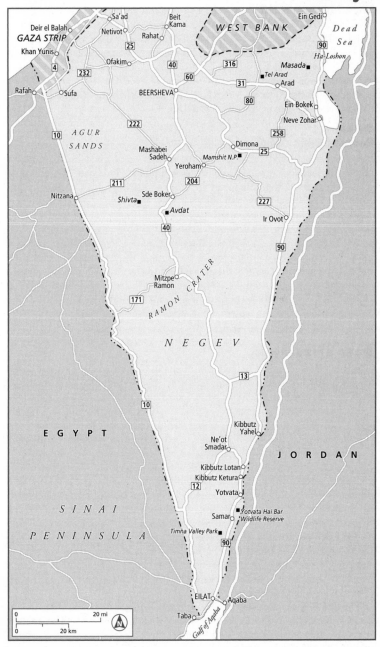

GAZA STRIP
Deir el Balah
Sa'ad
Beit Kama
Ein Gedi
WEST BANK
Dead Sea
Netivot
Rahat
Khan Yunis
25
Ha-Loshon
Ofakim
40
316
Masada
4
60
Tel Arad
Rafah
232
31
Arad
Sufa
BEERSHEVA
80
AGUR SANDS
10
Ein Bokek
Neve Zohar
222
258
Mashabei Sadeh
Dimona
25
Mamshit N.P.
Yeroham
211
204
Nitzana
Shivta
Sde Boker
227
Avdat
Ir Ovot
40
90
Mitzpe Ramon
171
RAMON CRATER
NEGEV
EGYPT
13
10
Kibbutz Yahel
Ne'ot Smadar
JORDAN
Kibbutz Lotan
Kibbutz Ketura
12
Yotvata
SINAI
Samar
Yotvata Hai Bar Wildlife Reserve
PENINSULA
Timna Valley Park
90
EILAT
Aqaba
Taba
Gulf of Aqaba

0       20 mi
0       20 km

427

# WHAT TO SEE & DO
## THE BEDOUIN MARKET

The famous Bedouin market is next to the municipal market, on the southeastern edge of downtown. The Thursday morning market, when the Bedouin tribes come in from the desert to buy and sell, is no longer the exotic event it once was, but you can still see Bedouins in long caftans bartering over sacks of flour and coffee and holding conferences on the dollar rate of exchange for hand-woven rugs and baskets. Most of the marketeering goes on between 5 and 7am.

## MUSEUMS

**Negev Museum Complex**    The museum's small collection combines antiquities, historical artifacts, and contemporary art, all presently housed in the turn-of-the-20th-century Turkish governor's house, set in a pleasant little park adjacent to Beer-sheva's Ottoman-Turkish mosque in the center of the Old City. Old photographs of pashas, provincial governors, staff officers in ancient motorcars, and early settlers provide a glimpse into Beersheva's early days as a municipality. You may also see displays about the Chalcolithic (3500 B.C.) civilization of the Negev, characterized by underground cities and houses, as well as 6th-century mosaics from the church of Kissufim in the Western Negev. As you approach the mosque, the most beautiful and interesting building in Beersheva, note the graceful *tughra* (the Ottoman sultan's monogram) in a medallion over the main door. After much of the area's Arab population fled during the 1948 war, the mosque housed the museum for a number of decades, but it has recently been restored and returned to its original status as a house of worship.

60 Ha-Atzma'ut St. (℃ 08/623-4338. Partially closed for renovation; call for admission fee and hours.

## MORE ATTRACTIONS

**Abraham's Well** is located at the southern end of Keren Kayemet Le-Israel Street, at the intersection of Derekh Hevron, down by the riverbed. Two large round stone walls, one open, the other covered by an arched stone roof, are surrounded by a stone courtyard, some desert date palm trees, and a wooden water wheel for drawing up the water. The wells are no longer in use, but you can still see the water far down below.

It may have been here that Abraham watered his large flocks almost 4,000 years ago and settled a dispute with Abimelech over rights to the water. Scholars still cannot decide whether "Beer-Sheva" means "Well of the Covenant" or "Well of the Seven" for the seven ewe lambs that Abraham gave Abimelech as a peace offering. *Tip:* Behind Abraham's Well, look for signs to the sporadic outdoor booths selling Ethiopian Jewish handicrafts. Their future at this location is not certain, so check with the tourist office. If they're around, craft lovers may find some of the choicest items in Israel.

**Ben-Gurion University of the Negev** is the pride of Beersheva. Its faculties include the humanities, the sciences, and a medical school. Many of the more than two dozen departments emphasize the development of the Negev. Some of the architecture is imaginative and combines an awareness of climatic conditions with the practical needs of the students and teachers.

**The Old Railway Station** on Tuviyahu Street is a local landmark. It was along the Beersheva line that ran to Egypt that Lawrence of Arabia played his train-blowing tricks against the Turks during World War I.

## The Taubel Center for the Preservation of Ethiopian Jewish Handcrafts (Finds)
This is a wonderful workshop where older immigrants produce utensils and sculptures

identical to those they made in Ethiopia. The goal of the center is preservation, but it's also a place where craftspeople and their traditions are honored. Visitors can see artisans at work and purchase unusual items.

50 Arlosoroff St., in the Gimel neighborhood. © 08/623-5882. Mon–Tues and Thurs 8:30am–12:30pm. Call manager Tova Mered to arrange a visit.

## ATTRACTIONS NEAR BEERSHEVA

**Desert Embroidery** ⚜ *Finds*   A second (separate) embroidery workshop that's also a women's collective concentrates on creating very beautiful new examples of traditional Bedouin cross-stitching art, applied to dramatic shawls, caftans, shoulder bags, pillow covers, dresses, and even modest eyeglass cases and bookmarks. Prices range from NIS 20 ($5/£2.50) and up. Both workshops help support a day-care center, lending library, and outreach education and leadership programs for Bedouin women.

At Rte. 31 near entrance to Lakiya. © 08/651-3208. Call project coordinator Hanna Deckel with inquiries and to arrange visit.

**Joe Alon Museum of Bedouin Culture** ⚜   This museum, located 24km (15 miles) north of Beersheva, is well worth a visit. Displays of Bedouin artifacts, photographs, and a video explain the way of life for Bedouin tribes in the Negev and the Sinai, and also the Jbaliyya (Jebaliya) tribe that has been associated for centuries with the Santa Katarina Monastery on Mount Sinai. There are folklore guides, lectures, and a traditional Bedouin tent where you can have spiced desert–style tea or coffee. Displays of Bedouin rugs, textiles, embroidery, jewelry, and tools will make you aware of the strikingly beautiful objects that were (and still are) part of the everyday life of these nomadic people. Today, of the 100,000 Bedouin living in the Negev, 60,000 have been settled into permanent housing, and the ancient Bedouin culture, so closely attuned to the nature of the Negev, is threatened with assimilation into the 21st century.

To get there, drive north from Beersheva on the road to Tel Aviv; after 24km (15 miles), you'll see a sign for Lahav, or Kibbutz Lahav, and the Joe Alon Center. Turn right here; go another 7km (4 miles) until you see the sign directing you uphill to the **Joe Alon Regional and Folklore Center;** the Bedouin museum is part of this center. As you go uphill, you'll go through part of the Jewish National Fund Forest, a shady place to stop for a picnic. There is no bus service.

Kibbutz Lahav. © 08/991-3322. www.lahavnet.co.il. Admission NIS 20 ($5/£2.50). Sun–Thurs 9am–4pm; Fri 9am–2pm.

**Lakiya Bedouin/Negev Weaving** ⚜ *Finds*   Here, more than 150 Bedouin women create rugs and weavings from handspun wool (some traditional, some employing new designs and color combinations), as well as traditionally embroidered textiles and clothing in a program designed and run by the women themselves. These women's empowerment projects preserve the crafts of an ancient culture, but also enable many families to enter the world of modern education and opportunities. A Bedouin Peace Tent and hospitality center are planned. Woven goods range from NIS 400 to NIS 4,000 ($100–$1,000/£50–£500); embroidered objects begin at around NIS 40 ($10/£5).

In the Bedouin town of Lakiya, off Rte. 31, 10km (6 miles) northeast of Beersheva. © 08/651-9883. www.lakiya.org. AE, DC, MC, V. Sun–Thurs 8:30am–5pm; Sat 10am–6pm; closed Fri.

**Monument to the Negev Fighters Brigade,** completed in 1969, commemorates the Palmach brigade that captured the Negev in an epic campaign during the 1948 War of Independence. Probably the most original and most evocative of the nation's many memorials, it is the work of Dani Caravan, one of Israel's most famous artists.

## The Negev Bedouin

It's estimated that 140,000 Bedouin live in Israel—most in the Negev, but there are smaller groups in the North. All are Israeli citizens, descendants of a nomadic culture that has existed in the Negev-Sinai-Jordanian desert region for at least 6,000 years. The customs and lifestyle of the Bedouin echo elements of Old Testament stories, especially those of the earliest patriarchs. The Bedouin are loyal to the State of Israel, and large numbers have served in the Israeli army with great distinction. However, as more and more of the Negev is developed, the once freewheeling Bedouin have been increasingly restricted to bleak permanent villages where their pastoral traditions and lifestyle cannot survive, and where schools, health services, and employment opportunities are minimal. A few Bedouin encampments still dot the countryside, with their large, black goat-hair communal tents (ecological marvels that are warm in winter, and cool in summer). With the help of the Ministry of Tourism and private organizations, cooperatives for Bedouin women's crafts are being developed, and Bedouin tourism projects, including desert treks, camping, and Bedouin dinner tents are a major Negev attraction.

The memorial, consisting of 18 symbolic sections, flows like a fantastic cement garden over the summit of a raw windy hill. Here the entire Negev campaign has been reduced to its essentials: a concrete tent wall, a bunker, a hill crisscrossed by communications trenches, a pipeline, and nine war maps engraved in the floor of the square. You can climb all over these structures and to the top of the tall cement tower (representing the watch and water towers on Negev kibbutzim that were under shelling during the war); you can also file singly through the inclined walls of the pass that lead into the Memorial Dome and enter the symbolic bunker. Sadly, this memorial to those who fell in the battle for the Negev is not always well maintained and has been vandalized with graffiti; nonetheless it remains a moving site. It's on the northeastern edge of the city, just off the road that leads northward to Hebron.

**Tel Beer Sheva National Park,** 3km (2 miles) northeast of Beersheva on Rte. 60 (© 08/646-7286), has been excavated by archaeological teams for many years. Patient work has unearthed an ancient city, possibly Israelite in its later period, dating from the 12th to the 8th centuries B.C., built over the ruins of earlier levels of habitation. A dominant feature of the Iron Age Israelite city is a circular street with rows of buildings on both sides. A massive, 27m-deep (89-ft.) well of great antiquity was found right outside the 3,000-year-old city gates—some speculate that this may actually have been the well of Abraham. A huge, four-horned ashlar altar was also found at the site—the original is now in the collection of the Israel Museum, and a reproduction is displayed near the entrance to the *tel.* Though a dramatic object, and central to the ancient religions of the area, this altar is made of carved stone, in violation of biblical law; it therefore was probably not an altar used by early Israelite worshipers. The *tel* is open Sunday to Thursday from 8am to 5pm, Friday 8am to 3pm, and Saturday 8am to 4pm. Admission is NIS 14 ($3.50/£1.75).

**The Israel Air Force Museum,** Rte. 233, 7km (4 miles) west of Beersheva (© 08/990-6890), contains at least 100 planes that played a role in Israel's history, ranging from one of the four Czech Messerschmitts that helped stop the Egyptian advance into Israel in 1948 to a Boeing 707 that was used in the famous 1976 rescue of Jewish passengers aboard an Air France plane that had been hijacked and taken to Entebbe, Uganda. A film about the rescue is shown inside the aircraft. An exhibit is in memory of Ilan Ramon, the Israeli astronaut and national hero killed in the *Columbia* space shuttle disaster. The museum is open Sunday to Thursday noon to 5pm and Friday 8am to noon. Admission is NIS 28 ($7/£3.50).

## OUTDOOR ACTIVITIES

**SWIMMING**    The **Golden Tulip Hotel** (© **08/640-5444**) has a heated pool, a children's pool, and a health club with dry and wet saunas and a Jacuzzi; call to check if it's open and for the most up-to-date nonguest fee. It is in the Old City.

## ORGANIZED TOURS

It is possible, while in Beersheva, to join a group tour for a visit to a **Bedouin encampment and a Bedouin-style dinner.** Ask at the tourist office across from the Central Bus Station. The cost will be anywhere from NIS 60 ($15/£7.50) for the "short visit," which consists of a chat with the sheik over coffee or tea, a camel ride, and Bedouin music, to about NIS 120 to NIS 150 ($30–$38/£15–£19) for the full "sunset visit" with Bedouin dinner, which includes the above as well as a typical rice, mutton, and fruit meal, eaten with the fingers or in pita. Prices include transportation, and can be higher if there are fewer than 25 people in the group. It is a good idea to phone ahead before reaching Beersheva to find out when the next group is going out.

## WHERE TO STAY

**Golden Tulip Negev Hotel**    Completed in 1996, this 15-story hotel is by far the best in Beersheva, within walking distance of the city hall, the municipal theater, and downtown restaurants (the few other hotels run from skuzzy to dreadful). Originally built as a lower-echelon Hilton, it is now part of a local Israeli chain that's been providing housing to families evacuated from settlements in Gaza (which tends to wear down facilities). There are standard rooms that are comfortable but contain few extra amenities; business rooms with additional amenities such as minibars, desks, safes, and hair dryers; and well-appointed minisuites with king-size beds. Some rooms are equipped for guests with disabilities.

Henrietta Szold St., Beersheva. © 08/640-5444. Fax 08/640-5445. 256 units. $135–$190 (£68–£95) double. AE, DC, MC, V. Parking (fee). **Amenities:** Dining room; cafe; bar; outdoor seasonal pool; basketball and volleyball courts; fitness center; Jacuzzi; sauna; salon; room service; massage; laundry service; synagogue; rooms for those w/limited mobility. *In room:* A/C, TV, minibar (some), hair dryer (some), safe (some).

## WHERE TO DINE

Beersheva has never had a stunning culinary reputation, but there are some places that are local institutions and are quite good. For an inexpensive meal, there are many quick-service counter restaurants in the pedestrian mall on Keren Kayemet Le-Israel Street. The air-conditioned Kanion Shopping Mall across from the Central Bus Station has a number of fast-food outlets and other places to grab a bite.

**Bet Ha-Fuul** HUMMUS/FALAFEL    Located near Ilie Steak Restaurant (see below), between Herzl, Ha-Histadrut, Ha-Avot, and Smilansky streets, this place is not much in terms of decor, but it's popular with the locals for its good food. A hearty lunch might include hummus or Egyptian *fool* beans with sauce and a boiled egg, assorted salads, and fresh, thick pita bread. The outside falafel counter is open daily until 8 or 10pm and serves a fine falafel.

In Gan Ha-Nassi Park. No phone. Light meals NIS 16–NIS 32 ($4–$8/£2–£4). Cash only. Sun–Thurs 10am–midnight; Fri 10am–3pm; Sat after Shabbat.

**Ilie Steak Restaurant** STEAK   What this place lacks in appearance it makes up for in good, fresh food. This restaurant is not fancy; the decor is mainly a meat-and-fish display. House specialties include Romanian kabobs, sirloin filet steak, and fresh fish grilled over charcoal. Regular customers even do the grilling themselves.

21 Herzl St. (C) 08/627-8685. Reservations not accepted. Main courses NIS 50–NIS 80 ($13–$20/£6.25–£10). AE, DC, MC, V. Sun–Thurs noon–midnight; Fri noon–3pm.

**Yakota** ⟨ MOROCCAN   For 40 years, Yakota has been serving some of the most authentic, home-style Moroccan food in Israel. The place is simple, and some of the dishes are fiery, but if you're willing to explore one of the world's great cuisines, Yakota is a treasure. The opening meze of hot and cold spicy salads is great—I especially love a dish of fried onions, okra, and rich, creamy eggplant. *Tagines,* or traditional clay pot stews cooked with dried fruits and spices, are the best main courses (all served with delicious couscous). Be adventurous and try the tender, slow-cooked oxtail *tagine* or the exotically seasoned calves' brain *tagine.* Lemon peel, marjoram, fennel, and cardamom abound in the sauces. The Moroccan desserts are very worthwhile.

27 Mordai Hagettaíot St., Old Town Center. (C) 08/623-2689. Reservations recommended. Main courses NIS 60–NIS 80 ($15–$20/£7.50–£10). MC, V. Sun–Thurs noon–midnight; Fri 11am–4pm; Sat after Shabbat.

## BEERSHEVA AFTER DARK
### PERFORMING ARTS
Beersheva is justifiably proud of its **Israel Sinfonietta** (© **08/623-1616**), which performs throughout the country. Tickets are by subscription, but you may be able to buy a ticket before the performance at the box office. The concerts start promptly at 8:30pm. Concerts are also given by the Beersheva Music Conservatory's Chamber Orchestra (© **08/627-6019**). Many superb musicians perform with these groups. The **Beersheva Theater** performs at Bet Ha-Am, in the Hever Community Center, the large white building in Gan Moshe Park. Performances are usually in Hebrew only. Check with the **Tourist Information Office** (© **08/623-4613**) for current programs. Tickets are approximately NIS 120 ($30/£15).

### PUBS & CAFES
Beersheva has a number of cozy, constantly changing pubs that spring up and close down, especially on the southern side of Old Town. Stroll around Trumpeldor and Smilansky streets and the little lanes of the neighborhood, listen to the music, and see the lights flood the streets from the open doors. **Hatzer Ha-Yayin Wine Bar** (© **08/ 623-8135**), in the Artists Quarter, is the classiest place around, serving wine and tapas at a pace that works well with quiet conversation.

## EN ROUTE FROM BEERSHEVA TO ARAD
As soon as you leave Beersheva, you'll see clusters of Bedouin tents and flocks—and also houses, for today the Bedouin are being strongly encouraged by the government of Israel to settle down.

At the first major intersection not far from Beersheva, take the right turn for Arad and The Dead Sea. A bit farther on you'll begin to see Bedouin villages—the Abu-Rabiya tribe has four such settlements between Beersheva and Arad, all fairly close together. Until the 1950s, the nomadic Bedouin roamed freely over the Negev, and some even continued to cross the borders into Egypt and Jordan, which at the time were still at war with Israel. Since then, there's been a slow program of restricting them to settled communities. The new Bedouin villages of the Negev consist largely of concrete huts and some planned housing projects. At times it may be possible to see a few traditional black goat-hair tents, which are amazingly cool in summer and warm in winter. Some villages may be quite large; others may be nothing more than three houses and five tents. Many of these settlements have not yet been recognized by the government, and so have no electricity, running water, schools, or medical or social services. Another thing to note is that the Bedouin here do a lot of farming, growing mostly wheat, but also other grains, fruits, and vegetables, most of which they sell in the Beersheva markets. A great deal of experimental agricultural work is being done along this road: Sisal is grown without irrigation; tamarisk, eucalyptus, and other trees are planted in small areas, where their growth is watched carefully by scientists who are planning to cultivate even more of Israel's desert.

When the road starts snaking around tight curves, you'll know you're approaching Arad.

## 2 Arad, Neve Zohar/Ein Bokek & Sodom

Arad: 46km (29 miles) E of Beersheva

### ARAD

The modern desert city of Arad, with a population of 25,000, is not a mirage, but rather a well-planned town located on the site of an ancient Israelite settlement—a concrete testimonial to the continuity of Jewish history. Arad is a logical place to stay if you're exploring the northern Negev. At 2,000 feet above sea level, the town's ultradry, mold-free climate is especially good for people who suffer from allergies or asthma, and hotels in Arad cater to such visitors.

Modern Arad was founded in 1961 and laid out, Western-style, with broad streets that bake in the Negev's summer sun. Today many believe an inventive city plan more rooted in desert tradition, with narrow, shaded, labyrinthine streets, might have been more successful. Arad's "development town" cityscape may seem bleak, but slowly Aradis have been reshaping the urban planner's 1960s concept of how to create a desert city. The Arad Artist's Quarter (see below) is a great example of recycled urban space.

### ESSENTIALS

**GETTING THERE    By Bus**    There is regular bus service from Jerusalem, Tel Aviv, and Beersheva; sheruts to Dead Sea, Ein Gedi, and Masada.

**By Car**    Main highways run east from Beersheva and west from the Jordan Valley at the southern end of The Dead Sea.

**VISITOR INFORMATION**    The Tourist Information Office is behind the Paz gas station in the industrial area at the entrance to town (© **08/995-4160**). Presently, it's open Thursday to Saturday from 9am to 5pm. You can e-mail ahead for information and advice at meida@arad.muni.il. The cafe at the gas station is open daily, and you'll find basic maps and hiking information there.

You will probably come into town from the north on Hwy. 31 **via Hebron Street.** The third cross street is **El'azar Ben-Yair** (named for the leader of the stronghold at Masada in A.D. 73). The corner of Hebron and Ben-Yair is the town's principal commercial center. The post office is at the corner of Hebron and Ben-Yair. Traveling toward Masada from Arad, you approach the dramatic site from the side of the evening sound-and-light show (but the road in the dark can be harrowing).

## WHAT TO SEE & DO

Most everything can be found at the commercial center, including food, clothing, cosmetics, stationery, banks, a hairdresser, pharmacy, and a photography store. Hiking and sightseeing are the main tourist activities, but even if you've come to Arad's high, dry location for relief from asthma, you should make the effort to see the spare landscape from the far eastern end of Ben-Yair/Moav Street. At the road's end, a path begins, heading out to a modern sculpture on the promontory.

Arad is such a friendly place that it's a good spot to meet area residents willing to participate in activities with tourists. Ask at the tourist office. *Evening tip:* A 30-minute drive down the road from Arad to Masada takes you to the side of Masada where the Sound and Light Show can be seen—a great way to spend an evening while based in Arad. You can book a seat and transport at the tourist office.

Many of the hangarlike buildings in the old Industrial Zone, now the **Artist's Quarter,** have been turned into artists' studios and galleries (some charge small entrance fees). Among the most interesting are Gideon Friedman's sculptural-fused glass creations at the Glass Museum (© **08/995-3388**) on Sadan Road, and Miri Leibovitch's unusual dolls made of pressed paper at the Doll Museum (© **052/239-8918**).

**Tel Arad,** a little more than 6km (4 miles) west of Arad, is a partially reconstructed 5,000-year-old Canaanite town with a 3,000-year-old Israelite fort. If you're with a well-informed guide, this can be a very interesting stop; otherwise, it is a must-see mainly for archaeology buffs. It's open October through March, Sunday to Thursday, from 8am to 4pm; until 5pm the rest of the year, closing an hour earlier, respectively, on Friday and holiday eves. The entrance fee is NIS 12 ($3/£1.50).

Local guide Giora Eldar (© **052/397-1774**) can take you around in his off-road vehicle on an itinerary that can include rappelling, mountain climbing, and observing the local hyraxes, deer, and vultures (with luck you may even spot a leopard). He can also set you up for your own hikes and take you to and from bike and hiking paths or to visit Bedouin still living in their tents. Dov Ponio (© **052/466-6056**) is recommended for escorted desert walks and hikes.

**Zman Midbar (Time in the Wilderness;** © **08/995-3108**) is a holistic center and spiritual retreat on the edge of the desert off Rte. 31 north of Arad (en route to Masada). It offers opportunities for desert meditation, as well as a dramatic locale for desert walks and personal solitude. Friday afternoons, there is a wonderful kaballat Shabbat (receiving the Sabbath) ceremony open to the public in the retreat's adobe-sand pavilion, built to create special acoustics. For further information on programs and events, go to www.zmanmidbar.net.

## WHERE TO STAY & DINE

Arad's three main hotels all cater to visitors with asthma and respiratory problems. The tourist office, with advance notice, can help set you up with a room in a private house or a B&B starting at $75 (£38) for two people. The town has few restaurants, but snack places can be found in the commercial center. **Max's,** 9 Maccabim St. (© **08/997-3339**), has the best pub/restaurant menu in town: You'll find skewers of meat, salads, pasta, and hummus, all served in generous portions. Open Monday to Saturday 8am to 11pm. **Muza,** located just behind the gas station at the Rte. 31 entrance to Arad (© **08/995-8764**), offers five plasma screens broadcasting a steady stream of Israeli and international sports, and a meat menu of lamb chops, entrecôte, hamburgers, and beer on tap. Open daily noon to after 2am.

**Inbar**  This is the newest (1998) of Arad's major hotels; a five-story, functional modern structure that's not fancy but offers the basic things you need after a day of desert hiking. Its facilities, including year-round Dead Sea–water and chlorinated swimming pools, are the best in town. The staff are friendly and the rooms compact. Minibars are available for standard rooms on request.

38 Yehuda St. ⒸⒸ **08/997-3303** or 997-3322. www.hotel-inbar.com. 103 units. $110–$140 (£55–£70) double. Rates include breakfast. MC, V. **Amenities:** Dining room; lobby bar; 2 swimming pools; wading pool; hot tub; exercise room; mineral spa; sauna; synagogue; free covered parking. *In room:* A/C, cable TV, minibar (suite), coffeemaker (suite), safe.

## SOUTHERN DEAD SEA: EIN BOKEK/NEVE ZOHAR, THE SPA HOTELS & SODOM

The Dead Sea is by far the lowest point on the face of the planet, the earth's most unworldly body of water. The northern coast along Hwy. 1 is the most beautiful, but it's farther south, near Ein Gedi and the hotels of Neve Zohar and Ein Bokek, that the water is most dense and believed to be very helpful for skin diseases such as psoriasis. These were Cleopatra's favorite waters for her beauty needs, and today the waters (and the mud) are said to be cleansing for the skin and scalp, improving skin texture and even smoothing wrinkles.

Experts came out here in the 1960s, had the waters analyzed by Hadassah technicians, and found that they contained the highest mineral content of any waters in the world: 300 grams per liter. As you bathe in The Dead Sea waters, you'll also be breathing the denser air of the below-sea-level atmosphere, which contains more than 10% more oxygen than at sea level. This is helpful for people with respiratory problems and heart disease. In addition, bromides evaporating into the air from the surface of The Dead Sea contribute to a relaxed feeling of well-being. It's not enough to space you out, but when tired or anxious people come here for a week, the atmosphere seems to help them unwind. The dense atmosphere also filters out harmful sun rays—psoriasis sufferers can stay out in the sun a bit longer without burning. At the area's hotels and spas, experts will tailor their treatment baths to your specific ailment. If you want a planned spa treatment, though, you'll have to have a medical okay. You can be examined by a resident physician, but a doctor's note certifying that your blood pressure can stand the stimulation of the waters and massage programs will suffice. In order to really get any benefit from The Dead Sea spas, you must stay here for at least 1 or 2 weeks. The four- and five-star hotels at Ein Bokek, though expensive, are the best way to really do an intensive program of spa treatments. *Tip:* An alternative to the big hotels is Kibbutz Ein Gedi's beautiful holiday village, on a hill overlooking The Dead Sea. Ein Gedi has its own beach area, and guests can use Ein Gedi's Sulfur Springs and Spa (p. 443).

### WHERE TO STAY

All hotels at The Dead Sea offer health and beauty programs, but these should not be your only reason for staying at a hotel in Neve Zohar or Ein Bokek; they also provide a very comfortable base for exploring the desert and enjoying The Dead Sea. Clientele is a mixture of long-term guests on health cures, and tourists sampling The Dead Sea for a day or two, except during summer and Israeli school holidays, when Israeli families pack in. At those times, some of the international chain hotels offer discos and teen activities at night, but otherwise, stargazing (if you can drive out of range of Ein Bokek's floodlights) is the night activity of choice.

## Expensive

**Crowne Plaza** ✿   Opened in 1997, the Crowne Plaza is half the size and not quite as dazzling as its rival, Le Méridien (see below), but it is a tasteful, state-of-the art hotel and spa, with every possible therapeutic, health, and resort program you could want. There are indoor and outdoor pools, and a wide range of sulfur, mineral, and mud baths. All rooms have Dead Sea views, and some are large enough for families. The glatt kosher breakfast, lunch, and dinner buffets are sumptuous, perhaps outdoing those at Le Méridien; and the Crowne Plaza has the added advantage of actual Dead Sea beachfront—a rarity on The Dead Sea hotel strip. Standard and deluxe rooms can fit two adults and two children; more pampering Crowne rooms on highest floors are only for adults. The pricey on-site Sato Bisrot, a mildly Asian fusion restaurant, is the best in the area.

Ein Bokek. ☎ **08/659-1919** or 03/539-0808 for reservations inside Israel. Fax 08/659-1911. www.h-i.co.il. 304 units. $270–$400 (£135–£200) double. Rates include breakfast. AE, DC, MC, V. **Amenities:** Restaurant; dining room; cafe; bar; indoor and outdoor heated pools; children's pool; fitness center; Jacuzzi; sauna; basketball and volleyball courts; playground; tour desk; business services; hairdresser; massage; laundry service; nonsmoking rooms. *In room:* A/C, TV, minibar, coffeemaker, hair dryer, safe.

**Golden Tulip Club Dead Sea Hotel**   Not to be confused with the Tulip Inn Dead Sea, this busy hotel, set by itself a few kilometers to the south of the main tourism center at Ein Bokek, has its own private beach and lagoon. For the past few years it's catered to an Israeli clientele as an all-inclusive hotel, with packages that include room plus three meals and 24-hour snacks, beverages, and bar. Many of the guest rooms overlook The Dead Sea. One-bedroom family rooms can house up to three children; there's a kids' club in season and water slide; and there are rooms for travelers with disabilities. With a large wing built in 1999 (the rest of the hotel was renovated at the same time), this hotel is livelier than many of its neighbors. Spa treatments are not included in the price.

Ein Bokek. ☎ **08/668-9444.** Fax 08/668-9400. www.nirvana-hotel.com. 388 units. $300–$400 (£150–£200) double, all-inclusive (food, beverages, and activities). Add up to $200 for Passover and Jewish holidays. AE, DC, MC, V. Free parking. **Amenities:** Dining room; bar; disco; seasonal outdoor pool; children's pool/water slide; children's activities; fitness center; spa; nonsmoking rooms; synagogue; rooms for those w/limited mobility. *In room:* A/C, TV, minibar, hair dryer, safe.

**Le Méridien Dead Sea** ✿   Built in 1996, and the largest spa hotel on The Dead Sea, this 17-story blockbuster (formerly the Hyatt Regency, but now managed by the local Israeli Fattal chain) is a climate-controlled world unto itself. There are heated indoor and outdoor swimming pools, including a lengthy serpentine swimming pool that winds through a palm-shaded patio (bathtub-warm in summer), beautiful sulfur pools, and Dead Sea mineral baths. There's also a Jacuzzi (too small for the number of guests), sauna, massage, Dead Sea mud treatments, a medical center offering a wide variety of services, and 14 separate facilities for beauty and health programs. Guest rooms are truly spacious and well-appointed; bathrooms have tubs and separate glazed shower stalls. The glatt kosher breakfast, lunch, and dinner buffets are average. There's a private Dead Sea beach for guests, but it's not easy to access from the hotel's grounds.

Ein Bokek. ☎ **08/659-1234.** Fax 08/659-1235. www.fattal.co.il. 600 units. $250–$400 (£125–£200) double. Rates include breakfast. AE, DC, MC, V. **Amenities:** Restaurant; dining room; cafe; bar; indoor and outdoor heated pools; Dead Sea water indoor pool; children's pool; fitness center; Jacuzzi; sauna; children's activities in season; business services; beauty treatments; room service; massage programs. *In room:* A/C, TV, minibar, hair dryer, safe.

**Prima Oasis Dead Sea**   This location of the moderate-price-range Prima Hotel chain is one of the few (somewhat) less-expensive hotels in the bustling resort center. Guest rooms are late 20th century but acceptable, however, public areas have been recently renovated and include a delightful Moroccan-decorated spa. The pace is leisurely (breakfast buffet is served until noon); the clientele is largely Israelis and older Europeans, but in summer and on school holidays, children's activities are offered. No private beach, but pleasant garden patios. A minimart is nearby.

Ein Bokek. ℂ **08/668-8666**. Fax 03/760-4434. www.prima.co.il. 143 units. $160–$260 (£80–£130) double. Rates include breakfast. AE, MC, V. Free parking. **Amenities:** Dining room; outdoor heated pool (seasonal); heated indoor Dead Sea water pool; wet and dry sauna; health club; spa; Jacuzzi; children's activities; massage programs; laundry service; synagogue. *In room:* A/C, cable TV, minibar or fridge, coffeemaker, hair dryer, safe.

**Sheraton Dead Sea** 🖈   Thanks to its own beach (where you can walk along the shoreline and feel The Dead Sea's serene mystery) and its manageable size, this well-run Sheraton, with an experienced staff, has a calmer atmosphere than some of the bigger hotels. Public areas sparkle with polished marble floors, food services keep to international standards, and guest rooms are spacious. The hotel is currently engaged in an ongoing renovation program: Floor six is the most recently renovated, and offers especially attractive rooms. There's a brand-new indoor health spa that's bright and pleasant, with a heated Dead Sea–water pool, Jacuzzi, wet and dry sauna, and an array of massage, beauty, and therapeutic treatment rooms. The isolated private beach, where you can really experience The Dead Sea, is a plus, as is the shaded children's playground. Hammocks are scattered around the lawns and gardens. All rooms have a sea view.

Neve Zohar, 4km (2½ miles) south of Ein Bokek. ℂ **08/659-1591**. Fax 08/658-4238. www.sheraton.co.il. 215 units. $225–$365 (£113–£183) double. AE, DC, MC, V. **Amenities:** Dining room; cafe; bar; large outdoor pool; tennis courts; health spa; children's club in season; playground; room service; nonsmoking rooms; synagogue. *In room:* A/C, TV, minibar, coffeemaker, hair dryer, safe.

## WHERE TO DINE

The in-house hotel restaurants offer the best possibilities for a major meal. Many visitors staying here hotel-hop to try out the different lunch or dinner buffets; they're all vast, and you're sure to find something interesting. Prices range from NIS 100 to NIS 200 ($25–$50/£13–£25). In the shopping mall at Ein Bokek, there are a number of cafes and restaurants where you can get inexpensive meals and light snacks. None of the choices, however, are standouts.

## SODOM

Driving south on Hwy. 90 from the hotels of Ein Bokek and Neve Zohar, you'll pass a number of places where minerals are harvested from the super salt waters. Mining Dead Sea minerals is lucrative, but is also a factor in The Dead Sea's shrinkage (dams allow almost no Jordan River water to flow into The Dead Sea anymore). Some studies indicate that in less than a century, The Dead Sea, one of the world's great natural wonders, will be gone, and its waters have already retreated far from the many hotel beaches.

Farther south along Hwy. 90, you'll reach the area where the legendary city of Sodom is said to have existed in the time of Abraham. There's nothing in terms of ruins to see. The wicked city of Sodom, the lowest inhabited place on earth, is no more (Gen. 19:12–29). Modern Sodom is now a potash concession, not a real town as such. A number of pillars of salt along the shore claim the title as Lot's wife. According to the biblical story of the destruction of Sodom and Gomorrah, angels intended to save Lot (nephew of Abraham) and his family, telling them to run for it and not to look back. Lot's wife, however, turned back in curiosity and was turned into a pillar of salt. On a hot day, the smell of sulfur in the air adds to the evil, forbidding feel of the place.

## 3 Qumran, Ein Gedi & Masada

Qumran: 45km (28 miles) SE of Jerusalem. Ein Gedi: 50km (31 miles) S of Jericho; 15km (9 miles) S of Ein Bokek

Your exploration of the Negev can start from Jerusalem eastward through the Judean desert to the outskirts of Jericho, and then south along the dramatic Dead Sea road via **Ein Gedi** and **Masada.** The route from Jerusalem south through the West Bank cities of Bethlehem and Hebron to Beersheva is not recommended at this time. Don't fail to see Masada and to take a dip in The Dead Sea at Ein Gedi. The road along The Dead Sea coast also passes the ruins of **Qumran,** near the caves where the first Dead Sea Scrolls were found in 1947.

### QUMRAN

In addition to the scrolls, hidden at the time of the First Jewish Revolt against Rome in A.D. 70, archaeological excavations during the early 1960s of the many caves in this region uncovered mysterious and beautiful copper ritual objects, used 5,000 to 6,000 years ago by members of a prehistoric civilization, as well as artifacts and personal documents and letters hidden by refugees from the Second Jewish Revolt against Rome in A.D. 135. Other caves in the area, their openings or interior reaches sealed by rockfalls over the centuries, may conceal still more treasures. A side road leads up to the ruins of Qumran. In a nearby cave, the world-famous Dead Sea Scrolls were found in 1947 by a Bedouin shepherd boy. These are the oldest existing copies of the Torah and other parts of the Bible. They also include previously unknown ancient Jewish writings.

### ESSENTIALS

**GETTING THERE     By Bus**     Buses will take you to Qumran from Egged's **Central Bus Station** in Jerusalem. For day tours from Tel Aviv or Jerusalem, check with Egged and United Tours.

**By Car**     From Jerusalem on Hwy. 1, bypass Jericho and turn right (south) onto Hwy. 90, the main road along the coast of The Dead Sea. Continue following the signs to Qumran and Ein Gedi.

### EXPLORING ANCIENT QUMRAN

This ancient site, excavated in the 1950s by a team headed by Père Roland de Vaux, has become the subject of a major archaeological controversy in recent years. De Vaux initially estimated that Qumran had been inhabited since the 8th century B.C., and that sometime in the 2nd century B.C., it had become the monastic desert retreat of the Essenes, an ascetic, mystical Jewish sect of the Second Temple period that may have influenced early Christianity. De Vaux and most archaeologists theorized that the Dead Sea Scrolls, found in nearby caves, were portions of the Essene community's library, hidden from the approaching Roman armies at the time of the First Revolt against Rome (A.D. 66–70). Qumran itself was destroyed by the Romans in A.D. 68. Structures uncovered at Qumran were interpreted in terms of the Essenes' collective religious community life as recorded by Flavius Josephus and the Roman historian Pliny the Elder, who wrote of an Essene settlement near The Dead Sea, "above Ein Gedi." In neither of these writings is the precise location of the Essene community named.

Although most scholars accept the theory that Qumran was an Essene monastic community and that the Dead Sea Scrolls are part of the Essenes' library, recent reinterpretations of Qumran's location and structures have led a few scholars to postulate that Qumran may have been a traders' inn and military and customs outpost rather

## The Shepherds, the Shoemaker, the Professor & the Scrolls

In the spring of 1947, a teenage Bedouin shepherd searching for a lost goat tossed a stone into a virtually inaccessible cave on the chance the goat might have somehow strayed into it. He heard the sound of pottery breaking. Pulling himself up to the cave's entrance, he saw giant terra-cotta jars in which he imagined there might be an Arabian Nights' treasure, but instead, found them filled with rolls of old leatherlike parchment. His family broke off some of the scrolls and took them to the shop of Kando, the shoe repairman in Bethlehem, who often sold oddities and ancient objects found by Bedouin in the desert. If nothing else, Kando might be able to use the old leather filled with strange writing for shoe repairs. Kando himself had no idea of the meaning and value of what the Bedouin had brought him.

Prof. E. L. Sukenick, of the Hebrew University in Jerusalem, noticed broken fragments of the scrolls while browsing at Kando's, and was shown some complete scrolls. The professor almost fainted in amazement. Acting on a feeling that the scrolls might be far, far older than any others known to be in existence, Professor Sukenick risked his life to return to Bethlehem a few weeks later and purchase as many of the scrolls as he could afford on the very day in November 1947 when the United Nations in New York was voting to partition Palestine into a Jewish and an Arab State. Rioting had erupted throughout British Mandate Palestine, and West Jerusalem was virtually under siege. According to his journal, when he stepped off the bus from Bethlehem in Jerusalem clutching the scrolls in a paper bag, Professor Sukenick said the prayer one recites on escaping death. He was probably the last Jew to visit Bethlehem until after the Six-Day War in 1967. During the Battle for Jerusalem, the scrolls remained in Professor Sukenick's house, while shells landed throughout the neighborhood. When Israel's War of Independence ended, the fragile scrolls were unraveled, in some cases using surgical instruments. Only then was it learned that the only scrolls of the Bible to survive from the time when The Temple stood in Jerusalem had been restored both to the Jewish people and to the world.

than the communal settlement of a religious sect. Qumran lies at a strategic point in an ancient trade route: Goods from Arabia and Africa were shipped up the Red Sea to Eilat, and then overland through the Arava Valley to the southern tip of The Dead Sea, where they were floated across to Qumran. At Qumran, cargo was unloaded and sent along the ancient Salt Road to Jerusalem. According to this theory, the otherworldly Essenes would not have settled at the crux of a major commercial route, but in a more remote location such as the caves in the mountains "above Ein Gedi." If this interpretation is correct, then the previously unknown writings found among the Dead Sea Scrolls may not be those of the Essenes at all, but a more mainstream sampling of extra-biblical literature from the time of the Second Temple, brought to the caves for safekeeping from Jerusalem. This heated debate is an example of the very partisan passions with which Israelis follow archaeological discoveries.

The excavated settlement includes trenches, pottery sheds, step-down baths, cisterns, bakery sites, and cemetery plots. You will also see the long, flat, tablelike structures that Père Roland de Vaux believed were the desks of the community's "scriptorium," where the Dead Sea Scrolls were written. Israelis love to debate whether these structures could or could not have been used as desks for ancient scribes of any normal human size. See what you think. You can view all the excavations from the top of the village tower. Near the ruins, signs direct you to the caves where some of the scrolls were found. It's a 10-minute walk, and you are permitted to visit the closest and most accessible cave. High above, you'll notice the mountains are dotted with many more caves. The **National Park at Qumran** (✆ **02/994-2235**) is open daily from 8am to 4pm and has an air-conditioned snack-bar facility. Admission is NIS 14 ($3.50/£1.75).

## BEACHES ON THE DEAD SEA

You can swim at **Einot Zuqim** (Ein Feshcha; ✆ **02/994-2355**), a large park with trees, picnic tables, freshwater pools, and a beach on The Dead Sea just 3km (2 miles) south of Qumran. Saturdays are packed, but fewer visitors come on the weekdays. The freshwater pools, fed by local springs, can get murky and sometimes have a fish or two swimming around. You can also take a dip in the lifeless Dead Sea, cover yourself with mineral-rich Dead Sea mud, or walk on the beach. Admission of NIS 30 ($7.50/£3.75) includes use of the shower facilities. Open March to November daily from 8am to 5pm; winter hours are variable.

## EIN GEDI ✪

Ein Gedi has been an Eden-like canyon oasis for millennia, attracting human beings for thousands of years before recorded time. More than 5,000 years ago, Chalcolithic people built a sanctuary amid the waterfalls and springs here—in the 1960s, Israeli archaeologists searching for Jewish scrolls (150 B.C.–A.D. 135) amid the crevasses and depths of inaccessible caves nearby came upon a cache of elegant, mysteriously designed copper wands, crowns, and scepters from 3000 B.C. that scholars believe were the sacred vessels of a long-forgotten prehistoric culture centered at Ein Gedi (the copper objects are now displayed at the Israel Museum). It was to Ein Gedi that the young David fled as a fugitive from the paranoid King Saul; here David had the chance to kill his pursuer, but he would not lay a hand on his king, the anointed of God. The "Song of Solomon" rhapsodized thus: "My beloved is unto me as a cluster of camphire from the vineyards of Ein Gedi." Rare herbs and spices grown at Ein Gedi from approximately the 6th century B.C. until the late 8th century A.D. were famous throughout the ancient world and used to produce the most exotic incense, lotions, and perfumes. The secret of these plantations was carefully guarded by the Ein Gedi

---

**⟨** *Warning* **A Sinking Feeling**

Because of the lowering level of The Dead Sea and of the underground water table, sinkholes have been appearing spontaneously in this area and throughout The Dead Sea shoreline. Areas of danger have been fenced off and posted with warning signs. *Do not enter these areas!* If you sense the ground underfoot is unstable, get to the main road as quickly as possible and report the situation to the authorities.

community until its demise in early Islamic times. Indeed, an inscription in the mosaic floor of a Byzantine-era synagogue discovered at Ein Gedi warns members of the community not to divulge the "secret of the town" to outsiders; many scholars believe this refers to the secret formulas for balm, incense, and perfumes. Modern romantics like to theorize that the "secret" the townspeople were pledged to protect may have been the knowledge of nearby caves in which the treasures of the Second Temple were hidden from the Romans. After more than 1,000 years of complete desolation, the region was resettled in 1949 by a group of pioneers who planted it with cotton, grapes, vegetables, and flowers. Beginning with nothing but rocky, barren land, the settlers created a beautiful kibbutz with stunning views of the wild, unearthly area, including the desert cascade of **Ein David Gorge,** where the water drops from a height of nearly 90m (295 ft.).

## ESSENTIALS

**GETTING THERE  By Bus**  There is service from Tel Aviv via Jerusalem and from Eilat four times daily. Ein Gedi is a request stop. Try to reserve your seat when you purchase your ticket at either end, as seats may be filled by passengers from Eilat or Jerusalem.

**By Car**  There are main roads to Eilat and Beersheva via Arad, and from Jerusalem via the Jordan Valley and The Dead Sea.

## WHAT TO SEE & DO

There is no modern town at Ein Gedi. The area now called Ein Gedi is spread out along 4.8km (3 miles) of the shore of The Dead Sea and divided into four basic sections, each with its own bus stop. If you're coming from Jerusalem by bus, the first (northernmost) stop at Ein Gedi is where you'll find the entrance to the **Nature Reserves,** the **youth hostel,** and the **SPNI study center/field school.** The second stop is the **bathing beach,** with its self-service restaurant and gas station. The third stop is for **Kibbutz Ein Gedi** and its kibbutz hotel. The fourth and southernmost stop is for the **Ein Gedi Spa.**

The spectacular waterfalls and hiking trails are within the **Ein Gedi Reserve's Nachal David and Nachal Arugot** canyons (© **08/658-4285**). Maps and suggested trail routes are available at the entrance; more-detailed maps and trail advice for hikes of several hours through these two neighboring canyon systems are available at the SPNI Center, near the hostel and the Nachal David entry gate. Follow the trail and the signposts, winding through tall pines and palm trees up and into the desert hills. You proceed between slits in the rock formations, under canopies of papyrus reeds, and after about 10 minutes of steady climbing, you'll hear the wonderful sound of rushing water. In another 5 minutes, your appetite whetted, you arrive at what is surely one of the wonders of the Judean desert—the **Nachal David–Ein Gedi waterfalls,** hidden in an oasis of vegetation that hangs in a canyon wall. A second trail involving a 30-minute climb takes you to the **Shulamit Spring** and then to the **Dodim Cave** at the top of the falls. A 20- to 30-minute walk to the left brings you to the fenced-in ruins of a **Chalcolithic sanctuary** dating from about 3000 B.C. Mysterious copper wands and crowns, probably belonging to this sanctuary and hidden in nearby caves for more than 5,000 years, are displayed in the antiquities section of the Israel Museum. Another walk leads to the ruins of Byzantine-era Ein Gedi's synagogue, with its marvelously intact mosaic floor. The reserve is open from 8am to 4pm; in summer until 5pm. You must make arrangements with the Nature Reserves Authority if you

## Eyes Wide Shut

The waters of The Dead Sea, though purportedly health giving, will burn open cuts and scrapes on your skin. It is most important not to let the water touch your eyes. Don't even think about plunging underwater. Backstroke is the way to go—the buoyancy of The Dead Sea is amazing, and most of your body will stay above the water level. If you get water in your eyes, shower with fresh water immediately.

plan to do any of the 5- to 6-hour hikes into the depths of the *nachal* (canyon) systems, especially if you plan to go beyond the **Hidden Falls.** Always carry at least 5 liters of water with you if you're planning a major hike in summer. From autumn to spring, it is important to be aware of the possibility of flash floods caused by rain in distant places. No food or cigarettes are allowed on the grounds. Admission to the reserve is NIS 24 ($6/£3). There is a snack kiosk at the entrance. *Tip:* Ein Gedi is impossibly hot midday in the summer. Worse yet, during school holidays, it will be overrun by school groups.

At the Ein Gedi National Antiquities Park, the ruins of **Ancient Ein Gedi** ⍟, one of Israel's most important archaeological sites, may be visited. Admission is NIS 12 ($3/£1.50). From First and Second Temple times until the end of the Byzantine era, Ein Gedi was a largely Jewish outpost famous throughout the ancient world for its production of rare spices; fragrant, intoxicating balsam oil; and priceless myrrh. Perhaps Ein Gedi was permitted to survive the tumultuous decades of wars and rebellions against Rome because its secret formulas for spice and incense production were not only beyond value, but also irreplaceable. At Ein Gedi, the **mosaic floor** of a 6th-century-A.D. synagogue has been uncovered. If you visit other mosaic synagogue floors discovered in the Jordan Valley and the Galilee, you'll find that a number of Byzantine-era synagogues (at Bet Alpha, Hammat Tiberias, and Zippori) contain a circle with a depiction of the zodiac as the centerpiece of their mosaic floors. Some scholars believe the zodiac was meant to represent the orderly patterns of God's universe. At Ein Gedi, in place of a zodiac circle, the mosaic floor is dominated by a central circle design of peacock chicks and adult birds, perhaps illustrating continuing patterns of birth and growth through which divine presence is revealed. It may be that the Jewish community at Ein Gedi, less influenced by outside cultures than the Jewish communities farther north, was reluctant to employ pagan motifs in the ornamentation of its synagogue.

The extraordinary personal papers, letters, and possessions found in The Dead Sea caves and dating from the Second Jewish Revolt against Rome (A.D. 135) belonged to Jewish inhabitants of Ein Gedi who attempted to escape the Roman armies by hiding in the region's almost inaccessible caves. Yigal Yadin's book, *Bar Kokhba,* details these dramatic finds.

Across The Dead Sea to the far left are the **Moab Mountains,** where Moses was buried and where Gad, Reuben, and half the Manasseh tribe settled after helping Joshua claim the rest of the Promised Land. To the right it seems the sea ends, but it's actually the **Ha-Loshon** (the **Tongue**)—a strip of peninsula from the Jordanian side that reaches across the middle of The Dead Sea.

The **Ein Gedi Beach** ⍟ is often mobbed with tour buses and weekending Israelis, but it's guarded and a fun place to try the experience of floating on The Dead Sea. There are showers on the beach and changing rooms available for NIS 5 ($1.25/60p).

This section of The Dead Sea does not purport to have the same healing properties as the more mineral-heavy waters farther south, but the super-buoyant experience is the same. The **Pundak Ein Gedi Cafeteria** (© **08/659-4761**), just beside the beach, is the only restaurant in the region and serves basic (kosher) chicken, meat, and vegetarian meals for under NIS 45 ($11/£5.60). It is open daily 10am to 6pm; an adjacent minimart is open daily 7:30am to 8pm.

About 3km (2 miles) south of Ein Gedi Beach is the often very busy, public **Ein Gedi Sulfur Springs and Spa** (© **08/659-4934**), housed in a modern building. Here you can soak in mineral-rich spring waters drawn from The Dead Sea. Admission to the spa costs NIS 65 ($16/£8.10) for adults Sunday to Monday and NIS 70 ($18/ £8.75) Saturday and holidays. Facilities include a total of six single-sex and coed indoor warm and hot mineral pools. There's a bland fish-and-dairy restaurant downstairs that serves lunch for NIS 50 to NIS 60 ($13–$15/£6.25–£7.50); you get a discount by presenting your receipt from the spa. The spa has its own Dead Sea swimming beach and plenty of the famous Dead Sea black mud to smear on your skin. Open daily from 8am to 6pm in summer; until 5pm in winter. Any bus to Ein Gedi will drop you here.

At Kibbutz Ein Gedi (© **08/658-4444**), you can visit the incredible **Botanical Gardens.** Members of the kibbutz were at first amazed to find that the rarefied soil and atmosphere produced lush gardens to rival the legendary ancient plantations of Ein Gedi. Over the years, they planted 900 species of rare and exotic trees, shrubs, flowers, and cacti, and have created an incredible internationally recognized botanical garden. Night tours are given Tuesday and Thursday at 8pm. Admission is NIS 28 ($7/£3.50) and is free for guests of the kibbutz.

## WHERE TO STAY
Ein Gedi is not a full-fledged resort with hotels, but Kibbutz Ein Gedi has a popular and dramatically sited guesthouse as well as an excellent youth hostel. Make sure to reserve in advance. Beds are scarce and in great demand.

### Moderate
**Kibbutz Ein Gedi Resort Hotel** ⟨⟨⟨ Dramatically located on a hill overlooking The Dead Sea, this kibbutz and its low-rise hotel units are set amid the exotic plantings of the only internationally registered botanical garden in which people live. Containing hundreds of species (including baobab trees and 900 types of cacti), the garden is the creation of the kibbutz, but it draws upon the ancient tradition of Ein Gedi's priceless trees and shrubs. For visitors, it's hard to believe that before 1949 there was nothing but barren rock here.

Rooms are simple but comfortable. A special upgraded group of rooms has recently been built; they offer a sleek decor not typical of a kibbutz. What makes this place special are the remarkable surroundings and an enthusiastic management that offers a program of desert excursions as well as great Bedouin evening barbecues. The rates for most guests include use of the Ein Gedi Spa, daily transportation to and from the sulfur springs, and use of the beach, plus movies, slides, and lectures about the kibbutz and the spa. The office is open from 8am to 8pm, and the kiosk for supplies opens twice daily. It is possible to arrive here by bus, as the kibbutz will transport you to the spa and the beach, but a car is virtually essential in order to stay and explore the area.

Kibbutz Ein Gedi, Mobile Post, Dead Sea 86980. © **08/659-4222**. Fax 08/658-4328. 120 units. $170–$300 ($85– £150) double. Discount available on Kibbutz Hotel Fly & Drive Package. Lowest rates in Jan–Feb and July. Reserve well in advance. AE, DC, MC, V. **Amenities:** 2 pools (indoor, outdoor); tennis courts; spa nearby; tour desk. *In room:* A/C, TV.

## Inexpensive

**Bet Sara Youth Hostel**    I highly recommend Bet Sara. Located off the main road, about 1.5km (1 mile) north of the kibbutz, this very clean, homey, and efficient hostel offers a fantastic view of the sea and mountains. There are four to eight beds per room, and each room has its own bathroom (shower only); if you reserve ahead, and the hostel is not at capacity, you may be able to rent a room as a double in the quieter (fewer school groups) Guest House section. The hostel has an outdoor cafe/bar and serves dinners for NIS 50 ($13/£6.25), as well as a convenient swimming beach off The Dead Sea. The snack bar, open from 5 to 8pm, sells simple supplies at higher than in-town prices, but you're far from civilization. There's no curfew or lockout; guests get 15% admission discount at Ein Gedi Nature Reserve.

Mobile Post, Dead Sea 86980. ⓒ **08/658-4165.** Fax 08/658-4445. 200 units. $38 (£19) per person double; $26 (£13) dorm bed. Take the bus from Beersheva via Arad, or from Jerusalem; ask the driver to stop near Bet Sara. AE, DC, MC, V. **Amenities:** Cafe; bar. *In room:* A/C, TV, minibar (some), fridge (some), coffeemaker.

## WHERE TO EAT

There's a nearby self-service restaurant at the Ein Gedi beach called **Pundak Ein Gedi.** The food is plain, but passable. Guests staying at Kibbutz Ein Gedi get a 15% discount. The air-conditioned restaurant serves breakfast, lunch, and "tea" until 6pm. Basic (kosher) chicken, meat, and vegetarian main courses are under NIS 45 ($11/£5.60). It's open daily 10am to 6pm; an adjacent minimart is open daily 7:30am to 8pm. Guests of Kibbutz Ein Gedi also get discounts for the Ein Gedi Spa restaurant and for the Ein Gedi Nature Reserve.

## MASADA ✸✸✸

It's a national tradition to make the ascent at least once, for Masada is the scene of what many believe is one of the most heroic and tragic incidents in Jewish history. Few non-Jews outside Israel had heard of Masada until the events were dramatized in a book and a subsequent television miniseries in 1981. The story of a small garrison that defied the Roman army, as the historian Flavius Josephus recorded and perhaps embellished it, is worth retelling.

King Herod had built a magnificent palace complex and fortress atop this nearly inaccessible desert plateau mountain around 30 B.C. Underground cisterns assured the fortress of a lavish water supply for the palace's baths and gardens, as well as for Herod's court. Most impressive was Herod's personal winter villa, the extraordinary hanging palace on the northern tip of Masada, calculated to catch the breathtaking vistas of the lake as well as the refreshing breezes from the north. He furnished the luxurious place with every comfort as well as storehouses of food and arms, protecting the entire establishment with impregnable fortifications. The audaciousness of such an undertaking tells much about Herod's personality. After Herod's death in 4 B.C., a small Roman garrison occupied the mount. However, during the Jewish Revolt against Rome in A.D. 66, a small band of Jewish zealots attacked and overtook the almost unattended fortress. They brought their families, lived off the vast storehouses of food, and had more than enough arms with which to defend themselves. The weapons were even put to use in raids on the surrounding countryside.

Finally, in A.D. 73, 3 years after the fall of Jerusalem and the end of the First Jewish Revolt, the Romans became so incensed with the Masada situation that they decided to put an end to this last pocket of Jewish resistance. They built a siege ramp up to the mountaintop, using captured Jews as slave laborers, knowing the defenders

# Masada

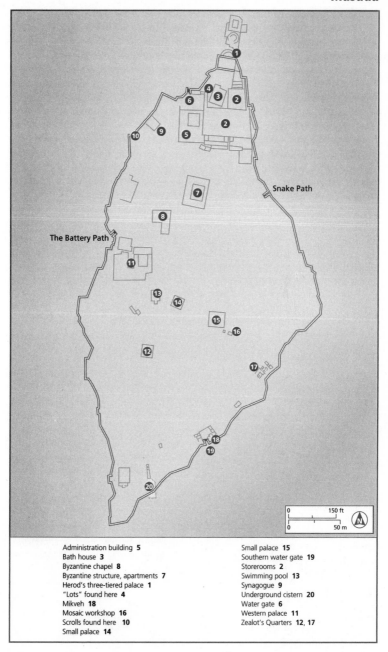

Snake Path

The Battery Path

| | |
|---|---|
| Administration building **5** | Small palace **15** |
| Bath house **3** | Southern water gate **19** |
| Byzantine chapel **8** | Storerooms **2** |
| Byzantine structure, apartments **7** | Swimming pool **13** |
| Herod's three-tiered palace **1** | Synagogue **9** |
| "Lots" found here **4** | Underground cistern **20** |
| Mikveh **18** | Water gate **6** |
| Mosaic workshop **16** | Western palace **11** |
| Scrolls found here **10** | Zealot's Quarters **12, 17** |
| Small palace **14** | |

0     150 ft
0     50 m

of Masada could not bring themselves to attack or harm their fellow countrymen. After a lengthy onslaught using siege engines, flaming torches, rock bombardments, and battering rams, the Masada fortress was still in Jewish hands. But with 10,000 Roman troops camped on the hillside and daily bombardments smashing at the walls, it became only a question of when the 900 defenders would succumb.

A brutal night attack spelled the end: Flaming torches thrown at the fort's wall were whipped by a wind into the midst of the defenders, and the garrison's gates caught fire. The Romans, seeing that Masada was practically defenseless, decided to wait until dawn and take it over in their own good time.

During that final night, the 900 men, women, and children who inhabited Masada held a desperate meeting. Their leader, Eliezer Ben-Yair, in a dramatic speech (as reported by the historian Flavius Josephus who, of course, was not actually present), persuaded his followers to accept death bravely, on their own terms. In the darkness at Masada nearly 2,000 years ago, one of history's great mass suicides occurred. Ten men were chosen as executioners. Members of families lay side by side and bared their throats. After all the families had been killed, one of the 10 executioners was chosen to kill the other nine; he then ran himself through on his own sword. Two women and five children survived, hiding in one of the caves on the plateau. The Romans, who had expected to fight their way in, were triply astonished at the lack of resistance, the eerie silence where they had expected to encounter battle, and at the "calm courage of [the defenders'] resolution . . . and utter contempt of death." So, Flavius Josephus wrote, ended the Jewish resistance against Rome. Like almost everything in Israel, the meaning of Masada has become a matter of controversy, with many contending that glorification of a political stand that resulted in mass suicide is not good for the national psyche.

## THE VISITOR CENTER & CLIMBING THE ASCENT

Masada is now a regional industry as well as a UNESCO World Heritage Site, and a new, air-conditioned state-of-the-art visitor complex has been set up at the entrance to the park, complete with a very useful history video and a model of ancient Masada, a small snack bar, and a souvenir shop. It doesn't fit in with the isolation and antiquity of Masada, but the air-conditioning and the chance to stock up here with bottled water will be most welcome. Portable audio guides can be rented here for NIS 24 ($6/£3). Park admission includes a pamphlet with a map of the Masada site.

From the parking lot at the foot of **Masada National Park** (© **08/658-4207;** www.parks.org.il), you've got two choices—climb on foot or ride the cable car that carries you almost to the summit. If you climb, especially in the summer months, be sure to start literally at the crack of dawn, or better yet, before. The heat is murderous by the middle of the day. Climbers are frantically urged by the National Parks Authority to wear hats and drink as much as possible before starting up. On days when the heat is too great, park rangers ban climbing, so in summer get to Masada before dawn if you are determined to make the climb.

Climbers have two choices: the route from The Dead Sea side, or the Roman siege ramp originally built in A.D. 73 on the side of the mountain facing in the direction of Arad (this Roman ramp path is only accessible by car from Arad). The route from The Dead Sea side requires from 30 minutes to an hour; it's called the **Snake Path** because of the steep, hairpin curves. The Snake Path opens approximately an hour before sunrise (so climbers can catch the sunrise) and closes at 3:30pm, and you must start down by then just to get to the bottom before dark. The same hours apply to the path up the other side. The mountainside path is called the **Battery,** after a battery the Romans

## Moments  Sunrise at Masada

The vistas from the top of Masada are awe-inspiring any time of day, but if you've made the climb up to the top in the predawn, you'll get to watch the sun coming up over the mountains of Jordan and its reflections in the other-worldly, sometimes mist-covered surface of The Dead Sea. There are many places to see dramatic sunrises in Israel, but sunrise at Masada holds special meaning and mystery for those who make their way to the plateau during the night. It's impossible not to think of the inhabitants of Masada, who made their way here after the fall of Jerusalem in A.D. 70, perhaps convinced they were the last hope for the survival of Judaism and belief in one god. In a quiet part of the plateau, you can understand the loneliness and despair they must have endured when it became clear defeat was certain, and you can almost touch the ghostly silence of the final dawn they never let themselves live to see.

built there. Getting to the top via that route takes only 15 to 30 minutes. Most visitors are happy to use the cable car to ascend and descend. *Note:* **Special access pathways** have been created on top of Masada for those with disabilities, and special arrangements can be made to help transport those with special needs to the top. Call for information and special help in advance.

The **Sound and Light Show,** lasting 45 minutes, is usually given Tuesday and Thursday evenings at an outdoor theater on the Arad (western) side of Masada. The theater is not accessible from Hwy. 90, which runs along The Dead Sea, so allow 45 minutes to get there by car (your hotel will give you the best directions). For exact time schedules and reservations, call © **08/995-9333.** Admission is NIS 50 ($13/£6.25). A historical narrative is given in Hebrew, but simultaneous translations can be rented.

Admission to Masada is NIS 25 ($6.25/£3.10) for adults and half-price for children; combined admission plus round-trip cable car is NIS 66 ($17/£8.25). Cable cars operate Sunday through Thursday from 8am to 4pm, on Friday and eves of holidays (including Sat) from 8am to 2pm. The cable car will deposit you about 45 very steep steps from the fortress top.

### THE RUINS OF MASADA

Masada excavations have unearthed perhaps the most exciting ruins in the entire country in terms of physical drama and historical mystique. Yigael Yadin's beautifully photographed book, *Masada,* carefully recounts the archaeological expedition that uncovered the original palace, walls, houses, straw bags, plaits of hair, pottery shards, stone vessels, cosmetic items, cooking utensils, synagogue, and important scroll fragments. Among the most intriguing finds are the ways the palace was adapted for use as a stronghold for guerrilla fighters and their families. Evidence from this period includes ritual baths *(mikvahs)* built by the observant defenders, and the ostraca marked with Hebrew names that might have been the very lots cast by the defenders in their final moments as they decided who among them would be chosen to kill the others rather than die at the hands of the Romans. You can also see the ruins of the Roman siege encampments, which provide an amazingly preserved visual lesson in Roman military field strategy. A later Byzantine chapel with a mosaic floor was built on Masada, and there are signs of Byzantine-era habitation in the ruined buildings of the palace. The desolation of the place in later centuries is testified to by archaeologists' discovery of the remains of a few human bones chomped on by hyenas and other wild beasts.

## WHERE TO STAY

**Masada Guest House and Youth Hostel** *(★ (Value*    This brand-new, dazzlingly contemporary complex offers air-conditioned rooms, each with its own private shower-only bathroom, TV, minifridge, and electric kettle. Everything is very simple, but well designed and fresh. With large terraces and lounges that overlook The Dead Sea and breathtaking desertscapes and sprawling wings that help separate guests reserving private rooms from larger, possibly noisy groups, the Masada Youth Hostel is a wonderful budget choice for those who want to explore The Dead Sea region without having to stay at an expensive, glitzy hotel. It's also especially useful for nature enthusiasts, hikers, and for travelers who want to make the traditional (strenuous) ascent up Masada in the cool predawn hours. Just tumble out of bed, and you're ready to make the climb. Otherwise, you'd have to leave your Tel Aviv or Jerusalem hotel at 2am and make the long, dark drive down to The Dead Sea for this unforgettable experience. Youth hostels in Israel are open to guests of all ages, and if you don't have a Hostel Association card, you can stay here for a rate that's only a few shekels more than members pay. As long as you're not traveling during summer, on weekends, or Jewish holidays, when the hostel is usually very busy, the management can generally arrange for two people or a family to be alone in a room (the price for a private double will be higher than for a dorm bed). When possible, student groups and individual travelers are booked into separate wings. At this super hostel, towels, sheets, soap, and shampoo are provided. Breakfast is included, and lunch and dinner or picnic meals can be arranged. All food services are kosher, and there's a synagogue on premises.

Masada National Park, Rte. 90. (C) **08/995-3222** or 599/510-511 in Israel. Fax 08/658-4650. www.iyha.org.il. 88 units, all with private shower. $76 (£38) double; $26 (£13) dormitory bed; $17 (£8.50) children 3–13 staying in parent's room. Rates include breakfast. MC, V. Free parking. Egged bus no. 444 from Jerusalem or Eilat or bus no. 384 from Beersheva via Arad (for both buses, ask driver for special stop at Masada hostel). **Amenities:** Synagogue. *In room:* A/C, TV, fridge, teakettle.

## 4 Into the Negev

Talmudic scholars say that Negev means "dry," and Old Testament experts claim it means "south." Both are correct—in literal terms. A vast wilderness of almost 10,360 sq. km (4,000 sq. miles), this desert is Israel's future—for population expansion, for chemical industries, and for farming. In fact, studies show that one-fifth of the desert can be used for some form of agriculture.

This region is a constantly varying landscape of red, black, and yellow, accented by valleys, deep craters, and burnt-brown mountains. Craggy limestone walls, mounds of sandstone, and red and green dunes of sand are everywhere strewn with great blocks of black volcanic silex. Saw-toothed mountain ridges, abruptly hollowed out by the wild gorges left from the Great Middle Eastern Earthquake, starkly point back to the day when these mountains just fell down and this desert opened its granite jaws to everything living on top of it. In this petrified desert world, temperatures can range from 125°F (52°C) during the day to 40°F (4°C) in a winter dawn.

There are two possible routes into the Negev. The faster route is Hwy. 90, along from Sodom to Eilat. Or you can go to Beersheva and take the older and slower but more interesting route through the heart of the Negev to the Port of Eilat on the Red Sea. If you choose the latter, there are several major points of interest along this bleak but fascinating road. If you're driving, stop the car at some uninhabited spot and listen to the almost frightening stillness. Equally mysterious are the secondary roads—cryptic paths winding their way into the flatlands and beyond the dunes, toward agricultural collectives. The Port of Eilat on the Red Sea is at the end of either route. Be sure to bring extra water, both for yourself and your car.

## SHIVTA

Shivta is an impressive site, but it's in the middle of nowhere, hard to get to, and has no facilities. If you have a car or plan to go on a tour, this can be a very worthwhile, atmospheric excursion—there's a good chance you'll have this ruined city all to yourself; otherwise spend your time at the other ruined Nabatean cities of Avdat or Mamshit.

Shivta is about 50km (31 miles) southwest of Beersheva, in the military zone about 8km (5 miles) off the Nizzana road. It's important not to get lost in the military zone, so here are explicit directions: From the highway, the Shivta road is two lanes and paved for the first 2.5km (1½ miles). It then narrows, and after another kilometer you pass a road, on the left, to the military installation. After passing this road, it's another 5km (3 miles) over a rough, curvy one-lane road to Shivta. There are few signs. Officially Shivta is a national park, but there is no office or telephone at this deserted location. Admission, if anyone is around to collect it, is NIS 12 ($3/£1.50) for adults and half-price for children 17 and under.

The Nabateans, a desert merchant people whose capital was the legendary city of Petra, in Jordan, established Shivta in the 1st century B.C., but Shivta (or Subeita) reached its high point during the time of Justinian the Great (6th c. A.D.), when Byzantine wealth and caravan trade were at their height. In addition to commercial wealth, Shivta's ingenious citizens built an elaborate irrigation and water-collection system that allowed them to farm the barren soil. Israelis are studying Nabatean irrigation techniques to this day.

Eventually trade routes slowly changed, and though Shivta survived as an Arab outpost for many centuries, by the 1100s it was a ghost town.

The ruins of Shivta remained in fairly good condition throughout the centuries because they were too far away from newer building sites to make pillage economical. As a result, the city, which dates from the 500s, is still somewhat intact. Restoration work began in 1958. Buildings restored include three churches, a mosque, a caravansary, two water-collection pools, and houses. Signs identify and discuss the principal buildings.

## SDE BOKER & AVDAT

About 50km (31 miles) due south of Beersheva, surrounded by sand and parched mountains, you suddenly come to a farm settlement—the famous Ben-Gurion kibbutz, Sde Boker. The settlement began in May 1952, at the prime minister's instigation, when the country was first encouraging settlers to populate the Negev. Ben-Gurion became a member of this kibbutz in 1953; he lived and worked here until his death in 1973, at the age of 87. He and his wife, Paula, are buried here, and his fascinating personal papers, photos, and eclectic collection of books on history, philosophy, and religion may be seen in the **Paula and David Ben-Gurion Hut** (© **08/ 655-0320** or 655-8444; www.bgh.org.il). The hut remains as it was when Ben-Gurion lived in it. Visiting hours are Sunday through Thursday from 8:30am to 3:30pm, on Friday, Saturday, holidays, and holiday eves from 8:30am to 2pm. Admission is NIS 12 ($3/£1.50).

Over the years Sde Boker began to thrive, as did several other young settlements in the Negev. A campus of the Ben-Gurion University of the Negev has been established at Sde Boker. A modern library, housing the **Ben-Gurion Institute and Archives** (📞 **08/655-5057**) and containing 750,000 documents associated with Israel's first chief of state, is located here. The institute also contains a **Research Center for Solar Energy** and a **Museum of Desert Sculpture,** a collection of art created from natural objects and materials found in the desert. The institute also serves as a center for the study of desert areas. It's open daily from 9am to 5pm; you must phone ahead for tours, which are given by appointment for NIS 10 ($2.50/£1.25).

**The graves of David and Paula Ben-Gurion** are 3km (2 miles) southwest of the Ben-Gurion House, to the right of the Gate of Sde Boker College. The site, chosen by Ben-Gurion, overlooks the dramatic Zin Valley, with the greenery of the Ein Avdat spring in the distance to the right.

**Avdat Archaeological Park** ✦, 20km (12 miles) south of the Paula and David Ben-Gurion Hut on Rte. 40 (📞 **08/655-0954**), was a major city built by the Nabateans in the 2nd century B.C. as a caravan post on a spice and trading route that ran from the Red Sea to the Nabatean capital at Petra, then to Avdat, Beersheva, and onward to Gaza on the Mediterranean coast. The city reached its peak of importance during Roman and Byzantine times and went into decline after the Roman conquest in the 7th century A.D.

Situated on a cliff 600m (1,969 ft.) above sea level, and with many partially restored structures, Avdat offers dramatic vistas across the desert; along with the ruined Nabatean city of Mamshit, it was used for location shots in the film *Jesus Christ Superstar.* The western half of Avdat's acropolis contains the ruins of two Byzantine churches; the eastern section is dominated by the city's fortress. Beyond the acropolis are a large Byzantine-era wine press and an olive press, evidence of the Nabateans' amazing ability to irrigate and farm the desolate Negev 1,500 years ago. Admission to the Avdat Archaeological Park is NIS 20 ($5/£2.50) for adults and half-price for those 17 and under. It is open from 8am to 5pm (until 4pm in winter). There is a small visitor center (📞 **08/658-6391**) at the entrance offering snacks, very good pamphlets with explanatory maps, and a brief video. Beside the ruins of Avdat, the Hebrew University has operated an experimental farm for the past 40 years in which Nabatean agricultural techniques, as uncovered by archaeologists, are being explored and redeveloped.

## WHERE TO STAY NEAR SDE BOKER & AVDAT

**Chan HaShayarot (Caravan Inn)** *Kids* This traveler's khan (a traditional Middle Eastern inn) consists of a gigantic, authentic Bedouin tent for dinner parties and communal sleeping, plus a group of modern, very simple but bright, clean private units for those not up to tenting. The Bedouin tent is an ecological wonder—warm in winter; cool and catching every possible desert night's breeze in the summer. Depending on your fellow travelers, the inn can be a quiet semicamping experience, with simple Bedouin meals, or it might consist of party groups and a Bedouin feast that you can join up with plus music and dance (the Bedouin entertainment is only available when ordered by large groups). There are central restroom and shower facilities; sleeping bags are provided in the tent. Tours with camels, off-road vehicles, and mountain bikes are offered as well as Bedouin hospitality and a night sky filled with galaxies and falling stars.

Rte. 40, between Sde Boker and Mitzpe Ramon. 📞 **08/653-5777.** Fax 08/653-5888. www.shayarot.com. 24 units, all with bathroom. $90 (£45) double, private indoor unit with bathroom; $55 (£28) for 2 people in tent. Bedouin dinner

$25 (£13) per person; must be ordered in advance. Rates include breakfast. MC, V. **Amenities:** Dining tent; organized tours. *In room:* A/C, kitchenette, fridge.

## MAMSHIT NATIONAL PARK

The ruins of Nabatean cities carry a certain aura of mystery and grandeur about them. This third ruined Nabatean city, 6km (4 miles) southeast of Dimona, is probably a few centuries older than Avdat and was built on a slightly more important trade route. It was a town of large caravansaries, warehouses, and accounting offices; by Roman times, the town sported large public bathhouses, villas with wall murals, and houses of pleasure. The two large, well-preserved Byzantine-era churches may have been converted to mosques after the Muslim conquest in A.D. 635, judging from Koranic verses inscribed on the walls of their ruins. However, the city seems to have been permanently abandoned not long after that time, and the inscriptions may have been made after the city was no longer inhabited. The ruins are set above Machtesh Ha-Gadol, one of the Negev's dramatic erosion craters. Mamshit National Park (© **08/655-6478**) is open daily 8am to 5pm; until 4pm in winter. Admission is NIS 20 ($5/£2.50).

## MITZPE RAMON ⟨⟩

Mitzpe Ramon (pop. 7,000) lies 139km (86 miles) south of Beersheva and appears to be a typical Negev development community if you approach it from the north. What you don't immediately see is the town's location right at the edge of the spectacular **Ramon Crater,** a vast, breathtakingly beautiful geologic depression formed by erosion that has exposed a virtual encyclopedia of fossils and geologic structures. Founded in 1954 as a clay-mining town and way station on the long road then being built through the desert to the isolated outpost of Eilat, Mitzpe Ramon was bypassed by the new, more direct road to Eilat built through the Arava Valley after the 1967 war.

Mitzpe Ramon struggled to survive as a viable economic community during the 1970s and 1980s. The Ramon Crater (which had not been picked up by aerial surveys during British Mandate times and was only discovered after the 1948 War of Independence) had not yet captured the imagination of travelers. It has only been since 1990, with the establishment of the Ramon Inn to accommodate middle- and upper-range visitors, that a tourism industry has begun to develop here. In the town's industrial area, artists' workshops and galleries have opened. A luxury resort is planned to overlook the sweeping site. The community has a great public spirit and gives you an opportunity to get a feel for day-to-day life in the kind of Negev community that Ben-Gurion envisioned as an important part of Israel's future. You can also feel the isolation and mystery of the Negev plateau. Sunsets and twilights at the edge of the crater usually bring out an extraordinary vista of changing colors as the landscape slowly sinks into darkness.

### WHAT TO SEE & DO

The **Mitzpe Ramon Visitors Center** (© **08/658-8620**) at the edge of the crater, housed in a large modern structure designed to resemble the spiral-shaped sea fossils embedded in the local rocks, is staffed by people trained by the Israel Nature Reserves Authority; the bookstore/gift shop is a good place to pick up background and hiking information as well as topographical maps. There are slide and film shows, and a museum exhibit of the area's geology, flora, and fauna, including the **Bio Ramon** habitat filled with local porcupines, scorpions, and lizards. Admission, including the Bio Ramon habitat, is NIS 44 ($11/£5.50). It is open Saturday through Thursday from 8am to 4pm and Friday 8am to 3pm.

The Ramon Crater is perhaps at its most accessible in the spring or fall, when it's not too hot or too bitterly cold. Whenever you happen to visit, it's worthwhile to invest in a professional tour or guide. There is a range of activities including 2- to 3-hour jeep and dune buggy tours that leave Mitzpe Ramon several times a day and cost NIS 160 ($40/£20) per person; full and overnight tours run roughly in the range of NIS 400 to NIS 800 ($100–$200/£50–£100). The visitor center and the Ramon Inn will have information on current guides and guiding tour companies; you can also arrange 2- and 3-day desert expeditions, including accommodations in Bedouin-style tents, camel tours, mountain-bike rentals, rappelling, escorted hikes, and Bedouin evenings complete with dinner. For a reputable local company, look into Negev Land Tours (www.negevland.co.il). At times, the **Society for Protection of Nature in Israel (SPNI)** offers excellent **Yarok** nature hikes that run about NIS 90 ($23/£11), as well as other tours, but you must book in advance. Serious hikers should get advice and maps at the Mitzpe Ramon SPNI Field School Information Center, located about a 2km (⅔-mile) walk beyond the southern end of Ben-Gurion St. (© **08/658-8615** or 658-8616). For more information and a schedule of Yarok tours, go to www.aspni.org.

For an overview of the Ramon Crater, turn left as you exit the visitor center and follow the 1km (½-mile) promenade alongside the crater's rim. Sunset is a good time for walking; with luck, you'll spot an ibex in the distance or an eagle aloft on the evening wind. In the opposite direction, you'll find the wonderful **Desert Sculpture Park,** with the sky and the crater as backdrop for works by a number of international and Israeli artists. To get there, drive out of the visitor center, make a left onto the main road, go past the gas station on the right, and make a right turn at the sign for Ma'ale Noah.

The **Alpaca Farm** ⚐ (© **08/658-8047;** www.alpaca.co.il) is 3km (1¾ miles) outside of town. Founded in 1987, this establishment raises both alpacas and llamas and produces fine alpaca and llama wool. The alpacas have a charm of their own, and after the Ramon Crater, they are the town's most memorable tourist attraction. Adorable, gentle, and fluffy, they quickly bond with anyone carrying a small paper bag of feed sold on the premises for NIS 6 ($1.50/75p). At times, they may spit (they are distantly related to camels), but they mean nothing personal. You can also visit the llama herd, but the llamas are not as whimsical. Kids can ride llamas at the farm for NIS 20 ($5/£2.50) for 15 minutes. Guided **llama treks** through the Ramon Crater can be arranged through the Alpaca Farm with gentle, intelligent llamas carrying your packs and serving as mounts for small children. The Alpaca Farm has an open-air snack bar serving light meals. Admission is NIS 28 ($7/£3.50). The farm is open daily 8:30am to 6pm and until 4:30pm in winter.

## WHERE TO STAY

**Isrotel Ramon Inn** ⚐    The Ramon Inn makes the Ramon Crater accessible to travelers unwilling to stay in a youth hostel or field school, and also brings hope of a genuine tourist industry to Mitzpe Ramon. The entire town is helping to make the project a success. A low-rise apartment block was totally rebuilt to create a modern inn composed of comfortable, tastefully decorated living room/bedroom suites with kitchenettes. The lobby sports a free-standing fireplace where guests gather on chilly desert nights; very helpful staff can plug you into local hiking and mountain biking; the inn's kitchen produces fabulous home-style buffet meals (see below); and the large, sunny indoor swimming pool and wet and dry saunas are just the thing after a day of trekking. Eco-friendly products are used throughout the hotel. Although this is not a kibbutz, you can book the Ramon Inn through the Kibbutz Hotel chain and get a considerable discount.

1 Aqev St., Mitzpe Ramon. ℂ **888/669-5700** or 08/658-8822. Fax 08/658-8151. www.isrotel.co.il. 96 units. $180–$220 (£90–£110) for 2–6 persons per room. Rates include breakfast. Half and full board can be arranged. Substantial discounts on Isrotel and Kibbutz Hotel chain plans. AE, DC, MC, V. Free parking. **Amenities:** Dining room; cafe; indoor heated pool; laundry service; nonsmoking rooms. *In room:* A/C, TV, kitchenette, minibar, coffeemaker, safe.

**Succah in the Desert** ℛ *Finds*    There's nothing like this in Israel—here you can experience the desert's immense silence, wind, and stars. Eight *succot* (simple shelters) dot the landscape around the central *succah,* which serves as a place for meals and guests to meet. Each *succah* is different, but all are made with walls of sheltering rocks and roofs of natural materials, and have areas open to the air. There are carpets covering earthen floors; comfortable mattresses, blankets, and bed linens; an enormous clay jar in which water is kept miraculously cool; copper vessels for washing; and ecologically sound solar-powered lamps and heaters. If you don't wish to blend totally into nature, there is a nonpolluting toilet and a solar shower near the main *succah.* You can do your own thing, but encampment is for meditation and spiritual renewal, so you are asked not to intrude on the quiet of others. Vegetarian meals are served.

PO Box 272, Mitzpe Ramon 80600 (7.5km [4½ miles] outside Mitzpe Ramon on the road to the Alpaca Farm). ℂ **08/658-6280** or 658-8267. Fax 08/658-6464. www.succah.co.il. 8 desert shelters, with shared bathrooms. Weekdays $130 (£65) double; Shabbat $160 (£80) double. Rates include half board; student discounts possible. AE, MC, V. **Amenities:** Dining room; meditation center; transportation to and from Mitzpe Ramon.

## WHERE TO DINE
**Hannah's Restaurant** *Value* ISRAELI    No frills or ambience, but the food at this cafeteria is good and has style. Soups, salads, schnitzel, and the house couscous (served Tues and Fri) are the best menu bets.

Next to Paz gas station near entrance to town. ℂ **08/668-8158.** Main courses NIS 36–NIS 48 ($9–$12/£4.50–£6). Cash only. Sun–Thurs 9am–6pm; Fri 9am–3pm.

**Ramon Inn Restaurant** ℛ *Finds* INTERNATIONAL    The dinner menu here is composed of family recipes contributed by the best local cooks and served in an all-you-can-eat buffet that varies from night to night; when it's good, it is one of the best meals you'll find in Israel. The choices represent traditions that range from Morocco and Yemen to Russia and Hungary. I strongly urge you to sample everything and then zero in on a dish with herbs, seasonings, or sauces that catches your fancy. Dessert, sometimes exotic, sometimes average, is included, as are coffee, tea, and other beverages. The restaurant also serves a buffet breakfast, with many special homemade jams, salads, pita bread made on the spot, and other unusual items. If you are a guest at the Ramon Inn and charge your meal to your room, the 15.5% VAT should be deducted from the price if you pay your bill in foreign currency. A meal here is a delicious way to end a winter's day of trekking the crater. Be at the dining room when the doors open—later things will be gone.

In the Ramon Inn. ℂ **08/658-8822.** Reservations necessary. Fixed-price meal NIS 120 ($30/£15). AE, DC, MC, V. Daily breakfast 7:30–9:30am; dinner 7–9pm.

## NORTH OF EILAT
As you travel down Rte. 90 toward Eilat, you'll pass a number of attractions that can be visited along the way or on day excursions from Eilat.

**Timna Valley Park** 𝒶    You'll need a car (or an organized tour from Eilat) to get around this vast park, but if you're driving to or from Eilat, it's a very worthwhile stop. At the entrance gate, you'll receive a road map with your admission fee. Not only is the landscape at Timna breathtaking (and not visible from Hwy. 90), but it's also historic. As you drive the byways of Timna, you can explore **ancient Egyptian copper mines** with sandstone arches, underground mining shafts, and galleries; about 3km (2 miles) from the mines, along a side road, is a parking area from which you make a short walk to see a **cliff wall carved with figures in chariots,** believed to be from Egyptian times. All these twists and turns are marked clearly by signs.

Along the roads you'll notice **"the Mushroom,"** a curious rock formation with a huge boulder resting on a column of sandstone, the result of erosion. But the most striking formation in the preserve is undoubtedly **Solomon's Pillars,** a series of vast sandstone fins jutting out of a rock face (and at times, the exotic background for wonderful outdoor moonlight concerts and dance performances in summer). Climb into the fins along a path with steps to see some **Egyptian rock carvings,** and then down the steps on the other side to the remains of a **small temple** dedicated to the Egyptian goddess Hathor.

The spare, clean air of the desert, the hot sun, and the quiet of the preserve are sure to make a lasting impression. You can get information on **hiking trails** from the staff at the main gate or at the visitor center. The development of Timna Valley National Park has become a major project of the Jewish National Fund of America. An artificial recreational lake and architecturally stunning **visitor center** have been built in the **Nechushtan Recreation Area** not far from Solomon's Pillars and the Sphinx. An outdoor Bedouin restaurant/cafe serves refreshments and simple meals (especially nice in the quiet of a hot summer night). The visitor center pavilion includes a cafeteria, a shop for traveling supplies, and a slide/video show on the history of Timna.

27km (17 miles) north of Eilat. ℂ 08/632-6555. Admission NIS 42 ($11/£5.60) adults; NIS 36 ($9/£4.50) children. Sept–June Sat–Thurs 8am–4pm, Fri 8am–1pm; July–Aug Sun and Fri 8am–1pm, Mon–Thurs and Sat 8am–1pm and 6–8:30pm. Tour buses leave from Eilat daily for Timna at 8am.

**Yotvata Hai Bar Wildlife Reserve** 𝒦𝒾𝒹𝓈    The purpose of this 3,200-hectare (7,907-acre) reserve is to save rare and endangered desert animals mentioned in the Bible, as well as other rare desert animals of western Asia and northern Africa, breeding them for eventual release into the wild. Among the 450 kinds of animals found here are the Nubian ibex, the Dorcas gazelle, the Persian onager, the scimitar-horned oryx, the addax antelope, and the Arabian gazelle, as well as wolves, hyenas, foxes, desert cats, caracal, leopards, cheetahs, wild donkeys, lots of ostriches, and many species of snakes, lizards, and even predatory birds. Many of these animals are nocturnal, due to the blistering desert heat, but a special dark room makes it possible to observe these creatures during your daylight visit. You can also ride around the reserve in special coaches (closed vehicles only) and observe the animals at close range. An interesting time to visit is 11am to 1pm, when the animals are getting their lunchtime feedings, though some children may be upset by the predators' eating habits.

You'll notice that the Hai Bar reserve has many acacia trees, signifying that water is lying below the arid desert. This area is known as the **Yotvata Oasis,** and it is believed that it was one of the places where Moses stopped as he brought the Children of Israel up out of Egypt.

*Note:* If you have no car, you can take a guided tour from Eilat, which takes about 2 hours.

35km (22 miles) north of Eilat. (C) **08/637-3057.** Admission, including guided tour, NIS 23 ($5.75/£2.90) for either wildlife reserve or predator center only. Sun–Thurs 8am–5pm; Fri–Sat 8:30am–4pm.

# ARAVA VALLEY
## THREE SPECIAL KIBBUTZIM ⊛

As Israel has solidified its position as a 21st-century, high-tech, business-savvy nation, it's become increasingly hard for travelers to find the idealistic, hardworking, "reclaiming-the-land" society that is so much a part of Israel's image. The once simple guest rooms of kibbutzim in the Galilee and central Israel have morphed into three- and four-star country hotels where travelers experience little interaction with the workings of the large and thriving kibbutz communities that manage them. However, three small desert kibbutzim in the dramatic Arava Valley—**Kibbutz Lotan, Kibbutz Yahel,** and **Kibbutz Ketura**—30 minutes by car north of Eilat, are becoming places where Israel's pioneering vision and spirit can still be shared.

Founded in the 1970s and 1980s, largely by Israelis from English-speaking countries (although now home to residents from a wide range of backgrounds), these kibbutzim, supported by the Movement for Progressive Judaism, are all involved in building creative, ecologically sensitive communities in the desert. In a time when most Israelis have forgotten Ben-Gurion's prediction that the country's future lies in the Negev, these kibbutzim are living his vision. Though minuscule in size, they are showing Israeli society how to recycle, live inventively, and create communities that are fun, filled with beauty, and in harmony with nature and the land. All offer very simple guest facilities and a wide variety of programs that allow travelers to interact with both the desert and the kibbutz experience. Again, guest facilities are *very* simple—this is the desert and you may find ants in your kitchenette and no pay TV movies in your room. But for travelers not into luxury, this is a chance to see a special side of Israel.

**Kibbutz Ketura**    This kibbutz is close to Lotan and offers the most comfortable guest accommodations of any of the three kibbutzim in the area (built with a grant from American supporters). The kibbutz is famous for its beautiful experimental orchards and is especially proud of the work of Dr. Elaine Soloway, who has brought to life a date sapling (named "Methusala"), spouted from 2,000-year-old seeds found at Masada. There's a family-oriented feel here. On Shabbat guests are invited to order the kibbutz Friday night dinner and join the evening service. The management is very helpful and hosts programs in Judaism, nature, eco-tours, massage, and relaxation therapy. Air-conditioned guest rooms contain new bathrooms and stocked kitchenettes; some two-room family suites with palm-frond shaded terraces are available.

Arava Rd. (C) **08/635-6658.** www.redseadesert.com. 44 units. $75–$100 (£38–£50) double; $125–$150 (£63–£75) family suite. Rates include breakfast. MC, V. **Amenities:** Dining room; pools (indoor, outdoor); massage; recreational facilities; playground. *In room:* A/C, cable TV, kitchenette, coffeemaker.

**Kibbutz Lotan** *(Finds)*    This is perhaps the most interesting of the three kibbutzim, with its Center for Eco-tourism and Creativity that includes programs in desert ecology, alternative building, permaculture, recycling, short and long desert hikes, birdwatching, and programs of holistic medicine and massage. You'll be amazed by Lotan's marvelous, inventive buildings, fashioned from recycled materials (all of Israel knows to send its outworn auto tires to Lotan). Tours of the region can be arranged, including Bedouin hospitality encounters, Red Sea snorkeling and diving, excursions to the nearby Timna National Park, or even to Petra, in Jordan. There are special programs designed for youth and others for families; at times the kibbutz hosts workshops on

Arab/Jewish understanding and intercultural communication. Lotan's Desert Birding programs are becoming world famous.

Accommodations at Lotan are very simple, but air-conditioned, either hostel-style or in private doubles that include kitchenettes and private shower-only bathrooms. Lunch and dinner can be arranged in the kibbutz dining hall, which serves kosher food (vegetables and salads are full of flavor, grown on Lotan's organic fields). There is a large outdoor kibbutz swimming pool, open from May to October. There's no TV in the rooms, but Wednesday and Friday are pub nights, with music, drinks, food, and good atmosphere; there's no smoking Friday after Shabbat begins. Other ways to spend a desert evening include the small heated indoor watsu treatment pool, relaxing with wine and refreshments under the stars at the outdoor pool (open May–Oct), or taking solar-heated tea in the vine-covered geodesic gazebo. Lotan is filled with enchanting places to gather and talk. For those who need to be connected, there's a TV lounge and free Internet access. Lunch, the day's main meal, is $11 (£5.50); the lighter dairy meal served at dinner is $6 (£3). If you arrange in advance and have a cellphone, pickup from Rte. 90 for guests traveling by bus is possible.

Arava Rd. ⓒ 08/635-6935. www.kibbutzlotan.com. 20 units. $95–$116 (£48–£58) double; add $16 (£8) for child in parent's room. Rates include breakfast. MC, V. **Amenities:** Dining room; lounge; pools (indoor, outdoor). *In room:* A/C, kitchenette, fridge, coffeemaker.

**Kibbutz Yahel**   Founded in 1976, this was the first Reform (Progressive) Jewish kibbutz in Israel. Like the others, it's small—30 families with approximately 70 children—and its economy is based on agriculture and simple desert tourism. Again, there is family atmosphere, and it is possible to arrange a Friday night dinner and to join services. The staff will also give out advice on arranging nature hikes and tours. Cheapest are 14 very simple hostel rooms; better are simple "country lodging" rooms with private shower-only bathrooms; best are 18 pleasant new "tourist" rooms with a feng shui design. Breakfast and a main meal at lunchtime and Friday night dinner are available (meal prices range $8–$15/£4–£7.50); no weeknight dinner is served unless ordered in advance by groups, but the kibbutz will lend you a barbecue grill, and you can prepare food in your kitchenette. No pickup from Rte. 90 for bus travelers is offered.

Arava Rd. ⓒ 08/635-7967. Fax 08/635-7051. www.redseadesert.com or www.kibbutzyahel.com. 42 units. Weekdays $60–$85 (£30–£43) double; weekend and holidays $70–$115 (£35–£58) double; additional child $16 (£8). AE, DC, MC, V. **Amenities:** Dining room; outdoor pool; tennis courts; basketball court; minimart; guided tours. *In room:* A/C, TV, kitchenette, coffeemaker, microwave (tourist room).

## 5 Eilat

243km (151 miles) S of Beersheva; 356km (221 miles) SE of Tel Aviv

This city of 70,000 at the southern tip of the Negev is the country's leading winter tourist resort. Eilat's chief claims to fame for the tourist are busy beaches with almost no wave action, coral reefs filled with exotic fish, and year-round sunshine. What was once a small, relaxed desert and Red Sea resort town now hosts 50 gargantuan upscale hotels and a downtown waterfront lined with jewelry shops, sneaker stores, and hawker's booths where visitors can while away their evenings. It's easygoing, fun, and mindless—and Israelis, both Jewish and Arab, flock here to forget the pressures of daily life. Lots of European package tourists jet directly into Eilat (and see nothing else in Israel), but most of the Scandinavian swimmers and snorkelers who were the mainstay of Eilat's winter season have moved on. The architectural style of Eilat's hotels and shopping malls has been agreed upon—new buildings are all of white concrete with

# Eilat

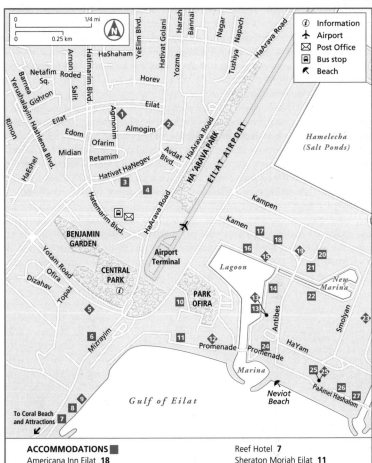

**ACCOMMODATIONS** ■

Americana Inn Eilat **18**
Club Hotel Eilat **6**
Crowne Plaza Eilat **16**
Dalia Hotel **10**
Dan Eilat Hotel Club **26**
Golden Tulip Eilat **17**
Herods Palace Hotel Complex **27**
Hilton Eilat Queen of Sheba Hotel **24**
Holiday Inn Eilat Patio **4**
Isrotel King Solomon's Palace **14**
Isrotel Lagoona All-Inclusive Hotel **13**
Isrotel Riviera Club **22**
Isrotel Royal Beach Hotel **25**
Le Méridien All Suite Hotel **8**
Marina Club Eilat **21**
Nova All Suite Hotel **3**

Reef Hotel **7**
Sheraton Moriah Eilat **11**
Vista **20**

**DINING** ◆

Agadir Burger Bar **19**
Casa do Brasil **2**
Denise Kingdom **23**
Eddie's Hideaway **1**
Ginger **5**
Pago Pago **15**
Red Sea Star Underwater
    Restaurant, Bar and
    Observatory **9**
Spring Onion Restaurant Cafe **12**
Tandoori **13**
Wang's Grill **25**

straight, crisp geometric lines; older hotels are being redesigned to conform to the light, airy look. There is a unity to the new Eilat, but from the outside, most hotels seem to vary only in size and shape. Planners have not emphasized the desert and Bedouin traditions of the region—instead they've aimed for the generic look of a gleaming white international resort, such as Cancún, Mexico. If you're hoping for a touch of regional color in your hotel, you'll have to try the Sinai or the new five-star establishments in Petra (Jordan).

Eilat is also a military outpost and shipping port—you'll see ample evidence of this all along the shoreline. The city's first-class hotel area is less than a mile from the Jordanian border, and you can see the Jordanian port city of Aqaba, with a population of 20,000, across the bay in a haze of desert sand, ringed by date palms. For almost 50 years, until Israel and Jordan signed a peace treaty in 1994, Aqaba seemed as unattainable as a mirage. There is now a border crossing for tourists just north of Eilat, and from Eilat you can also book excursions to Jordan's fabulous lost canyon city of Petra. For some time, Egypt, Israel, and Jordan have quietly been planning a regional coordinating committee and international park, which will protect the ecosystem of this end of the Red Sea, but this awaits a regional peace agreement. Meanwhile the area remains the most peaceful of Israel's borders. Even before the 1994 peace agreement with Jordan, when one of King Hussein's prize racehorses bolted and swam from Aqaba to Eilat, he was returned as if such incidents were an everyday occurrence. Saudi Arabia is 20km (12 miles) south of Aqaba—you can see it from the beaches in Eilat.

It was from the port of Eilat that King Solomon sent and received his ships from the land of Ophir, laden with gold, wood, and ivory. Dominating this exotic trade route with Solomon was Hiram of Tyre, Solomon's famous naval ally (Hiram was king of the Phoenician trading city of Tyre on the Mediterranean coast north of Israel). It is even thought by some that the Queen of Sheba landed at Eilat when she came to Jerusalem to see Solomon and "commune with him all that was in her heart." From 1000 to 600 B.C., Phoenician shipping from Eilat plied the shores of East Africa and at times developed trade with the coasts of India and even Southeast Asia. There is evidence that on occasion, Phoenician vessels circumnavigated the African continent. Today, the port is again bustling. This is an individualist's town, and it's also an entrepreneur's dream.

During summer, the outdoor afternoon heat in Eilat can exceed 110°F (43°C); it's best to stay in the shade between noon and 4pm to avoid sun poisoning. In winter, the thick dusty heat is gone and the air is cool and dry, but the water is warm enough for swimming, especially if you're used to the waters of the North Atlantic.

## ESSENTIALS

**GETTING THERE    By Plane**    Several daily **Arkia Airlines** flights (© **800/444-888** toll-free inside Israel, or 08/638-4888) arrive from points north. The downtown airport is right in the heart of town, next to the hotel district, and can receive only smaller aircraft; larger planes and international flights land at **Ouvda airport,** 60km (37 miles) north of Eilat. Aqaba's international airport, just on the border near Eilat, will be designed so that arriving planes will be able to taxi to either Israeli or Jordanian gates at the new Shalom-Salaam International Terminal. One-way flights from Tel Aviv or Jerusalem are approximately $160 (£80); if you fly both ways, you'll miss the Negev Desert close up, but there are good flight/hotel packages offered by Arkia. El Al passengers can also purchase an add-on to Eilat with their flight ticket to Israel. The bus ride from Ouvda to town can take an hour.

## Getting to Jordan

Bus service is now available from Eilat to Aqaba, Jordan, at the United Tours Terminal in Eilat. Fares are NIS 8 ($2/£1) each way. Buses stop at the hotel district, the airport, and the New Commercial Center in Eilat before continuing on to Aqaba via the Arava Crossing north of Eilat. Passengers must have a Jordanian entry visa and must pay a crossing fee of NIS 75 ($19/£9.40) from Israel into Jordan. For those coming from Aqaba to Eilat, the crossing fee is NIS 24 ($6/£3). As regulations are constantly being revised, check with the Eilat Tourist Information Center for the latest information.

If you arrive from inside Israel at Eilat's little **downtown airport,** you will be right at the bottom of the hill, where Hatmarim Boulevard meets Ha-Arava Road (the road north to Beersheva). It will be a 10-minute walk or a quick, inexpensive taxi ride to almost any Hatmarim Boulevard hotel or to hotels on the North Beach. All the local city buses (no. 1, 2, or 15) run every 20 to 30 minutes or so, from early morning until about 7 or 8pm, daily except Saturday, stopping early on Friday (about 3 or 4pm) in observation of Shabbat.

**By Bus**   There are a number of daily buses (except on Shabbat) from Jerusalem and Tel Aviv to Eilat. The trip takes about 4½ hours. If you arrive by bus, you will be planted in the center of town on the main street—Hatmarim (or Ha-Temarim) Boulevard. From there, hostel row, just around the corner on Ha-Negev Street, is within walking distance; local city bus no. 1 or 2 goes from the Central Bus Station to the North Beach area, around the lagoon, and down as far as the Jordanian border. You must take a taxi or city bus no. 15 if you're heading out to Coral Beach. There's a baggage checkroom at the bus station in case you have to seek out a hotel room. It is best not to even think about carrying luggage even short distances in Eilat's hot weather. For your return bus ride out of Eilat, the Egged information phone number is ℂ **08/636-5111.** Reserve your bus seat leaving Eilat at least 2 days ahead; on weekends, holidays, and summer vacations, 4-day advance reservations are necessary.

**By Car**   The trip takes approximately 4 hours by direct road from Tel Aviv and Jerusalem.

**VISITOR INFORMATION**   The **Eilat Tourist Information Center** (ℂ **08/630-9111;** zipiv@tourism.gov.il) is located in Bridge House, a small building on the North Beach Promenade not far from the Spring Onion Restaurant. Pick up an English-language map for NIS 5 ($1.25/60p) and free copies of other tourist brochures, including *Events in Eilat.* You can also get help and advice on booking accommodations and tours, as well as bus schedules, discount coupons, and schedules of events in the region. The staff here is often well attuned to the problems of budget travelers, and can also give advice about local travel agencies that specialize in area excursions, diving and snorkeling, and travel to Sinai and Jordan. The center accepts American Express, MasterCard, and Visa when booking rooms, travel tickets, and tours. In the same building, you'll find the **Eilat Tourist Information (E.T.I.) Attractions desk** (ℂ **08/637-0380;** fax 08/637-0434). At E.T.I., you can book tours of the Eilat region, diving cruises, and excursions to Sinai, as well as package tours to Petra and to Egypt. E.T.I. booking desks can be found at most major hotels. Hours for the Eilat

Tourist Information Center are Sunday through Thursday from 9am to 9pm and Friday, Saturday, and eves of holidays from 8am to 3pm.

Eilat has no VAT tax, but because many supplies have to be shipped in, prices tend to be higher. *Tip:* Gasoline for your car will be 15.5% cheaper in Eilat than in the rest of Israel, as there is no VAT in the city, so fill up before heading back north.

**ORIENTATION** There are three easily distinguishable areas in Eilat: the town itself, built atop hills that roll toward the sea; Coral Beach, with its great snorkeling, about 6km (4 miles) south of town on the western shore of the harbor; and North Beach, a 10-minute walk from the center of town on the eastern shore of the harbor. North Beach is the most central and busiest public beach, and where you'll find the most restaurants, bars, and better-quality accommodations. It is also the site of an elaborate marina system that started with the building of an artificial lagoon, cutting several hundred yards inland in back of the "hotel row" section. Around this lagoon are hotels, restaurants, and a promenade filled with pubs, discos, shops, and endless street vendors—a major way to spend a hot summer evening.

## SPORTS & OUTDOOR ACTIVITIES

**BEACHES** Although the waters around Eilat are safe, always take the elementary precaution of not going out too far alone, keeping in mind that depth is deceptive and that the numerous sharks are not particularly hungry for you; stepping on spiny sea urchins and getting your feet filled with their spines is the major danger.

**North Beach** is a stony/sandy beach that starts in front of the Sheraton Eilat Hotel, which extends as far eastward as the Dan Eilat Hotel and the Sheraton's Herods Palace Hotel complex; because it's relatively free of coral and sea urchins, this is a good beach for ordinary swimming. The nicer part of the beach is at the end near the Dan and Sheraton hotels. Water skis and boats can be rented, but make sure you know where you're going, because you don't have to ski very far to get into both Jordanian and hot water.

**Coral Beach** ⭐, which is a short drive or a no. 15 bus ride around the curve of the bay, is the beach for **snorkeling** and **diving.** It's blessed with coral reefs just offshore and lots of fish. Snorkeling equipment can be rented. Much of Coral Beach is now a nature preserve, perfect for both first-time and intermediate snorkeling and scuba diving. Best snorkeling is inside the actual Coral Beach Nature Reserve.

**Dolphin Reef** ⭐ is certainly the prettiest beach in Eilat, dotted with palm trees and thatched-roof *palapa* structures for shade. Once in the water, you'll find the area designated for humans, with its sandy floor, is also the best in Eilat for swimming. The dolphins are an added attraction. The reef's institute believes in informal, personal relationships between humans and dolphins. The dolphins are free to come and go to the open sea as they like, but for years have chosen to attach themselves to Dolphin Reef. As you swim and sun, you can watch them frolicking and being fed just beyond the roped-off human swimming zone; you can also walk out to a wooden observation pier in the dolphins' free-swimming area for a closer look. For about NIS 240 ($60/£30) per person, you can join a guided group of snorkelers for a 25-minute **swim among the dolphins.** (Advance reservations are necessary.) Sometimes, this can be an expedition of wonderful close encounters; at other times, the free-swimming dolphins (which are under no obligation to interact) keep their distance. You must be a good swimmer. There are no guarantees, refunds, or rain checks. More-advanced dives are also offered. Or, for NIS 110 ($28/£14), you can sit right on a raft while dolphins come up to the trainers for snacks and play sessions. Dolphin Reef also hosts a

---

## ⌒Warning Watch Your Feet!

Always be on the lookout for spiny sea urchins and sharp, burning corals when swimming at Coral Beach, and do your best to avoid them. Footwear or flippers are advisable when swimming here. Never put your feet down on the floor of the sea unless you can see that you will be standing on a clear, urchin-free space.

---

program of scientific studies, as well as a program in which people with medical or emotional problems may visit and interact with dolphins as part of their therapy. From time to time you may notice participants in these programs on the raft in the dolphins' free-swim zone. Also offered are sessions in the Dolphin Reef's three secluded **Relaxation Pools**—one is fresh water, one Red Sea water, and one heavy mineral water not unlike The Dead Sea. Sessions for up to 20 people last 2 hours and include New Age music, refreshments, and a botanical habitat for resting. The price is NIS 150 ($38/£19). Reservations are necessary. General admission to Dolphin Reef is waived for those entering with reservations for snorkeling/diving with dolphins and for the Relaxation Pools.

There is a reasonably priced cafeteria serving hot and cold drinks, snacks, and full meals on the premises, as well as a pub and a program of films on dolphins. The whole feel of the beach is friendly, easygoing, and interesting. Many evenings, when admission to the beach is free, there is live or disco music and dancing at the beach's pub. All in all, this is one of the best places in Eilat to spend a day or an evening.

Dolphin Reef is midway between North Beach and Coral Beach (✆ **08/630-0111** for activity reservations; www.dolphinreef.co.il). It's open daily from 9am to 5pm. Admission is NIS 54 ($14/£6.75) for adults and NIS 40 ($10/£5) for children. There's no admission fee after 7pm, when the pub/restaurant and beach stay open, but the dolphin sessions finish for the day. Bus no. 15.

**BOATING**    You can hire boats 24 hours a day at the North Beach marina and lagoon—boats for water-skiing and water parachuting, sailboats, fishing boats, paddleboats, motor sea-cycles, sail boards, and kayaks are all available.

**BIRD-WATCHING** 🕊🕊🕊    Eilat is one of the best places on earth for bird-watching, due to its prime location on the Jordan Valley–Red Sea–Great African Rift Valley migration path between Europe and Africa. Migration times are twice a year: From **September through November** the birds head south to Africa, and from **March through May** they head back north to Europe.

Eilat's **International Birding and Research Centre** (✆ **08/633-5339** or 050/211-2498 to reserve tours; fax 08/633-5319; www.birdsofeilat.com) is a storehouse for information and activities relating to bird-watching around Eilat. It conducts guided 2-hour bird-watching tours for NIS 150 ($38/£19) and 4-hour tours for NIS 220 ($55/£28); full-day tours can also be arranged. Between February 15 and May 15, a general spring census of birds is conducted, in which you may participate. The center will also offer advice on birding throughout the country. The International Birding and Research Centre is open Sunday through Thursday from 9am to 1pm and 5 to 7pm and Friday from 9am to 1pm. Also visit the bird-banding station during the morning hours on most days of the week. Similar activities take place again in the fall. Lectures, nature films, literature, and background material are also offered.

If you would like to be in Eilat at the best time for bird-watching, you should know that each year in March, the center hosts an **International Birdwatchers' Festival** of growing renown. Check the website for information about the many special programs and discounts on accommodations and car rentals at the time of the festival.

**GLASS-BOTTOM BOATS** 🐟   Boats leave from the jetty just north of Coral Beach or from North Beach near the Neptune Hotel. These boats offer a wonderful view of a fairy-tale marine world, with mounds of coral and clusters of rainbow-colored fish. **Israel Yam** (✆ **08/637-5528**) operates daily 1½-hour glass-bottom boat trips, leaving North Beach several times during the day for NIS 70 ($18/£8.75) for adults and NIS 50 ($13/£6.25) for children. You can book a boat ride through the E.T.I. attractions desks that operate at almost every Eilat hotel. Look for a 15% discount coupon, often available in the free Hebrew- and English-language tourist brochures. A newer state-of-the-art vessel that offers underwater vistas is the *Jules Verne Explorer* (✆ **08/637-7702**). The price is slightly higher than Israel Yam for a 2-hour tour, but for real underwater aficionados, it could be worthwhile. Mornings, when the sea is calm, usually provide the clearest water for viewing.

**SAILBOAT CRUISES** 🐟🐟   Several yacht and sailboat cruises will take you on a full-day (10am–5pm) excursion to **Taba**, on the Egyptian border, and on to the **Coral Island and the Fjord**—two points of interest along the Egyptian Sinai coast south of Eilat. The price for these cruises begins at $75 (£38) per person and includes a boxed or barbecue lunch; drinks and other refreshments are extra. *Note:* You must give your passport information ahead of time and carry a valid passport and Egyptian visa with you (the cruise company should help take care of visa procedures). Cruises anchor off Egypt's Coral Island for diving and snorkeling, and allow time to explore a ruined Crusader fort on the island. For a bit more money, you can also water-ski, go sail boarding, or book a cruise with a better quality lunch (several of the boats have kosher kitchens). Elsewhere at the marina, you can arrange a simple short sail for around NIS 80 ($20/£10). Special diving cruises can, of course, go above $75 (£38). Walk along the marina in front of the North Beach lagoon and see which boat or itinerary appeals to you; you can reserve in advance at most travel agencies, at the marina, or at large hotel desks, but it's worthwhile to do a bit of personal investigating and find the boat and cruise program you'll most enjoy. The Red Sea Sports Club, at the Ambassador Hotel (✆ **08/637-6569;** www.redseasports.co.il), manages one of the more affordable Coral Island cruises.

**SNORKELING & SCUBA DIVING** 🐟🐟🐟   *Note:* If you want to scuba dive, you must bring your certification from abroad or obtain a license in Israel.

The best-equipped firm for snorkeling and scuba diving are Aqua-Sport and Red Sea Sports Club. **Aqua-Sport** (✆ **08/633-4404;** www.aqua-sport.com), located across the highway from the Isrotel Ambassador Hotel on Coral Beach and with a branch at the Hilton Resort Hotel just across the border in Taba, Egypt, can fulfill your needs for masks, fins, and snorkels, as well as wet suits, weight belts, depth gauges, buoyancy compensators, cylinders, and other gear. Introductory dives are NIS 200 ($50/£25); diving lessons (in English), diving tours (half or full day), and even 3-day camping/diving or snorkeling safaris are also available. A 5-day diving course ($300/£150) leads to internationally recognized two-star diver certification; with 6 days' bed-and-breakfast at the divers' hostel, the cost comes to $400 (£200). Many other programs are also offered, including rentals and lessons in sail boarding. Bed-and-breakfast at the Aqua-Sport hostel is $27 (£13) per day in double or quadruple rooms. Aqua-Sport also has

## Dive In!

Eilat is a great place to pick up snorkeling and diving skills, and to sample the fabulous reefs of the Red Sea. But those who are really avid divers should schedule time to visit Dahab or Sharm el Sheik in Sinai, where the reefs and marine life are among the most extraordinary in the world. For a serious diver to come to Eilat and not go on to Sinai would be like visiting New York and never getting out of Kennedy airport.

a program of weeklong summer camps for kids ages 10 to 15 during July and August. Also operating through Aqua-Sport is the **School of Underwater Photography,** with half-day to 14-day programs on underwater video and still photography. In the evening, there's a pub, underwater video films, and occasional live entertainment and dancing. Aqua-Sport is open every day from 8:30am to 12:30am. Email Aqua-Sport for information on prices, programs, and to arrange for courses and trips. Aqua-Sport accepts Diners Club, MasterCard, and Visa.

**Red Sea Sport Club's Manta Dive Center,** located at the Red Sea Sport and Ambassador Hotel (② **08/633-3666;** www.redseasports.co.il), is another recommended diving center at Coral Beach. It offers facilities similar to those at Aqua-Sport, plus other activities including sailing, windsurfing, boating, deep-sea fishing, night cruises, organized diving trips to Sinai, desert safaris, horseback riding, camel treks, canoes and paddleboats, water-skiing, and bicycle rental, in addition to its diving and sail-boarding programs. There is even a special sauna facility for divers. It's open daily from 8:30am to 4:30pm in winter and until 6pm in summer. Red Sea Sport Club accepts all credit cards.

Snuba diving, tethered to an oxygen tank on a raft over the coral reef, is an easy, enjoyable way to dive without any extensive training. The **Snuba Diving Center** (② **08/637-2722;** www.snuba.co.il) will arrange a variety of snuba excursions for you. Prices start at NIS 180 ($45/£23) for 1½ hours and include training. Look for a discount coupon on the Snuba website.

**Coral Beach Nature Reserve** ★★   This is where you can explore Israel's small but fascinating chunk of the Red Sea's reef system, teeming with colorful, exotic fish and sea creatures of every description. Located south of the city, between downtown Eilat and the Egypt border, the reserve consists of a pleasant, unfrenzied beach dotted with shade structures. The sand here is the original coarse, beige sand of the shoreline—the imported, powdery white sand of North Beach tends to blow into the water and suffocate the coral. There are comfortable changing rooms with showers, and there's an open-air snack bar. Illustrated books about the reserve are for sale at the snack bar/gift shop.

The reserve will give you a flyer pointing out a number of underwater trails. For NIS 23 ($5.75/£2.90), you can rent a snorkel, mask, and fins, or you can bring your own gear. There is a refundable deposit of NIS 100 ($25/£13) for each snorkel set. There is a walkway to the water beyond the reef (which parallels the shore) so that coral is not broken underfoot by visitors. You enter at the northern end of the reef. Because the wind and current usually move southward, all you have to do is drift and paddle a bit to observe the reef through your mask. At the southern end of the reef, you can head for shore and walk back to the starting point for another round.

The nature reserve also operates a scuba program for novices called **snuba,** in which you can dive tethered to an oxygen tank on a floating dingy—the safest, easiest way

## Wings over Israel

After the Second Revolt against Rome in A.D. 135, Judea was left so desolate that olives, the ancient staple of the region, were not harvested again for more than a century, and according to legend, even birds avoided the once verdant hills. The loss of the birds must have been especially noticeable. Ninety-one resident species, 121 regularly migrating species, and more than 200 winter or summer residents—an amazing number and variety for so small an area—are found in Israel today. In ancient times, the variety and number of birds must have been even larger. Israel is located on the main migration route of the birds of Europe and Western Asia to and from Africa. For millions of years, migrating birds have followed the line of the below-sea Jordan Valley to the Great Rift Valley because they need warm air thermals to help them cover the distance between Europe and Africa. At times in the migration season—an amazing spectacle that includes overflights of 500 million birds—Israel hosts an estimated 85% of the world's stork population. Birds stop for several days' rest in the Galilee among the thriving kibbutz fishponds and farms along the Jordan River before continuing south across the Negev to Eilat.

The flight over the desert can be so difficult that exhausted birds commonly drop dead out of the sky in the Western Negev and Sinai, sometimes only a short distance from a watering hole on the fringe of Israeli agricultural land. Some migrants, including a dozen families of storks, have become so habituated to the lush agricultural scene developed in Israel over the past decades that they have begun to breed in Israel rather than their traditional European nesting areas. During migration season the skies can be so thick with birds that they are a major hazard to military and commercial flights in the area. Thanks to the peace agreements between Israel, Egypt, and Jordan, the governments of those countries have begun plans to build a network of migrating bird radar-tracking stations throughout the area in an effort to save the lives of both human passengers and the birds themselves. Over the next several years, this network will also be put to use for the benefit of worldwide bird enthusiasts who visit the region. Meanwhile, the first station of the network, the **Inter-University Institute for Research of Bird Migration**, is operational at Latrun, in the foothills of the Judean Mountains not far from Jerusalem. It operates in cooperation with the Hebrew University of Jerusalem, Tel Aviv University, and Haifa's Technion, and includes a research center, a museum, and an auditorium for screening films. The institute will join Eilat's International Birding and Research Centre, the Society for Protection of Nature in Israel, the Zipori Bird Park in Tel Aviv, and the Nature Reserve Center at northern Israel's Beit Ussishkin in Kibbutz Dan as a major resource for bird-watching enthusiasts traveling in Israel.

to dive. It costs NIS 180 ($45/£23) for 1½ hours, including instruction. There are showers and changing areas. **Warning:** Wear some sort of foot covering every time you enter the water here. Spiny sea urchins lurk almost everywhere you might want to stand.

Bus no. 15 runs from downtown Eilat to Coral Beach and back every half-hour.

© **08/637-6829.** www.parks.org.il. NIS 30 ($7.50/£3.75) adults; NIS 16 ($4/£2) children ages 5–18. Daily 9am–5pm. Closed Yom Kippur. Bus: 15.

**King's City** *Kids*    Part Arabian Nights fantasy, with a biblical and medieval touch thrown in, this castle of a theme park is filled with rides, games, multimedia activities and presentations, food courts, and other things to dazzle kids and empty pocketbooks. Frommer's 7-year-old expert, Lyne, was more into glass-bottom boats, checking out dolphins, the coral observatory, and snorkeling in the Coral Beach Nature Reserve, but she may be an exception. Still, it's a largely air-conditioned haven on a hot day and something to do when the weather is too cold for swimming.

East Lagoon North Beach. © **08/634-4444.** www.kingscity.co.il. NIS 125 ($31/£16). Sun–Fri 9am–1pm; call as hours may change.

**Coral World Underwater Observatory and Marine Park** *★★★ Kids*    Located just south of Coral Beach, this fascinating complex consists of three one-story buildings on the beach with distinctive rounded roofs and two underwater observatories, which are 90m (295 ft.) out to sea beside a picturesque reef called the Japanese Gardens. A pier binds the observatories to the coast. In addition to the underwater observatories, you'll also find the **Maritime Museum and the aquarium.** The aquarium is built so that you stand in the middle and the fish swim around you in a huge circular tank. The third building is a pleasant snack bar/cafe. There are also large outdoor observation pools—one for big sharks and another for sea turtles and rays. The tower of the observatory rises out of the sea to a height of 6m (20 ft.); inside, a spiral staircase of 42 steps leads down to the observatory itself. Since the water in the gulf is generally crystal clear, observation of the magnificent fish and coral life is unparalleled. For an additional NIS 10 ($2.50/£1.25), you can visit the Oceanarium, a high-tech simulated "dive" in a small theater that offers the sights and feel of going underwater. Kid-friendly and with lots of snack bars (and shops), the entire complex was reconstructed and redesigned in 2005.

*Tip:* The best time to visit the observatory is between 10am and 1pm, when the light is good and the water is usually calm and clear. Be sure not to miss feeding time, which is at 11:30am.

Off Derech Mitzraim. © **08/636-4200.** www.coralworld.com. Admission NIS 79 ($20/£9.90) adults; NIS 70 ($18/£8.75) children 5–16. Sat–Thurs 8:30am–4:30pm; Fri 8:30am–3:30pm. Bus: 15.

## WHERE TO STAY

If there is a low season here, it is from May to June. Europeans tend to come from October to April; Israelis come July to August and during the September to October holidays. Jewish and Christian holidays are also times when prices skyrocket even above high-season levels. In the past, winter was Eilat's high season, but with the prevalence of air-conditioning and the development of the town for tourism, it's become a popular year-round spot. Many hotels have developed their own systems for determining when to charge high- and low-season rates. Nobody in his right mind actually pays full price here. An Internet search or good travel agent or packager in Israel or abroad can get you fabulous deals. The Eilat Tourist Information Center can also help find you a room if you arrive midweek, during off season.

There are three main hotels areas:

**North Beach** is a lively (but noisy) hotel area packed with shops, restaurants, nightclubs, and discos, both attached to and separate from hotels. This area is within walking distance of the spread-out downtown part of Eilat, especially in the relative cool of the evenings. **Coral Beach** is a quieter, more spread-out hotel area near the Coral Beach National Park, several miles south of town. For those into exploring the reefs, this is a good choice, as North Beach is basically coral free. Bus no. 15 connects Coral Beach to North Beach and the bus station. The **downtown/bus station area** is about a 15-minute walk to North Beach and contains numerous private hostels; the Eilat Tourist Information Center is the place to check on which are currently up to standard. You can also gather information there about rooms in private homes and rental apartments. Less expensive hotels, most with pools, can also be found in this district. If you're just looking for an air-conditioned room from which to sample Eilat, or a place to crash en route to Jordan or Sinai, this is where to look.

## HATMARIN BOULEVARD, NEW TOURIST CENTER & NEAR THE BUS STATION
### Moderate
**Holiday Inn Eilat Patio**   Less fancy and in a less-prestigious area than the Crowne Plaza Eilat (p. 469), the Patio is one of a number of bright, moderately priced hotels with pools in the center of town, around the Central Bus Station. Its "kids are free" policy makes this a good base for families and offers generic, comfortable rooms but no beach or desert ambience. A pleasant outdoor dining terrace is a plus; service is uneven, but this is the way in Eilat.

3 Shifton Alley, Eilat. © **08/636-4364.** Fax 08/634-0118. www.ichotelsgroup.com. 115 units. $135–$170 (£68–£85) double. Rates include breakfast. Up to 2 children 18 and under stay free in parent's room. AE, DC, MC, V. Free parking. **Amenities:** Restaurant; heated outdoor pool; health club (fee); Jacuzzi; babysitting. *In room:* A/C, TV, minibar, safe.

**Nova All Suite Hotel**   Built in the mid-1990s, the one- and two-room suites of this six-story hotel overlook a swimming pool courtyard. Rooms are functional and simple, with rattan furniture and kitchenettes that help make a stay in Eilat a bit more economical. Atlas chain management means the Nova will be a bit better run than nearby competitors. Larger suites cost $50 (£25) more than standard suites. The cool underground parking lot keeps your car from becoming an oven.

6 Hativat Hanegev St., Eilat. © **08/638-2444.** Fax 08/638-2455. atlashot@netvision.net.il. 193 units. $127–$177 (£64–£89) standard suite; $177–$227 (£89–£114) large suite. Rates include breakfast. AE, DC, MC, V. Parking. **Amenities:** Restaurant; bar; pool; kids' club; room service; minimart. *In room:* A/C, TV, kitchenette.

## NEAR THE NEW TOURIST CENTER
The New Tourist Center (note that this neighborhood has nothing to do with the actual tourist information center, which is located elsewhere), right across (west of) the main highway from North Beach at the corner of Derech Ha-Arava and Derech Yotam, is a useful landmark and a prime nightlife area for Eilat's younger crowd.

### Expensive
**Club Hotel Eilat** *(Kids*   Built in 1997, this all-suite hotel, twice the size of any other in Eilat, is superfriendly to kids. It's 2 blocks inland from North Beach but offers seven swimming pools, a garden of more than 90,000 plants, and a mildly nautical decor that makes you feel like you're on a self-contained cruise ship. Recreational facilities include an entertainment center with video games, an Internet cafe, lots of shops, two

discos, and a "submarine" from which kids can view the adult swimming pool from underwater. The one- and two-bedroom suites are comfortable. Most rooms overlook the gardens and pools, but a few face a bleak parking lot—avoid them. Because many of the suites have been purchased as timeshares, the hotel is filled with Israeli families. It's lively, but not a romantic hideaway.

Ha-Arava St., Eilat. © 08/636-1666. Fax 08/632-2613. 135 units. $252–$480 (£126–£240) 1-bedroom suite; $332–$560 (£166–£280) 2-bedroom suite. July–Aug and Jewish and Christian holidays, add $150 (£75) per suite. Rates are for 4 adults or 2 adults and 3 children per suite. Breakfast $16 (£8) per person. AE, DC, MC, V. **Amenities:** 5 restaurants; bar; 7 pools; spa; volleyball and basketball courts; children's activities; business center; arcade; nonsmoking rooms; synagogue. *In room:* A/C, TV, kitchenette, fridge, microwave, hair dryer, safe.

## NORTH BEACH/NORTH SHORE AREA
This is the high-powered, high-priced hotel district covering the area from the northern shore of the Red Sea inland to the local Eilat airport. Most of the hotels here are mammoth blockbusters, although here and there a smaller holdover from pre-1993 Eilat has survived. An artificial lagoon has been created in the heart of this neighborhood, but it's not for swimming. A few hotels are right on the beach, but most hotels (including some of the most expensive) are anywhere from 1 to 4 blocks inland.

### Very Expensive
**Dan Eilat Hotel** ★★    Opened in 1995, this is the most inventively designed of the well-managed Dan Hotels. The location is excellent, on a prime, palm-dotted stretch of North Beach (beside the lavish Herods Palace) that's especially good for swimming. Adam Tihany, who did the interiors of trendsetting hotels and restaurants on three continents, decorated the public areas with elegant, lively reinterpretations of contemporary decor from the 1940s, 1950s, and 1960s that might be installations in a museum of design. People either love or ignore the intelligence and wit of the concept, but the Dan is not just another lavishly bland hotel. Rooms come in three categories: superior, deluxe, and family (with sleeping alcove); there are a variety of rooms and suites with spectacular private terraces overlooking the sea. Executive rooms have access to a business lounge and running light buffet. Food is terrific—the dinner buffet is the best in town. The gardened pools are large and attractive.

North Beach, Eilat. © 800/223-7773 for reservations in the U.S., 0171/439-9893 in the U.K., or 08/636-2222. Fax 08/636-2333. 378 units. $310–$500 (£155–£250) superior double. Rates include breakfast. AE, DC, MC, V. **Amenities:** 10 restaurants; cafe; bar; pool; children's pool; fitness center; Jacuzzi; sauna; watersports; squash courts; children's programs; concierge; business services; salon; 24-hr. room service; massage; nonsmoking rooms; nightclub; synagogue. *In room:* A/C, TV, dataport, minibar, coffeemaker, hair dryer, safe.

**Hilton Eilat Queen of Sheba Hotel** (Kids    Built in 2000, this high-rise Hilton offers a separate wing of family rooms equipped with kitchenettes (aimed largely at the Israeli market), which cuts down on noise for other travelers. The complex contains an excellent CYBEX fitness center, a large outdoor heated pool semisurrounded by the building's tall wings, and gardens that are maturing. It has no beachfront, but is about 150m (492 ft.) away from access to the good beachfronts of its neighboring competitors, the Dan Eilat and Herods Palace. Rooms are relatively fresh and well-appointed, as you would expect at a Hilton (though bathrooms are small and don't have the best water pressure); public areas are modern, airy, and sleek, with subtle decor touches that hint of ancient times. The entire hotel straddles the noisy, honky-tonk Queen of Sheba Shopping Mall. Rooms at the back get electrical generator noise, and no view.

North Beach, Eilat. ℭ **08/630-6666.** Fax 08/6306677. www.hiltonworldresorts.com. 479 units. $220–$290 (£110–£145) standard double; $320–$390 (£160–£195) family room. Rates higher on Jewish holidays. AE, DC, MC, V. Free parking. **Amenities:** Dining room; cafe; bar; outdoor heated pool; fitness center; basketball and volleyball courts; children's activities; business services; room service; nonsmoking rooms; synagogue. *In room:* A/C, TV w/pay movies, dataport, kitchenette (family room), minibar, coffeemaker, hair dryer, safe.

**Herods Palace Hotel Complex** ⭐⭐⭐    Herods is the place to come for pampering and luxury unequaled in Eilat, especially in the off season, when it's not packed to the brim. The complex is composed of three hotels: **Herods Palace,** which is the main hotel, encompassing 268 rooms and suites; **Herods Vitalis Health and Lifestyle Resort,** a high-rise spa par excellence (an absolute no-children zone) containing 64 balconied nonsmoking rooms, all with Jacuzzi bathtubs; and the **Herods Forum Convention Center,** a venue for special events and business meetings, with 104 rooms, suites, and cottages. Completed in 2000, this complex, with its own piece of prime, palm tree–studded beachfront, is the most expensive and lavish hotel in Israel. Visually, the towering ensemble of buildings, pools, and enormous, enclosed, light-filled space touched with Arabesque and Roman architectural elements looks like the stuff dreams are made of. There are domes, networks of bridges, waterfalls, and a Roman Cardo (colonnaded shopping street).

Guest rooms and bathrooms are spacious, tasteful, and equipped with comforts of a top hotel, but not all that unusual (try for Red Sea–view rooms; some simply face other towers in the complex). Swimming pools are vast and less crowded than those in other supersize hotels (replicas of ancient Egyptian cat statues spit water from the pool's edge). The **Vitalis Spa** is 21st-century glamour; in addition to massage and exercise rooms, it contains a perfumed garden, an adjustable waterfall massage, and a serpentine Jacuzzi that seats 20 people. The large children's pool is shaded by date palms and lattices; despite the hotel's august reputation, the staff is most welcoming to children. Tower floor rooms have access to the executive lounge, with the most lavish running snack buffet in Israel, including pastries, caviar, smoked salmon, and other delicacies to die for. Despite formidable rack rates, Internet and discounters' bargains abound.

North Beach, Eilat. ℭ **08/638-0000.** Fax 08/638-0100. www.sheraton.com. 468 units. $270–$490 (£135–£245) standard deluxe room; $560 (£280) double in Sky Tower; $590 (£295) double in Vitalis Spa. Add $150 (£75) per night during Passover. Rates include breakfast. AE, DC, MC, V. Free parking. **Amenities:** Restaurant; dining room; 3 pools; fitness center; spa; sauna; steam bath; watersports; children's sports; business services; shopping arcade; room service; laundry service. *In room:* A/C, TV w/pay movies, Wi-Fi (some), minibar, coffeemaker, hair dryer, safe.

**Isrotel Royal Beach Hotel** ⭐    Opened in 1994, this star of the Isrotel chain has a palm-shaded beach; airy, beautifully furnished public areas; and a sparkling swimming pool set amid rocks and artificial waterfalls. Architecturally, this is one of the best hotel buildings in the country, filled with light and soaring spaces; glass upper-story corridors look out onto wonderful vistas of Eilat and the desert mountains. Rooms are graceful, decorated with well-chosen works by Israeli artists, but some are a bit worn. Every room faces directly onto the Red Sea. There are standard, deluxe, and family rooms (which include a sleeping alcove for two children) as well as a variety of suites.

North Beach, Eilat. ℭ **08/636-8888.** Fax 08/636-8811. www.isrotel.co.il. 363 units. $260–$550 (£130–£275) double. Rates include breakfast. Internet discounts and packages available. AE, DC, MC, V. Free parking. **Amenities:** Restaurant; dining room; cafe; bar; heated pool; children's pool; fitness room; Jacuzzi; sauna; steam bath; business services; shops; 24-hr. room service; nonsmoking rooms; synagogue. *In room:* A/C, TV, coffeemaker, hair dryer.

**Le Méridien All Suite Hotel**    Another of the 1999 crop of Eilat hotels, Le Méridien offers style and (as a result of new Sheraton management) service. Location at the southern edge of North Beach is central, with vistas of the sea, but the beach is not for swimming. There are a number of one- and two-bedroom suites, all strikingly decorated; many have two bathrooms, making them great for families. All of the suites have balconies; some offer tanning beds where you can soak up the sun, others have Jacuzzi tubs. The large outdoor heated pool overlooks the Red Sea.

North Beach, Eilat. ✆ 08/638-3333. Fax 08/638-3300. www.sheraton.com. 245 units. $265–$530 (£133–£265) suite for 2 adults; add $30–$120 (£15–£60) per child (ages 2–18) per night staying in parent's room. Half board available. Rates include breakfast. AE, DC, MC, V. **Amenities:** Restaurant; dining room; bar; outdoor heated pool; children's pool; spa; children's activities; salon; basketball court; room service; laundry service; nonsmoking rooms; synagogue; nightclub. *In room:* A/C, TV, minibar, coffeemaker, hair dryer, safe.

## Expensive
### Crowne Plaza Eilat
On the Lagoon Waterfront Promenade, but a few blocks inland from the beach, this nine-story hotel is a beautiful structure that's constantly updated, though it can seem a bit jumbled at busy times in the lobby. Guest rooms are attractively decorated; an entire floor is reserved for nonsmokers. There are lots of activities that English-speaking kids can join.

North Beach, Eilat. ✆ 08/636-7777. Fax 08/633-0821. www.h-i.co.il. 290 units. $200–$350 (£100–£175) double. Rates include breakfast. AE, DC, MC, V. **Amenities:** Restaurant; dining room; bar; outdoor heated pool; spa; Jacuzzi; sauna; basketball court; children's activities; room service; laundry service; nonsmoking rooms; nightclub. *In room:* A/C, TV, minibar, coffeemaker, hair dryer, safe.

### Golden Tulip Club Eilat (Kids)
This all-inclusive (drinks, plus three meals a day and running snacks and activities) hotel is a sprawling three-story complex and a good choice on the lower end of the expensive price range. The hotel consists of a series of large atriums and courtyards connected by lattice-shaded outdoor passageways. Guest rooms resemble those in a standard American motel; most look out on a vast central swimming pool with a super water slide kids love. Top-priced garden-view rooms are the most desirable for adults without kids. The hotel's design is among the best in Eilat, but the location, inland from the beach, is a schlep with kids on a really hot day. Some rooms are equipped for travelers with disabilities, and some rooms have balconies or terraces.

North Beach, Eilat. ✆ 08/636-3636. Fax 08/636-3640. www.fattal.co.il. 282 units. $200–$440 (£100–£120) double. Add $50 (£25) per child up to 2 children. Rates include all meals, drinks, and watersports activities. AE, DC, MC, V. Parking (fee). **Amenities:** Restaurant; dining room; bar; lounge; heated pool; children's pool; tennis court; fitness room; Jacuzzi; sauna; children's activities; salon; babysitting; laundry service; nonsmoking rooms; synagogue; rooms for those w/limited mobility. *In room:* A/C, TV w/pay movies, minibar, hair dryer, safe.

### Isrotel King Solomon's Palace (Kids)
The first of Eilat's blockbuster hotels (built in the mid-1980s), this oft-renovated property has become one of the Isrotel chain's family-centered hotels. Guest rooms are larger than average and good for accommodating an extra child or two. Located right in the center of things on the Lagoon Waterfront Promenade (but, like many downtown hotels, a walk to the beach), the King Solomon is very comfortable and has perfected an amazing program of daytime and evening activities for kids, teens, and under- and over-25ers. The pool is gracefully shaped around an island and is heated in winter; you can join the daily poolside aerobics there or enjoy the open-air tropical snack bar. For kids, in addition to daytime activities, there's a well-organized Snoopy Disco from 5 to 9:45pm. Adult entertainment is from 10:30pm on, and the downstairs disco, with its laser sound-and-light system, is the acknowledged high-powered nightspot in town. The hotel's many restaurants are among the best in Eilat for quality kosher dining—the top-of-the-line

Brasserie is especially recommended. Five-person suites with large terraces and private Jacuzzis can be a viable choice if you're with a family or a group.

North Beach, Eilat. 🕐 **08/636-3444.** Fax 08/633-4189. www.isrotel.co.il. 420 units. $200–$400 (£100–£200) double. Rates include breakfast. Package discounts available. AE, DC, MC, V. **Amenities:** Restaurant; dining room; bar; outdoor heated pool; children's pool; tennis and basketball courts; health club; spa; Jacuzzi; sauna; children's activities; room service; laundry service; nonsmoking rooms; synagogue; nightclub. *In room:* A/C, TV, minibar, coffeemaker, hair dryer, safe.

**Isrotel Lagoona All Inclusive Hotel**    The Lagoona is an older but well-maintained hotel. It offers an economical way to enjoy Eilat without constantly reaching into your wallet. Located on the lagoon, beside the Isrotel King Solomon's Palace, the Lagoona is smaller and quieter than its more lavish neighbors, but comfortable and notable for its all-inclusive price—everything from meals to drinks to ice-cream cones is included in the rates. Luxurious the meals and extras may not be, but they're typical for a good middle-range Israeli hotel. There are special children's activities, and many loyal guests return here year after year.

North Beach, Eilat. 🕐 **08/636/6666.** Fax 08/633-1783. www.isrotel.co.il. 256 units. $250–$350 (£125–£175) double. Rates include meals, drinks, and snacks. AE, DC, MC, V. **Amenities:** Dining room; bar; heated pool; children's activities. *In room:* A/C, TV, minibar, coffeemaker, safe.

**Sheraton Moriah Eilat**    This property with glistening public areas ranks just below the Royal Beach, Dan, and Herods Palace as one of the more luxurious hotels on North Beach. The entire hotel was rebuilt in 1992. Polished-stone public areas lead out to meandering, natural-form swimming pools laid out amid rocks and small cascades. Staff and dining facilities are excellent. A light, attractive touch marks the guest rooms, most of which have balconies and water views. Sheraton maintains a high level of service here and has invested in updating. The very central location, on the beach and within walking distance of the city center, is a plus, but it faces a very busy part of the North Beach Promenade, and the beach (all beaches along the Promenade are public) is mobbed in season. Look for Internet bargains.

North Beach, Eilat. 🕐 **08/636-1111.** Fax 08/633-4158. www.sheraton.co.il. 296 units. $250–$420 (£125–£210) double. Rates include breakfast. AE, DC, MC, V. **Amenities:** Restaurant; dining room; cafe; bar; 2 pools; children's pool; health club; Jacuzzi; sauna; children's activities; business center; shopping arcade; salon; room service; laundry service; nonsmoking rooms; synagogue. *In room:* A/C, TV, minibar, coffeemaker, hair dryer.

## Moderate & Inexpensive

**Isrotel Riviera Club** *(Value*    Good for families or small groups, this busy, low-rise complex set around a pool and run by the efficient Isrotel chain is a good choice if you want an affordable place to stay in Eilat or as a way station if you plan to cross into Jordan and visit Petra. It offers pleasant, functionally furnished and decorated suites (many with garden terraces or balconies) with kitchenettes supplied with basic equipment (some have microwave ovens) and cleaning supplies. The feel is less formal than the big high-rise places in the area. Although not located on a kibbutz, this hotel is available at a discount rate through the Kibbutz Hotel chain. Also check specials through the Riviera's parent company, Isrotel.

North Beach, Eilat. 🕐 **888/669-5700** in the U.S. and Canada or 08/630-3666. Fax 08/633-3939. www.isrotel.co.il. 172 units. $140–$240 (£70–£120) suite for 2–4 persons. AE, DC, MC, V. **Amenities:** Heated pool; children's club; laundry service; minimarket. *In room:* A/C, TV, kitchenette, minibar, coffeemaker, safe.

**Marina Club Eilat** *(Value (Kids*    More than 20 years old, but bright and well maintained, the Marina offers one- and two-bedroom suites with living rooms that are ideal for families or small groups. Prices vary according to number of rooms, number of persons, and type of view (pool view is $20–$30/£10–£15 extra per suite), but each suite has its own kitchenette equipped with basics for producing anything from coffee to a full meal. There are accessible rooms for those with disabilities. The hotel surrounds a magnificent gardened pool (heated in winter) surrounded by mature date palms. The Marina Club has a barbecue area and a better-than-average children's activity program (during school holidays), and tries to create an easygoing, family atmosphere. They provide kayaks and pedal boats gratis, and also offer a free Internet desk. Prices can more than double during July, August, Jewish holidays, and Israeli school vacations, but at other times the hotel is an excellent deal for three- to six-person groups. Sunday to Thursday is the best time for bargaining a bit or finding a "special" rate. On weekends, prices go up $50 (£25) per suite. Bargain in off season or especially if you are only two people.

North Beach, Eilat 88141. © 08/633-4191. Fax 08/633-4206. www.marinaclub.co.il. 132 units. $200–$350 (£100–£175) suite up to 2 adults and 2 children. AE, DC, MC, V. **Amenities:** Outdoor pool; fitness center; volleyball court; children's activities; laundry service; billiards; rooms for those w/limited mobility. *In room:* A/C, TV, kitchenette, safe.

**Reef Hotel**    The Reef has a good reputation as a friendly, affordable choice. One of the few human-size hotels left in Eilat, the Reef also has a good location overlooking the water, just south of busy North Beach—walkable to shops, diving centers, and the North Beach Promenade. There's been updating, but don't expect chic rooms; they're comfortable but not exceptional. Most have sea views and refrigerators, and many have balconies. There's a medium-size pool surrounded by an attractive deck (with Jacuzzi) overlooking the sea, and direct access to the hotel's small slice of waterfront that serves as a launching pad into the sea, but it's not a great beach. The hotel can arrange a variety of watersports activities, including snorkeling and diving. There are two suites with Jacuzzi bathtubs.

North Beach, Eilat. © 08/636-4444. Fax 08/636-4488. www.reefhoteleilat.com. 79 units. $132–$200 (£66–£100) double. Rates include breakfast. Specials as low as $100 (£50) double. AE, DC, MC, V. **Amenities:** Dining room; pool; Jacuzzi; wet and dry sauna; fitness room. *In room:* A/C, TV, fridge, hair dryer, safe.

## Inexpensive
**Americana Inn Eilat** *(Value)*    This busy low-rise hotel, built in the 1970s, has a young, festive atmosphere and is one of the best deals in Eilat. The more recently refurbished rooms are situated around a large swimming pool/terrace; 36 rooms have private balconies, 50 have private kitchenettes. Films are shown daily in the TV room, and a new fitness room, sauna, and Jacuzzi are free to guests. It's a hike of a few blocks to the beach, which can be a problem on a really hot day. *Tip:* You can get incredible deals for this hotel on the Internet and from local travel agents in Jerusalem, Tel Aviv, or Eilat.

North Beach (PO Box 27), Eilat. © 08/633-3777. Fax 08/633-4174. www.americanahotel.co.il. 140 units. $132–$200 (£66–£100) double; add $9 (£4.50) for room with kitchenette; add $10 (£5) per person for Jewish holidays; add $10 (£5) for pool view. 10% discount for 7-night stay. AE, DC, MC, V. **Amenities:** Dining room; heated pool; children's pool; fitness room; Jacuzzi; sauna; watersports rentals; Ping-Pong tables; pool table; minimarket. *In room:* A/C, TV, kitchenette (some), fridge, hair dryer, safe.

**Dalia Hotel**    At the beginning of North Beach, close to the intersection of Durban and Arava roads, this well-located hotel, built in the early 1970s, has no view and offers utilitarian rooms. That said, renovations (in 1997) make it one of the more affordable choices in the lower-moderate price range if the season is busy and no special deals happen to be available elsewhere. Pluses include a small but pleasant swimming pool and a very reasonably priced all-you-can-eat, 24-hour buffet next door.

North Beach, Eilat. ☏ **08/633-4004**. Fax 08/633-4072. www.daliahotel.co.il. 63 units. $100–$180 (£50–£90) double. Rates include breakfast. AE, MC, V. **Amenities:** Pool. *In room:* A/C, TV, minibar, hair dryer, safe.

**Vista**   This relatively new hotel is in the area a few blocks inland from North Beach, a quiet location but not too far from the booming North Beach Promenade. Public areas and guest rooms are small but fresh and bright. The pool is medium-size; the breakfast is vast Israeli-style. If you're looking for less than luxury, and a bit of style but few frills, this is a good option. Through the Vista's website, you can at times find double rooms here for under $100 (£50).

Kamen St., North Shore, Kamen St., Eilat. ☏ **08/630-3030**. Fax 08/630-3040. www.vistaeilat.co.il. 84 units. $140–$220 (£70–£110) double. Rates include breakfast. DC, MC, V. Free parking. **Amenities:** Dining room; bar; outdoor heated pool; fitness room; laundry service; Wi-Fi in lobby; rooms for those w/limited mobility. *In room:* A/C, cable TV, minibar, coffeemaker, hair dryer, safe.

## CORAL BEACH & SOUTH TO THE BORDER
The hotels down here are away from the tourist crush of the downtown and North Beach sections of Eilat. They're convenient to the Coral Beach Nature Reserve and to smaller reefs good for snorkeling, as well as to a number of diving centers and a small group of restaurants. The no. 15 municipal bus brings you here from central Eilat.

### Very Expensive
**Eilat Princess Hotel** ⍟   Built in 1992, the Eilat Princess was for a time the snazziest hotel in town. Many guest rooms now need updating, but public areas and the lobby (dramatically built into the side of a desert cliff) remain sleek, and the large swimming pools laced with artificial cascades are fun. As the southernmost of Eilat's (and Israel's) hotels, 3.2km (2 miles) south of Coral Beach, the Princess is somewhat isolated unless you have a car, but there's a wide range of in-hotel upmarket dining choices. A small Red Sea–swimming beach is across the road, with a small offshore reef for snorkeling, but you're also not far from the Coral Beach Nature Reserve. Until renovating is done, bargain rates can often be found via the Internet.

Eilat. ☏ **08/636-5555**. Fax 08/637-6333. www.eilatprincess.com. 418 units. $220–$560 (£110–£280) double. Rates include breakfast. Internet and discount packages available. AE, DC, MC, V. Free parking. Bus: 15. **Amenities:** 6 restaurants; dining room; cafe; bar; 2 pools; 2 tennis courts; fitness room; spa; sports facilities; tour desk; shuttle into Eilat; 24-hr. room service; laundry service; synagogue. *In room:* A/C, TV, minibar, hair dryer, safe.

### Expensive
**Isrotel Ambassador** ⍟⍟   If you want to be close to snorkeling at the Coral Beach Nature Reserve, this hotel (built in 1997) offers the perfect location, less than a 5-minute walk across the road. On the hotel's property, you'll also find the excellent Red Sea Sport Club Diving Center, with a wide selection of scuba classes and excursions. Guest rooms are comfortable, though a bit small for the price, and surround a vast swimming pool. Service is relatively good.

Coral Beach, Eilat. ☏ **08/638-2222**. Fax 08/638-2200. www.isrotel.co.il. 170 units. $200–$380 (£100–£190) double. Rates include breakfast. AE, DC, MC, V. Free parking. Bus: 15. **Amenities:** Restaurant; dining room; cafe; bar; pool; tennis and basketball courts; billiards; fitness room; spa; children's activities; salon; massage; laundry service; synagogue; nightclub; diving center. *In room:* A/C, TV, minibar, coffeemaker, hair dryer, safe.

**Orchid Hotel and Resort**   This is one of Eilat's most unusual hotels, especially if you can conceive of a Thai resort transported to the barren, rocky desertscape of the Negev (a fire destroyed the hotel's tropical landscaping, but new plantings are growing in). With the exception of the beautiful Thai pavilion, housing a Thai restaurant, the rest of Orchid is faux Asian, but public areas are pleasant, surrounding a large, often busy pool.

Uphill are lines of wooden A-frame guest units with a double room and bathroom on the ground floor, and a sleeping loft reached by ladder/steps. A noisy golf cart shuttles guests up to their accommodations, which are decorated with non-Thai print curtains and bedspreads. Rooms in the "Shangri-la" wing are a bit more expensive and desirable. The Orchid is tranquil in the off season, but during school vacations is packed with Israeli families, which means screaming children. A beach is across the road.

South Beach, Eilat. ℂ 08/636-0360. Fax 08/637-5323. www.orchidhotel.co.il. 184 units. $280–$380 (£140–£190) double. Rates include breakfast. AE, DC, MC, V. Free parking. Bus: 15. **Amenities:** Restaurant; dining room; cafe; bar; heated pool; fitness room; spa; watersports; basketball and volleyball courts; business services; room service; massage; laundry service; synagogue. *In room:* A/C, TV, minibar, hair dryer, safe.

## JUST ACROSS THE BORDER: TABA, EGYPT

Just across the Israeli-Egyptian frontier at the southern edge of Eilat, Taba came under Israeli occupation, along with the rest of Sinai, at the end of the 1967 Six-Day War. When Israel returned the Sinai Peninsula to Egypt as part of the Camp David peace accords in the early 1980s, Taba remained in dispute. International arbitration in the late 1980s decided in favor of Egypt, but by then it had become a very valuable few acres, encompassing the site of the Taba Hilton, which visitors and residents alike had come to think of as a southern precinct of Eilat. Today, travelers from Eilat can pass across the border to the Taba Hilton for a few hours to visit the Taba Hilton's Casino without a visa—just show your passport at the crossing point. But to venture into Sinai beyond Taba requires a special visa. Guests at the Taba Hilton may and frequently do walk the few hundred feet across the border and taxi or bus into Eilat for shopping or dinner; however, Egyptian rental cars may not currently be taken across the border, nor can Israeli rental cars be taken out of Israel. *Note:* The Hilton (known also as the Taba Hilton Resort) was the victim of a terror bombing in 2004, probably because it was a favorite with Israelis and made an unusual and easy target just outside the protection of tight Israeli security (note that Egyptian security, even now, is not the equal of that in Israel).

**Taba Hilton Resort**    The informal, low-rise **Nelson Village** part of the Hilton Resort is spread along a beach with spacious, though older, rooms and gardens and terraces beside the sea for breakfasting with the birds. The **Taba Hilton** is a high-rise sharing the same reception office and facilities, with modern public areas and guest rooms, all newly (but rather economically) renovated after the 2004 bombing. Why stay here? The price is great, based on Egyptian standards; the ambience is different from Israel; the Egyptian staff is refreshingly polite; the snorkeling and diving center facilities and staff are exceptionally good, with a reef right off the private beach; and the hotel's gardens and palm trees are graceful and soothing. Unique attractions are the **casino** (easily visited by travelers from Eilat); the large saltwater swimming pool; and a small bazaar filled with interesting Egyptian crafts and souvenirs. Security is now *very* careful: Cars cannot approach the hotel, and baggage is inspected some distance from the building and shuttled over. Downside is el cheapo package tours that sometimes book here, but it's the same throughout Sinai. *Tip:* A restful day here and you're ready to plunge farther into Sinai at dawn without the hassle of the daybreak border ordeal.

Taba Beach, Sinai, Egypt. ℂ 069/353-0140 in Egypt or 08/632-6222 in Israel. Fax 62/578-7044 in Egypt. www. hilton.com. 326 units. $85–$200 (£43–£100) double. Half board and all-inclusive packages available. AE, DC, MC, V. **Amenities:** 4 restaurants; cafe; 3 bars; outdoor pool; 5 lighted tennis courts; diving and watersports center; windsurfing; jet-skiing; water-skiing; fitness center; children's club; tour desk; 24-hr. room service. *In room:* A/C, TV, minibar, coffeemaker, hair dryer.

## PRIVATE ROOMS, APARTMENTS & LAST-MINUTE HOTEL RESERVATIONS

Ask for referrals at the **Tourist Information Center** (✆ **08/630-9111**) at Bridge House, North Beach. It's best to use the tourist center for referral, as there have been complaints from people using other sources. Prices for a two-bedroom apartment (for four people or more) are about NIS 270 ($68/£34) per day during most of the year, and NIS 360 to NIS 450 ($90–$113/£45–£56) or more per day during high season (July–Aug and holidays). Especially for a group, this is one of the best ways to economize in Eilat.

## WHERE TO DINE
### INLAND, NORTH OF HATMARIM BOULEVARD

These choices are away from the almost wall-to-wall restaurants and fast-food places in North Beach, but it's worth the effort to get to them.

### Moderate

**Casa do Brasil** ✿ BRAZILIAN    This big, bustling place is a carnivore's paradise, and probably the best bottomless Brazilian meat restaurant in Israel. Everything here is delicious; only great self-discipline and the heat of Eilat's long, torrid summer will keep you from overeating. Meats are prepared on rotisserie grills imported from Brazil under the supervision of a Brazilian Israeli (whose family fled the Nazis in 1935), and his tasty Brazilian meatballs *(bolinho),* chorizo sausages, and *chimichurra* are all special. A cheerful serving staff brings appetizers, bread, olive tapenade, salad, rice, a little pot of Brazilian chili con carne, fries, and other treats to your table. Then the real parade begins: filet; baby lamb; beef ribs; chicken wings; gooseliver; aged, flavorful entrecôte; baby chicken basted in a sauce of honey, white wine, and soy; and duck breast. The menu varies at different times of day and season, but goes on and on. A less expensive luncheon parade offers less variety. Children's meals start at NIS 44 ($11/£5.50), and there's a selection of pastas and Brazilian-style pizza in case you manage to drag a vegetarian here. You can also order from an a la carte menu, but few do. Some nights there's Brazilian entertainment, and for those who can still move, excellent Brazilian desserts or refreshing fruit sorbets to finish.

3 Hativat Golani, near the Eilat Police Station. ✆ 08/632-3032. Reservations suggested. All-you-can-eat dinner NIS 100–NIS 130 ($25–$33/£13–£16); all-you-can-eat lunch from NIS 60 ($15/£7.50). AE, DC, MC, V. Daily noon–11pm.

**Eddie's Hideaway** ✿✿ CONTINENTAL    One of Eilat's very best restaurants, this quality establishment serves an enormous menu in a variety of inventive styles, yet manages to keep its prices reasonable and its customers very happy. Main courses, designed by Eddie himself, include such creations as Nairobi shrimp cooked in butter and hot paprika with onion, fresh mushrooms, and a touch of pineapple; moist, delicate Shanghai fish, smothered in a spicy soybean paste; or rich, heavenly gooseliver in a Middle Eastern date sauce. I'm also a fan of the homemade lasagna, the steaks, and the honey barbecued ribs. In addition, the menu includes lean, light dishes such as grilled sea bass or bream. A salad, vegetable, and potato are included with most main courses. A 10% service charge, which covers the tip, is automatically added to the bill. Because Eddie's is out-of-the-way, Eddie may deduct the price of your taxi (from any hotel in Eilat) from your bill—just give the waitress your receipt.

**Note:** Eddie's is aptly named. Not only is it far from the crush and glitz of the many semi-fast-food places on the North Beach Promenade, it is also not directly on Almogim

Street, and once you locate the building you must enter from around back. To find it, go up Hatmarim Street past the bus station, turn right on Almogim Street, and turn left at Peace Cafe.

68 Almogim St. ℂ 08/637-1137. Reservations required. Main courses NIS 40–NIS 100 ($10–$25/£5–£13). AE, DC, MC, V. Mon–Fri 6pm–midnight; Sat noon–4pm; closed Sun.

## NEW TOURIST CENTER
### Moderate
**Ginger** THAI/CHINESE/JAPANESE   Housed in a sleek, glassed-in upper-story pavilion, Ginger serves a Pan-Asian menu that's always interesting and a step above the many fast-food places on the North Beach Promenade. The Thai dishes are the strongest. There are pad Thai noodle dishes, both vegetarian and with meat; classic Thai dishes such as *omm olai* (chicken in a coconut, chili, and mint sauce); and my favorite, a spicy Beef Chang My Style, all of which the management will adeptly tone down in case you're not yet used to Thai seasonings. It's located at the edge of the New Tourist Center neighborhood facing Yotam Road. There is a nonsmoking section.

New Tourist Center. ℂ 08/637-0104. Reservations recommended. Main courses NIS 40–NIS 100 ($10–$25/£5–£13); business lunch from NIS 49 ($12/£6.10). AE, DC, MC, V. Daily 1–3:30pm and 6:30–11:30pm.

## NEAR NORTH BEACH
### Expensive
**Pago Pago** SEAFOOD/FRENCH   Moored in the North Beach Lagoon near the King Solomon Hotel, this floating restaurant, club, and bar offers a South Seas tropical ambience and a menu of exotic seafood, fresh fish, and meats prepared and served with flair. The light Thai seafood salad is a perfect dish for a hot Negev evening; or you might try *gratinée* of shrimps and calamari in cream sauce or the royal triple seafood platter for two (served in a giant ruffled clamshell). There are tropical drinks and mellow desserts (try the chocolate Pavlova mousse) served with chocolate liqueur coffee. A 10% service charge is added to the bill.

Eilat Laguna. ℂ 08/637-6660. Reservations recommended evenings. Main courses NIS 55–NIS 160 ($14–$40/£6.90–£20). AE, DC, MC, V. Daily 1pm–3am.

**Wang's Grill** 🍴🍴 ASIAN/CALIFORNIA FUSION   This elegant restaurant uses Asian cooking techniques to produce delicious dishes that have a Chinese influence, but are often far from standard Chinese food. Hot and cold appetizers (mostly in the NIS 32–NIS 54/$8–$14/£4–£6.75 range) include interesting variations of Asian crispy chicken salad and inventive California wonton soup, but you will also find ginger lamb dumplings with wild mushrooms, ginger, and garlic sauce, or tangerine duck with toasted almonds and crispy wontons on a bed of lettuce. A fusion grilled foie gras first course is NIS 90 ($23/£11). Main courses include grilled sirloin steak with a spicy Szechuan sauce and vegetables; grilled sea bass with sautéed Chinese cabbage and mustard vinaigrette; and a number of variations of Peking duck. Vegetable side dishes cost extra. Chocolate hazelnut terrine, poppy seed parfait, and a dynamite hot chocolate cake/brownie with a molten interior are among the dessert choices. Wang's has a kashrut certificate, and there's a NIS 41 ($10/£5.10) children's dinner not noted on the menu. *Tip:* Look for 10% discount coupons in tourist brochures or at **www.eluna.com**.

In Isrotel Royal Beach Hotel, North Beach Promenade. ℂ 08/636-8989. Reservations recommended. Main courses NIS 90–NIS 120 ($23–$30/£11–£15); all side dishes extra. AE, DC, MC, V. Sat–Thurs 7–11:30pm; Sat after Shabbat–11pm.

## Moderate & Inexpensive

**Agadir Burger Bar** ✦ INTERNATIONAL PUB  A delightfully eclectic place, both in menu and ambience, this is part of an idiosyncratic chain (no two locations are alike) that's been popping up all over the country. The burgers may be the best in Israel, with unbelievable toppings including portobello mushrooms, feta cheese, or spiced breast of goose. You'll also find everything from guacamole to tempura shrimp, spicy Moroccan merguez sausages, veal dumplings, and a choice of Israeli wines. The place morphs into a lively bar at night.

10 Kamon St., North Beach. ✆ 08/633-3777. Main courses NIS 40–NIS 60 ($10–$15/£5–£7.50). AE, DC, MC, V. Daily noon–3am.

**Denise Kingdom** *(Value (Kids* FISH  This very informal, busy restaurant is run by a local Eilat fish farm specializing in bream (dorade), a succulent white-meat sea fish, but it also serves sea bass and a few nonfarm choices. Kids will like the fish tanks, which they can visit between courses, as well as the chance to climb on the fish sculptures in the gardens beside the dining terrace. There are carefully deboned filets and nonfish plates on the children's menu. Adults will enjoy the ultrafresh whole fish or combo platters, which you can order steamed, poached, smoked, grilled, baked, or pan-fried. I especially like a dish of delicate fresh denise stuffed with lemon, chili, and spices. Main courses come with a baked potato and are preceded by a meze of Middle Eastern salads served with delicious fresh rolls, herbed butter, and olive tapenade—so although there's a choice of fish-centered appetizers, you probably won't want them. The pies, cakes, and cheesecakes are hefty in size and come with ice cream, another plus for kids.

North Beach, a block inland across from the entrance to Sheraton's Herods Palace. ✆ **08/637-9898.** Reservations recommended. Main courses NIS 70–NIS 85 ($18–$21/£8.75–£11). AE, DC, MC, V. Sun–Thurs noon–11pm; Fri noon–1 hr. before Shabbat; Sat after Shabbat–11pm.

## Moderate

**Red Sea Star Underwater Restaurant, Bar and Observatory** *(Kids* CONTINENTAL  This amazingly designed restaurant is 5m (16 ft.) below the surface of the Red Sea, with thick Plexiglas windows that give you an octopus-eye view of the surrounding fish, corals, and other creatures. The decor is fantasy oceanesque, with sand floors covered by a layer of clear epoxy; velvet, sea urchin cushions on the chairs; starfish lighting fixtures; and wavy blue underwater light filtering through the subsea pavilion from natural sources by day and artificial sources by night. It may sound campy, but the details are so well done that the effect is enchanting—you find your attention torn between the underwater vistas outside the windows, and the interior decor, overflowing with marine shapes and textures. The food is average, but the basic experience is fun. Denise, a fish from the Red Sea, leads the list of fish (though you may not feel comfortable dining on a sea creature while its family and friends glide past the windows). The restaurant becomes mostly a bar by 10pm. Both adults and kids enjoy the decor, but service can be slow enough to test the patience of visitors regardless of age. Tours come through and are led to an often worn-out buffet table—avoid it.

Next to the Le Méridien Hotel. ✆ **08/634-7777.** www.redseastar.com/restaurant-en.php. Reservations necessary. Main courses NIS 54–NIS 100 ($14–$25/£6.75–£13). AE, MC, V. Daily 7–10pm.

**Tandoori** ✦✦ INDIAN  Located in the Lagoona Hotel building, with its entrance on King's Wharf, this is one of frenzied Eilat's most calm and special restaurants.

Beautifully decorated with Indian artifacts, the restaurant serves a variety of Indian dishes, although it specializes in tandoori cooking. All traditional styles executed with a light, elegant touch (let them know if you want authentic, fiery spicing or prefer your dishes mild), and house creations, such as giant prawns in ginger marinade or South Indian lamb in spiced coconut milk sauce, are very much worth trying, as are the stuffed Indian breads and appetizers. Look into the reasonably priced luncheon specials, which include soup, breads, four choices of main course, plus vegetable curry, basmati rice, dessert, and a drink. Homemade desserts, such as the honeyed *gulab jamun,* are both exotic and delicious; and *lassi,* a yogurt-based drink, is a cool antidote to Eilat's torrid temperatures and clears the palate between hot courses.

On the Lagoona Hotel Promenade. 𝄐 **08/633-3879** or 633-3666. Reservations recommended. Main courses NIS 45–NIS 84 ($11–$21/£5.60–£11). AE, DC, MC, V. Daily noon–3pm and 6:30pm–midnight.

### Inexpensive
**Spring Onion Restaurant Cafe** VEGETARIAN/FISH    A favorite of Eilat vegetarians, with fresh, well-prepared food, this small modern place expands to a large outdoor terrace after the sun goes down, and is a great spot for people-watching as you dine. Salads are excellent, enormous, and can easily be shared by two. Pastas and fresh fish fill out the main courses, and there's also an assortment of wonderfully rich cakes for dessert. The sign is in English, but if you're asking directions from locals, the Hebrew name actually translates as "Green Onion."

North Beach Promenade near the bridge. 𝄐 **08/637-7434.** Main courses NIS 40–NIS 80 ($10–$20/£5–£10); light meals NIS 35–NIS 45 ($8.75–$11/£4.40–£5.60). AE, DC, MC, V. Daily 8am–after midnight.

## SOUTH OF TOWN & THE CORAL BEACH
### Moderate
**Last Refuge** ✦ SEAFOOD    Right across the street from the Ambassador Hotel, this rather expensive but good fish restaurant has weather-beaten nautical decor (not unlike something you'd find on Cape Cod or Long Island), tables both indoors and outside on a seaside deck, and generous portions of seafood and fish served in a variety of cream sauces. Simple, very fresh grilled fish is an excellent choice here.

Coral Beach. 𝄐 **08/6373-627.** Reservations recommended. Main courses NIS 69–NIS 100 ($17–$25/£8.60–£13). Add 10% service charge. AE, DC, MC, V. Daily 1–4:30pm and 6–11:30pm.

### Inexpensive
**Dolphin Reef Pub Cafe** SEAFOOD/PUB    This thatched-roof, tropical pavilion at the easygoing Dolphin Reef is a good place for lunch if you've paid admission to the Dolphin Reef's private beach for the day; it's also a congenial place to hang out in the evening, when admission to the Dolphin Reef is free and the management often provides live entertainment and dancing on the sand. The floor is sand, the bar is lively in the evening, and the menu choices range from cold yogurt and Greek salad to grilled whole fish or hamburgers.

Dolphin Reef. 𝄐 **08/637-1846.** Reservations suggested. Main courses NIS 65–NIS 100 ($16–$25/£8.10–£13); light meals and snacks NIS 20–NIS 40 ($5–$10/£2.50–£5). MC, V. Daily 11am–after midnight.

## EILAT AFTER DARK
In this sun-and-fun resort, the crowds move from beach to bar, disco, or club after the sun goes down. The Eilat Tourist Information Center's weekly bulletin, *Events in Eilat,* available for free at the tourist office, will let you know what's happening where.

Several of the major hotels have **nightclubs, piano bars,** and **discos.** These are some of the liveliest places in town, patronized by international tourists, Israelis, and native Eilatis alike. Of the discos, **Platinum,** in **King Solomon's Palace Hotel,** is popular, with spectacular laser and sound effects. Admission at top hotel discos runs NIS 60 to NIS 125 ($15–$31/£7.50–£16). My favorite for easygoing beach atmosphere and spirit is the **Dolphin Reef** (© 08/637-4292), with its thatched-roof, sandfloor cafe/bar. There's often dancing on the beach Monday and Thursday nights (cover charge is NIS 40/$10/£5), and Friday afternoon/evening there's a quiet *kaballat* Shabbat (receiving the Sabbath) ceremony, with the dolphins flipping offshore. Bus no. 15 will get you there. Call Dolphin Reef for more information. The **New Tourist Center** and the **North Beach Waterfront Promenade** also have a lot going on in the evening, with numerous pubs and indoor/outdoor cafes humming with activity. Check the blasting **Underground Pub** (© 08/637-0239; www.underground-pub. com), with cheap beer before 9pm and Wednesday night karaoke parties. The **Three Monkeys,** on the promenade near the Royal Beach Hotel, is Eilat's biggest, busiest spot for drinking and dancing, with live music every night, a dual-level indoor area, an outdoor section beside the water, and an international crowd, largely in the 25-to-30 age range. It opens every night at 9pm, gets busy toward midnight, and has a dress code: no shorts or flip-flops, and neat (preferably informal but stylish) clothing. Dining and dancing cruises with live music and stars or moonlight are offered in busy seasons: Call **Red Sea Sports Club** (© 08/637-9685), or check with the tourist desk at your hotel. Prices start at about NIS 120 ($30/£15).

Various Israeli **folklore evenings** are sponsored by the big hotels, usually beginning at 9:30pm several nights a week. Music for dancing, or a disco, often follows the performance. The fee (about NIS 25–NIS 35/$6.25–$8.75/£3.10–£4.40) includes a first drink, or perhaps wine and cheese. **Kibbutz Elot,** 5km (3 miles) north of Eilat, often offers Saturday evening performances of **Israeli Folk Dancing and Song.** The price, including transportation and a kibbutz-style buffet dinner, is NIS 160 ($40/£20).

The **Cinémathèque Club** screens films in English at the **Philip Murray Cultural Center** (© 08/633-2257), at the corner of Hatmarim Boulevard and Hativat Ha-Negev. Regular starting time seems to be around 9pm; admission is charged. The major hotels show films and videos about excursions in the Eilat area as well. Check the tourist office's *Events in Eilat* for details.

## SHOPPING

Eilat stones, a form of green and turquoise polished malachite, are sold throughout Israel in settings that range from contemporary to traditional Yemenite. They were popular in the 1960s and 1970s, less so now. Most hotel gift shops offer a selection of Eilat stone jewelry. You can visit **Malkit** (© 08/637-3372), an Eilat stone jewelry workshop in the Ha-Dekel part of town, Sunday to Thursday 8am to 7pm and Friday 8am to 1pm. The **Egyptian Bazaar** at the **Hilton Nelson Village** (p. 473) offers the chance to peruse Egyptian crafts and souvenirs you'd otherwise have to travel to Cairo to find. Some stock is tourist stuff; a few really beautiful crafts and objects will be found amid the stalls. It's easy to cross the border at the southern city limits of Eilat. Luxury shopping can be found at the Cardo Mall in Herods Palace; the North Beach Promenade runs the gamut from street fair booths to stylish shops that Israelis love because there's no VAT in Eilat.

## 6 Side Trips to Sinai

Sinai is a wild, awe-inspiring triangle of land that's mysterious and unforgettable. Its mountains are fringed with beaches and the crystal-clear waters of the Red Sea.

Mount Sinai and the ancient Byzantine **monastery of Santa Katarina** on its slope have been a destination for pilgrims for 16 centuries, almost miragelike in their sanctity. Over the past 30 years, the coast of the **Gulf of Aqaba** has become a second major Sinai attraction. It's a diver's and snorkeler's paradise, lined with some of the most beautiful and unusual coral-reef systems in the world. You can camp in simple huts along the beaches or pamper yourself in deluxe hotel complexes at prices that are incredible bargains.

### VISA REQUIREMENTS & TRAVEL PERMITS

Coming from Israel, there are two kinds of visas available, depending on what your travel plans may be. The first is a **Sinai Only Visa** (valid for 14 days; renewable inside Sinai), obtainable at the border crossing, which permits you to travel along the Gulf of Aqaba Coast to Nuweiba, Dahab, Na'ama Bay, and Sharm el Sheik, as well as to Mount Sinai and the Monastery of Santa Katarina. If you want to hike in the mountains near Santa Katarina; visit the extraordinary reefs at Ras Mohamed National Park, just south of Sharm el Sheik; or travel on to Cairo, you'll need a **standard All Egypt Visa,** which is more of a procedure and expense. You must obtain the standard visa ahead of time from the Egyptian Embassy in Tel Aviv, from the Egyptian Embassy in your own country, or from the Egyptian Consulate in Eilat.

Note that no tourists are allowed to hike or travel alone off the main roads and tourist centers in Sinai without a guide and **special permit.** Bedouin guides at the main tourist centers are always available, and can arrange the necessary permits for the itineraries you plan. Make sure your guide has the required permits. Escorted tours can be arranged from Eilat through most travel agencies there.

**Fast Facts**   Egypt (in Arabic: *Misr*)

Language: Arabic
County Telephone Code: 20
Sinai Area Code: 69
Currency: Egyptian Pound (LE, divided into 100 piasters.
$1=5.5LE; 1LE=18¢. £1=11LE; ILE=9p.

**WATER**   Drink bottled water only, except where hotels provide filtering systems.

**CROSSING THE BORDER**   **Taba Border Crossing** (Israeli side) ℂ **08/637-2104.** Open daily 24 hours at press time; check for hours during Jewish and Islamic

---

### ⟨Warning⟩ Travel Safety

Although peaceful and untouched by Middle Eastern wars and terror attacks for more than 30 years, Sinai was hit by a number of hotel bombings in 2004 and 2005, designed to destroy local tourism. At press time, Sinai remains the most mellow place in the Middle East, and Egypt has beefed up security, but check U.S. and U.K. government travel advisories before making plans to travel in Sinai.

holidays. The regulations, crossing schedules, and fees on both the Israeli and Egyptian sides of the border are constantly being revised. The Eilat **Tourist Information Center,** at Bridge House in North Beach (on the North Beach promenade), will give you current information and practical advice about what to expect in terms of regulations, fees, and ongoing bus connections. Do not plan to cross the border without checking there first. At press time, you can cross into Taba to visit the **Taba Hilton Resort and Casino** (located a short walk beyond the border) by going through border procedures but without getting a visa or paying fees. You will not be allowed to go farther into Sinai unless you have a visa in hand. *Note:* A visa stamp in your passport issued in Tel Aviv, Eilat, or at the Taba Border will preclude your entering Syria, Lebanon, and other countries at war with Israel. Check to see if visas can be issued on a separate piece of paper.

**CURRENCY EXCHANGE AT TABA BORDER**   Do your money-changing at the ATM at the Egyptian Border Pavilion—make an estimate of what amount of Egyptian currency you'll need. Banks and exchange offices in Sinai are few and far between except at Sharm el Sheik, and hours are iffy. There's also a Bank Misr office at the border, where you can change cash and traveler's checks; should it be closed, you can try at the Taba Hilton.

**TOURS & PACKAGES**   The **Eilat Tourist Information Center** (see above) is especially in touch with the tourist market in Sinai, and can advise you about tours of the Sinai leaving from Eilat. Check with **Red Sea Sports** (© 08/633-3666; www.redsea sports.co.il); **Desert Eco Tours** (© 052/276-5753; www.desertecotours.com); and the **Eilat Attractions Office,** all of which can book hotels (at times with considerable discounts) as well as hikes, jeep safaris, excursions to Santa Katarina, and diving packages on the Aqaba Coast. It's best to visit all three offices in person. Except on Jewish holidays, Sinai is not generally crowded and it's usually easy to find bargains and book at the last minute through these offices.

Tour packagers that offer a diving option include **Sinai Divers** (www.sinaidivers.com), **Dogsbreath Divers** (www.dogsbreathdivers.com), and **Desert Eco Tours** (www.desertecotours.com).

**BUS TRANSPORTATION**   **Egyptian buses** leave from the Egyptian side of the Israeli-Egyptian border at Taba, near Eilat, a number of times a day on routes southward to Nuweiba, Dahab, and Sharm el Sheik. There are also buses from Taba and Nuweiba to Santa Katarina and to Cairo. Schedules are generally unpredictable. Reserve a seat if possible, and arrive at the bus station more than an hour ahead of time. The Eilat Tourist Information Center can give you advice about current schedules and prices. The trip from Taba to Sharm el Sheik should be no more than $10 to $12 (£5–£6) on a scheduled bus.

**BY TAXI**   Private **Bedouin taxis** are often broken-down looking, but you won't have to wait endlessly for a bus. They'll take you all the way to Nuweiba, Dahab, and Sharm el Sheik. You have to bargain over the price: $60 (£30) from Taba to Sharm el Sheik is rock bottom. Look for others at the border to share your taxi. *Tip:* On the road, if things get too harrowing, offer to pay your driver a bonus if he drives slowly (and carefully). "*Shwayeh, shwayeh,*" is Arabic for "Slowly, slowly." Most drivers will understand what you mean. If you do drive or take a taxi, don't even think of being on unlit roads after dark.

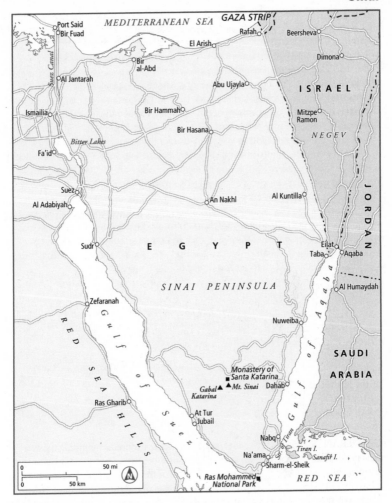

## MOUNT SINAI & SANTA KATARINA ✸✸✸

Located in the rugged interior of the peninsula, the place where Moses received the Ten Commandments is not the isolated pilgrimage site it once was; nevertheless it is a charismatic and powerful place. Nestled on the lower slopes of Mount Sinai (Gabal Mussa, or the Mountain of Moses in Arabic) is one of the world's greatest but least known treasures: the fortresslike **Monastery of Santa Katarina,** with origins reaching back to the times of the cave-dwelling monks of the 2nd century A.D. Much of the monastery is more than 1,500 years old; including its large wooden doors and carved ceiling beams. The library includes what is probably one of the most important collections of rare and ancient manuscripts outside of the Vatican.

The monastery's Church of the Burning Bush was built by command of the great Byzantine Emperor Justinian between A.D. 548 and A.D. 565. Mosaicists were probably

> ### *Tips* Ascending Mount Sinai
>
> The climb up steep pathways and staircases to the top of **Mount Sinai** ⚲⚲⚲ is arduous. In summer, most people do it in the cool (or cold) of night and enjoy the incredible sunrise. In winter, daylight hours are not as bitterly cold for climbing as the freezing predawn, but you miss the sunrise. The hike can take from 2 to 4 hours, depending on your strength. It's by no means an easy ascent—it's worthwhile to consider taking a Bedouin guide and renting a camel that will take you at least partway up the mountain at a cost of LE 70 ($12/£6) for the climb. Much bargaining may be involved; the Bedouin take all currencies (they're not going to lose a customer who will be gone tomorrow because he was short of Egyptian pounds; bring small bills—a man with a camel at 3am on Mount Sinai does not make change). The view from the summit (if you can get away from tour groups) is transcendent. If you can't make it all the way to the top, there are flat, camel-accessible way stations along the pathway, and the vistas from these places, containing chapels dedicated to Moses, Elijah, John the Baptist, and others, are very spiritual and dramatic. Remember, to ascend does not mean merely to climb.
>
> *Tip:* Six kilometers (3¾ miles) to the south is **Gabal Katarina (Mount Catherine),** the highest in Egypt. The path to the summit of this mountain is more beautiful and less trafficked by hordes of tourists than Mount Sinai; from the village of Milga the climb can take 6 hours. Although the tradition of identifying Mount Sinai as the place where the Ten Commandments were given to Moses is very strong, there are other traditions and theories attached to other mountains, and Gabal Katarina could possibly be the genuine place. There are a chapel and a source of water at the very top of the mountain. A guide is advisable.

sent from Constantinople to create the extraordinary mosaics surrounding the apse. The vast collections of ancient icons include some of the most beautiful examples of this art ever created. According to tradition, at the time of the church's construction, the actual Burning Bush (in its unfiery form) still stood just outside the apse, but was virtually destroyed over the centuries as pilgrims took away pieces as relics. What remained of the bush, a form of wild raspberry, was transplanted to a more protected spot in the monastery where it thrives to this day.

## WHERE TO STAY

The most atmospheric and economical choices is the **hostel inside the ancient (4th-c.-A.D.) Santa Katarina Monastery** ⚲⚲ (© 069/347-0353) on the left side of the monastery complex. Dorm rooms are hot and airless in summer, and rather cramped with up to eight beds to a chamber, but they are clean and the private rooms are pleasant. The place seems like a locale for an Indiana Jones adventure, and you'll always find interesting fellow travelers. Dorm beds are LE75 ($14/£7) a night; beds in rooms with three to four beds and a private bathroom are LE100 ($18/£9). If the hostel is not crowded, it is at times possible to rent a room as a private double for LE130 ($24/£12) per person; LE175 ($32/£16) single, breakfast and dinner included. Check-in is from

8am to 1pm and from 4 to 9pm. Very beautiful morning services are at 4am. You cannot enter the monastery after 9:30pm. Credit cards are not accepted.

## ALONG THE COAST BETWEEN TABA & DAHAB

This is some of the loveliest shoreline in the Gulf of Aqaba, dotted with isolated encampments and small hotels. They are inexpensive but tranquil places by day, and often crazy at night; most offer simple snorkeling and beaching, and can arrange hikes and jeep trips in the region as well as tours to Mount Sinai.

## NUWEIBA

Nuweiba is a small port and industrial center with beautiful beaches at its outskirts, and along the coast to the north of town. On busy days, the line of trucks waiting for the ferries to Jordan can stretch for 1km (½ mile). Separate from the port is Nuweiba's other incarnation as a beach resort—a mixture of sprawling camps and beach-hut hotels, especially to the north at **Tarabin**, where you can easily find a place in the $10-to-$20 (£5–£10) per person a night range. Tarabin is filled with little restaurants, cafes, and outdoor discos and pubs. From Nuweiba, there's a main road to Santa Katarina and Mount Sinai.

The Nuweiba coast's best hotel, located south of the port, is the **Nuweiba Hilton Coral Resort** ✶ (© **069/352-0320;** fax 069/352-0327; www.hilton.com). This sprawling, low-rise 200-unit complex is simple but relaxing and pleasant. It offers beautiful, isolated swimming and snorkeling beaches, pools, restaurants, and a PADI diving center. Doubles run $90 to $110 (£45–£55), but look for discounts. The more expensive, atmospheric bungalow rooms are worth the extra $30 (£15). Half board is available.

## DAHAB ✶✶

Once the flower child of the Aqaba Coast during the years of Israeli occupation, Dahab has grown into a laid-back resort town with the best diving in the area.

The **Nesima Hotel and Dive Center** (© **069/364-0320;** www.nesima_resort.com) offers friendly atmosphere, a full variety of courses and tours starting at 50€ ($79/£40), as well as multiday dive packages and snorkeling activities. Doubles start from 65€ ($102/£51), breakfast included. Scout out bargains and half-board deals. Prices are quoted in euros.

The most comfortable choice in town is the **Hilton Dahab Resort** ✶✶ (© **069/364-0310;** fax 069/364-0324; www.hilton.com), a mildly exotic low-rise village of whitewashed, desert design, with a fine beach, top-flight diving and windsurfing center, two outdoor pools, three restaurants, an excellent buffet, and three bars. Rates run $100 to $135 (£50–£68) for a double with meal plan, but there are packages and special deals that can get you in here for far less. Suites are $40 (£20) more.

As at Nuweiba, you'll also find lots of hutlike accommodations. They have no phone numbers—just ask about rooms at places that strike your fancy. There are tons of beachfront Bedouin restaurants, cafes, and discos.

## SHARM EL SHEIK ✶✶

At the southernmost point of the Sinai Peninsula, Sharm el Sheik is a sprawling center for commercial and industrial action as well as a mecca for divers.

**Na'ama Bay,** a low-rise resort offering beaches, snorkeling, and diving, is a 5-minute drive from commercial Sharm el Sheik. It's filled with inexpensive hotels, eateries and bars, and more than three dozen moderate and expensive hotel complexes catering largely to European visitors on package vacations. The better hotels are located directly on Na'ama Bay, and most have a slice of beach reserved for their guests. A pedestrian promenade runs along the beach, connecting all the hotel properties before terminating at the Na'ama Bay Shopping Mall.

Diving is good at Na'ama Bay, and the hotels and dive centers offer a large variety of snorkeling and diving options. The best diving and snorkeling, perhaps in the world, is just south of Sharm el Sheik, at the **National Park at Ras Mohamed** 𝕽𝕽𝕽. You must have the All Egypt Visa rather than Sinai Only Visa in order to enter this most elysian of the earth's coral reefs. Admission to the National Park is LE29 ($5.30/£2.60). The park is open daily from 8am to 5pm.

## WHERE TO STAY

The Na'ama Bay area, 7km (4½ miles) north of Sharm el Sheik, is filled with moderate and upper-level hotels, centered around an often crowded bathing beach.

### Expensive & Moderate

Located at the very center of the bay, with the choicest stretch of palm-shaded beach, the **Hilton Fayrouz Resort** 𝕽 (© 069/360-0136/7; www.hilton.com) is the most experienced of the international complexes at Na'ama Bay. The informal low-rise complex is set amid gardens that have had time to develop. Small swimming pools are hidden amid the gardens and terraces; facilities include a health club, several restaurants, and a nightclub. The staff are the most savvy in the region, and the diving, watersports, and other services are top class. All 150 units offer the standard amenities; doubles run $100 to $170 (£50–£85), not including tax and service charges. Rates include half board.

The most exclusive of all hotels in the area, the **Four Seasons** 𝕽𝕽𝕽, Sharm el Sheikh (© 069/360-3555; www.fourseasons.com), is located on a relatively pristine section of the sea, about 15 minutes by car from Na'ama Bay. The complex is filled with traditional Egyptian village and desert motifs that give the hotel an intimate, exotic charm, but also the luxury of a sprawling, whitewashed palace. Accommodations are the most luxurious in Sinai, and the personal attention is very pampering. A standard double costs $550 (£275), including breakfast, but look for bargain rates.

The modern, low-rise **Mövenpick Sharm el Sheikh Beach Resort,** Na'ama Bay (© 069/360-3200; www.moevenpick-hotels.com), is an outpost of a Swiss hotel chain that is a complete vacation enclave in its own right. The property has its own beach, diving center, and an 18-hole golf course. Special facilities include fresh- and saltwater swimming pools, tennis courts, a casino, and the best hotel shopping arcade in town. The chain is famous for its lavish buffet and in-house dining options. Doubles run from $160 (£80), including breakfast.

Located at the up-and-coming, sheltered Shark Bay, 15km (10 miles) north of Na'ama Bay, the **Sheraton Sharm Hotel Resort** (© 069/360-2070; www.starwood hotels.com) offers 835 relatively new rooms and suites, a location with clearer water than at Na'ama Bay, and numerous dining opportunities. There's an excellent (heated) pool complex and a fabulous spa center. Rooms run from $140 (£70) double, including breakfast. The downside: You must deal with taxis to get into town.

The **Hyatt Regency Sharm el Sheik,** The Gardens Bay (© 069/360-1234; www. hyatt.com), is an Egyptian desert fantasy, surrounded by artificial pools and set beside a genuine and especially good reef for snorkeling. The complex can get overloaded when fully booked, so a room at the Regency Club level—you get special services, a running snack buffet, and a separate swimming facility—could be worth the investment. Rates run $285 (£143) double, including breakfast.

Architecturally, the **Sonesta Beach Resort,** Na'ama Bay (© **800/766-3782** in the U.S., or 069/360-0725; www.sonesta.com), is the most interesting and beautiful complex on Na'ama Bay, located at the center of the swimming beach area. From a distance it looks like a whitewashed desert village filled with dome-roofed houses and arabesque arches. The Sonesta also offers full range of watersports and evening activities. Rates run $160 to $230 (£80–£115) double, including breakfast (but not the 20% tax and service charge); you can at times find package deals and Internet discounts that can lower the price to about $100 (£50) double.

### Budget

The **Pidgeon House Hotel** (© **069/360-0996;** fax 069/360-0995) is the best low-budget choice at Na'ama Bay, right across the road from the big, expensive hotels that line the beach. Standard doubles with shared bathrooms and fans, but no air-conditioning, are $20 (£10); and pleasant, new superior rooms with private bathrooms, air-conditioning, and a refrigerator are $36 (£18). Breakfast is included in the rates.

### WHERE TO DINE

Evening dinner options range from the lavish buffets that most deluxe hotels offer (usually around $22/£11 or less) to the under-$10 (£5) Italian, Middle Eastern, or Chinese dinners at restaurants in the shopping mall.

Two non-hotel restaurants in Sharm el Sheik that serve main courses in the LE50-to-LE100 ($9.10–$18/£4.50–£9.10) range deserve special mention. The **Sinai Star,** in Sharm el Sheikh, serves the best fresh grilled fish in the area, along with wonderful bread, salads, and chips. **Al Fanar,** overlooking the waterfront beside the lighthouse, has a Bedouin ambience but offers an Italian menu and serves alcohol. The pizza and the view are great. It's worth the taxi fare from Na'ama Bay into Sharm; every driver knows these places.

# 12

# A Side Trip to Petra

**P**etra, the legendary lost city carved into the walls of a hidden desert canyon, is the most famous of Jordan's many dazzling sites and a fascinating excursion from Eilat. There are escorted bus tours that leave Eilat early in the morning, get you to Petra before noon, and back to your hotel in Eilat by late afternoon. But Petra's antiquities, natural beauty, and ever-changing feel at different times of day are easily worth a stay of 1 to 3 nights or more. In addition, there are beautiful, amazing affordable desert resorts only a few minutes from Petra, which make this a good place to chill and relax.

We also encourage readers to look into adding more of Jordan to their travel plans. Since 1994, when the Hashemite Kingdom of Jordan and Israel signed a peace agreement ending a 46-year-long state of war, the Kingdom of Jordan has been host to a wave of international and Israeli tourists.

## 1 Planning a Trip to Petra

### VISITOR INFORMATION

The **Jordan Tourism Board** website (www.visitjordan.com) offers very thorough information about touring Jordan and Petra. Excellent information on Petra can be found at www.go2petra.com.

The **Royal Society for the Conservation of Nature** website (www.rscn.org.jo) has specific information about eco-tourism and hiking in **Petra; Wadi Rum** ✸✸, south of Petra; the wild, mountainous **Dana Reserve** ✸, north of Petra; as well as to other nature and wildlife reserves in the Kingdom of Jordan.

### TOUR OPERATORS

Reputable tour operators that run excursions to Petra (among other locations in Jordan) include **Abercrombie and Kent Jordan** (© **962-06/566-5465** in Amman; www.abercrombiekent.com); **Desert Eco Tours** (© **972-52/276-5753** outside Israel, or 054/276-5753 in Israel; www.desertecotours.com); and **Petra Moon Tourism** (© **962-03/215-6665** in Petra; www.petramoon.com). For further options, check with the Jordan Tourism Board (www.visitjordan.com).

### ENTRY REQUIREMENTS

You must have a valid passport that does not have an expiration date within 6 months of your planned visit. Travelers from the United States, Canada, the United Kingdom, Ireland, Australia, and New Zealand planning to enter Jordan overland from Israel can get their visas after paying a visa fee of JD 10 ($14/£7.15) for a single-entry visa or JD 20 ($28/£14) for a multiple-entry visa at the **Eilat/Aqaba Crossing.** There is also a departure fee from Israel of approximately NIS 90 ($23/£11). Jordan charges an exit fee of JD 5 ($7.05/£3.60) for leaving the country at any border crossing into Israel. If

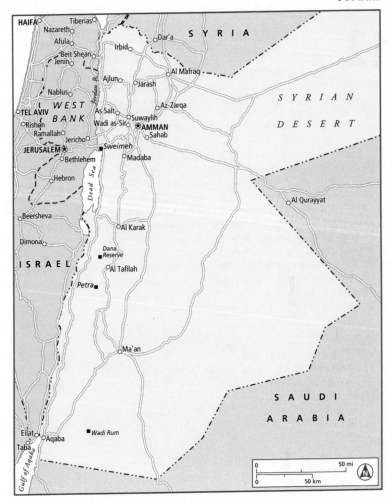

you enter Jordan via the Eilat/Aqaba Crossing, you can reenter Israel at the Eilat/ Aqaba crossing or at the Sheik Hussein crossing in northern Jordan near the Israeli town of Beit Shean, but you **cannot reenter Israel via the Allenby Bridge Crossing** into the West Bank near Jericho. If you have your Jordanian visa ahead of time, and you exited Israel via the Allenby Bridge (also called the King Hussein Bridge and *not* to be confused with the Sheik Hussein Bridge in the north), then you *can* reenter Israel via the Allenby Bridge. **Note:** The Allenby Bridge Crossing involves travel through the currently unstable West Bank, and can involve delays at the Allenby Bridge due to security and other considerations. I don't recommend using this route.

Most visas are issued for 15 days, renewable at local police stations without an additional fee; the renewable visa is usually good for an additional 3 months. Good travel agents and reputable tour companies can generally handle the arrangements for their

## A Look at Jordan's Past

The Hashemite Kingdom of Jordan encompasses boundaries defined by the Allied victors of World War I. Emir Abdullah, son of Sherif Hussein of Mecca, whose ancestry can be traced to the Prophet Muhammad, was awarded Trans-Jordan, the former Ottoman territories east of the Jordan River, in gratitude for Arab support during the war against the Ottoman Empire. Under British supervision, the Emirate of Trans-Jordan moved toward independence in 1946; with independence, Emir Abdullah became King Abdullah of Trans-Jordan. In 1949, with the annexation of the West Bank, the name of the country was changed to the Kingdom of Jordan.

In 1951, King Abdullah was assassinated in front of the Al Aqsa Mosque in Jerusalem by forces that felt the king was working for reconciliation with the new State of Israel. Abdullah's 14-year-old grandson, the future King Hussein, was at his side when he was struck down. Hussein ruled from 1953 until his death in 1999, bringing his country through more than 4 decades of wars and crises, walking a delicate tightrope between the larger powers in the Middle East. During this time, Jordan has absorbed and given citizenship to more than a million refugees from the 1948 and 1967 wars, as well as to more than 300,000 Palestinians expelled from Kuwait and other Gulf states in the wake of the 1991 Gulf War. In the last years of his life, King Hussein made the search for peace in the Middle East into a personal crusade. Few in the region will forget his committed words and presence at the funeral of Prime Minister Rabin or his personal condolence visits to the mourning Israeli families of Beit Shemesh, whose children had fallen victim to terrorism. Hussein's son, the Western-educated, innovative King Abdullah, has vowed to continue his father's work for peace.

In a land devoid of oil and with few natural resources, Jordan has created one of the most progressive and energetic societies in the Middle East, but the burden of absorbing so many refugees, largely without help from the outside world, has taken its toll on the nation's economy. The opportunities afforded by peace may turn this trend around. If it does, tourism will be an important element in Jordan's economic revival.

clients' visas. Visa fees are not included in most package tour prices, but there should be no charge for the service of obtaining the visa.

The Jordanian Embassy in the United States is at 3504 International Dr. NW, Washington, DC 20008 (② 202/966-2664); in Canada, 100 Bronson Ave., no. 701, Ottawa, Ont. KIR 6G8 (② 613/238-8091); in the United Kingdom, 6 Upper Philimore Gardens, London W8 7HB (② 020/937-36-85); and in Australia, 20 Roebuck St., Red Hill ACT 2603, Canberra (② 02/6295-9951). In Israel the Jordanian embassy is at 14 Aba Hillel Silva St., in Ramat Gan, a suburb of Tel Aviv (② 03/751-7722). If you book a tour to Jordan in Israel, the travel agency can usually arrange your visa paperwork for you.

To find the nearest Jordanian diplomatic mission to your location, go to the Jordanian Foreign Ministry website at **www.mfa.gov.jo.**

## MONEY

The Jordanian dinar is valued at approximately $1.40, 70p, and about NIS 6.30. So $1 = JD 0.71, and £1 = JD 1.40.

The **Jordanian dinar** (JD) is divided into 1,000 **fils:** 10 fils are 1 piaster; 500 fils are generally referred to as 50 **piasters.** Paper currency comes in denominations of JD 1, 5, 10, 20, as well as 500 fils (half a JD); there are silver coins for 25 fils, 50 fils, 100 fils, and 250 fils; copper coins are 5 and 10 fils.

## 2 Essentials

A 2- to 2½-hour drive north of Aqaba, Petra is the jewel in the crown of Jordan's attractions, and the main objective of many travelers to the country. The canyon city of Petra is vast, mysterious, and really demands a 1- or 2-night stay and 2 full days of exploring to get a feel for the atmosphere, to say nothing of the contents of the ruins. You could easily spend 3 or 4 very full days exploring Petra and the surrounding countryside. If you're staying at one of the luxury resort hotels near Petra, you can plan for a relaxing, exotic desert holiday amid marvelous surroundings, enjoying local foods, entertainment, and the opportunity to browse shops filled with tribal crafts. For those on a budget, the many less-expensive hotels at Wadi Musa, 5km (3 miles) from the entrance to Petra, are reasonably comfortable and offer the chance to meet interesting fellow travelers on the treks and tours of Petra. A hard day of exploring Petra will work up your appetite. In the evenings, many budget hotels offer very reasonably priced buffet dinners where travelers can meet to try traditional Middle Eastern dishes, make plans, and recount experiences. Many travelers buffet-hop and look for the most interesting and freshest deals being offered each night.

### GETTING THERE

After crossing from Eilat into Aqaba, it's easy to find taxis that will take you up to Petra. Some bargaining is required, but the general fare is around JD 50 ($70/£36). This is the fastest, safest, and most direct way to make the journey. Splitting a taxi to Petra with others you may meet at the border can make the fare per person very reasonable. A taxi to the Aqaba Bus Station plus bus fare up to Petra will be less than JD 7 ($9.85/£5), but there are few buses per day and there's virtually no schedule. If you want to avoid the hassle of bargaining with taxi drivers, ask your hotel in Petra to arrange for a pickup for you at the border crossing for an agreed price. Most Petra hotels in all price categories will be happy to do this—it ensures you won't be lured somewhere else. Again, the fare will be about JD 40 to JD 50 ($56–$70/£29–£36).

### *Moments* Local Experience

The Bedouin inhabitants of Petra are part of the Petra experience—their ancestors have camped in Petra for centuries, and they have an intuitive feel for the place and know its many secrets. I especially enjoy the children, even when they hawk souvenirs. Once, a teenage Bedouin girl who spoke English led a group of us up to the dramatic carved facade of "the Monastery" overlooking Petra and chanted into the late afternoon stillness so that the entire canyon echoed. "What does the chant mean?" we asked. "Nothing in words," she replied. "Just—it's beautiful."

## Tips  Petra by Night

To the dismay of romantics and adventurers, Petra National Park closes at sunset or earlier, even though this mysterious, long-hidden site is especially evocative in the evenings and was once a great place to camp at night. Camping is still forbidden, but recently, the park service has been offering Monday and Thursday night candlelight tours, starting at 8:30pm for JD 12 ($17/£8.60; children 11 and under are free)—a great way to spend the evening if you plan to be in Petra on those days. Night tours are also offered when there's a full moon. Check with the park authorities, and reserve in advance. In good weather, a Bedouin camp dinner in the mountains is another evening option. Not only do you get an interesting dinner, but you also get a feel for the beautiful, wild, countryside at night. Check with your hotel or the visitor center. The price is approximately JD 30 ($42/£21) for two people.

Travel agencies in Eilat can arrange for escorted, 1-, 2-, or 3-day tours, or unescorted packages to Petra that will include transportation arrangements. Petra is worth lots of time if you've got it, and it's best to stay at least 1 or 2 nights.

## VISITOR INFORMATION

The Jordanian Ministry of Tourism's excellent website, www.go2petra.com, is beautifully organized and filled with updated information about Petra National Park, as well as practical information about hotels, prices, and transportation.

The **visitor center** at the entrance to Petra (© 03/215-6029) is open Saturday through Thursday from 6:30am to 5pm. You can stay inside Petra until you are shooed out at sunset. Admission to Petra is JD 21 ($30/£15) for 1 day; JD 26 ($37/£19) for 2 days; and JD 31 ($44/£22) for 3 days. Children and students with international ID cards are half-price. The walk through the narrow Siq leading into Petra is very worthwhile, but you can also rent a horse-drawn carriage through the Siq for JD 20 ($28/£14) that will deposit you at the Treasury, the first building you encounter once inside the secret valley of Petra. If you ride horses, a horse ride through the Siq is included in the admission fee if a horse is available.

**Bedouin guides** can be arranged through the visitor center. The fee for a full day of guiding is JD 50 ($70/£36), but half-days can also be arranged. Or, once inside the park, if you feel you need a guide, you can easily find one to escort you to specific places. *Tip:* If you have hired a Jordanian guide before entering the park and the price of his admission is included in the arrangement, you should know that the admission price for Jordanians is JD 1 ($1.40/70p). At the visitor center, independent travelers can hire guides for JD 9 to JD 57 ($13–$80/£6.40–£40) per trip, depending on how long and how extensive you want your tour to be. Many of the guides are colorful, and although they may not have had formal training, most know their stuff (and have picked up great multilingual skills). It's a good idea to hire a guide, at least for your first foray into Petra, and especially if you plan to do a hike to some of the more remote parts of the city. A standard 2½-hour Petra city tour costs JD 15 ($21/£11).

At the visitor center, you'll also find a variety of books and maps of Petra for sale. A good guidebook and map are very useful investments, even if you hire a guide; most books make a basic self-guided tour of Petra quite easy, especially if you have a chance to read up before your visit. Officially, the park is open daily until 6pm, but in summer the guards usually let visitors stay a bit later in order to take in the sunset and twilight. It's a good idea to bring your own bottle of water when you enter Petra; as the day progresses you'll need to buy more bottled water from the Bedouins who until recently inhabited the site. A number of stands inside Petra sell refreshments and food. Prices will be high, but don't hesitate to shell out for water; keep drinking even if you're not especially thirsty to avoid the dangers of dehydration. In summer, you'll need four 1.5-liter bottles of water to get through the day.

## FAST FACTS: Petra

*American Express* The representative is **International Traders** (📞 06/560-7014) in the Shemaysani district, on Abdul Hamid Sharif Street, opposite the Ambassador Hotel. You can book tours here, and American Express cardholders can receive mail.

*Banks* The Arab Bank and the Housing Bank in the center of Wadi Musa, and the Cairo Amman Bank in the Mövenpick Hotel just outside the entrance to Petra, all change money. They also give Visa cash advances. Banking hours are Saturday to Thursday 8:30am to 12:30pm. The Housing Bank has an ATM connected to Cirrus and PLUS.

*Embassies* The U.S. Embassy (📞 06/592-0101; fax 06/592-0102) is in Abdoun near the Fifth Circle; the Canadian Embassy (📞 06/566-6124; fax 06/568-9227) is in Shemaysani, in the Philadelphia Bank Building Complex; the U.K. Embassy (📞 06/592-3100; fax 06/592-3293) is also in Abdoun, near the Fifth Circle and the Orthodox Club; the Australian Embassy (📞 06/593-0246) is near the Fourth Circle (in Jabal Amman, opposite the Embassy of Kuwait). The Israeli Embassy (📞 06/552-5407) is at Rabia, near the Embassy of China; it is open Sunday to Thursday 8am to 4pm. Always call first to confirm the hours the desk for visas to Israel will be open.

*Emergencies* Throughout Jordan, for police dial 📞 191 or 192; for an ambulance dial 📞 193.

*Hospitals* The **Petra Emergency Clinic** (📞 03/215-6694), across the parking lot from the Petra Forum Hotel, is not a hospital, but it has an X-ray machine, an operating room, and other modern equipment. It's open daily 8am to 8pm. In an emergency, your hotel or the police (📞 191) can help get you there.

*Pharmacies* The **Wadi Musa Pharmacy** (📞 03/215-6444) is on the main traffic circle in Wadi Musa, and is open daily 24 hours. The Modern Petra Pharmacy, a block from the Wadi Musa Traffic Circle, has an English-speaking staff and carries tampons, condoms, and other items not normally stocked by local pharmacies.

*Telephones* The country code for Jordan is **962**. The area code for Petra is **03**.

## 3 Exploring Petra ★★★

You enter Petra through the Siq, a narrow crevice-canyon lined with niches that once held statues of gods and spirits that protected the city. The incredible Siq winds its way through the rocks for almost a mile before opening to Petra's wonders of rock and light. Traditionally, visitors entered on horseback, or in special carts. Most visitors now walk from the entrance (beside the visitor center) through the Siq. As you proceed through the Siq, you feel as if you are in the prologue to a mysterious adventure. The Siq's dreamlike, sculptural turnings are almost hallucinatory and separate Petra from the outside, real world. Indeed, Petra was chosen as the location for the climatic sequence of the film *Indiana Jones and the Last Crusade* for its atmosphere. If you walk through the shadowed Siq at twilight, listen for the sound of the evening owl, once the symbol of the city.

The Nabataeans, who carved the elaborate palaces, temples, tombs, storerooms, and stables of their city into the solid rock of the cliffs, dominated the Trans-Jordan area from the 3rd century B.C. through Byzantine times. Little is known of the individual personalities who created Nabatean society. The Nabataeans, a Semitic people from northern Arabia, moved into the Negev and the southern portions of what is now Jordan in the 6th century B.C. They commanded the trade route from Damascus to Arabia; through here the great caravans passed, carrying spices, silk, jewels, gold, and slaves from as far away as Yemen and East Africa. As a trading people, the Nabataeans developed cosmopolitan tastes, and easily incorporated Hellenistic and Roman design into their architecture and into their lifestyle. The fabulous facades carved into the rose sandstone cliffs of Petra are exotically Hellenistic rather than classical Greek or even Roman, and reflect the mixture of Western and Eastern, Semitic and European influences in which Nabatean civilization developed.

**Nabatean religion** was centered around two deities: **Dushara,** the god of strength and masculine attributes, and **al-Uzza,** also known as Atargatis, the goddess of water and fertility. Slowly, these deities took on the characteristics of Greek and Egyptian gods; al-Uzza, especially, became associated with elements of Aphrodite, the Greek goddess of love, Tyche, the goddess of fortune, and the Egyptian mother goddess, Isis.

In addition to their hidden capital at Petra, the Nabataeans developed lucrative trading and caravan cities at **Avdat, Shivta,** and **Mamshit,** in the Negev (see chapter 11). Using careful methods of conserving dew and rainwater, and developing amazingly efficient methods of irrigation that are being studied by modern agronomists, the Nabataeans made the desert bloom and managed to sustain a population in the Negev and south Jordan far larger than the population of that region today.

Until the 1st century A.D., the mysterious Nabataeans skillfully maintained their independence from the Parthians, an Iranian people who ruled Mesopotamia to the east, as well as from the briefly successful Hasmonean Jewish Commonwealth (which lost its independence to Rome in 63 B.C.) and from the Hellenistic and Roman powers to the west. Nabatean neutrality and aloofness was legendary. In 40 B.C., the young Herod, who had recently been made governor of the Galilee and Judea by the Romans, was overthrown by Jewish insurgents. Desperate and pursued, Herod made his way with a small entourage across the desert to Petra to beg for sanctuary and reinforcements. Despite the fact that Herod's mother had been a Nabatean princess, the ever-cautious rulers of Petra denied him permission to enter the Siq and the confines of the city (the indefatigable Herod eventually made his way to Rome, obtained reinforcements, put down the rebellion, and ruled as Rome's "King of the Jews" until his death in 4 B.C.). In A.D. 106, the Nabataeans were finally annexed into the Roman Empire. The emperor Hadrian (who put down the Jewish Bar Kochba Revolt of A.D. 132 to 135, and who built the defensive wall separating Britain from Scotland) visited Petra in A.D. 130. Thereafter the city was known as Petra Hadriane in his honor; it

# Petra

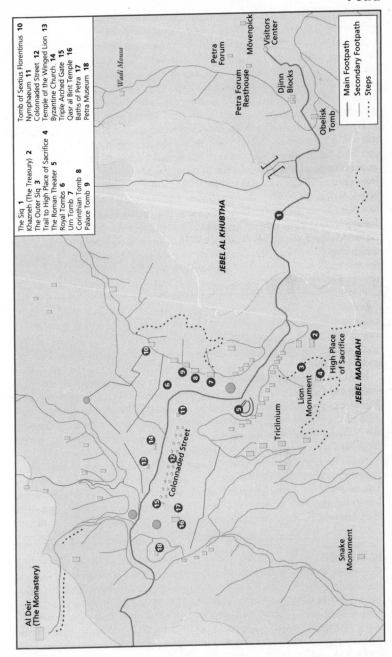

The Siq **1**
Khazneh (The Treasury) **2**
The Outer Siq **3**
Trail to High Place of Sacrifice **4**
The Roman Theater **5**
Royal Tombs **6**
Urn Tomb **7**
Corinthian Tomb **8**
Palace Tomb **9**
Tomb of Sextius Florentinus **10**
Nymphaeum **11**
Colonnaded Street **12**
Temple of the Winged Lion **13**
Byzantine Church **14**
Triple Arched Gate **15**
Qasr al Bint Temple **16**
Baths of Petra **17**
Petra Museum **18**

Main Footpath
Secondary Footpath
Steps

Visitors Center
Mövenpick
Petra Forum
Petra Forum Resthouse
Djinn Blocks
Obelisk Tomb

*Wadi Moussa*

**JEBEL AL KHUBTHA**

High Place of Sacrifice
Lion Monument
Triclinium

**JEBEL MADHBAH**

Colonnaded Street

Al Deir (The Monastery)

Snake Monument

493

continued to be the center of a highly profitable trading route, with connections to all parts of the Roman Empire.

In the early 4th century, Christianity became the dominant religion of the Nabataeans. Important churches were built in every Nabatean community; the bishops of Petra participated in ecumenical councils that helped shape the development of the early church. As the Roman Empire collapsed, and the amount of trade moving on the exotic desert routes through Petra shrank, the city's economy faltered. What trade there was tended to be shipped up the Red Sea to Egypt, bypassing the overland route through Nabatean territory. A series of earthquakes in late Byzantine times hastened the Nabataeans' decline. After Petra's conquest by the armies of the newly formed Muslim religion in A.D. 633, traditional trading routes changed, and the region became a forgotten backwater. Petra was briefly fortified by the Crusaders, but after its surrender to Saladin in 1189, it was abandoned and sank into almost total oblivion. Not until 1812, when the Swiss explorer Johann Ludwig Burckhardt (who had carefully studied Islamic rituals in order to disguise himself as a Muslim) bribed Bedouin tribesmen to take him to Petra, was the ruined, uninhabited city restored to the knowledge of the world. Only since 1958 has a careful exploration of the site been undertaken.

## WALKING TOUR　PETRA

| | |
|---|---|
| **Start:** | The Siq. |
| **Finish:** | Petra Museum. |
| **Best Times:** | Early morning, sunset. |
| **Worst Time:** | Midafternoon, when heat is at its worst. |

A guide (or a good guidebook) is necessary as you wander among the hidden city's monumental cliff edifices and sites ranging from prehistoric to Crusader times. It is important to remember that many of the sites and buildings at Petra were given fanciful names in modern times that have nothing to do with what we now know were their original functions. Also remember that once inside Petra, a fast but reasonably inclusive tour, without hikes to the sacred high places that overlook the city, can take 5 to 6 hours. Petra deserves at least 2 full days. Give yourself time to respond to the romantic mystery and beauty of the place, and to explore at your leisure. Every walk and hike will be filled with objects of interest and vistas that are remarkable. Petra changes dramatically as the light of day changes: The colors and mood of the city in early morning are different from the colors of Petra at noon or at sunset.

### ❶ The Siq

Beginning just near the visitor center, the winding 1.2km (¾-mile) walk through the narrow fissure, or canyonlike Siq, that leads into Petra can take from 45 minutes to 1½ hours, depending on your pace. The journey through this mysterious, highly sculptural passageway can be one of the most memorable parts of the Petra experience (especially in the soft twilight

as visitors depart from Petra for the night). At the entrance to the Siq and at various points throughout the passageway, you'll notice channels cut into the rock that once held pipes for the water system that carried the waters from the spring of Ain Musa into Petra. There is also a modern dam to prevent flash flooding during the winter rains; it is modeled after the ruins of an ancient Nabatean dam uncovered by archaeologists at this site. According to Nabatean and local Bedouin legend, Petra's water source, Ain Musa ("the Spring of Moses"), was created when Moses, leading the Israelites through the desert after the exodus from Egypt, struck a rock with his staff in despair as his people came close to death from thirst. The rocks burst forth with cool water. (Petra's Ain Musa is one of many springs in this part of the world that claims to be the site of this miracle.) Niches in the walls of the Siq once held the images of gods that protected the city, and that served to intimidate foreign visitors as they made their way into Petra.

### ❷ The Khazneh (Treasury)

Suddenly a turn in the Siq reveals the most famous structure in Petra, a royal tomb that has come to be known as the Treasury. Bedouins believed that the solid urn sculpted into the monument's facade was actually hollow and contained treasure; often they fired bullets at the urn in hopes of having the treasure spill out (you can detect their bullet marks across the magnificent facade). The Khazneh's stone facade changes color during the day: In the morning it's often a soft yellow-rose peach hue; by late afternoon it becomes a pure, sometimes jewel-like rose; at sunset, it turns an amazing intense red before slipping into the dusty twilight.

**Beyond the Khazneh (continuing to the right as you face the Khazneh), the Siq widens into what is called the:**

### ❸ Outer Siq

Here you'll encounter the busy modern denizens of Petra, sand artists, and water sellers. The outer Siq is lined with countless carved tomb facades in styles ranging from classical Roman to designs that echo Assyrian and nomadic desert influences. Honoring the dead was an important part of Nabatean culture. The outer Siq also contains caves inhabited until recently by Bedouins—the soft sandstone interiors are as wildly patterned as marbleized paper,

and are atmospheric spots to rest and shelter from the hot midday summer sun.

**To the left, opposite the Uneishu Tomb (which an inscription identifies as the tomb of the brother of a queen), is a flight of rough ancient stairs that leads to an uphill trail to the:**

### ❹ High Place of Sacrifice & the Tombs of Wadi Farasa

This can be an arduous hike for those out of shape, but it is a very worthwhile option to try at a later time. A hike to the High Place of Sacrifice and back down to the colonnaded main street of ancient Petra by a different route can take 1½ to 3 hours. It's wise to invest in a guide if you decide to make the excursion.

**Continuing on down what is now the main street of Petra, you come to the:**

### ❺ Roman Theater

Originally built by the Nabataeans, who were always adapting elements of other cultures into their way of life, the theater, facing the cliff-side facades of tombs, may have been used for religious ceremonies. In the 2nd century A.D., the theater was enlarged by the Romans, who apparently cared little for Nabatean traditions, and cut into nearby Nabatean tombs to create a vast 7,000-seat venue. The theater has been restored and, after a 1,500-year hiatus, will be used again for performances and other events.

**Farther along, on the opposite side of the canyon from the theater, are the:**

### ❻ Royal Tombs

The tombs are so named because of their elaborate facades, not because of any certainty that they were indeed created for royal burials.

**The first of these is the:**

### ❼ Urn Tomb

It's named for the carefully sculpted urn above its pediment. In A.D. 446, the Byzantines converted the inner chamber of this tomb into a church.

**A few facades beyond is the:**

### ❽ Corinthian Tomb

The tomb's facade actually includes a small-scale reproduction of the **Khazneh.**

**After the Corinthian Tomb is the:**

### ❾ Palace Tomb

Its two stories jut out from the side of the canyon. Part of the Palace Tomb was constructed of stone, rather than carved into the canyon rock.

**Around to the right is the heavily eroded:**

### ❿ Tomb of Sextius Florentinus

The tomb was built around A.D. 130 for a Roman governor of the Province of Arabia who so admired Petra's network of tombs that he asked to be buried in a tomb of his own design in this far outpost of the Roman Empire. A faint Latin inscription and a Roman eagle mark the tomb's facade. A route of processional staircases and corridors began here and wound uphill to sacred high places on the mountain beyond.

**Staying on the main path to the city center, you come to the:**

### ⓫ Nymphaeum

This two-story fountain, dedicated to the water nymphs, is a major landmark of Petra. How amazing to travelers from the desert this lavish structure of flowing water, piped in from Ain Musa, must have seemed. The Nymphaeum was a place of both refreshment and worship.

**The open water channel that fed the Nymphaeum continued on along the:**

### ⓬ Colonnaded Street

The street, built after A.D. 106 by the Romans, lay over the route of an earlier Nabatean thoroughfare. It was lined with shops, but also served as a civic and ceremonial route for processions.

**On a rise of land to the right (north) as you walk down the Colonnaded Street, is the:**

### ⓭ Temple of the Winged Lions

Named for the winged lions that serve as capitals for its columns, this was probably a temple dedicated to the worship of the female deity, al-Uzza. Built in A.D. 27, this was one of Petra's major temples until it was heavily damaged, apparently by fire, in the 2nd century. The structure was then used to house families until it was destroyed by an earthquake in 363. That the temple was not rebuilt as a religious structure after the fire in the 2nd century may indicate the old region of Petra had gone into decline under the Roman occupation. The temple is under excavation by an American-sponsored archaeological team.

**Also several hundred meters to the right of the Colonnaded Street is the:**

### ⓮ Byzantine Church

Here's a large structure with triple apses, and extremely beautiful and well-preserved mosaic floors that have been uncovered by the joint Jordanian-American team excavating the site. On both sides of the Colonnaded Street are the outlines of ruined buildings. According to some theories, the Roman forum of Petra would have been among the structures to the left (south) of the Colonnaded Street.

**At the end of the Colonnaded Street is the:**

### ⓯ Triple Arched Gate

The gate is adorned with carved panels containing bas-relief busts, animals, and geometric and floral designs. These monumental gateways would have borne wooden doors that opened to the *temenos,* or sacred precincts, of your next stop.

### ⓰ Qasr al Bint (Palace of the Pharaoh's Daughter) Temple

Perhaps the most important temple in Petra (again, despite its romantic name, the temple has nothing to do with a Pharaoh's daughter), this massive structure was built of stone, rather than carved from rock, and is the most impressive building in Petra. It faces north, toward the Sharra mountains, from which the name of the chief Nabatean god, Dushara ("he of Sharra") is derived, and may have been a sanctuary for the Dushara cult. This temple was built around the time of Jesus, and seems to have been destroyed late in the 3rd century.

Just to the south of the Arched Gate, but not accessible at present to visitors, were the:

**⑰ Baths of Petra**

These had access to a corner of the *temenos*.

Beyond the ruins of the Qasr al Bint Temple, you'll find the:

**⑱ Petra Museum**

There's a small collection of sculptural artifacts, jewelry, and pottery found at Petra. The museum building also houses the Petra Forum restaurant, as well as restrooms. A second part of the museum is housed in a nearby tomb.

## OTHER HIKES & EXCURSIONS AT PETRA

In addition to the hike up to the High Place of Sacrifice (see stop 4, above), a number of longer walks away from the center of Petra are very worthwhile and give you important vistas of this extraordinary place. These walks involve some amount of climbing as well as scrambling over rocks and ruined pathways; therefore, it's best to have some walking companions with you. Guides at Petra will escort you for about JD 35 to JD 50 ($49–$70/£25–£36). **Note:** You are required to have a guide with you when you go to more remote areas.

**Jabal Haroun** (the Mountain of Aaron, brother of Moses) is a climbing trek that can take as much as 4 to 8 hours depending on your route. The way passes **Ad Deir** (the Monastery), Petra's largest carved tomb monument, built in the 1st century A.D., with an interior adorned by carved and painted crosses from the Byzantine period. Across the canyon from Ad Deir is Jabal Haroun, the highest peak in the area. A small white church containing the **tomb of Aaron** stands at the top of the mountain. In winter, you might ask your guide to descend on the route that passes **Wadi Siyah,** where winter rains create a waterfall. This difficult but beautiful winter hike will take at least 3 hours, and a few additional hours if you return via Wadi Siyah. The Jabal Haroun trek requires a guide.

**Wadi Turkimaniya** is a pleasant 45-minute or so round-trip walk down the wadi that starts behind and to the left of the Temple of the Winged Lions. The easy road through the wadi supports rich vegetation in winter and leads to Petra's only tomb with a Nabatean inscription.

**Qasr Habis** (the Crusader's Castle) is a climb that takes you from near Petra's museum to the not very impressive ruins of Petra's Crusader stronghold; however, the pathway leads to wonderful vistas that overlook beautiful canyons. The round-trip can run from 1 to 1½ hours.

The **High Place of Sacrifice** is one of the most popular destinations for hikers, taking you to the great altars carved from rock (with drainage channels for the blood of sacrificial animals) far above the city. The panorama of Petra is dazzling; the round-trip hike can take from 1½ to 2½ hours and is not for visitors who are out of shape.

Additional treks to the **Snake Monument** and to **Jebal Numair** entail a minimum of 5 or 6 hours and require guides. There are also car tours and hikes available to **Al Madras** and **Al Barid,** nearby satellite towns of Petra. Al Barid is a kind of mini-Petra, entered through a smaller version of Petra's Siq, and is filled with carved canyon structures. Unlike at Petra, some of Al Barid's structures carved into cliff sides seem to have served as houses. Archaeology buffs can also take a taxi excursion (or hike with a Bedouin guide, about a 6-hr. round-trip) to the site of **El Beidha,** a Neolithic village from the 8th millennium B.C. A full-day or overnight-camping tour from Petra to the beautiful desertscapes of **Wadi Rum** is also highly recommended.

## 4 Where to Stay

*Note:* As at Israeli accommodations, hotel rates are almost exclusively quoted in dollars, and bargain rates (often steeply discounted) abound.

### EXPENSIVE

**Mövenpick Resort Petra** ★★★   This is the top hotel in town, and it has the best location as well—just steps from the entrance to Petra National Park. The public areas of the hotel seem to have been painted and furnished by master craftsmen from Cairo, Fes, and Marrakech; the dinner and lunch buffets are the best in town; and there's a wood-paneled library with reading material about Petra and Jordan. On the roof garden, guests can meet in the evenings and talk over their adventures amid the kind of camaraderie you seldom find in hotels of this class. The guest rooms have the usual array of amenities; some are equipped for travelers with disabilities.

PO Box 214, Petra. ☎ **800/344-6835** in the U.S., or 03/215-7111. Fax 03/215-7112. www.moevenpick-petra.com. 183 units. $130–$210 (£65–£105) double; $350 (£175) suite. Rates include breakfast, service charge, and tax. AE, MC, V. **Amenities:** Restaurant; bar; heated pool; fitness center; nonsmoking rooms; library. *In room:* A/C, TV, hair dryer, iron/ironing board.

**Taybet Zaman Hotel and Resort** ★★★   Atop a cliff 8km (5 miles) from Petra, Taybet Zaman is the most charming and unusual hostelry in Jordan. Rustic buildings of a 19th-century village have been renovated and decorated in a Bedouin-style chic that could easily grace the pages of *Architectural Digest;* the village lanes are now passageways for the hotel. The older rooms, created from village buildings, are each different and most interesting; the suites are amazing and great fun. A newer section offers rooms with sweeping views and Bedouin decor, but they're not as exotic. There is an attentive staff and spectacular vistas of the countryside. A sumptuous buffet dinner, often accompanied by traditional music, is offered April through November (and the rest of the year according to demand) for $21 (£11) per person. A drawback is the taxi ride from the hills down to Petra.

PO Box 2, Wadi Musa, Petra. ☎ 03/215-0111. Fax 03/215-0101. reservations@taybetzaman.com. 105 units. $130–$190 (£65–£95) double; $700 (£350) royal suite. Rates include breakfast. Add 13% tax and 10% service. AE, MC, V. Free parking. **Amenities:** Restaurant; 2 pools; fitness center; Jacuzzi; sauna; laundry service. *In room:* A/C, TV, fridge (on request).

### MODERATE

**Crowne Plaza Resort Petra**   Located close to the entrance to Petra, this hotel has a number of restaurants, comfortable rooms (most were renovated recently and in good shape) with views of the surrounding mountains, and an experienced staff.

PO Box 30, Wadi Musa, Petra. ☎ 03/215-6266. Fax 03/215-6977. www.petra.crowneplaza.com. 178 units. $140–$210 (£70–£105) double. Add 13% tax and 10% service charge. AE, DC, MC. **Amenities:** 4 restaurants; bar; outdoor heated pool; fitness center; Jacuzzi; sauna; concierge; room service; laundry; club-level rooms. *In room:* A/C, TV, minibar, coffeemaker, hair dryer, iron/ironing board.

**Golden Tulip Kings' Way Inn**   This modern choice with a terraced swimming pool is located at Ain Musa, 6.4km (4 miles) away from the entrance to Petra. Guest rooms are clean and comfortable, and there are good but comparatively pricey breakfast and dinner buffets.

Main St. (PO Box 71) Wadi Musa, Petra. ☎ 03/215-6799. Fax 03/215-6796. www.kingsway-petra.com. 77 units. $70–$100 (£35–£50) double. Add 13% tax and 10% service charge. AE, DC, MC, V. **Amenities:** Restaurant; bar; pool; club-level rooms. *In room:* A/C, TV, hair dryer.

**Petra Palace** ⭑  Located on the block of hotels and restaurants leading up to the entrance to Petra, this property is a comparative bargain. Guest rooms have the usual array of amenities; some overlook the mountains, others the pool.

PO Box 70, Wadi Musa, Petra. ✆ 03/215-6723. Fax 03/215-6724. www.petrapalace.com.jo. 83 units. $60–$80 (£30–£40) double. Add 13% tax and 10% service charge. AE, MC, V. Parking. **Amenities:** Restaurant; bar; heated pool; fitness room; business center. *In room:* A/C, TV, minibar, hair dryer.

## INEXPENSIVE

**Al Anbat 1 Hotel**  Attracting an upscale backpacking crowd and offering a great sunset, this hotel offers endless screenings of Indiana Jones films, rooms with balconies, a steam room and small pool (summer only), and free transportation to the entrance to Petra National Park. There's been a lot of upgrading, and half of the hotel was built in 2005. Breakfast and dinner buffets are good and very fairly priced. The newer Al Anbat 2 (✆ **03/215-7200;** fax 03/215-6888) is a small six-story tower with less expensive rooms and without the congenial atmosphere.

PO Box 43, Wadi Musa, Petra. ✆ 03/215-6265. Fax 03/215-6888. www.alanbat.com. 100 units. $40 (£20) double. Rates include tax and service. Breakfast $3 (£1.50). MC, V. Parking. **Amenities:** Restaurant; lounge; pool; Turkish bath; tour desk; laundry; dry cleaning. *In room:* A/C, satellite TV, fridge.

**Al Rashid Hotel** *(Value)*  In Wadi Musa, 5km (3 miles) from the entrance to Petra, the Al Rashid offers large, clean, carpeted rooms and free transport to Petra. Of the budget hotels, this is the best value and offers very good evening meals in its dining room.

Main Traffic Circle (PO Box 96), Wadi Musa, Petra. ✆ 03/215-6800. Fax 03/215-6801. Rashid@joinnet.com.jo. 40 units. $20 (£10) per person in a double room (no single supplement). Rates include breakfast. Add $8 (£4) per person for half board. DC, MC, V. **Amenities:** Restaurant. *In room:* A/C, TV.

## NORTH OF PETRA: JORDAN'S DEAD SEA SPAS

A 2-hour drive from Petra to the eastern shore of The Dead Sea brings you to **Sweimeh,** the area of the Jordanian side of The Dead Sea where a resort center has begun to develop. This side of The Dead Sea is far more tranquil than the booming high-rise resort center across the lake in Israel. The luxurious, new **Kempinski Ishtar Hotel,** the **Marriott Dead Sea,** and the less-expensive but attractive **Dead Sea Resort Spa** are very good, but the Mövenpick is the resort of choice for location, architectural design, and experienced staff. You'll find bargains at all hotels on a range of massage, health, beauty, and special Dead Sea mineral treatments.

**Mövenpick Dead Sea Resort and Spa** ⭑⭑ *(Finds)*  This beautiful top-quality resort, built in 1999, is an exotically designed, low-rise complex of arches, covered passageways, and vine-shaded terraces that create the feeling of a traditional Middle Eastern khan, or traveler's inn. There are large swimming pools and mineral baths, beautiful stretches of Dead Sea Beach, and an architecturally striking spa and fitness center offering a large variety of therapeutic, massage, and beauty treatments. Guest rooms are lovely and comfortable, with vistas of the mountains or of The Dead Sea; some are equipped for guests with disabilities. The restaurants here are all up to the Swiss Mövenpick chain's high standard of excellence, and the generous dinner buffet ($21/£11) is very worthwhile. You can arrange 3- to 7-night packages that include full board and spa treatments. Discount room rates off season can run as low as $130 (£65) for a double with breakfast.

Sweimeh, Jordan. ✆ 05/356-1111. Fax 05/356-1122. www.moevenpick-deadsea.com. 230 units. $200–$300 (£100–£150) standard double. Rate includes breakfast, tax, and service. Up to 2 children 15 and under stay free in parents room. AE, DC, MC, V. Parking. **Amenities:** 5 restaurants; cafe; 2 bars; pools (indoor, outdoor); tennis courts; health club; spa; Jacuzzi; sauna; kids' activities; car-rental desk; business center; 24-hr. room service; laundry; dry cleaning; nonsmoking rooms; currency exchange. *In room:* A/C, TV, dataport, minibar, hair dryer, safe.

## 5 Excursions North & South of Petra

### WADI RUM 👁👁 & DANA NATURE RESERVE 👁

You can obtain information about these extraordinary reserves for camping, escorted tours, and hiking by checking the **Royal Society for the Conservation of Nature** website (www.rscn.org.jo), which contains specific information about eco-tourism to the dramatic desert landscapes of **Wadi Rum** 👁👁, south of Petra, and about the wild, mountainous **Dana Reserve** 👁, north of Petra, as well as about other nature and wildlife reserves in the Kingdom of Jordan.

### AQABA

Aqaba is much quieter than Eilat, but at press time, it was going through the kind of frantic reconstruction of its tourism infrastructure that Eilat went through in the early 1990s. For the moment, the beaches are less friendly than Eilat's for women traveling alone, but that will likely change as Aqaba becomes more of an international tourism destination. The town has inexpensive, interesting restaurants, reefs are less damaged than in Eilat, and prices for accommodations are lower. Aqaba can be a relaxing stop for an overnight or a day or two en route between Petra and Eilat.

### WHERE TO STAY

The **Mövenpick Aqaba Resort** 👁 (© 962-03/203-4020; www.moevenpick-hotels. com), built in 2003, has 247 rooms and meets international luxury standards with a set of four swimming pools, plus a private beach, nine restaurants, a bar, and fitness and health facilities. Comfy rooms have an array of amenities ranging from high-speed Internet access to makeup mirrors in the bathrooms. Direct sea-view rooms cost extra, but are great for sunset watching. Rates are $184 to $240 (£92–£120) for a double (higher rates are for sea view).

The **Aqaba Intercontinental** 👁 (© 962-03/209-2222; www.ichotelsgroup.com) is the newest (2006) five-star hotel in town. The 255 rooms are fresh and stylish: There's a private beach and variety of pools and in-house dining choices. There may be nearby construction during the day. Rates are $160 to $235 (£80–£118) with breakfast included; without breakfast starting at $124 (£112).

### Moderate and Budget Hotels

Aqaba's hotels in the $90-to-$120 (£45–£60) moderate range are all very worn and poor value. Better to upgrade to the Mövenpick or Intercontinental, where you can at times find special deals, or opt for an inexpensive hotel.

A budget hotel choice is the centrally located (in town but not on the beach), 32-room **Shweiki Hotel,** Hammamat Street, town center (© **03/202-2657;** fax 03/202-2659). A standard double room is $45 to $60 (£23–£30), plus 13% tax and 10% service; all major credit cards are accepted. Guest rooms all have private bathroom, air-conditioning, minibar, and TV; guests receive a free voucher for the large pool at the nearby Aqaba Gulf Hotel. As at most Aqaba hotels, bargains are available.

### WHERE TO DINE

**Ali Baba Restaurant** 👁 ARABIC/INTERNATIONAL    With an outdoor dining terrace facing the central square, this is a meeting place for both Jordanians and foreign visitors. It has a large menu of Middle Eastern dishes, grilled meat and fish, pastas, and excellent curry. The grilled *shish taok* (garlic chicken) is a specialty. Wine and beer are served.

Town Center. ℂ 03/201-3901. Full meals JD 4–JD 11 ($5.60–$15/£2.80–£7.85). AE, DC, MC, V. Daily 8am–11pm.

**J Captain's Restaurant** ℱ SEAFOOD    Shaped like a ship, this tiny, busy place serves delicious fresh fish and seafood; chicken and meat dishes; and good, small, Arabic seafood and meze dishes. Soft drinks and nonalcoholic beer are served.

Next to Aquamarina II Hotel. ℂ 03/201-6905. Reservations essential for dinner. Main courses JD 3–JD 8 ($4.20–$11/£2.10–£5.70); set-menu dinners JD 9 ($13/£6.40). MC, V. Daily 9am–11pm.

**Royal Yacht Club** ℱ CONTINENTAL    Here's the best, most elegant restaurant in town, run by Jordan's top-quality Romero's of Amman. There is a spacious dining room, a terrace overlooking the marina, and a menu that includes excellent pastas, fish, and seafood. You can have a drink in the adjacent bar.

Town Center, at the Main Corniche. ℂ 03/202-2404. Reservations necessary. Full meals JD 8–JD 14 ($11–$20/£5.70–£10). MC, V. Daily 11:30am–3:30pm and 7:30–11:30pm.

## DIVING CENTERS
The **Royal Diving Center** ℱ is located 17km (11 miles) south of Aqaba (ℂ 03/201-7035; fax 03/201-7097). With a private beach beside a superb reef, this is the best-run snorkeling and diving center in Aqaba, offering equipment rentals, lessons, dives, and diving tours. It's open daily 9am to 5pm in summer; 9am to 4pm in winter. Admission is JD 2 ($2.80/£1.40); mask, fins, and snorkel rental is JD 3 ($4.20/£2.15). A taxi here from town costs JD 3 ($4.20/£2.15).

# Appendix A: Fast Facts, Toll-Free Numbers & Websites

**AMERICAN EXPRESS** Located in the El Al Building, corner of Ben-Yehuda and Shalom Aleichem streets (© **03/526-8888;** fax 03/777-8801).

**AREA CODES** Telephone area codes are 02 for Jerusalem; 03 for Tel Aviv; 04 for Haifa and the Galilee; 08 for Eilat, the Negev, The Dead Sea, and Rehovot; and 04 for Caesarea.

**ATM NETWORKS & CASHPOINTS** See "Money & Costs," p. 67.

**BUSINESS HOURS** Israel does not have a standard set of business hours. Government offices are open on weekdays, usually from 7:30 or 8am. Most are closed to the public on Friday, and all are closed on Saturday. In summer, they are open until 1 or 3pm; in winter, they remain open until 2 or 4pm. Banks are open Sunday, Tuesday, and Thursday 8:30am to 12:30pm and 4 to 5:30pm; on Monday and Wednesday 8:30am to 12:30pm only; and on Friday 8:30am to noon.

**CAR RENTALS** See "Toll-Free Numbers & Websites," later in this chapter.

**DRINKING LAWS** The legal age for purchase and consumption of alcoholic beverages is 18; proof of age is required and often requested at bars, nightclubs, and restaurants, so it's always a good idea to bring ID when you go out. Beer is available in most Israeli grocery stores; there are no closing times for bars inside Israel. Alcohol is forbidden and considered abhorrent by Islam. It is generally not available in Arabic communities inside Israel or in Jordan or the West Bank except at hotels for tourists. Do not drink or carry alcohol in public in these areas.

**DRIVING RULES** See "Getting There & Getting Around," p. 59.

**ELECTRICITY** The electric current used in Israel is 220 volts AC (50 cycles) as opposed to the 110-volt system used in America. If you bring an electric shaver or computer designed for 110 volts to Israel, you must use a proper transformer to convert the current. Cheap converters are not safe and sooner or later will cause damage. Do not use sensitive electronic items such as computers unless they have internal transformers that automatically convert to both 110 and 220 voltage systems, or you have an external transformer especially designed for your computer. You can buy 220-volt equipment at special shops that can be used in Israel. Sockets (or power points) are designed to accept plugs with either two or three round prongs. If your appliance doesn't have the right plug, you can buy a plug adapter in Israel quite easily for approximately NIS 3 (75¢/40p), or your hotel may have one to lend to you.

**EMBASSIES & CONSULATES** The **American Embassy** is at 71 Ha-Yarkon St., Tel Aviv (© **03/519-7575**). The **U.S. Consulate-General** in East Jerusalem is at 27 Nablus Rd. (© **02/628-7137**). Many services for U.S. citizens in Jerusalem are at the East Jerusalem consulate, so call first to check where you need to go.

The **Australian Embassy** is at 37 Shaul Ha-Melekh St., Tel Aviv (© **03/695-0451**).

The **Irish Embassy** is at 3 Daniel Frish St., 17th floor, Tel Aviv (℃ 03/696-4166).

The **New Zealand Embassy** is at 3 Daniel Frish St., Tel Aviv (℃ 03/695-6622).

The **British Embassy** is at 192 Ha-Yarkon St., Tel Aviv (℃ 03/725-1222). The **British Consulate-General** in East Jerusalem is in the Sheikh Jarrah neighborhood at 19 Nashashibi St. (℃ 02/671-7724 or 02/541-4100).

**Canadians** should contact the consular section of their new embassy in Tel Aviv at 3 Nirim St., Beit Hasepanut, Yad Eliahu (℃ 03/636-3300).

**EMERGENCIES**  For police, dial ℃ **100**; for fire, dial ℃ **102**; for medical emergency/ambulance, dial ℃ **101.**

**GASOLINE (PETROL)**  At press time, in Israel the cost of a liter of gasoline was moving toward NIS 8 ($2/£1) per liter, or approximately NIS 16 ($8/£4) per gallon. There is a small surcharge for buying gasoline on Shabbat and at night.

**HOLIDAYS**  For information on holidays, see "Israel Calendar of Holidays & Events," in chapter 3.

**HOT LINES**  The White Line for emotional counseling (℃ 03/732-5560) is open daily from 7:30 to 11:30pm. There are counselors who speak English.

**INSURANCE  Medical Insurance**  Although it's not required of travelers, health insurance is highly recommended. Most health insurance policies cover you if you get sick away from home—but check your coverage before you leave.

For travel overseas, most U.S. health plans (including Medicare and Medicaid) do not provide coverage, and the ones that do often require you to pay for services upfront and reimburse you only after you return home.

As a safety net, you may want to buy travel medical insurance, particularly if you're traveling to a remote or high-risk area where emergency evacuation might be necessary. If you require additional medical insurance, try **MEDEX Assistance** (℃ 410/453-6300; www.medex assist.com) or **Travel Assistance International** (℃ 800/821-2828; www.travel assistance.com; for general information on services, call the company's **Worldwide Assistance Services, Inc.,** at ℃ 800/777-8710).

**Canadians** should check with their provincial health plan offices, or call **Health Canada** (℃ 866/225-0709; www.hc-sc.gc.ca) to find out the extent of their coverage and what documentation and receipts they must take home in case they are treated overseas.

Travelers from the U.K. should carry their European Health Insurance Card (EHIC), which replaced the E111 form as proof of entitlement to free/reduced cost medical treatment abroad (℃ **0845 606 2030;** www.ehic.org.uk). Note, however, that the EHIC only covers "necessary medical treatment," and for repatriation costs, lost money and baggage, and cancellation coverage, travel insurance from a reputable company should always be sought (www.travelinsurance web.com).

**Travel Insurance**  The cost of travel insurance varies widely, depending on the destination, the cost and length of your trip, your age and health, and the type of trip you're taking, but expect to pay between 5% and 8% of the vacation itself. You can get estimates from various providers through **InsureMyTrip.com**. Enter your trip cost and dates, your age, and other information for prices from more than a dozen companies.

U.K. citizens and their families who make more than one trip abroad per year may find an annual travel insurance policy works out cheaper. Check **www.money supermarket.com**, which compares prices across a wide range of providers for single- and multi-trip policies.

## Tips  Etiquette & Customs

**Appropriate attire:** Israel, Jordan, and Sinai are informal places. A tie and jacket are rarely required for men at any restaurant or performance. Shorts are not appropriate for men or women in churches, synagogues, and mosques, and those wearing them may be refused entry. No bare arms, shoulders, or midriffs are allowed when visiting religious Jewish or Arabic neighborhoods or places of worship.

**Gestures:** In Muslim countries, do not offer your left hand in a handshake or offer or receive food with your left hand. The left hand is symbolically unclean. Israelis have a way of making a kissing sound, coupled with a slight upward nod of the head to indicate "no." A hotel reception person may respond with this gesture when you ask a question like: "Is the Israel Museum open this afternoon?" To many English speakers not familiar with the country, this looks and sounds like an obscenity, but in Israel, it just means a simple "no." Try not to take offense.

**Avoiding offense:** Obey *all* orders and rules at Muslim, Jewish, and Christian holy places without argument or question, and be especially respectful about closing times. Men must wear head coverings at Jewish synagogues and holy places; women must dress very modestly when visiting any religious site; shoes must be removed and left outside when entering a mosque; alcohol must not be carried or drunk in public in Muslim areas.

It can be very interesting to listen to the political views of Israelis or Palestinians you meet as you travel, but these days, it's a good idea not to respond with an opposing view or engage in political arguments—the more so if you visit Egypt, Jordan, or other Arabic areas. Similarly, it can be fascinating to

---

Most big travel agents offer their own insurance and will probably try to sell you their package when you book a holiday. Think before you sign. **Britain's Consumers' Association** recommends that you insist on seeing the policy and reading the fine print before buying travel insurance. The **Association of British Insurers** (② 020/7600-3333; www.abi.org.uk) gives advice by phone and publishes *Holiday Insurance,* a free guide to policy provisions and prices. You might also shop around for better deals: Try **Columbus Direct** (② 0870/033-9988; www.columbusdirect.net).

**Trip-Cancellation Insurance** Trip-cancellation insurance will help retrieve your money if you have to back out of a trip or depart early, or if your travel supplier goes bankrupt. Trip cancellation traditionally covers such events as sickness, natural disasters, and U.S. State Department advisories. The latest news in trip-cancellation insurance is the availability of **expanded hurricane coverage** and the **"any-reason"** cancellation coverage—which costs more but covers cancellations made for any reason. You won't get back 100% of your prepaid trip cost, but you'll be refunded a substantial portion. **Travel-Safe** (② 888/885-7233; www.travelsafe.com) offers both types of coverage. Expedia also offers any-reason cancellation coverage for its air-hotel packages. For details, contact one of the following recommended insurers: **Access America**

learn about the religious practices and beliefs of others, but ecumenicalism and tolerance are not strong points of any Middle Eastern society. Unlike in the West, people who are virtually strangers will often ask what religion you belong to. It's considered rude (or at least, suspect) to be evasive or not to respond, but it's a good idea not to go into detail about your own religious beliefs and practices.

**Eating and drinking:** If you're invited to dinner at the home of someone whose traditions you are not absolutely certain about, flowers are a safe gift. Even seemingly innocent gifts such as candy or bread may be made with ingredients that are not acceptable to observant Jewish or Muslim families, or may not be compatible with the kind of meal they are serving. Do not offer food or drink to any Muslim during the daylight hours of the month of Ramadan, when Muslims observe a daily dawn-to-dusk fast. During Ramadan, if you are in an Arabic area, it is considerate not to eat or drink in public places unless you are in a restaurant that is clearly open for business and serving foreigners. As Islam forbids the consumption of alcohol, a gift of a bottle of wine or chocolates containing alcohol would not be acceptable if you visit a Muslim home.

**Photography:** Be aware of restrictions about photographing military or police installations. In Israel, taking photographs is forbidden at the Western Wall on the Sabbath and many holidays. *Be aware that religious Jews, Muslims, and Christians usually do not want to have their pictures taken, especially when they are at prayer. Be very discreet if you want to include them in your photos.*

(© 866/807-3982; www.accessamerica.com), **Travel Guard International** (© 800/826-4919; www.travelguard.com), **Travel Insured International** (© 800/243-3174; www.travelinsured.com), and **Travelex Insurance Services** (© 888/457-4602; www.travelex-insurance.com).

**INTERNET ACCESS** Israel's cities are well supplied with Wi-Fi zones and cybercafes, but obviously you won't find these amenities in the remote Negev or in Sinai. Petra's adjacent town of Wadi Musa is also loaded with Internet cafes, and most hotels at the very least have an Internet desk.

**LANGUAGE** Hebrew and Arabic are the two official languages of Israel. English is widely spoken and understood; in major cities most street and business signs are in English as well as in Hebrew or Arabic. Highway signs are generally trilingual: Hebrew, English, and Arabic.

**LEGAL AID** For legal problems, international visitors should call their embassy or consulate.

**LOST & FOUND** Be sure to tell all of your credit card companies the minute you discover your wallet has been lost or stolen, and file a report at the nearest police precinct. Your credit card company or insurer may require a police report number or record of the loss. Credit card companies have an emergency toll-free number to call if your card is lost or stolen; they may be able to wire you a cash advance immediately or deliver an emergency credit card in a day or two. Visa's U.S. emergency number is ✆ **800/847-2911** or 410/581-9994. American Express cardholders and traveler's check holders should call ✆ **800/221-7282.** MasterCard holders should call ✆ **800/307-7309** or 636/722-7111. For other credit cards, call the toll-free number directory at ✆ **800/555-1212.**

In Israel, the emergency numbers for lost credit cards are as follows: **American Express** (✆ 800/940-3211), **Visa** (✆ 800/941-6384), and **MasterCard** (✆ 800/941-8873).

**MAIL** The Israeli Postal Service is dependable. Airmail letters and postcards can get to the United States in 3 to 5 days, except during holidays such as Rosh Hashanah or Passover when minor delays are possible. Postal rates are similar to those in the United States and the U.K. Packages must be brought to the post office unsealed for security inspection, and you must present your passport to the postal clerk.

**MAPS** Detailed city maps are generally in Hebrew, but for most purposes, maps given out by city tourist information offices and available at many hotels are sufficient. Full country maps of Israel handed out by rental car agencies are also good (in most places Israel is only 16km/10 miles wide and there are not many major roads in central Israel or in the Negev). In the Galilee, where you may want to freewheel and explore, the Tiberias branch of Steimatzky's Bookstore and the Tiberias Tourist Information Office sell a selection of regional road maps. In addition to standard road maps, look for Corazin Publishing's fold-out *Go Galilee,* and *Map of the Galilee, Golan and the Northern Valleys.* They cost about NIS 22 ($5.50/£2.75) each; Corazin also publishes a map of the *Northern Coast and Western Galilee* as well as a map of Israel. Corazin's **maps** are filled with details and explanations about historical and natural sites throughout Israel; they can be found at the gift shops and reading counters of Vered HaGalil Guest Farm (p. 393) and Kibbutz Ein Gev (p. 389).

**MEDICAL CONDITIONS** If you have a medical condition that requires **syringe-administered medications,** carry a valid, signed prescription from your physician; syringes in carry-on baggage will be inspected. Insulin in any form should have the proper pharmaceutical documentation. If you have a disease that requires treatment with **narcotics,** you should also carry documented proof with you.

**NEWSPAPERS & MAGAZINES** The English daily edition of *Ha'aretz,* Israel's most important Hebrew-language newspaper, comes free inside the daily *International Herald Tribune.* The Friday edition has a special section listing events and TV and radio schedules for the coming week throughout the country. The *Jerusalem Post* is an English-language newspaper that also carries a complete weekly events section in its Friday edition. Editorially, the *Post* is more right wing; *Ha'aretz* is more liberal. Newspapers are not published on Saturdays, so the "weekend" edition is the Friday edition. The *Jerusalem Report* is an English-language biweekly newsmagazine in the style of *Newsweek* and *Time,* focusing on Israeli, Middle Eastern, and Jewish issues.

**PASSPORTS** The websites listed below provide downloadable passport applications as well as the current fees for processing applications. For an up-to-date, country-by-country listing of passport requirements around the world, click on the "International Travel" tab on the U.S. State Department website at **http://travel.state.gov.**

**For Residents of Australia** You can pick up an application from your local post office or any branch of Passports Australia, but you must schedule an interview at the passport office to present your application materials. Call the **Australian Passport Information Service** at ✆ **131-232,** or visit the government website at www.passports.gov.au.

**For Residents of Canada** Passport applications are available at travel agencies throughout Canada or from the central **Passport Office,** Department of Foreign Affairs and International Trade, Ottawa, ON K1A 0G3 (✆ **800/567-6868;** www.ppt.gc.ca). *Note:* Canadian children who travel must have their own passport. However, if you hold a valid Canadian passport issued before December 11, 2001, that bears the name of your child, the passport remains valid for you and your child until it expires.

**For Residents of Ireland** You can apply for a 10-year passport at the **Passport Office,** Setanta Centre, Molesworth Street, Dublin 2 (✆ **01/671-1633;** www.irlgov.ie/iveagh). Those 17 and under age 18 and 66 and over must apply for a 3-year passport. You can also apply at 1A South Mall, Cork (✆ **21/494-4700**) or at most main post offices.

**For Residents of New Zealand** You can pick up a passport application at any New Zealand Passports Office or download it from their website. Contact the **Passports Office** at ✆ **0800/225-050** in New Zealand or 04/474-8100, or log on to www.passports.govt.nz.

**For Residents of the United Kingdom** To pick up an application for a standard 10-year passport (5-year passport for children 15 and under), visit your nearest passport office, major post office, or travel agency, or contact the **United Kingdom Passport Service** at ✆ **0870/521-0410** or search its website at www.ukpa.gov.uk.

**POLICE** Dial ✆ **100.**

**SMOKING** In **Israel,** smoking is not permitted indoors in public places including cafes, restaurants, and bars unless there is a specified area for smokers. This is a relatively new rule, and many Israelis ignore it, but violators are subject to fines, and at times angry confrontations. In Israeli Arab communities, in East Jerusalem, and in **Jordan** and **Egypt,** smoking is still ubiquitous, although some private places do restrict it to certain areas.

**TAXES** Israel has a value-added tax (VAT) of 15.5%, automatically included in all prices. These taxes will not appear on price tags. Certain tourist shops have forms that enable foreign travelers purchasing an item over $150 in value in foreign currency to apply for a VAT refund at Ben-Gurion Airport on departing from Israel. It's worth trying, but refund lines are often long; better to miss a refund than to miss a flight. Foreign visitors paying hotel bills in foreign currency (your credit card will do) are not subject to the 15.5% VAT, and that includes meals, drinks, and anything else you may charge on your hotel bill. In **Jordan** and Egypt, a tax is generally added to your hotel bill and there are no exemptions for foreigners paying in foreign currency.

**TELEPHONES** Israel's public telephones are mostly for phone cards only. A few public phones take one-shekel coins, and one-shekel coins are needed for pay phones in neighborhood groceries and restaurants. Many convenience groceries and newsstands sell **prepaid calling cards** in denominations ranging from NIS 18 to NIS 100 ($4.50–$25/£2.25–£13). Even if you've made cellphone arrangements, it can be a good idea to have a low-denomination calling card as backup.

For **reverse-charge or collect calls,** and for operator-assisted overseas or person-to-person calls, dial ✆ 188.

For **local directory assistance** ("information"), dial ✆ 144; 1-700 numbers are toll-free.

**To call Israel:** If you're calling from the United States:

1. Dial the international access code: 011.
2. Dial the country code: 972.
3. Dial the city or area code: (02 for Jerusalem, 03 for Tel Aviv, and so forth) *minus* the initial "0" and then the seven-digit local number. The whole number you'd dial for a telephone in Jerusalem would be **011-972-2-000-0000.**

If you're dialing from a city in Israel outside Jerusalem's 02 city code, the number you dial should look like this: **02-000-0000.** Within Jerusalem, just dial the local number without a prefix.

**To make international calls from Israel:** To make international calls from Israel, first dial 00 and then the country code (1 for the U.S. and Canada, 44 for the U.K., 353 for Ireland, 61 for Australia, 64 for New Zealand). Next you dial the area code and number. For example, if you wanted to call the British Embassy in Washington, D.C., you would dial **00-1-202-588-7800.** If you're calling from a pay phone with a phone card, the instruction card will tell you to dial 012, 013, or 014 for overseas; then dial your number starting with the country code.

**For directory assistance:** Dial ℂ **144** if you're looking for a number inside Israel, and dial ℂ **188** (overseas operator) for numbers to all other countries. For collect calls dial ℂ **142.**

**For operator assistance:** If you need operator assistance in making a call, dial ℂ 188 if you're trying to make an international call and if you want to call a number in another country.

**Toll-free numbers:** Numbers beginning with 1-800 and 1-177 within Israel are toll-free, but calling a 1-800 number in the United States from Israel is not toll-free—it costs the same as an overseas call.

When making a call from one area or city code to another inside Israel, it is necessary to use the area code of the number you are calling. If you're in Jerusalem, calling a number in Eilat, you must dial the 08 of the Eilat area code, plus the local number; for a number in Haifa, an initial 04 is required, and so on.

**Local pay phones are plentiful in Israeli cities.** Most require phone cards that can be purchased at newsstands, kiosks, and hotels for 20, 50, and 100 units. Best to buy the cards for a low number of units—you don't want to leave Israel with 90 unused units on a card. A local call from a pay phone eats up one unit for a 3-minute call, which means a fast local call is a reasonable 25¢. Rates are slightly lower after 9pm and during Shabbat, but daytime city-to-city calls gobble units very quickly. There are a very limited number of pay phones that accept shekels. These are hard to find, but most often located in restaurants or cafes.

**TELEGRAPH, TELEX & FAX** Most hotels have **fax machines** available for guest use (be sure to ask about the charge to use it). Many hotel rooms are wired for guests' fax machines. Your hotel will direct you to the easiest way to send a telegram from your location. Telegrams can be sent from central post offices in main cities.

**TIME** Israel is 2 hours ahead of Greenwich Mean Time, 7 hours ahead of Eastern Standard Time, and 10 hours ahead of Pacific Standard Time. When it's 7pm in Israel, it's noon in New York. Normally, Israel is 7 hours ahead of New York (Eastern Time), but because Israel has its own unique dates for going on and off daylight saving time, there is often a period of 1 or 2 weeks in the spring and a month in September or October when there's only a 6-hour time difference between New York and Israel. Palestinian areas, Jordan, and Egypt keep to their own dates for daylight saving time, and those areas of the West Bank not under direct Israeli control also keep to Egyptian/Jordanian time. This can make border crossings a disaster if both countries are not synchronized.

Jordan, Palestinian areas, and Egypt are normally 7 hours ahead of New York time, and 2 hours ahead of Greenwich Mean Time. In the past, because of religious and political considerations, the decision about when to begin and end daylight saving time has sometimes not been made until the last minute. For this reason, it is very important to reconfirm schedules at these times of year—you could miss your flight, or worse.

**TIPPING**   Tip 10% in restaurants or cafes, unless a service charge is already added to your bill. Taxi drivers do not expect tips unless they have helped you load or carry luggage. An extra NIS 5 ($1.25/60p) per bag is fair. Leave NIS 5 ($1.25/60p) per person per day for your hotel maid, more if she has given you extra help.

**USEFUL   PHONE   NUMBERS**   U.S. Department of State travel advisory ℂ 202/647-5225 (manned 24 hr.); U.S. passport agency ℂ 202/647-0518; U.S. Centers for Disease Control international traveler's hot line ℂ 404/332-4559.

**WATER**   Water is potable throughout Israel, except at The Dead Sea. Do not drink tap water in Egypt or Jordan under any circumstances.

## 2 Toll-Free Numbers & Websites

### MAJOR U.S. AIRLINES
(*flies internationally as well)

**American Airlines***
ℂ 800/433-7300 (in U.S. and Canada)
ℂ 020/7365-0777 (in U.K.)
www.aa.com

**Continental Airlines***
ℂ 800/523-3273 (in U.S. and Canada)
ℂ 084/5607-6760 (in U.K.)
www.continental.com

### MAJOR INTERNATIONAL AIRLINES

**Air France**
ℂ 800/237-2747 (in U.S.)
ℂ 800/375-8723 (in U.S. and Canada)
ℂ 087/0142-4343 (in U.K.)
www.airfrance.com

**Alitalia**
ℂ 800/223-5730 (in U.S.)
ℂ 800/361-8336 (in Canada)
ℂ 087/0608-6003 (in U.K.)
www.alitalia.com

**American Airlines**
ℂ 800/433-7300 (in U.S. and Canada)
ℂ 020/7365-0777 (in U.K.)
www.aa.com

**British Airways**
ℂ 800/247-9297 (in U.S. and Canada)

**Delta Air Lines***
ℂ 800/221-1212 (in U.S. and Canada)
ℂ 084/5600-0950 (in U.K.)
www.delta.com

**United Airlines***
ℂ 800/864-8331 (in U.S. and Canada)
ℂ 084/5844-4777 in U.K.
www.united.com

ℂ 087/0850-9850 (in U.K.)
www.british-airways.com

**Continental Airlines**
ℂ 800/523-3273 (in U.S. and Canada)
ℂ 084/5607-6760 (in U.K.)
www.continental.com

**Delta Air Lines**
ℂ 800/221-1212 (in U.S. and Canada)
ℂ 084/5600-0950 (in U.K.)
www.delta.com

**EgyptAir**
ℂ 212/581-5600 (in U.S.)
ℂ 020/7734-2343 (in U.K.)
ℂ 09/007-0000 (in Egypt)
www.egyptair.com

**El Al Airlines**
☎ 972/3977-1111 (outside Israel)
☎ *2250 (from any phone in Israel)
www.elal.co.il

**Iberia Airlines**
☎ 800/722-4642 (in U.S. and Canada)
☎ 087/0609-0500 (in U.K.)
www.iberia.com

**Israir Airlines**
☎ 877/477-2471 (in U.S. and Canada)
☎ 700/505-777 (in Israel)
www.israirairlines.com

**Lufthansa**
☎ 800/399-5838 (in U.S.)
☎ 800/563-5954 (in Canada)
☎ 087/0837-7747 (in U.K.)
www.lufthansa.com

**Olympic Airlines**
☎ 800/223-1226 (in U.S.)
☎ 514/878-9691 (in Canada)
☎ 087/0606-0460 (in U.K.)
www.olympicairlines.com

## CAR-RENTAL AGENCIES

**Avis**
☎ 800/331-1212 (in U.S. and Canada)
☎ 084/4581-8181 (in U.K.)
www.avis.com

**Budget**
☎ 800/527-0700 (in U.S.)
☎ 087/0156-5656 (in U.K.)
☎ 800/268-8900 (in Canada)
www.budget.com

## MAJOR HOTEL & MOTEL CHAINS

**Best Western International**
☎ 800/780-7234 (in U.S. and Canada)
☎ 0800/393-130 (in U.K.)
www.bestwestern.com

**Courtyard by Marriott**
☎ 888/236-2427 (in U.S.)
☎ 0800/221-222 (in U.K.)
www.marriott.com/courtyard

**Crowne Plaza Hotels**
☎ 888/303-1746 (in U.S.)
www.ichotelsgroup.com/crowneplaza

**Qantas Airways**
☎ 800/227-4500 (in U.S.)
☎ 084/5774-7767 (in U.K. and Canada)
☎ 13 13 13 (in Australia)
www.qantas.com

**South African Airways**
☎ 271/1978-5313 (international)
☎ 0861/FLYSAA (086/135-9122; in South Africa)
www.flysaa.com

**Swiss Air**
☎ 877/359-7947 (in U.S. and Canada)
☎ 084/5601-0956 (in U.K.)
www.swiss.com

**Turkish Airlines**
☎ +90 212/444-0 849 (international)
www.thy.com

**United Airlines***
☎ 800/864-8331 (in U.S. and Canada)
☎ 084/5844-4777 (in U.K.)
www.united.com

**Hertz**
☎ 800/645-3131 (in U.S.)
☎ 800/654-3001 (international)
www.hertz.com

**Thrifty**
☎ 800/367-2277 (in U.S.)
☎ 918/669-2168 (international)
www.thrifty.com

**Four Seasons**
☎ 800/819-5053 (in U.S. and Canada)
☎ 0800/6488-6488 (in U.K.)
www.fourseasons.com

**Hilton Hotels**
☎ 800/HILTONS (800/445-8667; in U.S. and Canada)
☎ 087/0590-9090 (in U.K.)
www.hilton.com

**Holiday Inn**
☏ 800/315-2621 (in U.S. and Canada)
☏ 0800/405-060 (in U.K.)
www.holidayinn.com

**Howard Johnson**
☏ 800/446-4656 (in U.S. and Canada)
www.hojo.com

**Hyatt**
☏ 888/591-1234 (in U.S. and Canada)
☏ 084/5888-1234 (in U.K.)
www.hyatt.com

**InterContinental Hotels & Resorts**
☏ 800/424-6835 (in U.S. and Canada)
☏ 0800/1800-1800 (in U.K.)
www.ichotelsgroup.com

**Marriott**
☏ 877/236-2427 (in U.S. and Canada)
☏ 0800/221-222 (in U.K.)
www.marriott.com

**Ramada Worldwide**
☏ 888/2-RAMADA (888/272-6232; in U.S. and Canada)
☏ 080/8100-0783 (in U.K.)
www.ramada.com

**Renaissance**
☏ 888/236-2427 (in U.S.)
www.marriott.com

**Sheraton Hotels & Resorts**
☏ 800/325-3535 (in U.S.)
☏ 800/543-4300 (in Canada)
☏ 0800/3253-5353 (in U.K.)
www.starwoodhotels.com/sheraton

# Appendix B:
# Useful Terms & Phrases

## 1 Hebrew Terms & Expressions

The Hebrew alphabet is, of course, entirely unlike our Latin ABCs. Fortunately for us, however, Israelis use the same numerals that we use: 1, 2, 3, 4, and so on.

Hebrew has a number of sounds that we don't use in English. They're difficult to communicate in writing, and until you hear them spoken correctly, you may not get the flavor of them. The first is the "ch" or "kh" sound, which you'll find repeatedly in many words throughout the vocabulary. This is not the sound of "ch" in either "change" or "champagne." We don't use this sound in English, and the closest to it are the "ch" sounds in the German exclamation "ach," and in the Yiddish "chutzpah." It's a raspy, hacking sound that comes from the back of the mouth.

Another difficult sound, and also very common in Hebrew words, is the "o" sound. The best advice for practicing this sound is to say the word "oh" and halfway through saying the word suddenly cut your voice off. That's what many call a short "o." You get an approximation with the "o" sound in the word "yoke." You just have to cut the "o" short, so when you say the Hebrew word *boker*, meaning "morning," you don't say *bowker*.

### USEFUL WORDS

hello **sha-*lom***

goodbye **sha-*lom***

good night ***lie*-la-tov**

I **ah-nee**

you **ah-tah**

he **hoo**

she **hee**

we **an-*nach*-noo**

where is? ***ay*-fo?**

there is **yesh**

there isn't **ain**

little **m'*aat***

much **har-*beh***

very **m'od**

so-so ***ka*-cha-*ka*-cha**

good **tov**

hot **chaam**

bad **rah**

see you later **le-hit-rah-*ott***

friend **cha-*vare***

excuse me **slee-*cha***

yes **kain**

no **lo**

please **be-vah-kah-*sha***

thank you **to-*dah* rah-*bah***

you're welcome **al low da-*vaar***

good morning ***bo*-ker tov**

good evening **erev tov**

I speak English **ah-*nee* m'dah-*behr* ahng-leet**

I don't speak Hebrew **ah-*nee* lo m'dah-*behr* ee-*vreet***

today **hah-*yom***

tomorrow **ma-char**

yesterday **et-*mohl***

right (correct) **na-*chon***

too much   yo-*tair* mee-die

patience   *sav*-la-*noot*

hands off   *blee* yah-*die*-im

what?   **mah?**

why?   *la*-ma?

how?   **aych?**

when?   **mah-tie?**

how long?   **kama-zman?**

pleasant   nah-*im*

excellent   met-soo-*yan*

wow, far out   **shiga-ohn**

crazy   me-shoo-g*ah*

healthy   ba-*ree*

sick   cho-*leh*

doctor   row-*feh*

dentist   row-*feh* shin-eye-yim

## POST OFFICE

post office   **dough-are**

postcard   **gloo-yah**

letter   **mich-tav**

stamp   **bool (pl. bool-im)**

airmail   **dough-are ah-*veer***

envelopes   ma-ata-*foth*

## SHOPPING & STORES

how much is it?   *ka*-mah zeh oh-*leh?*

manicure   *mah*-nee-koor

store   *cha*-noot

appointment   p'gee-*shah*

pharmacy   **bait mer-kay-*chat***

expensive   ya-*kar*

barber, hairdresser   **mahs-peh-*rah***

cheap   **zol**

shampoo   ha-fee-*fah*

## THE COUNTRYSIDE

sea   *yaam*

sand   **chol**

desert   mid-*bar*

forest   yah-*ar*

cold   **car**

village   **k'far**

road   *der*-ech

mountain   **har**

hill   **giv-*ah***

house   **bay-yit**

synagogue   **bait k-*ness*-et**

school   **bait *say*-fer**

newspaper   ee-*tahn*

spring, well   **ayn, ma-ay-in, ay-in**

farm   *mesh*-ech

valley   *ay*-mek

## HOTEL TALK

hotel   mah-*lon*

room   *che*-der

water   **my-im**

toilet   **bait key-*say*, no-*chi* yoot she-roo-*teem***

where is?   *ay*-fo?

key   maf-*tay*-ach

manager   min-ah-*hel*

accommodations   ma-*kom*

dining room   *che*-der oh-*chel*

bill   *chesh*-bon

Mr. (sir)   **ah-don-ee**

Mrs. (madam)   **g'ver-et**

money   keh-sef

bank   **bank**

do you speak English?   **ah-*tah* m'dah-*behr* ang-*leet?***

balcony   **meer-*pes*-et**

## LOCAL TRAVELING

station  **ta-cha-nah**

railroad  **rah-*keh*-vet**

airport  **sde t'u-*fah***

bus  **auto-boos**

bus stop  **ta-cha-naht ha-auto-boos**

which bus goes to . . . ?  **eh-zeh auto-boos no-say-ah le . . . ?**

taxi  **taxi**

shared taxi van (sherut)  **shay-*root***

trip  **tee-*yule***

straight ahead  **ya-*shar***

street  **re-*chov***

west  **m'ar-*av***

north  **tsa-*fon***

south  **da-*rom***

east  **miz-*rach***

near  **ka-*rov***

far  **rah-*chok***

central  **meer-ka-*zeet***

stop here  **ah-*tsor* kahn**

to the right  **yeh-*mean*-ah**

to the left  **smol-*ah***

wait  ***reg*-gah**

## RESTAURANT & MENU TERMS

to eat  **le-eh-*chol***

to drink  **lish-tot**

restaurant  ***miss*-ah-dah**

food  **o-chel**

cafe  **ca-*fe***

menu  **taf-*root***

breakfast  **ah-roo-*chat* bo-ker**

lunch  **ah-roo-chat tsa-ha-*rye*-im**

dinner  **ah-roo-*chat* erev**

waiter  **mel-*tsar***

ice cream  **glee-dah**

soup  **ma-rock**

wine  ***yah*-yin**

meat  **bah-sahr**

milk  **cha-*lav***

ice  **ker-*ach***

veal  **ay-*gel***

salt  **me-lach**

chicken  **tar-ne-*gol*-et**

sugar  **sue-*car***

fish  **dag**

omelet  **cha-vi-*tah***

tea  **tay**

sour  **cha-*muts***

coffee  **cafe**

apple  **ta-*poo*-ach**

orange  **tapooz**

tomatoes  ***ag*-von-ee-*oat***

cucumber  **mah-la-fe-*fon***

pepper  **pil-*pel***

vegetables  ***yeh*-rah-*koht***

butter  **chem-*ah***

cheese  **g'-vee-nah**

egg  ***bay*-tsa**

hard-boiled egg  **bay-*tsa* rah-*sha***

soft-boiled egg  **bay-*tsa* rah-*kah***

scrambled eggs  **bay-*tsim* m-bull-*bell*-et**

fried egg  **bay-*tsee*-ah**

sweet  **mah-*tok***

bread  ***lech*-hem**

salad  **sal-*at***

satisfy  ***sah*-vay-ah**

fruit  ***pay*-rote**

hungry  **rah-*ayv***

## DAYS & TIME

Sunday *yom* ree-shon
Monday *yom* shay-nee
Tuesday *yom* shlee-shee
Wednesday *yom* reh-vee-ee
Thursday *yom* cha-mee shee
Friday *yom* shee-shee
Saturday *sha*-baht

what time? *ma* ha-sha-*ah*?
minute da-*kah*
hour sha-*ah*
7 o'clock ha-sha-*ah shay*-va
day **yom**
week **sha-voo-*ah***
month *cho*-desh
year sha-*nah*

## NUMBERS

1 eh-*chad*
2 *shta*-yim
3 sha-*losh*
4 *ar*-bah
5 cha-*maysh*
6 shaysh
7 s*hev*-vah
8 sh-*mo*-neh
9 *tay*-shah
10 *ess*-er
11 eh-*chad* ess-ray
12 *shtaym*-ess-ray

20 ess-*reem*
21 ess-*reem* v'eh-*chad*
30 shlo-*sheem*
50 cha-mee-*sheem*
100 *may*-ah
200 mah-tah-*yeem*
300 shlosh may-*oat*
500 cha-*maysh* may-*oat*
1,000 elef
3,000 shlosh-*et* alaf-*eem*
5,000 cha-*maysh*-et alaf-*eem*

# 2 Arabic Terms & Expressions

## USEFUL TERMS

please **min fadlak**
thank you **shoo-khraan**
hello **a-halan, mahr-haba**
goodbye **salaam aleikum, ma-ah-salameh**
right **yemina**
left **she-mal**

straight **doo-ree**
today **il-yaum**
tomorrow **boo-kra**
what is your name? **shoo ismak?**
my name is . . . **ismay . . .**
how much is this? **ah-desh ha dah?**

## MEASURES & NUMBERS

one kilo **wahad kilo**
half kilo (500 grams) **noos kilo**
100 grams **mia gram**

1 **wa-had**
2 **ti-neen**
3 **talatay**
4 **ar-bah**
5 **ham-she**
6 **sitteh**

7 **sabah**
8 **tamanyeh**
9 **tay-sa**
10 **a-sha-rah**
50 **ham-seen**
100 **mia**

# Index

See also Accommodations and Restaurant indexes, below.

## Accommodations

## RESTAURANTS

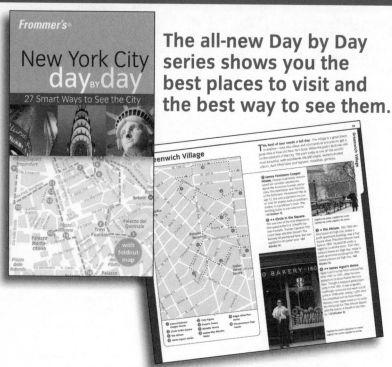